Leiths

BAKING BIBLE

Also in the Leiths series

Leiths Cookery Bible
Leiths Techniques Bible
Leiths Vegetarian Bible
Leiths Fish Bible

Leiths

BAKING BIBLE

SUSAN SPAULL and
FIONA BURRELL

BLOOMSBURY

First edition published in Great Britain in 2006

Copyright © Leiths School of Food and Wine, 2006

The moral right of the authors has been asserted

Bloomsbury Publishing Plc, 36 Soho Square, London W1D 3QY

A CIP catalogue record for this book is available from the British Library

ISBN 0 7475 8189 4
ISBN-13 9780747581895

10 9 8 7 6 5 4 3 2 1

Typeset by Hewer Text UK Ltd, Edinburgh
Printed in Singapore by Tien Wah Press

Photographs by Jason Lowe
Home economist: Susan Spaull with Marianne Lumb
Plate section design: Antigone Konstantinidou
Line drawings by Kate Simunek
Book design: Here + There

Contents

Acknowledgements

Writing a cookbook is a huge team effort. There are so many unsung heroes behind the scenes who labour late into the night to put the book together, the writing is the easy part. Many of this team work for Bloomsbury and we would like to credit Victoria Millar and Emily Sweet in particular, and their production team, for their patience and attention to detail.

We would also like to give a very great thanks to Caroline Waldegrave for her unwavering support and encouragement. In addition, she has overseen the testing of the recipes through Leiths School of Food and Wine. All the testing has been done in home kitchens in order to provide an environment that would be similar to that of our readers. Our recipe testers, Andrew Muir, Eithne Neame and Kate Hughes have been absolute stalwarts in working their way systematically through the recipes, providing suggestions and corrections along with invaluable feedback.

We would like to thank Jason Lowe who was hugely enthusiastic and efficient in producing the amazing photographs as well as key props and life-sustaining bacon sandwiches on sourdough bread. Marianne Lumb was a great help on the photo shoot and was responsible for producing many of the recipes shown in the photographs. Thank you also to Kate Simunek for the excellent drawings that are interspersed throughout the book.

Where possible, we have attempted to give credit to the source or inspiration for a recipe. Recipes for baked goods are necessarily formulaic and often will be similar to previously published recipes.

Susan Spaull would like to thank her mother, without whom baking would never have become such an intrinsic part of her life; she is an excellent and inspirational baker as well as a scientist who imparted to Susan the discipline needed to be able to bake successfully and to convey it in writing. Susan would also like to thank Robert, Rebecca and Guy for their help with recipe tasting and testing.

Fiona Burrell would like to thank her husband, Charles,Stevenson, for his never-ending support and her daughters, Evie, Isla and Lorna, for being enthusiastic tasters of recipes. They have thoroughly enjoyed coming home from school to find yet more cakes, biscuits and breads laid out for them to try.

Susan Spaull and Fiona Burrell

Foreword

Both Susan and Fiona have been teaching and demonstrating baking techniques at Leiths School of Food and Wine for years. For them to have encapsulated all their recipes in this latest Leiths Bible is a tremendous achievement and it gives me much pleasure to introduce it. The recipes were all tested in domestic ovens and then retested at Leiths School where many of them have become part of the curriculum of the Diploma course. This has meant that the smell of baking has permeated the building for the last 3 years, and now that the book is completed, it will be sorely missed. Where most people have pens, in my office I have knives, forks and spoons so that I can taste the constant stream of delicious food passing by, so I have already enjoyed eating my way through many of the recipes in this book. I hope that you enjoy them as much as I have.

Caroline Waldegrave O.B.E.

Introduction

Baking is as close to alchemy as you can get. The ingredients are put into the bowl, mixed and baked, filling the kitchen with wonderful, evocative aromas. Although it is easy to pull a loaf of bread or cake from the shelf at the supermarket, when you have baked it yourself you will know exactly what has gone into the finished product, when it was baked and how it should taste.

The Baking Bible is intended for both the enthusiastic, experienced baker and the nervous beginner. Baking is an enormous subject encompassing both savoury and sweet foods. *The Baking Bible* is a comprehensive collection of breads, cakes, pastries, meringues and biscuits, with traditional and modern British recipes as well as popular recipes from around the world.

At Leiths School of Food and Wine the students learn to make recipes from all categories of baking. In their first term the students begin with the more simple recipes: scones, soda bread, Swiss meringues, shortcrust pastry and brownies, and by the time they are in their third term they are making fougasse, puff pastry, Danish pastries and multi-layered Génoise cakes filled with buttercream and decorated with chocolate caraque. Along the way they are taught the theory behind what makes a recipe work and how to recognise what has happened when the recipe had not performed as expected. And most importantly, they learn the care and precision it takes to be a good baker. They also have a lot of practice. This book is written reflecting that approach.

It is divided into four main secions: pastry, biscuits, cakes and breads. In addition there are recipes for cheesecakes, meringues, and muffins and a section with recipes for gluten-free baking. In each section, advice is given on the best method to use and the key points to remember when making the recipes. 'What has gone wrong when . . .' pointers will help the novice baker avoid common pitfalls.

A few things to keep in mind when baking: it is important to measure ingredients carefully and have them at the correct temperature. Use the size of tin specified in the recipe if possible. If the tin size is different the baking time will be different and so will the results. Prepare the tin as specified before starting to mix.

An oven thermometer is a particularly useful piece of equipment as ovens vary in the way they heat as well as the way they are calibrated. All the recipes in the book were tested in ovens with an oven thermometer. If you have a fan oven read the tips in the *Baking Equipment* section (see page 23).

Medium size eggs weighing 55 g|2 oz were used for the recipes in this book, with a few exceptions where specified. A tablespoon measure equals 15 ml and a teaspoon measure equals 5 ml.

But above all remember that baking should be fun – both in the making and the eating.

Part One
BASICS

Baking Ingredients

Baking Powder

A mixture of sodium bicarbonate and acid, in the form of cream of tartar, used as a raising agent in baking. It is activated when it becomes wet. Baking powder from the US is also heat-activated so that a second chemical reaction occurs in the oven. This means it is less critical that the mixture is put into the oven immediately after mixing. It also produces a more reliable rise.

Butter

Butter is an essential ingredient in baking. It is important that it is fresh: butter can become rancid, which gives an 'off' flavour to baked products. Unsalted butter is thought to be fresher than salted butter as salt is a preservative. It is used when the flavour of the butter will predominate in the recipe, for example with puff pastry. In the US unsalted butter is known as sweet butter.

Butter was produced in early times as a method of preserving milk. Today butter is made from cream that has been ripened through the addition of lactic acid-producing bacteria. The cream is churned, which brings the fat molecules together with some of the water in suspension. Other liquid, the buttermilk, is drained away, then the butter is washed and worked to improve its texture. Salt is often added for flavour and to help preserve the butter. The type of cow, as well as the cows' diet, has a great influence on the flavour of the butter.

Butter, a water-in-oil emulsion, contains approximately 80 per cent fat, with the remaining 20 per cent consisting of milk solids and water. It is solid at room temperature and is a saturated fat, so it is best consumed in limited quantity.

Butter should be kept in the refrigerator, tightly wrapped and away from strong smelling foods as it will absorb their flavours. Most butter is marked with a 'use by' date; however, it will usually keep for about 1 week before developing a slightly 'off' flavour. Butter should not be left at room temperature. It quickly becomes rancid due to the oxidization of the fat and develops a noticeable sour smell and taste. Butter can be frozen for 1 month.

Buttermilk

Traditionally buttermilk was the liquid remaining after the butter has been churned from the cream. Today buttermilk is produced by adding bacteria to low-fat milk to thicken and slightly sour it. It has a fat content of about 2 per cent.

Buttermilk is primarily used in baking for recipes using bicarbonate of soda, such as *Soda Bread* (see page 238), pancakes and scones. The acidity from the buttermilk combines with the alkaline bicarbonate of soda to produce carbon dioxide, which raises the baked goods. If buttermilk is not available, milk can be substituted; however, a better result will be obtained if the milk is soured slightly by adding 1 tablespoon of lemon juice per 290 ml | 10 fl oz milk before using.

Chocolate

Plain chocolate varies tremendously in the amount of sugar and the amount of cocoa solids it contains. When choosing a chocolate to use in cooking, look for the percentage of cocoa solids on the list of ingredients. If the number is between 50 and 70 per cent the chocolate will have a rich taste that most people will find acceptable. Above 70 per cent cocoa solids the chocolate will be very dark and more bitter. Generally, the higher the percentage of cocoa solids, the more expensive the chocolate. As the flavour and texture of each brand of chocolate vary, it is important to taste your chocolate before using it for cooking to ensure it has the flavour you require.

Semi-sweet chocolate is a term used primarily in the US. It is similar to plain chocolate but contains slightly more sugar.

Couverture Couverture is a plain, dark chocolate with a relatively high proportion of cocoa butter. When melted it is more free-flowing than plain chocolate. Couverture is the best type of chocolate to use for confectionery, as it can be tempered easily – that is, the process of heating and cooling the liquid chocolate so that it becomes shiny when hard and breaks with a sharp snap. The word 'couverture' means 'blanket' or 'covering' in French.

Milk chocolate contains milk solids or cream as well as sugar. Milk chocolate should be melted to a slightly lower temperature than plain chocolate.

Unsweetened chocolate is widely available in the US and is commercially available in the UK, where it is also known as bitter or baking chocolate. It does not contain any sugar. In processing, the cocoa solids are ground very finely and an emulsifier such as lecithin is added.

White chocolate is not technically chocolate, but a manufactured concoction of milk solids, sugar, cocoa butter and vanilla.

Cocoa powder consists of cocoa solids and varying amounts of sugar. Cocoa powders vary tremendously in their intensity of chocolate flavour. Many recipes require the addition of boiling water to cocoa powder to release its chocolate flavour.

Certain brands of cocoa powder are described as being 'Dutch-processed'. This means that the cocoa powder has been treated with an alkaline solution to make it less bitter and the resulting powder is darker in colour. This type of cocoa powder is best for culinary use.

Melting chocolate
Chocolate has a sharp melting point which means that within a narrow temperature range it changes from solid to liquid. It is sensitive to heat and can change from melted to burnt within a matter of seconds. For this reason, chocolate is notoriously tricky to work with.

When melting chocolate, avoid dripping small amounts of water or other liquid into the chocolate. Small amounts of liquid, for example, drips from the underside of the bowl, will cause the chocolate to *seize* and harden into a solid, unworkable lump. If the chocolate seizes, it can be rescued by adding 1 teaspoon of flavourless oil per 55 g | 2 oz chocolate and then reheating the mixture. The result can still be used in cooking but cannot be tempered – only pure chocolate can be tempered (see below).

It is also very important not to overheat chocolate. As the temperature of the chocolate approaches 50°C | 120°F, the cocoa butter will start to separate from the cocoa solids. The cocoa solids will burn if the chocolate is overheated and the texture of the chocolate will be dry and crumbly. If the chocolate burns there is nothing that can be done to save it.

Melting Chocolate: Points to Remember

- Chocolate should be chopped into small pieces, no more than – 1cm | ½ in, before being melted.
- It should be stirred during melting to keep the temperature even throughout the mass.
- Half-fill a saucepan with water and heat until it simmers. Turn off the heat, then place a heatproof bowl containing the chopped chocolate over, but not touching, the water. Stir frequently until the chocolate has melted.
- Alternatively, place in a heatproof bowl – glass is ideal – then microwave on 50 per cent power for sessions of 30 seconds. Stir the chocolate after each session. Milk and white chocolate should be heated at 30 per cent power.
- Plain chocolate should be melted to a temperature of 30°C | 90°F for an optimum working temperature. It should not be heated any higher than 45°C | 115°F.
- Milk and white chocolate should be melted to 27°C | 87°F for an optimum working temperature.

Adding liquid to chocolate

Melted chocolate will seize with a small addition of water because the liquid combines with the dry cocoa solids. It is necessary to add a large enough quantity of liquid to cause these solids to form a solution.

If a recipe requires the addition of a small amount of liquid, add it to the chocolate before it is melted. If adding liquid to melted chocolate, ensure that the liquid measures at least 1 tablespoon per 55 g | 2 oz of melted chocolate. If possible, add the melted chocolate to the liquid ingredient. Do not add melted chocolate to cold ingredients as the cold could result in the cocoa butter solidifying.

NOTE: If your chocolate seizes, add more liquid and heat it, stirring, until it becomes smooth again.

Tempering chocolate

Tempering is a method of heating then cooling chocolate to a particular temperature so that when the chocolate cools and hardens, it has a shiny surface and breaks with a sharp snap. It is necessary to temper chocolate before using it to line moulds for filled chocolates, for coating and when making chocolate bands, curls and shapes. If it is melted, then used without tempering, it will have a dull, streaky appearance when it hardens.

Tempering changes the alignment of the molecules in the chocolate and results in the desired type of cocoa butter crystals remaining unmelted in the chocolate. It is best to work in a cool, dry environment when tempering chocolate.

Couverture, the dark chocolate with a high proportion of cocoa butter and cocoa solids, is the best chocolate to use for tempering. Good quality plain chocolate with a high proportion of cocoa solids can also be tempered successfully, as can good quality milk and white chocolate.

To temper chocolate, melt it by one of the methods described above so that it reaches a temperature of 45°C|115°F. Milk and white chocolate should be melted to a temperature 2° lower. At this temperature the cocoa butter will melt. An accurate and sensitive thermometer is necessary for tempering chocolate. Use a digital probe thermometer. Professional chocolatiers often use their upper lip for gauging the temperature of the chocolate because the upper lip is very sensitive.

The chocolate then must be cooled to 27°C|84°F, or 2° lower for milk or white chocolate. It must not become any cooler than 25°C|82°F or the chocolate will have to be reheated to 45°C|115°F. The chocolate can be cooled in one of the following ways:

- Add an additional 20 per cent of unmelted chocolate and stir constantly. This is called 'seeding'.
- Pour half the melted chocolate on to a cool, dry work surface. Spread the chocolate back and forth with a palette knife until it thickens and becomes difficult to spread. Stir this into the remaining melted chocolate. This is called 'tabling'.
- Place the bowl in a cool water bath and stir to keep the temperature even and to speed cooling.
- Use a tempering machine to melt the chocolate then add 20 per cent unmelted chocolate. The machine does the stirring.

To test if the chocolate has been tempered successfully, dip a palette knife into the chocolate and tap the knife on the edge of the bowl to remove the excess. Allow the chocolate on the palette knife to stand for up to 5 minutes. It should harden and have a shiny appearance. If the chocolate is not set and shiny, repeat the tempering process.

Storing chocolate

Keep chocolate in a cool, dry environment separated from strongly flavoured foods. Chocolate will keep for up to 1 year. Unless it is very hot, do not refrigerate chocolate.

Coffee

Coffee essence is something that can be made easily at home. Commercial coffee essence is sweetened and often flavoured with chicory. To make up your own coffee essence, take 1 tablespoon of instant coffee granules and add 1 tablespoon of boiling water. Mix well and add a little more water if necessary to ensure all the coffee has dissolved. (Each variety of coffee will vary.) Allow it to cool and then add the required amount to your mixture.

Cream

There are many types of cream available. Their fat content determines whether or not they can be whipped or heated and therefore their uses in cooking.

Single cream has a fat content of 18 per cent. It is used for pouring over desserts and for adding to coffee. It cannot be boiled without curdling and cannot be whipped.

Whipping cream has a fat content of 36 per cent. It can be used for pouring, heating or whipping. Although it can be heated or whipped, the lower fat content means that it is not quite as stable as whipped double cream. It is the best cream to use for ice cream.

Double cream has a fat content of 48 per cent. It is used for pouring and for whipping for filling cakes and buns. Whipped double cream is also used for decoration. Whipped cream is a foam stabilized by the protein and fat in the cream. Use a balloon whisk or an electric mixer. As soon as the cream starts to thicken, watch it carefully. When whipping cream it is important not to overwhip or the butterfat will become grainy, spoiling the texture and the appearance of the cream. If the cream reaches the stiff-peak stage (c) a little milk can be added to help soften it. If the cream is whipped further, the butterfat will start to clump together and separate from the whey, a thin liquid. At this point the cream is no longer usable.

Whipped cream: soft peak (a)

For both decorating and folding, the cream should be whipped to the soft-peak stage. (a) Overwhipped cream is difficult to fold into other mixtures. It tends to form clumps that won't combine into the base mixture.

When whipping cream in hot weather, above 25°C | 80°F, it is advisable to chill the bowl and beaters as well as the cream before starting to whip. If it is too hot the foam is unable to form.

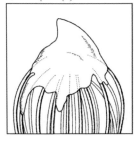

Whipped cream: medium peak (b)

Extra-thick cream has added stabilizing ingredients to make it spoonable without having to whip. It is used as a sauce for desserts. It does not whip well.

Soured cream is made from single cream that has been soured through the addition of lactic acid-producing bacteria to thicken it and give it a tangy flavour. It has a fat content of 18 per cent.

Crème fraiche, a speciality of the Normandy region in France, is traditionally made from unpasteurized milk that has been allowed to age. The bacteria present in the cream thicken it and give it a slightly tangy, nutty flavour. Today crème fraiche is made from pasteurized milk into which a bacterial culture has been introduced. Crème fraiche is often used as a substitute for whipped cream, as its slightly tangy flavour offsets the richness of the fat. With its high fat content (48 per cent), crème fraiche is often very thick when chilled but becomes softer at room temperature and when it is stirred. It can be served as an accompaniment to desserts or used in place of cream in quiche fillings. Full-fat crème fraiche can be boiled but low-fat crème fraiche tends to split or separate into lumps and liquid when boiled, so it does not make a good cream substitute if it is going to be heated to boiling point.

Whipped cream: stiff peak (c)

Clotted cream has a 55 per cent fat content. It is a speciality of the West Country made by heating cream to slightly concentrate it then allowing it to stand. The butterfat rises to the top, forming a thick, creamy crust that is skimmed off to use as a spread. It has a rich, creamy flavour and is traditionally served on scones with jam as part of a 'cream tea'. Clotted cream will keep for 5 days in the refrigerator.

Storing milk

Take into account cream's 'use by' date. Cream will keep for up to 3 days in the refrigerator once the container has been opened. Crème fraiche will keep for up to 7 days once the container has been opened. Whipping and double cream can be frozen for 1 month. Whip lightly then freeze in an airtight freezer container. Rewhisk slightly upon defrosting. Cream will not whip as firmly after freezing. Crème fraiche can be frozen for 1 month.

Dried Fruit

Dried fruits are produced from ripe fresh fruit and are classified into 2 groups: vine fruits and tree fruits. The moisture content is reduced by drying and the fruits change character completely, becoming dense, wrinkled and leathery. Their flavour is sweet and very concentrated. Approximately 1.8–2.3kg|4–5 lb fresh grapes will produce 450 g|1 lb sultanas, raisins or currants, whereas 2.7 kg|6 lb tree fruit will produce 450 g|1 lb dried tree fruit.

Dried fruit is often treated with sulphur dioxide to keep its colour and extend its shelf-life. The quantity of sulphur used is controlled and is helpful in stopping the formation of harmful bacteria. Fruit that has been treated with sulphur will be labelled as such and will keep for 18 months in a cool, well-ventilated, dry place. Once a packet has been opened the fruit should be kept in an airtight container. Unsulphured fruit is darker in colour; apricots, for example, are a mid-brown colour. The flavour of unsulphured fruit is not always superior, in fact it can taste bitter, but it can be a useful chemical-free option.

Dried fruit bought in packets needs no preparation as it has been washed and sorted for any grit or pips. However, if you are buying dried fruit from large bins in health-food shops or from market stalls, the fruit should be washed and dried before use. If the dried fruit has been in the cupboard for a while and is drier than it should be, it can be soaked in hot water for 15 minutes before use.

Weight for weight, dried fruit is higher in calories than fresh fruit but it is an extremely good source of dietary fibre and is nutritious. It contains a lot of fruit sugars – fructose and glucose – and therefore provides a constant source of energy.

Apples are available peeled, cored and sliced into rings or chunks. The apple has a tangy flavour and chewy texture. Origin: USA, Italy, China, Chile and South Africa.

Apricots are available halved or whole. They are usually bright orange but the unsulphured variety is dark brown. The small Hunza apricot is beige and has a very sweet, slightly caramel flavour when eaten unsoaked. They are grown in the wild in the valleys of Afghanistan and Kashmir. Many of the dried apricots found in the shops come from Turkey. They also come from the USA, Australia, South Africa and Iran.

Currants are mostly produced (89 per cent) in Greece and the remainder in South Africa, Australia and the USA. Currants are seedless black grapes. They all derive from the same type, the Corinth, and this is where the name 'currant' originated. The methods of drying vary depending on the climate and soil of the growing area, but it is said that keeping the grapes in the shade for the first stage of the drying process will produce the best quality currant. Currants are graded in 2 sizes: small and medium. The small ones are used by the baking industry, whereas the currants available in the grocery and health-food shops are generally the medium-sized variety.

Dates are the berry fruit of the date palm which grows up to 25 metres in height and has been grown in the dry desert-like regions of North Africa and the Middle East for at least 4,000 years. They are high in dietary fibre and contain potassium, iron and niacin but have virtually no vitamin C. Nowadays about three-quarters of the world's date crop is grown in the Middle East, mainly in Iraq, Iran and Israel, but the US grows large amounts in date gardens in California and Arizona. The Medjool date, which is a large date up to 5 cm | 2 in long, was originally from Morocco and is known as the king of dates as it was a favourite with the royal family and their honoured guests. The Deglet Noor date is the most readily available and can be obtained either pitted or unpitted. It is possible to buy blocks of chopped dates or chopped free-flowing dates. Fresh and dried dates should be smooth-skinned, glossy and plump. Avoid any that smell sour or have crystallized sugar on the surface. They should also not be rock hard. Semi-soft or fresh dates should be stored in the refrigerator in airtight plastic boxes so that they will not absorb other flavours or odours. If dried dates have become too dry soak them in hot water for 15 minutes prior to using.

Figs were one of the first fruits to be cultivated. Available whole or in blocks, dried figs are sweet and pale yellow-brown in colour. Apart from giving sweetness and richness to a cake, they also lend a slightly gritty texture. Origin: Turkey, US and Greece.

Peaches are available either in halves or in slices. They have a slightly sharp, tangy flavour and can give a traditional fruit cake a wonderful edge. Origin: USA, Australia, South Africa and China.

Pears are available in halves. They are a golden-yellow colour with a granular texture. Origin: USA, South Africa, Australia, China and Chile.

Prunes are dark, dried plums and are available whole or pitted. Like most tree fruits, they give extra moisture to a cake. Origin: California, eastern Europe, France, South America, South Africa and Australia.

Raisins are mainly produced in California, South Africa, Afghanistan, Chile and Australia, from unseeded or seeded black or white grapes. The word 'raisin' is derived from the Latin, *racemus*, which means 'a cluster of grapes or berries'. Raisins are generally dark brown and wrinkled, with a sweet, mellow flavour. The grapes are harvested when fully ripened and, like sultanas, are dried by different methods depending on the country of origin. Sometimes the grapes are dried on clean paper trays between the vines, or they are placed in specially made concrete drying areas. The clusters of grapes are spread out evenly and turned occasionally so that each grape gets the right amount of sun. The fruit lies in full sunlight for 2–3 weeks until the moisture content has been reduced to around 16 per cent. They are then packed in storage bins to keep them moist and are washed and oiled before export.

Sultanas are mainly produced in Turkey, Australia, Greece, Iran and South Africa, largely from seedless white grapes. They are amber-coloured and have a very sweet flavour. The majority are produced from the Thompson seedless grape, which contains 18–20 per cent fruit sugar. This helps to retain the plumpness of fruit after evaporation of its water content. There are different methods of drying sultanas, depending on their country of origin. One way is to spray the grapes with a vegetable-based drying oil prior to sun-drying. This will make the water evaporate more quickly from the fruit when exposed to the sun. In some places the fruit is dried on racks in partial shade, whilst in other countries the fruit is put in full sun on specially shaped concrete drying areas. Drying, until the moisture is reduced to approximately 16 per cent, takes a week to 10 days. The fruit is processed in factories where it is washed, cleaned and given a fine coating of vegetable oil. This keeps the sultanas moist and prevents them from sticking together.

Other dried tree fruits available include: nectarines, mangoes, bananas, pawpaw (or papaya), cherries, cranberries, blueberries and strawberries.

Eggs

The eggs used for the recipes in the book are medium-sized hens' eggs. A medium-sized egg weighs 55 g|2 oz.

To use other egg varieties in the place of chickens' eggs – such as goose eggs for a cake – weigh the goose egg and divide by 55 g|2 oz (the average weight of a hen's egg), in order to calculate how many hens' eggs the goose egg is replacing.

Storing eggs

Eggs are potentially hazardous as they are rich in nutrients and provide the ideal conditions for the growth of harmful bacteria such as salmonella, which is commonly found in the intestines of chickens. Most bacterial contamination is present on the shell of a dirty or cracked egg but can also be found inside the egg. Eggs that are dirty and/or cracked should be discarded.

To reduce the risk of salmonella poisoning, as well as to slow their rate of deterioration, store eggs at temperatures below 4°C|40°F. Eggs will age twice to three times as fast at room temperature as eggs kept in the refrigerator. Shop-bought fresh eggs are stamped with the 'best before' date set at 3 weeks from laying, provided they are kept in the refrigerator.

Egg whites can be refrigerated for up to 3 weeks, as they contain a natural bactericide, or frozen for up to 3 months. Yolks can be refrigerated for 2–3 days, covered with a little cold water and clingfilm to prevent a hard crust from forming. They can also be frozen for up to 3 months.

Egg dishes should also be stored below 4°C|40°F or above 63°C|145°F, or eaten within 1 hour of being prepared if held at room temperature.

Store eggs separately from other foods, as egg shells are porous and pervious to air, water and odours. To prevent the flavour of the eggs becoming tainted it is best to store eggs in their egg box, away from strongly flavoured, smelly foods. They will also keep better if they are stored standing upright on their pointed end so that the air sack, at the wide end, is facing upwards.

Essences and Extracts (see also *Vanilla*, page 21)

In baking, essences and extracts with flavours such as vanilla and almond are often used for cakes and biscuits. The words 'essence' and 'extract' are used almost interchangeably these days, which can be confusing. We recommend that you use only a *natural* essence, which is the same thing as an extract, rather than the products labelled 'flavouring'.

Flour

Flour is the finely ground and sifted meal of various edible grains, such as wheat, corn, rye or rice. Flour is also made from nuts, starchy vegetables and pulses, such as chestnuts, potatoes or chickpeas. Unless a type of flour is specifically called for, 'flour' in a recipe is assumed to be plain white wheat flour. Self-raising flour is a soft white flour that has chemical raising-agents added at the mill. It is used primarily for cakes and batters.

The importance of wheat in cooking lies in its combined proteins, glutenin and gliadin, which when mixed with water form an elastic substance called 'gluten'. It is the gluten in a dough which gives it body. All flours contain protein, starch, fat, water, fibre, vitamins and minerals in varying quantities. Millers mix flours from different wheat crops in order to produce a standard product.

Wheat that has a relatively high amount of protein is said to be 'hard'. Although there are over 30,000 different strains of wheat, the important distinguishing factor between them is the degree of hardness. The types of wheat can be put into three categories: hard, soft or durum. Flour with a protein content of 11.5 per cent or higher is said to be 'hard' or 'strong', and is best suited to bread-making. Flour with a protein content of 7–9 per cent is said to be 'soft' and is suitable for cakes, biscuits and some pastries. Durum wheat is very hard and is used for making dried pasta.

The structure of a grain of wheat looks something like this:

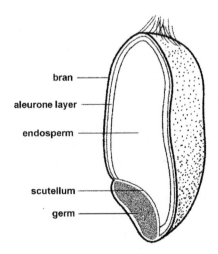

bran
aleurone layer
endosperm
scutellum
germ

Storing flour

Flour should be stored in a cool, dry place and will keep for about 6 months. It is best kept in an airtight container. Alternatively the bag of flour can be kept in a sealed plastic bag. Wholemeal flour will not keep as long due to its higher fat content. In hot climates it is best stored in the refrigerator.

The bran is the outer coating of the grain. It contains a high proportion of B vitamins and about 50 per cent of the mineral elements from the grain. Bran consists mainly of indigestible cellulose, which is a useful source of fibre (roughage) in the diet. It is separated from the grain during the milling process and is removed from white flour by sifting.

The germ is the embryo of the grain. It is rich in fats, proteins, B vitamins, vitamin E and iron. Most of the germ is lost during the milling process; however, wheat germ can be purchased as an individual food item from health-food shops. Due to its high fat content it goes rancid quickly, so is best stored in the refrigerator.

The scutellum is a membranous tissue that separates the germ from the endosperm. It is rich in thiamin.

The endosperm is the floury part of the grain, consisting mainly of starch and carbohydrate. It is very low in mineral elements and contains no vitamins. The endosperm contains the two proteins, glutenin and gliadin, which, when mixed with water, combine together to form gluten.

The aleurone layer is a single layer of cells surrounding the endosperm. It contains some proteins but is lost during the milling process.

Wholemeal flour/Wholewheat flour contains the whole of the cleaned wheat grain. 'Stone-ground' refers to the old method of grinding the wheat grain between two slowly moving stones. This process crushes the grain without generating heat or separating the germ from the grain. It contains a higher quantity of the bran and the germ than does white flour. Wheatmeal or brown flour contains 80–90 per cent of the cleaned wheat grain. This percentage is termed the 'rate of extraction'. It is the percentage of the whole grain that remains in the flour after milling.

Strong flour/Bread flour is milled from hard spring wheat which is grown in climates where the winter is very cold and the ground freezes to a depth of at least 20 cm | 8 in, primarily in Canada, the northern US and Russia. This wheat has a higher protein content, usually 11–15 per cent, than the wheat grown in warmer climates. This flour is used for bread-making because it forms a relatively large amount of gluten when made into a dough and kneaded.

Plain flour/All-purpose flour (US) is a fine-textured flour milled from the endosperm. White flour is usually made from 70–72 per cent of the cleaned wheat grain. It contains neither the bran nor the germ. It is milled from winter wheat that produces a flour with a protein content of 9–11 per cent, somewhat lower than strong flour. Plain flour is higher in starch than strong flour and absorbs less liquid. It is used for general cooking, particularly the thickening of sauces, and for making pastries, cakes and biscuits which do not require the tougher texture provided by the gluten in strong flour.

White flour in its natural state is a creamy colour, so it is often bleached to make it whiter. Unless a flour package is marked 'unbleached', it will have been bleached.

Self-raising flour is plain white or wholemeal flour to which raising agents have been added. It is used for cakes and other baked goods. The raising agent, which is usually baking powder, reacts with the liquid in the recipe to produce bubbles of carbon dioxide. Baking powder is a combination of bicarbonate of soda, an alkali, and cream of tartar, an acid. If bubbles of carbon dioxide are captured in the flour during baking, a risen effect will be produced. For best results, recipes using self-raising flour should be baked immediatley after mixing.

Plain flour can be converted to self-raising flour by the addition of 4 level teaspoons of baking powder per 225 g|8 oz plain flour. Too much raising agent will produce a sour, chemical taste in baked goods.

Cake flour is a white flour milled from soft wheat. It has been ground very finely and is particularly suitable for cakes.

Ciabatta flour is a rough flour produced in northern Italy. It has a high protein content and, when made into a very wet dough for ciabatta, enzymes in the flour create large bubbles.

Durum wheat flour/Pasta flour is a variety of hard wheat flour used to make pasta and gnocchi.

French white type 55 flour is produced from soft French wheat for making baguettes. It is a very white flour as 45 per cent of the wheat grain has been removed.

Gluten-free flour is a product manufactured for people who are intolerant to gluten. It is a blend of rice flour and potato flour, and sometimes buckwheat flour, tapioca flour and/or maize flour. It will not perform in the same way as wheat flour in leavened recipes, but it can be substituted for plain flour in other recipes, such as pastry, scones, pancakes and flour-based sauces.

Gluten-free flour can be converted to self-raising flour by adding 3 teaspoons baking powder per 200 g|7 oz flour. The gluten-free flour will absorb slightly more liquid than would plain wheat flour, so the liquid quantity in a recipe might need to be increased.

Semolina flour is a pale-yellow, grainy flour that is ground from durum wheat and is highly extensile when turned into a dough.

In Italy the durum wheat is ground into different degrees of fineness or 'types', 'tipo' in Italian. The very fine grind of '00' is commonly used for making pasta. It is a very white flour with a low ash content.

Spelt flour is made from the ancient grain, spelt, grown in southern Europe. It was popular with the Romans and was brought to England during the Roman occupation. Spelt has a light brown colour and nutty flavour. It is more digestible than wheat and is therefore tolerated better by people who are sensitive to wheat. In recipes, spelt flour can be substituted for wheat flour. It can be purchased in health-food stores.

Speciality Flours

Barley flour is a staple in Scotland and northern England. It is low in gluten and has a nutty flavour.

Besan flour is made by grinding dried chickpeas. This fine, golden-yellow flour is used primarily in Indian cooking for making chapatis. It is also known as gram flour.

Buckwheat flour is extracted from the seeds of a herb native to Asia and Russia. Light brown in colour with flecks of black, it is used for the Russian pancakes called blinis and for the large crêpes made in Brittany. It contains no gluten and has a nutty flavour. In recipes, it is usually mixed with a similar quantity of wheat flour.

Chestnut flour is made from dried, ground chestnuts. It has a distinct smoky flavour and is used in Europe, where it was once a staple in Corsica and the poorer areas of France and Italy. Chestnut flour can be used in cakes to give a nutty flavour.

Cornflour is a farinaceous thickening agent made from the starch of the corn. It is gluten-free. In addition to thickening sauces, it is used in baking in combination with wheat flour for shortbread.

Cornmeal/Maize flour is available in several degrees of fineness. As it does not contain gluten it is usually combined with wheat flour for use in baking.

Masa Harina is a finely milled and sifted cornmeal that has been treated with lime to make it digestible. It is used to make tortillas.

Oat flour is made from ground oat groats, the hulled oat grain. It does not contain gluten. The oat bran is particularly high in soluble fibre.

Polenta is a finely ground cornmeal used in Italian cooking.

Potato flour is the dried starch from potatoes. It is used as a thickening agent and in cakes to impart a light, dry texture. It does not contain gluten, so is a useful addition to gluten-free diets.

Rice is ground into rice flour, a very fine powder, and ground rice, a slightly gritty powder. It is mainly used for thickening puddings and for giving shortbread its characteristic sandy texture. It is particularly useful for gluten-free baking.

Rye flour is milled from a hardy cereal grass. It is a staple of central and eastern Europe, where the soil is too poor and the climate too harsh for growing wheat. Bread made from rye flour is a very dark brown. Although rye flour is high in protein, the type of protein it contains will not form gluten, so bread made from rye flour is dense and heavy. For bread-making, rye flour is best mixed with strong white flour. The type of bread called 'pumpernickel' is made using rye flour and black treacle (or molasses).

Soy flour is made from dried, ground soy beans. It is twice as high in protein as wheat flour. As it has a strong flavour, it is normally used in small quantities as a 'flour improver' to increase the protein content of wheat flour.

Glacé Fruits

Glacé fruits are preserved by cooking and soaking (macerating) in a strong sugar syrup. Small amounts of glacé fruit in a cake mixture, such as *Cherry Cake* (see page 346) have a tendency to sink to the bottom during baking. To avoid this, wash off the syrup, dry thoroughly and coat with flour before adding to the mixture. You can make your own glacé fruits, but this will take about 1 month from start to finish (see recipe below).

Glacé cherries are most commonly used in cakes. The variety most often seen is bright red, having been dyed to produce a rather unnatural colour. Undyed ones are also available and are a much darker red. Yellow and green (dyed) glacé cherries are useful for decoration, as in the *Old-Fashioned Boiled Fruit Cake* (see page 388).

Glacé citron is used in cakes and biscuits. It is made from a semi-tropical citrus fruit that looks like a large yellow-green lemon.

Mixed peel is a mixture of glacé or crystallized orange, lemon and lime peel. It is commonly available in diced form. More expensive glacé and crystallized citrus peel – lemon, orange, lime and grapefruit – is available in large pieces which have a far superior flavour to commercial chopped mixed peel.

Crystallized peel can be made at home. It will take about 1 month from start to finish. The result has a wonderful fresh flavour and will be much more economical than shop-bought peel.

peel of 6 oranges, lemons, limes or grapefruit, or a   340 g | 12 oz granulated sugar
mixture of any of these fruits

1 Wash the fruit well, peel and cut the peel into quarters. Cover with water in a saucepan and simmer for 1½–2 hours until quite tender. (If using grapefruit change the water twice, as the peel is very bitter.) Strain the liquid and make up to 290 ml | 10 fl oz with water.
2 Return the liquid to the pan, add 225 g | 8 oz of the sugar and heat gently until it has dissolved. Bring to the boil and add the peel, then remove from the heat, transfer to a bowl, cover and leave to macerate for 2 days in a cool place.
3 Strain the syrup into a saucepan, add the remaining sugar and dissolve over a low heat. Bring to the boil then add the peel and simmer over a low heat for about 20–30 minutes or until the peel is semi-transparent. Pour into a bowl and allow to cool. Cover and leave in a cool place for 2–3 weeks.
4 Remove the peel from the syrup, place on a wire rack and leave to dry out in an airing cupboard or other warm place where the temperature does not exceed 50°C | 120°F.
5 When the peel has lost its stickiness, store with waxed paper or baking parchment between the layers in a wooden or cardboard box. If put in a plastic box the fruit will go soggy, although it will still be usable.

NOTE: For a crystallized finish, dip the peel briefly in boiling water, drain thoroughly and roll in caster sugar. Leave to dry, then chop and finish as required.

Margarine

Margarine is a fat made from hydrogenated vegetable oil. Hydrogenation is a chemical process that changes a fat that is liquid at room temperature to a fat that is solid. Margarine is dyed to have a similar appearance to butter and the best quality margarine has 80 per cent fat, as does butter. Margarine can be substituted for butter in cakes and pastries. Low-fat spreads and margarines are not suitable for baking.

Milk

Whole milk with a fat content of 3.5 per cent can be used for extra creaminess in recipes.

Semi-skimmed milk, with a fat content of 1.5–1.8 per cent, can be substituted for whole milk in recipes without much noticeable difference.

Skimmed milk has a fat content of 0.3 per cent and is useful for a calorie-restricted diet. It seems watery in comparison to semi-skimmed milk but can be substituted for whole milk and semi-skimmed milk in recipes.

Scalding milk

To help prevent curdling, milk is scalded for many recipes, which means it is heated to just below boiling point. Heat the milk slowly to avoid scorching the casein and whey proteins on the bottom of the pan. Small bubbles form around the edge of the saucepan and steam rises from the milk. This helps to stabilize the milk.

Milk will curdle – that is, separate into hard lumps and runny liquid – when mixed with an acid such as lemon juice or partially cooked onions. It is therefore important that any acidic vegetables, such as onions, are cooked until they are very soft before adding milk.

Do not boil the milk, as this gives it a boiled flavour and results in a skin forming. This skin contains a large number of nutrients, which will be lost if it is discarded.

Storing milk

All milk should be stored in the refrigerator, away from light, as light destroys the vitamin content. Most milk today is sold stamped with a 'use by' date; however, if it is left at room temperature it can spoil before this date.

Nuts

Nuts are dry, edible kernels enclosed in a shell. Nutritionally dense with a high fat content, most nuts are delicious eaten as a snack. In addition they are used extensively in all areas of baking, adding flavour and texture.

Nuts are a good source of energy as they are high in protein, carbohydrate and fat. This means that they are high in calories, except for chestnuts, which are low in fat.

Many nuts are grown for their oil as well as their value as nut meat. These include, particularly, hazelnuts, walnuts, peanuts and almonds.

Most nuts are available all year round, although some are seasonal, such as chestnuts. Nuts that are available before drying are referred to as 'green' or, in the case of walnuts wet. Most are dried, which means they have a longer shelf life. Nuts in their shell should be heavy for their size and should not rattle if shaken. Avoid any with damp, mouldy shells, as they can contain toxins. If shelled, the nuts should be firm, not soft, and have a uniform colour. They go off quickly, so it is best to buy them in small quantities from a shop with a rapid turnover. Stale nuts will taste rancid and bitter. The more processed the nut, the quicker it will go off. Thus almonds in their shells will have a longer shelf life than ground, blanched almonds.

Storing nuts

Green nuts should be used within a few days of purchase or picking. Dried nuts have a low water content and keep well. Store them in an airtight container. Although nuts in their shell keep best of all, they are laborious to use. If packaged, consume by the 'use by' date; otherwise use within 4 months. Nuts can be frozen for up to 6 months. To freeze, double-wrap in plastic bags, excluding as much air as possible.

Toasting nuts

The flavour of nuts is always improved if they are roasted for a few minutes before being used:

1 Heat the oven to 180°C|350°F|gas mark 4.
2 Place the nuts in a single layer in a roasting tin or on a baking tray.
3 Bake for about 6–8 minutes until lightly browned, stirring once or twice. Allow to cool.

Skinning or blanching nuts

The skins of nuts can be bitter, so blanching is usually recommended.

To remove the skin from hazelnuts:

1 Roast at 180°C|350°F|gas mark 4 for 8–10 minutes or until the nuts are light brown.
2 Rub the nuts in a tea towel to remove the skins.

To remove the skins from almonds:

1 Immerse the nuts in boiling water to which 1 tablespoon of bicarbonate of soda per 290 ml|10 fl oz of water has been added.
2 Turn off the heat and allow the nuts to stand for 3 minutes. Drain.
3 Squeeze the nuts out of their skins.
4 Dry in a single layer for 30 minutes or toast as above.

Grinding nuts

Nuts that have been freshly ground will always have a better flavour than purchased ground nuts. A food processor is excellent for this job. Allow toasted nuts to cool before grinding. Place the nuts in a bowl and process in short bursts until the nuts are of a fine, uniform texture, rather like fresh breadcrumbs. Take care not to overprocess the nuts or they will become oily. If overprocessed nuts are used in cakes or pastry they will make them greasy and heavy. If processing for a recipe using sugar, add a couple of tablespoons of the sugar to the nuts while processing. It will absorb some of the oil and help keep the nuts free-flowing. Nuts can also be ground with a small hand-held grater or can be chopped finely with a large cook's knife.

Almonds are related to plums, peaches and apricots, and are grown commercially in many different parts of the world including California, Australia, North Africa, Spain, Italy and Portugal. There are 2 types: sweet and bitter. The most generally available are the sweet variety. Bitter almonds are used to flavour Italian Amaretti biscuits and to make Amaretto liqueur. Bitter almonds are poisonous if eaten raw but the toxins are destroyed by heat when cooked. Their sale is prohibited in some countries.

Almond kernels can be used with the skin on, as in praline, or can be used blanched. Almonds in cakes are used whole, flaked, nibbed or ground. They are probably the most used nut in cake-making and they form the base of marzipan. Ground almonds are sometimes used in place of flour to make moist cakes or biscuits such as macaroons. Their fat content is 50–54 per cent.

Brazil nuts are grown mainly in Brazil and its neighbouring countries. They are very high in fat and therefore go rancid quite quickly. They are large and fleshy, with a high fat content of 65–70 per cent, and can be used chopped or grated in cakes, or whole as part of a decorative topping.

Sweet chestnuts are grown in areas of temperate climate. The sweet chestnut is encased in a prickly green outer skin. Unlike most nuts, chestnuts bought in their shells are always in their fresh, undried state. Because of this they should be eaten quickly.

Preparing chestnuts

To prepare chestnuts, prick the shells and put them into a moderate oven for 10–15 minutes. Failure to prick the skins can cause the nuts to explode, which can be very dangerous. Remove from the oven and allow to cool slightly. Peel off the shell, beneath which the chestnuts are covered with a brown skin. To remove this, blanch the shelled nuts in boiling water for a couple of minutes and then pick off the skin. Alternatively, prick shells, simmer for 10–15 minutes, remove nuts one at a time from the hot water and peel. When this becomes difficult, re-heat the water and continue as before.

Ready-shelled and skinned chestnuts are available in vacuum packs. When used in cakes they are usually in a sweetened purée (available tinned), and they combine particularly well with chocolate. Chestnut flour, which is used in Indian, Corsican, Italian and Spanish cooking, is also available from health-food shops and specialist food stores. Chestnuts have a very low fat content of 2–3 per cent.

Coconut is generally freshly grated or bought desiccated for use in cake-making. Grated fresh coconut is particularly good in cakes and biscuits, its 35 per cent fat content adding good moisture. Coconut milk (available tinned) can be used in place of milk in a recipe to give a coconut flavour, and creamed coconut (available in blocks) can also be used if loosened with a little milk or water. Desiccated coconut is dried, grated fresh coconut, but it loses its flavour if stored for too long. Desiccated coconut is now available in sweetened form, which has a better flavour than the plain version.

Hazelnuts are also known as Barcelona nuts, cob-nuts, filberts or Kentish cob-nuts. Turkey is the largest producer of hazelnuts but the US, Italy and Spain also export them. Once hazelnuts have been roasted they should not be stored for very long. In cakes and biscuits, hazelnuts are used whole, chopped or ground. In breads they are usually used whole. Hazelnuts have an average fat content of 60–65 per cent.

Macadamia nuts are native to the woodlands of Australia but are also grown in California, Hawaii and Latin America. The shells are incredibly hard to crack and the nuts are round, white and quite high in fat (70–75 per cent). They are expensive but they give a special richness to cakes and biscuits, and a few go a long way.

Peanuts are also known as the groundnut or monkey-nut. They are not actually nuts but are legumes. Members of the pea family, they grow underground. Peanuts are very versatile and can be used whole, chopped or as peanut butter in cakes and biscuits. Groundnut or arachide oil is derived from peanuts, which contain 48 per cent fat.

Pecan nuts are native to the US and belong to the hickory family. The nut is inside a smooth shell and is in two halves, rather like a walnut but thinner and more tightly packed. The flavour is sweet and not at all bitter, and, at 70 per cent, pecans are quite high in fat. They are used in cakes, biscuits and sweet pies, as in the classic pecan pie (see recipes pages 125 and 126). They can also be used to replace walnuts in many recipes.

Walnuts are used in a large variety of cakes and biscuits and have an average fat content of 60–64 per cent. They need to be used quickly as rancid walnuts have a very bitter flavour. They combine very well with other flavours, particularly coffee, orange and chocolate.

Oats

Oatmeal is the cut-up or ground oat grain. The coarsest is pinhead, followed by rough, medium, fine and superfine. It is also possible to buy oat bran, which is the ground outer husk of the grain. If a recipe, for example oat cakes, asks for oatmeal and doesn't specify which type, use medium oatmeal.

Porridge oats are rolled oats or oat flakes (sometimes called jumbo oat flakes). They cook more quickly than oatmeal and are used in such recipes as flapjacks.

Sugar

Sugar, a simple carbohydrate, is a chemically stored energy source for all plants and animals. Although many different types of sugar are found in nature, only three are used in the kitchen: sucrose, glucose and fructose. Sucrose, the refined product of sugar cane or sugar beet, is the most widely used form of sugar. Table sugar is 99 per cent pure sucrose. Glucose and fructose are the major components of honey.

Honey is nature's sweetener and has been widely used in both cooking and religious ceremonies for centuries. From 2500 BC, when bees were first domesticated by the Egyptians, honey was widely used as the primary sweetener until the more easily-stored cane sugar became available in the 1500s.

Although the process of pressing the syrup from sugar cane and boiling it until it crystallizes into dark crystals was developed in India as early as 500 BC, sugar didn't arrive in Europe until it was brought from the Americas by Columbus in the 1500s. Sugar cane continued to be the only source of sugar until the nineteenth century, when it was discovered that sugar could be produced from beets. Napoleon promoted the use of sugar beet when the blockade of France during the Napoleonic wars meant that supplies of sugar from cane stopped. Sugar from beets now accounts for 40 per cent of world sugar production.

The process of refining sugar cane produces different kinds of cane sugar and syrups. However, the refining of sugar beet only produces white sugar. Although white and brown sugars often can be substituted for each other in recipes, the different flavours of each type of sugar will affect the flavour of the finished dish. Brown sugars, in particular muscovado sugars, are hydroscopic, which means that they retain moisture. This extra moisture will keep cakes and biscuits softer and moister than if they are made entirely with white sugar.

Brown sugars

Muscovado sugar/Barbados sugar is the darkest of the brown sugars. It has a high proportion of molasses residue and a strong caramel flavour. It is moist and hydroscopic and will make cakes and biscuits soft and moist, improving their keeping qualities. All moist brown sugars should be tightly wrapped in plastic then stored in an airtight container. If they dry out they become hard and unworkable. A piece of damp kitchen paper or a slice of apple can be stored with the sugar for a short time to rehydrate it.

Demerara sugar is more refined than muscovado sugar. Originally made in Demerara, Guyana, it has harder crystals than muscovado sugar. Much of what is sold today as demerara sugar is made by adding a little molasses to white sugar, resulting in a product with an insipid taste. It is used primarily as a sweetener for coffee.

Light brown sugar is further refined sugar with a much smaller proportion of molasses syrup remaining in the crystals. It has a small crystal, a moist texture and a subtle caramel flavour. It is used for biscuits and cakes. Store as for muscovado sugar.

Refined white sugars

These sugars are the result of a manufacturing process which removes the molasses and any impurities. They have been washed with lime and clean syrups to whiten them. All flavours have been removed other than their sweetness. White sugars should be stored in an airtight container to keep them free from moisture.

The white sugars are marketed in different crystal sizes: the size of the crystal will determine, for the most part, its use.

Preserving sugar has the largest crystal and will dissolve the fastest when added to a liquid. It is used for making jams and jellies. Pectin is sometimes added to the sugar, so it is best to check the label.

Granulated sugar has medium-sized crystals. Lump sugar is granulated sugar that has been formed into lumps through the addition of a little moisture. Granulated sugar is used for making sugar syrups as it dissolves readily in liquid.

Caster sugar/Superfine sugar (US) has very small crystals. It is known as caster sugar because it was designed to be used in a sugar caster (shaker). It is the most widely used sugar for baking and meringues. It is also used for making dry caramel and praline.

Golden caster sugar is unrefined, raw cane sugar that has a golden colour and a slight caramel flavour. It can be substituted for white caster sugar in recipes.

Icing sugar/Confectioners' sugar (US) has been ground until it is a white powder. Cornflour is often added to keep it free-flowing. It is used primarily for icings but is also useful for adding to sweet sauces where a granular texture is undesirable.

Treacles, Syrups and Honey

Black treacle/Blackstrap molasses is the dark, sticky syrup with a strong, caramel, slightly bitter flavour that is a by-product of sugar-refining. It is used in gingerbreads and cakes.

Light treacle/Golden syrup is a clear, golden, sticky syrup that is slightly more refined than black treacle. It is used to drizzle on to pancakes and for making treacle sponge, treacle tart and flapjacks.

Glucose syrup is a clear syrup that is used in confectionary to help avoid crystallization. It does not have a flavour other than its sweetness. Golden syrup can be substituted for glucose syrup in most instances, although golden syrup has a slight caramel flavour.

Corn syrups (white and dark) are sugar syrups made from maize in the US. Golden syrup is similar to dark corn syrup and can be used as a substitute. White corn syrup has no flavour other than its sweetness.

Honey Clear or runny honey is used in baking. The flavour of the honey is affected by the flowers the bees have gathered their nectar from, so choose a honey with a flavour you particularly like. Cloudy honey has some of the honeycomb stirred into it, which makes it much thicker than clear honey. Cloudy honey is not usually used for baking.

Measuring syrups and honey
To measure syrups accurately for use in cooking, warm your spoon in very hot water then dry it before measuring the syrup. For larger quantities, warm the syrup gently in a bowl placed over a pan of simmering water.

Vanilla

Vanilla beans are long pods from a tropical orchid plant that is a native of Mexico and is grown in Indonesia, Tahiti and the Indian Ocean islands of Madagascar, Comoros and Réunion, whose name used to be L'Ile Bourbon before the French Revolution. The unripe pods are picked and cured until they are dark brown. Vanilla pods are sold individually or in pairs in containers that look like test-tubes or cigar tins. They can be added to warm or hot milk, cream and sugar syrups to add flavour to custards, ice creams and desserts. To get more flavour, slice the pod in half lengthways and scrape out the sticky black seeds. The seeds can be added to desserts, biscuits, cakes and custards, but they are particularly good in vanilla ice cream, where they separate and disperse throughout. This is an expensive way to use vanilla but the pods, even when cut in half, can be reused until finally they can be put into jars of sugar, which will take up the vanilla flavour.

Vanilla essence comes in 2 forms: the extract from the seed pods and the cheaper synthetic flavouring. It takes up to 6 months to obtain pure vanilla extract. The beans are soaked in alcohol and the extract will eventually be 35 per cent alcohol by volume. Natural vanilla is an extremely complicated mixture of several hundred compounds, whereas synthetic vanilla is derived from phenol. In this book we recommend the use of natural vanilla extract or vanilla pods.

Vegetables

Vegetables such as carrots, parsnips, potatoes, sweet potatoes, pumpkin, courgettes, etc. are sometimes included in cakes, muffins and quick breads, particularly American-style recipes, to add extra texture, moisture and flavour. Carrots and parsnips, for example, have a great deal of natural sweetness which they give to a cake. They are usually included in a recipe either raw and grated or cooked and puréed.

Yeast

Yeast is a single-celled micro-organism of the fungus family, used as a leavening in bread and cakes (see **Bread**, page 477).

Yoghurt

Yoghurt is a fermented milk product made from cultured skimmed or whole milk. It has a fat content of between 0.5 and 4 per cent. It is made by heating milk to about $35°C | 110°F$ then adding *Lactobacillus bulgaricus* and *Streptococcus thermophilus*. The bacteria change the lactose into lactic acid, thickening the milk and giving it a sharp flavour.

Yoghurt is usually suitable for people who have lactose intolerance, because most of the lactose has been consumed by the bacteria. It has a reputation for being a healthy food as the live cultures in certain types of yoghurt are thought to help colonize bacteria in the intestines, aiding digestion. Some yoghurt is sweetened with sugar and flavoured with fruit.

Storing yoghurt

Cultured milk products should be stored, covered in their containers in the refrigerator, according to their 'use by' dates or for up to 2 weeks.

Greek yoghurt is made from either cows' or sheeps' milk. It has a higher fat content than commercial plain yoghurt, usually 10 per cent, because it has been strained and some of the water content has been lost. Sheeps' milk yoghurt has a tangier flavour than that made from cows' milk and is more stable in cooking.

Baking Equipment

Bread, Cake and Tart Tins

Tins should be strong and of a good weight. This prevents them from buckling in the heat of the oven and ensures that the heat is evenly conducted to the food. Most tins are made of aluminium: the thicker the metal the better the quality. Silicone non-stick tins are expensive but probably the best of the non-stick range and a worthwhile investment. Care should be taken when loosening the cakes in these tins with a knife, so as not to scratch the surface.

Some of the tins mentioned below, e.g. sandwich tins and deep cake tins, are available loose-bottomed. These are particularly useful for fragile cakes and cakes that cannot be turned out by inverting the tin.

Size as specified in the recipe is critical. If the tin is too big the mixture will cook unevenly and too fast. If it is too small the mixture may cook too slowly, develop an uneven texture, overflow or burn on the top whilst remaining uncooked inside. Tins for cakes should be between half and two-thirds full before baking.

Angel cake tin/Tube pan
A round, deep pan with a central tube used for baking angel cakes.

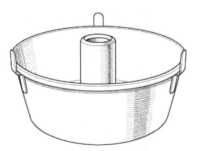

Brioche tin
A fluted, tinned-metal mould for baking brioche dough. They come in a variety of sizes to make large or individual brioches (see *Sweet Yeast Breads and Rolls*, page 591).

Deep cake tin (round or square)

Often used for fruit cakes. Heavy-duty tins are best as often these cakes are baked at a low oven temperature for a long time. It is useful to have a couple of different sizes, about 7.5 cm|3 in deep.

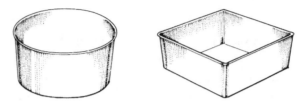

Flan ring

These are metal rings in varying diameters, usually 2.5 cm|1 in in depth. The ring is placed on to a baking sheet before being lined with pastry.

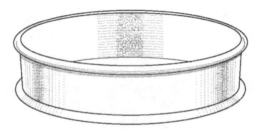

Flexible cooking moulds

Moulds are now available made from a blend of silicone rubber. They withstand temperatures of 220°C|425°F and need no greasing or lining as they are non-stick. They are available in muffin moulds, patty moulds, bread moulds and different shapes and sizes of cake moulds. Baking times for cakes and bread are slightly shorter when these moulds are used. They are becoming more common in the UK and are readily available in France and US.

Fluted tart tin

These tins are available in many different sizes. They vary in depth and are best made from strong metal with a removable base.

Gugelhopf mould or tin

This has a patterned edge and a funnel in the centre to allow the heat to reach the centre of the cake. This tin can also be used for angel cakes, although an angel cake is usually made in a tin with smooth sides.

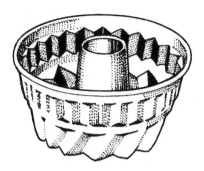

Loaf tin

A deep, rectangular tin used to mould and bake a loaf of bread or loaf cake. These are traditionally sold as 450 g | 1 lb (600 ml | 21 fl oz capacity) or 900 g | 2 lb (1.2 litre | 42 fl oz capacity), to contain dough of these weights. In practice, however, tins that are marketed as the same size can vary dramatically in capacity. For bread-making this is not a problem, but when baking loaf cakes the cooking time will vary depending on the actual size and shape of the tin. It is always best to check for doneness according to the recipe directions.

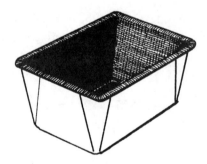

Moule à manqué

A classic French sponge tin, traditionally 20–23 cm | 8–9 in diameter, made from aluminium or tinned steel. The sides are about 5 cm | 2 in deep and slope gently outwards from the base to give the turned-out cake an attractive tapered shape when it is served upside down. It is often used for whisked sponge and Génoise.

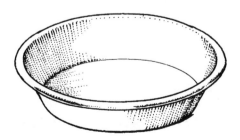

Patty tins/Bun tins

These usually contain 12 moulds, not all of which need to be filled. They are useful for small cakes, tartlets and individual Yorkshire Puddings. For small cakes paper cases can be put into the patty tins to line them. They are available in aluminium or with a non-stick coating. Muffin tins have deeper moulds with a capacity of 100 ml│3 ½ fl oz.

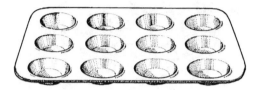

Sandwich tin

This is a shallow tin of which a pair is generally required. For a 2-egg Victoria Sandwich you will need 2 × 15 cm│6 in tins; for a 3-egg sponge 2 × 17 cm│7 in tins.

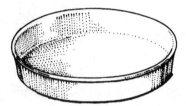

Spring-form tin

The base is separate from the sides, which have a clip to loosen them. These tins, which are useful for large, more delicate cakes and cheesecakes, are sometimes sold with an extra base with a funnel in it. The basic spring-form tin has a smooth, flat base without a central tube.

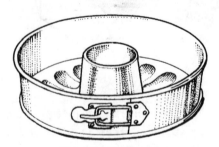

Swiss roll tin

This is usually 2.5 cm│1 in deep and about 35 × 25 cm│14 × 10 in. It should be reasonably heavy-duty as otherwise the heat of the oven will make it buckle and the cake's thickness will be uneven.

A container to make a Swiss roll can also be made using a double thickness of baking parchment and 4 paper clips. To make a paper case, cut a doubled piece of baking parchment 10 cm|4 in longer and wider than a sheet of A4 paper. Fold the parchment paper over over the edges of the A4 paper to form the sides. Remove the A4 paper. Fold the corners in and secure with paper clips. Place on a baking sheet.

Yorkshire Pudding tins
These are now available in a tray with 4 moulds and a non-stick coating. Each mould has a capacity of 100 ml|3½ fl oz. These tins can be used for baking small cakes and muffin tops.

Other Baking Equipment

Baking sheet
It is advisable to have a few of these in different sizes. Lipless ones are good if the article being baked is fragile and needs to be slid rather than lifted off. Lipped baking sheets are useful where there is a chance of an overflow. Sides that are bigger than 1 cm|½ in inhibit the flow of air. Large baking sheets should be at least 2.5 cm|1 in smaller than the oven all the way round. Do not buy thin, flexible baking sheets because they warp in the heat of the oven, which is likely to damage the baking food. Pale, dull sheets are best, as dark or shiny sheets can cause the food to overbrown.

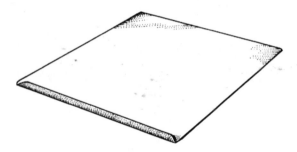

Biscuit/Cookie/Pastry/Scone cutters
These can be bought in sets and should have the top edge rolled to keep the shape rigid and to ensure your fingers don't get cut. They are available with plain or fluted edges and are used to cut pastry and biscuit dough into shapes. Sets of novelty shapes are also available and are particularly useful at Christmas time, when a star shape can be used to put on top of mince pies and gingerbread biscuits can be cut into festive shapes.

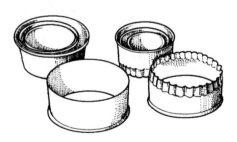

Blind-baking beans
These are usually dried pulses which are used specifically for the purpose. Also available are ceramic beads the size of small beans (see *Blind Baking*, page 44). Uncooked rice is also suitable.

Cake rack/Wire cooling rack
A large rack is most useful. It should be strong and 1–2.5 cm | ½–1 in high to allow air to circulate underneath to cool baked cakes effectively. A circular rack is ideal for cooling larger, heavier cakes as they are less likely to sag in the middle.

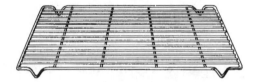

Dredger or sifter
A metal container with a close-fitting lid, perforated with small holes. It is filled with flour, turned upside down and shaken rhythmically to dust a work surface evenly or to coat the surface of food with flour to prevent sticking. It can also be filled with icing sugar or cocoa powder for dusting cakes and pastries.

Grater
Choose a sturdy grater with a selection of hole sizes, from a large half-moon to nail hole, to a fine nutmeg grater. Microplane graters are particularly good.

Grinder
A hand-held grater is excellent for grinding nuts and hard cheeses.

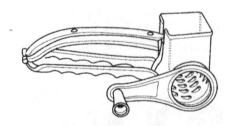

Icing bags
Nylon bags with sewn seams will last longer than plastic ones. However, if they are cheap some of the mixture can escape via the seams. The bags vary in size and it is good to have some of different sizes. They can be boiled to keep them fresh. Disposable plastic bags are

available either in rolls or in packs of 50. They are a good choice as they are hygienic and the end can be cut off to suit the nozzle size. For royal icing it is easier and cheaper to make your own greaseproof paper bags (see page 468).

Marble slab

A tile of marble measuring at least 45 × 60 cm | 18 × 24 in is useful for preparing foods that need to be kept cool during preparation, such as tempered chocolate, pastry and biscuit dough.

Mixing bowls

Wide-rimmed bowls with heavy bases and curved or sloping sides are used for mixing, beating and folding ingredients together. It is useful to buy mixing bowls in a number of sizes, as large bowls are used to beat or fold mixtures or to mix large quantities of ingredients together. Smaller bowls are useful for blending or emulsifying smaller volumes of ingredients. Stainless steel bowls are durable and have a curved lip for easy pouring. Mixing bowls also are available in plastic and toughened glass but are not so hard-wearing.

Non-stick baking liners

These liners are made from a non-stick material and therefore need no greasing. They can withstand temperatures of 260°C | 510°F and are wipe-clean. Various manufacturers make different types of these liners. Some are shaped to line baking sheets and others can be cut to line different size cake tins. They are particularly good for cooking meringues.

Oven gloves

A pair of gloves or gloves attached by a length of material used to protect the hands from hot cooking utensils. They are made of non-heat-conducting material such as layered, woven cotton or foil-lined foam in a cotton cover. Choose good quality, thick gloves as cheaper varieties are often not very effective and quickly fall apart.

Oven gloves made from flame-proof material used by firefighters are now available. They look similar to gardening gloves made from a woven material and are easy to use.

Oven thermometer

A thermometer that can be placed inside the oven to check the temperature is invaluable as ovens vary considerably. All the recipes have been tested in ovens with a separate thermometer.

An instant-read thermometer is a sharp probe with a dial attached to one end for inserting into food. It is useful for testing for doneness of breads and meat.

Palette knife

A palette knife is a long, flexible blade with a rounded end and no cutting edge, for easing under breads, cakes, biscuits and pâtisserie. It is also used for spreading icing on cakes. Off-set palette knives are particularly handy for pastry-making.

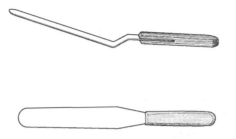

Pastry brush

A pastry brush has soft 2.5 cm|1 in bristles, usually made of nylon, set in a short wooden handle. They are used to brush off excess flour, to apply glazes or to wet the surface of rolled pastry so that smaller pieces of pastry can be stuck on for decoration. Make sure the bristles are securely bound so they don't work loose and stick to the food. It is useful to have a few pastry brushes: one for oil, one for egg and jam glazes and one for using with flour.

Rolling pin

Heavy, wooden rolling pins are the best. Choose one without handles as they are easier to use. Wipe clean after use.

Spatula

Flat, flexible rubber spatulas with a wooden or plastic handle are ideal for scraping out bowls. The rubber can retain odours, so it is best to reserve them for baking.

Whisks

A utensil made of stainless-steel wire bent into loops and held together in a handle. Whisks are used for different jobs and their designs differ accordingly.

Balloon whisk

Balloon whisks are designed specifically to whisk air into egg whites or cream. The flexible wire loops are arranged to produce a short, rounded balloon shape, held together by a wooden or metal handle.

Sauce whisk

A small metal whisk with tight loops of wire set in a spoon shape. It is used to beat and emulsify sauces and to beat lumps out of roux-thickened sauces.

Wooden spoons

Wooden spoons are used to stir and mix cooking foods, as they withstand heat well but do not conduct it. They come in a variety of sizes. Choose long-handled, heavy spoons as they are more practical to use over a high heat and will be more hard-wearing.

Specialist Bread-making Equipment

Baking/Pizza stone

A baking or pizza stone is a disc of unglazed ceramic, about 40 cm | 16 in in diameter, used for baking pizzas and hearth breads (see page 530). It should be placed in the oven before it is turned on so it can heat up with the oven. The uncooked bread or pizza is slid on to the stone using a *peel* (see page 32).

Banneton

A banneton is a basket made from willow twigs used for proving bread. The ridges in the basket leave indentations in the dough, giving the bread a striped appearance. Sometimes the baskets are lined with a floured linen cloth. If not, the basket itself needs to be heavily floured before use. They are available in different sizes and shapes, the most usual being round or oblong.

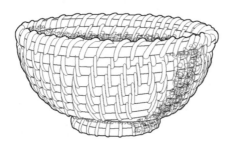

Baguette tins

These tins are made of perforated metal and are usually given a non-stick coating. They have 2 or 3 long, semi-circular moulds in order to support the baguettes during baking. The perforations give the baked baguettes a tell-tale dimpled appearance on their base.

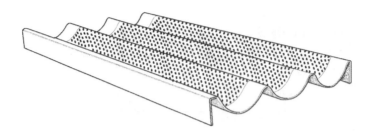

Bench scraper/Dough scraper

This is a rectangular metal tool about the size of an index card, with a grip along one long edge and a sharpened edge opposite the grip. It is used for scraping soft doughs from the work surface and for cutting soft doughs. A fish slice can be used instead.

Cloche

A cloche is a cover used when baking bread in order to imitate the conditions of a hearth oven. They can be obtained from specialist baking suppliers or one can be made by placing a new, unglazed terracotta pot over the dough being baked on the pizza stone. The terracotta pot should be wetted by running under the tap before using. A terracotta plant drip-tray can be used instead of a baking stone, but it is best to line it with baking parchment as the dough is liable to stick.

Dough slashers

Loaves that need to be slashed before baking will require either a single-edged razor blade or a very sharp, serrated knife.

Peel

A peel is the flattened, shovel-like tool used by bakers to slide pizza and artisan breads such as sourdough into the oven. They can be obtained from specialist baking suppliers or one can be approximated by heavily sprinkling a rimless baking sheet with rice flour or polenta. The dough is placed on the rice flour/polenta then is slid on to the hot baking stone once proved.

Plant mister

A plant mister is very useful for creating steam in the oven during bread-baking. Ensure that it never has been used for chemicals.

Specialist Cake-making Equipment

Cake boards
Cake boards should be 5 cm|2 in bigger than the cake, with the exception of the bottom tier of a wedding cake, which should have a cake board 10 cm|4 in bigger. Boards can be iced once the cake has been coated with the first layer of royal icing. The icing will need to be a little thinner than for the cake and once it has been iced do not move the cake until the icing is dry, otherwise it will crack. The sides of the board can be covered with ribbon.

Cake pillars
The best cake pillars are made from plaster of Paris, but plastic ones are more easily found. Square, round and octagonal pillars are available from specialist shops and are usually 7.5 cm|3 in high. Eight pillars are normally required for a 3 tier cake: 4 for each tier, or 5 to support the middle tier and 3 to support the top tier. When designing the decoration for the cake, bear in mind where the pillars are to be placed.

Piping nozzles and icing pipes
Piping nozzles come in plain or star shapes. The nozzles also come in different diameters. They are made of steel or plastic. A piping nozzle will be used in a piping bag to pipe cream, biscuits, choux pastry or meringues.

Icing pipes are smaller and are used with royal icing to decorate cakes. The best pipes are made of strong stainless steel and are unlikely to buckle and lose their shape. Metal pipes give a better definition than plastic. Most makes have numbers on their sides which signify their shape and size. As good quality pipes are expensive, it is advisable to build up a collection gradually. The most useful are writing pipes (thin, medium and thick) and star pipes (small, medium and large). Ribbon and petal pipes are useful once you have become more adept at icing.

Icing scraper and icing comb
An index-card-sized piece of plastic or metal, with a straight edge to smooth the sides of the icing on a cake and a serrated edge to drag through icing on the sides and top of a cake to make parallel lines.

Icing turntable

In general the more you spend on this the better it will be. To ice the heavy bottom tier of a wedding cake it is important to have a strong, stable and sturdy turntable, which will turn smoothly and easily. This will also serve for any other cake.

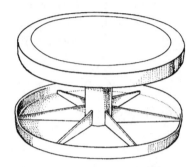

Straight-edge

A stiff metal or plastic ruler with smooth edges used for scraping royal icing on the top of cakes in order to create a smooth surface.

Measuring and Weighing Equipment

It is essential to have accurate weighing and measuring equipment for successful baking, especially when ingredients are measured for precisely calibrated recipes. Measurements are based on weight for dry ingredients and volume for liquids. It therefore is important to have several measuring devices, including scales and measuring jugs as well as liquid and dry measuring cups for American recipes. Always stick to either metric or imperial measurements when making a recipe. Do not swap between the systems.

Useful measuring charts can be found on page 653.

Scales

The 2 main types are spring–mechanism scales and balance scales.

Spring-mechanism scales have a flat tray used as a platform for the measuring bowl. As the ingredients are weighed, a spring mechanism moves the rotating dial marked with metric and imperial measurements. Spring-mechanism scales are also available in electronic models that display the weight on a digital screen. Choose scales that weigh in small units, i.e. 2 g|$\frac{1}{14}$ oz switch easily from metric to imperial and 'zero' easily, so you can weigh different items one after the other in the same bowl.

Balance scales are the more traditional model and use trays and free-weights counter-balance system, where weights are placed on one tray and ingredients are placed on the other until the trays balance, displayed by a marker. Although they can be very accurate, balance scales are more difficult to use than spring-mechanism scales.

American cup measures

American recipes measure dry and liquid ingredients by fractions of a 225 ml|8 fl oz cup. A set of American cups general measures 1 cup down to ¼ cup or 55 ml|2 fl oz.

Measuring jug

Used to measure liquids. Buy a large jug that will hold at least 1 litre of fluid, for measuring large quantities, and a small jug for small quantities, under 290 ml|½ pint. Large jugs are notoriously inaccurate for measuring small quantities. Water and milk can also be measured accurately by weighing as 10 ml = 10 g, etc. It is important that the jug features both metric and imperial measurements. 30 ml|1 oz demarcations are useful for measuring accurately.

Measuring spoons

A set of metal measuring spoons in 1 tablespoon, 1 teaspoon, ½ teaspoon, ¼ teaspoon and ⅛ teaspoon sizes is indispensable for baking. They can be used for measuring small volumes of dry and liquid ingredients. Always measure a level spoonful by running the straight edge of a knife over the rim of the spoon. Ensure that the tablespoon measure contains 15 ml and the teaspoon measure contains 5 ml, etc. Not all measuring-spoon sets sold in the shops are accurate.

Electrical Equipment

Food mixer

A food mixer consists of a motor that powers a rotating head at a selection of speeds, controlled by a dial, above a large metal bowl. A whisk, paddle or dough hook is fitted on to the rotating head to whisk cream and eggs or to beat cake mixtures and knead bread dough. Good for cakes, meringues, whipping cream and bread-making.

Food processor

Food processors consist of a motor that powers a revolving S-shaped blade in the base of a deep bowl fitted with a lid and funnel for dropping in ingredients. The food processor will only work if the lid is correctly fitted, for safety and to prevent spillage. The motor is powered by a selection of buttons so that the blade can chop ingredients both roughly and finely, as well as purée foods, emulsify sauces, liquidize soups and make pastry and bread. Disks can be used instead of the blade to slice, shred or julienne foods. The plastic blade can be used for kneading bread dough.

It is important to select a food processor with a powerful motor and a bowl large enough to hold a double recipe easily. Food processors with the bowl fitted directly over the motor are the most durable.

Hand-held whisk

An electric motor, fitted with plastic or steel whisking attachments. Electric whisks remove the physical effort and time involved when whisking by hand. Buy one with a heavy-duty motor for whisking larger quantities. Used for making cakes, meringues and whipping cream.

Liquidizer/Blender

A motor-driven, four-pronged blade sits in the base of a tall, cylindrical container of clear glass or reinforced plastic. A lid with a plugged hole, for adding ingredients, fits securely on to the container. Liquidizes foods such as soups and sauces to a smooth consistency but it is also used to blend batters, prepare smooth drinks and to emulsify sauces and dressings. Choose a machine with a large container and a lid that fits securely to prevent the food escaping whilst liquidizing is in progress.

Ovens

Conventional ovens

Conventional ovens are those which have a heat source that is either a gas flame at the back of the base of the oven or electric-heated filaments behind the walls of the oven. The oven temperature varies in that the top shelf of the oven is the hottest, while the bottom shelf is the coolest. In the UK, generally, the top shelf is good for pastries and biscuits (the hottest part of the oven), the middle of the oven is best for cakes and the bottom shelf is best for meringues (the coolest part of the oven). American ovens have the heat source in the base so these baking positions need to be reversed if using an oven from the US.

Although pastries, biscuits and meringues can be cooked perfectly in a conventional, fan or Aga oven, cakes, and particularly rich fruit cakes, are best cooked in a conventional oven.

Convection/Fan oven

Convection ovens use internal fans to circulate the air heated by either gas or electricity. This tends to cook foods more quickly and evenly. Convection ovens cook foods more quickly, so temperatures may need to be reduced by $10°C|25°F$ from those recommended for conventional ovens. Convection ovens can be tricky to bake with because the food tends to brown more quickly than it would in a conventional oven. For baking, it is best to choose an oven that has the option of turning the fan off or to cover the food when it becomes brown.

Aga

A heavy iron oven traditionally heated by solid fuel, but also by oil, electricity or gas. The Aga has a hot and cool oven, two covered hotplates and sometimes a warming oven. As the Aga loses heat rapidly when the hotplates are uncovered, it is mainly used for long, slow cooking and simmering in the ovens. Once understood, the Aga can be used successfully for baking and roasting. Although the Aga retains heat very efficiently for cooking purposes, enough heat is often radiated to warm the kitchen efficiently in winter.

Part Two
RECIPES

Types of Pastry

Shortcrust Pastry is a basic pastry made by the rubbing-in method. It is used for savoury flans, such as quiche. This pastry contains a small proportion of lard or vegetable shortening for crispness.

Rich Shortcrust Pastry is similar to Shortcrust Pastry but is made entirely with butter and includes an egg yolk for extra richness. It is used for sweet and savoury tarts.

Sweet Rich Shortcrust Pastry is the same as Rich Shortcrust Pastry with the addition of sugar. It is used for sweet tarts.

Pâte Sucrée is a French pastry enriched with egg yolks and sugar. It has a crisp, biscuit texture and is used primarily for fruit tarts.

Pâte Frollée is a French pastry enriched with egg yolks, sugar and ground almonds. It is used to make a flat base for fresh fruit or for almond biscuits.

Pâte Sablée is a French pastry enriched with egg yolks and icing sugar which is good made into biscuits then used in desserts.

Pâte à Pâte is a French pastry made with a high proportion of butter and enriched with egg yolks. This rich and crumbly pastry is used for encasing savoury meat pâtés.

Flaky Pastry, Rough Puff Pastry and Puff Pastry are all layered pastries, used for pie toppings, cooking meat and fish 'en croûte', feuilletée cases and other pastry cases.

Choux Pastry or Cream Puff Pastry makes light, crisp, hollow buns that are filled to make Profiteroles and Éclairs. When baked in a large ring then filled, the dish is known as a Gougère.

Filo or Strudel Pastry is stretched into thin sheets. Several layers are used to encase both sweet and savoury fillings.

Hot Water Crust is made with a high proportion of boiling water which gelatinizes the starch in the flour. It is used for containing moulded meat pies and has a firm texture.

Pastry

Pastry is a combination of flour, fat and usually a liquid to make a dough which, when baked, is used to hold or cover other ingredients. With a few exceptions, the fat content of pastry is at least half the weight of the flour, making it relatively high in fat. Few pastries are leavened, with the exception of yeasted layered pastries, such as croissants and Danish pastries (see page 162).

For many centuries in the western world, pastry functioned as a container in which meats, pâtés or fruit were baked. Usually the pastry was discarded after baking, having served its purpose of protecting the meat or fruit from the fierce heat of the oven and keeping the contents moist. In the fifteenth century techniques of pastry-making were refined and pastry was promoted, in France particularly, as both an art and a comestible in its own right. Today the maker of pastry, the pâtissier, has a separate section in the restaurant kitchen and has a pâtisserie shop in the high street.

Pastry: Points to Remember

- Work in a cool, dry kitchen. If you are planning to do other cooking it is usually best to make the pastry at the beginning of the cooking session, before the kitchen heats up.
- Use fresh, good quality butter or other fat and flour. The flavour of the fat will have a marked effect on the flavour of the pastry.
- Measure all the ingredients carefully and accurately. The proportions of the ingredients in relation to each other are important to produce the desired results. These proportions are difficult to alter once the paste has been mixed.
- Work quickly and lightly. Overworked pastry can be tough due to gluten development in the flour (see *Flour*, page 11).
- Use the minimal amount of extra flour on your work surface and avoid sprinkling additional flour on to the surface of the pastry. Additional flour can make the pastry dry.
- Heat the oven to the temperature specified in the recipe. Place the oven shelf in the required position in the oven. The sides of a tart case will collapse if the oven temperature is too low. The pastry might burn if it is too high.
- Before baking, chill the pastry until it is very firm so when the pastry is placed in the oven the flour will cook and hold the butter in position before it melts.

Pastry Yield Chart

For those times when you need to use bought pastry instead of making your own, use bought pastry in the following quantities to substitute for the recipes in the book:

Shortcrust Pastry	170 g|6 oz flour quantity	250 g|9 oz bought pastry
	225 g|8 oz flour quantity	340 g|12 oz bought pastry
Rich Shortcrust Pastry	170 g|6 oz flour quantity	300 g|10½ oz bought pastry
	225 g|8 oz flour quantity	400 g|14 oz bought pastry
Cream Cheese Pastry I	170 g|6 oz flour quantity	400 g|14 oz bought shortcrust pastry
Cream Cheese Pastry II	250 g|9 oz flour quantity	450 g|1 lb bought shortcrust pastry
Pate Sucrée	170 g|6 oz flour quantity	400 g|14 oz bought pastry
Flaky Pastry	225 g|8 oz flour quantity	500 g|1 lb 2 oz bought puff pastry
Rough Puff Pastry	225 g|8 oz flour quantity	500 g|1 lb 2 oz bought puff pastry
Puff Pastry	225 g|8 oz flour quantity	500 g|1 lb 2 oz bought puff pastry
Strudel Pastry	285 g|10 oz flour quantity	450 g|1 lb bought filo pastry

Making Pastry

How Much Pastry to Make

To determine the amount of pastry required to line a flan ring the general rule is to subtract 2 from the diameter of the flan ring as measured in inches. This will tell you the amount of flour to use in ounces. Therefore 15 cm|6 in flan ring will require a 115 g|4 oz flour quantity of pastry, an 20 cm|8 in flan ring will require a 170 g|6 oz flour quantity of pastry and so on.

Storing Pastry

Uncooked pastry can be stored in the refrigerator for 24 hours if tightly wrapped and may be frozen for up to 1 month if closely wrapped in a double layer of clingfilm. Baked pastry can be stored in an airtight container for up to three days or frozen for one month. To freeze, wrap tightly in clingfilm then overwrap. Pastry will absorb other flavours from the freezer unless tightly wrapped.

If baked pastry is chilled it will lose its crisp texture. However, once the pastry case has been filled, the filling will determine the method and length of storage.

Preparing a Pastry Case

Specific procedures are common to the types of pastries used for lining tart tins. These are described as follows:

Lifting pastry into a tart tin (a)

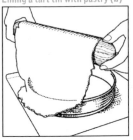

Rolling Out Pastry

To roll out pastry, sprinkle a work surface lightly with flour and rub the rolling pin with flour. Gently tap the surface of the pastry to ridge it, then roll with gentle strokes away from you. Give the pastry a quarter turn to ensure that the pastry is not sticking to the surface and to keep the pastry round. If necessary, use a palette knife to release the pastry from the work surface. Repeat the procedure until the pastry is the desired thickness. Generally, the smaller the pastry case, the thinner the pastry. A thickness of 3 mm|⅛ in, about the thickness of a £1 coin, is recommended for a 15–20 cm|6–8 in tart ring.

To make rolling out pastry easier, place the pastry between two sheets of clingfilm or greaseproof paper. Roll as described above to the desired thickness. After rolling remove the film from one side of the pastry and use the other side to help guide the pastry into place. Chill the pastry until firm then gently remove the uppermost piece of clingfilm or paper.

Lining a tart tin with pastry (b)

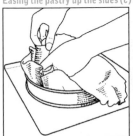

Easing the pastry up the sides (c)

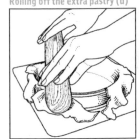

Lining a Tart Tin with Pastry

To line a tart tin, place the tin on to a baking sheet then drape the pastry over a rolling pin. (a) Gently lower the pastry into the tart tin, placing the side that was against the work surface uppermost. Allow the pastry to drape over the sides of the tin. (b) With the side of your finger, ease the pastry into the edges of the tart tin, then gently press the pastry against the side of the tin, taking care to avoid creasing or stretching the pastry. (c)

Use the rolling pin to remove the excess paste by rolling from the centre of the ring to the edge. The sharp edge of the tin will cut through the pastry. (d)

Run the side of your thumb along the top edge of the pastry and the tart tin to straighten the sides of the pastry case and ease the edge from the tin. (e) If the pastry overlaps the edge of the tin it will be impossible to remove the tin after the pastry is baked without breaking the pastry case.

Chill the pastry case until it is firm. This will take up to 30 minutes if the pastry is very soft and the kitchen is warm.

Rolling off the extra pastry (d)

Easing the pastry from the edge (e)

Blind Baking

If a recipe calls for blind baking, this means that the pastry needs to be baked completely before the filling is added. Heat the oven to the required temperature and place the oven shelf in the top third of the oven. Make a *cartouche* by cutting a round of greaseproof paper a little larger than the diameter of the pastry case. Crumple the paper to help it mould to the shape of the pastry, then line the pastry with the cartouche. Once the pastry case has been chilled, fill it with enough baking beans, either small ceramic beans or dried haricot beans used exclusively for the purpose of blind baking pastry cases, to support the sides of the pastry in the oven until they are firm. The base of the pastry case only needs a thin layer of beans, about 1 cm|½ in, to keep it from puffing up.

Place the pastry on the baking sheet in the top third of the preheated oven and bake for about 15 minutes or until the sides of the pastry have cooked through. The sides of the pastry will lose their grey tinge and become opaque and sand-coloured when cooked.

Using a large spoon, remove the beans from the pastry case and transfer them to a bowl to cool. Remove the greaseproof paper and return the pastry to the oven, placing it on the middle shelf. Continue to bake the pastry for about 5–10 minutes until the base of the pastry is a pale golden-brown and feels sandy to the touch. The pastry will have lost its grey appearance.

If the base of the pastry forms a hump it means that some air was trapped underneath the pastry when the tart tin was lined. While the pastry is still warm, gently press the hump with the back of a spoon to flatten the pastry against the baking sheet.

Shortcrust Pastry (Rubbing-in Method)

The basic pastry in the European kitchen is shortcrust pastry (Pâte Brisée), which is made by the rubbing-in method. The texture of good shortcrust can be described as both tender and crumbly, or 'short'.

Basic Shortcrust

This is a basic pastry recipe using half the amount of fat to flour. It is usually used for savoury fillings because of the lard content (see **Savoury Tarts**, page 69). The lard makes the pastry crisper and flakier than a pastry made entirely with butter. For vegetarians a similar pastry can be made by substituting solid vegetable fat for the lard.

FOR A 20 CM|8 IN TART TIN

170 g|6 oz plain flour
a pinch of salt
55 g|2 oz cold butter

30 g|1 oz lard
3 tablespoons ice-cold water

1 Sift the flour with the salt into a large bowl. Cut the fat into 1 cm|½ in pieces and toss into the flour. Cut the fat into the flour until it is the size of small peas, using 2 table knives, scissor-fashion.

2 Rub the fat into the flour by dipping your fingertips into the flour and gently rubbing the small pieces of fat in the flour between the tips of your thumbs and fingers to flatten them and incorporate them with the flour. Pull the flour up above the bowl as you do this to aerate it and keep the mixture cool as it falls back into the bowl. Continue this procedure until the mixture resembles fine breadcrumbs.

3 Shake the bowl occasionally to bring the pieces of fat to the surface of the flour. If at any point during the rubbing-in process the mixture starts to feel greasy or becomes yellow in colour, the fat has become too warm and the pastry will be greasy if it is not chilled. Place the bowl in the refrigerator to chill until the butter is cool and firm.

4 When the mixture resembles fine breadcrumbs, sprinkle half the water over the surface of the flour/fat mixture, then stir quickly with a table knife. The paste will start to form lumps. If any dry flour remains in the bowl, sprinkle a little more water over the dry part only and stir again with the flat blade of the table knife. It is important to add just enough liquid to bring the paste together; too much liquid will result in a hard pastry which will shrink when baked.

5 Using a wiping motion, bring the mixture together with your fingertips and squeeze gently to form an even-textured paste. If it is very soft, flatten it into a disc 1 cm|½ in thick, then wrap it closely with clingfilm and chill for at least 10 minutes. The paste should have the texture of plasticine for easy rolling. Line a tart tin as described above and chill until firm.

6 Heat the oven to 200°C|400°F|gas mark 6.

7 Blind bake the pastry case (see above). Use as required.

Using a food processor to combine fat and flour

The fat can be rubbed into the flour using a food processor, in a fraction of the time. It also means that the fat is kept cool, a real bonus if you have hot hands. Use the steel blade and the pulse button to chop the fat into the flour. The mixture should then be turned into a bowl and rubbed in by hand for about 30 seconds, to coat the flour grains with the fat. This helps to prevent gluten development when the liquid is added.

The liquid should also be added by hand as it is much easier to control the quantity of liquid and it is less likely that the paste will become overworked.

Rich Shortcrust

This pastry is richer and more tender than the Basic Shortcrust above. It has a slightly higher fat content. It can be used with either sweet or savoury fillings.

FOR A 20 CM|8 IN TART TIN

170 g|6 oz plain flour

a pinch of salt

100 g|3½ oz butter

1 egg yolk

2 tablespoons ice-cold water

Make the pastry by the same method described above. The egg yolk must be mixed with the water to avoid making the pastry streaky. Add the combined mixture in place of the water.

Sweet Rich Shortcrust: For a sweet pastry suitable for desserts, add 2 tablespoons caster sugar to the flour in the above recipe after the butter has been rubbed in. Bake as directed for the Basic Shortcrust recipe but be aware that the sugar in the pastry will make it brown more quickly. The edges of the pastry case can be protected with strips of kitchen foil, if necessary.

Wholemeal Pastry

Using a combination of wholemeal and white flours gives a lighter pastry that has all the flavour of wholemeal. If preferred, all wholemeal flour may be used.

FOR A 20 CM|8 IN TART TIN

85 g|3 oz wholemeal flour

85 g|3 oz plain flour

a pinch of salt

100 g|3 ½ oz butter

ice-cold water

1   Sift the flours with the salt into a large bowl and add the bran from the sieve. Rub in the butter until the mixture resembles fine breadcrumbs.
2   Add 1 ½ tablespoons water and mix to a firm dough, stiring first with a table knife and then with one hand. It may be necessary to add more water, but the pastry should not be damp.
3   Chill wrapped, in the refrigerator, for at least 30 minutes before using, or line the tart tin then allow the pastry to relax in the refrigerator before baking.

Sweet Wholemeal Pastry: To make sweet wholemeal pastry, mix in 2 tablespoons sugar once the butter has been rubbed into the flour.

Herb Wholemeal Pastry

FOR A 25–27 CM|10–11 IN TART TIN

115 g|4 oz plain flour

115 g|4 oz wholemeal flour

a pinch of salt

115 g|4 oz butter, chopped

1 tablespoon chopped fresh thyme

ice-cold water

1 Sift the flours with the salt into a large bowl and add the bran from the sieve.

2 Rub in the butter until the mixture resembles fine breadcrumbs. Add the thyme.

3 Add 2–3 tablespoons water and mix, to a firm dough, stirring first with a table knife and then with one hand. It may be necessary to add more water, but the pastry should not be damp.

4 Use as required.

NOTE: Any herb can be used in this recipe. Rosemary should be chopped finely.

Lemon Pastry

FOR A 20–25 CM|8–10 IN TART TIN

170 g|6 oz plain flour

a pinch of salt

1 teaspoon grated lemon zest

30 g|1 oz solid vegetable shortening

55 g|2 oz butter

ice-cold water, to mix

1 Sift the flour with the salt into a large bowl. Add the lemon zest.

2 Rub in the fats until the mixture resembles fine breadcrumbs.

3 Add 1½ tablespoons water to the mixture. Mix to a firm dough, stirring first with a table knife and then with one hand. It may be necessary to add more water, but the pastry should not be damp.

4 Use as required.

Walnut Pastry

FOR A 25–30 CM|10–12 IN TART TIN

225 g|8 oz plain flour

a pinch of salt

115 g|4 oz butter, chopped

140 g|5 oz ground walnuts

45 g|1½ oz sugar

1 egg, beaten

1 Sift the flour and salt into a large bowl. Rub in the butter until the mixture resembles fine breadcrumbs.

2 Stir in the walnuts and sugar and add enough beaten egg (probably half an egg) just to bind the mixture together. Pull together with your fingertips.

3 This pastry is crumbly so it will need to be pressed with your fingers into a tart tin. Chill in the refrigerator for 30 minutes before baking.

Chocolate Pastry

FOR A 20–25 CM|8–10 IN TART TIN

140 g|5 oz plain white flour

30 g|1 oz cocoa powder

a pinch of salt

15 g|½ oz caster sugar

85 g|3 oz butter

1 egg yolk mixed with 2 tablespoons cold water

1 Sift the flour, cocoa powder and salt into a large bowl or food processor. Mix in the sugar. Cut the butter into small cubes and toss into the flour.

2 Cut through the butter with 2 table knives, scissor-fashion, until the butter is the size of small peas. Rub in with your fingertips until the mixture resembles fine breadcrumbs or process in the food processor.

3 Mix the egg yolk with the water then drizzle over the mixture. Stir in with a table knife until the mixture starts to form lumps. Add a little more water if the mixture seems too dry. Bring together with your fingertips into a smooth paste.

4 Roll out on a lightly floured work surface to the thickness of a £1 coin then use to line a tart tin. Chill until firm. Use as required.

Polenta and Parmesan Pastry

FOR A 25–30 CM|10–12 IN TART TIN

170 g|6 oz plain flour

a pinch of salt

85 g|3 oz polenta

140 g|5 oz butter

30 g|1 oz Parmesan or Gruyère cheese, grated

1 egg, beaten

1 Sift the flour, salt and polenta into a large bowl. Rub in the butter until the mixture resembles fine breadcrumbs.

2 Add the cheese and enough of the egg to bind to a dough.

3 Roll into a circle 1 cm|½ in thick between 2 pieces of clingfilm or greaseproof paper. Chill until firm. Use as required.

Polenta and Chive Pastry

FOR A 20 CM|8 IN TART TIN

115 g|4 oz butter
2 egg yolks
140 g|5 oz plain flour
55 g|2 oz polenta

a pinch of salt
2 tablespoons fresh chives, chopped
2 tablespoons cold water

1 Cream the butter and egg yolks together.

2 Add the flour, polenta, salt and chives. Mix together and add the water. Mix to a firm dough.

3 Shape into a flattened circle, wrap in polythene and chill for 10–15 minutes before rolling.

Cream Cheese Pastry (I)

This pastry is used for *Maple Pecan Pie* (see page 126) and *Chocolate Pecan Tassies* (see page 152).

FOR A 23 CM|9 IN TART TIN

115 g|4 oz good quality full-fat cream cheese
115 g|4 oz butter, softened

170 g|6 oz plain flour
a pinch of salt

1 Mix together the cream cheese and the butter until just combined. Do not beat.

2 Sift the flour with the salt over the cream cheese/butter mixture and stir in. The pastry will be very soft.

3 Place the pastry between 2 sheets of clingfilm or greaseproof paper and roll out to the desired thickness. Chill for 15 minutes.

4 Remove one of the pieces of clingfilm or greaseproof paper, then use the other piece to ease the pastry into the tin. Chill until firm then remove the remaining clingfilm or greaseproof paper. If the recipe requires, blind bake as instructed on page 44.

Cream Cheese Pastry (II)

This pastry is very rich and can be a little tricky to handle. Do not allow it to get too warm whilst working with it and always chill both before and after rolling. This makes a firmer pastry than *Cream Cheese Pastry* (I) and can be used for free-form tarts and turnovers.

MAKES 4 TURNOVERS

85 g│3 oz butter   250 g│9 oz plain flour
85 g│3 oz cream cheese   a pinch of salt

1 Cream together the butter and cream cheese.
2 Sift the flour with the salt over the cream cheese/butter mixture and work together.
3 Wrap in clingfilm as a flat parcel and chill for 30 minutes before using.
4 Allow to soften slightly before rolling out to stop it from cracking.

Oatmeal Pastry

FOR A 20 CM│8 IN TART TIN

170 g│6 oz plain flour   55 g│2 oz oatmeal
a pinch of salt   cold water
115 g│4 oz butter

1 Sift the flour and salt into a large bowl.
2 Rub in the butter until the mixture resembles fine breadcrumbs.
3 Add the oatmeal and combine.
4 Add 2 tablespoons of water and mix to a firm dough, stirring first with a table knife and then with one hand. It may be necessary to add more water, but the pastry should not be too wet.
5 Chill for 30 minutes before using, or allow to relax after rolling out but before baking.

Shortcrust Pastry: What has gone wrong when . . .

The pastry has shrunk during baking.
- The pastry wasn't chilled until firm before baking.
- There was too much water in the pastry.
- The oven temperature wasn't hot enough.
- The pastry was stretched when the flan ring was lined.

- The pastry has not been cooked for long enough.
- The uncooked pastry has been kept for too long in the refrigerator.

- The pastry has been overcooked.
- The pastry was overworked and the fat became oily.

- The pastry has too much water added to it.
- The pastry has been overworked and the gluten has been developed.

French Flan Pastries

Pâte Sucrée, Pâte Frollée, Pâte Sablée and Pâte à Pâte are all types of French pastry that are used for tarts and biscuits. These are rich pastries that bake to a thin, crisp, biscuit texture. They are nearly always blind baked (see *Blind Baking*, page 44) before being filled. The first three pastries are sweet and are usually filled with fruit and/or cream or pastry cream (see *Crème Pâtissière*, page 458) or rich, egg-based fillings which require only a very short time in the oven.

The method for making these French flan pastries is described below in the recipe for Pâte Sucrée.

French Flan Pastries: Points to Remember

- Use good-quality butter that has been allowed to come to room temperature. Do not allow the butter to become oily.
- If your hands are warm, touch the pastry as little as possible. Use a food processor if possible.
- Roll the pastry very thinly, about 2 mm | ⅛ in thickness for a large tart case, thinner for individual serving-sized tins and canapé tins.
- Chill the pastry until firm before baking.
- Watch the pastry carefully during baking because it will colour quickly due to the high proportion of butter and sugar.
- For the best flavour, do not allow the pastry to take on any more than the palest colour during baking.
- After removing the baking beans from the pastry case, cover the sides of the pastry with strips of foil if they are beginning to brown.
- Remove the pastry from the tin whilst it is still warm. It will become crisp as it cools and will break if removed from the tin when cool.

Pâte Sucrée

Pâte Sucrée is used for lining tart tins, large or small, that are blind baked then filled with pastry cream and fruit. It is also used for *Tarte au Citron* or *Dark Chocolate Tart* (see pages 117 and 133). It is not suitable for fillings that require a long baking time because it becomes too brown and tastes bitter. It can be cut with a biscuit cutter to make small biscuits to accompany a mousse, fruit salad or ice cream.

FOR A 20–23 CM | 8–9 IN TART TIN

170 g	6 oz plain flour	3 egg yolks
a pinch of salt	85 g	3 oz caster sugar
85 g	3 oz unsalted butter, softened	2 drops of vanilla essence

1 Sift the flour with the salt on to a work surface. Scrape the flour away in the centre to make a circle of flour about 25 cm | 10 in in diameter.
2 Place the butter in the centre of the well, then place the yolks on top of the butter and the sugar and the vanilla on top of the yolks. (a)
3 Using a pecking motion with the fingertips of one hand, combine the butter, yolks and sugar until the mixture is completely smooth. (b)
4 Using a palette knife, scoop the flour on to the butter mixture. (c)
5 Hold the palette knife with each hand at either end and use the side of the palette knife to chop the flour into the butter. Continue chopping until there are no floury patches remaining and the mixture begins to stick together in larger lumps. (d)
6 Gather the pastry into a long narrow rectangle. Use the side of the palette knife again to smear the paste on to the work surface to bring it together into a smooth paste. This smearing is called to *fraiser* the pastry. (e)

Pecking the eggs, butter and sugar (a)

Ensuring there are no lumps of butter (b)

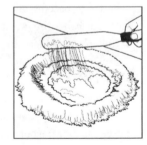

Scooping the flour over the mixture (c)

Chopping the flour into the butter mixture (d)

Fraiser the paste (e)

7 Wrap the pastry in clingfilm, pressing it into a flat disc.
8 Chill until pliable but not sticky before rolling out and lining the tart tin. Chill again until firm.
9 Heat the oven to 190°C|375°F|gas mark 5.
10 Line the pastry case with crumpled tissue paper and sufficient baking beans or uncooked rice to support the sides. Blind bake as directed above, protecting the edges of the pastry with strips of foil if they show signs of browning.
11 Allow the pastry to cool for about 2 minutes before removing it from the tin.

Pâte Frollée (Almond Pastry)

Pâte Frollée is a French flan pastry made with the addition of ground almonds. The almonds make it slightly less crisp than Pâte Sucrée. It is most suited for making a flat pastry disc to be covered with glazed soft fruit or for making biscuits.

FOR A 23 CM|9 IN DISC

115 g|4 oz plain flour
a pinch of salt
45 g|1½ oz ground almonds
85 g|3 oz unsalted butter, softened

45 g|1½ oz caster sugar
1 egg yolk
2 drops of vanilla or almond essence

The method is the same as for Pâte Sucrée, above, up to step 7 except that the almonds are scattered over the top of the flour at the end of step 1.

1 After the paste has chilled roll it into a 23 cm|9 in round, about 1 cm|½ in thick. Place the round on a baking sheet and crimp the edge. Place one forefinger on the surface of the pastry at the edge, without pressing down. Squeeze the pastry on either side of the forefinger, using the thumb and forefinger of your other hand to make a point. Repeat this action all the way round the edge of the pastry.
2 Prick the centre of the pastry through to the baking sheet and within 2.5 cm|1 in of the edge. Chill until firm.
3 Heat the oven to 190°C|375°F|gas mark 5. Bake the pastry until it is pale golden-brown in the centre and slightly darker around the edges.
4 Run a palette knife under the pastry immediately after it is removed from the oven, otherwise it will stick to the baking sheet. After 5 minutes transfer it to a wire rack to finish cooling.

Pàte Sablée

Pâte Sablée is a crisp, delicate pastry, much like very thin shortbread. It is particularly good made into biscuits, then layered with soft fruit and cream to make an elegant dessert.

140 g | 5 oz plain flour
a pinch of salt
115 g | 4 oz unsalted butter, softened

1 egg yolk
55 g | 2 oz icing sugar
2 drops of vanilla essence

Use the same method as for Pâte Sucrée, above.

To assemble into *Sablés au Fraises* (see page 131), make Pâte Sablée biscuits 5 cm | 2 in in diameter. Layer with sliced strawberries macerated with a small amount of raspberry coulis. Decorate with additional coulis, cream and a sprig of mint.

Pâte à Pâte

This is a savoury pastry made by the French method. It is used for tarts with savoury fillings and for raised pies.

FOR A DEEP 20 CM | 8 IN PIE
225 g | 8 oz plain flour
½ teaspoon salt
165 g | 5½ oz unsalted butter, softened

2 small egg yolks
2–3 tablespoons cold water

Make as for Pâte Sucrée, sprinkling the water over the flour after it has been scooped over the butter (step 4) but before you *fraiser* the paste (step 5). Use as required. Do not be tempted to leave out the water because the pastry will be too crumbly when baked.

French Flan Pastries: What has gone wrong when . . .

The pastry is hard and tough.
- It has been overworked at the *fraiser* stage.
- The pastry is overbaked.

The pastry is greasy.
- It has been overworked during the pecking stage and the butter has become too warm.

Layered Pastries: Basic Method

Flaky pastry, rough puff pastry and puff pastry are all known as layered pastries or laminated pastries. This type of pastry, where layers are formed in the paste during making through a process known as rolling and folding, became popular in France during the time of Catherine de Medici. Marzipan pastries made with flaky pastry were reputedly a favourite of Louis XIV.

The Détrempe

The base of each of these pastries is a mixture of flour, a little fat and water, called a 'détrempe'. The détrempe is made with plain flour and is manipulated very lightly to avoid gluten development which would make the pastry tough. The greater part of the fat is incorporated into the détrempe during the rolling and folding process. It is important that the fat be very fresh and cool yet pliable, so that it can be rolled thinly when the pastry is rolled. The fat should not be so warm that the surface of the fat becomes oily. Although the recipes for each type of pastry differ slightly and the method of incorporating of the fat varies, there are several common factors and techniques used to make layered pastries.

Ridging a layered pastry (a)

The Détrempe: Points to Remember

- The détrempe should be even in texture without any wet or dry patches. It should be soft but not sticky.
- The détrempe should be allowed to rest in a cool place for at least 10 minutes and preferably 30 minutes before the butter is added in order to relax any gluten that has been formed.
- The texture of the fat and the détrempe should be the same.

Rolling a layered pastry (b)

Rolling and Folding to Produce Layers

The technique of rolling and folding is used to produce layers of crisp pastry. As they bake, the water in these pastries turns to steam and the air trapped between the layers expands, causing them to separate and rise up. Puff pastry, which is given 6 rolls and folds, will have a total of 730 layers.

Folding a layered pastry (c)

The Technique of Rolling and Folding

1 Gently tap the pastry with the rolling pin to produce slight ridges. (a)
2 Lightly roll the pastry away from you. (b)
3 Run the palette knife under the pastry and tap the sides to keep them straight and the corners square.
4 Alternate the ridging and rolling until the pastry is 3 times as long as it is wide, about 12 cm × 36 cm|5 × 15 in.

5 Fold the bottom third of the pastry up and the bottom third down to make a parcel, rather like a business letter. This is 1 roll and fold. (c)

6 Press the edges of the pastry gently with the rolling pin to seal the air inside the layers.

Rolling and Folding: Points to Remember

- Ridge the pastry gently, then roll lightly along the length of the pastry.
- Use a palette knife to ensure the pastry is not sticking to the work surface and to keep the sides straight.
- Keep the sides of the pastry at right angles to each other, i.e. keep the angle of the corners at 90°.
- During the making of the pastry, only roll along its length, never from side to side.
- During the rolling and folding process the pastry may become noticeably elastic. If this occurs the pastry should be allowed to rest, either in the refrigerator or in a cool kitchen.
- Do not count the encasing of the butter as a roll and fold when making puff pastry.
- Do not give a layered pastry more than 7 rolls and folds or the layers will become too thin and will be liable to break.
- If at any time the fat is oozing out, the pastry should be wrapped closely and refrigerated until the fat has become firmer.
- Rest the pastry between every 2 rolls and folds to allow the gluten in the flour to relax.

Using Layered Pastry

These points should be followed whether the pastry is home-made or bought.

- Once all the rolls and folds have been completed, the pastry can be rolled from side to side and front to back in the same directions the pastry was rolled to make the layers. If a large, round shape is needed, roll the pastry into a square and cut out the round.
- Allow the pastry to sit for 5 minutes after rolling to relax before cutting into shapes.
- When cutting layered pastry, cut straight down through the pastry with a sharp knife. Do not drag the knife along the edge of the pastry as this will seal the layers together.
- Before baking a layered pastry, knock up the sides by lightly cutting into the edge of the pastry in the direction of the layers.
- When glazing a layered pastry, do not let the glaze run down the edges of the pastry, as this will seal the layers together.
- Never gather the pastry into a ball; you will ruin all your carefully made layers. Any leftover pieces can be piled up and brought together with a further roll and fold.

Flaky Pastry

Flaky pastry is used primarily for encasing a filling, as for Eccles Cakes, or to make a crisp pastry shell, as for Cream Horns. The fat is added to the détrempe in small pieces, producing a tender, flaky pastry, which should rise to double its original thickness.

225 g|8 oz plain flour

a pinch of salt

85 g|3 oz butter, cut into 1 cm|½ in pieces

6–9 tablespoons|85–140 ml cold water

85 g|3 oz lard, cut into 1 cm|½ in pieces

1 Sift the flour with the salt into a large bowl. Toss in half the butter.

2 Using 2 table knives, scissor-fashion, cut the butter into the flour until the pieces are the size of a small pea. Use your fingertips to rub the butter into the flour until the mixture resembles fine breadcrumbs.

3 Sprinkle 6 tablespoons of water over the flour and quickly stir with a knife until it starts to clump together. If necessary, sprinkle a little additional water over any dry flour remaining in the bowl.

4 Use your fingers to bring the mixture together into an even-textured paste.

5 This is the détrempe (see page 55). It should have a soft, pliable texture without being sticky. If it is too firm it will be difficult to roll out and the pastry will not rise well. Shape the paste into a rectangle 2 cm|¾ in thick, then wrap closely with clingfilm or greaseproof paper and place in the refrigerator for at least 10 minutes to allow the gluten in the flour to relax.

6 Flour a work surface lightly, then roll the paste into a long rectangle about 12 × 35 cm|5 × 15 in. Dot half the lard over the top two thirds of the paste.

7 Fold the bottom third of the paste up over the middle third, then fold again to make a parcel, rather like folding a business letter. Give the pastry a quarter turn so the closed edge is to your left, like a book. Gently press the open edges of the pastry parcel with the rolling pin.

8 Give the paste a roll and fold as detailed above in *The Technique of Rolling and Folding*. This roll and fold is called a blind roll and fold because no fat has been added to the paste in this roll and fold. Wrap the pastry again and chill it for at least 10 minutes to allow the gluten to relax and the lard to firm slightly.

9 Ridge and roll the paste again so it is 3 times as long as it is wide. Dot the remaining butter pieces over the top two thirds of the pastry. The butter should be pliable so that you can gently smear the lumps on to the paste.

10 Fold the bottom third of the paste up over the middle third, then again over the top third. Press the edges to seal.

11 Rotate the paste a quarter turn and ridge and roll the paste until it is 3 times as long as it is wide. Dot the remaining lard over the top two thirds of the paste and fold as before.

12 Give the paste another roll and fold without adding any fat. If the pastry is streaky with butter, make another roll and fold, but more than one additional roll and fold is not recommended because the layers of dough would then become too thin to keep the layers of fat separate.

To use the pastry for *Eccles Cakes* (see page 143), roll it to a thickness of about 3 mm | ⅛ in. For a pie top, roll the pastry 6 mm | ¼ in thick. The pastry must be chill until firm before baking. It can be glazed with beaten egg or with frothed egg white and sprinkled with a little sugar.

Puff Pastry (Pâte Feuilletée)

Of all the layered pastries, puff pastry is the most exacting and difficult to make. Depending on the use for the finished pastry, the amount of fat added can vary between 140 g | 5 oz and 200 g | 7 oz for a 225 g | 8 oz quantity of flour. The greater the quantity of butter used, the trickier it is to make this pastry.

   Due to the large proportion of butter in puff pastry, unsalted butter is traditionally used because it is thought to be fresher than salted butter and has a milder flavour. However, if you are confident of its freshness, either salted or unsalted butter can be used. Choose butter with a flavour that you like. If using salted butter, decrease the amount of salt added with the flour to 1 pinch.

225 g | 8 oz plain flour

3 pinches of salt

30 g | 1 oz lard

6–9 tablespoons | 85–140 ml iced water

140–200 g | 5–7 oz pliable unsalted butter

1 Sift the flour and the salt into a large bowl. Cut the lard into small pieces and toss into the flour. Rub in the lard with your fingertips or process in a food processor (see *Shortcrust Pastry*, page 44).

2 In one addition, sprinkle 6 tablespoons of the water over the flour. Quickly stir the water into the flour, using the blade of a table knife.

3 As the flour forms into clumps, pull them to one side, leaving any dry flour in the bottom of the bowl.

4 Sprinkle a little additional water over the dry flour to bring it together if necessary.

5 Using your fingers, pull the clumps of moistened flour together and fold the paste over, doubling 4–5 times to make it smooth. The détrempe should be soft but not sticky.

6 Shape the détrempe into a rectangle about 10 × 15 cm | 4 × 6 in. Wrap the détrempe in greaseproof paper or clingfilm and leave in a cool place for about 30 minutes to allow the gluten in the paste to relax and the moisture in the détrempe to become evenly distributed.

7 The butter needs to be the same texture as the détrempe so that it can be easily incorporated into the pastry. The butter should bend without breaking. If it is too firm, place it between 2 sheets of greaseproof paper and bash it with a rolling pin to soften it. The butter should not be oily, however. If the butter looks oily it has become too soft and needs to be chilled.

8 To incorporate the butter, roll the détrempe into a rectangle about 15 × 30 cm | 6 × 12 in. Use a table knife to shape the butter so that is a little less than half the size of the détrempe.

9 Place the butter on one half of the détrempe, leaving a margin of about 1 cm | ½ in around the edge of the détrempe. Fold these edges over the butter, (a) then fold the other half of the détrempe over the top of the butter to encase the butter completely. (b)

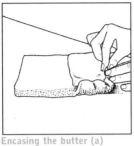
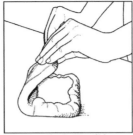

Encasing the butter (a)   Encasing the butter (b)

10 At this point, do not turn the paste. Give it 2 rolls and folds as directed under *The Technique of Rolling and Folding*, (see page 55). If at any time the butter breaks through it has become too soft, so wrap the pastry and chill immediately until the butter is firmer but still pliable. Wrap the pastry again and chill for about 10 minutes. If the paste is chilled for too long the butter will become hard and will break when the paste is rolled and folded again. If at any time you can feel the butter in hard lumps in the paste, leave it at room temperature until the butter softens so that it is pliable.

11 Give the paste a total of 6 rolls and folds, resting in the refrigerator between every 2 rolls and folds, or more frequently if the butter is breaking through. If streaks of butter still show in the paste, give it a 7th roll and fold, but no more than 7 as the layers of flour will become too thin to keep the layers of butter separate.

12 To use the pastry, see *Using Layered Pastry*, (see page 56). Roll to the thickness specified in the recipe and trim the about 1 cm|½ in from the edges to avoid an uneven rise. Shape the pastry as required, chilling well before baking in the top third of the oven, preheated to 200°C|400°F|gas mark 6.

Rough Puff Pastry

Rough puff pastry is a quick method for producing a layered pastry. It is often used for topping a savoury pie. It is important that the butter is cool yet pliable enough to be flattened when pressed. This pastry should rise to double in thickness when baked. The rise is likely to be somewhat uneven.

225 g|8 oz plain flour
a pinch of salt

140 g|5 oz pliable butter, cut into 1 cm |½ in cubes
6–9 tablespoon|85–140 ml ice-cold water.

1 Sift the flour with the salt into a large bowl. Using a table knife, toss the butter cubes with the flour.
2 Sprinkle 6 tablespoons of water over the flour and stir quickly with a table knife so that the paste clumps together.
3 Gather the lumps together with your fingertips, leaving any dry mixture in the bottom of the bowl.
4 If necessary, sprinkle additional water over any remaining dry flour to make it into a soft but not sticky paste.
5 Bring all the paste together and knead it lightly once or twice to bring it together into a smooth, even-textured paste.
6 Form the paste into a rectangle 2 cm ¾ in thick and wrap it in clingfilm or greaseproof paper. Chill for at least 10 minutes to allow any gluten formed to rest and for the paste to achieve an even texture. The butter must not be allowed to become hard or it will tear the paste when it is rolled out.
7 Give the paste a total of 4 rolls and folds following the instructions under *The Technique of Rolling and Folding* (see page 55). If the paste still looks streaky after 4 rolls and folds it can have one more before being used. Allow the pastry to relax for at least 10 minutes before using.

Vol-au-Vents

MAKES 4

225 g | 8 oz flour quantity puff pastry
(see page 58)

To glaze
1 egg, beaten

1 Heat the oven to 200°C|400°F|gas mark 6.
2 Roll out the pastry to 1 cm| ½ in thickness and cut into 4 rounds using as much of the pastry as possible. Place on a baking sheet.
3 Brush the tops of the vol-au-vents with the egg glaze. Use the back of a small knife to knock up the sides of the pastry to help the layers separate when baking.
4 Cut circles about 1 cm |½ in from the edge of the rounds, cutting halfway through the thickness of the pastry. Chill until firm.

5 Glaze the tops of the pastries again and bake in the top third of the oven for 20–25 minutes or until well-risen, golden-brown and firm to the touch.

6 Remove from the oven and carefully cut out the centres, reserving the lids. Scrape as much raw dough from the insides of the vol-au-vents as possible, then return them to the oven for 5 minutes to dry out the insides. Use as required.

Bouchée Cases

MAKES ABOUT 20

225 g | 8 oz flour quantity puff pastry (see page 58)   **To glaze**
1 egg, beaten

1 Heat the oven to 200°C|400°F|gas mark 6.

2 Roll out the pastry to 5 mm|¼ in thickness. With a 4 cm | 1½ in round pastry cutter, stamp it out in rounds. With a slightly smaller cutter, cut a circle in the centre of each round, but be careful not to stamp the pastry more than halfway through.

3 Gently tap the sides of the bouchée cases with a sharp knife to help separate the layers. Chill until firm.

4 Brush the tops with beaten egg, taking care not to get egg on the sides, which would prevent the pastry layers from separating and rising.

5 Bake in the oven for about 12 minutes, until brown and crisp.

6 Take off the pastry 'lids' and scrape out any raw pastry left inside. Return the bouchée cases to the oven for 4 minutes to dry out. Cool on a wire rack.

NOTE: Bouchée cases, if they are to be eaten hot, should be filled either while they are still very hot, with a cooked hot filling, or if they are cooked and cold with a cooked cold filling. Hot fillings will tend to make the pastry soggy during the reheating process. If both filling and pastry go into the oven cold, the pastry will have time to become crisp again before the filling is hot.

Feuilletée Cases

These boxes of puff pastry are classically served filled with poached seafood and a beurre blanc sauce.

MAKES 4

225 g | 8 oz flour quantity puff pastry

To glaze
1 egg beaten with a pinch of salt, then sieved

1 Fold a piece of paper in half, then in half again. Measure from the centre of the folds a point along one folded edge 6 cm from the centre. Along the other folded edge measure a point 5 cm away from the centre. Draw a line to join the two points, then cut along the line. Open out the paper for the template. (a)

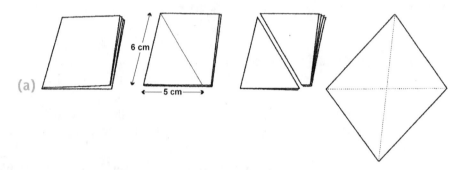

(a)

2 Roll the pastry just big enough to cut 4 cases from it after trimming the edges. When cutting puff pastry, do not drag the knife, cut straight down using a very sharp knife to prevent the layers from sealing together. (b)
3 Glaze the top of the pastry cases, taking care not to let the glaze drip down the sides, which could seal the layers together.
4 Cut a lid in the box using a small sharp knife, cutting halfway through the pastry. (c)

Cutting around template (b)

Cutting the lid (c)

5 Mark the edges of each box in a diamond pattern, using the back of the knife. (d) Mark the lid of the box into a grid pattern. (e)
6 Knock up the edges of the cases with a knife to help separate the layers. (f)
7 Chill the pastry cases until very hard before baking, to set the shape of the cases.
8 Heat the oven to 200°C | 400°F | gas mark 6.

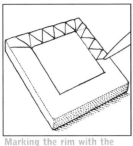

Marking the rim with the back of a knife (d)

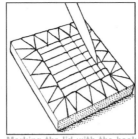

Marking the lid with the back of a knife (e)

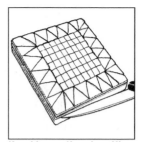

Knocking up the edges (f)

9 Glaze the tops of the pastry cases again before baking.

10 Bake in the top third of the oven for 25–30 minutes. Do not open the oven door until 15 minutes have elapsed as any cool draughts could cause the cases to collapse.

11 Before removing the cases from the oven, gently squeeze the sides to ensure that they are firm. If they still feel flexible, allow the pastry to cook for a further 5 minutes. If the cases are removed from the oven before the sides are set it is likely that they will fall.

12 When the cases are well-risen, golden-brown, with firm sides, remove them from the oven and use a sharp knife to cut out the lids.

13 Scrape the uncooked pastry from the inside the cases, taking particular care to remove it from the corners; use the pointed end of a teaspoon or the tines of a fork for this.

14 Return the cases and the lids to the oven to dry out and crisp. The lids will need to be removed from the oven after a minute or two as they tend to dry out more quickly. The cases should take about 5 minutes to dry out. If fat starts bubbling from the pastry, it is starting to overcook.

Layered Pastries: What has gone wrong when . . .

The pastry has not risen very much and the texture is crumbly rather than flaky.

- The butter broke through when rolling and folding so the layers have been lost.
- The lard was rubbed in too much at the beginning.
- The pastry has been rolled and folded too many times and the layers have been lost.

The layers are visible in the pastry but it has not risen very much.

- The pastry was removed from the oven before the sides had baked enough to hold its shape.
- The oven door was opened during the first 15 minutes of baking.

Fat has seeped out of the pastry.

- The pastry has been overbaked.
- The pastry was not chilled enough prior to baking.

The pastry is tough.

- Too much water was added when making the détrempe.
- The détrempe was overworked.
- The pastry was not allowed to rest enough between rolls and folds.

Choux Pastry

Choux is the light, crisp, hollow pastry used for profiteroles and éclairs. It may be so called because the individual buns look like little cabbages (*choux* in French) but it is possible that the term choux is a corruption of the word *chaud* (French for hot) – the pastry was originally called Pâte à Chaud.

Choux pastry can be used for either savoury or sweet dishes. It is the pastry used for Gougère (see page 101), a French dish consisting of a ring of choux pastry filled with soft fruit and whipped cream, served as a dessert, or with a sauced meat or vegetable preparation in a savoury version. Tiny choux buns with a little cheese added to the pastry make an easy canapé base.

Choux is one of the easiest types of pastry to make, because it involves little handling and is not greatly affected by the temperature in the kitchen. Careful measuring of ingredients and control of oven temperatures and timings will ensure successful results.

The method for making choux pastry is quite unlike that for any other pastry. The water and butter are brought to the boil and then the flour is stirred in to make the base of the pastry, called the *panade*. It is this mixture of flour and water that forms sheets of gluten. Eggs are then beaten into the *panade*, a little at a time, to make a soft, silky paste which should be of a reluctant dropping consistency. This means that a small amount placed on the end of a wooden spoon will fall off if the spoon is sharply jerked, and still hold a mounded shape. It is the eggs that cause the paste to puff up to three times the original size before the flour bakes to a thin, crisp shell.

Choux pastry is baked in a hot oven so that the incorporated water quickly turns to steam, which also leavens the paste. The egg bound to the gluten framework traps the steam to form a pastry-coated bubble. It is important that the oven door is not opened prematurely and that the pastry is not removed from the oven before it is completely firm or there is a danger that the pastry will collapse.

Choux Pastry

85 g | 3 oz butter, cut into small cubes
220 ml | 7½ fl oz water
105 g | 3¾ oz plain flour

a pinch of salt
3 eggs, beaten

1   Place the butter and the water in a saucepan over a low heat and allow the butter to melt.
2   Meanwhile, add the salt to the flour and sift the flour 3 times on to greaseproof paper to aerate it and ensure it is free of lumps.
3   When the butter has melted, turn the heat to high to bring the mixture to the boil.
4   As soon as the water comes to a fast boil, so that the liquid climbs the sides of the pan, turn off the heat and quickly tip the flour into the liquid.
5   Using a wooden spoon, stir the flour into the liquid until a firm, smooth paste has formed. Beat the paste until it comes away from the edges of the pan, forming a ball. Do not beat it any longer than it takes to come away from the sides of the pan or the baked choux will have a cracked, crazy-paving appearance.

6 Tip the paste on to a cold plate and smooth it into a thin layer. Leave it to cool for about 10 minutes, until it feels just warm to the touch.

7 Return the paste to the saucepan and beat in the eggs, a tablespoonful at a time, beating well after each addition.

8 Continue adding the egg until the mixture is a reluctant dropping consistency. The mixture will hold its shape and have a slight sheen.

9 The paste can now be used immediately or it can be refrigerated for 24 hours if tightly covered, or frozen for up to 1 month.

10 To bake choux buns or éclairs, heat the oven to 200°C|400°F|gas mark 6. For buns, pipe or spoon walnut-sized lumps on to lightly greased baking sheets. Bake in the top third of the oven for 20–30 minutes.

11 When the buns are golden-brown and firm, remove them from the oven. Make a small hole in the underside of the buns using the tip of a small knife. Lay the buns on the baking sheets so the holes are uppermost and return the buns to the oven for a further 5 minutes to allow the interiors to dry and crisp. Remove from the oven and place on a wire rack to cool completely before filling.

Piping an éclair

Using a piping bag with a 1 cm|½ in plain nozzle, pipe a line of choux pastry to the length of the finished éclair. Without stopping, pipe back over the line twice more, to create a flattened 'S' shape. Push down any pastry that is sticking out with a dampened finger.

Profiteroles and éclairs can be filled with whipped double cream sweetened with icing sugar or with *Crème Pâtissière* (see page 458). The filling can be flavoured with vanilla, coffee or chocolate.

Piping an éclair

Choux Pastry: What has gone wrong when . . .

The choux pastry was risen badly.

- The oven door was opened before the pastry had set or the pastry was removed from the oven too soon.
- Not enough egg was beaten into the pastry.
- The *panade* was too warm when the egg was added.

The surface of the choux pastry is crazed with many small cracks.

- The *panade* was beaten for too long after the flour was added.

Strudel Pastry

This type of pastry, which is similar to filo pastry, can be traced back to the Romans. It is made sheet by sheet and contains little fat. Although excellent pastry can be purchased, it is fascinating to make. Whether making your own pastry or using the bought filo, work quickly and keep the pastry covered and/or brushed with oil or melted butter because it will dry out quickly and crack.

285 g|10 oz plain flour
a pinch of salt
1 egg

150 ml|5 fl oz water
1 teaspoon oil

1 Sift the flour with the salt into a large bowl. Make a well in the centre.
2 Mix together the egg, water and oil. Stir enough of the liquid into the flour to make a soft dough.
3 Knead by throwing the paste on to a work surface from shoulder height for 15 minutes until it loses its stickiness and is so elastic that it can be stretched from one hand to the other to a length of about 50 cm|20 in.
4 Wrap the paste in clingfilm and leave at room temperature for at least 30 minutes for the gluten to relax.
5 Make the filling before stretching the dough.
6 When ready to use the pastry, cover a work surface measuring about 1.5 × 1 m| 60 × 39 in with kitchen paper or tea towels liberally dusted with flour, to keep the pastry from sticking to the surface.
7 Divide the paste in half. Keep one piece covered whilst rolling the other piece into a round of about 1 cm|½ in thickness.
8 The stretching is best done by 2 people working together. Before stretching the dough, remove any watches or rings. Pull the paste gently, using the backs of your hand and the tips of your fingers to stretch it. When it becomes transparent in the centre, place it on the floured surface and continue to stretch it until it is thin enough to read newsprint through. Take care not to tear the paste. If it does, it can be patched with a little extra paste. Work quickly so the paste doesn't become too dry.
9 To use, trim off the thick edges with scissors. Brush the pastry with oil or melted butter and use immediately.
10 Repeat the process to stretch the other piece of dough.

Strudel Pastry: What has gone wrong when . . .

The pastry will not stretch to a transparent sheet.
- The dough was too dry.
- The dough was not worked for long enough.
- The dough was not rested for long enough.

The pastry pulls into shreds.
- The dough has been stretched a little then left to stand. The gluten strands break down and the pastry cannot be pulled out thinly.

The pastry tears when stretched.
- A certain amount of tearing is likely. It usually will not show when the pastry is used. Take greater care when stretching the pastry.

The pastry cracks when it is rolled up.
- The pastry has become too dry. Keep it brushed with oil or butter or covered with clingfilm.

Hot Water Crust Pastry

Hot water crust pastry was originally made as a container for a raised meat pie. It was discarded before eating, but the recipe given overleaf produces pastry that is good enough to eat. It is used in *Veal and Ham Raised Pie* (see page 87).

Hot Water Crust: What has gone wrong when . . .

The paste is stretchy.
- Too much liquid was added to the flour.

The pastry is stiff, hard to mould and cracks when cooked.
- Not enough liquid was added to the flour.

The pastry is tough.
- Too much liquid was added to the flour.
- The pastry was overworked.

Hot Water Crust

40 g | 1¼ oz butter
40 g | 1¼ oz lard
85 ml | 3 fl oz water
225 g | 8 oz plain flour

½ teaspoon salt
1 egg, beaten

To glaze
1 egg, beaten

1 Wrap a soufflé dish approximately 15 cm | 6 in in diameter with clingfilm and then a double band of baking parchment secured with a paper clip.

2 Cut the butter and the lard into small pieces and place with the water in a small saucepan. Bring to the boil.

3 Meanwhile, sift the flour with the salt into a large bowl and make a well in the centre. Place the egg in the well and cover over with the flour.

4 Pour the boiling water and melted fat around the edge of the bowl and quickly stir in with a table knife.

5 Knead lightly until the pastry loses its streakiness and becomes smooth. Wrap in clingfilm and chill for 20–30 minutes.

6 Reserve one third of the pastry for the lid. Keep wrapped in clingfilm.

7 Roll the remaining pastry to 5 cm | 2 in larger than the base of the dish.

8 Invert the dish, place the pastry over the base and gently press the pastry down over the sides of the dish to a thickness of 6 mm | ¼ in. (a) Take care that the corners of the pastry do not become too thin.

9 Chill the pastry, uncovered, until firm.

10 Carefully remove the pastry from the dish. Place it on a baking sheet and wrap the baking parchment around the outside of the pastry to support it. Secure with a paper clip. Remove the clingfilm from inside the pastry. (b)

11 Fill the pastry with the meat.

12 Dampen the inside of the top edge of the pastry then roll the remaining pastry 6 mm | ¼ in thick. Place the pastry lid on top of the meat, bringing the lid pastry up the edge of the outer pastry. Trim to a depth of 1 cm | ½ in. Save the trimmings for decoration. Crimp the edge of the lid. (c)

  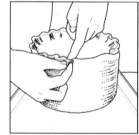

Drape the pastry over the inverted dish (a)

Remove the clingfilm (b)

Crimp the lid (c)

13 Glaze with beaten egg and decorate the top of the pie with the pastry trimmings. Glaze again and chill.

Savoury Tarts and Flans

Savoury tarts and flans are very versatile. They can be served as a main course for lunch or supper, accompanied by a salad and crusty bread. Smaller portions or individual tarts make an excellent first course.

A quiche is a classic savoury tart, the filling for which consists of an egg custard made with eggs, cream and/or milk and seasonings, mixed with other cooked ingredients and baked in a pastry case. Other dairy products such as crème fraiche, double cream or ricotta cheese can be used in place of the milk/cream mixture and set with eggs. Filling ingredients may include sautéed diced ham or bacon, fish or shellfish and vegetables such as sweated onions, mushrooms, blanched spinach, asparagus or broccoli. Strong-flavoured cheeses such as Gruyère or Cheddar are also added to flavour the custard. The filling ingredients should provide contrasting texture and flavour, without overpowering the delicate egg custard.

Do not make holes in the pastry case or prick the base as the filling, particularly if it is liquid, will leak out on to the baking tray. If possible, after blind baking allow the pastry to cool down before adding the filling, as this will help to stop the pastry base going soggy.

Quiche Lorraine

SERVES 4–6

170 g | 6 oz flour quantity rich shortcrust pastry (see
   Pastry, page 46)

For the filling

15 g | ½ oz butter
1 onion, finely chopped
115 g | 4 oz streaky bacon, diced
225 ml | 8 fl oz milk
225 ml | 8 fl oz single cream

3 eggs, beaten
3 egg yolks
85 g | 3 oz strong Cheddar or Gruyère cheese, grated
salt and freshly ground black pepper

1 Roll out the pastry and use to line a flan ring 20 cm | 8 in diameter, 4 cm | 1½ in deep. Chill until firm.

2 Heat the oven to 200°C | 400°F | gas mark 6. Blind bake the pastry case (see *Pastry*, page 44).

3 Melt the butter in a small saucepan and stir in the onion. Cover with a dampened piece of greaseproof paper and a lid. Cook over a low heat until the onion is soft but pale.

4 Remove the lid and the paper and stir in the bacon. Cook over a medium heat until the bacon is cooked through but not browned.

5 Remove the onion and the bacon from the pan with a slotted spoon and place in a sieve to drain away excess fat. Allow to cool.

6 Mix together the milk, cream, beaten eggs and yolks. Pass through a sieve to remove any eggy threads.

7 Stir in the onion and bacon mixture and the cheese. Season to taste.

8 When the pastry has cooked through, remove from the oven and turn the oven temperature down to 150°C | 300°F | gas mark 2.

9 Using a slotted spoon, remove the solids from the filling mixture and distribute evenly over the bottom of the baked pastry case. Pour enough of the cream mixture into the pastry case to fill it to the top.

10 Bake in the lower third of the oven for about 40 minutes until the filling has set and does not wobble. It should not take on a brown colour.

11 If the pastry is still very pale, the flan ring can be removed and the quiche returned to the oven for a further 5 minutes.

12 Serve warm or cold.

Spinach and Pine Nut Quiche

SERVES 4–6

170 g | 6 oz flour quantity rich shortcrust pastry (see
Pastry, page 46)

For the filling

30 g | 1 oz butter

1 medium onion, finely chopped

150 ml | 5 fl oz milk

150 ml | 5 fl oz single cream

3 eggs, beaten

340 g | 12 oz spinach, cooked, drained and finely
chopped

55 g | 2 oz strong Cheddar or Gruyère cheese, finely
grated

3 tablespoons pine nuts, toasted

freshly grated nutmeg

salt and freshly ground black pepper

1 Heat the oven to 200°C | 400°F | gas mark 6.

2 Roll out the pastry and use to line a 20 cm | 8 in diameter 4 cm | 1½ in deep flan ring. Chill until firm. Blind bake (see *Pastry*, page 44).

3 Turn the oven to 170° C | 325° F | gas mark 3.

4 Melt the butter in a small saucepan and stir in the onion. Cover with a piece of dampened greaseproof paper and a lid and cook over a low heat until the onion has softened. Allow to cool.

5 Mix together the milk, cream and eggs. Pass through a sieve to remove any eggy threads.

6 Stir the onion, spinach and cheese into the egg and cream mixture. Season to taste with nutmeg, salt and pepper.

7 Use a slotted spoon to remove the solids from the mixture and place in the baked pastry case. Pour over enough egg and cream mixture to fill the pastry case. Scatter the pine nuts over over the top.

8 Bake for 30–40 minutes in the lower third of the oven or until set. Serve warm or cold.

Smoked Haddock and Spinach Quiche

SERVES 4

For the pastry
85 g | 3 oz plain wholemeal flour
85 g | 3 oz plain white flour
¼ teaspoon salt
30 g | 1 oz vegetable fat
55 g | 2 oz butter
ice-cold water

For the filling
285 g | 10 oz smoked haddock fillet, skin on
150 ml | 5 fl oz milk
570 ml | 1 pint water
100 g | 3½ oz fresh young spinach
15 g | ½ oz butter
3 eggs, beaten
150 ml | 5 fl oz double cream
290 ml | 10 fl oz milk
55 g | 2 oz strong Cheddar cheese, grated
1 tablespoon fresh Parmesan, grated
ground paprika pepper
salt and freshly ground black pepper

1 For the pastry: sift the flours and the salt into a bowl or food processor. Add the bran in the sieve back to the flour. Cut the vegetable fat and butter into small cubes and toss into the flour.

2 Cut through the butter and flour with 2 table knives scissor-fashion, then rub in with your fingertips until the mixture resembles fine breadcrumbs, or pulse until smooth in the food processor.

3 Drizzle 1 tablespoon water over the flour and stir through with a table knife until the mixture comes together, adding more water if necessary. Use to line a 20 cm | 8 in diameter, 4 cm | 1½ in deep tart tin. Chill until firm.

4 Heat the oven to 200°C | 400°F | gas mark 6. Line the chilled pastry case with grease-proof paper and baking beans.

5 Bake the pastry for 15 minutes then remove the beans and paper and bake for a further 10 minutes, or until cooked through.

6 For the filling place the smoked haddock in a sauté pan and cover with the milk and water. Cover with greaseproof paper and cook over a medium heat for 10–15 minutes, or until the fish has turned opaque and flakes easily. Alternatively the fish can be placed in an ovenproof dish with the milk and water, then covered and baked in the oven until done (about 10 minutes).

7 Use a fish slice to remove the fish from the poaching liquid and place on a plate to cool.

8 Wash the spinach and remove any large stems. Heat the butter in a large sauté pan until golden-brown, then tip in the spinach and cook, stirring, until the spinach wilts. This will take about 30 seconds. Drain the spinach in a sieve.

9 Combine the eggs, cream and milk and pass through a sieve to remove any eggy threads. Stir in the cheeses then season to taste with salt and pepper.

10 Break the smoked haddock into large chunks, removing any skin and bones.

11 Place a thin layer of the egg mixture in the bottom of the cooked pastry case, then scatter the fish over it.

12 Pat the spinach dry on kitchen paper then drape over the fish. Pour over the remaining egg mixture and sprinkle with the paprika.

13 Turn the oven temperature to 170°C | 325°F | gas mark 3 and bake the quiche for 45–50 minutes, or until the centre has set. Use a table knife inserted in the centre to test that the custard is set.

14 Serve warm or at room temperature on the day it is made.

Caramelized Onion and Thyme Quiche

SERVES 6

170 g | 6 oz flour quantity rich shortcrust pastry (see **Pastry**, page 46)

For the filling

55 g | 2 oz butter

1 kg | 2¼ lb onions, sliced

1 teaspoon caster sugar

4 eggs

200 ml | 7 fl oz milk

200 ml | 7 fl oz single cream

4 tablespoons finely grated Parmesan cheese

2 teaspoons chopped fresh thyme, salt and freshly ground black pepper

1 Heat the oven to 200°C | 400°F | gas mark 6.

2 Roll out the pastry and use to line a 20 cm | 8 in diameter, 4 cm | 1½ in deep flan ring. Chill until firm, then blind bake (see **Pastry**, page 44).

3 Turn the oven temperature down to 170°C | 325°F | gas mark 3.

4 Melt the butter in a large sauté pan and stir in the onions. Cover with a dampened piece of greaseproof paper and cook over a low heat until softened, then remove the paper and stir in the sugar. Continue to cook until the onions are golden-brown. This can take up to 1 hour.

5 Beat the eggs in a large bowl and stir in the milk and cream. Strain through a sieve to remove any eggy threads, then stir in the cheese and thyme. Season to taste with salt and pepper.

6 Using a slotted spoon, remove the solids from the filling and place them in the bottom of the pastry case. Pour over enough of the egg and cream mixture to fill the pastry case to the rim.

7 Bake in the bottom third of the oven for about 40 minutes or until set.

8 Serve warm or cold.

Leek and Bacon Flan with Mustard

170 g | 6 oz flour quantity rich shortcrust pastry (see *Pastry*, page 46)

For the filling

55 g | 2 oz rindless bacon, finely chopped
15 g | ½ oz butter

300 g | 10 oz leeks, white part only, washed and finely chopped
1 egg, beaten
150 ml | 5 fl oz double cream
3 tablespoons freshly grated Parmesan cheese
2 tablespoons good quality coarse-grain mustard
salt and freshly ground black pepper

1 Roll out the pastry and use to line a 20 cm | 8 in flan ring. Chill until firm.
2 Heat the oven to 200°C | 400°F | gas mark 6.
3 Blind bake the pastry case (see *Pastry*, page 44). Remove from the oven and reduce the temperature to 170°C | 325°F | gas mark 3.
4 Cook the bacon, in its own fat, until it begins to brown.
5 Add the butter and leeks. Cover the mixture with a piece of dampened greaseproof paper and cook over a low heat until the leeks are soft. Drain well and allow to cool.
6 Mix together the egg, cream and cheese. Add the leeks and bacon. Season to taste with salt and pepper.
7 Spread a thin layer of mustard on the base of the flan and then pour in the filling. Bake in the oven for 40–45 minutes or until the filling is set.
8 Serve hot or at room temperature.

Courgette and Cheese Flan

SERVES 4

225 g | 8 oz flour quantity shortcrust pastry (see *Pastry*, page 44)

For the filling

375 g | 12 oz courgettes
55 g | 2 oz butter
1 clove of garlic, crushed
grated zest of 1 lemon

2 teaspoons lemon juice
2 level tablespoons flour
290 ml | 10 fl oz milk
115 g | 4 oz Cheddar cheese, grated
1 egg, separated
2 tablespoons fresh white breadcrumbs
fresh chives, to garnish
salt and freshly ground black pepper

1 Heat the oven to 190°C | 375°F | gas mark 5.
2 Make the pastry and line a 23 cm | 9 in flan ring. Chill, then blind bake (see *Pastry*, page 44).
3 Wash, trim and slice the courgettes. Place on a wire rack and sprinkle with a teaspoon of salt. Leave to degorge for 30 minutes to 1 hour, then rinse well.

4 Melt the butter in a large frying pan, then add the crushed garlic, lemon rind, courgettes, salt and pepper. Sauté for 2 minutes until the courgettes start to soften. Add the lemon juice, then lift out the courgettes and put them on a plate.

5 Stir the flour into the buttery juices in the pan, adding more butter if necessary. Cook the flour for a minute and add the milk gradually. Once all the milk is combined bring the sauce to the boil, reduce the heat and simmer for 2 minutes. Remove from the heat and add three quarters of the cheese. Season to taste with salt and pepper, then beat in the egg yolk.

6 Whisk the egg white stiffly, fold it into the sauce and then spread the mixture into the baked flan case. Place the courgettes on top and sprinkle with the remaining cheese, mixed with the breadcrumbs. Bake in the oven for 20–25 minutes or until set.

7 Serve hot or at room temperature, garnished with chopped chives.

Pea, Broad Bean and Goats' Cheese Flan

SERVES 4

170 g | 6 oz flour quantity shortcrust pastry (see *Pastry*, page 44)

For the filling

115 g | 4 oz broad beans
55 g | 2 oz peas
100 g | 3½ oz soft goats' cheese

2 tablespoons chopped fresh chives
1 egg
150 ml | 5 fl oz milk
2 tablespoons double cream
1 tablespoon grated Parmesan cheese
salt and freshly ground black pepper

1 Heat the oven to 200°C | 400°F | gas mark 6.

2 Roll out the pastry and line a 20 cm | 8 in flan ring. Chill, then blind bake (see *Pastry*, page 44). Reduce the oven temperature to 150°C | 300°F | gas mark 2.

3 Put the broad beans into boiling water and simmer for 5 minutes, then drain and refresh with cold water. Remove and discard the outer skins.

4 Put the peas into boiling water and simmer for 3 minutes, then drain and refresh with cold water.

5 Mix the goats' cheese, chives, egg, milk and cream together, then season with salt and pepper.

6 Place the peas and broad beans in the cooked pastry case, then pour over the goats' cheese and egg mixture. Scatter the Parmesan cheese over the top and bake for 25 minutes or until the filling has set.

7 Serve hot or cold.

Roasted Red Onion and Feta Cheese Tart

SERVES 6

170 g|6 oz flour quantity wholemeal pastry (see
  Pastry, page 46)

For the filling

2 red onions

2 tablespoons olive oil

4 rashers streaky bacon

3 eggs, beaten and sieved

150 ml|5 fl oz double cream

150 ml|5 fl oz crème fraiche

85 g|3 oz Gruyère or Cheddar cheese, grated

85 g|3 oz feta cheese, cut into 1 cm|½ in chunks

salt and freshly ground black pepper

1 Line a 25 cm|10 in diameter, 2 cm|¾ in deep tart tin with the pastry. Chill until firm.

2 Heat the oven to 200°C|400°F|gas mark 6.

3 Remove the skins from the onions and discard. Slice the onions into 8 from top to bottom. Place on a baking sheet in a single layer and drizzle with the olive oil. Place the bacon on the baking sheet with the onion.

4 Bake the bacon for 10–15 minutes then remove and crumble into small pieces. Continue baking the onions for a further 10–15 minutes or until soft right through and beginning to char on the edges.

5 Blind bake the pastry (see **Pastry**, page 44).

6 Mix together the eggs, double cream, crème fraiche and the Gruyère or Cheddar. Season to taste with salt and pepper.

7 Scatter the onions, bacon and feta cheese over the bottom of the pastry case then pour over the egg and cream mixture.

8 Place the tart on a baking sheet in the bottom third of the oven and turn the oven temperature down to 170°C|325°C|gas mark 3. Bake for 30 minutes or until the custard is set in the centre. Serve warm or at room temperature.

Potato, Olive and Onion Tart

SERVES 6–8

225 g|8 oz flour quantity shortcrust pastry (see
  Pastry, page 44)

For the filling

340 g|12 oz large new potatoes

2 tablespoons olive oil

2 onions, sliced

2 cloves of garlic, crushed

1 tablespoon chopped fresh thyme,

1 tablespoon chopped fresh oregano

85 ml|3 fl oz double cream

3 tablespoons tapenade (olive paste)

12 black olives, pitted and halved

1 tablespoon capers, rinsed

115 g|4 oz Gruyère cheese, grated

salt and freshly ground black pepper

1 Roll out the pastry and line a 27 cm | 11 in diameter, 2.5 cm | 1 in deep tart tin. Chill for 20 minutes. Heat the oven to 200°C | 400°F | gas mark 6.

2 Blind bake the pastry case (see **Pastry**, page 44) for 15 minutes, then remove the paper and beans and return to the oven for a further 5 minutes.

3 Scrub the potatoes and cook in boiling salted water until they are just cooked. Drain and pour cold water over them to stop the cooking and cool them down. Once cold, cut into slices approximately 1 cm | ½ in thick.

4 Heat the oil in a saucepan and add the onions. Stir and cover with a lid. Allow them to soften gently over a medium heat for about 15–20 minutes, stirring frequently to ensure they don't burn. Add the crushed garlic and cook for a further few minutes. Add the thyme, oregano and cream and remove from the heat. Season with salt and freshly ground black pepper.

5 Spread the tapenade over the pastry base. Scatter over the olives and capers. Cover with the sliced potatoes and then spread the onion mixture on top. Sprinkle the grated cheese evenly over the surface.

6 Place in the centre of the oven for 20–25 minutes or until the cheese has melted and the top is golden-brown. Serve warm or hot.

Artichoke and Green Olive Pie

SERVES 6–8

225 g | 8 oz flour quantity puff pastry (see **Pastry**, page 58)

For the filling

10 large globe artichoke hearts, cooked

30 g | 1 oz butter

10 shallots, finely diced

2 small cloves of garlic, crushed

1 teaspoon chopped fresh thyme

1 teaspoon chopped fresh sage

4 tablespoons dry white vermouth or white wine

150 ml | 5 fl oz double cream

170 g | 6 oz green olives, pitted and chopped

salt and freshly ground black pepper

To glaze

1 egg, beaten

1 Heat the oven to 190°C | 375°F | gas mark 5.

2 Cut the artichoke hearts into 5 mm | ¼ in cubes and cook slowly in the butter, with the shallots, garlic, thyme and sage, for 5 minutes.

3 Add the vermouth or wine and reduce by half, by boiling. Add the cream and reduce to a coating consistency. Stir the sauce every so often to prevent it from sticking.

4 Add the olives and season to taste with salt and pepper. Leave to cool.

5 Roll out the pastry and use half to line a 3 cm | 1¼ in deep 20 cm | 8 in tart tin. Pile in the artichoke and olive mixture and cover the pie with the remaining pastry.

6 Brush with beaten egg and bake in the centre of the oven for 15–20 minutes.

Aubergine Tart

225 g|8 oz flour quantity lemon pastry (see **Pastry**, page 47)

a pinch of chopped fresh thyme
a pinch of chopped fresh rosemary
a pinch of cayenne pepper
4 eggs

For the filling

1 medium (340 g|12 oz) aubergine, sliced
6 tablespoons olive oil
2 medium onions, thinly sliced
3 cloves of garlic, crushed
6 large tomatoes, peeled and chopped

150 ml|5 fl oz single cream
85 g|3 oz Cheddar cheese, grated
30 g|1 oz Parmesan cheese, freshly grated
12 black olives, pitted
salt and freshly ground black pepper

1 Sprinkle the aubergine slices lightly with salt and leave in a colander for 30 minutes to extract any bitter juices.

2 Roll out the pastry and use to line a tart tin about 27 cm|11 in in diameter. Chill until firm to allow the pastry to relax and prevent shrinkage during baking.

3 Heat the oven to 200° C|400° F|gas mark 6.

4 Blind bake the pastry case (see **Pastry**, page 44). Remove from the oven and turn the temperature down to 170° C|325° F|gas mark 3.

5 Rinse the aubergines well and pat dry. Fry them in about 2 tablespoons of the oil until golden-brown. Drain on kitchen paper.

6 Heat the remaining oil, add the onions and fry until lightly browned. Add the garlic and fry for a further 30 seconds. Add the tomatoes, thyme, rosemary, cayenne, salt and pepper. Cook for 5–6 minutes or until it forms a thick pulp. Allow to cool.

7 Beat the eggs and stir in the cream and cheeses. Mix with the tomato mixture. Season to taste with salt and pepper.

8 Spoon half the mixture into the baked tart case, cover with the fried aubergines and then spoon in the remaining tomato mixture with the olives. Bake in the oven for 40 minutes, or until set. Serve hot or at room temperature.

Watercress, Rocket and Feta Tart

SERVES 4

225 g|8 oz flour quantity shortcrust pastry (see **Pastry**, page 44)

2 eggs, beaten
150 ml|5 fl oz milk
4 tablespoons Greek yoghurt
2 tablespoons grated Parmesan cheese

For the filling

15 g|½ oz butter
2 shallots, chopped
100 g|3½ oz feta cheese

15 g| ½ oz watercress leaves (no stalks), chopped
15 g |½ oz rocket, chopped
salt and freshly ground black pepper

1 Heat the oven to 200°C| 400°F| gas mark 6.
2 Roll out the pastry and line a 20 cm | 8 in tart tin. Chill for 20 minutes and then blind bake (see **Pastry**, page 44). Remove and turn the oven down to 150°C| 300°F| gas mark 2.
3 Melt the butter in a small saucepan and add the chopped shallots. Cook gently over a low heat for 10 minutes. Do not allow them to brown.
4 Crumble the feta cheese and add the eggs, milk, yoghurt, half the Parmesan cheese, watercress, rocket, cooked shallots, salt and pepper.
5 Pour into the prepared pastry case. Sprinkle over the remaining Parmesan cheese. Bake for 30–35 minutes or until set. Serve hot or cold.

Metboukha Tartlets

This rich and spicy tomato and green pepper 'marmalade' has its origins in North Africa and can be served in tartlet cases as a first course or in smaller ones as a canapé.

SERVES 4

170 g|6 oz flour quantity shortcrust pastry (see
    Pastry, page 44)

For the filling
2 green peppers
340 g|12 oz tomatoes
2 tablespoons sunflower oil

1 red onion, chopped
1 clove of garlic, crushed
1 red chilli, chopped
½ teaspoon paprika
100 ml|3½ fl oz red wine
1 teaspoon sugar
salt

1 Heat the oven to 200°C| 400°F| gas mark 6.
2 Roll out the pastry and use to line patty tins. Blind bake for 10–15 minutes (see **Pastry**, page 44).
3 Heat the grill and cut the peppers into quarters, removing the seeds. Grill them skin-side up until they are blistered and blackened. Place in a plastic bag to cool. The steam will help loosen the skins. Remove the skins. Bring a pan of water to boil, add the skinned peppers and cook for 3 minutes. This should remove any bitterness. Drain and cut into small dice.
4 Peel the tomatoes and chop finely.
5 Heat the oil in a medium saucepan. Add the onion and sweat gently for 10 minutes. Add the garlic, peeled diced peppers, chopped red chilli and paprika and cook for 2 minutes.
6 Add the chopped tomatoes, red wine, sugar and a little salt. Bring to the boil and cook for 2 minutes. Reduce the heat, cover and cook gently for 30 minutes.
7 Remove the lid and evaporate any liquid. Taste and add more salt or sugar as necessary.
8 Divide the mixture between the tartlet cases and serve warm or cold.

Four Onion Tart with Polenta Pastry

SERVES 4

200 g│7 oz flour quantity polenta and chive pastry, (see **Pastry**, page 49)

For the filling

12 shallots, peeled and cut in half

2 tablespoons olive oil

1 onion, sliced

2 cloves of garlic, crushed

8 spring onions, trimmed, washed and sliced

1 egg

1 egg yolk

100 ml│3½ fl oz milk

55 ml│2 fl oz double cream

55 g│2 oz mature Cheddar cheese, grated

salt and freshly ground black pepper

1 Heat the oven to 200°C│ 400°F│ gas mark 6.

2 Roll out the pastry to line a 20 cm│8 in tart tin. Chill for 10 minutes. Blind bake for 15 minutes (see **Pastry**, page 44).

3 Meanwhile put the shallots in a roasting tin and add 1 tablespoon of olive oil. Turn the shallots over to coat them with oil. Put in the oven for 15–20 minutes or until they are softened and slightly caramelized. Remove from the oven and allow to cool. Turn the oven down to 170°C│ 325°F│ gas mark 3.

4 Heat the remaining tablespoon of olive oil in a saucepan, add the sliced onion, cover with a lid and sweat gently for 20 minutes or until soft but not coloured. Add the garlic and sliced spring onions. Cook for a further 5 minutes.

5 Mix together the egg, egg yolk, milk, cream, salt and pepper.

6 Put half the cheese on the base of the cooked pastry. Arrange the onions and shallots on top, then add the rest of the cheese. Pour over the egg and milk mixture. Bake for 20 minutes or until set. Serve hot or cold.

Red Onion and Pepper Polenta Tatin

SERVES 6–8

170 g│6 oz flour quantity polenta and Parmesan pastry (see **Pastry**, page 48)

For the topping

55 g│2 oz butter

900 g│2 lb red onions, thinly sliced

2 tablespoons white wine

2 cloves of garlic, crushed

1 tablespoon soft light brown sugar

¼ tablespoon chopped fresh rosemary

3 large red peppers

1 tablespoon capers, rinsed and drained

4 anchovies, slivered

1 Heat the oven to 190°C│375°F│gas mark 5.

2 To make the topping melt 30 g│1 oz of the butter in a heavy, ovenproof frying pan. Add the onions and cook, covered, for 15 minutes, until they begin to soften. Add the wine, garlic, rosemary and half the sugar and cook for 20 minutes. Turn up the heat and reduce, by boiling rapidly, until the liquid has evaporated and the onions start to fry. Turn on to a plate to cool.

3 Heat the grill to its highest setting. Cut the peppers into quarters, then remove the stalks, membrane and seeds. Grill the peppers, skin side uppermost, until the skin is black and blistered. Place in a plastic bag to cool. The steam will help loosen the skin.

4 Melt the remaining butter in a non-stick 20 cm|8 in frying pan, stir in the remaining sugar and remove from the heat. Peel the peppers and arrange them in the pan in a daisy pattern. Place the capers and anchovies between the peppers and cover with the cooked onions, taking care not to dislodge the peppers.

5 Place the pan over a high heat until the butter and sugar start to caramelize, which may take 5 minutes. Remove the pan from the heat and place it on a baking sheet.

6 Lay the polenta pastry on top of the onions and press down lightly. Bake for 25 minutes. Allow to cool slightly, then invert the pan over a plate and serve warm.

Mushroom and Ricotta Tart

SERVES 4–6

170 g|6 oz flour quantity herb wholemeal pastry
  (see *Pastry*, page 47)

For the filling
250 g|9 oz small flat mushrooms
1 clove of garlic, crushed
2 sprigs of thyme
250 g|9 oz ricotta cheese

3 eggs, beaten
45 g|1½ oz Parmesan cheese, grated
1 tablespoon chopped fresh parsley
1 tablespoon chopped fresh thyme
salt and freshly ground black pepper

1 Heat the oven to 200°C|400°F|gas mark 6. Blind bake the pastry (see *Pastry*, page 44).

2 Wipe any soil from the mushrooms using damp kitchen paper then remove the stems.

3 Place the mushrooms top side down on a baking sheet. Sprinkle with the garlic and season with salt and pepper. Bake for 10–15 minutes or until the mushrooms are tender and the juices have been given up and evaporated. Set aside.

4 Reduce the oven temperature to 180°C|350°F|gas mark 4.

5. Put the ricotta into a bowl and gradually beat in the eggs. Stir in the Parmesan and herbs, then season with salt and freshly ground black pepper.

6 Place half the ricotta mixture in the bottom of the baked tart case, then top with the mushrooms. Cover with the remaining ricotta mixture.

7 Place on a baking sheet and cook for 30 minutes or until set. Serve warm.

Wild Mushroom Tart with Oatmeal Pastry

SERVES 4

170 g|6 oz flour quantity oatmeal pastry (see
   Pastry, page 50)

For the filling

10 g|½ oz dried porcini mushrooms
150 ml|5 fl oz milk
15 g|½ oz butter
1 shallot, chopped

1 clove of garlic, crushed
115 g|4 oz oyster mushrooms, sliced
115 g|4 oz shiitake mushrooms, sliced
2 tablespoons chopped fresh sage
2 tablespoons chopped fresh parsley
2 eggs, beaten
2 tablespoons crème fraiche
salt and freshly ground black pepper

1 Heat the oven to 200°C| 400°F| gas mark 6.

2 Soak the dried porcini in the milk and leave for 15 minutes.

3 Roll out the pastry and line a 20 cm|8 in tart tin. Chill for 20 minutes and blind bake for 15 minutes or until the pastry is cooked (see *Pastry*, page 44). Reduce the heat to 170°C| 325°F| gas mark 3.

4 Melt the butter in a sauté pan, add the shallot and garlic and cook over a gentle heat for 5 minutes.

5 Drain the porcini mushrooms, reserving the milk. Turn up the heat and add the oyster mushrooms, shiitake mushrooms and porcini mushrooms to the pan and cook until they have softened, ensuring the shallot doesn't burn. Add the sage and parsley, then remove from the heat and allow to cool.

6 Mix the eggs with the porcini mushroom milk. Add the crème fraiche and season with salt and pepper. Add the cooled mushrooms.

7 Pour the filling into the baked pastry case and place on a baking sheet in the oven. Bake for 20–25 minutes or until the filling is just set in the middle.

8 Serve hot or at room temperature.

Savoury Pies

The pie descends from Roman times, when fish or meat was sealed into a paste made from flour, water and oil. The pastry cases were called 'coffyns,' 'coffers' or 'boxes' of pastry. They kept the filling moist and were discarded once cooked. In the Middle Ages cooks began to make pastry using flour, butter and lard. This was moulded into containers for the filling. By Elizabethan times a lot of fruit, dried fruit, spice and honey was added to the meat or fish, and savoury and sweet pies were difficult to tell apart. This development can be seen in modern-day mince pies, where all that is left of the meat is suet; in some mincemeat recipes suet is left out altogether.

Pies became more and more elaborate, with hand-raised pies decorated with gold leaf or painted with saffron. Some pies were made not for eating but as an amusement for diners. The pie would be brought to the table and cut open, and out would fly live birds. Hence the nursery rhyme about 'four and twenty blackbirds baked in a pie'.

The Georgians (1714–1836) made very good pastry and many of their recipes were recorded. At this time the pastry became an integral part of the dish. Later still, savoury pies were decorated with pastry leaves and flowers on the top, while sweet pies would be left plain so that it was easy to tell the difference between them when put side by side in the larder.

The pastries used in this section vary and the fillings can go towards producing a filling winter meal or a light and summery buffet-table pie. Strictly speaking a pie should always enclose the filling, either in pastry or sealing it in a dish.

When making a hot pie, ensure the filling is cold before topping it with pastry otherwise the underside of the pastry is likely to be soggy. Make slits in the pastry to allow the steam to escape, or use a 'pie-bird' to elevate the pastry above the filling. Remember to chill the pie until the pastry is firm before baking it. See page 42 for equivalent weights of bought and home-made pastry.

Steak and Kidney Pie

SERVES 4

225 g | 8 oz flour quantity rough puff pastry (see
   Pastry, page 60)

For the filling

675 g | 1½ lb chuck steak
225 g | 8 oz ox kidney
oil or dripping
1 onion, finely chopped

30 g | 1 oz plain flour
425 ml | 15 fl oz brown stock
1 tablespoon chopped fresh parsley
salt and freshly ground black pepper

To glaze

1 egg, beaten

1 Trim away the excess fat from the steak and cut the beef into cubes about 2.5 cm | 1 in square. Cut the kidneys into smaller cubes, discarding any sinew.

2 Heat the oil or dripping in a frying pan and fry a few cubes of beef and kidney at a time until browned all over, putting them into an ovenproof casserole as they are done. Once all the meat has been browned and removed, fry the onion in the same fat until soft and brown.

3 Stir in the flour and cook for 1 minute. Gradually add the stock, stirring continuously and scraping any sediment from the bottom of the pan. Bring to the boil, then simmer for 1 minute. Pour over the meat in the casserole, season with salt and pepper and simmer over a low heat until the meat is tender, about 2 hours. Add the parsley.

4 If the sauce is too greasy, skim off the fat; if it is too thin, remove the meat to a pie dish and boil the sauce rapidly until syrupy. Pour the sauce over the meat and leave until completely cold.

5 Heat the oven to 200°C | 400°F | gas mark 6.

6 Roll out the pastry to ¼ cm | ⅛ in thickness. Cut a long strip just wider than the rim of the pie dish, brush the lip of the dish with water and press down the strip.

7 Brush the strip with water and lay over the sheet of pastry. Press it down firmly. Cut away any excess pastry.

8 Cut a 1 cm | ½ in hole in the centre of the lid and disguise with a leaf-shaped piece of pastry (the hole is to allow the steam to escape).

9 Decorate the top with more pastry leaves. Brush all over with egg. Chill until the pastry is firm.

10 Bake in the oven for 30 minutes, or until the pastry is well-risen and golden-brown. Serve hot.

VARIATION

Steak and Mushroom Pie: Mushrooms can be substituted for the kidneys, if desired. Use 170 g | 6 oz field mushrooms cut into cubes. Fry as for the kidneys.

Flat Salmon Pie

SERVES 6

450 g│16 oz flour quantity pâte à pâte (see **Pastry**,
  page 54)

For the filling

55 g│2 oz Gruyère or Cheddar cheese, grated
30 g│1 oz Parmesan cheese, freshly grated
85 g│3 oz unsalted butter, melted
55 g│2 oz fresh white breadcrumbs
225 g│8 oz smoked salmon, chopped

2 tablespoons chopped fresh dill
1 large clove of garlic, crushed
140 ml│5 fl oz soured cream
lemon juice
freshly ground black pepper

To glaze

1 egg, beaten

1　Roll out the pâte à pâte into 2 rectangles, one to fit a Swiss roll tin, the other slightly larger. Chill for 20 minutes.
2　Heat the oven to 200°C│400°F│gas mark 6.
3　Lightly grease a baking sheet. Put the smaller rectangle of pastry on it and prick all over with a fork. Chill until firm. Bake for 25 minutes or until cooked. Loosen it on the baking sheet so that it does not stick. Leave to cool.
4　Mix together the Gruyère or Cheddar cheese, Parmesan, melted butter and breadcrumbs. Sprinkle half this mixture all over the pastry, leaving 1 cm│½ in clear round the edge.
5　Scatter the smoked salmon on top of the cheese mixture, then scatter over the dill.
6　Mix the garlic with the soured cream and spread all over the salmon. Season well with pepper but not salt.
7　Sprinkle evenly with lemon juice and top with the remaining cheese mixture. Wet the edge of the bottom piece of pastry lightly with beaten egg and put the top sheet of pastry in place, pressing the edges to seal it well.
8　Use any pastry trimmings to decorate the pie and brush all over with beaten egg.
9　Bake until the pastry is crisp and pale brown, about 25 minutes.
10　Serve hot or cold.

NOTE: Off-cuts and trimmings of smoked salmon are cheaper than slices and do well for this dish.

VARIATION

Flat Ham Pie: Substitute chopped cooked ham for the smoked salmon and chopped chives for the fresh dill.

Curried Chicken and Ham Pie

SERVES 4

225 g | 8 oz flour quantity wholemeal pastry (see
  Pastry, page 46)

For the filling

55 g | 2 oz butter

1 onion, chopped

2 teaspoons curry paste

½ teaspoon ground turmeric

45 g | 1½ oz plain flour

290 ml | 10 fl oz stock, reserved after cooking the
  chicken

150 ml | 5 fl oz creamy milk

1 teaspoon chopped fresh parsley

1 teaspoon chopped fresh mint

a pinch of crushed cardamom seeds

a pinch of dry English mustard

a squeeze of lemon juice

2 hard-boiled eggs, chopped

115 g | 4 oz ham, cut into 1 cm | ½ in dice

1 × 1.35 kg | 3 lb chicken, poached,
  boned and cut into large chunks

salt and freshly ground black pepper

To glaze

1 egg, beaten with a pinch of salt and a teaspoon of
  water and sieved

1 Heat the oven to 200°C | 400°F | gas mark 6.
2 Melt the butter in a saucepan and add the onion. Cover with a dampened piece of greaseproof paper and a lid. Cook gently until soft but not coloured.
3 Stir in the curry paste and turmeric and cook for 1 minute. Remove from the heat.
4 Add the flour, then return to a low heat and cook for 1 minute. Remove the pan from the heat. Add the stock gradually and stir well. Return to the heat and bring slowly to the boil, stirring continuously until the sauce is thick and shiny.
5 Add the milk and stir again until the sauce returns to the boil.
6 Add the parsley, mint, cardamom, mustard, salt and pepper. Simmer for 2–3 minutes.
7 Taste, adding more salt if necessary, and add the lemon juice. Allow to cool.
8 Stir in the hard-boiled eggs, the ham and the chicken. Pour the mixture into a pie dish.
9 Roll the pastry on a floured work surface to a rectangle about 5 mm | ¼ in thick.
10 Cut a band of pastry slightly wider than the edge of the pie dish. Brush the rim of the dish with water and press on the band of pastry. Brush with a little beaten egg or water and lay the pastry lid over the pie. Cut away any surplus pastry from the sides.
11 Press the pie edges together and mark a pattern with the point of a small knife, or pinch with the fingers into a raised border. Shape the pastry trimmings into leaves for decoration. Make a small hole in the pastry to allow the steam to escape.
12 Brush the pastry with beaten egg and decorate with the pastry leaves. Brush again with egg. Chill until the pastry is firm.
13 Bake for 30–35 minutes until golden-brown. Serve hot, straight from the oven.

NOTE: If the pie is not to be baked as soon as it has been assembled, it is essential that the curry sauce and the chicken are both completely cold before they are combined. Keep the pie refrigerated or frozen until ready to bake. If frozen, thaw in the refrigerator before baking.

Veal and Ham Raised Pie

The pastry case should be made at least 1 hour in advance of the filling. The finished pie must be left overnight for the aspic to set.

SERVES 4

450 g | 1 lb flour quantity hot water crust pastry (see **Pastry**, page 68)

For the filling
675 g | 1½ lb boned shoulder of veal
115 g | 4 oz ham
1 onion, chopped
2 tablespoons chopped fresh parsley
salt and freshly ground black pepper

For the jelly
290 ml | 10 fl oz aspic, flavoured with tarragon

To glaze
1 egg, beaten

1 Make the pastry and mould the pastry case (see **Pastry**, page 68).

2 Heat the oven to 190°C | 375°F | gas mark 5.

3 Cut the veal and ham into 1 cm | ½ in cubes. Trim away most of the fat and all the skin and gristle. Season with salt, pepper, the onion and parsley.

4 Fill the pie with the seasoned meat, making sure you press it firmly into the corners, then cover with the remaining pastry. Press the edges together. Make a neat hole in the middle of the lid. Secure a lightly buttered double piece of greaseproof paper around the pie with a paper clip.

5 Bake for 15 minutes. Reduce the oven temperature to 170°C | 325°F | gas mark 3. Bake for 1 further hour. When 30 minutes' cooking time remains, remove the paper collar and brush the pastry evenly all over with beaten egg. Remove the pie from the oven and allow to get quite cold.

6 Warm the aspic enough to make it just liquid but not hot. Using a funnel, fill up the pie with jelly. Plug any holes in the pastry with butter. Allow the liquid to set slightly and then add more, until you are sure that the pie is completely full. This will take some time. Leave in the refrigerator for the jelly to set.

NOTE: This is the classic English pie. However, a pâte à pâte crust can be used for a richer, more tender crust (see **Pastry**, page 54).

Cold Game Pie

This pie takes 2 days to complete.

SERVES 6–8

450 g | 1 lb flour quantity pâte à pâte (see **Pastry**, page 54)

For the filling

1 grouse
1 partridge
1 pigeon
2 hare joints
115 g | 4 oz venison
1 large carrot
2 large onions
2 sticks celery

115 g | 4 oz butter
4 tablespoons oil
290 ml | 10 fl oz red wine
1 litre | 1¾ pints white stock, made with chicken bones
4 bay leaves
a little fresh thyme
parsley stalks
30 g | 1 oz powdered gelatine
salt and freshly ground black pepper

To glaze

1 egg, beaten

1 Split the birds in half. Cut the venison into small cubes. Chop the carrot, onions and celery roughly.

2 Heat about 1 tablespoon each of butter and oil in a heavy frying pan, and when the butter is foaming, add the chopped vegetables. Keep the heat at a medium temperature – enough to fry and brown the vegetables without burning the butter. Keep turning the vegetables to get an even colour all over. When they are done, lift them out with a slotted spoon and transfer to a large, deep saucepan.

3 Add more oil and butter to the frying pan and brown the venison, the hare and finally the birds. If the bottom of the pan becomes sticky and brown, deglaze it with half a glass of the wine or stock: pour in the liquid and boil it, stirring with a metal spoon or fish slice and scraping the bottom of the pan to loosen the sediment. Tip this liquid in with the browned ingredients and continue frying the meats.

4 When all the ingredients are browned and transferred to the deep saucepan, deglaze the pan again, pouring the juices in with the meats. Add the remaining wine, the stock, and, if necessary, a little water (the ingredients must be just covered with liquid). Add the herbs, salt and pepper. Cover with a lid and simmer for 1½ hours or until everything is tender.

5 Strain off the liquid and leave until completely cold. Skim thoroughly, then transfer to a saucepan and boil to reduce to about 570 ml | 1 pint. Add the gelatine to the liquid and leave to soak.

6 When the meat is cool enough to handle, remove all the bones from the birds and hare and cut the flesh into small pieces (about the size of the cubes of venison). Discard the cooked vegetables, the bay leaves and parsley stalks. Let the meat cool completely.

7 Heat the oven to 190°C|375°F|gas mark 5. Lightly grease a 1.8 kg|4 lb pie mould or a loose-bottomed cake tin.

8 Roll two thirds of the pastry into a round big enough to cover the base and sides of the mould or tin. Dust the pastry with a little flour. Now fold it in half, away from you. Place one hand on the fold of the semicircle and, with the other, gently push and pull the sides so that you form a 'bag' roughly the shape and size of the pie mould or cake tin. Open out the bag and fit it into the greased mould or tin.

9 Fill the pie with the meat. Roll out the remaining pastry into a round big enough to cover the top of the pie. Dampen the bottom edge, then press this lid on to the pastry case, pinching the edges together.

10 Decorate with pastry trimmings, shaped into leaves, and make a neat pea-sized hole in the middle of the lid. Chill until the pastry is firm.

11 Brush with beaten egg. Bake for 40 minutes.

12 Remove the pie carefully from the mould or tin and stand it on a flat baking sheet. Brush the pie all over with beaten egg and return to the oven for a further 20 minutes. Remove and allow to cool.

13 Heat up the stock to melt the soaked gelatine. Allow to cool but not to set.

14 Using a small funnel, pour the cooled, but not quite set, stock into the pie through the hole in the pastry lid. Allow the liquid to seep down into the pie, then pour in some more: this can be a slow process, but the pie should take about 570 ml|1 pint of liquid, and it is important that you add it to prevent the filling becoming crumbly and dry.

15 Refrigerate for 4 hours or overnight to set the jelly before cutting.

NOTE: If buying such small quantities of hare and venison proves difficult, use 225 g|8 oz lean chuck steak instead.

Leek and Oyster Mushroom Pithivier

SERVES 4

225 g|8 oz flour quantity or 425 g |15 oz bought
   puff pastry

For the stock

½ onion, peeled and roughly chopped

1 medium carrot, peeled and roughly chopped

1 stick of celery, roughly chopped

1 clove of garlic, crushed

6 peppercorns

290 ml|10 fl oz water

150 ml|5 fl oz white wine

For the filling

30g|1 oz butter

225 g|8 oz leeks, washed and sliced

2 cloves of garlic, crushed

225 g|8 oz oyster mushrooms

150 ml|5 fl oz white wine

1 tablespoon chopped fresh sage

1 tablespoon chopped fresh thyme

2 tablespoons full-fat crème fraiche

1 teaspoon Dijon mustard

salt and freshly ground black pepper

To glaze

1 egg, beaten

For the sauce

150 ml|5 fl oz stock (see above)

150 ml|5 fl oz double cream

handful of watercress, sage and mint, stalks removed

lemon juice

1 tablespoon chopped fresh chives

1 Make the stock: place all the stock ingredients into a medium saucepan. Bring to the boil and simmer, uncovered, for 30–40 minutes until reduced to approximately 150 ml | 5 fl oz.

2 Meanwhile make the filling: melt the butter in a saucepan, add the leeks and garlic and sweat over a low heat, covered with a lid, for 15 minutes or until the leeks are soft. Stir occasionally to ensure the leeks do not brown.

3 Tear the oyster mushrooms into pieces and add to the leeks, then cook for 2–3 minutes. Add the wine and bring to the boil. Cook over a high heat until the wine has nearly evaporated. Add the sage, thyme, crème fraiche and mustard. Bring to the boil again and cook until the sauce just coats the leeks. Season with salt and pepper. Allow to cool.

4 Heat the oven to 200°C|400°F|gas mark 6.

5 Divide the puff pastry in half. Roll one piece into a sheet measuring 23 cm |9 in square. Using a template measuring 10 cm|4 in in diameter, cut out 4 circles.

6 Roll the second piece of pastry slightly larger than the first and cut out 4 circles measuring 12.5 cm|4½ in.

7 Divide the filling into four and place on the smaller circles, leaving a small border around the edge.

8 Wet the edges with a little water and place the remaining circles on top of the filling. Carefully press out any air bubbles and seal the edges together. Crimp the edges with finger and thumb and, using a blunt knife, mark a criss-cross pattern on the top of the pastry. Put on a baking sheet, brush with beaten egg and chill for 10 minutes.

9 Brush the pastry with egg again and bake for 20 minutes or until it has risen and is golden-brown.

10 Meanwhile make the sauce: put the stock and cream in a saucepan, bring to the boil and reduce by half. Pour boiling water over the watercress, sage and mint and then dip in cold water. Squeeze out any excess water. Chop roughly and put into a liquidizer. Pour over the reduced stock and cream and liquidize until a bright green sauce is achieved. Pour back into the pan, then add lemon juice, salt and pepper to taste. Stir in the chopped chives.

11 To serve, place the pithivier on a plate whilst still hot and pour a little sauce beside it.

Summer Vegetable Filo Pie

SERVES 4

6 sheets filo pastry

2 tablespoons olive oil

1 onion, sliced

1 red pepper, sliced

1 yellow pepper, sliced

1 bulb of fennel, sliced

1 clove of garlic

55 ml | 2 fl oz dry sherry

125 g | 4½ oz baby sweetcorn, cooked and cut into 2.5 cm | 1 in pieces

115 g | 4 oz baby carrots, topped, tailed, cooked and cut into 2.5 cm | 1 in pieces

grated zest of 1 lemon

2 tablespoons lemon juice

1 tablespoon chopped fresh chives

1 tablespoon fresh thyme leaves

200 ml | 7 fl oz crème fraiche

200 g | 7 oz baby courgettes, sliced and blanched in boiling water for 30 seconds

450 g | 1 lb new potatoes, boiled

30 g | 1 oz melted butter or 2–3 tablespoons olive oil

salt and freshly ground black pepper

To glaze

1 egg, beaten

1 tablespoon sesame or poppy seeds

1 Heat the oven to 190°C | 375°F | gas mark 5.

2 Heat the oil in a large saucepan and add the onion, red pepper, yellow pepper and fennel. Stir to coat with the oil, cover with a lid and cook gently for 30 minutes, stirring occasionally to prevent it from browning. Add the garlic and cook for a further minute.

3 Add the sherry and bring to the boil. Simmer for 2 minutes. Add the sweetcorn, carrots, lemon zest, lemon juice, chives, thyme and crème fraiche. Season with salt and pepper.

4 Put the courgettes in the bottom of a large, shallow, ovenproof dish. Season with salt and pepper. Cover the vegetables in sauce and arrange sliced boiled new potatoes on top.

5 Brush a sheet of filo pastry with the butter or oil and place over the top. Repeat with each piece of filo pastry, but brush the top layer with beaten egg. Trim the edges of the pastry and score a lattice pattern on the top. Scatter over the sesame seeds or poppy seeds.

6 Bake in the oven for 30 minutes. Serve hot.

Chicken and Coriander Filo Pie

This pie is based on the delicious dish from Morocco, the b'stilla.

SERVES 6

55 g | 2 oz fresh coriander

5 eggs, beaten

30 ml | 1 fl oz single cream

50 ml | 1¾ fl oz chicken stock

olive oil for brushing

4 skinless, boneless chicken breasts

lemon juice to taste

1 teaspoon cumin seeds

¼ teaspoon ground coriander

a pinch of ground cinnamon

400 g | 14 oz bought filo pastry, defrosted

30 g | 1 oz flaked almonds

salt and freshly ground black pepper

1 Finely chop the leaves and thin stems of the coriander. Mix with the eggs, cream and chicken stock.

2 Place a thin coating of olive oil in the bottom of a sauté pan. Place over a medium heat and cook the egg mixture, stirring constantly until it thickens like runny scrambled eggs. Do not allow it to overcook or it will separate into lumpy eggs in runny liquid.

3 As soon as the egg mixture is thick, like Greek yoghurt, turn it into a large bowl to cool.

4 Cut the chicken breasts into finger-sized strips and place in a bowl. Sprinkle the chicken with a little lemon juice, the spices and season with salt and pepper.

5 Heat the oven to 190°C | 375°F | gas mark 5.

6 Line a rectangular ovenproof dish with 5 layers of filo, allowing it to hang over the edges by 2.5 cm | 1 in. Brush each sheet of filo with a little oil as you go. Keep the rest of the filo covered with clingfilm.

7 Place half the cooled egg mixture into the bottom of the filo case then top with the chicken pieces. Cover with the remaining egg mixture.

8 Fold the edges of the filo pastry over the filling. Place the 4 remaining sheets of filo on the top, cutting it with scissors to fit the dish.

9 Brush the top with olive oil and sprinkle over the almonds.

10 Bake in the centre of the oven for 40 minutes or until the pastry is golden-brown. If you insert a skewer into the centre of the pie for 10 seconds it should come out hot.

11 Serve warm or at room temperature, with a yoghurt and cucumber salad.

Asparagus and Leek Filo Pie

SERVES 4

4 large sheets filo pastry

450 g | 1 lb asparagus

6 tablespoons olive oil

450 g | 1 lb trimmed leeks, sliced and washed

2 tablespoons plain flour

150 ml | 5 fl oz white wine

290 ml | 10 fl oz vegetable stock

2 tablespoons chopped fresh thyme

1 tablespoon lemon juice

85 g | 3 oz Emmental cheese

3 tablespoons double cream

1 tablespoon sesame seeds

salt and freshly ground black pepper

1 Heat the oven to 190°C | 375°F | gas mark 5.

2 Trim the ends off the asparagus and, using a potato peeler, peel the skin off the last 5 cm | 2 in of the stalks. Bring some water to boil in a large shallow pan. Put in the asparagus and cook for approximately 7 minutes or until just tender (depending on the thickness of the asparagus). Remove from the cooking water and put to one side.

3 Heat 2 tablespoons olive oil in a large saucepan, add the leeks and sweat gently for 10 minutes or until softened. Add the flour, cook for 30 seconds, add the wine and bring to the boil. Add the stock and bring back up to the boil. Simmer for 10–15 minutes or until it is quite a thick sauce. Remove from the heat and add the thyme, lemon juice, cheese, double cream, salt and pepper.

4 Cut the asparagus into 5 cm | 2 in lengths.

5 Pour half the sauce into a shallow, ovenproof dish. Cover with the asparagus and pour the remaining sauce on top.

6 Brush each sheet of filo pastry with olive oil and place on top of the vegetables in layers. Trim off the excess pastry, then brush the top with oil and score with a lattice pattern. Scatter with sesame seeds.

7 Bake for 20–25 minutes, turning the temperature down if the pastry gets too dark. Serve hot.

NOTE: The top can also be finished by placing 2 layers of pastry on the pie and then ripping the remaining sheets, crumpling them up slightly and laying them over the surface, to give more of a 3-D effect. Brush very carefully with oil and scatter over the sesame seeds. This pastry will brown quite quickly, so you may need to turn the oven down after 10 minutes.

Aubergine and Red Pepper Pie with a Brioche Crust

SERVES 4

full quantity of brioche dough (see page 600) using
    only 2 teaspoons sugar

For the filling

125 ml | 4½ fl oz olive oil

1 Spanish onion, sliced

2 aubergines

2 red peppers

1 bulb of fennel, sliced

2 cloves of garlic, crushed

100 ml | 3½ fl oz white wine

150 g | 5 oz cream cheese

1 tablespoon chopped fresh chives

lemon juice

5 medium tomatoes, skinned and sliced

2 tablespoons chopped fresh basil

salt and freshly ground black pepper

1 Heat 3 tablespoons of olive oil in a saucepan, add the onions and cook very slowly for 10 minutes, covered with a lid. Stir occasionally and do not allow to brown.

2 Slice the aubergines and sprinkle with salt. Lay on a wire rack and leave for 20 minutes. Cut the red peppers into quarters and remove the seeds.

3 Add the fennel to the onions and continue to cook slowly for 15 minutes. Add the garlic and cook for a further minute.

4 Heat the grill to its highest setting and heat the oven to 190°C | 375°F | gas mark 5.

5 Rinse the aubergine slices and lay them on the grill rack, brush with oil and grill. Once they are brown, turn over, brush with oil and grill again until brown.

6 Grill the red pepper quarters until the skin is black and blistered. Put into a bowl with a plate over the top. Leave for 10 minutes.

7 Add the wine to the fennel and onions and reduce by half. Remove from the heat, then add the cream cheese, chives and 1 tablespoon of lemon juice. Season with salt and pepper. Taste and add more lemon juice, salt and pepper as necessary.

8 Peel the peppers and cut into slices.

9 Put a layer of grilled aubergines in the base of a 1.75 litre | 3 pint pie dish. Cover with half the peppers and tomatoes, season with salt and pepper and basil. Put in all the onion and cream cheese mixture and cover with tomatoes, basil, peppers, salt and pepper and finally the remaining aubergines.

10 Roll out the brioche dough and cover the pie dish. Use the trimmings to decorate the pie and crimp the edges with thumb and forefinger.

11 Brush with beaten egg and bake for 10 minutes. Turn the oven down to 170°C | 325°F | gas mark 3 and continue to cook for a further 30 minutes.

12 Serve hot or at room temperature.

Savoury Pastries and En-croûte Dishes

The recipes in this section use a variety of pastry. Although most can be made easily at home, bought filo pastry is widely available both fresh and frozen. If using frozen pastry, give it enough time to thaw out before using it, otherwise it is likely to tear and form holes. Also, whilst working with filo pastry keep the remaining pieces covered, as it dries out very quickly.

Blue Cheese and Apple Filo Parcels

Any hard, blue-veined cheese can be used in this recipe. Serve as a first course with a green salad.

SERVES 4

4 large sheets filo pastry
55 g | 2 oz butter
2 shallots, finely chopped
1 clove garlic, crushed
225 g | 8 oz cooking apples
140 g | 5 oz blue cheese e.g. Stilton, Shropshire Blue
1 tablespoon chopped fresh sage

To glaze

1 egg, beaten
salt and freshly ground black pepper

1 Heat the oven to 200°C | 400°F | gas mark 6.
2 Melt 15 g | ½ oz butter in a saucepan, add the shallots and garlic and sweat over a low heat for 5 minutes, without letting them colour.
3 Peel, quarter and core the apple. Cut into very small dice. Chop the cheese into small pieces and combine with the apple. Add the sage, salt, pepper and sweated shallots.
4 Melt the remaining butter and brush it over a sheet of filo pastry. Cut it in half lengthways. Put a spoonful of the filling at one end of each strip. Form a triangle by folding the right hand corner over to the opposite side and then fold across from the left hand corner to the right edge. Continue folding until the pastry is used up. Place on a baking sheet and brush well with beaten egg. Continue with the remaining filling to make 8 parcels in all.
5 Bake for 10–15 minutes and serve warm.

Spinach and Ricotta Strudels

These strudels can be made easily with bought filo pastry.

SERVES 6

140 g|5 oz flour quantity strudel pastry (see **Pastry**, page 66) or 6 sheets of ready-made filo pastry

For the filling

450 g|1 lb fresh spinach, cooked and finely chopped
170 g|6 oz ricotta cheese
1 egg, lightly beaten
freshly grated nutmeg
melted butter
salt and freshly ground black pepper

1 Heat the oven to 200°C|400°F|gas mark 6.

2 Mix the spinach with the ricotta cheese, egg, nutmeg, salt and pepper to taste.

3 Cut the strudel sheets into 13 cm|5 in squares. Brush each square immediately with melted butter. Lay 2 or 3 squares on top of each other.

4 Put a spoonful of the spinach mixture on each piece of pastry. Fold the sides of the pastry over slightly to prevent the filling escaping during cooking, then roll the strudels up rather like a Swiss roll.

5 Brush with more melted butter, place on a greased baking sheet and bake in the oven for 15 minutes. Serve warm.

NOTE: Alternatively, the pastry can be cut into long strips, a spoonful of the filling placed in the top right-hand corner and the pastry folded into successive triangles.

Pumpkin and Lentil Strudel

SERVES 4–6

140 g|5 oz flour quantity strudel pastry (see **Pastry**, page 66) or 6 sheets of ready-made filo pastry

For the filling

1 tablespoon olive oil
4 shallots, sliced
675 g|1½ lb pumpkin, peeled, deseeded and cut into 2.5 cm|1 in cubes
115 g|4 oz brown lentils, cooked
1 large clove of garlic, crushed
1 × 400 g|14 oz can of tomatoes

1 teaspoon chopped fresh thyme
1 bay leaf
½ teaspoon sugar
85 g|3 oz butter, melted
1 tablespoon very finely chopped fresh parsley
salt and freshly ground black pepper

To glaze

1 egg, beaten
1 tablespoon sesame seeds

1 Heat the oil in a large saucepan. Add the shallots and cook until soft and transparent.

2 Stir in the pumpkin and lentils. Then add the garlic and cook for a further minute.

3 Add the tomatoes, thyme and bay leaf. Cook for 20 minutes or until the pumpkin and lentils are soft but still hold their shape. The mixture should be moist but not runny. Season to taste with the sugar, salt and pepper. Remove from the heat and leave to cool. Remove the bay leaf.

4 Heat the oven to 200°C|400°F|gas mark 6. Grease a large baking sheet.

5 If using home-made strudel pastry, stretch it on a floured tea towel. If using ready-made filo pastry, arrange overlapping sheets on the tea towel.

6 Brush the pastry with the melted butter.

7 Place the pumpkin and lentil filling in a line at one end of the pastry and scatter with parsley. Using the tea towel to help, roll up the pastry as for a Swiss roll, trying to maintain a fairly tight roll. Lift the cloth and gently tip the strudel on to the prepared baking sheet. Bend into a crescent.

8 Brush with beaten egg and sprinkle with sesame seeds.

9 Bake on the middle shelf of the oven for 30 minutes or until golden-brown. Serve hot.

Mushroom Turnovers with Cream Cheese Pastry

MAKES 4

For the filling

250g|9oz flour quantity cream cheese pastry (II)
  (see **Pastry**, page 50)

2 tablespoons olive oil

2 shallots, chopped

450g|1lb mushrooms, chopped

1 teaspoon plain flour

100ml|3½ fl oz soured cream

1 tablespoon chopped fresh dill

salt and freshly ground black pepper

To glaze

1 egg, beaten

1 Heat the olive oil in a sauté pan, add the shallots and cook for 5 minutes. Add the chopped mushrooms and cook rapidly until all their liquid has evaporated, about 5 minutes.

2 Stir in the flour and cook for 1 minute, add the soured cream, bring to the boil and remove from the heat. Add the dill and season with salt and pepper. Allow to cool completely.

3 Heat the oven to 200°C|400°F|gas mark 6.

4 Cut the pastry into 4 pieces and roll each piece to approximately 15 cm | 6 in in diameter. Use a saucer or small plate to cut out a circle.

5 Put the filling into the centre of each circle. Brush around the edge with water. Carefully bring the sides up and over the filling and seal the edges together. Using a finger and thumb, crimp the edges. Place on a baking sheet, brush with beaten egg and chill for 10 minutes.

6 Brush again with beaten egg. Bake near the top of the oven for 20 minutes. Serve hot.

Canapé Cornish Pasties

MAKES 20

For the cheese pastry

115 g | 4 oz plain flour
55 g | 2 oz butter
15 g | ½ oz Parmesan cheese, freshly grated
a pinch of cayenne pepper
a pinch of dry English mustard
½ egg, beaten
cold water

For the filling

225 g | 8 oz lean minced beef
1 small onion, finely
  chopped
1 small potato, diced
1 small carrot, diced
1 teaspoon plain flour
stock to moisten
a few drops of Worcestershire sauce
salt and freshly ground black pepper

To glaze

1 egg, beaten

1 Sift the flour into a mixing bowl and rub in the butter. Add the Parmesan, cayenne and mustard. Bind to a firm dough with the beaten egg and a little water, then chill.

2 Brown the mince, onion, potato and carrot in a non-stick saucepan. Add the flour and cook over a low heat for 1 minute. Add the stock, Worcestershire sauce, salt and pepper and cook until the vegetables are just soft. Remove from the heat and allow to cool.

3 Heat the oven to 200°C | 400°F | gas mark 6.

4 Roll out the pastry thinly and stamp out rounds using a 4 cm | 1½ in pastry cutter.

5 Divide the filling between the pastry rounds. Brush the edges of the pastry with beaten egg and fold over into pasties. Seal the edges well. Brush the pastry with beaten egg and place the pasties on a greased baking sheet. Bake for 10–15 minutes or until golden-brown.

Traditional Cornish Pasties

MAKES 4

225 g | 8 oz flour quantity shortcrust pastry (see
  Pastry, page 44)

For the filling

115 g | 4 oz chuck steak, finely diced
1 onion, finely chopped

1 baking potato, finely diced
2 tablespoons water
salt and freshly ground black pepper

To glaze

1 egg, beaten

1 Divide the pastry into 4 equal pieces and roll each piece into discs 2 mm | ⅛ in thick. Place between sheets of greaseproof paper and chill.

2 Heat the oven to 200°C|400°F|gas mark 6.

3 Mix together the filling ingredients.

4 Place the pastry circles on to a baking sheet and mound the filling into the centre of each. Brush water around the outside edge then bring the edges together in the centre like a closed purse. Crimp.

5 Brush with the beaten egg and chill for 10 minutes.

6 Bake in the top third of the oven for 15 minutes then turn the oven temperature down to 180°C|350°F|gas mark 4 and bake for a further 45–50 minutes. Cover the pasties if they are becoming too brown.

Butternut Squash and Feta Pasties

SERVES 4–6

225 g|8 oz flour quantity shortcrust pastry (see
Pastry, page 44)

For the filling

1 tablespoon olive oil

1 onion, chopped

1 × 400 g|14 oz can of tomatoes

a pinch of caster sugar

675 g|1½ lb butternut squash, peeled, deseeded and
cut into 1 cm|½ in chunks, steamed

115 g|4 oz Puy lentils, cooked

1 tablespoon chopped fresh parsley

55 g|2 oz feta cheese, cubed

salt and freshly ground black pepper

To glaze

1 egg, beaten

1 Heat the oil in a large saucepan. Add the onion and cook until soft and transparent. Add the tomatoes and the sugar. Cook for 15 minutes or until thick and dry, stirring frequently.

2 Stir in the squash, lentils and parsley. Allow to cool.

3 Stir in the feta cheese then season with salt and pepper to taste.

4 Heat the oven to 200°C|400°F|gas mark 6. Grease a large baking sheet.

5 Divide the pastry into 8 equal pieces and roll each piece into a 15 cm|6 in round.

6 Divide the filling between the pastry rounds and fold the pastry over the centre, crimping the edges together to make a pasty.

7 Place on the baking sheet and brush with the beaten egg. Chill until firm.

8 Brush with egg again.

9 Bake on the top shelf of the oven for 25–30 minutes or until golden-brown. Serve hot.

Empanadas

These Spanish and Mexican pastries are similar to Cornish pasties, but spicy.

MAKES 8

For the pastry

225 g | 8 oz flour quantity shortcrust pastry (see
 Pastry, page 44)
1 teaspoon paprika
1 egg, beaten

For the filling

2 tablespoons vegetable oil
1 small onion, chopped

1 clove of garlic, crushed
450 g | 1 lb minced beef
150 ml | 5 fl oz water
1 teaspoon Cajun spice
a pinch of ground cinnamon
a pinch of ground cayenne pepper
200 g | 7 oz chopped fresh tomatoes
salt and freshly ground black pepper

1 Make the shortcrust pastry according to the directions on page 44, with the addition of the paprika to the flour. Divide into 8 equal pieces and roll each into 15 cm | 6 in rounds. Wrap with clingfilm and chill.

2 For the filling, place half the oil in a sauté pan and stir in the onion. Cover with a dampened piece of greaseproof paper and cook over a low heat until softened, about 10–15 minutes. Remove the paper and turn up the heat slightly to brown the onions. Stir in the garlic and cook for a further 30 seconds. Remove from the pan and set aside.

3 Place the remaining oil in the sauté pan and brown the beef over a medium heat. Remove with a slotted spoon and place in a sieve over a bowl to drain away any excess fat. Remove any excess fat from the pan.

4 Add the water to the hot pan and scrape the bottom to remove the brown colour. Return the meat to the pan, stir in the spices and cook for a further minute, then add the tomatoes and the water. Add the onions and garlic.

5 Place in a small saucepan and simmer for 1 hour or until the meat is tender and the sauce is no longer watery. Season with salt and pepper. Allow to cool.

6 Heat the oven to 200°C | 400°F | gas mark 6. Lightly grease 2 baking sheets.

7 Lay the pastry circles on the work surface in a single layer. Brush 1 cm | ½ in of the edges with beaten egg.

8 Divide the filling between the pastry rounds then fold over to make half-moon shapes. Crimp the edges.

9 Place the pastries on to the baking sheet and brush with the egg. Chill until firm.

10 Brush again with egg and bake for 25 minutes or until golden-brown. Serve warm.

Chicken and Mushroom Gougère

SERVES 4

1 × 3 egg quantity of choux pastry (see **Pastry**, page 64)

For the filling

1.35 g|3 lb chicken, cleaned but not trussed
1 small onion, thickly sliced
1 bay leaf
6 peppercorns
2 parsley stalks
1 slice of lemon
4 springs fresh thyme

55 g|2 oz butter
225 g|8 oz button mushrooms, sliced
40 g|1½ oz plain flour
2 tablespoons double cream
1 tablespoon chopped fresh parsley
salt and freshly ground black pepper

To finish

2 tablespoons finely grated Parmesan cheese
2 tablespoons dried breadcrumbs

1 To poach the chicken, place it breast-side up in a large saucepan and add the onion, bay leaf, peppercorns, parsley stalks, lemon and thyme. Pour enough cold water into the pan to leave the breasts standing slightly proud of the water. Cover with greaseproof paper and a lid.

2 Cook over a medium heat until the occasional bubble comes to the surface, then turn the heat down to maintain the temperature. Do not allow the liquid to boil. Poach for 1¼–1½ hours or until the drumstick feels wobbly and the juices run clear from the thigh. Remove the chicken from the pan and set aside to cool.

3 Strain the poaching liquid then boil to reduce to 570 ml|1 pint.

4 To make the sauce, melt 15 g|½ oz of the butter in a large sauté pan and stir in the mushrooms. Cook over a medium heat until the mushrooms give up their juices and start to fry. Remove them with a slotted spoon and set aside.

5 Add the remaining butter to the pan and stir in the flour. Cook, stirring, for about 2 minutes or until straw-coloured. Remove the pan from the heat and stir in the reduced stock to make a smooth sauce. Bring to the boil and boil for 2 minutes. Stir in the cream and allow to cool.

6 When the chicken is cool, remove the skin and discard. Cut the meat into chunks.

7 Mix together the sauce, chicken, mushrooms and parsley. Season to taste.

8 Heat the oven to 200°C|400°F|gas mark 6.

9 Heap the pastry around the edge of a 25 cm|10 in ceramic flan dish, leaving a space of about 10 cm|4 in in the centre. Bake in the oven for 20–25 minutes or until golden-brown.

10 Remove from the oven and make a slit horizontally in the pastry ring. Remove any uncooked pastry from the inside of the ring then pile the filling in the centre of the dish and underneath the pastry.

11 Sprinkle with the Parmesan cheese and breadcrumbs and return to the oven for 20 minutes to heat the filling through. Serve immediately.

Prosciutto and Aubergine Gougère

MAKES 4

For the pastry

2 egg quantity choux pastry (see *Pastry*, page 64)

55 g | 2 oz freshly grated Parmesan cheese

½ teaspoon dry English mustard

butter for greasing

For the filling

1 small aubergine, cut into 1 cm | ½ in dice

1 tablespoon olive oil

85 g | 3 oz prosciutto, cut into shreds

1 teaspoon chopped fresh basil

4 tablespoons double cream

1 tablespoon freshly grated Parmesan cheese

salt and freshly ground black pepper

1 Heat the oven to 200°C|400°F|gas mark 6 and lightly butter 4 ramekins.

2 Beat the cheese and the mustard into the choux pastry.

3 Using a 1 cm|½ in plain piping nozzle, pipe the pastry around the insides of the ramekins, leaving a space in the middle.

4 Fry the aubergine in the oil until soft then add the prosciutto, basil and cream. Season.

5 Spoon the filling into the centre of the ramekins and sprinkle over the remaining cheese.

6 Place on a baking sheet and bake in the top third of the oven for 15–20 minutes or until risen and well-browned. Serve hot.

Individual Smoked Haddock and Spinach Gougères

SERVES 8

1 × 3 egg quantity choux pastry (see *Pastry*, page 64)

55 g | 2 oz Gruyère cheese, coarsely grated

For the topping

2 tablespoons freshly grated Parmesan cheese

2 tablespoons dried breadcrumbs

For the filling

15 g | ½ oz butter

250 g | 9 oz baby spinach, washed and destalked

225 g | 8 oz smoked haddock, cooked and flaked

100 ml | 3½ fl oz crème fraiche

freshly grated nutmeg

salt and freshly ground black pepper

1 Lightly butter 8 × size 1 ramekins (150 ml|5 fl oz capacity).

2 Heat the oven to 200°C| 400°F| gas mark 6.

3 Melt the butter in a sauté pan and when it starts to brown stir in the spinach. Cook until wilted, about 1 minute, then place in a sieve to drain.

4 Squeeze the spinach dry then mix with the smoked haddock and crème fraiche. Season with nutmeg, salt and pepper.

5 Stir the cheese into the choux pastry. Place the pastry into a piping bag fitted with a 1 cm | ½ in plain nozzle. Pipe the pastry around the insides of the ramekins.

6 Pile the filling into the centre of the ramekins and sprinkle with the Parmesan cheese and breadcrumbs.

7 Place the ramekins on to a baking sheet and bake in the top third of the oven for 15–20 minutes or until well-risen and brown. Serve hot.

Steak Wellington

SERVES 4

225 g | 8 oz flour quantity rough puff pastry (see **Pastry**, page 60)

85 g | 3 oz chicken liver pâté
salt and freshly ground black pepper

For the filling

4 × 170 g | 6 oz fillet steaks or tournedos
Worcestershire sauce
30 g | 1 oz beef dripping or 1 tablespoon oil
55 g | 2 oz flat mushrooms, chopped

To glaze

1 egg, beaten

To garnish

watercress

1 Heat the oven to 220°C | 425° F | gas mark 7. Trim any fat or membranes from the steaks. Season with pepper and a few drops of Worcestershire sauce.

2 Heat the dripping or oil in a frying pan and brown the steaks quickly on both sides. The outside should be brown, the middle absolutely raw. Reserve the frying pan, unwashed. Leave the meat to cool on a wire rack (this is to allow the fat to drip off the steaks rather than cooling and congealing on them).

3 Cook the mushrooms in the frying pan. Tip into a bowl. Allow to cool.

4 Beat the mushrooms into the pâté. Check the seasoning. Spread one side of each steak with the mixture. Roll out the pastry until it is about the thickness of a £1 coin. Cut into 4 × 17 cm | 7 in squares.

5 Place each steak, pâté-side down, on a piece of pastry. Brush the edges with water and draw them together over the steak, making a neat and well-sealed parcel. Place them on a damp baking sheet, pâté side up, and brush with beaten egg. Make a small slit in the top of each parcel so that the steam can escape. Decorate with leaves made from the pastry trimmings. Brush these with egg too. Chill for 30 minutes to allow the pastry to become firm.

6 Brush the parcels with a little more beaten egg. Bake for 15 minutes, or until the pastry is golden-brown and the meat pink.

7 Serve hot, garnished with watercress.

Salmon en Croûte

SERVES 10

450 g | 1 lb flour quantity puff pastry (see **Pastry**, page 58)

a few tablespoons fine semolina

For the filling

1 × 2.3 kg | 5 lb salmon, filleted and skinned

lemon juice to taste

1–2 tablespoons chopped fresh tarragon leaves

salt and freshly ground white pepper

To glaze

1 egg, beaten

For the sauce

55 g | 2 oz butter

20 g | ¾ oz plain flour

290 ml | 10 fl oz fish stock

55 ml | 2 fl oz dry white wine

1 teaspoon chopped fresh tarragon or parsley

2 tablespoons double cream

salt and freshly ground white pepper

1 Heat the oven to 220°C | 450°F | gas mark 7.

2 Roll out one third of the pastry into a long, narrow rectangle about the thickness of a £1 coin. Cut it to roughly the size and shape of the original salmon.

3 Place on a baking sheet and prick all over with a fork. Chill for 15 minutes. Bake in the oven until the pastry is brown and crisp. If when you turn it over it is soggy underneath, put it back in the oven, upside down, for a few minutes. Allow to cool.

4 Sprinkle semolina over the cooked pastry to prevent the fish juices making it soggy.

5 Reassemble the salmon fillets on the cooked pastry, sprinkling with lemon juice (to taste), tarragon, salt and white pepper. Trim away the excess cooked pastry, leaving a border of 1 cm | ½ in.

6 Roll out the remaining pastry into a large sheet, slightly thinner than the base, and lay it over the salmon. Cut around the fish, leaving a good 2.5 cm | 1 in border beyond the edge of the bottom layer of pastry. Carefully tuck the top sheet under the cooked pastry, shaping the head and tail of the fish carefully.

7 Brush with beaten egg. Mark the pastry to represent fish scales, using the rounded end of a teaspoon. Cut some pastry trimmings into fine strips and use them to emphasize the tail fins and gills, and use a circle of pastry for the eye. Brush again with beaten egg.

8 Bake in the oven for 15 minutes to brown and puff up the pastry, then turn down the oven temperature to 180°C | 350°F | gas mark 4 for a further 20 minutes to cook the fish. Cover the crust with damp greaseproof paper if the pastry looks in danger of overbrowning. To test if the fish is cooked, push a fine skewer through the pastry and fish from the side: it should glide in easily. Slide on to a serving dish.

9 Melt half the butter in a saucepan, remove from the heat and add the flour. Return to the heat and cook, stirring, until the butter and flour are a pale, biscuit colour. Remove from the heat then gradually add the stock and wine. Return to the heat and stir until boiling and smooth. Boil rapidly until you have a sauce of coating consistency.

10 Add the tarragon or parsley and the cream. Season to taste. Beat in the remaining butter, piece by piece, then pour into a warmed sauceboat.

Fillet of Beef en Croûte

SERVES 8–10

340 g|12 oz flour quantity puff pastry (see **Pastry**, page 58)

For the filling

1.8 kg|4 lb piece of fillet from the thick end
Worcestershire sauce (optional)
30 g|1 oz beef dripping or 2 tablespoons oil

30 g|1 oz butter
115 g|4 oz flat mushrooms, very finely chopped
115 g|4 oz chicken liver pâté
freshly ground black pepper

To glaze

1 egg, beaten

1 Heat the oven to 230°C|450°F|gas mark 8.
2 Trim the fillet and season well with pepper and Worcestershire sauce, if using. Heat the dripping or oil in a roasting pan and, when hot, add the meat and brown on all sides. Roast for 20 minutes for rare beef, 30 minutes for medium beef and 35 minutes for well done beef. Allow to cool.
3 Remove the fillet from the roasting pan and allow to cool on a wine rack.
4 Take one third of the pastry and roll it out on a floured work surface until it is a little more than the length and breadth of the fillet. Place it on a damp baking sheet, prick all over with a fork and bake in the oven for about 20 minutes, until golden-brown. Do not turn the oven off. Place the pastry on a wire rack and leave to cool on a wire rack.
5 Melt the butter in a frying pan and fry the mushrooms quickly. Allow to cool. Mix with the pâté and spread the mixture over the cooked pastry base. Place the cold fillet on top of this and, with a sharp knife, cut away any pastry that is not covered by the fillet.
6 Roll out the remaining pastry on a floured board into a 'blanket' large enough to cover the fillet easily. Lift up the blanket and lay it gently over the fillet. With a sharp knife, cut off the corners and reserve these trimmings.
7 Lift one edge of the pastry blanket and brush the underside with beaten egg. With a palette knife, lift the base and tuck the blanket neatly underneath it. Repeat with the other 3 sides. Shape the pastry trimmings into leaves. Brush the pastry with beaten egg. Decorate with the pastry leaves and brush again with beaten egg. Chill until the pastry feels hard.
8 Bake the fillet in the oven for 20 minutes, or until the pastry is very dark brown.
9 Serve hot or cold. If served hot, the fillet should be carved at the table or the juices will be lost and the meat may have a grey, unappetizing look.

NOTE: This dish may be prepared in advance up to the final baking. It should be stored in the refrigerator on the baking sheet, loosely covered with clingfilm or kitchen foil. It is important that the mushrooms and pâté should be completely cold before mixing together, and that the meat should be cold before covering with the pastry.

Pâté en Croûte

For the filling

1 shallot, very finely chopped

15 g | ½ oz butter

115 g | 4 oz chicken livers, cleaned

2 tablespoons brandy

170 g | 6 oz lean veal, minced

170 g | 6 oz lean pork, minced

170 g | 6 oz pork fat, minced

1 egg, beaten

30 g | 1 oz fresh white breadcrumbs

1 teaspoon dried mixed herbs

1½ teaspoons ground allspice

1 pig's caul, about 45 cm | 18 in square

salt and freshly ground black pepper

For the garnish

115 g | 4 oz lean ham

115 g | 4 oz lean veal

2 tablespoons brandy

1 tablespoons chopped fresh thyme

For the pastry

450 g | 1 lb plain flour

1 teaspoon salt

225 g | 8 oz butter, cut into cubes

1 egg, beaten

2–3 tablespoons ice-cold water

To glaze

1 egg, beaten

To finish

290 ml | 10 fl oz aspic, seasoned with Madeira or tarragon vinegar

1 Make the filling: sweat the shallot in the butter until soft but not coloured. Add the chicken livers and sauté gently.

2 Warm the brandy in a ladle, set alight with a match and then pour over the chicken livers and allow to *flambé* until the flames subside.

3 Whizz the mixture in a food processor until smooth, then set aside to cool.

4 Mix all the meats together with the pork fat, egg, breadcrumbs, herbs, allspice and seasoning. Mix in the liver purée. Leave to marinate overnight in the refrigerator.

5 Meanwhile, prepare the garnish: cut the ham and veal into strips 1 cm | ½ in thick and marinate in the brandy with the thyme overnight in the refrigerator.

6 Make the pastry: sift the flour with the salt into a bowl. Rub in the fat until the mixture resembles fine breadcrumbs.

7 Beat the egg with 2–3 tablespoons of water. Stir into the flour with a knife and bring together to form a stiff but not dry dough, adding more water if necessary.

8 Roll out a large rectangle no thinner than a £1 coin. Chill for 20 minutes.

9 Assemble the pâté: cut a long strip 10 cm | 4 in wide from the edge of the pastry and reserve for the top. Place the remaining rectangle of pastry on a baking sheet.

10 Lay the piece of pig's caul over the pastry, to cover it entirely.

11 Take one third of the meat filling and lay it in a neat rectangle about 7.5 × 20 cm | 3 × 8 in on the pastry. Arrange half the garnish strips of ham and veal on top and season

with salt and pepper. Repeat with another layer of meat. Arrange the remaining garnish on top and cover with the remaining meat.

12 Cut the corners out of the pastry, wet the edges and lift the pastry up to the sides of the meat, forming a terrine shape. Seal at the corners and crimp. Cut the reserved strip of pastry down to the exact size and lay over the top. Decorate the edges by crimping. Make 4 steam holes in the pastry on top.

13 Heat the oven to 220°C|425°F|gas mark 7.

14 Glaze the pastry all over with beaten egg. Garnish with pastry trimmings cut into decorative shapes. Chill for 30 minutes.

15 Glaze the pastry again with beaten egg. Bake in the top of the oven for 15 minutes, then turn down the oven temperature to 170°C|325°F|gas mark 3, transfer the pâté en croûte to the bottom of the oven and bake for a further 1–1½ hours. It is cooked when a skewer inserted into the centre of the terrine comes out hot. Remove from the oven and place on a cooling rack until completely cold.

16 Using a plastic baster, drip the aspic into the steam holes to fill up any air pockets inside the pastry. If there are any holes in the pastry before adding the aspic, block them with softened butter.

17 Chill the pâté en croûte again for at least 4 hours before serving.

NOTE: Pig's caul is available from good butchers, although it may need to be ordered in advance. It should be soaked for 5 minutes in cold water before use to soften it.

Salmon Koulibiac

SERVES 4

170 g | 6 oz flour quantity rough puff pastry (see
   Pastry, page 60)

For the filling
115 g | 4 oz long-grain rice
55 g | 2 oz butter
1 onion, finely diced
30 g | 1 oz mushrooms, chopped

1 tablespoon chopped fresh parsley
juice of half a lemon
285 g | 10 oz cooked salmon, flaked
2 hard-boiled eggs, roughly chopped
salt and freshly ground black pepper

To glaze
1 egg, beaten with a pinch of salt

1   Heat the oven to 200°C | 400°F | gas mark 6.
2   Cook the rice in a large saucepan of boiling water for 10–12 minutes. Drain in a colander or sieve and refresh with cold water. Stand the colander on the draining board. With the handle of a wooden spoon, make a few draining holes through the pile of rice to help the water and steam escape. Leave until cool.
3   Roll a third of the pastry into a rectangle 2 mm | ⅛ in thick. Chill for 10 minutes.
4   Place the pastry on a baking sheet. Prick lightly all over with a fork. Bake in the oven for about 15 minutes, until golden-brown. Transfer to a wire rack and leave to cool but do not turn the oven off.
5   Melt the butter over a medium heat and add the onion. When nearly cooked, add the mushrooms and cook gently for 5 minutes. Allow to cool.
6   Put the cooked rice into a bowl and fork in the onion, mushrooms, parsley, lemon juice, salmon, eggs and plenty of salt and pepper.
7   Place the cooled pastry base on the baking sheet and pile on the rice mixture. Shape it with your hands into a neat mound, making sure that it covers all the pastry base.
8   Roll the remaining pastry into a blanket large enough to cover the mixture with an overlap of 2.5 cm | 1 in. Using a sharp knife, cut the corners off the blanket at right angles to the cooked base. Working carefully with a palette knife, lift the base and tuck the pastry blanket underneath it. Brush with beaten egg to seal. Repeat with the other sides. Chill until the pastry is firm.
9   Meanwhile, shape the discarded pastry corners into leaves, making the veins and stem with the back of a knife.
10 Brush the koulibiac with more beaten egg, decorate with the pastry leaves and brush again with egg. Bake in the oven for 30 minutes, until the pastry is golden-brown.
11 Serve hot or cold.

NOTE: If a sauce is required, serve plain soured cream, seasoned with salt and pepper.
   This is also delicious made with cooked chicken instead of salmon.

Egg and Spinach Kouliabiac in a Brioche Crust

Brioche dough makes a good pastry to contain this pie. The secret of successfully rolling it into shape is not to 'knock it back' after its initial rising, i.e. do not re-knead it but take it straight from the bowl to roll it out.

SERVES 4

450 g | 1 lb flour quantity brioche dough, using only 2 teaspoons sugar (see **Bread**, page 600)

For the filling

2 tablespoons olive oil

340 g | 12 oz leeks, washed and sliced into rings

1 clove of garlic, crushed

115 g | 4 oz long-grain rice

75 ml | 2½ fl oz white wine

290 ml | 10 fl oz vegetable stock

1 tablespoon fresh thyme leaves

1 bay leaf

200 g | 7 oz fresh leaf spinach

4 hard-boiled eggs, chopped

30 g | 1 oz flaked almonds, toasted

150 ml | 5 fl oz crème fraiche

salt and freshly ground black pepper

To glaze

1 egg, beaten

1 Make up the brioche dough and leave in a warm place, covered, to rise for 45 minutes.

2 Heat the olive oil in a large saucepan, add the leeks and cook for 10 minutes. Do not allow them to colour. Add the crushed garlic and cook for a further 2 minutes.

3 Add the rice and stir over a low heat until it is opaque and glossy. Add the wine and bring to the boil. Boil for 2 minutes and then add the stock, thyme, bay leaf, salt and pepper. Bring back up to the boil, cover and reduce the heat. Cook for 15 minutes or until the liquid has been absorbed and the rice is cooked. Add more water if necessary.

4 Meanwhile cook the spinach. Wash it well and remove the thick stalks. Put into a pan and cover with a lid. Put over a medium heat and cook until it has just wilted. Remove from the pan, squeeze the excess moisture from it and chop finely.

5 Once the rice is cooked, remove the bay leaf and add the spinach, eggs, almonds and crème fraiche. Season well with salt and pepper.

6 Heat the oven to 190°C | 375°F | gas mark 5.

7 Roll out one third of the brioche dough into a rectangle measuring 20 × 25 cm | 8 × 10 in. Place onto a greased, lipless baking sheet. (If your baking sheet has a lip turn it over.) Brush a little beaten egg over the surface of the dough.

8 Place the rice mixture on the dough, leaving a 2.5 cm | 1 in border all the way around. Brush the border again with beaten egg.

9 Roll out the remaining piece of brioche dough to approximately 1½ times the size of the original piece, i.e. approximately 30 × 37.5 cm | 12 × 15 in. Lift the dough carefully with a rolling pin and lay it over the filling. Press down gently, removing any air bubbles, and seal it. Trim off the excess dough. Crimp the edges with a thumb and forefinger. Brush with beaten egg and decorate the top by scoring a lattice pattern over it with the back of a knife.

10 Bake in the oven for 25–30 minutes or until the brioche is golden-brown. Serve immediately.

Seafood Feuilletées with Spinach

SERVES 4

225 g|8 oz flour quantity puff pastry (see **Pastry**,
    page 58)
1 egg, beaten, to glaze

For the filling

400 g|14 oz fresh very young spinach
30 g|1 oz butter
290 ml|10 fl oz fish stock
85 g|3 oz raw tiger prawns
3 small sole fillets, cut into strips
340 g|12 oz peeled, cooked prawns
115 g|4 oz scallops, prepared
freshly grated nutmeg
salt and freshly ground white pepper

For the sauce

2 shallots, finely chopped
225 g|8 oz unsalted butter, chilled
100 ml|3½ fl oz dry white wine
1 tablespoon double cream
juice of ¼ lemon
salt and freshly ground white pepper

1 Heat the oven to 220°C|425°F|gas mark 7.

2 Shape the pastry into feuilletée cases (see page 62).

3 Bake the pastry cases for 20–30 minutes, or until puffed up and brown. Using a knife, outline and remove the lids and scoop out any uncooked dough inside. Return to the oven for 5 minutes to dry out.

4 Transfer the cases and lids to a wire rack and leave to cool. Reduce the oven temperature to 130°C|250°F|gas mark 1.

5 Wash the spinach very well and remove the stalks. Fry quickly in half the butter until just beginning to wilt. Drain well.

6 Put the fish stock into a large shallow pan. Bring up to scalding point (just below boiling), add the tiger prawns and poach for 1 minute, then add the sole fillets and peeled, cooked prawns and poach for 1 further minute. Remove the fish from the pan with a slotted spoon. Strain the stock and reduce to a glaze. Reserve. Fry the scallops in the remaining butter until just cooked. Keep warm.

7 To make the sauce, sweat the shallots very slowly in 15 g|½ oz of the butter in a saucepan. Add the fish glaze and white wine. Strain. Add the cream and reduce again. Cut the remaining cold butter into small pieces and gradually whisk it into the pan over a low heat. Remove the pan from the heat from time to time so that the butter thickens the sauce without melting. Work fairly quickly, however, as otherwise you may find that the sauce is only just warm (it does not reheat well). Add the lemon juice. Taste, add extra fish glaze if necessary and season with salt and white pepper.

8 While the sauce is being made the feuilletées can be assembled and reheated. Place the pastry cases in the oven. Reheat the spinach in the butter and season with salt, pepper

and nutmeg. Pile some spinach inside each pastry case. Arrange the seafood, including the peeled, cooked prawns, on the spinach.

9 Just before serving, spoon a generous tablespoon of sauce over each feuilletée. Set a lid on top. Serve the remaining sauce separately in a warmed sauce boat.

Sweet Tarts

A tart has a pastry crust with shallow sides to hold a filling. It does not have a top crust. The filling may be cooked along with the pastry, as in Treacle Tart, or it can be placed in a baked pastry case and cooked again, as with Lemon Meringue Pie. Baked pastry cases are also filled with crème patissière (see *Crème Patissière*, page 458) and fresh fruit.

Shortcrust, rich shortcrust and sweet shortcrust are the pastries most commonly used for tarts that are going to be baked with added filling. Pâte sucrée is used after being baked blind for fresh fruit tarts or with fillings that only need a short time in the oven, as the pastry browns easily and becomes hard.

Sweet tarts are served for dessert or with a cup of coffee or tea at any time. They are best eaten on the day of making. Tarts should be kept at room temperature, so long as the filling will not spoil; otherwise they must be refrigerated. Pastry stored in the refrigerator, however, will lose its crispness within a few hours.

Custard Tart

SERVES 6

170 g | 6 oz flour quantity rich shortcrust pastry (see **Pastry**, page 46)

For the filling
4 eggs
55 g | 2 oz caster sugar
290 ml | 10 fl oz milk
290 ml | 10 fl oz single cream
a few drops of vanilla essence
freshly grated nutmeg

1 Heat the oven to 200°C | 400°F | gas mark 6. Roll out the pastry and use to line a 20 cm | 8 in tart tin then blind bake (see **Pastry**, page 44).
2 Turn the oven temperature down to 170°C | 325°F | gas mark 3.
3 Beat the eggs with the sugar. Pour on the milk and cream and add the vanilla essence.
4 Place the pastry case on a baking sheet then strain the custard into the case. Sprinkle lightly with grated nutmeg.
5 Bake for 1 hour, or until the custard has set.

Plum Streusel Tartlets

MAKES 4

For the pastry

170 g|6 oz plain flour
a pinch of salt
85 g|3 oz butter

For the topping

115 g|4 oz plain flour
55 g|2 oz butter
45 g|1½ oz soft light brown sugar
15 g|½ oz porridge oats
1 teaspoon ground cinnamon

For the filling

340 g|12 oz ripe plums, stoned and cut into
    1 cm |½ in chunks
4 teaspoons soft light brown sugar

1 Heat the oven to 200°C|400°F|gas mark 6.

2 Make the pastry by sifting the flour into a bowl with the salt. Rub the butter into the flour until it resembles fine breadcrumbs. Add approximately 2 tablespoons of very cold water and bring together until it forms a dough.

3 Cut the pastry into 4 even pieces. Roll each piece out on a lightly floured surface until it is large enough to line an individual tartlet tin 10 cm |4 in in diameter. Repeat with the other three pieces and chill for 15 minutes.

4 Meanwhile prepare the topping. Sift the flour into a bowl, rub in the butter until it resembles fine breadcrumbs. Add the sugar, oats and cinnamon.

5 To assemble, put the chopped plums into the pastry cases and sprinkle a teaspoon of sugar over each tartlet. Add the topping and press very lightly. Use a fork to roughen the top.

6 Place on a baking sheet in the oven and bake for 10 minutes. Reduce the heat to 180°C| 350°F| gas mark 4 and continue cooking for 20 minutes or until the topping has browned and the plums are cooked.

7 Serve with cream, crème fraiche or custard.

Treacle Tart

SERVES 8

170 g | 6 oz flour quantity sweet rich shortcrust
pastry (see **Pastry**, page 46)

For the filling
450 g | 1 lb golden syrup

grated zest of ¼ lemon
1 teaspoon lemon juice
½ teaspoon ground ginger
3 eggs, lightly beaten
115 g | 4 oz fresh white breadcrumbs

1 Heat the oven to 190°C | 375°F | gas mark 5. Place a baking sheet in the middle of the oven.
2 Line a 20 cm | 8 in tart tin with the pastry and chill until firm.
3 Mix the golden syrup with the lemon zest and juice. Add the ginger, eggs and breadcrumbs.
4 Carefully ladle the mixture into the pastry case and bake in the top third of the oven for 30 minutes.
5 Reduce the oven temperature to 150°C | 300°F | gas mark 2 and bake for a further 30–40 minutes in the bottom third of the oven, until set.
6 Serve warm.

Swiss Lemon Tart

SERVES 6–8

170 g | 6 oz flour quantity sweet rich shortcrust
pastry (see **Pastry**, page 46)

For the filling
4 eggs
115 g | 4 oz caster sugar
290 ml | 10 fl oz whipping cream
grated zest and juice of 4 small lemons

1 Heat the oven to 200°C | 400°F | gas mark 6.
2 Roll the pastry and use to line a 23 cm | 9 in diameter, 2 cm | ¾ in deep tart tin. Chill until firm then blind bake (see **Pastry**, page 44). Reduce the oven temperature to 150°C | 300°F | gas mark 2.
3 Beat the eggs well with a fork then pass through a sieve to remove any eggy threads.
4 Mix in the sugar, cream, lemon zest and juice. The lemon juice will cause the cream to thicken.
5 Pour into the baked tart case and bake in the lower part of the oven for 30 minutes or until just set in the centre. Serve warm or at room temperature.

Mincemeat Tart

SERVES 8

225 g | 8 oz flour quantity rich shortcrust pastry (see **Pastry**, page 46) or pâte sucrée (see **Pastry**, page 52)

For the filling

1 small cooking apple
55 g | 2 oz butter
85 g | 3 oz sultanas
85 g | 3 oz raisins
85 g | 3 oz currants

45 g | 1½ oz chopped mixed peel
45 g | 1½ oz almonds, chopped
grated zest of 1 large lemon
½ teaspoon ground mixed spice
1 tablespoon brandy
85 g | 3 oz soft light brown sugar
1 banana, coarsely mashed

To finish

caster sugar for sprinkling

1 Heat the oven to 200°C | 400°F | gas mark 6.

2 Roll out the pastry and use to line a 25 cm | 10 in tart tin, keeping the pastry trimmings for the lattice decoration, and blind bake (see **Pastry**, page 44).

3 Prepare the mincemeat: grate the unpeeled apple. Melt the butter and add it, with all the remaining filling ingredients, to the apple. Mix well.

4 Fill the tart case with the mincemeat. Cut the pastry trimmings into thin strips and lattice the top of the tart with them, sticking the ends down with a little water. Brush the lattice with water and sprinkle with caster sugar. Return to the oven for 10–12 minutes, removing the tart ring after 5 minutes to allow the sides of the pastry to bake to a pale brown.

Lemon Meringue Pie

SERVES 8

170 g | 6 oz flour quantity sweet rich shortcrust
pastry (see **Pastry**, page 46)

For the filling

4 level tablespoons cornflour

225 g | 8 oz caster sugar

290 ml | 10 fl oz water

3 egg yolks

1 egg, beaten

zest of 2 large, unwaxed lemons

115 ml | 4 fl oz lemon juice

For the meringue

3 tablespoons water

2 teaspoons cornflour

3 egg whites

85 g | 3 oz caster sugar

To finish

a little extra caster sugar

1 Make the pastry and use to line a 20 cm | 8 in diameter, 4 | 1½ in deep tart tin. Chill until firm then blind bake (see **Pastry**, page 44). Reduce the oven temperature to 180°C | 350°F | gas mark 4.
2 Place the cornflour and sugar in a saucepan and add the water.
3 Stir over a medium heat and cook until the mixture boils. It will become thick and translucent.
4 Whisk in the egg yolks and beaten egg into the hot mixture then pass through a sieve to remove any eggy threads.
5 Whisk in the lemon juice and zest.
6 Pour the hot filling into the warm pastry case and place in the middle of the oven for 10 minutes.
7 For the meringue topping: place the water and cornflour in a small saucepan and whisk over a medium heat until the mixture is thick and translucent. Remove from the heat.
8 Whisk the whites until stiff peaks form then gradually whisk in the caster sugar. Whisk in the warm cornflour gel.
9 Pile the meringue on top of the filling, starting at the edge next to the pastry case then moving towards the middle. Mound the filling slightly in the centre.
10 Use a knife to make peaks on the meringue then sprinkle with a little extra sugar.
11 Place in the oven for 15 minutes until the topping is light brown.
12 Allow to cool before serving or chill if keeping overnight.

Smoked Haddock and Spinach Quiche

Sifting the flour

Chopping through with two knives

Rubbing in

Adding liquid

Stirring in liquid

Bringing the pastry together

Rolling out

Rotating the pastry

Placing pastry in the tin

Lining the tart tin

Rolling off excess pastry

Blind baking

Strawberry and Mascarpone Tart

Metboukha Tartlet

Upside-down Apricot and Cranberry Tart

Making Almond Pastry

Pecking the butter, sugar and egg yolk

Scooping over the flour and almonds

Chopping through with a palette knife

Fraisering the paste

Crimping the pastry

Almond Pastry Fruit Tart

Free-form Plum and Almond Pie (uncooked)

Free-form Plum and Almond Pie

Trimming the baked base

Cutting pastry for the top

Covering the base with slatted pastry

Apple and Raisin Jalousie

Stretching strudel dough

Rolling a strudel

Rhubarb and Blueberry Strudel

Maple Pecan Pie

Tarte au Citron

SERVES 6

170 g|6 oz flour quantity pâte sucrée (see **Pastry**, page 52)

200 g|7 oz caster sugar
150 ml|5 fl oz double cream
grated zest and juice of 2 lemons

For the filling
4 eggs
1 egg yolk

To finish
icing sugar, sifted

1 Heat the oven to 190°C|375°F|gas mark 5.
2 Line a 20 cm|8 in tart tin with the pâte sucrée. Chill until firm, then blind bake (see **Pastry**, page 44). Remove the lining paper and beans. Turn the oven temperature down to 150°C|300°F|gas mark 2.
3 Mix the eggs and egg yolk with the sugar until smooth. Pass through a sieve and stir in the cream. Add the lemon zest and juice: the mixture will thicken considerably.
4 Pour the lemon filling into the pastry case. Bake in the oven for 50 minutes until almost set.
5 When the tart is cooked, remove the tart tin and leave to cool
6 To serve, dust thickly and evenly with sifted icing sugar.

Apple Flan Ménagère

SERVES 4

170 g|6 oz flour quantity rich shortcrust pastry or pâte sucrée (see **Pastry**, pages 46 and 52)

For the filling and topping
1 kg|2 lb 4 oz medium-sized dessert apples
1–2 tablespoons caster sugar
6 tablespoons warm apricot glaze (see page 474)

1 Heat the oven to 190°C|375°F|gas mark 5.
2 Roll out the pastry and use to line a 20 cm|8 in tart tin. Chill until firm, then blind bake (see **Pastry**, page 44).
3 Peel, quarter and core the apples. Using a stainless steel knife, thinly slice them into the pastry case (the apples will shrink considerably during cooking, so make sure that it is well-filled). Arrange the top layer of apple slices very neatly in overlapping circles.
4 Dust the apples well with caster sugar and bake for about 25 minutes until the apples are soft.
5 When the tart is cooked, brush with warm apricot glaze and slide on to a wire rack to cool.

Tarte Normande

SERVES 8–10

170 g | 6 oz flour quantity sweet rich shortcrust
   pastry (see *Pastry*, page 46)

4 teaspoons Calvados or Kirsch

200 g | 7 oz blanched almonds, ground

4 tablespoons plain flour

3–4 ripe dessert apples

For the frangipane

200 g | 7 oz unsalted butter, softened

200 g | 7 oz caster sugar

2 eggs, beaten

2 egg yolks

To finish

150 ml | 5 fl oz warm apricot glaze (see page 474)

1 Make the pastry (see *Pastry*, page 46) and wrap and chill for at least 30 minutes.

2 Heat the oven to 200°C | 400°F | gas mark 6.

3 Roll out the pastry and use to line a 30 cm | 12 in tart tin. Chill again until firm, then blind bake (see *Pastry*, page 44). Allow the pastry case to cool.

4 Make the frangipane: cream the butter in a bowl, gradually beat in the sugar and continue beating until the mixture is pale and fluffy. Gradually add the eggs and egg yolks, beating well after each addition. Add the Calvados or Kirsch, then stir in the ground almonds and the flour. Spread the frangipane into the pastry case.

5 Peel the apples, halve them and scoop out the cores. Cut the apples crosswise into very thin slices and arrange them on the frangipane like the spokes of a wheel, keeping the slices of each half-apple together. Press them down gently until they touch the pastry base.

6 Bake the tart near the top of the oven for 10–15 minutes until the pastry is beginning to brown. Lower the oven temperature to 180°C | 350°F | gas mark 4 and bake for a further 30–35 minutes, or until the apples are tender and the frangipane is set.

7 Transfer to a wire rack to cool. Brush the tart with the apricot glaze and serve at room temperature.

NOTE: This tart is best eaten the day it is baked, but it can also be frozen. Just before serving, reheat in a low oven. If using red apples, they need not be peeled.

Individual Apple Tarts

MAKES 6

170 g | 6 oz flour quantity sweet rich shortcrust
   pastry (see *Pastry*, page 46)

For the filling and topping

3 dessert apples

2 tablespoons caster sugar

6 teaspoons Calvados

warm apricot glaze (see page 470)

1 Heat the oven to 200°C | 400°F | gas mark 6.

2 Roll out the pastry and shape into 6 equal discs.

3 On a floured work surface roll out each piece of pastry into a 12.5 cm | 5 in circle, place on a baking sheet and chill for 20 minutes.

4 Peel the apples, if desired. Cut in quarters and carefully remove the cores.

5 Slice the apples very thinly and arrange the slices of half an apple on each circle of chilled pastry. Take care to pack the apples tightly to allow for shrinkage during cooking.

6 Sprinkle each tart evenly with 1 teaspoon caster sugar.

7 Bake on the top shelf for 20 minutes, or until the pastry is golden-brown. If the apples are not quite brown, place them under a hot grill for 1–2 minutes.

8 Sprinkle with a little Calvados and brush with warm apricot glaze.

Puff Pastry Apple Tartlets with Calvados Crème Anglaise

SERVES 4

225 g | 8 oz flour quantity puff pastry (see **Pastry**, page 58)

4 dessert apples

caster sugar

To glaze

1 egg, beaten

warm apricot glaze (see page 474)

To serve

1 tablespoon Calvados

290 ml | 10 fl oz crème anglaise (see page 474), chilled

1 Heat the oven to 200°C | 400°F | gas mark 6.

2 Roll out the pastry 2 mm | ⅛ in thick and cut into 4 circles 12.5 cm | 5 in in diameter. Place on a baking sheet. Using a sharp knife, trace an inner circle about 1 cm | ½ in from the edge of each pastry circle. Do not cut all the way through the pastry.

3 Peel, core and thinly slice the apples and arrange in concentric circles within the border of each pastry tart.

4 Sprinkle lightly with caster sugar. Brush the rim of each pastry circle with beaten egg, taking care not to let it drip down the sides of the pastry.

5 Flour the blade of a knife and use this to knock up the sides of the pastry. Chill until firm.

6 Bake for 20 minutes. Remove from the oven and leave to cool slightly, then brush liberally with warm apricot glaze.

7 Add the Calvados to the crème anglaise. Serve the tarts warm with the cold custard.

Pear Tarte Tatin with Spiced Caramel

The addition of spices to the caramel makes this tarte tatin particularly exotic.

SERVES 8

For the pastry

140 g|5 oz plain flour

30 g|1 oz ground rice

a pinch of salt

115 g|4 oz cool butter, cut into 1 cm|½ in cubes

1 egg, beaten

For the caramel

115 g|4 oz granulated sugar

55 ml|2 fl oz warm water

1 pod star anise

1 stick of cinnamon

1 teaspoon cardamom pods

30 g|1 oz cold butter

1 kg|2 lb 4 oz firm ripe pears

1 To make the pastry: sift the flour, ground rice and salt into a large bowl. Cut in the butter using 2 table knives, scissor-fashion. When the lumps of fat are the size of small peas, use your fingertips to rub in the butter until the mixture resembles fine breadcrumbs.

2 Drizzle the beaten egg over the flour and stir quickly with a knife to combine. Bring together with your fingertips. If the flour seems too dry, sprinkle a little cold water over the dry part and mix. Gather into a flat disc and wrap in clingfilm. Chill.

3 To make the caramel, place the sugar, water and spices in a sturdy saucepan and melt the sugar over a low heat. When the sugar has dissolved, turn the heat to high and cook until it is a rich caramel, about 5 minutes. Remove from the heat and carefully add the butter. Pour the caramel into a warmed 25 cm|10 in ceramic flan dish. Remove the spices. Take care not to touch the caramel or allow it to splash on to your skin as it is very hot.

4 Heat the oven to 200°C|400°F|gas mark 6.

5 Peel and halve the pears, removing the stems and cores. Place rounded side down over the caramel.

6 Roll the pastry on a lightly floured surface until large enough to cover the flan dish. Use the rolling pin to lift the pastry on to the pears. Trim the edges of the pastry then tuck them around the edges of the pears.

7 Bake in the top third of the oven for 30 minutes or until the pastry is golden-brown and cooked through.

8 Carefully invert the tart on to a lipped serving dish whilst still hot.

Upside-down Apricot and Cranberry Tart

SERVES 8

170 g|6 oz flour quantity sweet rich shortcrust
   pastry (see **Pastry**, page 46)

For the filling

55 g | 2 oz butter, melted

85 g | 3 oz soft, light brown sugar

340 g | 12 oz dried whole apricots

30 g | 1 oz dried cranberries

1 Roll the pastry between two sheets of clingfilm into a round disc 23 cm|9 in in diameter. Chill.

2 Heat the oven to 200°C|400°F|gas mark 6.

3 Place the melted butter in the bottom of a 20 cm|8 in ceramic flan dish and sprinkle over the sugar. Arrange the apricots in a single layer over the mixture. Push the cranberries into the spaces between the apricots.

4 Remove the clingfilm from the pastry. Place the pastry on top of the apricots, tucking it in between the apricots and the edge of the dish.

5 Bake the tart in the top third of the oven for 25 minutes or until the pastry is golden-brown. Carefully invert on to a lipped serving dish while still hot. Serve warm or at room temperature.

Higgledy-piggledy Fruit Tart

SERVES 8–10

225 g|8 oz flour quantity walnut pastry (see **Pastry**,
   page 48)

For the filling

full quantity crème pâtissière (see page 458)

soft seasonal fruit, such as 1 mango, 1 punnet
   strawberries, 1 banana, 2 kiwis, fruits, 1 punnet
   blueberries, 1 punnet raspberries

115 g | 4 oz seedless grapes

warm apricot glaze (see page 474)

1 Line a 25 cm|10 in tart tin with the pastry, pressing it in. Chill for 30 minutes.

2 Heat the oven to 190°C|375°F|gas mark 5.

3 Blind bake the pastry case (see **Pastry**, page 44). Leave to cool.

4 Spread the crème pâtissière into the pastry case in an even layer.

5 Prepare the fruit as for fruit salad and arrange in a higgledy-piggledy way in the tart case.

6 Brush or spoon the warm apricot glaze over the top.

Rhubarb Tart

675 g | 1½ lb trimmed rhubarb
1 tablespoon caster sugar

For the pastry
225 g | 8 oz plain flour
a pinch of salt
55 g | 2 oz butter
55 g | 2 oz lard
1 teaspoon caster sugar

For the filling
2 eggs
125 g | 4½ oz caster sugar
150 ml | 5 fl oz crème fraiche or single cream

1 Cut the rhubarb into 2.5 cm | 1 in lengths and sprinkle with sugar.

2 Place the rhubarb and sugar in a shallow saucepan and cook over a low heat until the rhubarb softens slightly but still holds its shape. Remove from the heat and allow to cool.

3 Heat the oven to 190° C | 375° F | gas mark 5.

4 Sift the flour with the salt into a medium bowl. Rub in the fats until the mixture resembles fine breadcrumbs. Stir in the sugar. Add enough cold water to bind the pastry together.

5 Roll out the pastry and use to line a 25 cm | 10 in tart tin. Chill for 30 minutes.

6 Blind bake the pastry case (see **Pastry**, page 44). Turn the oven temperature down to 150° C | 300° F | gas mark 2.

7 Mix the filling ingredients together and pass through a sieve to remove any eggy threads.

8 Arrange the rhubarb, without its juice, carefully in the baked tart case. Pour over the filling mixture and bake in the oven for 20–30 minutes until just set. This tart is best served cold but not chilled.

Banoffee Pie

This popular pie is decorated with extravagant chocolate curls but if time is short use grated chocolate to decorate it instead. It was invented by the Hungry Monk Restaurant in Somerset.

SERVES 8

For the crust

170 g | 6 oz digestive biscuits

85 g | 3 oz butter, melted

1 tablespoon caster sugar

For the filling

115 g | 4 oz butter

115 g | 4 oz light muscovado sugar

1 × 400 g | 14 oz tin sweetened condensed milk

1 large banana, sliced

1 teaspoon lemon juice

To decorate

200 g | 7 oz good quality plain chocolate

For the topping

150 ml | 5 fl oz double cream

1 tablespoon icing sugar, sifted

a few drops of vanilla essence

1 For the crust: place the digestive biscuits in a sturdy plastic bag and bash with a rolling pin to make crumbs. Place in a bowl. Stir into the melted butter and sugar. Press into a buttered 23 cm | 9 in pie plate. Chill for 10 minutes.

2 Heat the oven to 200°C | 400°F | gas mark 6.

3 Bake the crumb crust for 10 minutes or until lightly browned.

4 For the filling, place the butter, sugar and condensed milk into a saucepan over a low heat and warm until the butter melts and sugar dissolves.

5 Turn the heat up to boil the mixture, stirring until it becomes a golden caramel. Dip the base of the pan into a sink of cold water to stop the cooking. Be careful not to touch the caramel as it remains hot for a very long time. Remove from the water and leave to stand at room temperature while making the chocolate curls.

6 Melt the chocolate in a bowl set over, but not in, steaming water. Spread a couple of tablespoons of chocolate over the pastry base, then allow the remaining chocolate to cool until it starts to thicken. Spread into a thin layer over a marble or granite surface. Let it stand until nearly set and dry-looking on the surface, then scrape a thin sharp knife through the chocolate at a 45° angle to produce long curls. The chocolate curls will keep in an airtight container for several weeks. Set aside.

7 Toss the banana with the lemon juice then stir the sliced banana into the caramel mixture. Spread into the pastry case. Chill until set.

8 For the topping, whip the cream with the icing sugar and vanilla until medium peaks form. Pile on top of the pie and decorate with the chocolate curls.

Mango and Pawpaw Tart with Passion-fruit Sauce

SERVES 4

For the crust

170 g | 6 oz digestive biscuits, crushed

70 g | 2½ oz butter, melted

For the filling

1 ripe medium mango

1 ripe pawpaw

2–3 tablespoons lime juice

2 tablespoons caster sugar

290 ml | 10 fl oz double cream

For the sauce

4 ripe passion-fruit

1 tablespoon caster sugar

30 ml | 1 fl oz orange juice

1 Heat the oven to 150°C | 300°F | gas mark 2.

2 Mix together the crushed biscuits and melted butter. Line the base and sides of a 20 cm | 8 in tart tin with the mixture. Bake for 10 minutes. Allow to cool completely.

3 Peel the mango and cut the flesh away from the stone. Cut half into small dice and put the other half, roughly chopped, into a food processor.

4 Peel the pawpaw, cut in half and scoop out and discard the seeds. Cut one half into small dice and put the other half, roughly chopped, into the food processor.

5 Process the fruit until smooth and add 2 tablespoons of lime juice and the caster sugar.

6 Whip the double cream until it holds its shape. Add the mango and pawpaw purée and mix in well. It should be thick enough to hold its shape. Fold in the diced mango and pawpaw. Taste and add more lime juice or sugar as necessary. Pile into the cooled biscuit case.

7 To make the sauce: cut the passion-fruit in half and scoop the seeds into a bowl. Add the sugar and orange juice.

8 Serve slices of the tart with some passion-fruit sauce drizzled over them.

Free-form Plum and Almond Pie

This free-form pie is very easy to make and doesn't require lining a tart tin. Peaches or nectarines can be substituted for the plums, if desired.

SERVES 8

340 g | 12 oz flour quantity shortcrust pastry (see **Pastry**, page 44)

For the filling

675 g | 1½ lb ripe plums, halved and stoned

2 teaspoons ground ginger

2 teaspoons cornflour

4 tablespoons caster sugar (or to taste)

1 tablespoon raspberry jam

2 tablespoons ground almonds

1 egg white, lightly beaten

2 tablespoons flaked almonds

2 tablespoons granulated sugar

1 Roll the pastry into a disc of 30 cm | 12 in in diameter, then chill for 15 minutes.
2 Make the filling: mix together the fruit, ginger, cornflour and sugar.
3 Heat the oven to 200°C | 400°F | gas mark 6. Place a baking sheet on a rack in the top third of the oven.
4 Place the pastry on to a second, cold baking sheet.
5 Spread 20 cm | 8 in of the centre of the pastry with the jam then sprinkle with the ground almonds. Pile the fruit on top then fold the edges of the pastry over the fruit, leaving a gap of about 10 cm | 4 in in the centre. Chill until firm.
6 Brush the pastry with the egg white. Sprinkle with the flaked almonds and sugar.
7 Place the baking sheet with the pie on it on to the hot baking sheet and bake in the top third of the oven for 35 minutes or until golden-brown. The pie may need to be covered with greaseproof paper after 20 minutes in the oven, to prevent overbrowning.
8 When then pie is cooked, release from the baking sheet by running a palette knife underneath. Cool on the baking sheet for at least 20 minutes before transferring to a serving plate. Serve warm or cold.

Chocolate Pecan Pie

SERVES 6–8

225 g | 8 oz flour quantity shortcrust pastry (see
  Pastry, page 44)

For the filling
200 g | 7 oz pecan nuts, roughly chopped
85 g | 3 oz dark chocolate, roughly chopped
2 eggs
115 g | 4 oz caster sugar

55 g | 2 oz golden syrup
55 g | 2 oz clear honey
30 g | 1 oz unsalted butter, melted
icing sugar for dusting

To serve
vanilla ice cream or whipped cream

1 Heat the oven to 200°C | 400°F | gas mark 6.
2 Roll out the pastry and line a 23 cm | 9 in tart tin. Chill for 20 minutes and then blind bake (see **Pastry**, page 44). Allow the pastry case to cool. Reduce the oven temperature to 170°C | 325°F | gas mark 3.
3 Put the pecan nuts and chopped chocolate into the baked tart case. Mix together the eggs, sugar, syrup, honey and butter and pour over the nuts and chocolate.
4 Place on a baking sheet in the centre of the oven for 40–45 minutes or until the filling is just set.
5 Remove from the oven and allow to cool. Just before serving, dust with icing sugar. Serve with vanilla ice cream or whipped cream.

Maple Pecan Pie

SERVES 8

170 g | 6 oz flour quantity cream cheese pastry (see
   Pastry, page 49)

For the filling

200 g | 7 oz pecan nuts
55 g | 2 oz butter
115 g | 4 oz soft dark brown sugar

150 ml | 5 fl oz pure maple syrup
150 ml | 5 fl oz golden syrup
1 teaspoon vanilla essence
4 eggs, beaten

To serve

290 ml | 10 fl oz double cream

1 Roll the pastry between two sheets of clingfilm or greaseproof paper to a circle large enough to line a 23 cm | 9 in tart tin. Remove one sheet of clingfilm or greaseproof paper and use the other piece to help ease the pastry into the tin. Chill until firm.

2 Place a baking sheet in the oven and heat to 200°C | 400°F | gas mark 6.

3 To make the filling, reserve 115 g | 4 oz of the pecan nuts, choosing the whole nuts for the top of the tart. Chop the remaining nuts.

4 Melt the butter and sugar then stir in the syrups, chopped nuts and vanilla. Leave to cool to room temperature then stir in the eggs.

5 Remove the hot baking sheet from the oven and place the pastry-lined tin on it. Pour in the filling then arrange the reserved nuts on top.

6 Return to the oven and bake for 15 minutes, then reduce the oven temperature to 180°C | 350°F | gas mark 4 and bake for a further 30 minutes or until the centre is just set.

7 Serve warm or at room temperature with the double cream.

Pine Nut Tart

SERVES 6–8

170 g | 6 oz flour quantity sweet rich shortcrust
   pastry (see *Pastry*, page 46)

For the filling

3 tablespoons cherry or seedless raspberry jam
100 g | 3½ oz butter, softened
100g | 3½ oz caster sugar

½ teaspoon vanilla essence
100 g | 3½ oz ground almonds
2 tablespoons plain flour
55 g | 2 oz pine nuts

To serve

½ tablespoon icing sugar

1 Roll the pastry to 3mm, the thickness of a £1 coin, and use to line a 23 cm | 9 in diameter, 2.5 cm | 1 in deep tart tin. Chill until firm.

2 Heat the oven to 200°C | 400°F | gas mark 6.

3 Line the pastry with paper and baking beans and blind bake (see *Pastry*, page 44). Allow to cool.

4 Turn the oven temperature down to 180°C|350°F|gas mark 4.

5 Spread the jam over the pastry base.

6 To make the filling: beat the butter and sugar together until light. Stir in the vanilla, almonds and flour. Spread into the pastry case.

7 Sprinkle with the pine nuts.

8 Bake for about 25 minutes or until golden-brown and set.

9 Cool on a wire rack. Sift over the icing sugar to serve.

Sweet Potato Tart

This tart is made in the southern states of the US during the harvest season. The recipes vary greatly from family to family but the common denominators are sweet potato, spices and egg.

SERVES 6–8

225 g|8 oz flour quantity shortcrust pastry (see **Pastry**, page 44)

For the filling

400 g|14 oz sweet potatoes, peeled, boiled and drained

115 g|4 oz soft light brown sugar

grated zest and juice of 1 orange

3 eggs

200 ml|7 fl oz double cream

1 teaspoon ground cinnamon

½ teaspoon ground ginger

½ teaspoon ground cloves

½ teaspoon ground allspice

¼ teaspoon ground nutmeg

To serve

whipped cream

grated nutmeg

1 Roll out the pastry to 5 mm|¼ in thick and use to line a 27 cm|11 in tart tin (approximately 3 cm|1½ in deep). Chill for 20 minutes. Heat the oven to 200°C|400°F|gas mark 6.

2 Blind bake the pastry for 15 minutes (see **Pastry**, page 44). If the pastry is set at the sides remove the paper and beans and bake for a further 5 minutes. Remove from the oven and allow to cool on the baking sheet. Reduce the oven temperature to 170°C|325°F|gas mark 3.

3 Put the potato flesh, sugar and the zest and juice of orange into a food processor and process until smooth. Add the eggs, cream and spices and process again until well mixed. Pour into the pastry case and bake for 45–60 minutes or until the centre is set.

5 When cold, dust with a little grated nutmeg and serve with whipped cream.

Spiced Pumpkin and Orange Pie

Pumpkin pie is served as the dessert for a traditional American Thanksgiving meal.

SERVES 6–8

For the pastry

170 g | 6 oz plain flour

a pinch of salt

a pinch of ground cinnamon

115 g | 4 oz butter

1 tablespoon caster sugar

1 egg yolk mixed with 2 tablespoons water

grated zest and juice of 1 small orange

75 ml | 2½ fl oz double cream

2 large eggs, beaten

30 g | 1 oz plain flour

1 teaspoon mixed spice

1 teaspoon ground ginger

¼ teaspoon ground nutmeg

For the filling

140 g | 5 oz canned pumpkin purée

75 g | 2½ oz soft light brown sugar, sifted

140 g | 5 oz full-fat cream cheese, at room temperature

To garnish

200 ml | 7 fl oz double cream, whipped

a little grated nutmeg

julienne of orange peel

1 For the pastry: sift the flour, salt and cinnamon into a large bowl. Cut the butter into small cubes and toss into the flour. Using 2 table knives, scissor-fashion, cut the butter into the flour until it is the size of small peas. Then, using your fingertips, rub the butter into the flour until the mixture resembles fine breadcrumbs. Stir in the sugar.

2 Mix the egg yolk with the water and drizzle over the flour. Stir in with a knife until the mixture starts to come together. Pull together with your fingertips into a smooth paste then roll out and use to line a deep 20 cm | 8 in tart tin or a shallow 23 cm | 9 in pie dish. Chill until firm.

3 Heat the oven to 200°C | 400°F | gas mark 6. Line the pastry with greaseproof paper and baking beans and blind bake (see **Pastry**, page 44). Reduce the oven temperature to 150°C | 300°F | gas mark 2.

4 Meanwhile, make the filling. Beat the pumpkin purée, sugar and cream cheese until smooth. Beat in the orange zest and juice, cream and eggs. The filling can be made in the food processor if desired.

5 Sift together the flour and spices and stir into the cream-cheese mixture.

6 Place in the baked pastry case and bake for 35–45 minutes or until the filling is just set and does not wobble when gently shaken.

7 Serve at room temperature or chilled, decorated with rosettes of whipped cream and garnished with the nutmeg and the orange julienne.

St Clement's Tart

SERVES 8–10

For the pastry

250 g | 9 oz plain flour

170 g | 6 oz butter, cut into pieces

85 g | 3 oz caster sugar

100 g | 3½ oz toasted hazelnuts, finely chopped

1 egg, beaten

For the filling

6 eggs

juice and grated zest of 3 medium oranges

juice and grated zest of 1 lemon

115 g | 4 oz caster sugar

290 ml | 10 fl oz Greek yoghurt

1 Heat the oven to 190°C | 375°F | gas mark 5.

2 Make the pastry: sift the flour into a large bowl. Add the butter and rub in with the fingertips until the mixture resembles fine breadcrumbs. Add the sugar, hazelnuts and beaten egg. Bring it together with your hands.

3 Roll out the pastry and line a 27 cm | 11 in tart tin. (If the pastry is too soft, press it into the tin.) Chill until firm.

4 Blind bake the pastry (see **Pastry**, page 44), then remove the paper and beans after 10 minutes. Bake for a further 10 minutes or until the pastry looks dry and pale brown. Reduce the oven temperature to 150°C | 300°F | gas mark 2.

5 Meanwhile make the filling: gently beat the eggs, but do not make them too frothy. Sieve to remove any eggyy threads. Add the orange juice and zest, lemon juice and zest, sugar and yoghurt, taste and add more sugar if necessary.

6 Pour the filling into the baked tart case and place in the centre of the oven. Bake for 50 minutes or until the filling is just set. Serve cold.

Almond Pastry Fruit Tart

SERVES 6–8

115 g | 4 oz flour quantity almond pastry (see **Pastry**, page 53)

a selection of fruit, such as 2 small oranges, 2 kiwi fruits, 1 banana, strawberries, raspberries, blueberries, grapes

4 tablespoons apricot glaze (see page 474)

1 Heat the oven to 190°C | 375°F | gas mark 5.

2 On a baking sheet, roll or press the pastry into a 23 cm | 9 in disc. Decorate the edges with a fork or by pinching between fingers and thumb. Prick lightly all over with a fork. Chill until firm.

3 Bake for about 15–20 minutes until a pale, biscuit colour. Loosen from the baking sheet with a palette knife and allow to cool slightly and harden on the baking sheet. Slip on to a wire rack and leave to cool completely.

4 Prepare the fruits, leaving any that discolour until you assemble the tart.

5 Brush the pastry with some of the apricot glaze (this helps to stick the fruit in place and prevents the pastry from becoming too soggy).

6 Arrange the fruit, taking care to get contrasting colours next to each other. Brush with apricot glaze as you go, especially on apples, pears and bananas. When all the fruit is in place, brush with the remaining glaze.

NOTE: This tart should not be assembled too far in advance as the pastry will become soggy in about 2 hours.

Strawberry and Mascarpone Tart

SERVES 8

170 g | 6 oz flour quantity pâte sucrée (see **Pastry**, page 52)

For the filling

250 g | 9 oz mascarpone cheese
85 ml | 3 fl oz plain Greek yoghurt
icing sugar, to taste
2 drops of vanilla essence
500 g | 1 lb 2 oz strawberries
170 g | 6 oz redcurrant jelly

1 Heat the oven to 190°C | 375°F | gas mark 5.

2 Line a 20 cm | 8 in loose-based tart tin with the pastry. Chill until firm then blind bake (see **Pastry**, page 44). Cool on a wire rack.

3 Beat the mascarpone with the yoghurt, icing sugar and vanilla to combine. Spread in the pastry case.

4 Wash, hull and dry the strawberries. Slice in half from top to bottom and arrange in overlapping concentric circles over the filling.

5 Heat the redcurrant jelly to melt it and pass through a fine sieve. Brush the strawberries with a generous layer of the jelly.

Strawberry Tartlets

MAKES 20

170 g | 6 oz flour quantity pâte sucrée (see **Pastry**, page 52)

For the filling

250 g | 9 oz mascarpone cheese
55 g | 2 oz caster sugar
450 g | 1 lb strawberries, hulled
4 tablespoons redcurrant jelly, melted

1 Heat the oven to 190°C | 375°F | gas mark 5.
2 Roll out the pastry thinly and use to line 20 tartlet tins. Blind bake (see **Pastry**, page 44) until it is a pale biscuit colour. Remove the beans and lining papers. If the pastry is not quite cooked, return to the oven for 5 minutes. Carefully remove the pastry cases from the tins and leave to cool on a wire rack.
3 Beat the cheese with the sugar and place a teaspoonful of the mixture at the bottom of each case. Arrange the strawberries, cut in half if necessary, on top of the cheese and brush lightly with warm, melted redcurrant jelly.

Sablés aux Fraises

SERVES 6

290 g | 10 oz flour quantity pâte sablée (see **Pastry**, page 54)
675 g | 1½ lb strawberries, hulled and sliced

425 ml | 15 fl oz raspberry coulis (see page 475)
55 g | 2 oz icing sugar, sifted, for dusting

1 Heat the oven to 190°C | 375°F | gas mark 5.
2 Divide the chilled dough into 2 pieces to make rolling easier.
3 Roll out each piece to the thickness of a 20p coin and cut into a total of 18 × 7.5 cm | 3 in circles. Chill to relax for 10 minutes. Bake for 8 minutes or until pale golden. Transfer to a wire rack and leave to cool.
4 Save a few whole strawberries for garnish, then thickly slice the remainder. Mix the sliced strawberries with enough raspberry coulis to coat them. Leave to macerate.
5 Place a pastry base on each of 6 plates. Arrange a few macerated strawberries on top. Cover with a second pastry base and more strawberries. Cover with a third piece of pastry and dust generously with icing sugar. Serve immediately once assembled.
6 Serve the remaining raspberry coulis separately or poured around the sablés.

Danish Strawberry Shortcake

SERVES 4

For the pastry

85 g|3 oz plain flour

a pinch of salt

55 g|2 oz butter

30 g|1 oz caster sugar

30 g|1 oz ground hazelnuts, browned

For the glaze

4 tablespoons redcurrant jelly

1 tablespoon lemon juice

450 g|1 lb strawberries

1 Heat the oven to 190° C|375° F|gas mark 5.

2 Sift the flour with the salt into a bowl. Rub in the butter until the mixture resembles fine breadcrumbs. Stir in the sugar and ground hazelnuts. Knead to form a stiff dough.

3 On a lightly greased baking sheet, roll or press the pastry into a flat 20 cm|8 in disc. Prick with a fork through to the baking sheet. Chill until firm.

4 Bake for 10–15 minutes until pale brown all over. Loosen the pastry from the baking sheet with a palette knife and leave to cool and harden on the sheet.

5 Make the glaze: melt the redcurrant jelly with the lemon juice, but do not allow it to boil. Keep warm.

6 Place the baked shortcake on a serving dish, arrange the strawberries neatly over the top and brush thickly with the redcurrant glaze.

Dark Chocolate Tart

Choose a good quality chocolate that you like the flavour of when eaten plain. If the chocolate is too bitter, the resulting tart will be inedible.

SERVES 10

225 g | 8 oz flour quantity pâte sucrée (see **Pastry**, page 52)

2 egg yolks
85 g | 3 oz caster sugar
1 teaspoon vanilla essence

For the filling

200 g | 7 oz plain chocolate, chopped into small pieces
100 g | 3½ oz unsalted butter
3 eggs, beaten

To serve

1 punnet fresh raspberries
single cream

1 Line a 27 cm | 11 in tart tin with the pâte sucrée. Chill until firm then blind bake (see **Pastry**, page 44).

2 Reduce the oven temperature to 180°C | 350°F | gas mark 4.

3 Melt the chocolate and butter in a bowl placed over, but not touching, steaming water. Stir to combine and allow to cool to warm room temperature.

4 Place the eggs, yolks and sugar in a large mixer bowl and beat until light and fluffy. Stir in the vanilla.

5 Fold in the chocolate/butter mixture.

6 Turn into the pastry case and bake for 15 minutes until nearly set.

7 Remove from the oven and allow to cool. Serve garnished with raspberries and accompanied by single cream.

Crumbles and Cobblers

Traditionally crumbles and cobblers are simple, country desserts made using fruit cooked with a topping. These desserts are made quickly with whatever fruit is to hand or in the garden, hence the proliferation of recipes for apple crumbles and cobblers.

Crumbles are a British pudding that have a lumpy, pastry-like topping made from flour, butter and sugar. The topping is made by the rubbing-in method and is scattered over the top of soft or stewed fruit. Although crumbles are most often made in the autumn and winter, soft summer fruits such as peaches and plums make delicious crumbles.

Cobblers are topped with scone dough which is cut into rounds and placed in an overlapping pattern on top of the filling. The topping is said to resemble cobbles. Cobblers can be either savoury or sweet.

Two other close relatives of crumbles and cobblers are crisps and brown betties. Bread or biscuit crumbs are mixed with butter and sugar then used as a topping for cooked fruit to make a crisp. When the buttered crumbs are layered with the fruit before baking the dessert is called a brown betty.

Dessert crumbles and cobblers can be served with pouring cream, crème anglaise (see page 474) or ice cream.

The following recipes have been expanded to use savoury fillings and toppings as well as the traditional cooked-fruit fillings. Variations to the toppings, as well as the fillings, have been made with the addition of oats, herbs, dried fruits and/or nuts. The topping of a savoury crumble or cobbler becomes the starch portion of the meal, so these dishes are suitable for an informal supper or lunch when served with vegetables or a green salad.

Chicken and Mushroom Cobbler

SERVES 4–6

For the filling

1.35 kg | 3 lb chicken, cleaned but not trussed

1 small onion, thickly sliced

1 bay leaf

6 peppercorns

2 parsley stalks

1 slice of lemon

4 springs of fresh thyme

70 g | 2½ oz butter

225 g | 8 oz closed-cap mushrooms, sliced

45 g | 1½ oz plain flour

1 tablespoon double cream

1 tablespoon chopped fresh parsley

salt and freshly ground black pepper

For the topping

225 g | 8 oz plain flour

a pinch of cayenne pepper

a pinch of salt

2 teaspoons baking powder

½ teaspoon bicarbonate of soda

85 g | 3 oz butter, cut into small cubes

150 ml | 5 fl oz milk

To glaze

1 egg, beaten

1 To poach the chicken, put it breast-side up in a large saucepan and add the onion, bay leaf, peppercorns, parsley stalks, lemon and thyme. Pour enough cold water into the pan to leaves the breasts standing slightly proud of the water. Cover with greaseproof paper and a lid.

2 Place over a medium heat until the occasional bubble comes to the surface, then turn the heat down to maintain the temperature. Do not allow the pot to boil. Poach for 1¼–1½ hours or until the drumstick feels wobbly and the juices run clear from the thigh. Remove the chicken from the pan and set aside to cool.

3 Strain the poaching liquid then boil to reduce to 570 ml | 1 pint.

4 To make the sauce, melt 15 g | ½ oz of the butter in a large sauté pan and stir in the mushrooms. Cook over a medium heat until the mushrooms give up their juices and start to fry. Remove with a slotted spoon and reserve.

5 Add the remaining butter to the pan and stir in the flour. Cook, stirring, for about 2 minutes or until straw-coloured. Remove the pan from the heat and stir in the reduced stock to make a smooth sauce. Return to the heat. Bring to the boil whilst stirring and boil for 2 minutes. Stir in the cream and allow to cool.

6 When the chicken is cool, remove the skin and discard. Cut the meat into chunks.

7 Mix together the sauce, chicken, mushrooms and parsley. Season with salt and pepper then turn into a 20 cm | 8 in square, 1.7 litre | 3 pint ovenproof dish.

8 Heat the oven to 200°C | 400°F | gas mark 6.

9 To make the topping, sift the flour with the cayenne pepper, salt, baking powder and bicarbonate of soda into a large bowl. Toss in the butter then rub in with your fingertips until the mixture resembles fine breadcrumbs. Add enough milk to make a soft but not sticky dough. Pat into a 1¼ cm | ½ in thick disc on a floured work surface and cut into 16 rounds with a floured 4 cm | 1½ in cutter (you will need to reroll the scraps).

10 Overlap the rounds on top of the filling, taking care to cover it completely. Brush the topping with the beaten egg. Place the dish in the top third of the oven for about 35 minutes or until the topping is well-risen and golden-brown and the filling is piping hot. Serve immediately.

Salmon and Leek Cobbler

SERVES 4

For the filling

500 g│1 lb 2 oz salmon fillet

55g│2 oz butter

40 g│1½ oz plain flour

570 ml│1 pint milk

225 g│8 oz small leeks, cut into chunks and steamed

1 tablespoon chopped fresh parsley or dill

salt and freshly ground black pepper

For the topping

225 g│8 oz plain flour

a pinch of cayenne pepper

a pinch of salt

2 teaspoons baking powder

½ teaspoon bicarbonate of soda

85 g│3 oz butter, cut into small cubes

150 ml │ 5 fl oz milk

beaten egg for glazing

1 Heat the oven to 190°C│375°F│gas mark 5.

2 To cook the salmon, place skin-side up in an ovenproof dish and cover with water. Cover with greaseproof paper. Bake for 20 minutes or until the salmon is opaque and the flesh flakes easily. Allow to cool.

3 To make the sauce: melt the butter in a large sauté pan and stir in the flour. Cook over a medium heat until it bubbles, then remove from the heat and gradually stir in the milk to make a smooth paste.

4 Return to the heat and cook, stirring, until boiling. Boil for 2 minutes. Allow to cool.

5 When the salmon is cool, remove the skin and discard. Break into chunks.

6 Mix together the sauce, leeks and parsley or dill. Season with salt and pepper then turn into a 20 cm│8 in square, 1.7 litre│3 pint ovenproof dish.

7 Heat the oven to 200°C│400°F│gas mark 6.

8 To make the topping: sift the flour with the cayenne pepper, salt, baking powder and bicarbonate of soda into a large bowl. Toss in the butter then rub in with your fingertips until the mixture resembles fine breadcrumbs. Add enough milk to make a soft but not too sticky dough. Pat into a 1¼ cm│½ in thick disc on a floured work surface and cut into 16 rounds with a floured 4 cm│1½ in cutter (you will need to reroll the scraps).

9 Overlap the rounds on top of the filling, taking care to cover it completely. Brush the topping with the beaten egg. Place the dish in the top third of the oven and bake for about 35 minutes or until the topping is well-risen and golden-brown and the filling is piping hot. Serve immediately.

Aubergine and Tomato Cobbler

This is a good winter supper dish. Although the vegetable layers can be prepared in advance and chilled, the scone dough must be cooked immediately after mixing and shaping.

SERVES 4

For the filling

3 medium aubergines

7 tablespoons olive oil

1 large red onion, chopped

2 red peppers, cut into slices

1 clove of garlic, crushed

450 g | 1 lb fresh ripe tomatoes, peeled and chopped

1 tablespoon chopped fresh oregano

1 tablespoon chopped fresh basil

½ teaspoon sugar

55 g | 2 oz stale brown bread, cut into 1 cm | ½ in cubes

200 ml | 7 fl oz Greek yoghurt

salt and freshly ground black pepper

For the cobbler

200 g | 7 oz self-raising flour

45 g | 1½ oz butter

55 g | 2 oz Cheddar cheese, grated

1 tablespoon chopped fresh basil

150 ml | 5 fl oz milk

1 Cut the aubergines into slices and degorge by sprinkling with salt and laying on a wire rack over a tray.

2 Heat the oven to 200°C | 400°F | gas mark 6.

3 Heat one tablespoon of oil in a medium saucepan. Add the onion and cover with a lid. Allow to soften for 10 minutes, stirring occasionally to prevent it from browning. Add the sliced peppers and cook for a further 5 minutes.

4 Add the garlic, tomatoes, oregano, basil, sugar, salt and pepper. Cover again and cook until the tomatoes are soft. Add the brown bread and remove from the heat.

5 Heat the grill. Rinse the aubergines and pat dry. Place the slices on the grill rack and brush with oil. Grill until brown, turn over, brush with oil and grill again until brown and softened.

6 Layer the aubergines and tomato mixture in a 2.3 litre | 4 pint casserole dish, starting with a layer of aubergines. Cover with a third of the tomatoes and spread half the yoghurt on top. Add another layer of aubergines, tomato and yoghurt and finish by covering the yoghurt with a final layer of aubergines and topping those with tomatoes. There should be three layers of aubergines, three layers of tomatoes and two layers of yoghurt.

7 To make the cobbler, sift the flour into a large bowl and rub in the butter until it resembles fine breadcrumbs. Add the cheese and herbs. Make a well in the centre of the mixture, pour in all of the milk and mix to a soft, spongy dough with a knife.

8 On a floured surface, knead the dough very lightly until it is just smooth. Roll or press out to about 1.5 cm | ½ in thick and use a biscuit cutter to stamp out 5 cm | 2 in rounds.

9 Put the scones on top of the tomato mixture and bake for approximately 25–30 minutes or until the scones are risen and brown. Serve immediately.

NOTE: If the filling is made in advance and chilled, assemble and cook the cobbler as above, then, to make sure the filling is heated through, turn the oven down to 170°C | 325°F | gas mark 3 and continue to cook for another 15–20 minutes or until it is very hot.

Quorn Herb Crumble

For the filling

3 tablespoons sunflower oil

1 onion, chopped

1 stick of celery, chopped

1 red pepper, chopped

115 g|4 oz carrot, chopped

1 clove of garlic, crushed

350 g|12½ oz Quorn mince

2 tablespoons plain flour

1 × 400 g|14 oz tin chopped tomatoes

150 ml|5 fl oz vegetable stock

1 tablespoon tomato purée

For the crumble

170 g | 6 oz plain flour

85 g | 3 oz butter

3 tablespoons fresh chopped herbs, e.g. parsley, mint, thyme and rosemary

55 g|2 oz Cheddar cheese, grated

salt and freshly ground black pepper

1 Heat 2 tablespoons of oil in a frying pan. Add the onion, celery and pepper and fry for 2 minutes, then add the carrot and garlic and cook over a low heat for 3 minutes. Put into a clean saucepan.

2 Heat 1 tablespoon of oil in the frying pan and add the Quorn mince. Fry for a few minutes and add to the vegetables in the pan.

3 Add 2 tablespoons of flour to the Quorn and vegetables and mix well. Add the tomatoes, stock and tomato purée and bring to the boil, stirring all the time. Season with salt and pepper, reduce the heat and cook gently for 15 minutes. Allow to cool.

4 Meanwhile, make the crumble topping. Rub the butter into the flour until it resembles fine breadcrumbs. Mix in the herbs, cheese, salt and pepper.

5 Heat the oven to 180°C|350°F| gas mark 4.

6 Put the Quorn mixture into a pie dish and cover with the crumble topping. Place on a baking sheet and cook for 25–30 minutes.

Peach and Almond Crumble

SERVES 6

For the topping

170 g|6 oz plain flour

a pinch of salt

85 g|3 oz butter, cut into small cubes

55 g|2 oz ground almonds

85 g|3 oz caster sugar

¼ teaspoon vanilla or almond essence

30 g|1 oz flaked almonds

For the filling

8 ripe peaches, peeled and thickly sliced

2 tablespoons caster sugar

2 teaspoons cornflour

½ teaspoon cinnamon

1 To make the topping: sift the flour with the salt into a bowl.
2 Toss in the cubes of butter then rub in with your fingertips until the mixture resembles fine breadcrumbs. You can also use the food processor.
3 Stir in the ground almonds, sugar and vanilla or almond essence.
4 Continue to rub in the mixture until it begins to form clumps. Chill.
5 Heat the oven to 190°C|375°F|gas mark 5.
6 To prepare the filling: place the peach slices in a bowl. Mix together the caster sugar, cornflour and cinnamon. Sprinkle over the peaches and toss them to coat with the mixture. Place in a shallow ovenproof dish.
7 Sprinkle the crumble topping over the fruit. Scatter over the flaked almonds.
8 Bake in the top third of the oven for 35–40 minutes or until golden-brown.

Blackberry and Apple Crumble

SERVES 4

For the crumble
170 g|6 oz plain flour
a pinch of salt
115 g|4 oz butter
55 g|2 oz porridge oats
55 g|2 oz caster sugar

For the filling
675 g|1½ lb cooking apples
140 g|5 oz blackberries
115 g|4 oz caster sugar
½ teaspoon ground cinnamon
1 teaspoon cornflour

For the topping
1 tablespoon demerara sugar

1 To make the crumble: sift the flour with the salt into a large bowl. Cut the butter into small cubes and toss into the flour. Rub in with your fingertips until the mixture resembles fine breadcrumbs. Stir in the oats and sugar. Rub in a little more until the mixture begins to clump together. Chill whilst making the filling.
2 Heat the oven to 190°C|375°F|gas mark 5.
3 Peel and core the apples and cut into chunks. Place in a bowl with the blackberries.
4 Combine the sugar, cinnamon and cornflour. Sprinkle over the fruit and toss to coat. Place the fruit in a shallow ovenproof dish, leaving a 2.5 cm|1 in space for the topping.
5 Scatter the crumble mixture over the fruit and sprinkle with the demerara sugar.
6 Place on a baking sheet in the top third of the oven and bake for about 40 minutes or until the crumble is golden-brown and the fruit is soft when tested with a skewer.

Apple and Orange Crumble

SERVES 4

For the crumble
170 g | 6 oz plain flour
a pinch of salt
115 g | 4 oz butter
55 g | 2 oz caster sugar

For the filling
3 oranges
900 g | 2 lb cooking apples
3 tablespoons demerara sugar
a good pinch of ground cinnamon

1 To make the crumble: sift the flour with the salt into a bowl. Cut the butter into small pieces and rub in using your fingertips. When the mixture resembles fine breadcrumbs stir in the sugar. Rub in a little more so that the mixture begins to form clumps. Chill whilst making the filling.
2 Heat the oven to 200°C | 400°F | gas mark 6.
3 Peel the oranges using a sharp, serrated knife, removing all of the white pith. Cut the oranges into segments over a bowl, discarding the membranes but reserving the juice.
4 Peel and core the apples. Cut into chunks and mix with the orange segments. Add the sugar and cinnamon then tip into an ovenproof dish.
5 Sprinkle over the crumble topping then place on a baking sheet in the top third of the oven for 35–45 minutes or until well-browned on top. Serve warm.

Plum and Blackberry Cobbler

SERVES 4

For the filling
12 Victoria plums or similar, halved and stoned
140 g | 5 oz blackberries
30 g | 1 oz soft light brown sugar
2 tablespoons cornflour
½ teaspoon ground cinnamon

For the topping
170 g | 6 oz plain flour
a pinch of salt
2 teaspoons baking powder
½ teaspoon bicarbonate of soda
85 g | 3 oz butter
45 g | 1½ oz caster sugar
100 ml | 3½ fl oz plain yoghurt
extra caster sugar for sprinkling

1 Heat the oven to 200°C | 400°F | gas mark 6.
2 Cut the plums into quarters. Place in a bowl with the blackberries.
3 Mix together the sugar, cornflour and cinnamon. Toss with the fruit. Place the fruit in a shallow ovenproof baking dish with a diameter of about 17 cm | 7 in.
4 To make the topping: sift the flour with the salt, baking powder and bicarbonate of soda into a large bowl. Cut the butter into small cubes and toss into the flour. Rub in using

your fingertips until the mixture resembles fine breadcrumbs. Stir in the caster sugar. The topping can be made in a food processor up to this point.

5 Stir the yoghurt into the flour mixture to make a soft, slightly sticky dough. Turn the dough on to a floured work surface and pat into a 1 cm|½ in thick disc. Cut into 3.5 cm|1½ in rounds using a floured scone cutter. Place the 'cobbles' on to the fruit, slightly overlapping. Sprinkle with caster sugar.

6 Bake in the top third of the oven for 30–35 minutes or until the topping is golden-brown and the fruit is bubbling. Serve warm.

Apple and Hazelnut Brown Betty

SERVES 6

200 g|7 oz fresh breadcrumbs, preferably wholemeal	½ teaspoon ground cinnamon
	¼ teaspoon ground nutmeg
85 g|3 oz butter, melted	grated zest of 1 lemon and some of the juice
100 g|3½ oz hazelnuts, toasted and chopped	900 g|2 lb cooking apples, peeled and cored
85–115 g|3–4 oz caster sugar	1 tablespoon demerara sugar

1 Heat the oven to 190°C|375°F|gas mark 5. Butter a 1.4 litre|2 pint ovenproof dish.
2 Toss the breadcrumbs with the butter and mix in the hazelnuts. Sprinkle one third of the mixture on the bottom of the dish.
3 Mix together the caster sugar, cinnamon, nutmeg and lemon zest.
4 Cut the apples into chunks in a bowl then toss with the sugar mixture and a little lemon juice.
5 Place half of the apples on top of the breadcrumbs in the dish then top with another third of the topping. Repeat with the remaining apples and breadcrumbs.
6 Cover with buttered foil and bake for 30 minutes. Remove the foil and sprinkle over the demerara sugar. Bake for a further 20 minutes or until the apples are tender when pierced with a skewer and the top is browned and crisp. Serve warm.

Amaretti Pear Crisp

SERVES 4

6 firm, ripe pears

3 tablespoons butter

2 tablespoons caster sugar

2 tablespoons rum or brandy

To serve

150 ml | 5 fl oz single cream

½ teaspoon ground cinnamon

1 teaspoon cornflour

For the topping

115 g | 4 oz plain flour

85 g | 3 oz butter

2 tablespoons caster sugar

1 teaspoon ground cinnamon

4 pairs amaretti biscuits, finely crushed

1 Heat the oven to 190°C | 375°F | gas mark 5.

2 Peel the pears and cut into eighths lengthways, removing the cores.

3 Melt the butter over a medium heat in a large sauté pan, then cook the pears for about 5 minutes or until slightly softened. Sprinkle over the sugar, cinnamon, cornflour and the rum and stir to coat. Place the pears in a shallow ovenproof dish.

4 To make the topping: place the flour in a bowl. Cut the butter into the flour using 2 table knives, scissor-fashion, until the pieces are no bigger than currants.

5 Stir in the remaining topping ingredients and sprinkle over the pears.

6 Bake in the top third of the oven for 20–25 minutes or until the crisp is lightly browned.

7 Serve warm with the cream.

Pâtisserie

Pâtisserie is a French word that is used for both the art of pastry and cake-making as well as the shop in which the pâtisserie can be purchased, often along with a cup of *café au lait* or *chocolat chaud*.

The famous French chef La Varenne wrote the first book of pastry-making in 1655. Before this time cakes and pastries were baked almost as an afterthought in the large ovens used for baking bread. Small ovens, called *petits fours*, began to be used to bake the pastries. Today the miniature forms of pâtisserie served at the end of a formal meal are still called petits fours, after the ovens.

A pâtisserie today will sell a range of pastries, biscuits and meringues, ranging from simple sugar biscuits to intricately decorated cakes, as well as breads and savoury tarts.

Eccles Cakes

MAKES 6

225 g | 8 oz flour quantity rough puff pastry (see **Pastry**, page 60)

For the filling

15 g | ½ oz butter
55 g | 2 oz soft light brown sugar
115 g | 4 oz currants
30 g | 1 oz chopped mixed peel

½ teaspoon ground cinnamon
¼ teaspoon freshly grated nutmeg
¼ teaspoon ground ginger
grated zest of ½ lemon
1 teaspoon lemon juice

To finish

1 egg white
caster sugar

1 Heat the oven to 220°C | 425°F | gas mark 7.
2 Roll the pastry to the thickness of a £1 coin. Cut 6 × 12.5 cm | 5 in rounds. Chill.
3 Melt the butter in a saucepan and stir in all the other filling ingredients. Cool.
4 Place a good teaspoon of filling in the centre of each pastry round. Pull the pastry around the filling and squeeze to seal. Trim away any excess pastry. Turn the balls over and place on a baking sheet. Flatten lightly with a rolling pin until the fruit begins to show through the pastry.
5 Beat the egg white lightly with a fork, until frothy. Brush the tops of the cakes with this and sprinkle with sugar. With a sharp knife, make 3 small parallel cuts on the top.
6 Bake for 20 minutes, or until lightly browned.

Apple Turnovers

MAKES 8

225 g | 8 oz flour quantity puff pastry (see **Pastry**, page 58)

45 g | 1½ oz unsalted butter

30 g | 1 oz caster sugar

4 sharp dessert apples, peeled, cored and cut into 1 cm | ½ in cubes

grated zest of 1 lemon

3 teaspoons lemon juice

½ teaspoon ground cinnamon

1 egg, beaten

1 Roll out the puff pastry to about 6 mm | ¼ in thick. Cut out 8 × 12 cm | 5 in circles and roll each one into an oval shape measuring approximately 12 × 20 cm | 5 × 8 in. Put them on to a baking sheet and chill.

2 Melt the butter and add the sugar. Cook for 1 minute and add the apples. Cook them over a medium heat for 5 minutes, stirring occasionally to prevent them from burning. Add the lemon zest, lemon juice and cinnamon. Stir well. Pour in 100 ml | 3½ fl oz water and cook the apples until the water has evaporated and the apples are pulpy. Some apples take longer than others, so if necessary add a little more water to continue the cooking process. Allow to cool completely.

3 Heat the oven to 200°C | 400°F | gas mark 6. Place baking parchment paper on 2 baking sheets. Put the ovals of pastry on a lightly floured work surface. Brush beaten egg around the edges of each oval. Divide the apple between the pastries and fold each one very carefully in half. Try to exclude as much air as possible from each one before sealing the edges. Knock up the edges and mark into a scallop design with your finger and the back of a knife.

4 Place the turnovers on the lined baking sheets, brush carefully with the beaten egg and make a lattice design on the tops with the back of a knife. Bake in the top of the oven for 15 minutes.

Poppy Seed Jalousie

Jalousie is French for a shutter, which this pastry resembles.

SERVES 6

1 recipe Danish pastry (see page 163) or 225 g|8 oz flour quantity puff pastry (see **Pastry**, page 58)

15 g|½ oz dry breadcrumbs
30 g|1 oz raisins
30 g|1 oz mixed peel
¼ teaspoon ground cinnamon

For the filling

100 g|3½ oz poppy seeds, ground
170 ml|6 fl oz milk
55 g|2 oz caster sugar
1 tablespoon unsalted butter

To finish

1 egg, beaten
caster sugar

1 To make the filling: place the poppy seeds, milk, sugar and butter in a small saucepan and bring to the boil. Simmer, stirring continuously, until the mixture is thick, rather like molten tar.

2 Remove from the heat and stir in the breadcrumbs, raisins, peel and cinnamon. Allow to cool.

3 Heat the oven to 200°C|400°F|gas mark 6. Place a baking sheet to heat in the top third of the oven.

4 Roll the pastry to the size of an A4 piece of paper. Place on an ungreased baking sheet. Make slits on the angle from both of the long sides toward the middle, leaving the middle third of the pastry uncut.

5 Spread the filling down the central, uncut pastry. Fold over the strips, alternating from side to side. Glaze with the beaten egg. Chill until firm.

6 Glaze the pastry again and sprinkle over the caster sugar. Place the pastry, still on the baking sheet, on top of the baking sheet heating in the oven (the bottom heat will help the underside of the pastry to cook). Bake in the top third of the oven for 20–25 minutes or until the pastry is golden-brown.

NOTE: A coffee-grinder is ideal for grinding the poppy seeds.

Apple and Raisin Jalousie

SERVES 4

225 g|8 oz flour quantity rough puff pastry (see
  Pastry, page 60)

For the filling

225 g|8 oz dessert apples
30 g|1 oz unsalted butter
55 g|2 oz soft light brown sugar

squeeze of lemon juice
1 tablespoon brandy
55 g|2 oz raisins

To finish

milk
caster sugar

1 Heat the oven to 220°C|425°F|gas mark 7.

2 Roll the pastry into 2 thin rectangles. One should be smaller, measuring around 13 × 20 cm|5 × 8 in, and the other should be 17 × 25 cm|7 × 10 in. Prick the smaller rectangle all over with a fork. Chill until firm.

3 Meanwhile, make the filling. Quarter and core the apples and cut into large chunks. Melt the butter with the sugar and stir in the apples and lemon juice. Cover with a lid and cook until the apples are tender but not mushy. Stir in the brandy and allow to cool. Stir in the raisins.

4 Bake the smaller piece of pastry until crisp and brown. Remove from the oven and turn over on to a baking sheet. Allow to cool. Spread the apple filling all over the cooked piece of pastry.

4 Lay the larger pastry rectangle on a board, dust it lightly with flour so that nothing sticks and fold it in half lengthways, gently. Using a sharp knife, cut through the folded side of the pastry in parallel lines, at right angles to the edge, as though you were cutting between the teeth of a comb. Leave an uncut margin about 2.5 cm|1 in wide, all round the other edges, so that when you open up the pastry you will have a solid border.

5 Now lay the cut pastry on top of the pastry covered with apple filling and tuck the edges underneath. Brush the top layer carefully all over with milk. Sprinkle well with sugar.

6 Bake for about 20 minutes, until well-browned. Serve warm or cold.

Choux à la Crème

The choux pastry can be made in advance, spooned on to the baking sheet and frozen before it is baked. The choux buns can then be baked from frozen. Once the choux à la crème have been assembled, they will last for about 1½ hours before going soggy.

The choux pastry can also be piped into fingers to make éclairs. Fill with sweetened whipped cream and coat with chocolate or coffee glacé icing.

SERVES 8–10

For the pastry
55 g | 2 oz butter
150 ml | 5 fl oz water
70 g | 2½ oz plain flour, sifted
a pinch of salt
2 eggs, beaten

For the filling
425 ml | 15 fl oz double cream
icing sugar, sifted
225 g | 8 oz fresh fruit, such as strawberries,
   raspberries, peaches, apricots, washed and sliced
   as necessary

1 Heat the oven to 200°C | 400°F | gas mark 6.
2 Cut the butter into cubes and put into a saucepan with the water. Bring slowly to the boil so that by the time the water boils, the butter is completely melted.
3 As soon as the mixture is boiling really fast, tip in all the flour with the salt and remove the pan from the heat.
4 Working as fast as you can, beat the mixture hard with a wooden spoon: it will soon become thick and smooth and leave the sides of the pan. Do not overbeat at this stage. Leave to cool.
5 When the mixture is cool, beat in the eggs gradually until it is soft, shiny and smooth. If the eggs are large, it may not be necessary to add all of them. The mixture should be of a dropping consistency.
6 Place spoonfuls of the mixture 5 cm | 2 in apart on a baking sheet. Bake in the top of the oven for about 30 minutes or until the buns are brown and crisp.
7 Remove from the oven and make a hole in the side of each bun to let the steam escape. Return to the oven for 5 minutes to dry the insides out. Transfer to a wire rack and leave to cool completely.
8 Meanwhile, whip the cream until just stiff and sweeten with 1–2 tablespoons icing sugar.
9 Split the buns in half and place a spoonful of the whipped cream and some fruit inside. Dust the tops with sifted icing sugar.

Paris–Brest

This is a ring-shaped pastry that was invented by an enterprising Parisian pastry chef in 1891. His pâtisserie was on the route of the bicycle race that went from Paris to Brest in Brittany. The idea was that it was shaped like a bicycle wheel.

SERVES 8–10

2 egg quantity choux pastry (see **Pastry**, page 64)

1 egg, beaten

45 g | 1½ oz flaked almonds

For the praline

115 g | 4 oz granulated sugar

a pinch of cream of tartar

55 g | 2 oz almonds

For the filling

1 full quantity crème pâtissière (see page 458)

icing sugar

1 Heat the oven to 200°C | 400°F | gas mark 6. Line a large baking sheet with baking parchment and draw a circle in pencil round a dinner plate measuring 25–27 cm | 10–11 in. Turn the paper over so that the circle is on the underside but visible. The pastry ring will expand a bit, so make sure you have a baking sheet that is big enough.

2 Make the choux pastry and put it into a piping bag fitted with a 1 cm | ½ in plain or star nozzle. Pipe a large circle, using the pencil line as your guide, on to the baking sheet. If any parts of the choux are sticking up, push them down using a wet finger. Lightly brush some beaten egg over the top of the ring. Make sure it doesn't drip down the sides as it may stop it rising evenly. Scatter the flaked almonds around the top. Place in the oven for 35 minutes or until crisp and golden in colour. Make a few holes in the side of the ring and put back in the oven for about 5 minutes. This allows the steam to escape and stops the pastry ring from going soggy. Put on a wire rack to cool down completely.

3 Make the praline: grease a baking sheet with oil. Put the sugar and cream of tartar in a heavy pan and place over a low heat. It will start to liquefy and turn brown. If this happens too quickly, take it off the heat for a few seconds. Once all the sugar has melted, add the almonds and cook in the caramel for a few seconds. Do not allow it to burn. Pour it out on to the baking sheet and leave until it has cooled down completely. Take care not to touch the caramel as it is very hot. Once cold, break into pieces and either crush finely with a rolling pin or whizz in a food processor. Mix it with the prepared crème pâtissière.

4 To assemble: use a bread knife to split the pastry ring in half. Fill a piping bag fitted with a 1 cm | ½ in plain or star nozzle with the crème pâtissière and praline. Pipe into the bottom half of the pastry and replace the top half. Alternatively you could spoon the filling around the ring. Dust with a little icing sugar and serve.

NOTE: This will also make 6 individual 7.5 cm | 3 in rings. For a quicker filling you can use 290 ml | 10 fl oz lightly whipped double cream mixed into 3–4 tablespoons of chocolate hazelnut spread. Continue to whip until it just holds its shape. Do not overwhip.

Chocolate Profiteroles

MAKES ABOUT 27

3 egg quantity choux pastry, cooked as in recipe (see *Pastry*, page 64)

For the filling

570 ml|1 pint double cream

1–2 tablespoons icing sugar, sifted

225 g|8 oz plain chocolate, chopped into small pieces

15 g|½ oz butter

2 tablespoons water

1 Whip the cream until it just holds its shape, then sift over and fold in the icing sugar.
2 Using a ½ cm|¼ in plain nozzle and a piping bag, pipe the cream into the choux buns through the hole made during baking. Fill until the cream begins to squeeze out.
3 Place the chocolate with the butter and water in a small bowl over, but not touching, steaming water. Melt the chocolate, stirring occasionally.
4 One at a time, hold the base of each choux bun and dip the tops in the melted chocolate, rotating the buns to coat as much of the top as possible without coating your fingers. Place the buns on a serving plate.
5 Serve as soon as possible. Do not chill unless the kitchen is very hot or the chocolate will lose its sheen and the pastry will become soggy.

Gâteau St-Honoré

SERVES 10

170 g | 6 oz flour quantity pâte sucrée (see *Pastry*, page 52)

3 egg quantity choux pastry (see *Pastry*, page 64)

2 x quantity crème pâtissière (see page 458)

170 g | 6 oz granulated sugar

1 Heat the oven to 190°C | 375°F | gas mark 5. Line a 20 cm|8 in flan ring with the pâte sucrée. Chill until firm. Bake blind until biscuit-coloured (see *Pastry*, page 44).
2 Make the profiteroles: increase the oven temperature to 200°C|400°F|gas mark 6.
3 Put rounded teaspoonfuls of the choux pastry on to 2 lightly greased baking sheets and bake for 25 minutes until firm and pale brown.
4 Using a skewer, make a hole the size of a pea in the base of each choux bun and return to the oven for 5 minutes to allow the insides to dry out. Leave on a wire rack to cool.
5 Put the crème pâtissière into a piping bag fitted with a plain nozzle and pipe into the profiteroles through the holes made by the skewer. Spread the remaining crème patissière in the bottom of the pastry case, then pile the profiteroles into a pyramid on top.
6 Heat the sugar in a heavy saucepan over a low heat until it caramelizes. Remove from the heat and dip the base of the saucepan into cold water, taking care not to touch the caramel as it is very hot. Pour the caramel over the profiteroles.

Apricot Gougère

SERVES 6

3 egg quantity choux pastry (see **Pastry**, page 64)

For the filling
225 g|8 oz fresh apricots
150 ml|5 fl oz sugar syrup (see page 475)
2 tablespoons apricot jam
290 ml|10 fl oz double cream, whipped

To finish
140 g|5oz icing sugar, sifted
30 g|1 oz almonds, toasted

1 Heat the oven to 200°C|400°F|gas mark 6.
2 Wash and halve the apricots and remove the stones. Poach in the sugar syrup until just tender (about 15 minutes). Drain well and leave to cool.
3 Spoon the pastry into a circle about 20 cm|8 in in diameter on a lightly greased baking tray. Bake for about 30 minutes until brown and crisp. Allow to cool.
4 Split horizontally with a bread knife. Scoop out any uncooked pastry and discard. Leave the choux ring on a wire rack to cool completely.
5 Place the base of the choux ring on a serving dish. Heat the jam and spread it on the base of the choux ring.
6 Mix 30 g|1 oz of the icing sugar with the cream and layer the cream and apricots on the base of the ring.
7 Mix the remaining icing sugar with a little boiling water until just runny. Coat the top of the choux ring with the icing and, while still wet, sprinkle with browned almonds.

Apple Pecan Choux Ring

SERVES 6–8

3 egg quantity choux pastry (see **Pastry**, page 64)

For the filling

6 dessert apples, such as Granny Smith

170 g│6 oz granulated sugar

30 g│1 oz butter

100 g│3½ oz pecan nuts, toasted

For the icing

1–2 tablespoons boiling water

115 g│4 oz icing sugar, sifted

a few drops of vanilla essence

1 Heat the oven to 200°C│400°F│gas mark 6. Lightly grease a baking sheet.

2 Spoon the choux pastry on to the baking sheet in a ring about 25 cm│10 in diameter.

3 Bake in the top third of the oven for 25 minutes or until golden-brown and firm to the touch.

4 Slice the ring in half horizontally and scrape any uncooked mixture from the inside. Return the ring to the oven, cut sides up, for a further 5 minutes to dry out the interior.

5 Cool on a wire rack then place the base of the ring on a serving dish.

6 For the filling, core and slice the apples into eighths but do not peel.

7 Place the granulated sugar in a sauté pan and pour over 100 ml│3½ fl oz warm water. Place over a low heat to melt the sugar then bring to the boil.

8 When the sugar starts to turn brown, add the apples, turning to coat them in the caramel. Take care not to touch the caramel as it will be extremely hot.

9 When the apples are just soft, stir in the butter and half the pecans. Pile the mixture into the base of the choux ring. Allow to cool.

10 For the icing, place 1 tablespoon of boiling water into a small bowl and gradually stir in the icing sugar to make a smooth icing the consistency of cream. Add additional water as required. Flavour with the vanilla.

11 Place the top of the choux ring over the apples then drizzle the icing over the top. Sprinkle over the remaining pecans whilst the icing is still wet. Allow to set but serve within 4 hours.

Chocolate Pecan Tassies

The word 'tassie' is a Scottish term for little cup. These little pastries are excellent after dinner or as something sweet at a drinks party.

MAKES 24

For the pastry

55 g | 2 oz good quality full-fat cream cheese

55 g | 2 oz butter, softened

85 g | 3 oz plain flour

a pinch of salt

For the filling

75 g | 2½ oz golden syrup

30 g | 1 oz dark chocolate, chopped into small pieces

15 g | ½ oz butter

15 g | ½ oz soft light brown sugar

½ teaspoon instant coffee granules

2 teaspoons boiling water

½ teaspoon vanilla essence

1 egg, beaten

2 tablespoons cocoa powder

55 g | 2 oz pecan nuts, finely chopped

1 Mix together the cream cheese and butter until just combined. Do not beat.
2 Sift over the flour with the salt and stir into the cream cheese/butter mixture. The pastry will be very soft.
3 Place the pastry between 2 sheets of clingfilm or greaseproof paper and gently roll out to a 2 mm | 1/10 in thickness.
4 Chill for 15 minutes.
5 Remove 1 piece of the clingfilm or greaseproof paper and cut out 5 cm | 2 in rounds with a biscuit cutter. Re-roll the pastry once. Ease the pieces of pastry into mini-muffin tins. Chill until firm.
6 Heat the oven to 190°C | 375°F | gas mark 5.
7 For the filling, place the golden syrup, chocolate, butter and sugar in a heatproof bowl set over but not in steaming water, until the chocolate has melted.
8 Mix the coffee granules with the boiling water to dissolve, then stir into the chocolate mixture. Add the vanilla. Remove the bowl from the water and allow to cool until just warm.
9 Stir in the egg. Sift over the cocoa powder then stir in. Fold in the pecan nuts.
10 Fill each pastry case to the brim, then return to the centre of the oven for 20 minutes or until the filling is set. It should soufflé slightly when done.
11 Serve warm or at room temperature. Store in an airtight container for up to 4 days.

Raspberry Rugelach

These pastry crescents using cream-cheese pastry are a Hanukkah tradition. They keep well for several days.

MAKES 24

For the pastry

200 g | 7 oz good quality cream cheese, at room
temperature
200 g | 7 oz butter, softened
2 tablespoons clear honey
250 g | 9 oz plain flour

For the filling

115 g | 4 oz seedless raspberry jam or preserve
50 g | 1¾ oz walnuts, toasted and finely chopped

For the topping

1 tablespoon caster sugar
1 teaspoon ground cinnamon
1 egg, beaten and sieved
50 g | 1¾ oz walnuts, toasted and finely chopped

1 Beat the cream cheese and butter until just combined. Take care not to overmix or the mixture will become too runny. Stir in the honey.

2 Gently fold the flour into the butter mixture. Divide the dough into 2 equal portions and roll between 2 sheets of baking parchment or clingfilm into 2 flat discs, about 30 cm | 12 in in diameter. Chill until firm.

3 Remove the baking parchment or clingfilm from the pastry and spread the jam over the pastry discs. Sprinkle the nuts over the jam.

4 Cut each disc into 12 equal segments, making the cuts like the spokes of a wheel, and gently roll up. Roll into crescents. Place the individual pastries on to 2 baking sheets lined with baking parchment. Chill until firm.

5 Heat the oven to 180°C | 350°F | gas mark 4.

6 For the topping, mix together the caster sugar and the cinnamon. Brush the pastries with the egg wash, then sprinkle with the nuts and the cinnamon sugar.

7 Bake in the top third of the oven for 20 minutes or until a deep golden-brown. Cool on a wire rack.

VARIATION

Apricot and Pistachio Rugelach: Substitute apricot jam for the raspberry jam and shelled chopped pistachios for the walnuts. The pistachios do not need to be toasted.

Chocolate and Hazelnut Rugelach

These pastries are particularly easy to make and will keep for several days.

MAKES 24

For the pastry

200 g | 7 oz good quality cream cheese, at room
  temperature
200 g | 7 oz butter, softened
2 tablespoons caster sugar
250 g | 9 oz plain flour

For the topping

1 tablespoon caster sugar
1 teaspoon cocoa powder
1 egg, beaten and sieved
50 g | 1¾ oz hazelnuts, chopped and toasted

For the filling

200 ml | 8 tablespoons chocolate hazelnut spread, at
  room temperature
50 g | 1¾ oz hazelnuts, chopped and toasted

1 Beat the cream cheese and butter until just combined. Take care not to overmix or the mixture will become too runny. Stir in the sugar.

2 Gently fold the flour into the butter mixture. Divide the dough into 2 equal portions and roll between clingfilm into 2 flat discs, about 30 cm | 12 in in diameter. Chill until firm.

3 Remove the clingfilm from the pastry and spread the chocolate over the pastry discs. Sprinkle the nuts over the chocolate.

4 Cut each disc into 12 equal segments, making the cuts like the spokes of a wheel, and gently roll up. Shape into crescents. Place the individual pastries on to 2 baking sheets lined with baking parchment. Chill until firm.

5 Heat the oven to 180°C | 350°F | gas mark 4.

6 For the topping, mix together the caster sugar and the cocoa powder. Brush the pastries with the egg wash. Sprinkle with the hazelnuts, then sieve over the sugar and cocoa powder mixture.

7 Bake in the top third of the oven for 18–20 minutes or until a deep golden-brown. Cool on a wire rack.

Apple Strudel

SERVES 6

285 g | 10 oz flour quantity strudel pastry (see page 66), or 400 g | 14 oz quantity bought filo pastry

To finish

85 g | 3 oz butter, melted

icing sugar, sifted

For the filling

900 g | 2 lb cooking apples

a handful of currants, sultanas and raisins

55 g | 2 oz soft light brown sugar

½ teaspoon ground cinnamon

a pinch of ground cloves

3 tablespoons browned breadcrumbs (dry white crumbs)

grated zest and juice of ½ lemon

1　Heat the oven to 200°C | 400°F | gas mark 6. Grease a baking sheet.

2　Prepare the filling: peel, core and cut the apples into chunks and mix together with the dried fruit, sugar, spices, breadcrumbs, lemon zest and juice. Taste the apples and add more sugar if required.

3　Flour a large tea towel. If using home-made pastry, stretch to a rectangle of at least 40 × 60 cm | 16 × 24 in on the tea towel. Bought filo should be laid out to a rectangle of the same size. Use several overlapping layers.

4　Brush with melted butter. Place the filling at one end of the pastry. Using the tea towel, gently roll up the strudel.

5　Place on the greased baking sheet and curve into a horseshoe shape. Brush with melted butter.

6　Bake in the top third of the oven for 30–40 minutes or until golden-brown. Insert a skewer into the strudel to check that the apples are tender. Sift over the icing sugar and serve warm or at room temperature.

Rhubarb and Blueberry Strudel

SERVES 6

140 g | 5 oz flour quantity strudel pastry (see page
    66) or 250 g | 9 oz bought filo pastry
30 g | 1 oz unsalted butter, melted

To finish

2 tablespoons icing sugar

For the filling

100 g | 3½ oz caster sugar

3 tablespoons cornflour

½ teaspoon ground cinnamon

40 g | 1½ oz fresh white breadcrumbs

600 g | 1 lb 5 oz trimmed rhubarb, cut into chunks

200 g | 7 oz blueberries, washed

1 Heat the oven to 200°C | 400°F | gas mark 6.

2 Combine the caster sugar, cornflour, cinnamon and breadcrumbs, then toss in with the rhubarb and blueberries.

3 Lay 2 sheets of filo pastry on a clean work surface with the long edges slightly overlapping, creating a rectangle about 25 × 45 cm | 10 × 18 in. Brush with a little of the melted butter. Place 2 more pastry sheets over the top and brush with more butter. Place another 2 pastry sheets over the top to make a total of 3 layers.

4 Arrange the fruit mixture in a log shape along the edge of the pastry, leaving a 2.5 cm | 1 in border at each end. Fold over the edges of the pastry to keep the fruit from falling out.

5 Carefully roll up the strudel and place it on a large baking sheet, seam-side down. If the strudel is too long to fit on the baking sheet, curve it into a horseshoe shape. Brush the remaining melted butter over the strudel. If making ahead, store in the refrigerator at this point.

6 Bake the strudel in the top third of the oven for 20 to 25 minutes, until golden-brown.

7 Mix 1 tablespoon of icing sugar with 2 teaspoons cold water in a small cup and brush over the top of the strudel.

8 Return to the oven and continue to cook for 5 minutes, then allow to cool.

9 Dust with the remaining icing sugar and serve warm or at room temperature.

NOTE: When rhubarb is not is season, substitute cooking apples or pears for the rhubarb.

Gâteau Pithiviers

SERVES 6–8

225 g | 8 oz flour quantity puff pastry
  (see *Pastry*, page 58)
1 egg, beaten with ½ teaspoon salt

To finish

icing sugar, sifted

For the filling

125 g | 4½ oz butter, softened
125 g | 4½ oz sugar
1 egg
1 egg yolk
125 g | 4½ oz whole blanched almonds
15 g | ½ oz plain flour
2 tablespoons rum

1 Chill the puff pastry.
2 Make the almond filling: cream the butter in a bowl, add the sugar and beat thoroughly. Beat in the egg and egg yolk; then stir in the ground almonds, flour and rum.
3 Roll out just under half the puff pastry to a circle about 27 cm | 11 in in diameter. Using a pan lid as a guide, cut out a 25 cm | 10 in circle from this with a sharp knife. Roll out the remaining pastry slightly thicker than for the first round and cut out another 25 cm | 10 in circle. Set the thinner circle on a baking sheet and mound the filling in the centre, leaving a 2.5 cm | 1 in border. Brush the border with beaten egg. Set the second circle on top and press the edges together firmly.
4 Scallop the edge of the gâteau by pulling it in at intervals with the back of a knife. Brush the gâteau with beaten egg and, working from the centre, score the top in curves like the petals of a flower. Do not cut through to the filling. Chill the gâteau until firm.
5 Heat the oven to 220°C | 425°F | gas mark 7.
6 Bake the gâteau in the oven for 30–35 minutes, or until firm, puffed and brown.
7 Heat the grill to its highest setting.
8 Dust the gâteau with icing sugar. Place under the grill until lightly glazed.

Millefeuilles

SERVES 4–6

225 g│8 oz flour quantity rough puff pastry (see *Pastry*, page 60) or puff pastry (see *Pastry*, page 58)

225 g│8 oz strawberries, hulled and sliced

290 ml│10 fl oz double cream, whipped

225 g│8 oz icing sugar, sifted

1 Heat the oven to 220° C│425° F│gas mark 7.

2 On a floured board, roll the pastry into a thin rectangle about 20 × 30 cm│8 × 12 in. Place on a baking sheet. Prick all over with a fork. Chill until firm.

3 Bake in the oven for about 20 minutes, until brown. Remove and allow to cool.

4 Cut the pastry into 3 neat strips, each measuring 10 × 20 cm│4 × 8 in. (Keep the trimmings for decoration.) Choose the piece of pastry with the smoothest base and reserve. Sweeten the cream with 1 tablespoon of the icing sugar. Spread the other 2 strips with cream, top with strawberries and sandwich together. Cover with the third, reserved piece of pastry, smooth side uppermost. Press down gently but firmly.

5 Mix the icing sugar with boiling water until it is thick, smooth and creamy. Be careful not to add too much water. Coat the top of the pastry with the icing and, while still warm, sprinkle crushed cooked pastry trimmings along the edges of the icing. Allow to cool before serving.

NOTE: To 'feather' the icing, put 1 tablespoon warmed, sieved liquid jam in a piping bag fitted with a 'writing' nozzle. Pipe parallel lines of jam down the length of the newly iced millefeuilles, about 2 cm│¾ in apart. Before the icing or jam is set, drag the back of a knife across the lines of jam. This will pull the lines into points where the knife crosses them. Repeat this every 5 cm│2 in the same direction, then drag the back of the knife in the opposite direction between the drag-lines already made.

Millefeuilles are also delicious covered with fresh strawberries and glazed with warm, melted redcurrant jelly instead of icing.

Summer Fruit Feuilletées

SERVES 4

225 g│8 oz flour quantity puff pastry (see *Pastry*, page 58)

1 egg, beaten

For the coulis

250 g│9 oz blackcurrants

115 g│4 oz redcurrants

115 g│4 oz caster sugar

45 ml│3 tablespoons crème de cassis

For the filling

8 tablespoons Greek yoghurt, sweetened with 2 teaspoons icing sugar

a selection of summer fruits, such as 115 g│4 oz raspberries, 115 g│4 oz strawberries, hulled, and 115 g│4 oz blueberries

To serve

icing sugar, sifted

1 Roll the pastry to 1 cm|½ in thickness. Cut out 4 star shapes, each 8.5 cm|3½ in across. Chill until firm, about 30 minutes.

2 Heat the oven to 200°C|400°F|gas mark 6.

3 Place the pastry stars on a baking sheet. Brush the tops with beaten egg and bake in the top third of the oven for 15–20 minutes or until risen and golden-brown. Leave to cool on a wire rack.

4 Prepare the coulis: de-stalk the blackcurrants and redcurrants and place in a saucepan with the sugar. Cook over a low heat for 15 minutes or until the fruit is pulpy.

5 Press the pulp and juice through a sieve. Taste for sweetness and add more sugar if necessary. Stir in the crème de cassis.

6 Using a sharp knife, split each pastry star in half horizontally. Spoon 2 tablespoons of yoghurt on to each of the 4 bases.

7 Arrange the summer fruits of your choice on top. Spoon 2 teaspoons of coulis on to the fruit and cover with the pastry lids. Dust the top of the lids with icing sugar.

8 Spoon a layer of coulis on to 4 individual plates and place a feuilletée on each plate.

Feuilletée de Poires Tiède

SERVES 4

340 g|12 oz flour quantity puff pastry (see **Pastry**, page 58)

290 ml|10 fl oz double cream, lightly whipped

55 ml|2 fl oz Poire William liqueur

icing sugar, to taste

For the filling

2 William pears

290 ml|10 fl oz sugar syrup (see page 475)

To finish

icing sugar, sifted

1 Peel the pears, cut into quarters and remove the cores. Poach in the sugar syrup until translucent.

2 Heat the oven to 220°C|425°F|gas mark 7.

3 On a lightly floured work surface, roll the pastry into 4 neat rectangles, each measuring 6 × 10 cm|2½ × 4 in. Chill for 20 minutes.

4 Bake the pastry for 15 minutes until brown. Split in half horizontally, remove any uncooked dough and return to the turned-off oven to dry out. Remove from the oven.

5 Flavour the cream with the liqueur and icing sugar to taste.

6 Sandwich the pastry slices together with the cream mixture and slices of warm poached pear. Dust the pastry lightly with icing sugar.

Baklava

This recipe has been taken from Claudia Roden's *A New Book of Middle Eastern Food.*

SERVES 6

170 g|6 oz unsalted butter, melted
1 × 400 g|14 oz packet filo pastry (24 sheets)
340 g|12 oz pistachios, walnuts or almonds, ground
   or finely chopped

For the syrup

450 g|1 lb granulated sugar
290 ml|10 fl oz water
2 tablespoons lemon juice
2 tablespoons orange-blossom water

1 Make the syrup: put the sugar, water and lemon juice into a saucepan, dissolve over a low heat and then simmer until thick enough to coat the back of a wooden spoon. Add the orange-blossom water and simmer for a further 2 minutes. Remove from the heat and leave to cool, then chill.

2 Heat the oven to 170°C|325°F|gas mark 3.

3 Brush melted butter on the base and sides of a deep 20 × 25 cm|8 × 10 in baking tray. Put half the filo sheets into the tray, brushing each sheet with melted butter and overlapping or folding the sides over where necessary.

4 Spread the nuts evenly over the pastry, spoon over 4 tablespoons of the sugar syrup and then cover with the remaining sheets of filo, brushing each one as you layer it up. Brush the top layer with butter. Cut diagonally through to the bottom into diamond shapes with a sharp, serrated knife.

5 Bake for 45 minutes, then turn the oven temperature up to 220°C|425°F|gas mark 7 and bake for a further 15 minutes or until well-risen and golden-brown.

6 Remove from the oven and pour the chilled syrup over the hot baklava. Leave to cool.

7 When cold, cut into diamond shapes and place on a serving dish.

Konafa

Konafa pastry is shredded filo dough. It looks like vermicelli and is available fresh or frozen from specialist delicatessens.

SERVES 8

450 g | 1 lb konafa pastry
225 g | 8 oz unsalted butter, melted

For the syrup

450 g | 1 lb granulated sugar
290 ml | 10 fl oz water
2 tablespoons lemon juice
2 tablespoons orange flower water

For the filling

6 tablespoons ground rice
4 tablespoons caster sugar
1 litre | 1¾ pints milk
150 ml | 5 fl oz double cream

1 To make the syrup, put the sugar, water and lemon juice into a saucepan, dissolve over a low heat and then simmer until thick enough to coat the back of a wooden spoon. Add the orange-flower water and simmer for a further 2 minutes. Remove from the heat and leave to cool, then chill.

2 Mix the ground rice and sugar to a smooth paste with 150 ml | 5 fl oz of the milk. Bring the remaining milk to the boil and gradually add the ground rice paste, stirring vigorously. Simmer until very thick, stirring to prevent the mixture from catching on the bottom of the pan. Remove from the heat and allow to cool, then add the cream and mix well.

3 Heat the oven to 170°C | 325°F | gas mark 3.

4 Put the konafa pastry into a large bowl. Pull out and separate the strands as much as possible with your fingers so that they do not stick together too much. Pour in the melted butter and work it in very well. Put half the pastry into a large, deep, ovenproof dish. Spread the filling evenly over and cover with the remaining pastry. Flatten it with the palm of your hand.

5 Bake for 1 hour. Then turn the oven temperature up to 220°C | 425°F | gas mark 7 and bake for a further 10–15 minutes or until golden-brown.

6 Remove from the oven and pour the cold syrup over the hot konafa.

NOTE: Konafa can be made with a variety of fillings, such as curd cheese, nuts and cinnamon or sliced bananas. They can also be made as individually rolled pastries instead of one large pastry.

Yeasted Layered Pastries

Croissants and Danish Pastries are yeasted layered pastries. They are made using a combination of bread-making and pastry-making techniques and are considered to be among the most difficult types of pâtisserie to make well. They are rewarding to make but are very time-consuming and require great skill and care. The home-made product is invariably much richer and fresher-tasting than most store-bought equivalents.

Before attempting either Croissants or Danish Pastries the cook should have made puff pastry and bread successfully. The **Pastry** and **Bread** sections should be read as a reminder of the principles of yeast cookery and the making of layered pastries.

Yeasted Layered Pastries: Points to Remember

- Work in a cool kitchen to prevent the yeast from working too rapidly and to keep the butter from oozing out of the pastry.
- The butter needs to be soft in order to form a layer between the dough. It should be the same texture as the dough.
- If the butter starts to ooze out between the layers or breaks out from the dough, chill the pastry immediately.
- Allow the shaped pastries to prove in a cool environment. Normal room temperature of about 20°C|70°F is ideal. If the pastries are proved in too hot an environment, the butter will seep out of the pastries, making them greasy.
- Chill the pastries after proving and before baking to set the shape and chill the butter so it is less likely to run out during baking.

Danish Pastries

The technique of interleaving a yeasted dough with butter and folding it to create layers is thought to have originated in Turkey. The technique spread throughout the Austro-Hungarian empire before being brought to Denmark by an Austrian chef in the 1800s, which is why these pastries are called Wienerbrot or Vienna Bread in Denmark. The pastries can be eaten for breakfast or for a snack throughout the day with a cup of tea or coffee.

Plain flour is used in this recipe to give the pastries a cake-like, tender texture. Strong flour can be used for a more open, chewy texture.

This pastry should be shaped when cold, therefore it is best to spread the making of the pastries over 2 days.

Danish pastries can be filled with an almond paste filling or a cinnamon filling. Dried fruits, such as apricots or prunes, are sometimes placed inside the pastries. The pastries can be decorated with toasted flaked almonds. The glacé icing should not be made up until the pastries are baked.

Danish Pastries

MAKES 6 LARGE OR 12 SMALL PASTRIES

15 g | ½ oz fresh yeast*

1 tablespoon caster sugar

115 ml | 4 fl oz lukewarm milk

225 g | 8 oz plain flour

a pinch of salt

1 egg, beaten

115 g | 4 oz unsalted butter, softened

1 egg, beaten, to glaze

For the almond paste filling

45 g | 1½ oz butter, softened

45 g | 1½ oz icing sugar

30 g | 1 oz ground almonds

2 drops of vanilla essence

For the glacé icing

115 g | 4 oz icing sugar

boiling water, to mix

1 Cream the yeast with 1 teaspoon of the sugar and 2 tablespoons of the milk.

2 Sift the flour and remaining sugar with the salt into a large bowl and make a well in the centre. Pour the yeast mixture, the remaining milk and the egg into the well and stir to make a soft dough.

3 Turn the dough on to a work surface and knead once or twice to make a smooth dough. Roll into a rectangle about 1 cm | 1½ in thick and 12 × 36 cm | 5 × 15 in. Cover with clingfilm and chill for at least 30 minutes to rest.

4 Place the chilled dough on a lightly floured work surface. Divide the butter into hazelnut-sized pieces and dot it over the top two-thirds of the dough, smearing it into the dough slightly but leaving gaps between the pieces of butter.

5 Fold the dough into 3, bringing the bottom third up, then folding the middle third up to encase the butter. Press the edges together lightly.

6 Give the dough a quarter turn so that the folded edge of the dough is on your left.

7 Repeat steps 5 and 6, then chill the pastry in an oiled plastic bag for 10 minutes.

8 Repeat steps 5 and 6 twice more so that the pastry has had a total of 4 rolls and folds. If the pastry looks streaky, give it another roll and fold. Chill for 15 minutes.

9 Roll the pastry into a rectangle 20 × 60 cm | 8 × 24 in. Place on a lightly floured baking sheet, cover with clingfilm and chill overnight.

10 To make the almond paste, beat the butter with the icing sugar, then stir in the almonds and vanilla. Chill.

11 The following day, cut the pastry into the desired size and shape, as shown overleaf.

12 Allow the pastries to rise up until pillowy, then chill for 20 minutes before baking.

13 While the pastries are chilling, heat the oven to 200°C | 400°F | gas mark 6.

14 Glaze the pastries with the beaten egg and bake for 20 minutes or until golden-brown.

15 Cool the pastries on a wire rack whilst you make the glacé icing. Sift the icing sugar into a bowl. Add boiling water a little at a time to achieve the consistency of single cream. Make a piping bag out of greaseproof paper (see *Making an Icing Bag*, page 468) and use it to drizzle the icing over the pastries in a zig-zag motion.

*If using fast-action or dried yeast, see page 480.

Almond Squares

1 Put a spoonful of filling into the centre of each square.
2 Bring each of the corners to the middle of the filling and press down lightly to seal.

Making Danish Pastries:
Almond Squares

Crosses

1 Cut through 2 opposing corners at right angles, about 1 cm|½ in from the edge. (a)
2 Bring the outside edge of the 2 strips to match the edge of the central square. (b)
3 Place a little filling in the hollow in the centre of the cross. (c)

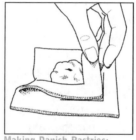

Making Danish Pastries:
Crosses (a)

Making Danish Pastries:
Crosses (b)

Making Danish Pastries:
Crosses (c)

Pinwheels

1 Place a spoonful of filling in the centre of each square.
2 Cut a diagonal from each corner to meet the filling in the centre. (a)
3 Bring the right point of each triangle to meet in the centre of the filling. (b)
4 Press the point down lightly to seal.

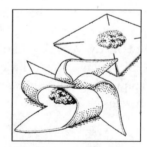

Pinwheels (a)

Pinwheels (b)

Comb

1 Place a line of filling down the centre of each pastry square.

2 Fold the edges over like a book. (a)

3 Cut several slits from the open edge towards the filling. Curve the pastry backwards to open out the cuts. (b)

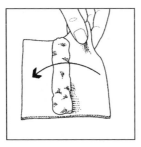

Danish Pastries: Comb (a)

Making Danish Pastries: Comb (b)

Apricot Danish Pastries

MAKES 6

1 quantity Danish pastry (see page 163)

½ quantity crème pâtissière, without cream (see page 458)

6 dried apricots

1 quantity apricot glaze (see page 474)

3 tablespoons flaked almonds, toasted

1 Make the pastry and shape into 6 crosses (see above).

2 Place on a baking sheet. Place 1 tablespoon cooled crème patissière in the centre of each cross then top with a dried apricot.

3 Cover with oiled clingfilm and allow to prove at cool room temperature until puffy.

4 Chill until firm, about 20 minutes.

5 Meanwhile, heat the oven to 200°C | 400°F | gas mark 6.

6 Bake the pastries in the top third of the oven for about 25 minutes or until golden-brown. Place on a wire rack.

7 While the pastries are still warm, glaze with the apricot jam and sprinkle over the toasted almonds.

Pains au Raisin

MAKES 12

1 quantity Danish pastry dough (see page 163)

For the filling

55 g|2 oz butter, softened

55 g|2 oz caster sugar

2 teaspoons ground cinnamon

3 tablespoons raisins

1 tablespoon chopped mixed peel

1 Cream the butter and sugar, then stir in the cinnamon.

2 Roll the Danish pastry dough into a rectangle 25 × 20 cm|12 × 8 in.

3 Spread the cinnamon paste over the pastry then sprinkle with the fruit.

4 Roll the pastry from the short end and then pinch the edges to seal.

5 Cut the roll into 12 rounds. Place them on a baking sheet then press lightly with a floured hand to flatten them to 1 cm|½ in thick. Cover with oiled clingfilm.

6 Allow to prove then chill for 20 minutes.

7 Heat the oven to 200°C|400°F|gas mark 6.

8 Bake in the top third of the oven for 20–25 minutes or until golden-brown.

9 Cool on a wire rack.

Danish Pastries: What has gone wrong when . . .

The pastries are flat and greasy.

- The dough was rolled too thinly.
- The butter broke through the layers during rolling and folding.
- The pastries were overproved and collapsed
- The pastries were overbaked.
- The pastries underproved.

The pastries are tough.

- The dough was overworked when it was mixed together.
- Too much flour was used during rolling and folding.

Lardy Cake

Lardy cake is a traditional English pastry made with a similar method to Danish pastries.

MAKES 20 SQUARES

For the dough
450 g | 1 lb plain flour
1 teaspoon salt
20 g | ¾ oz fresh yeast*
290 ml | 10 fl oz lukewarm water
melted lard for greasing

For the filling
115 g | 4 oz lard, cut into small pieces
115 g | 4 oz sultanas
115 g | 4 oz caster sugar
1 teaspoon ground mixed spice

To finish
oil for brushing
2 tablespoons caster sugar

1 Sift the flour with the salt into a large mixing bowl. Cream the yeast with the water. Make a well in the centre of the flour and add the yeast mixture. Mix to a soft but not sticky dough. Knead until the dough is smooth. Place in a large, clean bowl, cover with oiled clingfilm or a clean, damp cloth, and leave in a warm place to rise until doubled in volume. This will take about 1 hour.

2 Heat the oven to 200°C | 400°F | gas mark 6. Grease a 20 × 25 cm | 8 × 10 in roasting tin.

3 Place the risen dough on a floured work surface and roll out to a 45 × 15 cm | 18 × 6 in rectangle.

4 Dot one third of the lard over the top two-thirds of the dough. Toss the sultanas with the sugar and spice and sprinkle one third of the mixture over the larded dough. Fold the dough into 3, bringing the bottom, uncovered third up over the centre section first, and then the top third down over it.

5 Allow the dough to rest for 10 minutes.

6 Roll out again and cover with the second third of the lard, fruit, spice and sugar as in step 4. Fold into 3 as before.

7 Allow the dough to rest for 10 minutes.

8 Roll out again and cover with the remaining third of the lard, fruit, spice and sugar as in step 4. Fold into 3 as before.

9 Roll the dough out to fit the prepared tin. Place in the tin, cover and leave at room temperature to rise until 1½ times its original volume.

10 Brush with a little oil and sprinkle with the 2 tablespoons sugar. Using a large knife, make a criss-cross pattern on the top.

11 Bake in the centre of the oven for 20 minutes, then turn the oven temperature down to 180°C | 350°F | gas mark 4 and bake for about 1–1¼ hours or until the cake sounds hollow when tapped on the underside. Transfer to a wire rack to cool.

* If using fast-action or dried yeast, see page 480.

Croissants

The French word *croissant*, meaning crescent, describes the shape of these yeast-raised layered pastries. Although the making of pastries in crescent shapes can be traced back to Turkey, it is thought that the croissant as we know it was developed in France in the twentieth century.

The quality and flavour of croissants varies dramatically depending on the amount of butter layered into the dough. With the recent popularity of filled croissants, bakers have started using less butter or substituting margarine for butter. Two types of croissants are now available in the shops, *croissant au beurre*, which must be made with butter, and croissants containing other types of fat. The versions with less butter tend to have a more bread-like texture that make them ideal for dunking into coffee or hot chocolate.

To make croissants the cook must be familiar with the techniques of bread-making and the making of layered pastries. Read the notes above under *Yeasted Layered Pastries: Points to Remember*. The texture of the détrempe should be slightly softer than the détrempe for puff pastry. The butter must be very malleable and of the same texture as the détrempe.

It is recommended that the making of croissants be spread over a period of 2–3 days.

Butter Croissants and Pains au Chocolat

The détrempe should be made at 12–24 hours in advance to allow the flavours to develop.

MAKES 10–12 CROISSANTS AND 4 PAINS AU CHOCOLAT.

45 g | 1½ oz caster sugar
1 teaspoon salt
290 ml | 10 fl oz cold milk
15 g | ½ oz fresh yeast*
500 g | 1 lb 2 oz strong white flour
285 g | 10 oz unsalted butter

For the glaze
1 egg yolk, beaten with 1 tablespoon milk

For the pains au chocolat
4 small pieces plain chocolate

1　Dissolve the sugar and the salt into one third of the milk. In a separate bowl, whisk the yeast into the remaining milk.
2　Sift the flour into a large bowl and mix in both the liquids. Mix to a smooth, soft dough but do not knead.
3　Cover the dough with lightly oiled clingfilm and leave in a warm place until doubled in size, about 1 hour.
4　Knock back the dough by patting it firmly. Do not work the dough. Cover with lightly oiled clingfilm and chill overnight.
5　Shape the dough into a ball and cut a cross into the top halfway through the centre of the dough. Pull each quarter lobe away from the dough ball and roll into a thin flap. (a)
6　Place the butter in the centre, then fold over the flaps to encase the butter. (b)
7　Lightly flour the work surface, then ridge the dough to form a 40 × 75 cm | 16 × 30 in rectangle. Brush off the excess flour and fold the dough into 3, like a business letter.

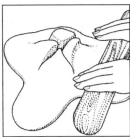

Making croissants (a)

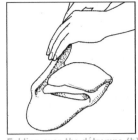

Folding over the détrempe (b)

Cutting croissants using
a template (c)

8 Give the dough a quarter turn so the folded edge of the dough is on your left. Repeat step 7.

9 Wrap the dough in clingfilm and chill for 20 minutes.

10 Repeat steps 7 and 8 until the dough has had 4 rolls and folds and is no longer streaky.

11 Roll out the dough into a 40 × 75 cm | 16 × 30 in rectangle. Place on a baking sheet covered with greaseproof paper, then cover the dough with clingfilm. Chill until firm.

12 Using a large knife, trim the edges of the dough, then cut it lengthways into two equal strips. Using a template, cut the dough into triangles. (c)

13 Place the triangles one at a time on the work surface with the longer point towards you. Stretch out the two shorter points, (d) then roll the triangle up loosely. (e) The tip should fold over the top of the croissant and touch the baking sheet but it should not be underneath the croissant.

Stretching the corners (d)

Rolling the croissant (e)

14 Place the shaped croissants on a baking sheet, curving them into a crescent shape (f) and leaving enough space for them to double in size without touching. The point should be facing towards the middle of the baking sheet to help prevent them from burning. (g)

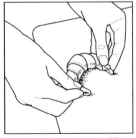

Curving into a crescent (f)

Croissants on baking sheet (g)

15 For the pains au chocolat, stack the offcuts of dough and roll and fold to combine them into one piece. Roll out the dough to ½ cm|¼ in thickness. Cut into 4 rectangles. Place a piece of chocolate in the centre of each and fold over. Place seam-side down on a baking sheet.

16 Cover all the pastries with lightly oiled clingfilm and prove at normal room temperature, 20°C|70°F, until they are very puffy. Chill for 20 minutes to set the shape.

17 Heat the oven to 230°C|450°F|gas mark 8.

18 Glaze the pastries with the egg yolk and milk and bake in the hottest part of the oven for 10 minutes, then turn the oven down to 190°C|375°F|gas mark 5 and bake for a further 20 minutes or until the pastries are a deep brown. Cool on a wire rack.

* If using fast-action or dried yeast, see page 480.

Almond Croissants

MAKES 10

1 recipe croissants, baked (see page 168)

For the filling
85 g | 3 oz butter, softened
85 g | 3 oz icing sugar

55 g | 2 oz ground almonds
2 drops of vanilla essence
1 egg, beaten
5 tablespoons flaked almonds, toasted

To finish
icing sugar, sifted

1 For the filling, mix the butter, icing sugar and ground almonds and flavour with a little vanilla extract.

2 Split the croissants in half horizontally and divide the filling between them.

3 Cover with the top half then brush with the beaten egg. Sprinkle with the toasted almonds then sift over a generous coating of icing sugar. Warm in a 150°C|300°F|gas mark 2 oven for 10 minutes.

Croissants: What has gone wrong when . . .

The croissants are badly risen.
- The dough was rolled too thinly.
- The butter broke through the layers when rolling and folding.
- The croissants were not proved for long enough.
- The croissants were overproved and collapsed in the oven.

The croissants are greasy.
- The butter was too soft when added to the détrempe.
- The croissants were not chilled for long enough before baking.
- The croissants were proved at too high a temperature.
- The croissants were overbaked.

The middle of the croissants is doughy.
- The croissants are underbaked.
- The croissants were underproved.

Making Meringues: Points to Remember

- Use clean, grease-free equipment. Do not use plastic bowls or spatulas as they tend to retain traces of grease on their surfaces. Rinse and dry equipment thoroughly.
  Ensure the whites are free from any yolk.
- If possible, do not make meringues on a damp or rainy day. It is difficult for them to dry them out sufficiently.
- Older egg whites are easier to whisk than fresh egg whites. Egg whites can be kept in the refrigerator for up to 3 weeks. However, if they start to smell, throw them away.
- Allow egg whites to come to room temperature before using them. They will whisk more easily.
- If the whites are very fresh, add a tiny pinch of salt before beginning to whisk, to help break the thread of the whites.
- Begin by whisking slowly, then increase your speed as the egg whites begin to foam.
- Do not add any sugar before the egg whites are very stiff. This can be tested by holding a small amount of white upright on the end of your whisk; the white should stand straight up without bending.

- Avoid overwhisking egg whites or they will lose their elasticity and will not expand well when cooked. If whites are overwhisked their volume will begin to decrease. A sign that the whites have been whisked too much is a lumpy, cottonwool-like texture around the edge of the bowl. Continuing to whisk can lead to collapse.
- Acid, in the form of cream of tartar, can be added to stabilize the foam. Although it has no effect on the volume of foam produced, it makes it less prone to overwhisking and collapse. Only a tiny amount is needed to make a significant difference – about $\frac{1}{16}$th teaspoon per egg white.work surface   Use baking parchment (silicon-treated paper) to line the baking sheets and tins.

Meringues

Meringues, the snowy confection of egg whites and sugar, were first made in Europe in the 1600s. Some cookery historians believe that a Swiss pastry chef, Gasparini, who practised his art in the small town of Meringen, invented meringues, hence the name. Meringues were soon adopted by the French court.

There are three types of crisp meringue: Swiss meringue, Italian meringue and *meringue cuite*, or cooked meringue, in addition to the soft meringue which is used principally as a topping for pies, such as lemon meringue pie.

The first part of this section covers crisp meringues.

Meringue is a combination of an egg-white foam and sugar which has been dried in a low oven until the moisture content has been reduced enough to stabilize the mixture. As the egg whites are whisked, the proteins stretch. When they are stiff and the proteins have been stretched as far as possible, sugar is beaten in. The sugar attracts the water in the egg whites and forms a syrup which coats the stretched proteins. When the meringue is baked the water evaporates, leaving a dry coating of sugar on the coagulated egg protein. Egg whites are notoriously temperamental so it is necessary to abide by the rules at the beginning of this section when making meringues.

Using Copper Bowls to Whisk Meringues

Egg whites whisked in a copper bowl will be more stable and have more volume when baked. The foam will have a greater elasticity, which will give a lighter result. This is due to the chemical reaction that takes place between the egg whites and the copper.

The bowl must be cleaned before each use. To do this, rub the inside of the bowl with the cut edge of half a lemon and a teaspoon of salt until any oxidation disappears. Rinse with clean water and dry with kitchen paper.

Swiss Meringue

Swiss meringue is used for making individual meringues sandwiched together in pairs with cream, for Petits Fours and for Vacherin, which is assembled from 2 or 3 discs of piped meringue layered together with cream. It is named after the French cheese, which it resembles in shape and colour.

Swiss meringue is made with twice the weight of caster sugar to egg white. One medium egg white weighs 30 g | 1 oz with a volume of 30 ml | 1 fl oz so for each egg white use 55 g | 2 oz caster sugar. If whisking by hand it is relatively easy to whisk up to 4 whites at a time; more than that becomes very tiring. Standard electric mixers can usually whisk up to 8 whites. Refer to the manufacturer's instructions for capacity.

Swiss meringue will liquefy if left to stand for any time, so be prepared to use the mixture immediately upon making; have the oven preheated and the baking sheets lined with baking parchment.

Flavouring meringues: Finely ground nuts, such as almonds or hazelnuts, are traditionally added to a Swiss meringue mixture and baked in round, flat discs to produce a Dacquoise or a Hazelnut Meringue. The discs are layered with whipped cream and the confection is served as a cake, usually with a sharp fruit coulis. Cocoa powder or coffee essence can be folded into a meringue mixture before baking.

It is important to add the flavouring ingredients after all the sugar has been incorporated. Fold the ingredients into the meringue mixture quickly and avoid over folding: the added ingredients tend to break down the egg-white foam and could cause the meringue to collapse. 30 g | 1 oz finely ground nuts per egg white is recommended. Mix 1 tablespoon of the sugar with the nuts when grinding to absorb some of the oils and make the nuts more free-flowing.

Swiss Meringues

MAKES 50 MINIATURE OR 12 LARGE MERINGUES

4 egg whites

225 g | 8 oz caster sugar

For the filling

290 ml | 10 fl oz double cream, lightly, whipped

1 Heat the oven to 110°C | 225°F | gas mark ½.

2 Line 2 baking sheets with baking parchment.

3 Whisk the egg whites until stiff but not dry.

4 Gradually whisk in half of the sugar until very stiff and shiny.

5 Fold in the remaining sugar, using a large metal spoon.

6 Drop the meringue mixture on to the lined baking sheets in spoonfuls set fairly far apart or pipe as shown below. Use a teaspoon for tiny meringues or a dessertspoon for larger ones.

7 Bake for about 1½–2 hours until the meringues are dry right through and will lift off the paper easily.

8 When cold, sandwich the meringues together in pairs with whipped cream.

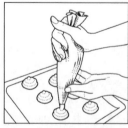

Piping individual meringues

Swiss Meringues: What has gone wrong when . . .

The egg whites will not whisk to a stiff peak.

- The whites contain some oil or yolk or the equipment was not clean of grease or washing-up liquid.

The meringue mixture is too soft.

- The sugar was added before the whites came to a stiff peak.
- The mixture was beaten for too long once the sugar was added.
- The mixture was overfolded when the sugar was added and started to collapse.

Melted sugar oozes from the cooked meringues, the meringues weep.

- The meringues were cooked for too long.
- The meringues were cooked at too high a temperature.

The meringues do not dry out.

- The meringues have not been cooked for long enough.
- The weather is too damp.

Pavlova

SERVES 6–8

For the meringue

4 egg whites

225 g | 8 oz caster sugar

1 teaspoon cornflour

1 teaspoon vanilla essence

1 teaspoon white wine vinegar or lemon juice

For the filling

1 tablespoon icing sugar

290 ml | 10 fl oz double cream, lightly whipped

450 g | 1 lb soft fruits

1 Heat the oven to 140°C | 275°F | gas mark 1.
2 Line a baking sheet with baking parchment.
3 Whisk the egg whites until stiff. Gradually add half the sugar, then fold in the remainder with a large metal spoon.
4 Fold in the cornflour, vanilla and vinegar or lemon juice.
5 Pile half the mixture on to the prepared baking sheet, shaping into a 20 cm | 8 in circle. Pile the remaining meringue around the edges to form walls. Bake for 1–1½ hours. The meringue is cooked when the outer shell is a pale, biscuit colour and hard to the touch. Remove from the oven and leave to cool completely on a wire rack.
6 When cold, place on a serving dish. Stir the icing sugar into the cream. Layer the whipped cream and fruit in the centre.

Raspberry Vacherin

SERVES 8

For the meringue
4 egg whites
225 g|8 oz caster sugar

For the filling
290 ml|10 fl oz double cream
250 g|9 oz fresh raspberries
icing sugar, to taste

1 Heat the oven to 140°C|275°F|gas mark 1. Place 3 shelves in the oven.
2 Line 3 baking sheets with baking parchment. Draw 20 cm|8 in circles on one side of each of the papers and place the marked side down on the baking sheet.
3 Whisk the egg whites until stiff, then whisk in half the caster sugar one teaspoonful at a time. Using a large metal spoon, fold in the remaining sugar.
4 Put the meringue into a piping bag fitted with a 1 cm|½ in plain nozzle and pipe on to the baking parchment to make 3 flat discs (see page 178).
5 Bake in the oven for 45 minutes, then reverse the position of the trays and bake for a further 30–45 minutes. The meringues will peel off the paper easily when done and will feel firm to the touch in the centre.
6 Cool the meringues on a wire rack.
7 To fill, whisk the cream to soft peak and whisk in 1–2 tablespoons icing sugar.
8 Place one meringue disc on to a serving dish. Reserve a small amount of cream for rosettes and 8 raspberries if you wish, for decoration.
9 Spread half the cream on the disc. Top with half the raspberries. Place the second disc of meringue on top, pressing down lightly.
10 Spread with the remaining cream and top with the remaining raspberries. Place the final meringue disc on top and decorate with cream rosettes and raspberries, if desired. Serve within one hour of filling.

Hazelnut Meringue Cake with Raspberry Coulis

SERVES 6–8

For the meringue

115 g | 4 oz hazelnuts

225 g | 8 oz caster sugar

4 egg whites

a drop of vanilla essence

½ teaspoon white wine vinegar

For the coulis

225 g | 8 oz raspberries

icing sugar, sifted

a squeeze of lemon juice

For the filling

290 ml | 10 fl oz double cream

icing sugar

1 Heat the oven to 190°C | 375°F | gas mark 5. Line 2 × 20 cm | 8 in cake tins with lightly oiled kitchen foil or non-stick baking-parchment paper cases.

2 Place the hazelnuts on a baking sheet and roast in the oven until brown. Remove the skins by rubbing the nuts in a tea towel. Leave until completely cold. Set aside 6–8 nuts and grind the remainder with 1 tablespoon of the caster sugar. Do not overgrind or they will become greasy and make the meringue heavy. Add half the remaining caster sugar.

3 Whisk the egg whites until stiff, then gradually whisk in the remaining caster sugar one tablespoon at a time, whisking until very stiff. Very gently fold in the nuts, sugar, vanilla and vinegar, using a large metal spoon. Pile the mixture into the prepared tins, spreading evenly with a spatula.

4 Bake in the oven for 40 minutes. Remove from the oven and allow to cool for 5 minutes. Lift out the meringues in the foil, then carefully peel away the foil. Leave the meringues to cool completely on a wire rack.

5 Meanwhile, liquidize the raspberries in a blender with icing sugar and lemon juice to taste. Push through a sieve and taste for sweetness. If very thick, add a little water.

6 To decorate: whip the cream and sweeten to taste with icing sugar. Sandwich two meringues together using two thirds of it. Dust the top with icing sugar. Pipe 6–8 large rosettes of cream round the edge of the top of the meringue and decorate each rosette with a reserved hazelnut. Serve the raspberry coulis separately.

Almond Dacquoise with Apricot Purée

SERVES 6–8

For the meringue

5 egg whites

a large pinch of cream of tartar

285 g|10 oz caster sugar

115 g|4 oz ground almonds

For the filling

290 ml|10 fl oz double cream

115 g|4 oz dried apricots

icing sugar

To decorate (optional)

100 ml|3½ fl oz double cream, whipped

2 tablespoons flaked almonds, toasted

1 Heat the oven to 140°C|275°F|gas mark 1. Line 3 baking sheets with baking parchment and mark with 23 cm|9 in circles and place the marked side down on the baking sheet.

2 Add the cream of tartar to the egg whites and whisk them until stiff with an electric whisk, then whisk in half the caster sugar one tablespoonful at a time.

3 Mix the remaining caster sugar with the grounds almonds and fold in carefully.

4 Fill a piping bag fitted with a 1 cm|½ in plain nozzle with the meringue and pipe into the marked circles.

Piping a meringue disc

5 Bake in the lower third of the oven for 1 hour until the baking parchment will peel away easily. Cool on a wire rack.

6 While the meringue is cooking, make the apricot purée. Place the dried apricots in a saucepan and add just enough water to cover. Place over a medium heat and simmer until the apricots are pulpy and the water has nearly evaporated. Allow to cool then purée in a liquidizer.

7 To fill the meringue: whip the cream until soft peaks form and flavour with the purée and the icing sugar.

8 Sandwich the two meringue discs with the apricot cream. If desired, decorate with rosettes of whipped cream and a few toasted flaked almonds.

Chocolate Fruit and Nut Meringue

This is a very rich pudding. Serve with fruits such as strawberries or raspberries in the summer, or a compote of dried apricots and dried cherries in the winter.

SERVES 10

For the meringue
6 egg whites
225 g | 8 oz caster sugar
140 g | 5 oz toasted almonds, chopped
30 g | 1 oz dried apricots, chopped
55 g | 2 oz raisins
30 g | 1 oz dried cherries

For the icing
200 g | 7 oz low-fat curd cheese
200 ml | 7 fl oz double cream
225 g | 8 oz plain chocolate, grated
2 tablespoons Tia Maria or Glayva liqueur (optional)

To decorate
85 g | 3 oz white chocolate, coarsely grated
85 g | 3 oz plain chocolate, coarsely grated

1 Heat the oven to 150°C | 300°F | gas mark 2. Line the base and sides of a 23 cm | 9 in spring-form tin with baking parchment.

2 Using an electric whisk, whisk the egg whites until they form stiff peaks. Gradually add the sugar, beating well between each addition. Fold in the almonds, fruit and half the chocolate carefully, using a large metal spoon. Spoon into the prepared tin and place in the oven for 1¼–1½ hours or until firm. Remove from the oven but leave in the tin until cold.

3 Beat the curd cheese and cream together until slightly thickened and smooth. Add the grated chocolate and liqueur, if using.

4 Remove the meringue carefully from the tin and spread the cream and chocolate mixture over the top and sides. If the meringue breaks, use some of the chocolate mixture to stick it back together.

5 Mix the dark and white chocolate together and carefully cover the top and sides of the meringue.

Pistachio Pavlovas with Rhubarb and Raspberries

SERVES 6

For the meringue

3 egg whites

170 g | 6 oz caster sugar

1 teaspoon cornflour

100 g | 3½ oz shelled pistachio nuts, ground

1 teaspoon raspberry or white wine vinegar

For the filling

3 stalks of young rhubarb, cut into 2.5 cm | 1 in pieces

250 g | 9 oz frozen raspberries, defrosted

6 tablespoons icing sugar

290 ml | 10 fl oz double cream

1 Heat the oven to 130°C | 250°F | gas mark 1. Mark 6 × 7.5 cm | 3 in circles on a piece of baking parchment large enough to cover a baking sheet. Place the baking parchment on the baking sheet with the markings on the underside.

2 Whisk the egg whites in a large, clean bowl until they form stiff peaks. Whisk in half the caster sugar one tablespoon at a time, whisking well between each addition.

3 Stir together the remaining sugar, the cornflour and the ground pistachios, then fold into the meringue along with the vinegar.

4 Divide the meringue between the 6 circles, making a well in the centre of each meringue.

5 Bake in the bottom of the oven for 1 hour or until the meringues will easily lift from the baking parchment. Leave to cool.

6 To make the filling, heat the oven to 190°C | 375°F | gas mark 5. Place the rhubarb on a baking sheet and bake for 20 minutes or until tender. Leave to cool, then stir together with the raspberries, the juice from the raspberries and 4 tablespoons of the icing sugar.

7 Whip the cream to medium–soft peaks and fold in the remaining icing sugar. Place the pavlovas on individual dessert plates. Divide the cream between the pavlovas and top with the rhubarb and raspberry mixture. Serve immediately.

Brown Sugar Meringues with Chocolate and Ginger

MAKES ABOUT 30

For the meringues

4 egg whites

30 g | 1 oz caster sugar

200 g | 7 oz soft light brown sugar

1 teaspoon ground ginger

For the filling

100 g | 3½ oz good quality plain chocolate

150 ml | 5 fl oz double cream

2 pieces stem ginger, very finely chopped

1 Heat the oven to 140°C | 275°F | gas mark 1. Line 2 baking sheets with baking parchment.

2 Whisk the egg whites until just stiff then whisk in the caster sugar. Mix the ginger into the brown sugar and quickly fold in. Put into a piping bag fitted with a 1 cm | ½ in plain nozzle.

3 Pipe golf-ball-size meringues on to the baking parchment.

4 Bake in the lower third of the oven for 1 hour or until the meringues peel away from the paper easily. Cool on a wire rack.

5 Chop the chocolate into small pieces and melt in a bowl placed over, but not touching, steaming water.

6 Dip the bases of the meringues into the chocolate and return to the paper to set.

7 To fill, whisk the double cream until soft peaks form, then fold in the stem ginger. Use to sandwich the meringues in pairs. Pile on to a serving dish and serve within 1 hour.

Lemon Meringue Roulade

SERVES 6–8

For the meringue

4 egg whites

225 g | 8 oz caster sugar

1 teaspoon cornflour

1 teaspoon vanilla essence

1 teaspoon white wine vinegar or lemon juice

For the filling

290 g | 10 oz lemon curd

290 ml | 10 fl oz double cream, lightly whipped

To serve

450 g | 1 lb strawberries

1 Heat the oven to 140°C | 275°F | gas mark 1 and line a Swiss roll tin with baking parchment.

2 Whisk the egg whites until stiff. Gradually add half the sugar, beating well between each addition, then fold in the remainder with a large metal spoon.

3 Fold in the cornflour, vanilla and vinegar or lemon juice.

4 Spread the mixture on to the prepared tin. Bake for about 1 hour. The meringue is cooked when the outer shell is a pale, biscuit colour and hard to the touch. Remove from the oven and leave to cool completely on a wire rack.

5 When cold, invert on to a sheet of greaseproof paper. Spread with the lemon curd and cream then roll from the short end. Place on a serving dish and decorate with the strawberries.

Coconut Meringues

These meringues are dipped in chocolate before serving. Alternatively, sandwich them together with cream, or do both.

MAKES 50 SMALL OR 12 LARGE MERINGUES

4 egg whites

225 g│8 oz caster sugar

85 g│3 oz desiccated coconut

115 g│4 oz plain chocolate, chopped into small pieces

1 Heat the oven to 110°C│225°F│gas mark ½ and line 2 baking sheets with baking parchment.

2 Using an electric whisk, whisk the egg whites until stiff but not dry.

3 Whisk in three quarters of the sugar gradually with the electric whisk, one spoonful at a time.

4 Mix the remaining sugar with the coconut and carefully fold into the meringue mixture with a large metal spoon.

5 Drop spoonfuls of the meringue mixture carefully on to the baking parchment; use a teaspoon for small meringues and a dessertspoon for larger ones. Make sure they are set fairly far apart.

6 Place in the oven and bake for 1½–2 hours (depending on the size) or until they will lift easily from the baking parchment. Put on a wire rack to cool. Keep the parchment.

7 When the meringues are cold, melt the chocolate in a bowl set over, but not touching, a pan of steaming water.

8 Spread a little chocolate on the base of each meringue and allow to set on the parchment paper. Alternatively, drizzle chocolate on the top and sandwich the meringues together with whipped cream.

Baked Alaska

SERVES 8

1 × 2 egg quantity baked Victoria sponge cake 17 cm | 7 in round (see page 286)

570 ml | 1 pint good quality ice cream

2–3 tablespoons raspberry jam

3 egg whites

170 g | 6 oz caster sugar

1 Heat the oven to 230°C | 450°F | gas mark 8.

2 Place the sponge on a baking sheet. Spread with the jam.

3 Invert the ice cream on to the cake. It should cover the top of the cake leaving a margin of 1 cm | ½ in.

4 Whisk the egg whites until stiff. Gradually whisk in the sugar.

5 Put the meringue into a piping bag fitted with a 1 cm | ½ in fluted nozzle and pipe the meringue over the cake and ice cream, ensuring that they are totally covered.

6 Sprinkle with a little caster sugar and place in the oven for about 10 minutes or until the meringue has turned golden-brown. Serve immediately.

Batons Maréchaux

MAKES 80 PAIRS

5 egg whites

115 g | 4 oz caster sugar

30 g | 1 oz plain flour

115 g | 4 oz ground almonds

85 g | 3 oz nibbed almonds or chopped hazelnuts

apricot jam, for filling

1 Heat the oven to 180°C | 350°F | gas mark 4.

2 Whisk the egg whites until stiff but not dry. Gradually whisk in half the sugar and whisk again until very stiff and shiny.

3 Sift together the remaining sugar, flour and ground almonds, then fold into the meringue.

4 Place the meringue in a piping bag fitted with a ½ cm | ¼ in plain nozzle and pipe 4 cm | 1½ in lengths on to 3 baking sheets lined with baking parchment.

5 Sprinkle with nibbed almonds or chopped hazelnuts.

6 Allow the meringues to dry slightly before baking for 30 minutes or until a pale golden-brown. The meringues will feel slightly soft when removed from the oven but will crisp on cooling.

7 Sandwich the biscuits together in pairs with apricot jam.

NOTE: Instead of sandwiching with jam, melted chocolate can be used. Or use apricot jam to sandwich and dip the end of the pairs in melted chocolate. Approximately 100 g | 3½ oz plain chocolate will be required.

Italian Meringue

Italian meringue uses the same proportions of sugar to egg white as Swiss meringue, but the sugar is made into a syrup which is brought to the firm ball stage before being added to the stiffly whisked egg whites. This method produces a meringue mixture that is very stable once mixed and can be stored uncooked, tightly covered with clingfilm, in the refrigerator for up to 2 days.

Italian meringue cooks more quickly than Swiss meringue and produces a chalkier, more powdery, brilliant white meringue. It is excellent for making piped meringue baskets because it holds its shape well during cooking and is sturdy enough to hold up well when filled. Italian meringue is also used as a base for ice cream.

Italian Meringue

225 g | 8 oz granulated or lump sugar   4 egg whites
6 tablespoons water

1 Put the sugar and water into a heavy saucepan over a low heat.
2 If using, place a sugar thermometer in the pan. Bring slowly to the boil without stirring. Wash down the sides of the pan with a pastry brush dipped in water to remove any sugar crystals stuck to the sides of the pan.
3 The syrup is ready when the temperature reaches 120°C | 248°F. Alternatively, test for the firm ball stage (see page 645).
4 While the sugar is boiling, whisk the egg whites to stiff peaks.
5 Pour the boiling syrup on to the whites in a thin, steady stream while whisking. Take care not to allow the syrup to pour on to the beaters as it could stick if it comes in direct contact with them.
6 Once all the syrup has been added, continue to whisk until the mixture is stiff, shiny and stable. When the whisk is lifted, the meringue should not move at all.
7 Keep covered with clingfilm or a damp cloth if not using immediately.

Italian Meringue: What has gone wrong when . . .

The mixture fails to thicken or increase in volume.
- The sugar syrup was not hot enough when poured on to the whites.

The mixture collapses.
- The mixture was overwhisked.
- The sugar syrup was boiled to too high a temperature.

Noix au Café

These little 'nuts of coffee' make wonderful petits fours. They are made using Italian meringue.

MAKES ABOUT 80 PAIRS

225 g|8 oz granulated sugar

6–7 tablespoons water

2 teaspoons coffee essence

4 egg whites

1 Heat the oven to 140°C|225°F|gas mark 1. Line 2 baking sheets with baking parchment.

2 Put the sugar, water and coffee essence into a heavy saucepan. Warm over a low heat to dissolve the sugar then turn up the heat to boil the syrup, without stirring, until the mixture reaches 120°C|248°F on a sugar thermometer (firm ball stage).

3 Meanwhile, whisk the egg whites with an electric whisk until stiff. Pour the boiling sugar syrup in a steady stream on to the whites while whisking, taking care that the syrup does not get poured on to the beaters, as it might set solidly. Whisk until the meringue is completely cool.

4 Reserve a teacupful of the mixture for filling, then place the meringue into a piping bag fitted with a ½ cm|¼ in nozzle. Pipe tiny cherry-sized meringues on to the baking parchment,

5 Bake for 1–1½ hours. The meringues will still feel sticky but if they are left at room temperature for 1 minute they should become crisp (test 1 meringue first to see if it is done).

6 Cool on a wire rack and use a little of the uncooked mixture to stick two meringues together, bottom to bottom. Place in small paper petits fours cups to serve.

Meringue Cuite

Meringue cuite, or cooked meringue, is a professional chefs' meringue used for icings, cake fillings and meringue baskets. Meringue cuite is finer and chalkier-textured than Italian or Swiss meringue. Like Italian meringue, meringue cuite is very stable in the oven, hardly swelling at all, and is unlikely to cook out of shape.

Meringue cuite can be kept for up to 4 hours in the refrigerator before baking, if closely covered. The proportion of sugar to whites is the same as for most meringues, i.e. 55 g | 2 oz, sugar per egg white, but the sugar used is icing (confectioners') sugar, rather than caster sugar.

An electric hand-held whisk is necessary to make this type of meringue as it can require up to 15 minutes of whisking.

Meringue Cuite

4 egg whites   3 drops of vanilla essence
225 g | 8 oz icing sugar, sifted

1 Place the whites into a heatproof bowl that will fit snugly over a saucepan of simmering water. The base of the bowl should not come into contact with the water. Whisk the egg whites to stiff peaks.
2 Sift the icing sugar over the whites, then set the bowl over the pan of water. Whisk slowly at first to avoid the icing sugar billowing out of the bowl.
3 Continue whisking until the mixture is thick and stable. It needs to reach a temperature of 49°C | 120°F.
4 Remove the bowl from the water and continue whisking for up to 5 minutes, until the mixture and the bowl feel cool. The meringue should be thick enough to hold a teaspoon vertically.
5 Whisk in the vanilla. Keep covered with a damp cloth or clingfilm if not using immediately.

Meringue Cuite: What has gone wrong when . . .

In addition to the problems listed above under Swiss meringue and Italian meringue, the following can occur:

The meringue does not become stiff enough during whisking.
- The mixture has not been whisked enough or it has been overwhisked.
- The water under the bowl was not hot enough.

Strawberry Meringue Basket

This recipe uses meringue cuite because it is the most stable of the three types of crisp meringue. Make one large basket for a spectacular centrepiece for a buffet or make individual baskets for a smart dinner party. Two quantities of meringue cuite are needed. Make the second batch while the first batch is baking.

SERVES 8

For the filling

425 ml | 15 fl oz double cream, lightly whipped

450 g | 1 lb strawberies, hulled and sliced in half lengthways

1 Heat the oven to 140°C|275°F|gas mark 1.
2 Line 2 baking sheets with baking parchment. For a large basket, mark 3 × 17 cm|7 in circles on the underside of the paper. For individual baskets, mark 24 × 8 cm|3 in circles.
3 Make the first batch of Meringue Cuite as directed in the recipe above.
4 Using a 1 cm|½ in plain nozzle for the large basket or a 6 mm|¼ in nozzle for the small baskets, pipe a circular base for each of the baskets. Start piping in the centre of the circle. Hold the piping bag vertically and allow the meringue to drop from the nozzle on to the paper while guiding the meringue into the correct shape. If there are any gaps between the lines, gently lift the edge of the paper to tilt the lines together. Cover half the paper circles with piped meringue.
5 Pipe hoops over the remaining circles.
6 Bake the meringue base and hoops for 45–60 minutes or until dry and crisp. Cool on a wire rack.
7 Make up the second batch of meringue cuite.
8 Place the cooked base on a baking sheet. Use the uncooked meringue to glue the hoops over the base. Don't worry if the hoops break, just stick them together with the uncooked meringue.
9 Fill a piping bag with a 1 cm|½ in star nozzle for the large basket or a 6 mm|¼ in nozzle for the small baskets.
10 Pipe in straight lines from the base of the meringue over the top edge. Carefully trim the points from the inside of the basket with a knife to make a smooth edge. If desired, pipe scrolls over the top edge of the meringue.
11 Bake for 45–60 minutes until set and crisp.
12 Cool on a wire rack then remove the paper.
13 Layer with strawberries and cream in the basket no more than 1 hour before serving. Reserve the best strawberries for the top. The strawberries can be glazed with cooled, melted redcurrant jelly if desired.

Cheesecakes

Cheese has been made from cows', goats' and sheep's milk for thousands of years: jars used for the storage of cheese have been found dating back to 6,000 BC. In ancient Greece the cheese was mixed with a little flour and eggs and baked to form a type of cheesecake. The Romans later brought their version to Western Europe and England. By Tudor times there were recipes for cheesecakes, although they are not quite what we would recognize by that name today.

Taken to America by immigrants from Europe, the cheesecake became very popular in New York in the early 1900s, where it was made using a new type of cheese known as Philadelphia cream cheese. This product was developed by the Empire Cheese Company, New York, in the late 1800s while they were trying to imitate the French Neufchatel. In 1912, James L. Kraft perfected the pasteurization of cream cheese and so it became a commodity that was easy for people to buy.

Today there are many different recipes for cheesecakes, but the common ingredient is the cheese. This is usually a cream cheese, curd cheese, ricotta or Neufchatel. Although some cheesecakes are set with gelatine, in this book we have included only the baked type. When baking a cheesecake, the temperature of the oven must be low: if it is too hot the cheesecake will soufflé and the liquid from the cheese will separate, making it watery, while the top will become leathery and the eggs rubbery. If you have a fan oven, turn off the fan or turn the oven down by 30°C|50°C. A cheesecake is done when it wobbles only very slightly in the centre when shaken. It will need to cool completely to obtain its correct, creamy consistency, either in the turned-off oven, at room temperature or in the refrigerator overnight. Individual recipes give the necessary cooling instructions.

Cheesecakes can be frozen for 1 month, although there may be some deterioration in texture. Wrap closely with clingfilm when cool then store in a sturdy plastic container. Alternatively, if the cheesecake is very soft, freeze it before wrapping (open-freeze) then wrap when frozen solid. Cheesecake can be defrosted in the refrigerator overnight.

Baked Cheesecake

For the crust

12 digestive biscuits (200 g | 7 oz), crushed

85 g | 3 oz butter, melted

For the filling

225 g | 8 oz good quality cream cheese, at room
   temperature

75 ml | 2½ fl oz double cream

1 egg, beaten

1 egg yolk

1 teaspoon vanilla essence

30–55 g | 1–2 oz sugar

For the topping

70 ml | 2½ fl oz soured cream

ground cinnamon

1 Heat the oven to 150°C | 300°F | gas mark 2.

2 Mix together the ingredients for the crust and press the mixture into the base of a
   shallow 20 cm | 8 in pie plate or tart tin.

3 Bake in the oven for 10 minutes, or until firm to the touch.

4 Beat the cream cheese and then add the remaining filling ingredients. Beat well until
   smooth and pour into the crust.

5 Return to the middle of the oven and bake until the filling has set, about 30 minutes.

6 Remove from the oven and allow to cool.

7 Spread with the soured cream and dust with the cinnamon before serving.

New York Cheesecake

This crustless cheesecake is cooked in a bain-marie, which gives it an extra smooth texture. It is gluten-free.
Serve small wedges with a combination of fresh strawberries and raspberries tossed in a little caster sugar.

SERVES 10

85 g | 3 oz unsalted butter, softened

600 g | 1¼ lb good quality cream cheese, at room
   temperature

115 g | 4 oz caster sugar

1 teaspoon vanilla essence

1 teaspoon lemon zest

1 tablespoon lemon juice

3 eggs, beaten, at room temperature

280 ml | 10 fl oz soured cream, at room temperature

1 Generously butter a 20 cm | 8 in spring-form tin using some of the butter from the recipe.
   Line the base of the tin with a circle of baking parchment. Wrap the outside of the tin
   with foil so that the water from the bain-marie cannot get into the cheesecake (use wide
   foil or a double layer of foil).

2 Place a roasting tin half-filled with water in the centre of the oven and heat the oven to
   170°C | 325°F | gas mark 3.

3 Place the butter, cream cheese, caster sugar, vanilla, lemon zest and juice in a large bowl and beat until just combined and smooth. Do not overbeat or the mixture will become too runny.

4 Gradually beat in the eggs, then stir in the soured cream.
5 Pour into the prepared tin and place in the bain-marie.
6 Bake for 30–45 minutes or until the centre is set and the edges have pulled away from the sides of the tin. Turn off the oven and leave for 1 hour, then remove the cheesecake from the bain-marie.
7 Place on a wire rack to cool completely then chill for at least 4 hours to finish setting.
8 Before serving, allow the cheesecake to stand at room temperature for 30 minutes.

Marbled Chocolate and Grand Marnier Cheesecake

SERVES 4

For the crust
85 g|3 oz butter
10 plain chocolate digestive biscuits, crushed

For the filling
200 g|7 oz cream cheese
100 ml|3½ fl oz double cream
2 eggs

1 egg yolk
2 tablespoons caster sugar
85 g|3 oz plain chocolate
2 tablespoons Grand Marnier

For the topping
140 ml|5 fl oz soured cream
1 tablespoon cocoa powder

1 Heat the oven to 150°C|300°F|gas mark 2.
2 Melt the butter and remove from the heat, add the crushed biscuits and mix well.
3 Press into the bottom of a 20 cm|8 in removable-based cake tin. Bake for 10 minutes. Remove from the oven and allow to cool.
4 Beat the cream cheese and gradually add the cream, eggs, egg yolk and sugar. Beat out any lumps.
5 Melt the chocolate in a medium-sized bowl set over, but not touching, steaming water. Add two thirds of the cream-cheese mixture and mix well.
6 Add the Grand Marnier to the remaining third of the cream-cheese mixture.
7 Pour the chocolate mixture, which will be quite thick, on to the crust. Pour over the Grand Marnier mixture and gently stir with a fork to give a marbled effect. Place on a baking sheet in the centre of the oven. Bake for 30 minutes or until set. Remove from the oven and allow to cool.
8 Once the cheesecake has cooled, remove it from the tin, spread over the soured cream and sift cocoa powder over the surface just before serving.

Marbled Mocha Cheesecake

SERVES 8

For the crust

170 g | 6 oz bought double chocolate cookies,
  crushed
55 g | 2 oz butter, melted

For the filling

675 g | 1½ lb full-fat cream cheese, at room
  temperature
170 g | 6 oz caster sugar
3 eggs, beaten
4 tablespoons double cream
1 teaspoon vanilla essence
3 tablespoons cocoa powder
½ teaspoon instant coffee granules

1 Heat the oven to 140°C | 275°F | gas mark 1.

2 Combine the crushed biscuits with the butter in a bowl and press the mixture into the base of a 20 cm | 8 in removable-based, deep cake tin. Chill until required.

3 Beat the cream cheese and sugar together until very soft, then beat in the eggs a little at a time. Stir in the cream and the vanilla essence and divide between two bowls.

4 Mix the cocoa powder and coffee granules to a paste with 4 tablespoons warm water and beat into one of the cream-cheese mixtures.

5 Pour alternating cupfuls of the two mixtures slowly into the centre of the crust.

6 When both mixtures are in the tin, pull a skewer from the centre through the filling to form a swirled pattern.

7 Bake for 50 minutes, then turn off the oven and leave the cheesecake in it for a further hour.

8 Remove, cool and chill overnight before serving.

Pink Grapefruit Cheesecake

SERVES 8

For the crust

85 g | 3 oz butter, melted
200 g | 7 oz digestive biscuits, crushed

For the filling

200 g | 7 oz cream cheese
100 ml | 3½ fl oz double cream
grated zest of 1 pink grapefruit
1 egg
1 egg yolk
1½ tablespoons caster sugar

To decorate

3 pink grapefruit

1 Heat the oven to 150°C |300°F|gas mark 2.
2 Mix together the melted butter and crushed biscuits and use to line the base of a shallow 20 cm|8 in removable-based sandwich tin, pressing down well and pushing it up the sides.
3 Bake for 10 minutes.
4 Beat the cream cheese and then add the remaining filling ingredients. Beat well until smooth and pour on to the crust.
5 Place on a baking sheet and return to the middle of the oven and bake until the filling has set, about 25 minutes.
6 Remove from the oven and allow to cool completely.
7 Peel the grapefruit with a serrated-edged knife, removing all the pith. Cut out the grapefruit segments, leaving behind the membranes.
8 Arrange the segments neatly over the top of the cheesecake.

Cheesecakes: What has gone wrong when . . .

The cheesecake is cracked.
- The cheesecake was cooked for too long.

The cheesecake does not set.
- The cheesecake was underbaked.
- The cheesecake has not been chilled sufficiently.
- The recipe does not contain enough egg.

The cheesecake has souffléd in the centre and is watery.
- The cheesecake is overbaked.
- The oven temperature was too hot.

Biscuits: Points to Remember

- Use very little extra flour when rolling biscuits. Too much will make them dry.
- Do not reroll the dough more than once.
- Arrange the biscuits in staggered rows on the baking sheet to aid even cooking.
- Use flat, dull, heavy metal baking sheets with no or very low edges in preference to dark-coloured trays with lips. Covering the tray with baking parchment can stop biscuits from singeing around the edges and give a more even colour.
- When baking a batch of certain biscuits, it is worthwhile to bake a single biscuit as a test before baking a whole tray. If baking brandy snaps, for example, it is possible to alter the mixture slightly if you discover after test-baking that there is too much or too little flour.
- Remove the biscuits from the baking tray as soon as they are set, usually within about 1 or 2 minutes after removing from the oven. It depends on the type of biscuit.
- Cool the biscuits on wire racks.
- Cool completely before storing in an airtight container.

Biscuits and Cookies

Biscuits are, generally, easy to make and can be varied by the addition of different flavourings and ingredients. It is important, as with most baking, to measure the ingredients carefully to get a good result. They can also overcook and burn easily due to their high sugar content, so time them carefully.

The first evidence of biscuits was hardtack – hard, thin biscuits that were taken around the globe on ships. These biscuits had a very long storage life and could last for months or even years; when the fresh food ran out there were always the ships' biscuits to eat. The commercial manufacture of biscuits really took off in the 1800s with the availability of inexpensive flour and sugar and the invention of chemical raising agents, such as baking powder and bicarbonate of soda.

In Britain and France the word 'biscuit' means a small, crisp pastry, either sweet or savoury. Biscuit actually means twice-baked in French, derived from the Latin *bis coctum*. In Italy they are called *biscotti*, which has the same meaning. In America the word 'cookie' is used to describe both crisp biscuits and soft and/or chewy small cakes. This is derived from the Dutch word *koekje*, the diminutive word for cake.

Originally biscuits were twice-baked, i.e. they were cooked in the oven to colour them, then the oven was turned off and the biscuits went back in to dry out further without burning. It made the biscuits very hard and meant that they kept well before airtight containers were invented. Biscotti are still made in this way: the dough is cooked in a roll, then the roll is sliced up and cooked again in a low oven until crisp and hard.

Biscuits are served as a snack either at mid-morning or at teatime. A crisp biscuit, for example a shortbread, may be served as an accompaniment to a dessert such as fruit salad. Savoury crisp biscuits, called crackers, are served with cheese.

Methods of Making Biscuits and Cookies

There are many different methods used for making biscuits and cookies. They are similar to the ones used in cake-making. The method used, along with the ingredients in the recipe, will affect the finished texture of the biscuit.

Creaming Method

The fat and sugar are beaten together until just blended or, if air is needed in the dough, until light and fluffy. Then the other ingredients are added. Biscuits made using this method include Almond and Gin Biscuits, Chocolate Kisses and Refrigerator Biscuits. Always bring the butter out of the refrigerator in advance so that it is soft and easy to beat. If soft enough, the mixing can be done easily with a wooden spoon. However, if you are going to beat in eggs, it is probably better to use an electric mixer. Food processors can be used for creamed biscuits, but be careful if adding dried fruit to the mixture to ensure that the fruit doesn't get cut up by the blades. You can do this by pulsing the mixture a couple of times. Eggs should also be at room temperature because they are more likely to curdle the creamed fat and sugar mixture if very cold.

Rubbing-in Method

This method is not used so often now. Shortbread is often made by the rubbing-in method but it can also, as in this book, be made by quickly mixing the butter and sugar together before mixing in the flour. If a recipe uses the rubbing-in method the butter should be firm and cold, although if it comes straight out of the refrigerator it will prove difficult to rub into the flour. A food processor is very good for this method, although you may need to tip the rubbed-in mixture into a bowl and mix by hand for a minute or two before adding the liquid or eggs. Too much liquid can make the biscuits tough.

Melting Method

Biscuits and cookies such as Gingernuts, Brandy Snaps and Flapjacks use this method. The fat, sugar and/or syrup are melted together in a saucepan and not allowed to get too hot. The dry ingredients are then added and the dough is either rolled out, spooned on to baking sheets or pressed into a tin. A characteristic of these biscuits are that they cool quickly and can harden and stick to the baking sheet if not removed quickly. This is due to their high sugar content.

Whisking Method

These biscuits are made by adding the flour and other ingredients to a whisked mixture of eggs and sugar, or egg whites and sugar. This is used for Macaroons, Tuiles and Sponge Fingers. There is often very little or no fat in these recipes.

Storing Biscuits

Crisp biscuits should always be stored in an airtight container, separately from soft cakes. Keep in a cool, dry cupboard. If it is likely that the biscuits will stick together, interleave them with layers of greaseproof paper. Most biscuits will keep for up to 5 days, but some crisp biscuits, such as shortbread, will keep for up to 1 month. Biscuits that are high in fat and/or dried fruit or that have a low moisture content, such as biscotti, usually keep the best.

Biscuits can be frozen, if tightly wrapped, for up to 1 month. Unbaked dough can be kept in the refrigerator for 3 days and in the freezer for up to 1 month.

Most biscuits can be refreshed by putting them in a single layer on a baking sheet in a 150°C|300°F|gas mark 2 oven for 5 minutes. This treatment will also improve shop-bought biscuits.

Biscuits: What has gone wrong when . . .

The biscuits are tough and dry.
- The biscuits were overbaked.
- The dough was overworked when the flour was added.
- There is too much flour in the recipe or too much flour was used when rolling out.

The biscuits lose their definition and spread whilst baking.
- The butter was overbeaten, incorporating too much air.
- The dough was not chilled for long enough before baking.
- The biscuits contain too much butter or sugar. Add a little more flour.

The biscuits are not evenly browned.
- The baking trays were not rotated during baking.
- The oven temperature was too high.

The biscuits are greasy.
- The biscuits were not chilled for long enough before baking.
- The dough was overworked.
- The biscuits were underbaked.

The biscuits are hard.
- The biscuits were overbaked.
- The eggs were too large.

The biscuits are too thick and cakey.
- The biscuits contain too much flour.
- The oven temperature was too high.
- The biscuits were poorly shaped.

Shortbread

MAKES 2 ROUNDS OF 6–8

115 g | 4 oz butter, softened

55 g | 2 oz caster sugar

115 g | 4 oz plain flour

55 g | 2 oz ground rice

To finish

caster sugar

1 Heat the oven to 170°C | 325°F | gas mark 3.
2 Beat the butter until soft, stir in the sugar.
3 Sift in the flours and ground rice. Work to a smooth paste.
4 Place a 15 cm | 6 in flan ring on a baking sheet and press half the shortbread dough into a neat circle with the back of a metal spoon. Remove the flan ring and repeat with the rest of the dough. Crimp the edges. Mark each round of the shortbread into 6 wedges and prick all over with a fork. Chill until firm.
5 Sprinkle lightly with a little extra caster sugar and bake for 20 minutes until a pale, biscuit colour. Leave to cool for 2 minutes and then lift on to a cooling rack to cool completely.

VARIATIONS

Orange shortbread: Add the finely grated zest of 2 oranges to the creamed butter and sugar before adding the flour.

Ginger shortbread: Add 1 teaspoon of ground ginger and 55 g | 2 oz chopped crystallized stem ginger with the flour.

Almond Shortbread

MAKES ABOUT 16

115 g | 4 oz butter, softened

55 g | 2 oz caster sugar

¼ teaspoon almond essence

30 g | 1 oz ground rice

30 g | 1 oz ground almonds

115 g | 4 oz plain flour

a pinch of salt

55 g | 2 oz toasted almonds, chopped

To finish

caster sugar

1 Heat the oven to 170°C | 325°F | gas mark 3.
2 Stir the butter, caster sugar and almond extract together.
3 Stir in the ground rice and ground almonds then the flour and salt. Work in the chopped

almonds. You might need to use your fingers to pull the mixture together as it will be quite dry, but take care not to overwork.

4 Shape into a log 4 cm | 1¾ in diameter and wrap in clingfilm. Chill until firm. Slice into ½ cm | ¼ in rounds and place on an ungreased baking sheet.

5 Bake for about 20 minutes or until pale golden on the edges.

6 Sprinkle the biscuits with caster sugar. Use a palette knife to loosen from the baking sheet. Stand on the baking sheet for 2 minutes then move to a wire rack to cool completely.

7 Store in an airtight container.

Chocolate Shortbread Biscuits

MAKES 16

115 g | 4 oz butter, softened
55 g | 2 oz caster sugar
115 g | 4 oz plain flour
30 g | 1 oz cocoa powder

30 g | 1 oz cornflour
70 g | 2½ oz chocolate drops

To finish
caster sugar

1 Heat the oven to 180°C | 350°F | gas mark 4.

2 Mix together the butter and caster sugar.

3 Sift together the flour, cocoa powder and cornflour.

4 Stir into the butter mixture then add the chocolate drops. Pull together with your fingers to make a smooth dough.

5 Divide into 16 equal pieces, roll into balls and place on an ungreased baking sheet. (If the dough is too soft you may need to chill it briefly at this point.)

6 Flatten the balls with your fingers or the base of a glass to ½ cm | ¼ in thick.

7 Sprinkle with caster sugar and chill for 10 minutes.

8 Bake for 15 minutes or until dry around the edges.

9 Remove from the baking sheet whilst warm and place on a wire rack to cool.

Toasted Pecan Shortbread

MAKES ABOUT 16

115 g | 4 oz butter, softened

55 g | 2 oz caster sugar

¼ teaspoon vanilla essence

55 g | 2 oz ground rice

115 g | 4 oz plain flour

a pinch of salt

55 g | 2 oz pecan nuts, toasted and chopped

To finish

caster sugar

1 Stir the butter, caster sugar and vanilla together.

2 Stir in the ground rice then the flour and salt. Work in the pecans. You may need to use your hands to pull the mixture together as it will be quite dry, but take care not to overwork.

3 Roll into a 4 cm | 2 in diameter log and wrap in clingfilm. Chill until firm.

4 Heat the oven to 180°C | 350° | F | gas mark 4.

5 Slice ½ cm | ¼ in rounds from the dough. Place on an ungreased baking sheet.

6 Bake for about 20 minutes or until pale golden at the edges.

7 Sprinkle with caster sugar. Use a palette knife to loosen from the baking sheet.

8 Allow to stand on the baking sheet for 2 minutes then move to a wire rack to cool completely.

9 Store in an airtight container.

Cinnamon Shortbread

MAKES 16–20

170 g | 6 oz butter, softened

85 g | 3 oz soft light brown sugar

1 teaspoon vanilla essence

170 g | 6 oz plain flour

85 g | 3 oz rice flour (or ground rice)

3 teaspoons ground cinnamon

1 Heat the oven to 170°C | 325°F | gas mark 3. Line 2 baking sheets with baking parchment.

2 Cream the butter and sugar together, using an electric beater, until pale and fluffy. Add the vanilla essence.

3 Sift the plain flour, rice flour and ground cinnamon together and add to the butter mixture. Mix together to form a dough.

4 Divide the mixture into 2 pieces and, on a lightly floured work surface, roll each one into a log measuring 6 cm | 2½ in in diameter.

5 Wrap in either clingfilm or greaseproof paper and chill until firm (approximately 3 hours).

6 Cut the logs into slices about 1 cm | ½ in thick and place on to the baking sheets. Leave a gap between the biscuits as they may spread a little. Bake for 15–20 minutes. Allow the biscuits to cool for a few minutes on the baking sheet before transferring to a wire rack to cool completely.

Greek Almond Shortbread

MAKES 30

225 g|8 oz unsalted butter, softened

85 g|3 oz icing sugar

1 tablespoon brandy

1 teaspoon vanilla essence

115 g|4 oz blanched almonds, finely chopped

450 g|1 lb plain flour

1 teaspoon baking powder

To finish

rose-water

icing sugar

1 Cream the butter and icing sugar with an electric beater until pale and fluffy. Beat in the brandy and vanilla essence.

2 Mix the almonds into the flour and baking powder and add to the butter mixture. Mix to a dough. It will take time to bring together. Cover and chill for 30 minutes.

3 Heat the oven to 170°C|325°F|gas mark 3. Line 2 baking sheets with baking parchment.

4 Using your hands, roll tablespoonfuls of the mixture into 7.5 cm|3 in logs. Shape them into crescents or S shapes and place on the baking sheet, 5 cm|2 in apart. Bake for 20–25 minutes until a pale, golden colour. Do not overcook. Allow to cool for a few minutes on the baking tray before removing to a wire rack to cool completely.

5 Whilst cooling, sprinkle with a little rose-water and dust with icing sugar.

Sponge Fingers

MAKES 30

6 eggs

140 g|5 oz caster sugar

115 g|4 oz flour

30 g|1 oz arrowroot

1 Heat the oven to 200°C|400°F|gas mark 6. Line 2 large baking sheets with baking parchment. Draw parallel lines 12.5 cm|5 in apart on the parchment.

2 Separate 5 of the eggs. Beat the yolks with the whole egg and 115 g|4 oz of the sugar in a large bowl until the mixture is nearly white.

3 Whisk the egg whites until stiff, then gradually whisk in the remaining sugar until stiff and shiny. Fold the egg whites into the yolk and sugar mixture, using a large metal spoon. Sift the flour with the arrowroot and fold in carefully.

4 Fit a 5 mm|¼ in plain nozzle on to a piping bag and fill the bag with the mixture. Pipe 12.5 cm|5 in fingers between the parallel lines on the baking parchment. The fingers should be just touching.

5 Bake in the top of the oven for about 10 minutes or until risen and biscuit-coloured.

6 Remove the sponge fingers from the oven, invert on to a clean tea towel and immediately and carefully peel off the paper. Turn on to a wire rack and leave to cool completely.

Hazelnut Sablés

MAKES ABOUT 24

225 g | 8 oz butter

115 g | 4 oz icing sugar, sifted

2 egg yolks

340 g | 12 oz plain flour

55 g | 2 oz ground hazelnuts

1 Heat the oven to 180°C | 350°F | gas mark 4.
2 Cream the butter and icing sugar together until pale and fluffy. Beat in the egg yolks.
3 Sift the flour and mix with the ground hazelnuts. Stir into the butter mixture and bring together to form a dough.
4 Roll out the dough to the thickness of a 50p coin and stamp out biscuits with a small round pastry cutter. Place on a baking sheet and chill for 10 minutes.
5 Bake the biscuits for 20 minutes, or until golden-brown.

Passion-fruit Shortcake

MAKES 22

170 g | 6 oz butter

85 g | 3 oz caster sugar

pulp of 3 passion-fruit

170 g | 6 oz plain flour

85 g | 3 oz cornflour

To finish

caster sugar

1 Cream the butter and sugar together until pale and fluffy. Add the passion-fruit pulp.
2 Sift together the flour and cornflour and add to the butter and sugar mixture. Mix to a dough.
3 Roll the dough out between two pieces of clingfilm. Make into a square or rectangle approximately 1 cm | ½ in thick. Chill for 45 minutes.
4 Heat the oven to 170°C | 325°F | gas mark 3. Line a baking sheet with baking parchment.
5 Remove the dough from the clingfilm. Trim the edges and cut into squares 5 × 5 cm | 2 × 2 in. Cut each square in half to form triangles. Place on the baking sheet and bake in the centre of the oven for 20–25 minutes. Remove from the oven and dust with caster sugar.
6 Place on a wire rack to cool.

Coffee Kisses

MAKES 12

170 g | 6 oz self-raising flour
85 g | 3 oz butter, cut into pieces
85 g | 3 oz caster sugar
1 egg, beaten
1 tablespoon coffee essence

For the buttercream

55 g | 2 oz butter, softened
115 g | 4 oz icing sugar, sifted
2–3 teaspoons coffee essence

1 Heat the oven to 180°C | 350°F | gas mark 4. Line 2 baking sheets with baking parchment.
2 Sift the flour into a large mixing bowl. Add the butter and rub into the flour until it resembles fine breadcrumbs. Stir in the sugar.
3 Stir in the egg and coffee essence and mix well until it forms a dough.
4 Make into 24 balls the size of large cherries. Place on the baking sheet and flatten very slightly. Bake for 15 minutes, then remove to a wire rack to cool.
5 Meanwhile, make the coffee buttercream: put the butter into a bowl and cream it with a wooden spoon. Add the icing sugar, mix well and add coffee essence to taste.
6 When the biscuits are cold, sandwich together with the buttercream.

Lime Kisses

MAKES 12

170 g | 6 oz self-raising flour
85 g | 3 oz butter, cut into pieces
85 g | 3 oz caster sugar
grated zest of 1 lime
1 egg, beaten
1 tablespoon lime juice

For the buttercream

55 g | 2 oz butter
115 g | 4 oz icing sugar
grated zest of ½ lime
2–3 teaspoons lime juice

1 Heat the oven to 180°C | 350°F | gas mark 4. Line 2 baking sheets with baking parchment.
2 Sift the flour into a large bowl and rub in the butter with your fingertips until it resembles fine breadcrumbs. Add the caster sugar and lime zest.
3 Mix the egg and lime juice into the mixture and bring together to form a soft dough.
4 Take teaspoonfuls of the mixture and shape into balls the size of cherries using your hands. Place on the baking sheets and flatten slightly. Bake for approximately 15 minutes. Remove from the baking sheet to a wire rack to cool completely.
5 Make the buttercream: soften the butter with a wooden spoon. Add the sifted icing sugar and mix well. Add the lime zest and enough juice to taste.
6 Sandwich the cold biscuits together with the buttercream.

Chocolate Kisses

MAKES 15

115 g | 4 oz butter, softened
115 g | 4 oz caster sugar
1 egg, beaten
225 g | 8 oz plain flour
½ teaspoon baking powder
3 tablespoons cocoa powder

For the buttercream

85 g | 3 oz butter, softened
170 g | 6 oz icing sugar
1 tablespoon cocoa powder

1 Heat the oven to 180°C | 350°F | gas mark 4. Line 2 baking sheets with baking parchment.
2 Cream the butter and sugar with an electric beater until pale and fluffy. Add the egg, a little at a time, beating well between each addition.
3 Sift the flour, baking powder and cocoa together and add to the butter mixture. Mix well with a wooden spoon to form a dough.
4 Take teaspoons of the mixture and roll with your hands into 30 balls the size of cherries. Place on the baking sheet and flatten slightly, leaving a gap between them as they will spread. Bake for 15 minutes. Allow to sit on the baking sheet for a couple of minutes before removing to a wire rack to cool.
5 Meanwhile, make the chocolate buttercream: put the butter into a bowl and cream it with a wooden spoon. Sift the icing sugar and cocoa together and add to the butter. Mix well. Add more sifted cocoa to taste.
6 When the biscuits are cold, sandwich together with the buttercream.

Chocolate Oaties

MAKES 16

115 g | 4 oz butter
115 g | 4 oz soft light brown sugar

200 g | 7 oz porridge oats
170 g | 6 oz plain chocolate

1 Grease a shallow, square 20 cm | 8 in cake tin, or line with baking parchment. Heat the oven to 170°C | 325°F | gas mark 3.
2 Melt the butter and add the sugar and oats. Mix well and press into the prepared cake tin.
3 Place in the centre of the oven and bake for 25–30 minutes.
4 Remove from the oven and allow to cool in the tin for 5 minutes. Cut into squares and remove to a wire rack to cool.
5 Carefully melt the chocolate in a bowl over, but not touching, a pan of steaming water. When the biscuits are cold, spread the chocolate over half of each biscuit. Allow to set.

Anzac Biscuits

These biscuits were made by the wives and mothers of the Australian and New Zealand Army Corps to send to them whilst away from home. They keep well, and if you don't like coconut you can leave it out and add an extra 45 g|1½ oz oats.

MAKES 24

70 g|2½ oz plain flour

a pinch of salt

100 g|3½ oz porridge oats

55 g|2 oz desiccated coconut

115 g|4 oz butter, softened

55 g|2 oz caster sugar

2 tablespoons golden syrup

½ teaspoon bicarbonate of soda

1 tablespoon hot water

1 Heat the oven to 170°C|325°F|gas mark 3. Line a baking sheet with baking parchment.

2 Mix the flour, salt, oats and coconut together in a bowl. In another bowl, cream the butter and sugar together with the syrup.

3 Dissolve the bicarbonate of soda in the hot water and add to the butter mixture. Add the dry ingredients and mix to a dough.

4 Take teaspoonfuls of the mixture and roll into balls. Place on the baking sheet, leaving a 5 cm|2 in gap between them, and bake for 12–15 minutes. Cool on a wire rack.

Muesli Biscuits

MAKES ABOUT 40

225 g|8 oz porridge oats

55 g|2 oz raisins

55 g|2 oz hazelnuts, toasted and chopped

55 g|2 oz almonds, toasted and chopped

115 g|4 oz dried apricots, chopped

115 g|4 oz self-raising flour

115 g|4 oz soft light brown sugar

55 g|2 oz sesame seeds

1 tablespoon clear honey

2 eggs, beaten

170 g|6 oz butter, melted and cooled

1 Heat the oven to 180°C|350°F|gas mark 4. Grease 3 baking sheets.

2 Combine all the dry ingredients in a large bowl.

3 Mix together the honey, eggs and butter and add to the dry ingredients. Mix very well.

4 Put large teaspoons of the mixture on to a baking sheet, flattening them slightly and allowing 5 cm|2 in between them for spreading.

5 Bake in the oven for 10–15 minutes or until firm to the touch. Transfer to a wire rack and leave to cool completely. Store in an airtight container.

Refrigerator Biscuits

These biscuits are so called because the dough can be kept in the refrigerator (well-wrapped) for 1 week or in the freezer for 3 months, and the biscuits can be cut and baked as required. Change the flavouring by leaving out the lemon zest and adding either orange zest, 1 teaspoon ground cinnamon, 1 teaspoon ground ginger or 1 tablespoon cocoa powder.

MAKES 18–20

140 g｜5 oz butter	grated zest of 1 lemon
140 g｜5 oz caster sugar	1 egg, beaten
1 teaspoon vanilla essence	225 g｜8 oz plain flour

1 Cream the butter and sugar together until pale and fluffy. Beat in the vanilla essence, lemon zest and egg. Mix in the flour and bring together to a dough.
2 Knead lightly and wrap in clingfilm. Chill for 30 minutes.
3 Remove from the refrigerator and roll into a sausage shape approximately 5 cm｜2 in in diameter and 20 cm｜8 in long. Wrap in greaseproof paper and put back in the refrigerator for at least 30 minutes.
4 Heat the oven to 190°C｜375°F｜gas mark 5. Line a baking sheet with baking parchment.
5 Cut 1 cm｜½ in slices from the roll of dough and place on the baking sheet. Bake in the centre of the oven for 12–15 minutes. Allow the biscuits to cool for a few minutes before lifting them with a palette knife on to a wire rack to cool completely.

Gingernuts

MAKES 20–25

30 g｜1 oz demerara sugar	115 g｜4 oz plain flour
55 g｜2 oz butter	½ teaspoon bicarbonate of soda
85 g｜3 oz golden syrup	1 heaped teaspoon ground ginger

1 Heat the oven to 180°C｜350°F｜gas mark 4. Grease a baking sheet.
2 Melt the sugar, butter and syrup together slowly, without boiling. Make sure the sugar has dissolved, then remove from the heat and allow to cool.
3 Sift the flour with the soda and ginger into a bowl. Make a well in the centre.
4 Pour the melted mixture into the well and knead until smooth. Roll into balls and flatten, on the prepared baking sheet, into biscuits about 3.5 cm｜1½ in in diameter.
5 Bake for 20–25 minutes, or until golden-brown. Leave on a wire rack to crisp and cool.

Pecan, Almond and Hazelnut Biscuits

MAKES 16–20

225 g|8 oz butter, softened
115 g|4 oz caster sugar
1 teaspoon vanilla essence
85 g|3 oz pecan nuts, chopped
55 g|2 oz blanched almonds, chopped

55 g|2 oz blanched hazelnuts, chopped
340 g|12 oz plain flour, sifted

To finish
icing sugar

1 Cream the butter and caster sugar with an electric beater until pale and fluffy. Add the vanilla essence. Using a wooden spoon, add the nuts and flour and combine to form a dough.

2 Divide into 2 pieces and roll into logs that measure approximately 5 cm|2 in in diameter. Wrap in clingfilm or greaseproof paper and chill until firm (approximately 2 hours).

3 Heat the oven to 170°C|325°F|gas mark 3. Line 2 baking sheets with baking parchment.

4 Using a sharp, warm knife, cut the logs into 1 cm|½ in slices and place on the baking sheets.

5 Bake for 20–25 minutes or until a very pale golden-brown. Allow them to sit on the baking sheets for 2 minutes to firm up, then remove them with a palette knife to a wire rack to cool down.

6 Whilst they are still warm, dust with sifted icing sugar.

Orange Polenta Biscuits

MAKES 20

225 g|8 oz butter, softened
170 g|6 oz icing sugar
1 teaspoon vanilla essence
grated zest of 2 oranges

70 g|2½ oz polenta
340 g|12 oz plain flour

To finish
caster sugar

1 Line 2 baking sheets with baking parchment.

2 Beat the butter and sugar together with an electric beater until pale and fluffy. Add the vanilla essence and the orange zest. Beat again for 30 seconds.

3 Mix the polenta with the flour and add to the mixture, combining carefully.

4 Gently knead the dough on a floured work surface until it has come together and is smooth. Roll out to a thickness of 1 cm|½ in and cut into 5 cm|2 in biscuits using a plain cutter. Place on the baking sheets and chill for 1 hour.

5 Heat the oven to 180°C|350°F|gas mark 4. Bake the biscuits for about 10–15 minutes or until they are a pale golden colour.

6 Cool on the baking sheet for 5 minutes. Sprinkle each biscuit with some caster sugar whilst hot. Remove to a wire rack to cool completely and store in an airtight container.

Almond and Gin Biscuits

These biscuits have a wonderfully crisp texture and a delicious taste, with a very slight hint of juniper.

MAKES 14

115 g | 4 oz butter, softened
85 g | 3 oz caster sugar
2 tablespoons gin

140 g | 5 oz plain flour, sifted
85 g | 3 oz flaked almonds, chopped

1 Heat the oven to 180°C|350°F|gas mark 4. Grease 2 baking sheets.
2 Cream the butter and sugar together until pale and fluffy. Beat in the gin.
3 Mix together the sifted flour and almonds and stir into the butter mixture. Bring the dough together, first with a wooden spoon and then with the fingers of one hand.
4 Shape into 14 balls the size of a ping-pong ball.
5 Place on the baking sheets, allowing 5 cm|2 in between them for spreading. Press your thumb into the centre of each, to make a dimple.
6 Bake in the top of the oven for 15–20 minutes or until golden-brown. Transfer to a wire rack and leave to cool completely.

Afghan Biscuits

MAKES 24–26

200 g | 7 oz butter, softened
85 g | 3 oz caster sugar
170 g | 6 oz plain flour
30 g | 1 oz cocoa powder
55 g | 2 oz cornflakes

For the icing

115 g | 4 oz icing sugar
1 tablespoon cocoa powder
boiling water

to decorate

walnut halves

1 Heat the oven to 180°C|350°|gas mark 4. Line a baking sheet with baking parchment.
2 Cream the butter with an electric beater, add the sugar and beat until pale and fluffy.
3 Sift the flour with the cocoa powder and add to the mixture. Finally add the cornflakes.
4 Put teaspoonfuls shaped into rounds on to the prepared baking sheets and bake for approximately 15 minutes.
5 Remove the biscuits to a wire rack to cool down and make the icing. Sift the icing sugar and cocoa powder together into a bowl. Add 1 tablespoon of boiling water or enough to make a thick icing.
6 Decorate the cold biscuits with the icing and place a walnut on top of each, if desired.

Viennese Biscuits

MAKES ABOUT 40

225 g | 8 oz unsalted butter, softened

115 g | 4 oz icing sugar

2 egg yolks

1 teaspoon vanilla essence

340 g | 12 oz plain flour

a pinch of salt

4–6 tablespoons single cream

To finish

caster sugar

1 Heat oven to 190°C | 375°F | gas mark 5.

2 Beat the butter with the icing sugar until pale and fluffy.

3 Beat in the egg yolks and the vanilla.

4 Sift the flour and salt over the butter and stir to combine.

5 Stir in the single cream to make a pipeable dough.

6 Fill a piping bag fitted with a 1 cm | ½ in star nozzle and pipe 5 cm | 2 in S-shaped biscuits, pushing closed any gaps in the Ss.

7 Sprinkle with caster sugar and bake for 10–12 minutes or until beginning to brown.

8 Cool on a wire rack. Store in an airtight container when cool.

Chocolate Melting Moments

MAKES 18–20

115 g | 4 oz butter, softened

85 g | 3 oz caster sugar

1 teaspoon vanilla essence

140 g | 5 oz self-raising flour

2 tablespoons cocoa powder

7–10 tablespoons porridge oats

1 Heat the oven to 180°C | 350°F | gas mark 4. Line 2 baking sheets with baking parchment.

2 Cream the butter and sugar together using an electric beater until pale and fluffy. Add the vanilla essence.

3 Sift the flour and cocoa together and work into the butter mixture. Bring it together to form a dough.

4 Take teaspoonfuls of the mixture and roll into balls, then roll lightly with wet hands and roll in the oats.

5 Place on the baking sheets 5 cm | 2 in apart and press down to flatten slightly. Bake for 12–15 minutes. Remove from the baking sheets and place on a wire rack to cool completely.

Carrot and Date Biscuits

MAKES 18

115 g | 4 oz butter, softened
115 g | 4 oz soft light brown sugar
1 egg, beaten
115 g | 4 oz plain flour
1 teaspoon baking powder

1 teaspoon ground cinnamon
½ teaspoon ground nutmeg
a pinch of ground ginger
55 g | 2 oz carrot, grated
85 g | 3 oz dried dates, chopped

1 Cream the butter and sugar together using an electric beater until pale and fluffy. Add the egg a little at a time, beating well between each addition.
2 Sift together the flour, baking powder and spices. Add to the mixture with the carrot and dates. Bring together, to form a dough.
3 Place the mixture in the refrigerator for 1 hour.
4 Heat the oven to 190°C | 375°F | gas mark 5. Line 2 baking sheets with baking parchment.
5 Shape the mixture into golf-ball-sized rounds and place on the baking sheet approximately 5 cm | 2 in apart. Flatten slightly and bake for 10–15 minutes.
6 Cool for 5 minutes before removing to a wire rack to cool completely.

Chocolate Refrigerator Cookies

The dough for these cookies needs to be well chilled before cutting, but this means that you can just cut as many as you need. The dough will keep in the refrigerator for about 1 week or in the freezer for up to 3 months.

MAKES 35

170 g | 6 oz butter, softened
85 g | 3 oz soft light brown sugar
1 teaspoon vanilla essence
55 g | 2 oz plain chocolate, chopped into small pieces

250 g | 9 oz plain flour
1 tablespoon cocoa powder
85 g | 3 oz white chocolate drops

1 Cream the butter and sugar together using an electric beater until pale and fluffy. Add the vanilla essence.
2 Put the plain chocolate in a small, heatproof bowl, over but not in a pan of steaming water. Heat until the chocolate has just melted. Remove from the heat.
3 Sift the flour and cocoa powder together. Mix the melted chocolate into the butter and sugar, followed by the flour, cocoa powder and white chocolate drops. Mix well to form a dough.
4 Divide the dough in half and shape into 2 long rolls measuring 5 cm | 2 in in diameter. Wrap well in clingfilm or aluminium foil and chill for 2 hours.
5 Heat the oven to 190°C | 375°F | gas mark 5. Line 2 baking sheets with baking parchment.
6 Remove the dough from the refrigerator and cut into 5 mm | ¼ in slices with a sharp knife. Place on the baking sheet and bake for 10 minutes. Transfer the cookies to a wire rack to cool.

Macadamia and White Chocolate Cookies

MAKES 18–20

170 g | 6 oz butter, softened
115 g | 4 oz soft light brown sugar
225 g | 8 oz plain flour
½ teaspoon bicarbonate of soda

55 g | 2 oz white chocolate, chopped into small pieces
55 g | 2 oz macadamia nuts, chopped to the same size
  as the chocolate pieces

1 Heat the oven to 180°C | 350°F | gas mark 4. Line 2 baking sheets with baking parchment.
2 Cream the butter and sugar together using an electric beater until pale and fluffy.
3 Sift the flour and bicarbonate of soda together and add to the butter mixture along with the chocolate and nuts. Bring together to form a dough.
4 Roll large teaspoonfuls into balls and place on the prepared baking sheets about 5 cm | 2 in apart. Flatten them lightly with your hand.
5 Bake for about 15–20 minutes. Allow to cool slightly on the baking sheets before moving them, with a palette knife, to cool down on a wire rack.

Banana, Apple and Coconut Cookies

MAKES 36

170 g | 6 oz butter, softened
85 g | 3 oz caster sugar
85 g | 3 oz soft light brown sugar
1 egg, beaten
3 medium bananas, mashed

1 teaspoon vanilla essence
170 g | 6 oz dried apple pieces, chopped
55 g | 2 oz desiccated coconut
250 g | 9 oz plain flour
1 teaspoon baking powder

1 Heat the oven to 180°C | 350°F | gas mark 4. Line a baking sheet with baking parchment.
2 Cream the butter and sugar together until pale and fluffy, then beat in the egg.
3 Stir in the mashed bananas, vanilla essence, apple pieces and coconut.
4 Sift in the flour and baking powder and mix to form a sticky dough.
5 Cover the bowl with clingfilm and chill for 30 minutes.
6 Place teaspoonfuls the size of ping-pong balls on the baking sheet, 5 cm | 2 in apart. Flatten with a fork.
7 Bake for 20 minutes. Cool on the baking sheet for 5 minutes before removing them to a wire rack to cool completely.

Carrot and Apricot Cookies

These cookies will be soft and slightly chewy when cooked.

MAKES 18

115 g | 4 oz butter, softened

115 g | 4 oz soft light brown sugar

1 egg, beaten

55 g | 2 oz grated carrot

115 g | 4 oz chopped apricots

3 tablespoons sunflower seeds

115 g | 4 oz plain flour

1 teaspoon baking powder

1 teaspoon ground cinnamon

a pinch of nutmeg

1 Beat the butter and sugar together until pale and fluffy. Add the egg and beat well.

2 Add the carrots, apricots and sunflower seeds.

3 Sift the flour, baking powder, cinnamon and nutmeg into the mixture and mix together to form a dough. Wrap in clingfilm and chill for 2 hours.

4 Heat the oven to 180°C | 350°F | gas mark 4. Line 2 baking sheets with baking parchment.

5 Roll the dough into pieces the size of a ping-pong ball and place on the baking tray 5 cm | 2 in apart. Flatten with your hand.

6 Bake for 15–20 minutes. Cool for 5 minutes on the baking tray before moving to a wire rack to cool completely.

Chocolate Chip Cookies

MAKES 36

115 g | 4 oz butter, softened

85 g | 3 oz caster sugar

85 g | 3 oz soft light brown sugar

1 teaspoon vanilla essence

1 egg, beaten

140 g | 5 oz plain flour

¼ teaspoon bicarbonate of soda

a pinch of salt

100 g | 3½ oz walnuts, coarsely chopped

170 g | 6 oz chocolate chips

1 Heat the oven to 170°C | 350°F | gas mark 4.

2 Cream the butter and sugars until pale and fluffy. Stir in the vanilla.

3 Gradually add the egg, beating between each addition.

4 Sift together the flour, bicarbonate of soda and salt. Stir into the butter mixture.

5 Stir in the walnuts and chocolate chips.

6 Place tablespoons of dough on to ungreased baking sheets, leaving the space of one mound between each cookie to allow for spreading.

7 Bake in the middle of the oven for 8–10 minutes until pale golden and set in the centre. Rotate the tray from back to front halfway through the cooking time.

8 Cool on the baking sheet for 1 minute then place on a wire rack to cool.

Peanut Butter Cookies

MAKES ABOUT 40

140 g | 5 oz butter, softened
115 g | 4 oz caster sugar
115 g | 4 oz soft light brown sugar
1 large egg, beaten
115 g | 4 oz crunchy peanut butter

½ teaspoon vanilla essence
200 g | 7 oz plain flour
½ teaspoon salt
1 teaspoon baking powder
caster sugar, for sprinkling

1 Heat the oven to 180°C | 350°F | gas mark 4.
2 Cream the butter and sugars together until smooth and soft. Beat in the egg, then the peanut butter, and add the vanilla essence.
3 Sift the flour, salt and baking powder into the mixture and stir until smooth. Do not overbeat or the dough will be oily.
4 Roll the mixture into small balls using your fingers and place well apart on 3 ungreased baking sheets. Flatten with the prongs of a fork. Sprinkle with caster sugar.
5 Bake for 10–15 minutes to an even, not too dark, brown.
6 While hot, ease off the baking sheets with a palette knife or fish slice and cool on a wire rack. Once completely cold and crisp, store in an airtight container.

Mocha Chocolate Chip Cookies

MAKES 24

170 g | 6 oz butter, softened
115 g | 4 oz soft light brown sugar
1 tablespoon strong coffee essence

225 g | 8 oz plain flour
½ teaspoon bicarbonate of soda
100 g | 3½ oz plain or milk chocolate chips

1 Heat the oven to 180°C | 350°F | gas mark 4. Line 2 baking sheets with baking parchment.
2 Cream the butter and sugar together using an electric beater until pale and fluffy, then beat in the coffee essence.
3 Sift the flour and bicarbonate of soda together and add to the butter mixture along with the chocolate chips.
4 Roll large teaspoonfuls of the mixture into balls and place on the baking sheets about 5 cm | 2 in apart. Flatten them slightly with your hand.
5 Bake for about 12–15 minutes. Allow to cool slightly on the baking sheets before moving them, with a palette knife, on to a wire rack to cool completely.

Triple Chocolate Cookies

MAKES ABOUT 40

115 g | 4 oz butter

100 g | 3½ oz plain chocolate, chopped into small pieces

1 teaspoon instant coffee granules

140 g | 5 oz caster sugar

140 g | 5 oz soft light brown sugar

2 eggs, beaten

2 teaspoons vanilla essence

250 g | 9 oz plain flour

30 g | 1 oz cocoa powder

½ teaspoon baking powder

140 g | 5 oz milk or plain chocolate chips

1 Melt butter and plain chocolate over a low heat, then stir in the coffee granules.

2 Heat the oven to 180°C | 350°C | gas mark 4.

3 Cool the butter mixture until barely warm, then stir in the sugars, eggs and vanilla.

4 Sift together the flour, cocoa powder and baking powder. Fold into the butter mixture then stir in the chocolate chips. The mixture will be very stiff so you may need to squeeze it together with your fingers.

5 Place rounded tablespoons on to lightly greased baking sheets.

6 Bake in the centre of the oven for 10 minutes. The cookies will still be soft in the centre but will set when cool. Do not overbake or the cookies will be too hard.

7 Cool on the baking sheets for 1 minute then transfer to a wire rack to cool completely.

Snickerdoodles

MAKES ABOUT 24

140 g | 5 oz caster sugar

85 g | 3 oz butter, softened

30 g | 1 oz vegetable fat

1 egg, beaten

½ teaspoon vanilla essence

200 g | 7 oz plain flour

1 teaspoon cream of tartar

½ teaspoon bicarbonate of soda

a pinch of salt

¼ teaspoon freshly grated or ground nutmeg

¼ teaspoon ground cinnamon

To finish

1 teaspoon sugar

a pinch of ground cinnamon

1 Beat the caster sugar, butter and vegetable fat together then gradually beat in the egg and vanilla.

2 Sift together the flour, cream of tartar, bicarbonate of soda, salt, nutmeg and cinnamon. Stir into the butter mixture.

3 Wrap the dough in clingfilm and chill until firm enough to shape, about 30 minutes.

4 Heat the oven to 190°C | 375°F | gas mark 5.

5 Mix the caster sugar and cinnamon together in a small bowl. Roll tablespoons of the dough into balls then roll in the cinnamon sugar.

6 Place on ungreased baking sheets (the cookies spread a little) and bake in the centre of the oven for 12–13 minutes. Leave to stand on the baking sheet for 1 minute then remove to a wire rack to cool completely.

Macaroons

MAKES 20

115 g | 4 oz ground almonds

170 g | 6 oz caster sugar

1 teaspoon plain flour

2 egg whites

2 drops of vanilla essence

To decorate

split blanched almonds

1 Heat the oven to 180°C | 350°F | gas mark 4. Line a baking sheet with rice paper or baking parchment.
2 Mix together the almonds, sugar and flour.
3 Add the egg whites and vanilla. Beat very well.
4 Place teaspoonfuls of the mixture on the baking sheet, allowing 5 cm | 2 in between them for spreading. Place a split almond on each macaroon.
5 Bake in the oven for 20 minutes or until the macaroons are firm to the touch and the almonds are golden-brown. Transfer to a wire rack and leave to cool completely. If using rice paper, trim the excess paper from around the macaroons.

Pine Nut Macaroons

MAKES ABOUT 24

115 g | 4 oz ground almonds

170 g | 6 oz caster sugar

2 drops of vanilla essence

1 teaspoon plain flour

2 egg whites

100 g | 3½ oz pine nuts

1 Heat the oven to 180°C | 350°F | gas mark 4. Line 2 baking sheets with rice paper or baking parchment.
2 Mix together the almonds, sugar, vanilla essence and flour. Stir in the egg whites and beat well.
3 Spoon teaspoonfuls of the mixture on to the rice paper or baking parchment, then gently press the nuts on the top of each pile.
4 Bake in the centre of the oven for 20 minutes until golden, then transfer to a wire rack to cool.
5 If using rice paper, tear off and discard excess paper from around the edges of each biscuit.

Chocolate Macaroons

MAKES ABOUT 30

3 egg whites
170 g|6 oz icing sugar
85 g|3 oz ground almonds
15 g|½ oz cocoa powder

To finish
extra cocoa powder

1 Heat the oven to 140°C|275°F|gas mark 1. Line 2 baking sheets with baking parchment.
2 Whisk the egg whites until stiff peaks form, then gradually whisk in half the icing sugar. Sift together the remaining sugar, ground almonds and cocoa powder, then fold into the meringue mixture.
3 Drop teaspoonfuls on to the baking parchment. Sift over a little cocoa powder to coat.
4 Bake in the bottom third of the oven for 1½ hours or until the meringues peel off the baking parchment easily. Cool on a wire rack then store in an airtight container.

Amaretti Biscuits

MAKES 85

170 g|6 oz ground almonds
1 teaspoon cornflour
115 g|4 oz icing sugar
3 egg whites
a pinch of cream of tartar

170 g|6 oz caster sugar
2 teaspoons almond essence

To finish
crystal coffee sugar (optional)

1 Heat the oven to 150°C|300°F|gas mark 2. Line 2 baking sheets with baking parchment.
2 Mix the ground almonds, cornflour and icing sugar together. Put the egg whites and cream of tartar into a large bowl and whip with an electric beater until they form stiff peaks.
3 Beat in about a quarter of the sugar until the mixture is stiff and shiny. Continue beating in the rest of the sugar gradually. It will probably take about 5 minutes in all. Add the almond essence.
4 Carefully fold in the almond mixture using a large metal spoon.
5 Put into a piping bag with a 1 cm|½ in plain nozzle. Pipe little mounds about 2.5 cm|1 in in diameter. Use a damp finger to press down any peaks and sprinkle with a little crystal coffee sugar, if desired.
6 Bake for 30–40 minutes or until lightly browned. Turn the oven off and allow them to cool in the oven for a further 15 minutes. Transfer to a wire rack to cool down completely.

Tuiles

The word 'tuile' means tile, and these biscuits are so called because they look very similar to roof tiles. Tuiles are shaped biscuits that are made using the melting method. To shape them quickly and evenly, make a stencil. Cut a circle (7.5 cm|3 in for biscuits and 10 cm|4 in for baskets) out of the lid of a plastic box, such as an ice-cream container and, using a palette knife, spread the mixture over the stencil to fill the circle in a thin, even layer, then remove to make the next biscuit.

MAKES 20

55 g|2 oz butter

2 egg whites

115 g|4 oz caster sugar

55 g|2 oz plain flour

1 Heat the oven to 190°C|375°F|gas mark 5.
2 Line 2 baking sheets with baking parchment, each sheet cut into 4 equal squares.
3 Melt the butter and allow it to cool to room temperature.
4 Beat the egg whites with a fork to break them up, then stir in the sugar.
5 Stir in the butter and then the flour.
6 Spread the mixture into very thin rounds on the parchment squares.
7 Bake for 5–7 minutes or until lightly browned. Lift the biscuits using the paper to protect your hand and drape over a rolling pin. Alternatively, the biscuits can be wrapped around the handle of a wooden spoon. Allow to cool.

Lime and Coconut Tuiles

MAKES 10–12

30 g|1 oz butter

1 egg white

55 g|2 oz caster sugar

30 g|1 oz plain flour

grated zest of 1 lime

2 tablespoons desiccated coconut

1 Melt the butter and leave to cool.
2 Heat the oven to 190°C|375°F|gas mark 5. Line a baking sheet with baking parchment.
3 In a large bowl, whisk the egg white until stiff, then whisk in the caster sugar.
4 Fold in the other ingredients, including the cooled butter.
5 Spread the mixture on to the baking sheet in very thin, 10 cm|4 in rounds.
6 Bake in the oven for 5–6 minutes or until golden-brown around the edges and opaque in the centre.
7 Drape each biscuit over a lightly oiled rolling pin, one by one. When set, transfer them to a wire rack to finish cooling.

Tuiles à l'Orange

MAKES 20

2 egg whites

115 g | 4 oz caster sugar

55 g | 2 oz butter, melted and cooled

55 g | 2 oz plain flour, sifted

grated zest of 1 orange

1 Heat the oven to 190°C | 375°F | gas mark 5. Line a baking sheet with baking parchment.

2 Whisk the egg whites until frothy. Add the sugar and whisk to combine.

3 Add the butter to the meringue mixture, by degrees, with the flour. Fold in the orange zest.

4 Spread out teaspoonfuls of the mixture very thinly on the prepared baking sheet, keeping them well apart to allow for spreading during cooking. Bake for 5–6 minutes or until golden-brown.

5 Oil a rolling pin or the handle of a large wooden spoon. Loosen the tuiles from the baking sheet while still hot. While they are still warm and pliable, curl them over the rolling pin or round the wooden spoon handle. When they are quite firm, slip them off.

6 Leave to cool completely on a wire rack.

Tuiles Amandines

MAKES 25

30 g | 1 oz blanched almonds

2 egg whites

115 g | 4 oz caster sugar

55 g | 2 oz plain flour

½ teaspoon vanilla essence

55 g | 2 oz butter, melted and cooled

1 Heat the oven to 180° | 350°F | gas mark 4. Lightly grease a rolling pin and line baking sheets with baking parchment.

2 Cut the almonds into fine slivers or shreds.

3 Place the egg whites in a bowl. Beat in the sugar with a fork. The egg white should be frothy. Sift in the flour and add the vanilla essence. Mix with the fork.

4 Add the melted butter to the mixture. Stir well.

5 Place teaspoonfuls of the mixture at least 13 cm | 5 in apart on the prepared baking sheets and spread very thinly. Sprinkle with the almonds.

6 Bake for about 6 minutes until a pale, biscuit colour in the middle and a good brown at the edges. Remove from the oven and cool for a few seconds.

7 Carefully lift off the biscuits using a palette knife. Lay them over the rolling pin, while still warm and pliable, to form them into a slightly curved shape. Leave on a wire rack to cool completely.

Langues du Chat

'Langues du chat' or 'cats' tongues' are thin, crisp biscuits that are ideal for serving with a dessert mousse.

MAKES 30–40

100 g | 3½ oz butter, softened
100 g | 3½ oz caster sugar
a few drops vanilla essence

3 egg whites
100 g | 3½ oz plain flour

1 Heat the oven to 200°C | 400°F | gas mark 6. Line a baking sheet with baking parchment.
2 Beat together the butter and sugar until pale and fluffy. Stir in the vanilla.
3 Whisk the egg whites with a fork to break them up, then beat gradually into the butter mixture.
4 Sift the flour over the top of the mixture and fold in.
5 Place the mixture in a piping bag fitted with a ½ cm | ¼ in plain nozzle. Pipe fingers 5 cm | 2 in long on to the parchment, leaving 3.5 cm | 1½ in between each biscuit.
6 Tap the baking sheet on the underside to release any air bubbles.
7 Bake for 5–7 minutes or until a pale, biscuit colour in the middle and golden at the edges.
8 Leave on the baking sheet for 2 minutes before removing to a wire rack to cool completely.

Cracked Black Pepper Biscuits

These sweet biscuits are delicious served with strawberries.

MAKES 12–14

115 g | 4 oz butter, softened
55 g | 2 oz caster sugar
115 g | 4 oz plain flour
55 g | 2 oz cornflour

1 teaspoon black peppercorns, crushed in a pestle and mortar

To finish
caster sugar

1 Heat the oven to 170°C | 325°F | gas mark 3.
2 Beat the butter until soft, then add the sugar and beat until pale and fluffy.
3 Sift in the flours, add the peppercorns and work to a smooth dough.
4 Roll out to the thickness of a £1 coin and stamp into rounds using a pastry cutter. Place on an ungreased baking sheet and chill for 10 minutes.
5 Bake for 15–20 minutes. Remove from the oven, put on a wire rack to cool and dust with caster sugar whilst still hot.

NOTE: If you don't have a pestle and mortar, the peppercorns can be crushed in a saucepan using the end of a rolling pin.

Brandy Snaps

Brandy snaps can be served as small biscuits with ice cream or can be moulded over a timbale or ramekin to form a cup for ice cream, sorbet or fruit salad.

The mixture contains a high proportion of sugar and golden syrup. The ratio of the ingredients to each other is important, so measure carefully. To measure golden syrup, dip the measuring spoon into very hot water and then into the syrup. Make sure the syrup is level in the spoon. The syrup should slide off the warm spoon.

The dough can be kept overnight in the refrigerator. When firm, shape the mixture into cherry-sized balls and place on to baking parchment to cook.

MAKES APPROXIMATELY 10 LARGE OR 18 SMALL BISCUITS

115 g | 4 oz caster sugar   2 tablespoons lemon juice or brandy
115 g | 4 oz butter   115 g | 4 oz plain flour
4 tablespoons golden syrup   a large pinch of ground ginger

1 Heat the oven to 190°C|375°F|gas mark 5. Cover a baking sheet with baking parchment then cut it into 4 equal squares. This will make it easier to shape the biscuits.

2 Melt the sugar, butter and syrup together. Stir in the juice or brandy and cool to room temperature.

3 Sift together the flour and ginger. Stir into the sugar mixture.

4 Bake one test biscuit to see if the mixture is the correct consistency – it should be thin and lacy. If the biscuit is too thick, add more golden syrup. If it is too lacy, add more flour.

5 Place teaspoonfuls of the mixture on to the centre of each square of paper and bake for 5–7 minutes or until golden-brown. Remove the baking sheet from the oven.

6 Use the paper to lift the biscuits from the baking sheet and drape over a rolling pin, one by one. Alternatively the biscuits can be wrapped around the handle of a wooden spoon or can be draped over an upturned ramekin to make a cup for ice cream or fruit. Allow the biscuits to cool. They will firm as they cool.

Florentines

MAKES 20

55 g | 2 oz butter

55 g | 2 oz caster sugar

2 level teaspoons clear honey

55 g | 2 oz plain flour

45 g | 1½ oz chopped mixed peel

45 g | 1½ oz glacé cherries, finely chopped

45 g | 1½ oz blanched almonds, finely chopped

85 g | 3 oz plain chocolate, melted

1 Heat the oven to 180°C | 350°F | gas mark 4. Line 2 baking sheets with baking parchment.
2 Melt the butter, sugar and honey in a saucepan. Allow to cool to room temperature.
3 Stir in the flour, then the peel, cherries and almonds.
4 Drop teaspoonfuls of the mixture on to the baking sheets, leaving plenty of room for them to spread. Bake for 8–10 minutes, until pale brown. Leave on the sheets for 2 minutes then transfer to a wire rack to cool completely.
5 Spread the bottom of the biscuits with a thin layer of chocolate. It is best that the chocolate is tempered (see *Baking Ingredients*, page 5) so it will dry quickly. Place in the refrigerator to set, then spread another slightly thicker layer on to the first. Allow almost to set, then scrape a fork across the chocolate to make the characteristic wavy pattern. Allow to set completely.

Tommies

MAKES ABOUT 20

70 g | 2½ oz caster sugar

115 g | 4 oz butter, softened

85 g | 3 oz ground toasted hazelnuts

140 g | 5 oz plain flour

clear honey

225 g | 8 oz plain chocolate, chopped into small pieces

1 Heat the oven to 180°C | 350°F | gas mark 4.
2 Cream the sugar and butter together until pale and fluffy.
3 Stir in the hazelnuts and flour.
4 As soon as the mixture becomes a paste, wrap it in clingfilm and chill for 30 minutes.
5 Roll out thinly and cut into 2.5 cm | 1 in rounds using a biscuit cutter.
6 Place on a baking sheet and bake for 12 minutes. Transfer to a wire rack to cool.
7 When cool, spread honey on half the biscuits, then sandwich them with the others.
8 Meanwhile, place the chocolate into a bowl over, but not touching, a saucepan of steaming water until it is melted and smooth.
9 Place the biscuits on a wire rack, then spoon the chocolate over the biscuits to cover them completely.
10 Leave until set. If there is enough melted chocolate left, place in a small piping bag fitted with a writing nozzle and pipe a design over the set chocolate.

Festive Biscuits

Biscuits as well as cakes are eaten at festival and holiday times. They are often flavoured with spices such as ginger, cinnamon and cloves, all of which were highly prized and expensive in days gone by. Festive biscuits are often elaborately decorated. They can also be used as decorations in their own right – for example, ginger biscuits can be hung on the Christmas tree.

Cinnamon Stars

MAKES 24

55 g | 2 oz unsalted butter, softened
55 g | 2 oz caster sugar
1 egg, beaten
3 drops vanilla essence
170 g | 6 oz plain flour
a pinch of salt
¼ teaspoon ground cinnamon

For the topping

1 egg white, beaten to a froth
1 tablespoon caster sugar
½ teaspoon ground cinnamon
24 whole pieces flaked almonds

1 Heat the oven to 180°C | 350°F | gas mark 4.
2 Mix together the butter, sugar, beaten egg and vanilla until smooth.
3 Sift together the flour, salt and cinnamon, then stir into the butter mixture. Once the flour has been added the mixture will be dry, so you will need to pull it together with your hands.
4 Divide the dough into two then roll out as thinly as possible between 2 sheets of greaseproof paper. Chill until firm. Remove the greaseproof paper then cut into biscuits, rerolling the scraps once only. Place on a lightly greased baking sheet.
5 For the topping, mix the caster sugar with the ground cinnamon.
6 Brush the uncooked biscuits with the frothy egg white then sprinkle with the cinnamon sugar. Place a piece of flaked almond in the centre of each biscuit.
7 Bake in the centre of the oven for 5–6 minutes. The biscuits are done when the edges are very lightly browned.
8 Transfer to a wire rack to cool.

Lebkuchen

Lebkuchen, meaning 'honey cake', is a traditional holiday treat in Germany and Austria.

The dough improves from being made in advance and allowed to 'ripen' in the refrigerator for 2–3 days. Once the cakes are baked they will keep for up to 3 weeks in an airtight container.

Biscuits can be made from this dough as well. Roll the dough 3 mm | 1/8 in thick between 2 sheets of greaseproof paper and cut with lightly floured biscuit cutters. Bake at 180°C | 350°F | gas mark 4 for 10 minutes.

MAKES A 25 × 30 CM | 10 × 12 IN CAKE | 45 BISCUITS

170 ml | 6 fl oz clear honey

225 g | 8 oz light muscovado sugar

55 g | 2 oz butter

grated zest of 1 lemon

450 g | 1 lb plain flour

2 teaspoons ground cinnamon

1 teaspoon ground ginger

½ teaspoon ground cardamom

¼ teaspoon ground nutmeg

½ teaspoon bicarbonate of soda

2 eggs, beaten

170 g | 6 oz dried currants

85 g | 3 oz mixed peel or citron peel, finely chopped

100 g | 3½ oz chopped almonds

To ice

55 g | 2 oz icing sugar, sifted

1 tablespoon boiling water

½ teaspoon lemon juice

1 Place the honey, sugar and butter in a large saucepan and heat slowly until the sugar is melted. Do not allow to boil. Set aside to cool slightly. Add the lemon zest.

2 Sift the flour with the spices and the bicarbonate of soda into a large bowl.

3 Gradually stir the flour into the honey mixture, adding it alternately with the eggs.

4 Stir in the currants, peel and almonds.

5 Place the warm dough (it will be a bit sticky but will firm up when cool) in a plastic bag and tie to exclude air, then store in the refrigerator for 2–3 days.

6 Heat the oven to 170°C | 325°F | gas mark 3. Line a 25 × 30 cm | 10 × 12 in shallow baking tin with baking parchment.

7 Press the dough into the tin then bake in the centre of the oven for 25–30 minutes or until golden-brown and firm to the touch.

8 Make the icing by gradually mixing the icing sugar into the water and lemon juice. It will be very runny. Brush over the warm cake or biscuits and allow to cool.

Gingerbread Cookies

These traditional Christmas biscuits are good to have on hand during the holidays. They can be tied on to the Christmas tree with a small piece of ribbon if a small hole is made in the top just before baking.

MAKES ABOUT 48

225 g | 8 oz butter, softened

170 g | 6 oz light muscovado sugar

1 tablespoon molasses

1 egg, beaten

340 g | 12 oz plain flour

1 teaspoon bicarbonate of soda

2 teaspoons ground cinnamon

1 teaspoon ground ginger

½ teaspoon salt

½ teaspoon ground cloves

To finish

icing sugar

1 Beat the butter, sugar and molasses in a bowl until fluffy. Gradually add the egg, beating well between each addition.

2 Sift together all the remaining ingredients, except the icing sugar, into a bowl. Stir into the butter mixture.

3 Press the dough into a flat layer between 2 sheets of greaseproof paper. Chill for about 1 hour until firm.

4 Heat the oven to 190°C | 375°F | gas mark 5.

5 On a lightly floured surface, roll out the dough to 5 mm | ¼ in thick for slightly soft cookies, or thinner for very crisp cookies. Cut out cookie shapes and place on a lightly greased baking sheet, leaving 4 cm | 1½ in between each cookie. Chill until firm.

6 Bake in the middle of the oven for 8–10 minutes or until the edges of the cookies are lightly browned. Cool for 1 minute, then transfer to a wire rack to cool completely.

7 Dust with icing sugar before serving. Store in an airtight container.

Panforte

This is a rich, chewy Italian delicacy. It is a cross between a cake and a biscuit and is traditionally served with strong black coffee, often at Christmas. Store in an airtight container for up to 2 weeks.

MAKES 1.2 KG | 2½ LBS

rice paper

115 g | 4 oz granulated sugar

115 g | 4 oz clear honey

115 g | 4 oz blanched almonds

85 g | 3 oz walnuts, chopped

85 g | 3 oz hazelnuts, chopped

85 g | 3 oz dried figs, chopped

85 g | 3 oz dried pears, chopped

55 g | 2 oz glacé cherries, chopped

55 g | 2 oz dried apricots, chopped

85 g | 3 oz plain flour

30 g | 1 oz cocoa powder

1 teaspoon ground cinnamon

¼ teaspoon freshly grated nutmeg

To finish

1 tablespoon icing sugar

½ teaspoon ground cinnamon

1 Heat the oven to 180°C|350°F|gas mark 4. Line the base and sides of a 23 cm|9 in sandwich tin with rice paper, cutting it to fit exactly.

2 Heat the sugar and honey together gently, stirring all the time until the sugar dissolves. Bring to the boil, then reduce the heat and simmer for 2 minutes. Remove from the heat and allow to cool slightly.

3 Mix together the chopped nuts and fruit. Sift together the flour, cocoa powder and spices and mix with the nuts and fruit. Add the cooled syrup and knead well to combine thoroughly. The mixture should be kneaded firmly to incorporate the fruit and nuts.

4 Press the mixture into the prepared tin, cover with another piece of rice paper and flatten the top.

5 Bake in the centre of the oven for 45–60 minutes or until fairly firm to the touch but not solid.

6 Remove from the oven and allow to cool in the tin for 20 minutes, then carefully ease out of the tin and transfer to a wire rack. Leave to cool completely.

7 Sift the icing sugar and cinnamon together over the top before serving.

Pecan Snowballs

These rich biscuits are Christmas favourites. They keep well in an airtight container for up to 1 month.

MAKES ABOUT 22

115 g|4 oz unsalted butter, softened
45 g|1½ oz icing sugar, sifted
½ teaspoon vanilla essence
170 g|6 oz plain flour, sifted

a pinch of salt
115 g|4 oz pecan nuts, finely chopped

To finish
extra icing sugar

1 Stir together the butter, icing sugar and vanilla, then stir in the flour and salt.

2 Work the pecan nuts into the mixture.

3 Using a scant tablespoon of the mixture, form into balls with your hands. You may need to flour your hands if the dough is very soft.

4 Place on a baking sheet lined with baking parchment and chill until firm, about 1 hour.

5 Heat the oven to 170°C|325°F|gas mark 3.

6 Bake the biscuits until just starting to brown on the undersides, about 15–20 minutes.

7 Sift a layer of icing sugar on to a plate and place the warm biscuits on top. Sift additional icing sugar over the biscuits.

8 Transfer to a wire rack to cool. Roll again in sifted icing sugar before storing.

Stained-glass Biscuits

These biscuits are not really meant to be eaten, although they can be if you wish – they are designed to decorate the Christmas tree. The crushed boiled sweets melt when baked to give a stained-glass effect.

MAKES ABOUT 20

115 g|4 oz butter, softened

115 g|4 oz caster sugar

1 egg, beaten

a few drops of vanilla essence

285 g|10 oz plain flour

a pinch of salt

a selection of different colours of boiled sweets

To finish

thin ribbon or glittery string to tie

1 Heat the oven to 190°C|375°F|gas mark 5.
2 Beat the butter until soft, add the sugar and beat until pale and fluffy. Gradually beat in the egg. Add the vanilla essence.
3 Sift the flour with the salt and mix it into the butter, sugar and egg mixture.
4 Roll the dough out to the thickness of a £1 coin and cut out the desired shapes using biscuit cutters. Place on a baking sheet lined with baking parchment.
5 Cut smaller shapes out of the biscuits using tiny cutters or a knife.
6 Crush the boiled sweets, one colour at a time, with a mortar and pestle.
7 Sprinkle the crushed sweets into the gaps in the biscuits to make a stained-glass effect. Make a small hole near the edge of each biscuit for the ribbon.
8 Bake for 8–10 minutes until just beginning to brown at the edges. Leave to cool on a wire rack.
9 Once cool, thread the ribbon through the hole and tie to create a loop for hanging.

Easter Biscuits

MAKES 8

55 g|2 oz butter, softened

55 g|2 oz caster sugar

grated zest of ½ lemon

½ egg or 1 egg yolk

115 g|4 oz plain flour

½ teaspoon caraway seeds

55 g|2 oz currants

30 g|1 oz granulated sugar

1 Heat the oven to 180°C|350°F| gas mark 4. Line a baking sheet with baking parchment.
2 Cream together the butter, caster sugar and lemon zest. Beat in the egg.
3 Fold in the flour, caraway seeds and currants.
4 Roll out the dough to 5 mm|¼ in thick on a floured board. Cut into 7.5 cm|3 in rounds and carefully lift them on to the baking sheet. Prick with a fork and sprinkle with granulated sugar.
5 Bake for 10–15 minutes until set and a pale, golden-brown.
6 Leave on a wire rack to crisp and cool.

Paintbrush Biscuits

Children love to decorate these biscuits.

MAKES ABOUT 20

115 g | 4 oz butter, softened
115 g | 4 oz caster sugar
1 egg, beaten
a few drops of vanilla essence
290 g | 10 oz plain flour
a pinch of salt

For the 'paint'

1 egg yolk
red and blue food colouring
small paintbrushes

1 Heat the oven to 190°C | 375°F | gas mark 5.

2 Beat the butter and sugar until pale and fluffy. Gradually beat in the egg and vanilla.

3 Sift the flour with the salt and stir into the butter mixture.

4 Roll out the dough on a floured surface to 2 mm | ⅛ in thickness, then cut into shapes using floured biscuit cutters. Place on a lightly greased baking sheet.

5 Chill until firm.

6 To decorate, divide the egg yolk between individual ramekins. Mix a couple of drops of water and food colouring into the yolk to make red 'paint' and green 'paint'. Leave one pot plain for yellow. Brush the 'paint' on to the biscuits to decorate.

7 Bake in the centre of the oven until just beginning to brown on the edges, about 8–10 minutes.

8 Cool for 1 minute, then transfer to a wire rack to cool completely.

Biscotti

These long, crisp biscuits have become very popular in recent years and are ubiquitous in chains of urban coffee bars. Translated literally from the Italian, 'biscotti' means 'twice-cooked', although in Italy the term is often used generically to denote any crisp biscuit. 'Hard tack', the dry ships' biscuits of the 1500s, are the ancestors of biscotti but the modern, sweetened version is thought to have originated in Prato, Tuscany.

Most recipes for biscotti require 2 bakings: the first, at a high temperature, browns the outside while the second, at a lower temperature, dries them out completely. During the first baking the dough is baked in a log shape that flattens somewhat as it cooks. The log should then be allowed to stand for 10 minutes before being sliced on an angle and turned on each side to dry out at a lower oven temperature. The standing time before slicing helps the dough to settle, making the biscotti less crumbly when cut. Using a sharp, serrated knife, cut the log on an angle of about 45° into individual biscuits. The individual biscotti can be sliced thinly or up to 1 cm | ½ in thick, depending on personal preference.

Traditionally biscotti are made with both ground and whole almonds and are cut quite long and thick (about 10 cm | 4 in long and 1 cm | ½ in thick) and they are served to dunk into a cappuccino or latte. Smaller biscotti, called *cantucci*, are dipped in *vin santo*, the sweet Italian wine. Because they are well dried-out, these biscuits keep for a very long time in an airtight container.

Chocolate Chip Macadamia Nut Biscotti

MAKES ABOUT 60

115 g | 4 oz butter
285 g | 10 oz plain flour
a pinch of salt
1 tablespoon baking powder
3 eggs

200 g | 7 oz caster sugar
½ teaspoon vanilla essence
100 g | 3½ oz macadamia nuts, roughly chopped
200 g | 7 oz chocolate chips

1 Heat the oven to 180°C | 350°F | gas mark 4.
2 Place the butter in a small saucepan over a medium heat until golden-brown. Pour into a heatproof bowl to cool.
3 Sift the flour with the salt and baking powder into a large bowl.
4 Beat the eggs, then stir in the butter, sugar and vanilla.

5 Stir the egg/butter mixture into the flour, then stir in the chopped macadamia nuts and chocolate chips. The mixture will be very soft, but do not bother to chill the dough. Add a little flour if necessary.

6 Shape the mixture into 4 equal-sized logs, about 20 cm | 8 in long and 3 cm | 1½ in wide. Place on 2 baking sheets lined with baking parchment, keeping the logs well separated.

7 Bake in the centre of the oven for 30 minutes or until the logs feel firm when pressed lightly. They will be golden-brown and will have nearly doubled in size.

8 Place on a wire rack to cool for 30 minutes.

9 Slice the logs on a 45° diagonal into 1 cm | 1½ in slices, using a serrated knife.

10 Place the individual biscotti cut-side up on to 2 baking sheets and return to the oven for 15 minutes. Turn the biscotti over and bake for a further 15 minutes. The biscotti should be a deep golden-brown. If they are too pale they will have a bland flavour.

11 Cool on a wire rack and store in an airtight container.

Fruit and Nut Biscotti

MAKES ABOUT 60

500 g | 18 oz plain flour

500 g | 18 oz unrefined caster sugar

1 tablespoon baking powder

5 eggs, lightly beaten

100 g | 3½ oz sultanas

100 g | 3½ oz dried apricots, chopped

100 g | 3½ oz pitted dates, chopped

100 g | 3½ oz shelled pistachio nuts

100 g | 3½ oz whole blanched almonds

100 g | 3½ oz hazelnuts

grated zest of 2 lemons

1 Heat the oven to 180°C | 350°F | gas mark 4.

2 Mix the flour, sugar and baking powder in a large bowl. Add half the beaten eggs and mix well, then add half of what is left and mix again. Now add the last quarter, a little bit at a time, until the dough takes shape but isn't too wet (you may not need to use all of the eggs).

3 Add the fruit, nuts and lemon zest and mix well.

4 Divide the dough into 6 and roll into sausage shapes about 3 cm | 1 in in diameter and place, at least 6 cm | 2 in apart, on baking trays lined with baking parchment. Wetting your hands when rolling these out helps to prevent the dough sticking.

5 Lightly flatten the 'sausages' and bake until golden-brown, about 20–30 minutes. Remove from the oven and leave for 10 minutes to cool and firm up.

6 Reduce the oven temperature to 140°C | 275°F | gas mark 1.

7 With a serrated knife, cut the biscotti on a 45° angle into 5 mm | ¼ in slices and place these on the baking trays. Return them to the oven and cook for 12 minutes, then turn the biscotti over and cook until they are a pale, golden colour (another 10–15 minutes).

8 Remove from the oven and cool on wire racks. Store in an airtight container.

Pine Nut Biscotti

MAKES 24

100 g | 3½ oz blanched almonds
100 g | 3½ oz pine nuts
225 g | 8 oz plain flour
a pinch of salt
½ teaspoon baking powder
85 g | 3 oz caster sugar

2 eggs, lightly beaten
55 g | 2 oz butter, melted and cooled

To glaze
1 egg white

1 Heat the oven to 190°C | 375°F | gas mark 5. Grease a baking sheet.
2 Place the almonds and pine nuts on the baking sheet and bake for 8 minutes or until golden-brown. Remove from the oven and cool. Chop roughly.
3 Sift the flour, salt and baking powder into a large bowl. Mix in the nuts and sugar.
4 Make a well in the centre and add the eggs and butter. Mix to a firm dough.
5 Divide the dough into 2 equal pieces and roll into long, sausage shapes, about 2 cm | ¾ in wide and 20 cm | 8 in long.
6 Place the rolls at least 5 cm | 2 in apart on the baking sheet.
7 Lightly whisk the egg white and brush over the rolls.
8 Bake for 20 minutes.
9 Remove the rolls and turn the oven temperature down to 80°C | 175°F | gas mark ¼. Cut the rolls at a 45° angle into 1 cm | ½ in slices. Place on the baking sheet cut-side up.
10 Bake for a further hour, turning over halfway through the baking.
11 Cool on a wire rack then store in an airtight container.

Toasted Almond and Orange Biscotti

MAKES ABOUT 40

115 g | 4 oz whole blanched almonds
2 eggs, beaten
grated zest of 1 orange
140 g | 5 oz caster sugar
½ teaspoon vanilla essence

¼ teaspoon almond essence
170 g | 6 oz plain flour
55 g | 2 oz polenta
¼ teaspoon salt
½ teaspoon bicarbonate of soda

1 Heat the oven to 180°C | 350°F | gas mark 4. Line 2 baking sheets with baking parchment.
2 Place the almonds in a single layer on the baking sheet and bake for 8 minutes or until golden-brown. Place on a plate to cool.
3 In a large mixing bowl beat together the eggs, orange zest, sugar and vanilla and almond essences.

4 Sift the dry ingredients, except the almonds, over the egg mixture. Stir to combine then work in the almonds using your hands.

5 Divide the dough into 2 pieces and shape into logs measuring about 7 × 25 cm│3 × 12 in on the baking sheet. Flour your hands if the dough is sticky.

6 Bake for 20 minutes or until golden and slightly risen.

7 Cool on a wire rack for 10 minutes then slice on the diagonal into 1 cm│½ in slices. Place the biscuits on their sides on 2 baking sheets then return to the oven for 15 minutes. Turn the biscuits over and bake for a further 15 minutes

8 Cool on a wire rack and store in an airtight container.

Chocolate Hazelnut Biscotti

MAKES ABOUT 30

100 g│3½ oz skinned hazelnuts, toasted
100 g│3½ oz caster sugar
200 g│7 oz plain flour
30 g│1 oz cocoa powder
2 teaspoons baking powder
85 g│3 oz butter, melted and cooled
2 eggs, beaten

1 teaspoon vanilla essence
200 g│7 oz plain chocolate chips

To glaze

1 egg white, lightly beaten
caster sugar

1 Heat the oven to 190°C│375°F│gas mark 5. Line 2 baking sheets with baking parchment.

2 Grind half the hazelnuts to a fine powder with the caster sugar and chop the remainder coarsely.

3 Place the ground hazelnuts and sugar in a large bowl and sift over the flour, cocoa powder and baking powder.

4 Mix together the butter, eggs and vanilla and stir into the flour mixture. When nearly combined, add the chopped hazelnuts and the chocolate chips. The mixture is dry, so you will need to bring it together by squeezing it with your hands.

5 Form the mixture into 2 long logs measuring 3 cm│1½ in in diameter and place on the baking sheet. Brush with the beaten egg white and sprinkle with caster sugar.

6 Bake in the centre of the oven for 20 minutes, then remove and turn the oven down to 150°C│300°F│gas mark 2.

7 Slice both logs into pieces 1 cm│½ in thick using a sharp serrated knife at an angle of 45°. Place the pieces on the baking sheet so that the cut sides are uppermost.

8 Return to the oven to bake for a further 10 minutes. Turn the slices over and bake for an additional 10 minutes to dry out.

9 Cool on a wire rack before storing in an airtight container.

Spiced Almond Biscotti

This recipe makes long biscotti. For smaller biscotti, divide the dough into 4 logs and use 2 baking sheets to bake the logs. Although the amount of baking powder seems a lot, it makes these biscotti particularly light.

MAKES ABOUT 40

100 g | 3½ oz whole blanched almonds

115 g | 4 oz butter

285 g | 10 oz plain flour

a pinch of salt

1 tablespoon baking powder

2 teaspoons ground cinnamon

½ teaspoon ground nutmeg

3 eggs, beaten

200 g | 7 oz caster sugar

½ teaspoon almond essence

½ teaspoon vanilla essence

1 Heat the oven to 180°C | 350°F | gas mark 4.

2 Place the almonds on a baking sheet and toast for 7–8 minutes or until pale brown. Allow to cool then chop roughly. Set aside.

3 Place the butter in a small saucepan over a medium heat until golden-brown. Pour into a heatproof bowl to cool.

4 Sift the flour with the salt, baking powder, cinnamon and nutmeg into a large bowl.

5 Beat the eggs then stir in the butter, sugar and essences.

6 Stir the egg/butter mixture into the flour then stir in the chopped almonds. The mixture will be very soft. Do not bother to chill the dough.

7 Shape the mixture into 2 equal-sized logs, about 40 cm | 16 in long and 5 cm | 2 in wide. Place on a baking sheet lined with baking parchment, keeping the logs well separated.

8 Bake in the centre of the oven for 30 minutes or until the logs feel firm when pressed lightly with your finger. They will be golden-brown and will have nearly doubled in size.

9 Place on a wire rack to cool for 30 minutes.

10 Slice the logs on a 45°diagonal into 1 cm | 1½ in slices, using a serrated knife.

11 Place the individual biscotti cut-side up on to 2 baking sheets and return to the oven for 15 minutes. Turn the biscotti over and bake for a further 15 minutes. The biscotti should be a deep golden-brown. If they are too pale they will have a bland taste.

12 Cool on a wire rack and store in an airtight container.

Savoury Biscuits

The biscuits in this section can be served with drinks, with cheese or simply eaten as a snack.

Hungarian Cheese Biscuits

This recipe is from Katarina Diezinger, who is a marvellous hostess and cook. These little biscuits are very easy to make and are ideal to serve with a glass of wine. In Hungary they are topped with caraway seeds, but these can be difficult to find in the UK, so grated Parmesan has been used as a substitute.

MAKES ABOUT 30

250 g | 9 oz softened butter
250 g | 9 oz plain cottage cheese
250 g | 9 oz plain white flour
¼ teaspoon salt

To glaze

1 egg, beaten
3 tablespoons grated Parmesan cheese
paprika

1 Mix together the butter and cottage cheese.
2 Sift over the flour and salt and stir to combine.
3 Spread on to a piece of clingfilm in a 1 cm | ½ in thick rectangle.
4 Wrap entirely in clingfilm and chill until firm, about 2 hours or overnight.
5 Fold the dough into thirds, like a business letter, then roll out on a floured surface to 1 cm | ½ in thickness.
6 Cut with a floured 2 cm | ¾ in cutter and place on a baking sheet.
7 Brush with the beaten egg and sprinkle with the Parmesan cheese and a little paprika.
8 Bake in the top third of the oven for 25 minutes or until golden-brown. Cool on a wire rack.

Cheddar Herb Biscuits

MAKES 48

170 g|6 oz butter, softened

170 g|6 oz strong Cheddar cheese, finely grated

1 egg, beaten

300 g|10½ oz plain flour

½ teaspoon salt

¼ teaspoon cayenne pepper

½ teaspoon dry English mustard

2 teaspoons dried herbes de Provence

1 Heat the oven to 170°C|325°F|gas mark 3.

2 Mix together the butter and cheese. Beat in the egg.

3 Sift together the flour, salt, cayenne pepper and mustard. Add the dried herbs then work into the butter mixture.

4 Roll into a log 3 cm|1¼ in in diameter then cut into ½ cm|¼ in slices. Place on a baking sheet and chill until firm.

5 Bake for 35–40 minutes or until just starting to brown. Cool on a wire rack.

Rice and Cheese Biscuits

MAKES 25–30

170 g|6 oz plain flour

a pinch of salt

115 g|4 oz butter, cut into small pieces

a pinch of cayenne pepper

85 g|3 oz Cheddar cheese, grated

85 g|3 oz Rice Krispies

1 Heat the oven to 190°C|375°F|gas mark 5. Line 2 baking sheets with baking parchment.

2 Sift the flour and salt into a large bowl. Rub in the butter until the mixture resembles fine breadcrumbs. (This can be done in a food processor but it must be removed to a bowl before adding the rest of the ingredients.)

3 Mix in the cayenne pepper, cheese and Rice Krispies. Form into little balls the size of a ping-pong ball, or smaller if wished. Place on the baking sheet and flatten with a fork. They will only spread a little, so leave gaps between them.

4 Bake in the oven for 15–20 minutes.

NOTE: For a change, mix 1 tablespoon sesame seeds or poppy seeds into the dough before shaping into balls.

Oatcakes

These oatcakes are cooked in the oven, although they can be cooked on a griddle on top of the stove. Some recipes for oatcakes use rendered bacon fat instead of butter.

MAKES 16

140 g|5 oz medium oatmeal
15 g|½ oz butter
a pinch of salt

125 ml|4 fl oz boiling water
extra oatmeal for rolling

1 Heat the oven to 180°C|350°F|gas mark 4. Grease a baking sheet or line with baking parchment.

2 Put the oatmeal in a bowl. Put the butter and salt in the boiling water. Allow the butter to melt and pour over the oatmeal. Leave it to stand for at least 5 minutes so that it becomes cool enough to handle. This will also allow the oatmeal to swell.

3 Dust a work surface with oatmeal. Divide the dough in 2 and roll each piece out to a thin circle about 17 cm|7 in in diameter. Place on the baking sheet and cut each one into 8 wedges. Bake in the oven for 20–30 minutes. Cool on a wire rack.

Savoury Quick Breads and Scones

Quick breads are made without yeast. The doughs require no kneading and do not have to rise before being baked. Instead of yeast, chemical raising agents such as bicarbonate of soda, cream of tartar and/or baking powder are used in these breads. Quick breads have a close, cake-like texture and tend to stale more quickly than yeast-raised breads, so they are best eaten on the day they are made.

Brown or Irish soda bread is the most common of these types of bread, and many of the recipes in this section are variations of this type. Cornbread is also a quick bread and can be made either savoury or sweet.

For a well-risen quick bread, it is important to get the mixture into the oven as soon as it is made in order to capture the gas given off by the chemical raising agents. The oven must be preheated and the tins prepared before mixing begins.

The chemical raising agents used are sodium bicarbonate (an alkali) and cream of tartar (an acid). Occasionally soured milk or buttermilk is used as the acid in place of cream of tartar. When the alkali and acid combine with each other and liquid is added, carbonic acid is formed. This gas, along with the conversion of liquid in the dough to steam and the expansion of the eggs, serves to raise the bread. Baking powder, the mixture of an acid (cream of tartar) with an alkali (sodium bicarbonate), was developed in England around 1835. Commercial baking powder became available in 1850.

It is very important to sift the ingredients well with the flour, several times to ensure they are properly combined. Badly mixed raising agents show up in the bread as yellow deposits in the crumb.

A soft dough will make a lighter bread or scone. Try to handle the dough as little as possible to prevent it from becoming tough.

As a raising agent for quick breads, baking powder can be substituted for bicarbonate of soda and cream of tartar. To make self-raising flour, use 4 level teaspoons baking powder per 250 g|9 oz plain flour.

Soda Bread

This is the traditional soda bread marked with a cross. The cross was said to let the devil out.

MAKES 1 LOAF

225 g | 8 oz wholemeal flour

225 g | 8 oz plain white flour

1½ teaspoons salt

2 teaspoons bicarbonate of soda

45 g | 1½ oz butter

1 tablespoon caster sugar

290–425 ml | 10–15 fl oz buttermilk

1 Heat the oven to 190°C | 375°F | gas mark 5. Oil a baking sheet.
2 Sift the flours, salt and bicarbonate of soda together 3 times. Reserve any bran left in the sieve.
3 Cut the butter into small pieces, then rub into the flour using your fingertips.
4 Stir in the sugar.
5 Make a well in the centre. Stir in enough buttermilk to make a soft dough.
6 Knead lightly to bring together into a round.
7 Place on the baking sheet and sprinkle with the reserved bran.
8 Using a wooden spoon handle, make a deep cross in the centre of the bread nearly all the way down to the baking sheet.
9 Bake for about 40 minutes or until well-risen and browned. The cross in the centre of the bread should not seem damp.
10 Transfer to a wire rack and leave to cool.

NOTE: If buttermilk is not available, use regular milk plus 1 tablespoon lemon juice per 290 ml | 10 fl oz milk and add 1 teaspoon cream of tartar to the flour at step 2.

Seeded Soda Bread

MAKES 1 LOAF

225 g | 8 oz wholemeal or malted brown flour

225 g | 8 oz strong white flour

1½ teaspoons salt

1 tablespoon caster sugar

2 teaspoons bicarbonate of soda

55 g | 2 oz butter

6 tablespoons mixed seeds, such as linseed, sesame, sunflower or poppy

425–475 ml | 15–17 fl oz buttermilk or acidulated milk (see note)

1 Heat the oven to 190°C | 375°F | gas mark 5. Lightly flour a baking sheet.
2 Sift the flours with the salt, sugar and bicarbonate of soda into a large bowl. Reserve any bran remaining in the sieve.

3 Cut the butter into small pieces and toss into the flour. Rub in with your fingertips. Stir in the seeds.

4 Stir in enough of the milk to make a soft but not sticky dough.

5 Knead for 5 seconds then place on the baking sheet. Using the floured handle of a wooden spoon, press a cross into the dough. Sprinkle with the reserved bran.

6 Place immediately in the top third (the hottest part) of the oven. Bake for 35–45 minutes or until golden-brown. The cracks in the bread should no longer appear damp when the bread is done.

7 Cool on a wire rack.

NOTE: If buttermilk is not available, use the equivalent volume of regular milk soured with 1 tablespoon lemon juice per 290 ml | 10 fl oz of milk *or* add 1 teaspoon of cream of tartar to the flour at step 2.

Lemon and Coconut Soda Bread

This can be made to taste more of coconut by substituting some of the milk with coconut milk; however, it will push up the fat content of the finished loaf. If preferred, it can be cooked as 1 loaf, which will take 35–40 minutes.

MAKES 2 LOAVES

170 g | 6 oz plain flour

170 g | 6 oz wholemeal flour

1½ teaspoons bicarbonate of soda

55 g | 2 oz butter, cut into pieces

115 g | 4 oz porridge oats

55 g | 2 oz desiccated coconut

½ teaspoon salt

grated zest of 1 lemon

juice of 1 lemon

290–350 ml | 10–12 fl oz milk

1 Heat the oven to 200°C | 400°F | gas mark 6. Oil a baking sheet.

2 Sift the flours and bicarbonate of soda into a large mixing bowl. Tip any bran left in the sieve into the bowl. Rub the butter into the flour using your fingertips. Add the oats, coconut, salt and lemon zest. Mix well.

3 Add the lemon juice and milk. Mix quickly to form a soft but not sticky dough, adding more flour if necessary.

4 Put the dough on to a floured work surface and form into 2 round loaves. Place both loaves on the baking sheet. Using the floured handle of a wooden spoon, make deep crosses in the centre of each loaf.

5 Bake in the centre of the oven for 20–25 minutes. They are ready when they sound hollow when tapped on the underside. Remove from the baking sheet immediately and cool on a wire rack.

Oat and Yoghurt Soda Bread

MAKES 2 LOAVES

450 g | 1 lb wholemeal plain flour

2 teaspoons bicarbonate of soda

1 teaspoon salt

85 g | 3 oz coarse oatmeal

290 g | 10 fl oz natural yoghurt

150 ml | 5 fl oz water

To finish

2 tablespoons coarse oatmeal

1 tablespoon sesame seeds (optional)

1 Heat the oven to 200°C | 400°F | gas mark 6. Grease a baking sheet.

2 Sift the flour with the bicarbonate of soda and salt into a large mixing bowl. Tip any bran left in the sieve into the bowl. Add the oatmeal.

3 Add the yoghurt and water and mix quickly to a soft dough. If the dough is too wet add a little more flour, but it should be soft.

4 Put the dough on a floured work surface and divide into 2. Shape into round loaves. Place on to the baking sheet and use the floured handle of a wooden spoon to make a deep cross in the centre of each loaf.

5 Mix the extra oatmeal and sesame seeds, if using, and sprinkle over the top of the loaves. Place in the centre of the oven and bake for 30–40 minutes. If the loaves are getting too dark and are not quite cooked, turn the oven down. The loaves should sound hollow when tapped on the underside.

6 Remove from the baking sheets straightaway and put on to wire racks to cool.

Mint and Thyme Soda Rolls

MAKES 8

340 g | 12 oz wholemeal flour

115 g | 4 oz plain flour

1 teaspoon salt

1 teaspoon bicarbonate of soda

2 teaspoons cream of tartar

1 teaspoon sugar

30 g | 1 oz butter

2 tablespoons chopped fresh mint

1 tablespoon chopped fresh thyme

290 ml | 10 fl oz milk

1 Heat the oven to 190°C | 375°F | gas mark 5. Oil a baking sheet.

2 Sift all the dry ingredients together into a large bowl and rub in the butter using your fingertips.

3 Add the mint and thyme and make a well in the centre of the flour.

4 Pour in all the milk and mix together, first with a knife and then with one hand, to form a soft dough. Add more milk if necessary.

5 Divide the dough into 8 pieces and shape each one very quickly into a roll. Put on the greased baking sheet.

6 Using the floured handle of a wooden spoon, mark a deep cross in each roll.

7 Put in the centre of the oven and bake for 15 minutes. Remove and cool on a wire rack.

Wheat and Oat Soda Bread

MAKES 1 LOAF

115 g|4 oz wholemeal flour

225 g|8 oz plain flour

1½ teaspoons salt

2 teaspoons bicarbonate of soda

170 g|6 oz coarse oatmeal, plus extra for dusting

45 g|1½ oz butter, melted

2 tablespoons lemon juice

290 ml|10 fl oz milk

1 Heat the oven to 190°C|375°F|gas mark 5. Oil a baking sheet.

2 Sift the flours together with the salt and bicarbonate of soda into a bowl. Add any bran left in the sieve to the bowl. Add the oatmeal and mix well. Make a well in the centre.

3 Mix together the butter, lemon juice and milk and add to the well. Add more milk if necessary to make a soft but not wet dough.

4 Shape quickly into a round. Place on the baking sheet. Sprinkle with a little extra oatmeal.

5 Using the floured handle of a wooden spoon, make a deep cross in the centre of the bread nearly all the way down to the baking sheet.

6 Bake for about 35 minutes or until well-risen and browned. It will sound hollow when tapped on the underside.

7 Transfer to a wire rack to cool.

Chilli Cornbread

This bread is quick to make and is a good accompaniment to chilli con carne.

MAKES 1 LOAF

2 red Kenyan chillis, deseeded and finely chopped

2 green Kenyan chillies, deseeded and finely chopped

115 g | 4 oz polenta

225 g | 8 oz plain flour

1 tablespoon baking powder

¼ teaspoon cayenne pepper

1 tablespoon caster sugar

½ slightly rounded teaspoon salt

1 egg, beaten

4 tablespoons olive oil

150 ml | 5 fl oz soured cream

150 ml | 5 fl oz milk

4 tablespoons freshly grated Parmesan cheese

1 Heat the oven to 180°C | 350°F | gas mark 4. Line the base and sides of a 10 × 20 cm | 4 × 8 in loaf tin with baking parchment. Lightly oil the paper.

2 Mix the chillies, polenta, flour, baking powder, cayenne pepper, caster sugar and salt in a large bowl. Make a well in the centre.

3 Mix the egg, olive oil, soured cream, milk and 3 tablespoons cheese. Pour into the well in the dry ingredients and mix quickly to combine.

4 Pile into the loaf tin and sprinkle with the remaining cheese.

5 Bake in the centre of the oven for 50–55 minutes or until well-risen and golden-brown. Cool in the tin for 5 minutes then turn out on to a wire rack and cool for a further 20 minutes.

Cheese Cornbread

MAKES 1 LARGE LOAF

115 g | 4 oz plain flour

1 tablespoon baking powder

½ teaspoon salt

a good pinch of cayenne pepper

115 g | 4 oz polenta or coarse cornmeal

55 g | 2 oz Cheddar cheese, grated

55 g | 2 oz Gruyère cheese, grated

2 eggs, beaten

290 ml | 10 fl oz milk

55 g | 2 oz butter, melted

1 Heat the oven to 200°C | 400°F | gas mark 6. Grease a 675 | g | 1½ lb loaf tin.

2 Sift the flour, baking powder, salt and cayenne pepper into a large bowl, then add the polenta and cheeses. Mix together.

3 Make a well in the centre and add the beaten eggs, milk and melted butter. Mix well and pour into the prepared tin.

4 Place in the centre of the oven and bake for 40–45 minutes or until, when turned out of its tin, the bottom of the loaf sounds hollow when tapped. Cool on a wire rack.

Gruyère Spoonbread

Spoonbread is served in America as an accompaniment to roasted meats. It has a soft consistency, similar to a soufflé. This recipe is particularly good served with baked gammon.

SERVES 4

570 ml | 20 fl oz milk	½ teaspoon freshly grated nutmeg
150 ml | 5 fl oz double cream	1 teaspoon paprika
115 g | 4 oz cornmeal or polenta	½ teaspoon Dijon mustard
55 g | 2 oz butter	170 g | 6 oz Gruyère cheese, coarsely grated
1 teaspoon salt	4 eggs, separated

1 Heat the oven to 180°C | 350°F | gas mark 5. Butter a 1.2 litre | 2 pint ring mould.
2 Bring the milk and cream to the boil in a saucepan then remove from the heat and gradually whisk the cornmeal.
3 Return to the heat and cook over a medium heat, stirring continuously, until the mixture comes to the boil.
4 Remove from the heat and stir in the butter, salt, nutmeg, paprika, mustard, cheese and egg yolks. The mixture should be well-seasoned.
5 Whisk the egg whites to medium peaks and fold into the cornmeal mixture.
6 Spoon into the ring mould and bake in the centre of the oven for 35–40 minutes or until well-risen and golden-brown. The top should be crusty and the centre soft.
7 Loosen the edges of the spoonbread from the tin and turn on to a plate to serve. Serve hot.

Courgette and Cheese Picnic Bread

This bread is ideal for slicing up and taking on picnics as it is very portable and fairly substantial. However, it is equally good served slightly warm with soup.

MAKES 1 LARGE LOAF

225 g | 8 oz self-raising flour	3 eggs, beaten
½ teaspoon salt	85 g | 3 oz butter, melted and cooled
a pinch of cayenne pepper	55 ml | 2 fl oz milk
115 g | 4 oz Cheddar cheese, grated	225 g | 8 oz courgettes, grated

1 Heat the oven to 180°C | 350°F | gas mark 4. Oil a 900 g | 2 lb loaf tin and line the base with a piece of baking parchment, cut to fit.
2 Sift the flour with the salt and cayenne pepper into a large bowl. Stir in the cheese.
3 Make a well in the centre and add the eggs, butter and milk.
4 Mix in the courgettes to make a thick mixture. Spoon into the loaf tin and spread flat. Bake for 45–50 minutes or until a knife inserted into the centre comes out clean.

Curried Pumpkin Bread

This is delicious bread quick to make and goes very well with a chunky vegetable soup for lunch. If tinned pumpkin purée is not available then steam approximately 900g|2 lb pumpkin or butternut squash until it is very soft and purée in a blender or food processor. Weigh the purée before use.

MAKES 2 LOAVES

225 g|8 oz plain flour

225 g|8 oz polenta or coarse cornmeal

2 teaspoons baking powder

1 teaspoon bicarbonate of soda

45 g|1½ oz caster sugar

85 g|3 oz unsalted butter

2 onions, finely chopped

½ teaspoon ground turmeric

½ teaspoon ground coriander

½ teaspoon ground cumin

⅛ teaspoon cayenne pepper

2 teaspoons salt

20 g|¾ oz cumin seeds, toasted lightly and cooled

1 × 425 g|15 oz can pumpkin purée

3 eggs

150 ml|5 fl oz buttermilk (or natural yoghurt)

1 Heat the oven to 180°C|350°F|gas mark 4. Grease and line the bases of 2 × 450 g|1 lb loaf tins with a piece of baking parchment cut to fit.

2 Sift together the flour, cornmeal, baking powder, bicarbonate of soda and sugar.

3 Melt 30 g|1 oz of the butter in a frying pan and add the onion. Cook over a low heat for 5 minutes until the onion has softened a little. Add the turmeric, coriander, ground cumin, cayenne pepper and salt. Cook over a low heat for 5 minutes, stirring all the time. Let the mixture cool and add the cumin seeds. Melt the rest of the butter in a saucepan.

4 Put the pumpkin purée, eggs, buttermilk, melted butter and onion mixture into a large bowl and whisk together.

5 Make a well in the flour mixture and add the pumpkin and onion mixture, stirring well to form a batter. Pour into the prepared loaf tins.

6 Place in the centre of the oven for 40–45 minutes or until the breads spring back when touched with a finger.

7 Remove from the tins and allow to cool on a wire rack. Serve warm or cold.

Swiss Meringues

Selkirk Bannock

Iced Cinnamon Swirl Bread

Sticky Toffee Ginger and Date Muffins

Fruit and Nut Biscotti

Blueberry Crumble Muffins

New York Cheesecake

Challah

Baked Challah

Baked Challah with Honey

Pecan Sticky Buns

Orange Scented Rolls

Black and White Sesame Bread Sticks

Salmon and Leek Cobbler

Butternut Squash and Feta Pasties

Pine Nut Macaroons

Chocolate Melting Moments, Pine Nut Macaroons,
Almond and Gin Biscuits, Carrot and Date Biscuits

Brownies, Blondies and Chocolate Almond Squares

Savoury Bread

This is a delicious recipe that can be varied by adding different ingredients. It can be made vegetarian by omitting the bacon and using vegetarian cheese.

MAKES 1 FLAT LOAF

1 tablespoon olive oil

1 large onion, sliced

55 g|2 oz bacon lardons

1 clove of garlic, crushed

2 eggs

150 ml|5 fl oz white wine

100 ml|3½ fl oz olive oil

225 g|8 oz self-raising flour

140 g|5 oz Emmental (or Cheddar), coarsely grated

3 tablespoons pitted green olives, rinsed and lightly chopped

1 tablespoon capers, rinsed

1 tablespoon chopped fresh thyme

1 tablespoon chopped fresh oregano

salt and freshly ground black pepper

1 Heat the oven to 200°C|400°F|gas mark 6. Grease a roasting tin measuring approximately 20 × 30 cm|8 × 12 in (or line with baking parchment).

2 Heat the olive oil in a sauté pan. Add the onions and gently cook, covered with a lid, until they are soft and have taken on a little colour. Add the bacon lardons and cook through. Add the garlic and cook for 2 more minutes. Put aside to cool down.

3 Beat the eggs with the white wine and olive oil.

4 Sift the flour into a large bowl and make a well in the centre. Add the liquid ingredients to the well and incorporate with the flour, gradually, beating well to get rid of any lumps.

5 Add the onion mixture, cheese, olives, capers and herbs. Season with salt and pepper. The mixture should be of a reluctant pouring consistency, so if necessary add a little more wine.

6 Pour it into the prepared tin, make sure it is level and bake for approximately 40 minutes or until it is brown and a knife comes out clean when pushed into the centre. Serve warm.

Australian Damper

This bread was made by bush settlers in Australia and was either baked over the coals of an open fire or in a Dutch oven (a large, lidded cast iron pot). The dough can also be wrapped around a stick and suspended over the coals of a camp fire. There are many variations to the recipe.

MAKES 1 LOAF

370 g|13 oz strong white flour
115 g|4 oz wholemeal flour
4 teaspoons baking powder
1 teaspoon salt

1 teaspoon sugar
400 ml|14 fl oz milk
30 g|1 oz unsalted butter, melted

1 Heat the oven to 220°C|425°F|gas mark 7. Grease a baking tray.
2 Sift the flours, baking powder and salt together and make a well in the centre.
3 Add the milk and butter to the well. Mix first with a knife and then with the fingers of one hand to bring to a soft but not wet dough. Shape quickly into a round loaf and place on the greased baking tray.
4 Brush with milk and dust with wholemeal flour. Cut a deep cross into the top of the loaf and bake for 15 minutes. Turn the oven down to 180°C|350°F|gas mark 4 and bake for a further 20–25 minutes. It is ready when it sounds hollow if tapped on the underside. Put on a wire rack to cool.

Oat Scones

These scones are particularly good with cheese and chutney.

MAKES 8

115 g|4 oz plain flour
a pinch of salt
2 teaspoons baking powder

55 g|2 oz butter, chopped into pieces
115 g|4 oz porridge oats
75–85 ml|2½–3 fl oz milk

1 Heat the oven to 200°C|400°F|gas mark 6. Grease a baking sheet.
2 Sift the flour, salt and baking powder into a mixing bowl. Rub in the butter using your fingertips and add the oats.
3 Add enough milk to make a soft dough.
4 Put on to a floured surface and quickly shape into a 17 cm|7 in diameter circle. Put on the baking sheet and mark into 8 wedges with a large sharp knife.
5 Bake in the oven for 20 minutes. Put on a wire rack to cool and cover with a clean tea towel to soften the top. Serve slightly warm.

Potato Scones

MAKES 8

15 g | ½ oz butter, melted
225 g | 8 oz cooked potatoes, mashed and cooled
½ teaspoon salt

55 g | 2 oz plain flour
½ teaspoon baking powder

1 Grease a griddle or heavy frying pan.
2 Add the melted butter to the potatoes in a mixing bowl and season with salt.
3 Sift together the flour and baking powder and work into the potatoes to make a soft, pliable dough.
4 Divide the dough in half. Roll out each half on a lightly floured board to a thin 15 cm | 6 in diameter circle. Mark into quarters.
5 Heat the prepared griddle until moderately hot and add the scones. Cook for about 3 minutes on each side, until golden-brown. Keep warm in the folds of a clean tea towel while cooking the remaining scones in the same way.
6 Serve warm with butter. The scones can be reheated by being placed under a hot grill.

Parmesan and Chive Scones

MAKES 12

225 g | 8 oz self-raising flour
½ teaspoon salt
½ teaspoon bicarbonate of soda
30 g | 1 oz butter
30 g | 1 oz Parmesan cheese, finely grated

1 tablespoon finely chopped fresh chives
150 ml | 5 fl oz buttermilk

To glaze
1 egg, beaten

1 Heat the oven to 220°C | 425°F | gas mark 7. Flour a baking sheet.
2 Sift the flour, salt and bicarbonate of soda into a large bowl.
3 Cut the butter into small pieces and rub into the flour using your fingertips then stir in the Parmesan and chives.
4 Make a well in the mixture, pour in the buttermilk and mix to a soft dough using a table knife. Knead lightly on a floured surface until smooth.
5 Roll out the dough to 2.5 cm | 1 in thick and cut into rounds using a small, floured scone-cutter. Place the rounds on the floured baking sheet and brush the tops with beaten egg.
6 Bake in the top of the oven for 12–14 minutes or until risen and browned. Serve warm.

Cheddar Muffins

Quick to make, these muffins can be served in place of bread with a soup or stew.

MAKES 12

115 g|4 oz plain flour

30 g|1 oz wholemeal flour

85 g|3 oz polenta

1 scant teaspoon salt

1 tablespoon baking powder

¼ teaspoon bicarbonate of soda

¼ teaspoon dry mustard

1 teaspoon caraway seeds

1 egg, beaten

4 tablespoons vegetable oil

225 ml|8 fl oz milk

85 g|3 oz Cheddar cheese, finely grated

1 Heat the oven to 190°C|375°F|gas mark 5. Lightly butter 12 muffin tins.

2 Sift the flours, polenta, salt, baking powder, bicarbonate of soda and mustard into a bowl. Stir in the caraway seeds.

3 Mix together the egg, oil and milk in a separate bowl and stir in all but 4 tablespoons of the cheese.

4 Make a well in the centre of the flour mixture, pour in the milk mixture and stir quickly to make a batter. Spoon into the tins. Sprinkle the reserved cheese over the top.

5 Bake for 20 minutes or until the muffins are well-risen and golden. Cool for 5 minutes, then remove from the tins and transfer to a wire rack to cool completely.

Sweet Scones

Traditionally, sweet scones are served at teatime. Scones are at their best if mixed and cooked quickly, as any raising agent in them will start to work once the liquid is added. A soft mixture will produce a better scone. Ideally they should be served still warm from the oven.

Scones

MAKES 6

225 g | 8 oz self-raising flour
½ teaspoon salt
55 g | 2 oz butter

30 g | 1 oz caster sugar (optional)
150 ml | 5 fl oz milk
1 egg, beaten

1 Heat the oven to 220°C | 425°F | gas mark 7. Flour a baking sheet.
2 Sift the flour with the salt into a large bowl. Rub the butter until the mixture resembles breadcrumbs. Stir in the sugar, if using.
3 Make a deep well in the flour, pour in the milk and mix to a soft, spongy dough with a knife.
4 On a floured surface, knead the dough very lightly until it is just smooth. Roll or press out to about 2.5 cm | 1 in thick and stamp into rounds with a samll pastry cutter. Gather the scraps together and cut into more scones
5 Brush the scones with beaten egg for a glossy crust, sprinkle with flour for a soft one or brush with milk for a light gloss and soft crust.
6 Bake the scones at the top of the oven for 15–20 minutes, or until well risen and brown. Leave to cool on a wire rack, or serve hot from the oven.

VARIATIONS

Fruit scones: Add 115 g | 4 oz raisins with the sugar.

Apricot scones: Add 115 g | 4 oz chopped dried apricots with the sugar.

Treacle scones: Warm the milk and add 3 tablespoons treacle. 30 g | 1 oz extra flour may need to be added to the mixture.

Cheese scones: Add 115 g | 4 oz grated Cheddar cheese, ¼ teaspoon dry English mustard and a pinch of cayenne pepper after the butter has been rubbed in. Omit the sugar.

Plain savoury scones: Omit the sugar.

Sweet Damper

The recipe for this traditional Australian 'bread' is from a former Leiths teacher, Chris Bailey. It is best eaten warm or toasted.

MAKES 8 PIECES

softened butter for greasing	2 tablespoons caster sugar
225 g	8 oz self-raising flour	150 ml	5 fl oz milk
a pinch of salt	a handful of dried fruit, such as sultanas or currants

1 Heat the oven to 220°C|425°F| gas mark 7. Liberally butter a small Le Creuset casserole or similar covered, ovenproof pan.
2 Mix all the dry ingredients together.
3 Add enough milk to form a softish dough. Roll into a rough ball shape.
4 Place in the casserole and cover. Bake in the centre of the oven for 30 minutes or until well-risen and golden-brown. The damper can be removed from the casserole and returned to the oven on a baking sheet for 5 minutes to brown the top, if desired. Serve warm.

Griddle Scones

Baking scones and cakes on a flat griddle or girdle is an ancient form of baking and you must control the heat carefully to get the best results. The griddle has to heat up before any cooking takes place. Then, when the scones or cakes are put on to cook, the heat should be turned down to ensure that they are cooking but not burning. Use a griddle or a thick, flat-based frying pan.

Drop Scones

MAKES 30

225 g	8 oz plain flour	**To serve**
½ teaspoon salt	butter
4 teaspoons baking powder	jam
2 eggs, separated	
290 ml	10 fl oz milk	
2 tablespoons butter, melted and cooled	

1 Sift the flour with the salt and baking powder into a large bowl.
2 Make a well in the centre of the mixture and add the egg yolks and a quarter of the milk.
3 Mix with a wooden spoon and gradually draw in the flour from the sides of the bowl,

making a smooth batter. Add the remaining milk gradually until the batter is the consistency of thick cream.

4 Fold in the melted butter.

5 Whisk the egg whites until stiff but not dry and fold into the batter.

6 Meanwhile, lightly grease a heavy frying pan or griddle iron and heat it. When really hot, drop 2 spoonfuls of butter on to the surface, keeping them well separated.

7 Cook for 2–3 minutes. When the undersides of the pancakes are brown and bubbles rise to the surface, lift them with a fish slice, turn over and brown the other side.

8 Keep warm, covered with a clean tea-towel, and serve with butter and jam.

Strawberry Shortcake

Strawberry shortcake is a popular American dessert.

MAKES 6

225 g│8 oz self-raising flour
a pinch of salt
55 g│2 oz butter, softened
55 g│2 oz caster sugar
150 ml│5 fl oz milk

For the filling

400 g│14 oz fresh strawberries
2 tablespoons caster sugar
150 ml│5 fl oz double cream
1 tablespoon icing sugar
¼ teaspoon vanilla essence

1 Heat the oven to 200°C│400°F│gas mark 6. Lightly grease a baking sheet.

2 Sift the flour and salt together into a large bowl.

3 Cut the butter into sugar-lump-sized pieces. Stir into the flour then rub in lightly with your fingertips. Leave the butter in flakes. If the butter is well-chilled it can be grated on a coarse garter and mixed directly with the flour. Stir in the sugar.

4 Quickly stir in enough milk to make a soft dough. Turn out on to a floured surface and knead gently to bring together. Pat or roll to a thickness of 2 cm│¾ in.

5 Cut into 6 cm│2½ in rounds using a floured scone cutter.

6 Place on to the baking sheet and bake in the top third of the oven for 10–12 minutes or until risen and golden-brown. Cool on a wire rack.

7 Hull and wash the strawberries. Slice thickly into a bowl and toss with the caster sugar.

8 Whip the cream with the icing sugar and vanilla essence to soft peaks.

9 To serve, split the shortcakes in half. Place the bases on individual serving plates and layer over some of the strawberries. Place the top of the shortcakes over the strawberries and decorate with a dollop of cream.

10 Serve immediately with the remaining strawberries and cream served separately.

Singin' Hinny

This griddle cake comes from Northumberland and is supposed to hiss and sing while cooking, hence its name.

MAKES 8

225 g | 8 oz self-raising flour

½ teaspoon salt

30 g | 1 oz ground rice

55 g | 2 oz lard

55 g | 2 oz caster sugar

85 g | 3 oz currants

125 ml | 4 fl oz milk

1 egg, beaten

1 Sift the flour, salt and ground rice together into a large mixing bowl. Cut the lard into pieces and rub into the flour with the fingertips. Add the sugar and currants and make a well in the centre.

2 Mix together the milk and egg and pour into the well. Bring the mixture together, first with a round-bladed knife and then with the fingers of one hand. Knead very lightly to a soft dough.

3 Roll out on a floured board to a large circle about 1.25 cm | ½ in thick. Prick the top well with a fork.

4 Grease and heat a griddle or a thick frying pan. Place the dough on the hot griddle and cook for about 5 minutes on each side over a low to medium heat or until a deep golden-brown.

5 Cut into wedges, split in half and serve warm, spread liberally with butter.

Welsh Cakes

MAKES 16

225 g | 8 oz self-raising flour

55 g | 2 oz caster sugar

1 teaspoon mixed spice

115 g | 4 oz butter

85 g | 3 oz sultanas

1 large egg, beaten

75 ml | 2½ fl oz milk

lard, for greasing

1 Sift the dry ingredients into a large bowl. Rub in the butter and mix in the fruit. Add the egg and mix to a dough, adding milk if necessary.

2 Roll out on a floured surface to about 5 mm | ¼ in thick and cut into 6 cm | 2½ in rounds. Grease a thick frying pan (or flat griddle) with lard and heat until the pan is very hot. Cook the cakes, in batches, for about 2–3 minutes each side. Control the heat very carefully or the cakes will burn on the outside. Put them into a clean tea towel whilst cooking the rest. Add more lard to the pan as necessary.

NOTE: If using a non-stick pan it may not be necessary to add any lard.

Muffins: Points to Remember

- Weigh and measure all ingredients before beginning to bake. Heat the oven to the correct temperature and line the muffin tins with paper cases or brush with oil and line with small circles of baking parchment.
- Mix quickly. Overmixing produces tough muffins riddled with tunnels. The best tool for mixing muffins is a large wire whisk used with a stirring motion. It will mix the batter quickly.
- Only mix the wet and dry ingredients together sufficiently to moisten the flour. It is better to have a few sprays of flour visible than to overmix.
- To keep added fruit or nuts from sinking to the bottom, dredge them with a little flour or fold them in with softly beaten egg white.
- Fill the muffin cups quickly, as once the wet ingredients are mixed into the dry ingredients the chemical raising agents will be activated and the batter will start to rise. To capture this rise in the muffins, the mixture needs to be baked as soon as possible.
- To tell when the muffins are done, insert a wooden cocktail stick into the centre of the muffin all the way to the bottom: it should come out clean. Alternatively, press the muffin lightly in the centre: it should spring back.
- For soft tops, cover the muffins with a clean tea towel during cooling.

Muffins

The muffin recipes in this chapter are for American muffins, the individual cakes that are baked in tins with cup-like indentations lined with fluted paper cases, rather like fairy cakes. American muffins are made from a mixture similar to a quick bread that is leavened using chemical raising agents such as baking powder and/or bicarbonate of soda and baked in the oven. Their texture is similar to a cake but coarser.

English muffins are griddle cakes that are made with a yeast-raised batter enriched with milk and butter. They are fried in a pastry cutter to give them a round shape (see recipe, page 563). They are not usually sweetened and have a bread-like texture. These muffins are normally split in half across the middle then toasted and spread with butter.

It is thought that the word 'muffin' is a derivative of the French *moufflet*, meaning 'soft' when referring to bread. English muffins can be traced back to the mid-1700s and are described by cookery writer Hannah Glasse as having a 'honeycomb' texture. Muffins were sold on the street by 'muffin men' until the 1840s, when a law was passed prohibiting their sale (most likely due to the nuisance of the muffin man's bell).

Although American muffins can be savoury and served with a soup or first course, they are most likely to be sweet. These muffins often contain fresh or dried fruits, such as blueberries or raisins, and are served with a cup of coffee for breakfast, elevenses or at teatime.

Traditionally muffins are made by sifting together all the dry ingredients then combining all the wet ingredients in a separate bowl. The two mixtures are then combined quickly, using no more than about 20 strokes. Muffins can also be made by the creaming method (see *Methods of Cake-making*, page 278). This method will produce muffins with a finer, more cake-like texture. Miniature muffins can be made by baking the mixture in mini-muffin tins lined with small paper cases. A 250g|9oz flour quantity will make about 36 miniature muffins. They need to be baked for about 12 minutes.

Muffins are best eaten warm from the oven or on the day of baking. They can be reheated by being placed in a 150°C|300°F|gas mark 2 oven for 5 minutes or in a microwave for 1 minute on a medium setting. Muffins can also be frozen for 1 month. Wrap each muffin in clingfilm then place in a freezer bag or box.

Lemon and Poppy Seed Muffins

MAKES 12

250 g | 9 oz plain flour

2 teaspoons baking powder

½ teaspoon bicarbonate of soda

a pinch of salt

115 g | 4 oz butter, melted and cooled

115 g | 4 oz soft light brown sugar

2 eggs, beaten

85 ml | 3 fl oz milk

grated zest and juice of 2 small lemons

2 tablespoons poppy seeds

1 Heat the oven to 190°C | 375°F | gas mark 5. Line 12 muffin tins with paper muffin cases or brush the tins with oil and line with greaseproof paper discs.

2 Sift the flour, baking powder, bicarbonate of soda and salt together and set aside.

3 In a large bowl, mix together the butter, sugar, eggs, milk, lemon zest and juice.

4 Fold the flour into the wet mixture in the bowl, using no more than 20 strokes.

5 Stir in the poppy seeds. Do not overmix.

6 Quickly fill the muffin tins, using an ice-cream scoop or small cup. They will be full to the top. Do not level.

7 Bake in the centre of the oven for 20 minutes or until the muffins are well-risen and golden-brown and a wooden skewer inserted into the centre comes out clean. Cool on a wire rack.

Blueberry Muffins

These muffins are very easy to make. If blueberries are hard to find, try fresh or frozen raspberries or blackcurrants.

MAKES 12

340 g | 12 oz plain flour

3 teaspoons baking powder

½ teaspoon salt

115 g | 4 oz caster sugar

290 ml | 10 fl oz milk

1 egg, lightly beaten

55 g | 2 oz butter, melted and cooled

225 g | 8 oz blueberries (fresh or frozen)

1 Heat the oven to 200°C | 400°F | gas mark 6. Grease 12 muffin tins or put 12 muffin cases on to a baking sheet.

2 Sift the flour, baking powder, salt and sugar together into a large mixing bowl. Make a well in the centre.

3 Mix together the milk, egg and butter. Pour the mixture gradually into the well, mixing with a wooden spoon and incorporating the flour as you stir to make a smooth batter.

4 Mix in the blueberries lightly and spoon into the muffin tins or cases, filling each one by no more than two thirds.

5 Bake in the centre of the oven for 25–30 minutes or until well-risen and brown.

6 Transfer the muffins to a wire rack and leave to cool.

Blueberry Crumble Muffins

MAKES 12

For the topping

85 g│3 oz plain flour

a pinch of salt

55 g│2 oz butter

55 g│2 oz caster sugar

For the muffins

250 g│9 oz plain flour

2 teaspoons baking powder

½ teaspoon bicarbonate of soda

1 teaspoon ground cinnamon

a pinch of salt

115 g│4 oz butter, melted and cooled

115 g│4 oz soft light brown sugar

2 eggs, beaten

1 teaspoon grated lemon zest

140 g│5 oz soured cream

200 g│7 oz blueberries

1 Make the topping: sift the flour into a bowl with the salt, then cut the butter into small cubes and toss in the flour. Cut in the butter using two table knives, scissor-fashion, then rub in with your fingertips until the mixture resembles fine breadcrumbs. Stir in the sugar and chill.

2 For the muffins, heat the oven to 190°C│375°F│gas mark 5. Line 12 muffin tins with paper muffin cases or oil the tin well and line with greaseproof paper discs.

3 Sift the flour with the baking powder, bicarbonate of soda, cinnamon and salt into a large bowl.

4 In a separate bowl, combine the butter, sugar, eggs, lemon zest and soured cream.

5 Stir the wet ingredients into the dry ingredients, taking care not to overstir. Add the blueberries after about 10 strokes. Do not use more than 20 strokes altogether or the muffins will be tough.

6 Divide the mixture between the muffin cases and sprinkle over the topping.

7 Bake in the centre of the oven for 20 minutes or until well-risen and golden-brown. A skewer inserted into the centre will come out clean.

8 Remove the muffins from the tin and cool on a wire rack.

Raspberry Streusel Muffins

MAKES 12

For the topping

55 g | 2 oz plain flour

1 teaspoon mixed spice

30 g | 1 oz butter, cut into pieces

2 tablespoons soft light brown sugar

For the muffins

300 g | 10½ oz self-raising flour

170 g | 6 oz defrosted frozen raspberries

1 medium apple, peeled and grated

150 g | 5½ oz soft light brown sugar

3 eggs, beaten

75 ml | 2½ fl oz vegetable oil

75 ml | 2½ fl oz natural yoghurt

1 Heat the oven to 200°C | 400°F | gas mark 6. Put 12 paper muffin cases into muffin tins or grease the tins well and line with greaseproof paper discs.

2 Make the topping: sift the plain flour with the spice, rub in the butter and stir in the sugar. Put to one side.

3 Sift the flour into a large bowl, then stir in the raspberries, apple, sugar, eggs, oil and yoghurt. Mix well and put into the prepared cases. Scatter over the streusel topping.

4 Bake for 20 minutes. The muffins are cooked if the tops spring back when pressed lightly with a finger.

Rhubarb Muffins

MAKES 16–18

450 g | 1 lb self-raising flour

225 g | 8 oz soft light brown sugar

2 teaspoons ground cinnamon

115 g | 4 oz butter, melted but not hot

200 ml | 7 fl oz milk

2 eggs, beaten

200 g | 7 oz cooking apples, coarsely grated

1 × 540 g | 1 lb 3 oz tin of rhubarb (245 g | 9 oz drained weight)

1 Heat the oven to 190°C | 375°F | gas mark 5. Put 16–18 paper muffin cases into muffin tins or grease the tins well and line with greaseproof paper discs.

2 Sift the flour, sugar and cinnamon together into a large bowl. Make a well in the centre.

3 Add the butter, milk and eggs to the well and combine carefully with the flour. Add the apple and drained rhubarb, taking care not to break the rhubarb up too much.

4 Spoon into the prepared cases and bake for 30–35 minutes. These muffins are best served slightly warm.

Carrot and Orange Muffins

MAKES 12

300 g | 10½ oz self-raising flour

85 g | 3 oz wholemeal flour

115 g | 4 oz caster sugar

340 g | 12 oz carrot, grated

2 eggs, beaten

115 g | 4 oz butter, melted

125 ml | 4½ fl oz milk

grated zest of 1 large orange

115 ml | 4 fl oz orange juice

1 Heat the oven to 200°C | 400°F | gas mark 6. Place 12 paper muffin cases into muffin tins or grease the tins well and line with greaseproof paper discs.

2 Sift the flours together into a large bowl and add the sugar. Mix together the carrot, eggs, butter, milk, orange zest and orange juice. Add this to the flour and mix well.

3 Spoon the mixture into the cases and bake in the centre of the oven for 25 minutes. The muffins are ready when the tops spring back when pressed lightly with your finger.

Carrot and Pineapple Muffins

These muffins are perfect for lunch boxes. It is easy to make a double quantity, freeze them and put them whilst still frozen into the lunch box. They will have defrosted by lunchtime.

MAKES 10–12

115 g | 4 oz plain flour

115 g | 4 oz plain wholemeal flour

1 teaspoon baking powder

¾ teaspoon bicarbonate of soda

1½ teaspoons ground cinnamon

225 ml | 8 fl oz sunflower oil

85 g | 3 oz caster sugar

2 eggs, beaten

125 g | 4½ oz grated carrots (approx. 2 medium-sized carrots)

1 × 225 g | 8 oz tin crushed pineapple, drained

45 g | 1½ oz dried apricots, chopped

115 g | 4 oz raisins

1 Heat the oven to 180°C | 350°F | gas mark 4. Place 12 paper muffin cases into muffin tins or grease the tins well and line with greaseproof paper discs.

2 Sift together the flours, baking powder, bicarbonate of soda and cinnamon.

3 Beat the oil, sugar and eggs together until well-blended. Add the grated carrots, pineapple, apricots and raisins.

4 Make a well in the centre of the flour mixture and pour in the wet ingredients. Mix well, beating a little if necessary to remove any lumps of flour.

5 Put the mixture into the cases and bake for 20–25 minutes or until the tops spring back when pressed lightly with a finger. Cool on a wire rack.

Plum and Oat Muffins

When making these muffins, choose ripe but not overripe plums.

MAKES 10–12

340 g | 12 oz ripe plums

170 g | 6 oz self-raising flour

115 g | 4 oz wholemeal self-raising flour

½ teaspoon mixed spice

½ teaspoon ground cinnamon

85 g | 3 oz porridge oats

115 g | 4 oz unrefined soft light brown sugar

115 g | 4 oz butter, melted

150 ml | 5 fl oz milk

1 egg, beaten

For the topping

2 tablespoons porridge oats

1 tablespoon unrefined soft light brown sugar

¼ teaspoon ground cinnamon

1 Heat the oven to 190°C | 375°F | gas mark 5. Place paper muffin cases into a muffin tins or grease the tins well and line with discs of greaseproof paper.
2 Cut the plums in half and carefully remove and discard the stones. Chop the flesh into even dice.
3 Sift the flours and spices into a large bowl, then add the oats and sugar. Make a well in the centre and add the butter, milk and egg. Mix well and add the diced plum flesh.
4 Spoon carefully into the paper cases until they are three quarters full.
5 Mix together the extra oats, sugar and cinnamon and sprinkle on the tops of the muffins.
6 Bake in the centre of the oven for 20–25 minutes. They are cooked if the top springs back when lightly pressed with a finger. Transfer to a wire rack to cool.

Butternut and Peach Muffins

MAKES 12

370 g | 13 oz self-raising flour

225 g | 8 oz caster sugar

2 eggs, beaten

55 ml | 2 fl oz milk

125 ml | 4 fl oz sunflower oil

115 g | 4 oz raw butternut squash, grated

4 tinned peach halves, rinsed and chopped

85 g | 3 oz dried peaches, chopped

1 Heat the oven to 190°C | 375°F | gas mark 5. Put 12 paper muffin cases into muffin tins or grease the tins well and line with discs of greaseproof paper.
2 Sift the flour into a large bowl and add the caster sugar. Make a well in the centre.
3 Combine the eggs, milk and sunflower oil. Pour into the well and combine with the flour and sugar. Mix in the squash and peaches.
4 Spoon into the muffin cases and bake in the centre of the oven for 20–25 minutes. The muffins are cooked if the tops spring back when lightly pressed with a finger.

Banana and Strawberry Muffins

MAKES 12

250 g│9 oz strawberries

1 large ripe banana (115 g│4 oz peeled weight)

140 g│5 oz caster sugar

85 g│3 oz butter, melted and cooled

2 eggs, beaten

225 g│8 oz self-raising flour

½ teaspoon bicarbonate of soda

demerara sugar, for sprinkling

1 Heat the oven to 190°C│375°F│gas mark 5. Line a muffin tin with 12 paper muffin cases.

2 Wash and hull the strawberries and place on kitchen paper to dry. Cut into ½ cm│¼ in dice. Place 55 g│2 oz strawberries in a large bowl with the peeled bananas and set the rest aside.

3 Mash the strawberries and banana coarsely (a potato masher is good for this).

4 Stir in the sugar, butter and eggs.

5 Sift the flour and bicarbonate of soda over the wet mixture and fold in, using no more than 20 strokes. Overfolding will make the muffins tough.

6 Stir in the diced strawberries. Divide the mixture between the muffin cases and sprinkle with demerara sugar.

7 Bake in the centre of the oven for 20–25 minutes or until a cocktail stick inserted in the centre comes out without any wet batter sticking to it.

8 Serve warm or at room temperature.

Chocolate and Banana Muffins

MAKES 12–14

225 g│8 oz self-raising flour

55 g│2 oz cocoa powder

½ teaspoon bicarbonate of soda

225 g│8 oz caster sugar

2 ripe bananas, mashed

85 g│3 oz plain chocolate chips

1 egg, beaten

30 g│1 oz unsalted butter, melted

225 ml│8 fl oz milk, warmed to blood temperature

1 Heat the oven to 190°C│375°F│gas mark 5. Line a muffin tin with paper muffin cases or grease the tin well and line with greaseproof paper discs.

2 Sift the flour, cocoa powder and bicarbonate of soda together into a big bowl. Add the sugar. Make a well in the centre and add the banana, chocolate chips, egg, butter and milk. Mix well and pour into the muffin cases.

3 Bake for 20–25 minutes or until the tops spring back when pressed lightly with a finger. Cool on a wire rack.

Triple Chocolate Muffins

MAKES 12

285 g | 10 oz self-raising flour

55 g | 2 oz cocoa powder

225 g | 8 oz soft light brown sugar

1 egg, beaten

85 g | 3 oz butter, melted

175 ml | 6 fl oz milk

100 ml | 3½ fl oz soured cream

55 g | 2 oz white chocolate chips

55 g | 2 oz dark chocolate chips

85 g | 3 oz milk chocolate chips

1 Heat the oven to 180°C | 350°F | gas mark 4. Place 12 paper muffin cases in a muffin tin or grease the tin well and line with greaseproof paper discs.

2 Sift together the flour and cocoa. Add the sugar. Make a well in the centre.

3 Add the egg, butter, milk and soured cream to the well and mix carefully into the flour mixture. Add the chocolate chips.

4 Spoon into the cases, filling them about three-quarters full. Bake in the centre of the oven for 20–25 minutes. The muffins are cooked when the top springs back when lightly pressed with a finger.

5 Transfer to a wire rack to cool.

Milk Chocolate and Marmalade Muffins

MAKES 12

250 g | 9 oz plain flour

2 teaspoons baking powder

½ teaspoon bicarbonate of soda

a pinch of salt

115 g | 4 oz butter, melted and cooled

115 g | 4 oz soft light brown sugar

2 eggs, beaten

150 ml | 5 fl oz milk

½ teaspoon vanilla essence

115 g | 4 oz milk chocolate drops

4 tablespoons marmalade

1 Heat the oven to 180°C | 350°F | gas mark 4. Line a muffin tin with 12 paper muffin cases or oil the tin well and line with greaseproof paper discs.

2 Sift together the flour, baking powder, bicarbonate of soda and salt. Set aside.

3 In a large bowl mix together the butter, sugar, eggs, milk and vanilla.

4 Fold the flour into the butter mixture.

5 Fold in the milk chocolate drops. Do not overmix.

6 Use half the mixture to half-fill the muffin cups. Place a teaspoon of marmalade in the centre of each, then cover with the remaining batter. The cases should be full to the top.

7 Bake for 20–25 minutes or until risen and golden-brown. Cool slightly before eating as the marmalade will be very hot.

Chocolate and Walnut Muffins

MAKES 12

200g | 7 oz self-raising flour
55 g | 2 oz cocoa powder
1 teaspoon bicarbonate of soda
a pinch of salt
115 g | 4 oz butter, melted and cooled

115 g | 4 oz soft light brown sugar
2 eggs, beaten
150 ml | 5 fl oz milk
½ teaspoon vanilla essence
100 g | 3½ oz walnuts, chopped

1 Heat the oven to 190°C | 375°F | gas mark 5. Line a muffin tin with 12 paper muffin cases or oil the tin well and line with greaseproof paper discs.

2 Sift the flour, cocoa powder, bicarbonate of soda and salt together and set aside.

3 In a large bowl, mix together the butter, sugar, eggs, milk and vanilla.

4 Fold the flour into the wet mixture in the bowl, using no more than 20 strokes.

5 Stir in the walnuts. Do not overmix.

6 Quickly fill the muffin tins, using an ice-cream scoop or small cup. They will be full to the top. Do not level.

7 Bake in the centre of the oven for 20 minutes until the muffins are well-risen and golden-brown and a wooden skewer inserted into the centre comes out clean. Cool on a wire rack.

Chocolate Chip Muffins

MAKES 12

250 g | 9 oz self-raising flour
½ teaspoon bicarbonate of soda
a pinch of salt
115 g | 4 oz butter, melted and cooled
115 g | 4 oz soft light brown sugar

2 eggs, beaten
150 ml | 5 fl oz milk
½ teaspoon vanilla essence
100 g | 3½ oz chocolate chips

1 Heat the oven to 190°C | 375°F | gas mark 5. Line a muffin tin with 12 paper muffin cases or oil the tin well and line with greaseproof paper discs.

2 Sift the flour, bicarbonate of soda and salt together and set aside.

3 In a large bowl, mix together the butter, sugar, eggs, milk and vanilla.

4 Fold the flour into the wet mixture in the bowl using no more than 20 strokes.

5 Stir in the chocolate chips. Do not overmix.

6 Quickly fill the muffin tins, using an ice-cream scoop or small cup. They will be full to the top. Do not level.

7 Bake in the centre of the oven for 20 minutes or until the muffins are well-risen and golden-brown and a wooden skewer inserted into the centre comes out clean. Cool on a wire rack.

Applesauce Raisin Muffins

MAKES 12

2 eggs

250 ml | 9 fl oz sweetened chunky applesauce

115 g | 4 oz butter, melted and cooled

115 g | 4 oz caster sugar

225 g | 8 oz self-raising flour

½ teaspoon bicarbonate of soda

2 teaspoons ground cinnamon

115 g | 4 oz raisins

1 Heat the oven to 190°C | 375°F | gas mark 5. Line a muffin tin with 12 paper muffin cases or brush with oil and line the bases with greaseproof paper discs.

2 Break the eggs into a large bowl and beat with a fork. Stir in the applesauce, butter and sugar.

3 Sift together the flour, bicarbonate of soda and cinnamon.

4 Fold the dry mixture into the applesauce mixture. Stir in the raisins, taking care not to overstir.

5 Divide the mixture between the muffin cases.

6 Bake in the centre of the oven for 18 minutes or until a cocktail stick comes out clean. Cool on a wire rack.

Apple and Coconut Muffins

MAKES 12

340 g | 12 oz self-raising flour

140 g | 5 oz soft light brown sugar

1 teaspoon ground cinnamon

2 tablespoons desiccated coconut

1 egg, beaten

200 ml | 7 fl oz natural yoghurt

115 ml | 4 fl oz sunflower oil

2 dessert apples, peeled and grated

100 g | 3½ oz dried apples, chopped

1 Heat the oven to 190°C | 375°F | gas mark 5. Place paper muffin cases in muffin tins or grease the tins well.

2 Sift the flour into a large bowl, add the sugar, cinnamon and coconut. Make a well in the centre.

3 Combine the egg, yoghurt and oil and pour into the well. Mix well and add the grated and dried apple. Spoon into the muffin cases.

4 Bake in the centre of the oven for 20 minutes. They are cooked if the tops spring back when pressed lightly with a finger.

Lemon Curd and Coconut Muffins

MAKES 12

250 g | 9 oz self-raising flour

1 teaspoon bicarbonate of soda

a pinch of salt

115 g | 4 oz butter, melted and cooled

140 g | 5 oz caster sugar

2 eggs, beaten

85 ml | 3 fl oz milk

grated zest and juice of 2 small lemons

115 g | 4 oz sweetened desiccated coconut

100 g | 3½ oz bought lemon curd

extra coconut, to sprinkle

1 Heat the oven to 190°C | 375°F | gas mark 5. Line a muffin tin with 12 paper muffin cases or oil the tin well and line with greaseproof paper discs.

2 Sift the flour, bicarbonate of soda and salt together and set aside.

3 In a large bowl, mix together the butter, sugar, eggs, milk, lemon zest and juice and coconut.

4 Fold the flour into the wet mixture in the bowl, using no more than 20 strokes.

5 Working quickly, as the mixture will be rising at this point, place slightly more than half the mixture in the bottom of the muffin tins.

6 Divide the lemon curd between the cases, placing the lemon curd in the centre of the batter at the bottom of each case. Top with the remaining muffin mixture, taking care to cover over the lemon curd.

7 Sprinkle the tops of the muffins with a little extra coconut.

8 Bake in the centre of the oven for 18–20 minutes or until the muffins are well-risen and golden-brown. Cool on a wire rack.

Pumpkin and Orange Muffins

MAKES 10

225 g | 8 oz self-raising flour

½ teaspoon ground cinnamon

½ teaspoon mixed spice

85 g | 3 oz soft light brown sugar

85 ml | 3 fl oz vegetable oil

2 eggs, beaten

200 g | 7 oz cooked pumpkin or butternut squash, mashed (or ½ × 425 ml | 15 oz can of puréed pumpkin)

grated zest of 1 orange

55 ml | 2 fl oz orange juice

1 Heat the oven to 190°C | 375°F | gas mark 5. Place paper muffin cases in a muffin tin or oil the tin well and line with greaseproof paper discs.

2 Sift together the flour, cinnamon and spice into a large bowl. Add the sugar, oil, eggs, pumpkin, orange zest and orange juice. Mix well and spoon into the muffin cases.

3 Bake in the centre of the oven for 20–30 minutes. The muffins are cooked if the tops spring back when pressed lightly with a finger. Transfer to a wire rack to cool.

Coconut, White Chocolate and Pineapple Muffins

MAKES 12

340 g | 12 oz self-raising flour

1 teaspoon baking powder

55 g | 2 oz desiccated coconut

115 g | 4 oz caster sugar

55 g | 2 oz butter, melted

200 ml | 7 fl oz coconut milk

1 egg, beaten

1 teaspoon vanilla essence

100 g | 3½ oz white chocolate chips

85 g | 3 oz dried pineapple pieces, soaked in boiling water for ½ hour, drained and chopped

1 Heat the oven to 190°C | 375°F | gas mark 5. Place paper muffin cases in a muffin tin or oil the tin well and line with greaseproof paper discs.

2 Sift the flour and baking powder together into a large bowl. Add the coconut and sugar.

3 Mix the butter, coconut milk, eggs and vanilla essence together and add to the dry ingredients. Mix well and add the chocolate chips and pineapple pieces.

4 Spoon into the cases and bake in the oven for approximately 25 minutes. The muffins are ready when the tops spring back when lightly pressed with a finger.

Cinnamon Raisin Muffins

MAKES 12

115 g | 4 oz butter, melted

150 ml | 5 fl oz milk

2 eggs, beaten

115 g | 4 oz soft light brown sugar

2 tablespoons caster sugar

125 g | 4½ oz self-raising flour

125 g | 4½ oz wholemeal plain flour

2 teaspoons baking powder

½ teaspoon bicarbonate of soda

1 teaspoon ground cinnamon

30 g | 1 oz porridge oats

170 g | 6 oz raisins

To finish

1 tablespoon porridge oats

1 Heat the oven to 190°C | 375°F | gas mark 5. Line a muffin tin with paper muffin cases or grease the tin well and line with greaseproof paper discs.

2 Mix together the butter, milk, eggs and sugars.

3 Sift the flours, baking powder, bicarbonate of soda and ground cinnamon into a large bowl. Stir in the oats and make a well in the centre.

4 Stir in the wet ingredients, taking care not to overstir. Fold in the raisins.

5 Divide between the muffin cases then sprinkle over the extra oats.

6 Bake in the centre of the oven for 18–20 minutes or until a cocktail stick inserted in the centre comes out clean. Cool on a wire rack.

Sticky Toffee Ginger and Date Muffins

These muffins are served warm with the sauce poured over the top at the last minute. They can be served as a pudding or a teatime treat. The muffins and sauce can be cooked in advance and reheated.

MAKES 16

140 g | 5 oz dried dates, chopped
75 ml | 2½ fl oz orange juice
¼ teaspoon bicarbonate of soda
285 g | 10 oz self-raising flour
140 g | 5 oz self-raising wholemeal flour
2 teaspoons ground ginger
1 teaspoon mixed spice
200 g | 7 oz soft dark brown sugar
2 teaspoons grated orange zest

1 egg, beaten
290 ml | 10 fl oz natural low-fat yoghurt
150 ml | 1¾ fl oz sunflower oil

For the sauce

200 g | 7 oz soft dark brown sugar
290 ml | 10 fl oz double cream
55 g | 2 oz unsalted butter

1 Heat the oven to 200°C | 400°F | gas mark 6. Put 16 muffin cases on to a baking sheet or grease 16 muffin tins.
2 Put the dates into a small saucepan with the orange juice, bring to the boil and add the bicarbonate of soda. Allow to stand for 3 minutes.
3 Sift the flours and spices into a large bowl. Add the sugar, date mixture, orange zest, egg, yoghurt and oil. Mix together well and spoon into the prepared tin.
4 Bake for 15–20 minutes, or until the muffins spring back when pressed with a finger.
5 Meanwhile, make the toffee sauce. Put the sugar, cream and butter into a saucepan and heat gently. Once the sugar has dissolved, bring it to the boil and simmer for 3–4 minutes or until it has thickened slightly.
6 Put a warm muffin on a plate, remove the paper case and pour some of the warm sauce over the top.

Raisin Bran Muffins

MAKES 12

200 ml | 7 fl oz semi-skimmed milk
115 g | 4 oz butter
100 g | 3½ oz All-Bran cereal (strands)
115 g | 4 oz soft light brown sugar
2 eggs, beaten
170 g | 6 oz self-raising flour

1 teaspoon baking powder
½ teaspoon bicarbonate of soda
½ teaspoon ground cinnamon
140 g | 5 oz raisins
extra All-Bran cereal, for sprinkling

1 Heat the oven to 190°C | 375°F | gas mark 5. Line a muffin tin with 12 paper muffin cases.

2 Warm the milk and the butter in a saucepan to melt the butter.

3 Place the cereal and sugar in a bowl then stir in the milk and melted butter.

4 Allow to cool to lukewarm then stir in the eggs.

5 Sift together the flour, baking powder, bicarbonate of soda and cinnamon. Stir into the cereal mixture. Stir in the raisins. Use only about 20 strokes to fold in as overfolding will cause the muffins to be tough.

6 Divide the mixture between the muffin cases. Sprinkle a little extra cereal over the tops.

7 Bake in the top third of the oven for 18–20 minutes. A wooden cocktail stick will come out clean when done. Cool on a wire rack.

Orange and Raisin Muffins

MAKES 16

340 g | 12 oz plain flour
1 teaspoon bicarbonate of soda
grated zest of 2 oranges
225 g | 8 oz caster sugar

2 eggs, beaten
115 g | 4 oz butter, melted and cooled
290 ml | 10 fl oz natural yoghurt
115 g | 4 oz raisins

1 Heat the oven to 200°C | 400°F | gas mark 6. Put 16 muffin cases on to a baking sheet or grease 16 muffin tins.

2 Sift the flour with the bicarbonate of soda into a large mixing bowl. Add the orange zest and sugar. Make a well in the centre.

3 Put the eggs, butter and yoghurt into the well and gradually incorporate all the flour, mixing to a smooth batter.

4 Stir in the raisins and spoon into the muffin tins or cases, filling each by no more than two thirds.

5 Bake in the centre of the oven for 20–25 minutes or until the muffins spring back when pressed lightly with a fingertip. Cool on a wire rack.

Coffee and Date Muffins

MAKES 12

140 g|5 oz dried dates, chopped
½ teaspoon bicarbonate of soda
1 teaspoon instant coffee granules
150 ml|5 fl oz boiling water
225 g|8 oz soft light brown sugar

115 g|4 oz butter, melted
2 eggs, beaten
250 g|9 oz self-raising flour
100 g|3½ oz walnuts, chopped

1 Place the dates in a heatproof bowl with the bicarbonate of soda and coffee granules. Pour over the boiling water and stir. Allow to stand for 10 minutes.

2 Heat the oven to 190°C|375°F|gas mark 5. Line a muffin tin with 12 paper muffin cases or brush the tin with oil and line the bases of each with discs of greaseproof paper.

3 Stir the sugar, butter and eggs into the date mixture.

4 Fold in the flour until just combined, then fold in the walnuts.

5 Divide the mixture between the prepared muffin cases. Bake in the centre of the oven for 20 minutes. A skewer inserted in the centre should come out clean.

6 Remove the muffins from the tin and place on a wire rack to cool. Cover with a clean tea towel during cooling to keep the tops soft.

Maple Syrup and Pecan Muffins

MAKES 12

340 g|12 oz self-raising flour
55 g|2 oz soft dark brown sugar
115 g|4 oz pecan nuts, chopped
1 teaspoon ground cinnamon

290 ml|10 fl oz buttermilk (or natural yoghurt)
100 g|3½ oz butter, melted but not hot
1 egg, beaten
75 ml|2½ oz maple syrup

1 Heat the oven to 200°C|400°F|gas mark 6. Place paper muffin cases in a muffin tin or grease the tin well and line with greaseproof paper discs.

2 Sift the flour into a large bowl. Add the sugar, pecan nuts and cinnamon. Make a well in the centre.

3 Pour the buttermilk, melted butter, egg and maple syrup into the well and combine with the dry ingredients. Mix well and pour into the prepared muffin cases.

4 Bake in the oven for 20 minutes or until the tops spring back when pressed lightly with a finger. Cool on a wire rack.

Sweet Potato and Apple Muffins

MAKES 12

340 g | 12 oz sweet potato
115 ml | 4 fl oz water
225 g | 8 oz cooking apples
225 g | 8 oz plain flour
1 teaspoon bicarbonate of soda
1 teaspoon ground cinnamon

½ teaspoon grated nutmeg
140 g | 5 oz caster sugar
115 g | 4 oz butter
1 egg, beaten
85 g | 3 oz dried apricots, chopped

1 Heat the oven to 180°C | 350°F | gas mark 4. Grease a muffin tin and line with grease-proof paper discs or place 12 paper muffin cases in the tin.

2 Peel the sweet potato and cut into small dice. Put into a saucepan with the water. Bring to the boil, cover with a lid and cook over a very low heat for 5–10 minutes, stirring occasionally. Do not let it dry out and add more water if necessary.

3 Peel and core the apples and cut into small dice. Add to the softened sweet potato. Cook over a low heat until the apple is soft. Ensure that the mixture does not dry out and add more water if necessary. Mash with a fork or potato masher to remove any lumps. Allow to cool.

4 Sift together the flour, bicarbonate of soda, cinnamon and nutmeg into a large bowl. Add the sugar.

5 Melt the butter and allow to cool.

6 Add the egg to the sweet-potato mixture. Add the cooled butter and chopped apricots.

7 Make a well in the centre of the flour and pour in the sweet-potato mixture. Mix quickly and well, using a hand whisk or a fork.

8 Pour into the muffin cases and bake in the centre of the oven for 30 minutes or until the cakes spring back when touched lightly with a finger.

9 Transfer to a wire rack to cool.

Pear and Ginger Muffins

MAKES 10

115 g | 4 oz butter
55 g | 2 oz clear honey
140 g | 5 oz soft light brown sugar
2 medium pears, peeled, cored and roughly chopped
70 g | 2½ oz pecan nuts, roughly chopped
225 g | 8 oz plain flour

1 teaspoon bicarbonate of soda
1 teaspoon ground cinnamon
½ teaspoon freshly grated nutmeg
½ teaspoon ground cloves
a pinch of salt
2 small eggs, beaten

1 Heat the oven to 180°C | 350°F | gas mark 4. Line 10 muffin cups with paper cases or grease 10 muffin tins.

2 Melt the butter in a saucepan with the honey and sugar. Do not allow to boil.

3 Toss the pears and nuts in the butter and honey mixture.

4 Sift together the flour, bicarbonate of soda, spices and salt.

5 Add the eggs to the butter and pear mixture. Fold in the flour. Fill the muffin tins or cases to the top with the mixture.

6 Bake in the top of the oven for 35–40 minutes or until the muffins spring back when pressed lightly with a fingertip. Transfer to a wire rack and leave to cool.

Banana Pecan Muffin Tops

Muffin tops are baked in individual Yorkshire Pudding tins and are for those who like the tops of muffins best.

MAKES 8

For the topping	For the muffins
85 g⎮3 oz plain flour	170 g⎮6 oz ripe bananas (peeled weight)
a pinch of salt	140 g⎮5 oz caster sugar
55 g⎮2 oz butter	85 g⎮3 oz butter, melted and cooled
45 g⎮1½ oz caster sugar	2 eggs, beaten
50 g⎮1¾ oz pecan nuts, chopped	225 g⎮8 oz self-raising flour
	½ teaspoon bicarbonate of soda
	55 ml⎮2 fl oz milk
	50 g⎮1¾ oz pecan nuts, chopped

1 For the topping, sift the flour with the salt into a large bowl. Cut the butter into 1 cm⎮½ in cubes and toss into the flour. Rub in with your fingertips until the mixture starts to clump together then stir in the sugar and nuts. Set aside.

2 Heat the oven to 190°C⎮375°F⎮gas mark 5. Lightly oil 8 × 10 cm⎮4 in Yorkshire Pudding tins and line the bases with baking parchment.

3 Mash the banana with a potato masher or fork in a large bowl. Stir in the sugar, butter and eggs.

4 Sift the flour and bicarbonate of soda over the banana mixture and fold in along with the milk. Fold in the nuts. Take care not to overstir the mixture.

5 Divide the batter between the Yorkshire Pudding tins and smooth the tops. Sprinkle with the topping mixture.

6 Bake in the centre of the oven for 15–18 minutes or until risen and golden-brown. A skewer inserted in the centre should come out clean.

7 Cool on a wire rack for 5 minutes, then run a knife around the edge of each muffin to release it from the tin. Place on to a wire rack to cool.

NOTE: If all the tins will not fit on one shelf at the same time, place some on the lower shelf then transfer these to the centre shelf to finish baking when the first tray of muffins is done.

Cakes: Points to Remember

- Set the oven to the correct temperature before starting to mix the cake.
- Turn the oven fan off if possible.
- Place the oven shelf at the right level, in the middle of the oven.
- Place an oven thermometer in the middle of the oven.
- Use the size of tin called for in the recipe and prepare it as specified.
- Weigh and measure all the ingredients.
- Ensure your ingredients are at the correct temperature. Use room-temperature eggs.
- Sift the flour with the raising agents.

Cakes

Since the most primitive people in the world first discovered how to mill flour they made cakes, although these are not cakes we would recognise today. Grain was roughly crushed, mixed with water or milk, shaped and cooked on a hot stone. Oatcakes are a good example of this: although they are called cakes, they are more recognisable to us today as biscuits. The words bread and cake are of Anglo-Saxon origin, and indeed cakes and bread were interchangeable, the smaller breads often being called cakes.

By the middle of the eighteenth century eggs were used in cakes as a raising agent rather than yeast. For a long time, cakes had been baked for special occasions, and the wealthier you were the more often you would eat cake. However, after the industrial revolution baking ingredients became more affordable and readily available because of mass production and better communications. Bicarbonate of soda and baking powder were introduced as raising agents. Easy access to sugar, butter, flour and eggs meant that classic cakes like the Victoria Sandwich made frequent appearances at the tea table. Before tea was introduced in Britain in the mid-1600s the main meals were breakfast and dinner, but in the early 1800s the Duchess of Bedford decided to invite friends to join her for tea at five o'clock in the afternoon, where sandwiches, small cakes and tea would be served. Other society hostesses started adopting this practice and afternoon tea was born as a separate meal.

A cake mixture is essentially a batter with a high proportion of fat, sugar and eggs in relation to flour. Careful weighing and measuring, using the correct utensils and equipment, not rushing the process, precise oven temperatures and careful timing all contribute towards good results. When the cake mixture goes into the oven the air beaten into it will expand and the raising agents, for example baking powder, will form carbon dioxide gas. As the cake bakes, strands of protein called gluten, present in the flour, are stretched by the gas given off until the heat cooks and firms the cake. The amount of enriching ingredients such as fat, sugar and eggs will soften the gluten, causing cakes to have a tender texture. Fatless cakes, such as Swiss rolls, have a more open and tougher texture than a Victoria Sandwich, which has a high proportion of fat.

Before starting to make the cake, always weigh out all the ingredients, prepare the cake tin and heat the oven. Cakes are better cooked in a conventional, non-fan oven. A fan can drive the moisture from a cake and give a dry result. So, if possible, turn the fan off or refer to the manufacturer's instructions as to what temperature to use. It may need to be set 10, 20 or even 30 degrees lower than a conventional oven. If this is not possible, buy an oven thermometer to ensure accuracy. They are relatively inexpensive. If the cake is to be cooked for a long time in the oven, protect it by wrapping several layers of newspaper around the outside of the tin and, if you are using a small oven which has a tendency to get hot on the bottom, place the cake on a newspaper whilst baking. This will help to stop the bottom from burning.

If substituting a round tin for a square tin, or vice versa, always allow a difference of 2.5 cm | 1 in. That is, if going from square to round, use a round tin that is 2.5 cm | 1 in bigger than the square tin mentioned in the recipe, if using a square tin rather than a round tin, use one that is 2.5 cm | 1 in smaller.

Cake Ingredients

Fats

Fats have the effect of shortening the cake mixture. This means that when the fat is distributed throughout the mixture it shortens the strands of gluten by coating the flour molecules. This protects the protein in the flour from the liquid in the batter which causes the gluten to form long strands.

Butter gives the best flavour to cakes. It should be used softened, but not melted for creamed cakes. In this way the fat will hold air. Margarine, particularly the soft tub variety, can be used for speed and is also cheaper, but it doesn't have the flavour of butter. Spreads and low-fat margarines cannot be used in cakes. Vegetable shortenings are flavourless but give a light result.

Lard produces a crumbly and soft result. It is rarely used in cakes but there are some notable exceptions such as Lardy Cake. Lard is also the best fat to use for greasing tins (see page 276).

Vegetable oil is sometimes used in cake-making, particularly in American recipes. It can give a very tender result and the cakes have a moist but dense crumb. This is because the oil cannot be beaten to incorporate air into the cake.

Flour (see also *Flour*, page 11)

The best type of flour to use in cake-making is plain white flour or self-raising flour, as specified in the recipe. Cake flour, a low-gluten flour, is available in some countries and is ideal for both cakes and shortcrust pastries. The high proportion of low-gluten wheat in European flour makes it particularly suitable for cake-making. Too high a content of gluten in the flour would produce a tough chewy, cake, so strong bread flour is unsuitable to use in cake-making. Self-raising wholemeal flour can be used in cake making. It is often combined in the recipe with white self-raising flour. If it is the only flour in the recipe it will produce a very dense, heavy cake.

Kneading or beating a dough or mixture strengthens or toughens the gluten. Whilst this is important in bread-making it is not wanted in cake-making. When mixing the cake, the flour should be folded in gently so as not to strengthen the gluten. Vigorous mixing of the cake once the flour has been added, or over folding of the flour will produce a cake with a tough texture.

Self-raising flour has raising agents added to it and should only be used when specified in a recipe. All flour, even if labelled 'ready-sifted', should be sifted before use to eliminate lumps and to incorporate air.

Eggs

Unless otherwise specified, the eggs used in this book are medium eggs weighing 55 g| 2 oz. Eggs give flavour, colour and volume to a cake. They also constitute part of the liquid. Eggs, when beaten with sugar, help the cake to rise. Sponges made by this method are usually very light. However, when eggs are used in creamed or melted cakes other forms of chemical raising agents are necessary.

Eggs should be used at room temperature. If used straight from the refrigerator, they cool the butter and cause the mixture to curdle. This will result in a badly risen cake that is coarse and tough in texture. If the eggs are too cold, bring them up to room temperature by putting them, in their shells, in a bowl of warm but not hot water for a few minutes before using.

Raising Agents

Beating butter and sugar together, whisking eggs or sifting flour incorporates air into the cake mixture. The liquid in the wet batter turns to steam during the baking process. Both the expansion of the beaten-in air and the liquid turning to steam help the cake to rise. However, sometimes this will not be enough for the cake to rise sufficiently. This depends on the mixture of ingredients in the recipe and the method used to make the cake. So a chemical leavening can be used.

Bicarbonate of soda

Bicarbonate of soda is a white powder which is an alkali. When it is mixed with an acid it produces carbon dioxide gas. This causes the cake to rise in the oven and the heat in the oven sets the structure of the cake. When the cake cools the carbon dioxide is replaced by air. Other ingredients in a cake that will cause this chemical reaction when mixed with bicarbonate of soda are cream of tartar, sour milk, buttermilk, vinegar, soured cream, natural yoghurt and the natural acids in honey, treacle and fresh milk.

When using bicarbonate of soda, it is important to get the cake into the oven as quickly as possible in order to capture this chemical reaction in the cake and make it rise. Too much bicarbonate of soda can give an unpleasant flavour as well as an orangey-yellow colour. For this reason bicarbonate of soda is usually used in strong-tasting cakes such as gingerbread.

Baking powder

Baking powder in its commercial form is a white powder that is a mixture of sodium phosphate, an acid (usually cream of tartar) and a filler such as cornflour to keep the mixture dry. The chemical reaction created by baking powder is activated when it is mixed with liquid, so cakes made with baking powder also need to be mixed quickly and put into the oven immediately. In the US, a double-action baking powder, which has a second, heat-activated reaction, is available.

Too much baking powder in a recipe will produce a cake with an 'off' taste. The amount used should not exceed 2 teaspoons per 115 g|4 oz flour. Baking powder is perishable, so if in doubt about its efficacy, mix 1 teaspoon with 55 ml|2 fl oz hot water. It should bubble vigorously.

To make self-raising flour, add 4 level teaspoons baking powder to 250 g|9 oz plain flour.

Yeast

Yeast is used in some cakes as a raising agent. It is particularly popular in Germanic or Eastern European cakes, but is also found in some British cakes such as Lardy Cake or Tea Cakes. However, these are classified as sweetened, enriched breads (see **Sweet Yeast Breads and Rolls**, page 591, and **Pâtisserie**, page 143).

Sugars

Sugar sweetens a cake and helps it to brown. It also interferes with the development of gluten and so keeps the cake tender.

Caster sugar is the best sugar for creamed cakes. It produces a light texture when creamed with the fat to produce air. Granulated sugar can give a speckled appearance to the finished cake, but can be ground down in a food processor or liquidizer and then used. Icing sugar is not suitable as the smooth surface of the individual grains cannot hold tiny air bubbles.

Golden caster sugar, an unrefined, raw cane sugar, will give a richer, slightly caramelized flavour to a cake. The darker brown sugars, such as the soft brown sugars (light or dark), give colour and flavour to gingerbreads or rich fruit cakes, but would give a sponge cake too strong a taste of caramel. Muscovado sugar (also available as light or dark) is made from unrefined (raw) cane sugar and has a fine flavour.

Cakes made by the melting method are often sweetened with golden syrup, treacle, molasses or honey instead of sugar. They are baked quite slowly as they can caramelize and burn at higher temperatures.

Preparing a Cake Tin

All tins, even non-stick ones, should be greased and/or lined to prevent the food from sticking or burning around the sides or on the base. Melted lard is the best fat to use for greasing, as it is clean and unlikely to stick. Vegetable oil can also be used, but it does tend to leave a yellow deposit on the tin which needs to be cleaned well to avoid build-up. Butter is sometimes suggested to help form a crust on the sides of the cake.

Always melt solid fats before using for greasing, because much less will be required and it will form a more even layer. Thickly greased cake tins have a tendency to 'fry' cakes on their outside crust. Use a pastry brush or a piece of absorbent paper dipped into fat or oil to get a thin layer.

Loaf tins only need to be greased, although it is occasionally suggested that the tins are dusted with flour as well or lined with baking parchment.

Creamed cakes or melting-method cakes should be put into tins which have been greased and the base lined with a piece of greaseproof paper or baking parchment cut to fit. To cut the paper accurately, draw around the tin (a) and cut just inside the line. (b) Whisked cakes are put into tins which have been greased and lined then dusted with a layer of caster sugar and flour.

Lining a cake tin (a)

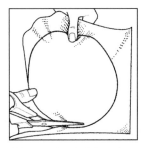
Lining a cake tin (b)

For fruit cakes and other cakes that are to be baked for a long time and need extra protection, line the base and sides with greaseproof paper or baking parchment as follows:

1 Cut 2 pieces of greaseproof paper or baking parchment to fit the base of the tin.
2 Cut 2 pieces of greaseproof paper or baking parchment long enough to go right round the sides of the tin and to overlap slightly. They should be 3.5 cm | 1½ in deeper than the height of the cake tin.
3 Place 1 long strip on top of the other and fold one long edge of this double strip over 2.5 cm | 1 in all the way along its length.
4 Cut snips at 45° angles from the edge to the folded line, about 2.5 cm | 1 in apart, all along the long, folded side. The snips should just reach the fold. (a)
5 Grease the tin with melted lard or oil, place 1 paper base in the bottom and grease again.
6 Fit the long strip inside the tin with the folded, cut edge on the bottom (the flanges should overlap slightly) and the main, uncut part lining the sides of the tin. Press well into the base (and corners if using a square tin).
7 Grease the paper and lay the second base on top of the flanges of paper. (b)
8 Brush the base again with more lard or oil.

Lining a fruit cake tin (a)

Lining a fruit cake tin (b)

9 Once the cake mixture is in the tin it is wise to wrap several layers of newspaper around the outside of the tin and secure it with string. The newspaper should come 2.5 cm | 1 in above the tin. This extra wrapping may mean that the cake will take longer to bake, but it will be less likely to burn.

Instead of using greaseproof paper it is possible to use non-stick baking paper, baking parchment or silicone non-stick paper. These are all names of paper that can be used without the need to grease, however some recipes require greased greaseproof paper rather than silicone-coated baking parchment (see *Whisking method*, page 281). The cakes will come off easily and, as there is no need to grease the tins, the washing-up is easier too. However, you may find that if using baking parchment for a rich fruit cake where the tin needs to be lined as described above, greasing the tin first will help the paper to stick to the tin.

Also available on the market now are parchment liners for both loaf tins and round cake tins. These work well but, because they are fluted, can give the finished cake a 'shop-bought' look. Ready-cut parchment circles in different diameters are also available. For something more permanent, reusable tin liners can be used, washed and used again.

Methods of Cake-making

There are 4 main different methods used in making cakes. All give a different texture to the finished cake.

Rubbing-in Method

The fat is rubbed into the flour as for pastry. This can be done with the fingertips or with a food processor. Eggs and sometimes milk are added. The raising agent will usually be either self-raising flour, baking powder or bicarbonate of soda. The resulting cake has a crumbly, dense texture, for example scones and rock cakes.

Rubbing-in Method Cakes: Points to Remember.

- The fats should be cold, as for pastry.
- Add the liquid quickly.
- Put into the oven as quickly as possible.

Rubbed-in Method Cakes: What has gone wrong when . . .

The cakes are heavy and badly risen.

- The cakes were not put into the oven quickly enough.
- The mixture was too dry.
- The cakes are tough.
- The mixture was overworked.

Melting Method

The fat, sugar and/or syrup are heated gently in a saucepan and then allowed to cool. The flour and other dry ingredients are sifted together into the cooled, melted mixture and any other liquids, for example milk and eggs, are stirred in carefully. The raising agent is often bicarbonate of soda. These cakes are very easy to make and have a moist, heavy texture. They have excellent keeping qualities, for example *Black Sticky Gingerbread* (see page 322).

Melting-method Cakes: Points to Remember

- Let the melted sugar and fat cool to room temperature before adding the eggs or the eggs will cook in the heat.
- Sift the dry ingredients together thoroughly.
- Work quickly when folding the dry ingredients into the wet ingredients and put the cake into the oven as quickly as possible.

Melting-method Cakes: What has gone wrong when . . .

The cake sinks in the middle.
- The oven door was opened before the cake was set.
- The cake is underbaked.

The surface of the cake is covered with little holes.
- The cake was not placed into the oven quickly enough.
- The oven temperature was too low.
- The bicarbonate of soda was not mixed into the flour well enough.

The top of the cake is thick and crusty.
- The oven temperature was too high.
- The cake is overbaked.

The top of the cake is domed and cracked.
- The oven temperature was too high.

The cake has a sour flavour and/or a greenish tinge.
- Too much bicarbonate of soda was used.

Creaming Method

Softened butter and sugar are beaten together to form a light, creamy consistency, then eggs are beaten in gradually; if they are added too fast the mixture can curdle. If the mixture has curdled it will look separated and lumpy. A badly curdled mixture will affect the finished texture of the cake, making it coarser. Use eggs that are at room temperature, as cold eggs straight from the refrigerator will cool the butter and make the mixture more likely to curdle. If there are signs that this is happening, add a tablespoonful of the measured-out flour. However, if attempts at rescuing the cake are failing then add the flour quickly and get the cake in the oven, as if the curdled mixture is left to stand it will continue to separate. Finally the flour is folded in. A creamed cake mixture ready to bake is often described as 'of dropping consistency'. This means that a tablespoon of the mixture will fall off the spoon rather reluctantly and in a single blob. If it runs off the spoon it is too wet, and if it will not fall off, even when the spoon is jerked slightly, it is too dry. Add a little more flour if it is too wet and a little warm water if it is too dry.

All-in-one cakes are an adaptation of creamed cakes. All the ingredients are beaten together with a strong electric mixer. Ensure the butter is soft before use or use tub margarine. In creamed cakes the raising agents are the air beaten into the cake, the raising agent in the self-raising flour and the expansive properties of the eggs. Examples are *Victoria Sandwich* (see page 286) and rich fruit cakes.

Creaming-method Cakes: Points to Remember

- Make sure the butter is softened and the eggs are at room temperature.
- Cream the butter and sugar very well before adding the eggs.
- The eggs must be added a little at a time to give the mixture less chance to curdle.
- Fold in quickly with a large metal spoon.
- If dividing into sandwich tins, make sure the mixture is divided evenly and spread flat.

Creaming-method Cakes: What has gone wrong when . . .

The cake has risen a little but has a dense, heavy texture.
- The eggs were added too quickly and the mixture has curdled.
- The mixture was overfolded when the flour was added.

The cake is flat and dense.
- No raising agent was included in the mixture.

The cake has tiny holes on the surface.
- The cake was not put into the oven quickly enough.
- The oven temperature was too low.

The base and sides of the cake are damp and soggy.
- The cake was left in the tin to cool.

The cake is domed and/or cracked in the centre.
- The oven temperature was too high.
- The tin size was too small.
- Too much raising agent was used.

The cake has sunk in the middle.
- The cake was underbaked.
- The oven door was opened before the cake was set.

The edges of the cakes are thick and crunchy.
- Too much oil was used to coat the tin.

Whisking Method

The eggs and sugar are whisked together, sometimes over heat, until the mixture is light and thick and leaves a ribbon trail once the beaters are lifted. If it is being whisked over steaming water it is important not to allow the water to touch the bowl or the eggs will become too hot and the protein in them will start to cook. They then lose all their elasticity. The gentle heat speeds up the dissolving of the sugar and slightly thickens the eggs, encouraging the mixture to hold thousands of tiny air bubbles. The mixture gets lighter and lighter both in texture and colour and will increase to about 4 times its original volume. Once this stage is reached, the bowl should be removed from the heat and the whisking continued until the bowl and the mixture have cooled down. If the flour is added when the mixture is too hot, the flour will cook on contact and a very thick mixture will be produced that will not rise and will look like a large biscuit once cooked.

The raising agent is the trapped air which causes the cake to rise in the heat of the oven. The simplest whisked sponge contains no fat. Sifted flour is gently folded into the whisked eggs and sugar so that as much air as possible is retained. For a *Génoise* (see page 296), some melted – but not hot – butter is folded into the mixture. In a lighter but more complicated whisked sponge, the eggs are separated and the whites are whisked in a separate bowl, sometimes with a little sugar added to make a meringue. This is then folded into the yolks, remaining sugar and flour to make a more stable mixture. An angel cake is made using egg whites and does not contain any fat.

If the mixture is underwhisked, the cake will not rise well. If it is overwhisked the cake will be tough. Folding in the flour is important too: use a large metal spoon for this. The thin edge cuts through the mixture, knocking out little volume. If overfolded, the air will be knocked out, resulting in a flat cake; if underfolded, pockets of flour will remain, spoiling the finished cake. The mixture is poured into the tin and should find its own level. Put it into the centre of the oven to bake and do not disturb for 25 minutes. Whisked sponges are the most likely to collapse if the oven door is opened too early. When the cake is cooked it should look risen, golden-brown and slightly wrinkled around the edges. It will spring back when touched in the centre by a fingertip, and you will hear a slight popping or creaking sound coming from the cake. Once the cake is out of the oven, loosen the sides and turn it upside down on to a wire rack. Leave the tin over it for 10 minutes. This allows the texture of the cake to set. Once the tin is cool enough to touch, remove it and peel away the lining paper to allow the steam to escape. If the cake has been cooked in a *moule à manqué* tin, the cake is served upside down, i.e. the side with the smallest diameter at the top.

Occasionally whisked sponges include a little baking powder to ensure success, but a classic whisked sponge or *Génoise* has only the whisked in, trapped air as its raising agent. Whisked sponges are light and springy but they go stale quickly. A *Génoise*, because of the butter, will keep for a day or two longer. Both cakes freeze successfully.

- Line the tin with a disc of greaseproof paper cut to fit and lightly greased with oil and dusted wth caster sugar and flour.
- Sift the flour at least 3 times to get in as much air as possible.
- Whisk the eggs and sugar over heat until very light in colour and texture.
- Allow the mixture and the bowl to cool off the heat while continuing to whisk.
- Once the mixture is holding a trail and has cooled down, fold in the flour quickly using a large metal spoon and figure-of-eight movements. Do not overfold.
- Pour into the prepared tin and move the tin to level the cake. Don't spread the mixture as it will lose volume.
- Put into the oven as quickly as possible.
- Leave the oven door closed until just before the cooking time is up. Opening the door too early will cause the cake to collapse.

Whisking-method Cakes: What has gone wrong when . . .

The egg and sugar mixture fails to double in volume.
- The water underneath the bowl is not hot enough.
- The mixture has not been whisked for long enough.

The egg and sugar mixture cooks around the edge of the bowl.
- The water underneath the bowl is too hot.

The cake has bubbles on the surface.
- The oven was not hot enough.

The cake is badly risen.
- The eggs weren't whisked enough or they were whisked too much and collapsed before the flour was added.
- The mixture was overfolded when the flour and/or butter were added.

The cake is badly risen and has a very hard crust.
- The egg and sugar mixture was too hot when the flour was folded in.

There are pockets of flour in the cake.
- The flour was not folded in well enough.
- The butter was not folded into the cake before the flour, so the flour formed lumps with some of the butter.

The cake has a greasy, dense layer at the bottom.
- The eggs and sugar weren't whisked enough before the butter was added.
- The butter wasn't folded in well enough.
- The butter was too cool and thick.

Other Methods

Boiling method

This is an old-fashioned method used for fruit cakes. It does not mean the cake itself is boiled rather than baked, but that some of the ingredients are brought to the boil together prior to baking. Usually butter, sugar, dried fruit and any liquid are brought to the boil and then allowed to cool before any other ingredients are added. Then the eggs, flour and spices are simply stirred in. This method produces a very rich cake with plump fruit which has good keeping qualities. An example of this type of cake is *Old-fashioned Boiled Fruit Cake* (see page 388).

Yeast method

Many European-style cakes use yeast to raise the cake. They often have a high fat, sugar and fruit content. Because both butter and sugar affect the rising effect (proving) of the yeast, the texture of these cakes will be both closer to and softer than that of bread. The mixture often takes a while to rise or prove in the tin but once put in the oven will give a final fast rise before the yeast is killed by the heat. Examples of cakes using yeast are *Gugelhopf*, *Panettone* and *Stollen* (see pages 603, 615 and 613).

To Test When a Cake is Cooked

When checking whether a cake is done, test it while the cake is still in the oven and as quickly as possible. If a cake is removed from the oven before it is ready it will sink in the middle.

A sponge cake is ready when the sides have shrunk away slightly from the sides of the tin and the cake feels firm to the touch and springs back when pressed lightly with a fingertip. It should not be necessary to insert a skewer or knife.

A rich fruit cake is ready when the top feels firm to the touch and when a small sharp knife or skewer inserted at an angle into the centre of the cake to the base comes out clean. The knife or skewer should be moist but have no uncooked mixture on it.

A melted-method cake can be tested by pressing with a fingertip and inserting a knife or skewer.

A whisked cake should be risen, golden-brown and slightly coming away from the edges. If you listen carefully you can hear creaking or popping noises coming from the cake. If pressed lightly on the top with a fingertip, the top should spring back.

A yeast-risen cake is ready when it sounds hollow when tapped on the underside, although something like a gugelhopf can be tested by inserting a knife or skewer.

Cooling Cakes

Most cakes benefit from being left in the tin for a few minutes before they are turned out. This helps to prevent the possibility of the cakes collapsing. However, sponge cakes will become soggy if they are left to cool completely in the tin and should be turned out on to a wire rack after 5–10 minutes. Rich fruit cakes should be cooled completely in the tin as they are heavy and fragile when hot. Placing the tin on a wire rack will speed up the cooling process. Yeast cakes, cakes and buns cooked on a baking sheet can be removed immediately and placed on a wire rack to cool.

Turning Out Cakes

If the tin is properly greased and lined or baking parchment has been used there should be no problem with turning out the cake. With sponge cakes, after the initial cooling in the tin, run a round-bladed knife carefully around the edge, avoiding cutting into the crust. Invert the tin and turn the cake out, then quickly but carefully peel off the lining paper and put the cake the right way up (crust side on top) on to a wire rack.

A rich fruit cake can be left in its lining paper after turning out, if it is to be stored for any length of time.

A cake baked in a *moule à manqué* tin is always served upside down (with the crust on the bottom).

A cake baked in a loose-bottomed tin can be removed by placing the tin on top of a container of a smaller diameter. The sides of the cake tin will fall down, leaving the cake just on the base. Simply remove the base with the aid of a palette knife.

A spring-form tin has a clip on the side which when unclipped loosens the sides away from the cake, making it easier to lift off. Make sure no part of the cake is sticking to the sides before doing this, then remove the base with a palette knife.

In most cases, if a cake is to be cooled quickly the lining paper can be removed immediately, but it will not matter if it is left on until the cake is cold.

Splitting a Cake into Layers

Some cake recipes require a cake to be split into 2 or 3 layers before sandwiching together with a filling. This can be tricky if the cake is thin and fragile. The following points should help to achieve neat and even layers:

1 Use a large bread knife or a serrated-edged knife.
2 Place the cake on a board or flat surface (not a plate).
3 Cut a horizontal groove in the side of the cake and place two cocktail sticks in the side, one above the groove and one below it. This will help to line up the cake later.
4 Place your hand flat over the surface of the cake and, using the centre of the blade of the knife, cut through very carefully with a sawing action. Use a long knife so the pointed end of the knife can be seen on the far side of the cake. Do not turn the cake around as you work.
5 A day-old *Génoise* can be cut into layers using a long piece of cotton thread (a fresh Génoise will tear instead of cut with this method). Cut a groove as described above and place the thread in the groove and around the cake. Cross the ends over and pull gently.

Freezing and Storing Cakes

All cakes can be stored for a time in a tin or plastic box. Depending on the type this will vary from a couple of days to a couple of weeks. Whisked fatless sponges stale the quickest but can be stored in the freezer. Creamed cakes also begin to stale after a few days but can be frozen very successfully. This is very handy if batch-baking. Most cakes freeze well. However, if an iced cake is frozen, the icing can weep a little when it defrosts. It is not advisable to freeze cakes covered with fondant icing or royal icing. Cakes with glacé icing can be frozen but they will lose their glossy finish when defrosted.

Rich fruit cakes wrapped and stored in an airtight tin keep perfectly well and so do not require freezing. Generally cakes made using the melting method will improve with keeping and will keep in an airtight container for up to 2 weeks. They will also freeze very successfully.

Any cake that is to be frozen can be open-frozen first, that is placed in the freezer uncovered. Once the cake has frozen it must be put into a freezer bag, wrapped in kitchen foil or placed in a plastic freezer box. It should be well-wrapped to prevent the cold air in the freezer getting to it and causing freezer burn. All cakes can be kept in the freezer for up to 3 months, after which they will start to become dry.

Classic Cakes

This section is made up of classic, basic recipes, some more elaborate ones for special occasions and a selection of old favourites. It is impossible to include every classic cake, but these are among the best.

Victoria Sandwich

This basic recipe for a creamed sponge cake can also be used to fill individual paper cake cases or tins for fairy cakes and butterfly cakes.

MAKES A 15 CM|6 IN CAKE

115 g|4 oz butter, softened
115 g|4 oz caster sugar
2 room-temperature eggs, beaten
115 g|4 oz self-raising flour, sifted
1–2 tablespoons water

To finish
2 tablespoons seedless raspberry jam
caster sugar

1 Heat the oven to 190°C|375°F|gas mark 5.

2 Lightly grease 2 × 15 cm|6 in sandwich tins and line the base of each with a disc of baking parchment.

3 Cream the butter and sugar together in a mixing bowl until pale and fluffy.

4 Beat the eggs gradually into the creamed mixture, beating well after each addition. Add 1 tablespoon of the flour if necessary, to prevent the mixture from curdling.

5 Using a large metal spoon, fold in the remaining flour, adding enough water to bring the mixture to a reluctant dropping consistency. Divide the mixture between the prepared tins.

6 Bake in the centre of the oven for about 20 minutes or until the cakes are well-risen, golden and feel spongy to the fingertips.

7 Remove the cakes from the oven and allow them to cool in the tins for a few minutes, then turn out on to a wire rack and leave to cool completely.

8 When the cakes are cold, sandwich them together with raspberry jam. Dust the top with caster sugar.

NOTE: For more information on creaming-method cakes, see page 279.

Battenburg Cake

This old-fashioned cake, named after Prince Henry of Battenburg, is really worth making. It is far better than the shop-bought variety, which tends to be rather dry.

MAKES A 20 CM│8 IN LOAF

170 g│6 oz self-raising flour, sifted
1½ teaspoons baking powder
170 g│6 oz butter, softened
170 g│6 oz caster sugar
3 large room-temperature eggs, lightly beaten

3 tablespoons lukewarm water
red food colouring
1 recipe marzipan paste (see page 000)
4 tablespoons apricot jam

1 Heat the oven to 190°C│375°F│gas mark 5. Grease 2 × 450 g│1 lb loaf tins and line the base of each with a piece of baking parchment.

2 Sift the flour with the baking powder. Cream the butter in a mixing bowl, add the sugar and beat together until pale and fluffy. Add the eggs gradually, beating well after each addition. Using a large metal spoon, fold in the remaining flour with the baking powder and add the water to achieve a softish dropping consistency.

3 Divide the mixture in half. Place one half in one of the prepared tins. Add 4–6 drops of red food colouring to the other half until the mixture is very pink. Place in the other prepared tin.

4 Bake in the centre of the oven for about 35 minutes or until the sides of the cakes start to shrink away from the tins and the tops spring back when pressed lightly.

5 Remove the cakes from the oven and allow to cool in the tins for 5 minutes, then turn out on to a wire rack and leave to cool completely.

6 Meanwhile, make the marzipan paste.

7 When the cakes are cold, trim them and cut each in half lengthways, to give 4 pieces all the same size.

8 Spread each piece with apricot jam and sandwich together in pairs, to give a chequer-board effect. Spread the long sides but not the ends of the cake with jam.

9 Roll out the marzipan quite thinly. Cut to size and encase the cake with the marzipan. Leave the ends uncovered. Trim neatly.

NOTE: For more information on creaming-method cakes, see page 279.

Madeira Cake

MAKES A 17 CM | 7 IN CAKE

170 g | 6 oz unsalted butter, softened

170 g | 6 oz caster sugar

grated zest and juice of 1 lemon

a pinch of ground cinnamon

3 room-temperature eggs, beaten

115 g | 4 oz self-raising flour

55 g | 2 oz ground almonds

milk (optional)

1 Grease a 17 cm | 7 in cake tin and line the base with a disc of baking parchment.
2 Heat the oven to 170°C | 325°F | gas mark 3.
3 Cream the butter in a mixing bowl until soft. Beat in the sugar until pale and fluffy. Add the lemon zest and cinnamon.
4 Add the eggs gradually, beating well after each addition. Add a little of the flour if necessary to prevent the mixture from curdling. Add the lemon juice.
5 Using a large metal spoon, fold in the remaining flour and the ground almonds.
6 Add enough milk to bring the mixture to a dropping consistency (it should drop rather than run off the spoon).
7 Spoon the mixture into the prepared tin and spread out evenly with a palette knife or spatula.
8 Bake in the centre of the oven for 1¼ hours or until the top springs back when pressed lightly with a fingertip. Remove the cake from the oven and allow to cool in the tin for 10 minutes, then gently ease it out on to a wire rack and leave to cool completely.

NOTE: For more information on creaming-method cakes, see page 279.

Sand Cake

MAKES A 450 G | 1 LB LOAF

8 ratafia or amaretti biscuits, crushed

115 g | 4 oz butter, softened

115 g | 4 oz caster sugar

grated zest of 1 lemon

2 room-temperature eggs, beaten

115 g | 4 oz cornflour

15 g | ½ oz ground rice

½ teaspoon baking powder

To finish

icing sugar for dusting

1 Heat the oven to 180°C | 350°F | gas mark 4. Prepare a 450 g | 1 lb loaf tin by greasing well with melted butter and dusting with crushed ratafia biscuits.
2 Cream the butter and sugar together until pale and fluffy. Add the lemon zest.
3 Add the eggs a little at a time, beating well between each addition.
4 Sift the cornflour, ground rice and baking powder together and add to the cake mixture.

Fold in carefully and turn into the prepared tin. Bake in the centre of the oven for 20 minutes. Turn the oven down to 170°C│325°F│gas mark 3 and cover with a piece of damp greaseproof paper. Continue to cook for another 25–30 minutes. It is ready when the top springs back when lightly pressed.

5 Remove from the oven and leave to cool in the tin for 5 minutes before turning out to cool on a wire rack. When cold, dust with sieved icing sugar.

NOTE: For more information on creaming-method cakes, see page 279.

Seed Cake

MAKES A 20 CM│8 IN CAKE

225 g│8 oz butter, softened
170 g│6 oz caster sugar
3 room-temperature eggs, beaten
225 g│8 oz self-raising flour
½ teaspoon ground mace

½ teaspoon freshly grated nutmeg
2 teaspoons caraway seeds
2 tablespoons brandy (optional)
1½ tablespoons water

1 Heat the oven to 180°C│350°F│gas mark 4. Grease a deep 20 cm│8 in cake tin and line the base with a disc of baking parchment.

2 Cream the butter and sugar together in a mixing bowl until pale and fluffy. Add the eggs gradually, beating well after each addition. Add a little of the flour if necessary, to prevent the mixture from curdling.

3 Sift together the remaining flour, mace and nutmeg and fold into the cake mixture, using a large metal spoon. Stir in the caraway seeds and brandy, if using, and water. Turn the mixture into the prepared cake tin and spread out evenly.

4 Bake in the centre of the oven for about 45 minutes or until the sides of the cake start to shrink away from the tin and the top springs back when pressed lightly with a fingertip.

5 Remove the cake from the oven and allow to cool in the tin for a few minutes, then turn out on to a wire rack and leave to cool completely.

NOTE: For more information on creaming-method cakes, see page 279.

American Carrot Cake

MAKES A 2-LAYER 20 CM|8 IN CAKE

250 ml|9 fl oz vegetable oil

4 room-temperature eggs, beaten

225 g|8 oz soft light brown sugar

140 g|5 oz carrots, peeled and finely grated

225 g|8 oz self-raising flour

½ teaspoon bicarbonate of soda

1½ teaspoons ground cinnamon

½ teaspoon ground ginger

140 g|5 oz walnuts, chopped

For the icing

45 g|1½ oz unsalted butter, softened

170 g|6 oz good quality full-fat cream cheese

300 g|10½ oz icing sugar

1 teaspoon vanilla essence

lemon juice to taste

To decorate (optional)

8 walnut halves

1 Heat the oven to 180°C|350°F|gas mark 4. Line 2 × 20 cm|8 in sandwich tins with baking parchment.

2 In a bowl, stir together the oil, eggs, sugar and carrots.

3 Sift the flour, bicarbonate of soda, cinnamon and ginger into a large bowl.

4 Fold the 2 mixtures together then fold in the walnuts.

5 Divide between the 2 tins and bake in the centre of the oven for 25 minutes or until the cakes spring back when pressed lightly in the centre.

6 Cool on a wire rack for 10 minutes in the tin, then turn out and cool completely.

7 To make the icing, beat the butter and cream cheese together until smooth. Sift the icing sugar over the top and stir in. Flavour with vanilla and lemon juice.

8 Use the icing to fill the cake and ice the top. Decorate with walnut halves, if desired.

Marmalade Cake

The flavour of this cake will vary depending on which marmalade is used. A thick-cut, old-fashioned marmalade is recommended. To vary it even more, try using a lemon or lime marmalade and put lemon or lime zest and juice in the cake instead of orange.

MAKES A 20 CM|8 IN CAKE

170 g|6 oz butter, softened

85 g|3 oz soft light brown sugar

2 room-temperature eggs, beaten

grated zest of 1 orange

2 tablespoons orange juice

6 level tablespoons marmalade

115 g|4 oz raisins

225 g|8 oz self-raising flour

1 Heat the oven to 180°C|350°F|gas mark 4. Grease and line the base of a deep 20 cm|8 in round tin with a disc of baking parchment.

2 Using an electric beater, cream the butter and sugar together until pale and fluffy. Add

the eggs gradually, beating well between each addition. Mix in the orange zest and juice.

3 Add the marmalade and raisins and finally fold in the sifted flour. Tip the mixture into the prepared tin and spread flat. Place in the centre of the oven for 1 hour. A small, sharp knife inserted into the centre should come out clean when it is cooked. Leave the cake in the tin for 15 minutes before turning it out on to a wire rack to cool completely.

NOTE: For more information on creaming-method cakes, see page 279.

Plum Cake

Plum cake sounds like it should contain plums or at least prunes; however, in the seventeenth century plums referred to raisins or other fruit. This is an old-fashioned fruit cake that can be used as a Christmas cake.

MAKES A 20 CM | 8 IN CAKE

225 g | 8 oz butter, softened
225 g | 8 oz soft dark brown sugar
3 room-temperature eggs, beaten
225 g | 8 oz currants
225 g | 8 oz raisins
55 g | 2 oz ground almonds
55 g | 2 oz flaked almonds

115 g | 4 oz mixed peel
grated zest of 1 lemon
225 g | 8 oz plain flour
1 teaspoon ground cinnamon
½ teaspoon ground mace
½ teaspoon grated nutmeg
55 ml | 2 fl oz sherry

1 Heat the oven to 170°C | 325°F | gas mark 3. Line the base and sides of a 20 cm | 8 in cake tin with a double layer of baking parchment.
2 Cream the butter and sugar together until pale and fluffy. Add the eggs, a little at a time, beating well between each addition. Add the currants, raisins, ground and flaked almonds, mixed peel and grated lemon zest.
3 Sift the flour and spices and add to the cake mixture. Stir in the sherry.
4 Turn into the prepared cake tin and cook for 1½ – 2 hours. It is ready when a sharp knife inserted into the centre comes out clean. Leave the cake in the tin for 15 minutes before turning out on to a wire rack to cool completely.

NOTE: For more information on creaming-method cakes, see page 279.

Guards Cake

340 g | 12 oz plain flour

170 g | 6 oz butter, cut into cubes

115 g | 4 oz currants

115 g | 4 oz soft brown sugar

1 teaspoon ginger

1 teaspoon mixed spice

1 teaspoon cream of tartar

1 teaspoon bicarbonate of soda

a pinch of salt

1 room-temperature egg, beaten

200 ml | 7 fl oz milk

1 Grease and line a 20 cm | 8 in cake tin with a disc of baking parchment. Heat the oven to 170°C | 325°F | gas mark 3.

2 Rub the flour and butter together until they resemble fine breadcrumbs.

3 Add all the other dry ingredients and add the beaten egg and milk to make a slack dough.

4 Pour into the cake tin and bake in the centre of the oven for 50–60 minutes. It is cooked when a knife inserted into the centre comes out clean. Allow to cool in the tin for 5 minutes before turning out on to a wire rack to cool completely.

NOTE: For more information on rubbing-in method cakes, see page 278.

Honey Cake

MAKES A 900 G | 2 LB LOAF

140 g | 5 oz butter

85 g | 3 oz soft light brown sugar

140 g | 5 oz clear honey

2 room-temperature eggs, beaten

225 g | 8 oz self-raising flour, sifted

15 g | ½ oz flaked almonds

1 Heat the oven to 170°C | 325°F | gas mark 3. Grease a 900 g | 2 lb loaf tin and line the base with a piece of baking parchment.

2 Put the butter, sugar and honey into a medium saucepan and melt over a low heat. Remove from the heat and allow to cool. Beat in the eggs. Fold in the flour carefully, using a large metal spoon.

3 Pour into the prepared tin and spread out evenly. Sprinkle the surface with the almonds.

4 Bake in the centre of the oven for 45 minutes or until the top springs back when pressed lightly with a fingertip.

5 Remove from the oven and allow to cool in the tin for 10 minutes, then turn out on to a wire rack and leave to cool completely.

NOTE: For more information on melting-method cakes, see page 279.

Angel Cake

There are special angel cake tins available on the market but any cake tin can be used. A spring-form tin with a funnel base is good. An angel cake should be very light and airy, rather like a soufflé.

MAKES A 20 CM | 8 IN CAKE

85 g | 3 oz plain flour
170 g | 6 oz caster sugar
6 egg whites
1 teaspoon cream of tartar
1 teaspoon vanilla essence

To decorate (optional)

1 egg white quantity American frosting (see page 453)

1 Heat the oven to 170°C | 325°F | gas mark 3. Line the base with a disc of baking parchment of a 20 cm | 8 in spring-form tin with a funnel base.
2 Sift the flour 3 times. Sift the sugar separately. Mix together the flour and 40 g | 1½ oz sugar and sift well together.
3 Whisk the egg whites with the cream of tartar until very stiff. Add the vanilla and 2 tablespoons of the remaining sugar and whisk again until stiff and shiny. Whisk in the remaining sugar gradually until the egg whites form stiff peaks.
4 Fold the flour and sugar mixture very carefully into the egg whites, using a large metal spoon. Get rid of any large bubbles or pockets of flour, but do not overfold. Turn the mixture into the prepared tin.
5 Bake in the centre of the oven for 40 minutes or until the top springs back when pressed lightly with a fingertip.
6 Once cooked, turn the cake upside down immediately on to a wire rack. Leave to cool in the tin for 30 minutes, then remove very carefully. The cake will probably cling to the sides a little, so use a fork or knife to pull it away carefully. Leave to cool completely.
7 When the cake is cold, cover with American frosting (see page 000), if liked, or serve plain.

NOTE: For more information on whisking-method cakes, see page 281.

Lemon and Almond Angel Cake

This is a lovely light cake from Katarina Diezinger. It is low in fat.

SERVES 8–10

70 g│2½ oz blanched almonds
9 egg whites
a pinch of salt
250 g│9 oz caster sugar

125 g│4½ oz plain flour
grated zest of 1 lemon
70 g│2½ oz sultanas

1 Slice about half of the almonds and reserve for garnish. Chop the remainder finely.

2 Heat the oven to 190°C│375°F│gas mark 5. Grease and flour an angel cake tin or a 1 litre│2 lb loaf tin.

3 Beat the egg whites with the salt until stiff peaks form. Gradually beat in half the caster sugar.

4 Stir together the remaining sugar with the flour, lemon zest, sultanas and finely chopped almonds. Fold into the egg-white mixture.

5 Pile into the prepared tin and sprinkle with the sliced almonds.

6 Bake in the centre of the oven for 30–35 minutes or until golden-brown. A wooden skewer will come out clean when inserted into the cake. Cool on a wire rack in the tin for 10 minutes then loosen the edges of the cake from the tin with a sharp knife. Turn out on to a wire rack to continue cooling.

7 Slice with a serrated knife to serve.

NOTE: For more information on whisking-method cakes, see page 281.

Whisked Sponge

MAKES A 20 CM│8 IN CAKE

3 room-temperature eggs
85 g│3 oz caster sugar
1½ tablespoons lukewarm water

85 g│3 oz plain flour, sifted
a pinch of salt

1 Heat the oven to 180°C│350°F│gas mark 4. Grease a 20 cm│8 in *moule à manqué* tin and line the base with a disc of greased greaseproof paper. Dust lightly with sugar and then flour. Tap out the excess.

2 Place the eggs, sugar and water in a large, heatproof bowl and fit it over, but not in, a saucepan of gently steaming water. Whisk with an electric beater until the mixture is light, thick and fluffy.

3 Remove the bowl from the heat and continue whisking until slightly cooled.

4 Sift the flour again with the salt and, using a large metal spoon, fold it into the mixture, being careful not to beat out any of the air. Turn the mixture into the prepared tin.

5 Bake in the centre of the oven for about 30 minutes or until the sides have shrunk away from the tin slightly and look crinkled, and the cake feels firm but spongy when pressed lightly with a fingertip and sounds 'creaky'.

6 Turn the cake out on to a wire rack and leave to cool completely.

NOTE: For more information on whisking-method cakes, see page 281.

Swiss Roll

MAKES A 20 CM|8 IN ROLL

85 g|3 oz plain flour, sifted

a pinch of salt

3 room-temperature eggs

85 g|3 oz caster sugar

1½ tablespoons lukewarm water

2–3 drops of vanilla essence

To finish

caster sugar

3 tablespoons seedless jam, warm but not hot

1 Heat the oven to 190°C|375°F|gas mark 5. Grease the base and sides of a Swiss roll tin. Line the base with a piece of greased greaseproof paper. Dust lightly with caster sugar and then flour. Tap out the excess.

2 Sift the flour with the salt.

3 Place the eggs, sugar, water and vanilla essence in a large heatproof bowl and fit it over but not in a saucepan of steaming water. Whisk with an electric beater until the mixture is light, thick and fluffy.

4 Using a large metal spoon, fold the flour into the egg mixture and pour into the prepared tin.

5 Bake in the centre of the oven for 12–15 minutes until the sides have shrunk very slightly away from the tin and no impression remains when the top is pressed lightly with a fingertip.

6 Lay a piece of greaseproof paper on the work surface and sprinkle it evenly with caster sugar. Using a knife, loosen the edges of the cake, then turn it out on to the sugared greaseproof paper. Remove the lining paper and trim the edges of the cake neatly.

7 While the cake is still warm, spread it with the jam.

8 Using the paper under the cake to help you, roll the cake up tightly from one end. Making a shallow cut across the width of the cake just where you begin to roll helps.

9 Dredge the cake with caster sugar. Transfer to a wire rack and leave to cool completely.

NOTES: If the Swiss roll is to be filled with cream, it must be cooled. Roll the cake up, unfilled, and keep it wrapped in greaseproof paper until cool. Unroll carefully, spread with whipped cream and roll up again.

For more information on whisking-method cakes, see page 281.

Génoise Commune

MAKES A 20 CM|8 IN CAKE

4 room-temperature eggs

125 g|4½ oz caster sugar

55 g|2 oz butter, melted and cooled

125 g|4½ oz plain flour, sifted

1 Heat the oven to 190°C|375°F|gas mark 5. Grease a 20 cm|8 in *moule à manqué* or deep sandwich tin. Line the base with a disc of greased greaseproof paper. Dust with caster sugar and then flour. Tap out the excess.

2 Break the eggs into a large, heatproof bowl. Add the sugar. Fit the bowl over but not in a saucepan of gently simmering water. Whisk with an electric beater until the mixture has doubled in volume and will leave a ribbon trail on the surface when the whisk is lifted. Lift the bowl off the heat and continue to whisk until cool. Fold in the butter quickly; if you work slowly the cake will collapse.

3 Sift the flour over the mixture and fold it in thoroughly but gently, using a large metal spoon. Turn the mixture into the prepared tin.

4 Bake in the centre of the oven for 30–35 minutes until the top springs back when pressed lightly with a fingertip.

5 Remove the cake from the oven and allow to cool in the tin inverted on to a wire rack and leave to cool completely.

NOTE: For more information on whisking-method cakes, see page 281.

Chocolate Génoise

MAKES A 20 CM|8 IN CAKE

4 room-temperature eggs

125 g|4½ oz caster sugar

55 g|2 oz unsalted butter, melted and cooled

85 g|3 oz plain flour, sifted

30 g|1 oz cocoa powder, sifted

1 Heat the oven to 190°C|375°F|gas mark 5. Grease a 20 cm|8 in *moule à manqué* tin and line the base with a disc of greased greaseproof paper. Dust with caster sugar and then flour. Tap out any excess.

2 Place the eggs and sugar in a large, heatproof bowl and fit over, but not in, a saucepan of steaming water. Whisk with an electric beater until the mixture is light, thick and fluffy.

3 Remove the bowl from the heat and continue whisking until the mixture is cool and a ribbon trail is left when the whisk is lifted. Do not overwhisk, and stop if the mixture begins to lose bulk. Fold in the butter quickly; if you work slowly the cake will collapse.

4 Sift the flour and cocoa powder together on to the mixture and fold in, using a large metal spoon. Turn into the prepared tin and tap it lightly on the work surface to get rid of any large air pockets.

5 Bake in the centre of the oven for 25–35 minutes or until the top springs back when pressed lightly with a fingertip.

6 Remove the cake from the oven and allow to cool in the tin inverted on to a wire rack and leave to cool completely.

NOTES: For more information on whisking-method cakes, see page 281.

Génoise Fine

MAKES A 20 CM | 8 IN CAKE

4 room-temperature eggs

125 g | 4½ oz caster sugar

100 g | 3½ oz butter, melted and cooled

100 g | 3½ oz plain flour

1 Heat the oven to 190°C | 375°F | gas mark 5. Grease a 20 cm | 8 in *moule à manqué* or deep sandwich tin. Line the base with a disc of greaseproof paper and dust lightly with caster sugar and then flour. Tap out the excess.

2 Break the eggs into a large, heatproof bowl and add the sugar. Fit the bowl over, but not in, a saucepan of steaming water and whisk with an electric beater until the mixture is light, fluffy and doubled in bulk. Remove from the heat and continue whisking until cool. Fold in the butter quickly; if you work slowly the cake will collapse.

3 Sift the flour over the mixture and fold it in thoroughly but gently, using a large metal spoon. Turn the mixture into the prepared tin.

4 Bake in the centre of the oven for 30–35 minutes until the top springs back when pressed lightly with a fingertip.

5 Remove the cake from the oven and allow to cool in the tin inverted on to a wire rack and leave to cool completely.

NOTE: This is sometimes called a 'butter sponge'. However, this description is not culinarily correct, as a true sponge contains no fat.

For more information on whisking-method cakes, see page 281.

Chocolate Cakes

Chocolate cake is popular with almost everyone. The cakes in this section vary from having just a touch of chocolate to being very rich and chocolatey indeed. Some are very quick and easy to make, whereas others are more complicated and suitable for special occasions.

Chocolate can sometimes be tricky to work with, but by following a few simple rules there should be no problems. When melting chocolate by itself, always place it in a bowl set over a saucepan of steaming water. The bowl containing the chocolate should not be touching the water. Chocolate can also be successfully melted in a microwave on the defrost setting, but you must be careful not to allow it to get too hot. If chocolate is allowed to get too hot it will become dull and grainy. If it gets so hot that the oil comes out of the chocolate, it is impossible to use and should be thrown away. When melting chocolate with other ingredients, a heavy-bottomed saucepan can be used if the recipe specifies.

Make sure to add the other ingredients before beginning to melt the chocolate. If liquid is added to melted chocolate it likely seize and become very thick. This is very difficult to correct. Quite a lot of hot water added to it will make the chocolate liquid again but will alter the properties of the liquid in the cake.

There is more information on chocolate in the *Baking Ingredients* section (see page 4).

Chocolate Fudge Cake

SERVES 8

115 g | 4 oz butter, softened
115 g | 4 oz caster sugar
115 g | 4 oz soft light brown sugar
4 room-temperature eggs, beaten
170 g | 6 oz self-raising flour
55 g | 2 oz cocoa powder
1½ teaspoons bicarbonate of soda
a pinch of salt

6 tablespoons crème fraiche or soured cream
1 teaspoon vanilla essence

For the icing
225 g | 8 oz plain chocolate, chopped into small pieces
225 g | 8 oz crème fraiche or soured cream
1 tablespoon caster sugar

1 Heat the oven to 180°C | 350°F | gas mark 4. Line 2 × 17–20 cm | 7–8 in sandwich tins with baking parchment.

2 Cream the butter and sugars until pale and fluffy. Beat in the eggs gradually.

3 Sift together the flour, cocoa powder, bicarbonate of soda and salt, then fold into the butter/sugar mixture alternately with the crème fraiche. Stir in the vanilla.

4 Divide between the tins. Bake in the middle of the oven for 25–30 minutes or until the cake is risen and springs back to the touch when pressed in the centre.

5 Cool on a wire rack for 10 minutes then turn out and allow to cool completely.

6 Make the icing: melt the chocolate over a bowl placed over, but not in, steaming water. Stir in the crème fraiche or soured cream and sugar. Allow to stand to thicken if necessary, then use to sandwich and ice the cake.

NOTE: For more information on creaming-method cakes, see page 279.

Chocolate Coffee Layer Cake

MAKES A 17 CM | 7 IN CAKE

170 g | 6 oz butter, softened
170 g | 6 oz caster sugar
3 room-temperature eggs, beaten
200 g | 7 oz self-raising flour
45 g | 1½ oz cocoa powder
30 g | 1 oz ground almonds
1–2 tablespoons milk

To finish

coffee custard buttercream, using 115 g | 4 oz butter
   and 225 g | 8 oz icing sugar (see page 451)
glacé icing, using 225 g | 8 oz icing sugar, (see page
   455), mixed with 2–3 teaspoons coffee essence
55 g | 2 oz almonds, toasted and chopped (optional)

1 Heat the oven to 190°C | 375°F | gas mark 5. Grease and line 2 × 17 cm | 7 in straight-sided sandwich tins with discs of baking parchment cut to fit.

2 Cream the butter and sugar together until pale and fluffy. Add the eggs a little at a time, beating well between each addition.

3 Sift the flour and cocoa powder together and mix into the cake mixture with the ground almonds. Add enough milk to create a dropping consistency.

4 Divide the cake mixture between the two tins and spread flat. Place in the centre of the oven and bake for approximately 35–40 minutes. The cakes are ready when the tops spring back when lightly pressed with a finger.

5 Turn out of the tins and allow to cool completely.

6 Meanwhile, make the buttercream and glacé icing (which should be thick, so be careful not to add too much liquid).

7 Once the cakes are cold, carefully split them in half horizontally. Sandwich the four pieces together with the coffee buttercream and coat the top with coffee glacé icing. Whilst the icing is still wet, sprinkle the nuts over the top.

NOTE: For more information on creaming-method cakes, see page 279.

Chocolate and Orange Cake

MAKES A 20 CM | 8 IN CAKE

85 g│3 oz plain chocolate, chopped into small pieces
340 g│12 oz soft light brown sugar
115 g│4 oz butter
grated zest of 1 orange
225 g│8 oz plain flour
2 room-temperature eggs, beaten
1 teaspoon bicarbonate of soda
290 ml│10 fl oz milk, warmed

For the filling

290 ml│10 fl oz double cream, whipped
2 tablespoons icing sugar
grated zest of 1 orange

For the icing

115 g│4 oz plain chocolate, chopped into small
   pieces
4 tablespoons milk

1 Heat the oven to 180°C│350°F│gas mark 4. Grease a deep 20 cm│8 in cake tin and line with a disc of baking parchment.

2 Put the chocolate, sugar and butter into a small saucepan and melt over a gentle heat, stirring until quite smooth. Remove from the heat, add the orange zest and allow to cool.

3 Sift the flour into a mixing bowl. Make a well in the centre and add the eggs and melted chocolate mixture. Add the bicarbonate of soda to the milk and add to the well. Mix carefully, gradually incorporating the flour, and beat to a thick, smooth batter. Pour into the prepared tin.

4 Bake in the centre of the oven for about 1 hour or until the sides have shrunk away from the tin slightly and the top springs back when pressed lightly with a fingertip.

5 Remove the cake from the oven and allow to cool in the tin for 20 minutes, then turn out on to a wire rack and leave to cool completely.

6 Make the filling: mix the cream with the sugar and orange zest.

7 Make the icing: put the chocolate and milk into a saucepan and melt over a gentle heat until smooth. Remove from the heat and allow to cool to a thick coating consistency.

8 When the cake is cold, split horizontally into 3, very carefully. Sandwich the layers together with the cream. Pour the chocolate icing evenly over the top. Allow to set.

NOTE: For more information on melting-method cakes, see page 279.

Chocolate and Orange Marbled Cake

MAKES A 20 CM|8 IN CAKE

225 g|8 oz butter, softened

225 g|8 oz caster sugar

4 room-temperature eggs, beaten

225 g|8 oz self-raising flour

2 tablespoons cocoa powder

grated zest of 2 oranges

For the icing, optional

115 g|4 oz plain chocolate, broken into small pieces

115 g|4 oz butter

225 g|8 oz icing sugar, sifted

grated zest of 1 orange

To finish, optional

30 g|1 oz white chocolate, coarsely grated

30 g|1 oz plain chocolate, coarsely grated

1 Heat the oven to 180°C|350°F|gas mark 4. Grease and line a deep 20 cm|8 in round cake tin with a piece of baking parchment cut to fit.

2 Cream the butter and sugar together until pale and fluffy, then beat in the eggs a little at a time, beating well between each addition. If the mixture starts to curdle, beat in a little of the measured flour.

3 Sift the flour and fold into the cake mixture. Divide the cake mixture in half and put one half into another bowl. Sift the cocoa powder into one half and mix the orange zest into the other half.

4 Put alternate spoons of the chocolate and orange mixtures into the cake tin. Swirl a clean knife through it gently, once, and smooth the top carefully. Place the cake in the centre of the oven and bake for 45–55 minutes. It is cooked when the top springs back when pressed lightly with a finger. Leave in the tin for 5 minutes before turning out to cool on a wire rack.

5 To make the filling: melt the chocolate in a bowl set over, but not in, a pan of steaming water. Once melted, allow it to cool down. Cream the butter until soft and gradually beat in the sifted icing sugar. Add the cooled but melted chocolate and the orange zest.

6 When the cake is cold, split it in half horizontally. Spread one third of the icing inside the cake and use the rest for the top and sides, spreading it neatly. Finish by scattering over a mixture of grated white and dark chocolate.

NOTE: For more information on creaming-method cakes, see page 279.

Chocolate Marmalade Cake

MAKES A 20 CM|8 IN CAKE

225 g|8 oz butter, softened

225 g|8 oz caster sugar

5 room-temperature eggs, separated

2 tablespoons dark, coarse-cut marmalade

170 g|6 oz plain chocolate, melted

225 g|8 oz plain flour

2 teaspoons baking powder

55 g|2 oz ground almonds

For the filling

140 g|5 oz plain chocolate

140 ml|5 fl oz soured cream

1 tablespoon dark, coarse-cut marmalade

1 tablespoon Grand Marnier (optional)

To finish

cocoa powder

1 Heat the oven to 170°C|325°F|gas mark 3. Grease a deep 20 cm|8 in round cake tin and line with a piece of baking parchment cut to fit.

2 Cream the butter and sugar together until pale and fluffy, then beat in the egg yolks, one at a time.

3 Cut up any large pieces of marmalade and stir into the mixture with the melted chocolate.

4 Sift the flour and baking powder together and fold in with the ground almonds.

5 Whisk the egg whites until they form medium peaks. Fold 1 tablespoon into the cake mixture to loosen it, then carefully fold in the rest.

6 Pour the cake mixture into the prepared tin and bake for 50–60 minutes or until the top springs back when lightly pressed with a finger. Allow it to stand in the tin for 10 minutes before turning out on to a wire rack to cool completely.

7 To make the filling: break up the chocolate and put it into a bowl with the soured cream. Place over, but not in, a pan of steaming water. Stir until the chocolate has melted and is well-amalgamated with the cream. Remove from the hot water and allow it to cool, stirring occasionally. Cut up any large pieces of marmalade and add to the filling with the Grand Marnier, if using. Mix well.

8 When the cake is cold, split in half horizontally and spread with the filling. Finish by dusting the cake with cocoa powder.

NOTE: For more information on creaming-method cakes, see page 279.

German Chocolate Cake

This is a light-textured cake made from milk chocolate. The icing is an extravagant combination of milk chocolate, coconut and pecan nuts. This cake is adapted from a classic American recipe by its creator, Samuel German.

MAKES 12 PIECES

170 g|6 oz good quality milk chocolate, chopped
   into small pieces
225 g|8 oz self-raising flour
1 teaspoon bicarbonate of soda
a pinch of salt
225 g|8 oz unsalted butter, softened
300 g|10½ oz golden caster sugar
5 room-temperature eggs, separated
1 teaspoon vanilla essence
140 ml|5 fl oz soured cream

For the icing

170 g|6 oz good quality milk chocolate, chopped
   into small pieces
170 g|6 oz unsalted butter, softened
150 ml|5 fl oz soured cream
170 g|6 oz sweetened desiccated coconut
100 g|3½ oz pecan nuts, chopped

1 Heat the oven to 180°C|350°F|gas mark 4. Line the base and sides of a 23 × 33 cm| 9 × 13 in roasting tin with baking parchment.

2 Place the milk chocolate to melt in a bowl set over, but not in, steaming water. Set aside to cool slightly.

3 Sift together the flour, bicarbonate of soda and salt.

4 Beat the butter with half the caster sugar until thick, then beat in the egg yolks, one at a time. Beat in the vanilla.

5 Beat the egg whites until stiff, then gradually beat in the remaining caster sugar to make a thick meringue.

6 Using a large metal spoon, fold the chocolate into the butter mixture.

7 Fold the flour into the butter mixture alternately with the soured cream. Fold in the egg whites.

8 Gently spread into the prepared tin then bake in the centre of the oven for 45 minutes or until a cocktail stick inserted into the centre of the cake comes out clean.

9 Cool on a wire rack in the tin.

10 For the icing: melt the chocolate in a bowl set over, but not touching, steaming water. When melted, remove from the heat and gradually beat in the butter.

11 Stir in the soured cream then fold in all but a couple of tablespoons of the coconut and the pecan nuts.

12 Spread the icing over the cake and scatter over the reserved coconut and pecan nuts. When it has set, cut into squares.

Chocolate and Almond Cake

MAKES A 17 CM | 7 IN CAKE

115 g | 4 oz butter, softened

115 g | 4 oz caster sugar

2 room-temperature eggs, beaten

115 g | 4 oz self-raising flour

2 tablespoons golden syrup

30 g | 1 oz ground almonds

a pinch of salt

30 g | 1 oz cocoa powder

For the icing

115 g | 4 oz granulated sugar

125 ml | 4 ½ fl oz milk

140 g | 5 oz plain chocolate, chopped into small pieces

55 g | 2 oz butter

2 tablespoons double cream

2 teaspoons vanilla essence

1 Heat the oven to 180°C | 350°F | gas mark 4. Grease a deep 17 cm | 7 in cake tin and line the base with a disc of baking parchment.

2 Cream the butter in a mixing bowl until soft. Add the sugar and beat until pale and fluffy.

3 Add the eggs gradually to the creamed mixture, beating well after each addition. Beat in 1 teaspoon of the flour if necessary, to prevent the mixture from curdling.

4 Stir in the syrup and ground almonds. Sift together the flour, salt and cocoa powder and fold into the mixture, using a large metal spoon, to achieve a reluctant dropping consistency. If it is too stiff, add a little water or milk. Turn into the prepared tin and spread out evenly.

5 Bake in the centre of the oven for 40 minutes or until the cake is well-risen and feels spongy to the touch. Turn out on to a wire rack and leave to cool.

6 Meanwhile, make the icing: put the sugar and milk into a saucepan over a low heat. Allow the sugar to dissolve, then bring up to the boil. Simmer, without stirring, for 8 minutes.

7 Remove the pan from the heat and stir in the chocolate, then add the butter, cream and vanilla essence. Stir until completely melted. Put into a bowl, cover and chill for 2 hours or until the icing is spreadable.

8 When the cake is cold, split in half horizontally and sandwich together with one quarter of the icing. Spread the remaining icing on the top and sides of the cake, swirling it to give a frosted appearance. Allow to set.

NOTE: For more information on creaming-method cakes, see page 279.

Very Rich Chocolate Cake

This cake should be moist and soft in the centre, but be careful not to overbake as it becomes very dry.

MAKES A 20 CM|8 IN CAKE

55 g|2 oz sultanas, chopped finely
55 ml|2 fl oz brandy
3 room-temperature eggs
140 g|5 oz caster sugar
200 g|7 oz plain chocolate, chopped into small
  pieces
2 tablespoons water

115 g|4 oz unsalted butter
55 g|2 oz plain flour, sifted
85 g|3 oz ground almonds

For the icing

140 g|5 oz plain chocolate, chopped into small pieces
150 ml|5 fl oz double cream

1 Soak the sultanas in the brandy overnight.
2 Heat the oven to 180°C|350°F|gas mark 4. Grease a *moule à manqué* or 20 cm|8 in cake tin. Line the base with a disc of baking parchment.
3 Separate the eggs. Beat the egg yolks and sugar until pale and mousse-like.
4 Put the chocolate and water into a heatproof bowl fitted over but not in a saucepan of steaming water. Stir until melted, then stir in the butter piece by piece until the mixture is smooth. Allow to cool slightly, then stir into the egg-yolk mixture.
5 Fold the flour carefully into the egg-yolk and chocolate mixture with the ground almonds, sultanas and brandy, using a large metal spoon.
6 Whisk the egg whites until stiff but not dry and fold into the chocolate mixture. Turn into the prepared tin.
7 Bake in the centre of the oven for 35–40 minutes (the centre should still be moist).
8 Remove the cake from the oven and allow to cool completely in the tin, then turn out on to a wire rack.
9 Make the icing: heat the chocolate and cream in a small saucepan. Stir until all the chocolate has melted and the mixture is smooth. Allow to cool and thicken to a coating consistency.
10 When the cake is cold, pour over the icing and allow to set for at least 2 hours.

NOTE: For more information on whisking-method cakes, see page 281.

Chocolate Yoghurt Cake

This cake improves with keeping and is excellent for children's birthday cakes, as it is easy to cut into shapes.

MAKES A 20 CM|8 IN CAKE

3 room-temperature eggs

150 ml|5 fl oz sunflower oil

150 ml|5 fl oz natural yoghurt

4 tablespoons golden syrup

85 g|3 oz caster sugar

225 g|8 oz self-raising flour

4 tablespoons cocoa powder

½ teaspoon bicarbonate of soda

1 Heat the oven to 170°C|325°F|gas mark 3. Grease a deep 20 cm|8 in cake tin and line the base with a disc of baking parchment.

2 Beat together the eggs, oil, yoghurt, syrup and sugar in a mixing bowl.

3 Sift together the flour, cocoa powder and bicarbonate of soda and fold into the egg mixture, using a large metal spoon. Pour into the prepared tin.

4 Bake in the centre of the oven for about 1¼ –1½ hours or until the top springs back when pressed lightly.

5 Remove the cake from the oven and allow to cool in the tin for 10 minutes, then turn out on to a wire rack and leave to cool completely.

NOTE: This cake can also be baked in a roasting tin measuring approximately 20 × 25 cm|8 × 10 in. It will then take only 45–60 minutes to bake.

Chocolate Ginger Cake

SERVES 8

200 g|7 oz good quality plain chocolate, chopped into small pieces

2 tablespoons brandy (optional)

1 tablespoons syrup from preserved stem ginger

115 g|4 oz butter, diced

140 g|5 oz caster sugar

3 room-temperature eggs, separated

100 g|3½ oz ground almonds

55 g|2 oz self-raising flour

2 pieces preserved stem ginger, chopped

For the glaze

140 g|5 oz good quality plain chocolate, chopped into small pieces

1 tablespoon brandy

45 g|1½ oz butter, diced

1 piece preserved stem ginger, cut into fine strips

1 Heat the oven to 180°C|350°F|gas mark 4. Line the base of a 20 cm|8 in spring-form tin with baking parchment.

2 Put the chocolate in a bowl with the brandy or 2 tablespoons of water and the syrup and set over a pan of steaming water. When the chocolate has just melted, take it off the heat and stir in the butter.

3 Whisk the sugar and egg yolks in a large bowl until pale and thick, stir in the chocolate mixture and then fold in the ground almonds, flour, ginger and 2 tablespoons of warm water.

4 Whisk the egg whites until just stiff. Fold 1 tablespoonful into the chocolate mixture, then fold in the remainder.

5 Turn the mixture into the tin and bake in the centre of the oven for 40 minutes (cover with greaseproof paper if browning too quickly). The cake will feel firm when done.

6 Leave the cake in the tin on a wire rack to cool, then remove the tin and place the cake on the rack for glazing.

7 Make the glaze: melt the chocolate with the brandy then stir in the butter. Quickly smooth the glaze over the cake. Arrange small heaps of stem ginger around the top of the cake and leave until the glaze has set.

Devil's Food Cake

This sticky, rich chocolate cake can be served plain, or the centre can be filled with whipped cream and/or fruit.

MAKES A 1.2 LITRE│2 PINT RING CAKE

225 g│8 oz caster sugar
55 g│2 oz cocoa powder
225 ml│8 fl oz buttermilk
115 g│4 oz plain flour
1 teaspoon baking powder
a pinch of salt

55 g│2 oz butter, softened
1 room-temperature egg, beaten
½ teaspoon vanilla essence

For the filling (optional)
1 tablespoon icing sugar
150 ml│5 fl oz double cream

1 Heat the oven to 180°C│350°F│gas mark 4. Grease a 1.2 litre│2 pint ring mould very well (preferably with lard).

2 Mix together 115 g│4 oz of the sugar, the cocoa powder and 75 ml│2½ fl oz of the buttermilk in a bowl. Leave to stand for 10 minutes.

3 Sift together the flour, baking powder and salt.

4 Cream the butter and remaining sugar in a mixing bowl until light and fluffy. Gradually add the egg, beating well after each addition.

5 Fold in the flour mixture carefully, using a large metal spoon, and mix in the remaining buttermilk and the vanilla essence. Finally, fold in the cocoa mixture. Pour into the prepared ring mould.

6 Bake in the centre of the oven for 30 minutes or until firm to the touch.

7 Remove the cake from the oven and allow to cool in the ring mould for 5 minutes, then turn out on to a wire rack and leave to cool completely.

8 Whip the icing sugar and cream together until soft peaks form then pile into the centre of the cake.

NOTE: This cake can be frozen very successfully without the cream.

Chocolate Roulade

This classic cake is gluten-free. It can be decorated to resemble a 'yule log' for Christmas by curling a small strip of the cake into a knot for the log.

SERVES 6

225 g | 8 oz plain chocolate, chopped into small pieces
85 ml | 3 fl oz water
1 teaspoon strong instant coffee granules
5 room-temperature eggs
140 g | 5 oz caster sugar

For the filling

200 ml | 7 fl oz double cream
icing sugar

To dust

icing sugar

1 Take a large roasting tin and cut a piece of non-stick baking parchment to fit the base and sides of the pan; don't worry if the edges stick up untidily round the sides. Heat the oven to 200°C | 400°F | gas mark 6.

2 Put the chocolate, water and coffee granules into a heavy saucepan and melt over a low heat. Stir occasionally during melting. Remove from the heat when smooth.

3 Separate the eggs and beat the yolks and all but 1 tablespoon of the caster sugar until pale and mousse-like. Fold in the cooled melted chocolate.

4 Whisk the whites until stiff but not dry then whisk in the remaining caster sugar. With a large metal spoon, stir a small amount thoroughly into the chocolate mixture to loosen it. Fold the remaining whites in gently. Spread the mixture evenly into the tin.

5 Bake for 12–15 minutes or until the top is slightly browned and firm to touch. Do not overbake or the cake will crack badly when rolled.

6 Slide the cake and parchment out of the roasting pan and on to a wire rack. Cover immediately with a damp tea towel and leave to cool.

7 Dust thickly with icing sugar a piece of greaseproof paper or baking parchment large enough to cover the cake. Using the wire rack to hold the cake, quickly flip the cake on to the sugar-covered paper. Carefully peel away the baking parchment.

8 Whip the cream to the soft-peak stage and flavour with a little icing sugar. Spread it evenly over the cake. Roll up like a Swiss roll from one of the short sides, peeling away the parchment as you go. Put the roll on to a serving dish, seam-side down, and sift a little icing sugar over the top just before serving.

NOTE: The cake is very moist and inclined to break apart, but this does not matter. Just stick it together with the cream when rolling it up; the last-minute sifted icing sugar will do wonders for its appearance.

If this cake is used as a Yule log its tendency to crack is a positive advantage, so do not cover it with a tea towel when leaving to cool. Before filling, flip the whole flat cake over on to a tea towel. Carefully peel off the lining paper then fill with cream and roll up. The firm skin will crack, very like the bark of a tree. A dusting of icing sugar will look like snow.

Victoria Sandwich

Creaming the butter and sugar

Beating until pale and fluffy

Adding the egg gradually

Sifting over the flour

Folding in the flour

Spreading into cake tins

American Carrot Cake

Berry Tea Loaf

St Clement's Cake

Fairy Cakes and Butterfly Cakes

Whisking the eggs

Whisking the eggs and sugar

Thick and mousse-like

Sifting over the flour

Folding in the flour

Spreading into the tin

Assembling a Swiss Roll

Baked cake

Spreading with jam

Rolling up the cake

Swiss Roll

Toasted Almond Roulade with Strawberries and Cream

Squashy Rhubarb Cake

Chocolate and Orange Marbled Cake

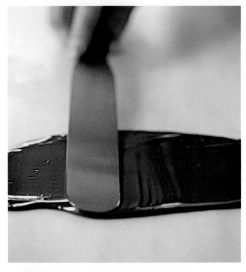

Spreading chocolate for curls

Scraping curls with a knife

Finished chocolate curls

Chocolate Ruffle Cake

Old-fashioned Boiled Fruit Cake

Warm Chocolate Puddle Cakes

These little cakes are served warm and slightly undercooked so that the runny middle becomes a chocolate sauce for the cake. Serve with plenty of vanilla ice cream.

MAKES 4

1 tablespoon butter, melted, for greasing

2 tablespoons cocoa powder, sifted

170 g | 6 oz plain chocolate, chopped into small pieces

55 g | 2 oz unsalted butter

2 room-temperature eggs

1 egg yolk

45 g | 1½ oz caster sugar

½ | teaspoon vanilla essence

30 g | 1 oz plain flour

To serve

vanilla ice cream

1 Heat the oven to 190°C | 375°F | gas mark 6.
2 Butter 4 × 150 ml | 5 fl oz capacity timbale moulds and dust with the sifted cocoa powder.
3 Put the chocolate in a bowl set over, but not in, a saucepan of steaming water. When melted, stir in the butter. Remove from the heat when the butter has just melted.
4 Put the egg, egg yolk, sugar and vanilla into a large bowl and whisk until thick and mousse-like.
5 Fold in the chocolate mixture and then sift over the flour. Fold in the flour gently.
6 Divide between the timbale moulds (it will only fill them about halfway), then place on a baking sheet and bake in the centre of the oven for 8–10 minutes. The surface should look cooked but should have a slight wobble.
7 Turn on to individual plates and serve immediately with ice cream.

Tiramisu Cake

This cake, based on a classic *Génoise* recipe, makes a wonderful, rich, dinner-party dessert.

MAKES A 20 CM|8 IN CAKE

4 large room-temperature eggs

125 g|4½ oz caster sugar

2 teaspoons instant coffee, dissolved in hot water

55 g|2 oz butter, melted and cooled

100 g|3½ oz plain flour

½ teaspoon baking powder

For the syrup

30 g|1 oz granulated sugar

5 tablespoons water

1 tablespoon Marsala

For the filling

2 teaspoons Marsala

250 g|9 oz mascarpone or cream cheese

2 teaspoons icing sugar

To finish

cocoa powder

1 Heat the oven to 180°C|350°F|gas mark 4.

2 Oil a 20 cm|8 in *moule à manqué* or round cake tin and line the base with a disc of oiled baking parchment. Dust first with caster sugar and then with flour. Tap out the excess.

3 Break the eggs into a heatproof bowl, add the sugar and fit the bowl over but not in a saucepan of steaming water. Whisk with an electric beater until the mixture has doubled in volume. Remove from the heat, add the coffee and continue whisking, off the heat, until the mixture has cooled.

4 Using a large metal spoon, quickly fold in the butter and the flour, sifted with the baking powder. If you work too slowly the cake will collapse. Turn into the prepared tin and spread out evenly.

5 Bake in the centre of the oven for about 30–35 minutes or until the top springs back when pressed lightly with a fingertip.

6 Remove from the oven and allow to cool slightly in the tin, then turn out on to a wire rack and leave to cool completely.

7 Make the syrup: put the sugar and water into a heavy saucepan and stir over a low heat without boiling until the sugar has dissolved completely. Bring to the boil and boil until syrupy. Remove from the heat, allow to cool slightly and add the Marsala.

8 When the cake is cold, split it in half horizontally, brush with half the syrup and leave on a wire rack to get cold.

9 Mix together the filling ingredients and spread on the bottom layer of the cake. Sift over a thin layer of cocoa powder and cover with the top layer of the cake. Brush with the remaining syrup.

10 Just before serving, dust with sifted cocoa powder.

NOTE: For more information on whisking-method cakes, see page 281.

Chocolate Polenta Cake

This delicious cake can also be served as a pudding and is perfect with fresh raspberries and Greek yoghurt or crème fraiche. It is gluten free.

MAKES A 20 CM|8 IN CAKE

225 g|8 oz plain chocolate, chopped into small pieces
115 g|4 oz unsalted butter
5 room-temperature eggs

140 g|5 oz caster sugar
3 tablespoons dark rum
85 g|3 oz fine polenta

1 Heat the oven to 180°C|350°F|gas mark 4. Grease a 20 cm|8 in *moule à manqué* or a 23 cm|9 in sandwich tin. Line the base with a disc of baking parchment. Dust lightly with caster sugar and then potato or rice flour. Tap out the excess.
2 Put the chocolate into a saucepan with the butter. Melt gently over a low heat. Remove from the heat and allow to cool slightly in a bowl.
3 Separate the eggs. Beat the yolks with 85 g|3 oz of the sugar. Add 1 tablespoon of the rum and continue beating until thick and pale.
4 Fold the melted chocolate mixture into the egg and sugar mixture.
5 Whisk the egg whites until thick and holding a medium peak. Gradually whisk in the remaining sugar until thick and glossy.
6 Fold the remaining rum and polenta into the chocolate mixture, using a large metal spoon, and finally fold in the egg whites. Pour into the prepared tin.
7 Bake in the centre of the oven for 40–50 minutes or until a sharp knife or skewer inserted into the centre comes out clean.
8 Remove the cake from the oven and allow to cool in the tin for 10 minutes, then turn out on to a serving plate and leave to cool completely.

NOTE: The cake is turned directly on to a plate as it is fragile and can break if it is moved.

Rich Chocolate Squash Cake

MAKES A 900 G | 2 LB LOAF

225 g | 8 oz raw gem squash or courgettes, grated
115 g | 4 oz unsalted butter, softened
55 ml | 2 fl oz sunflower oil
85 g | 3 oz soft dark brown sugar, sifted
2 large room-temperature eggs
55 g | 2 oz cocoa powder
115 g | 4 oz plain flour
1 teaspoon baking powder
1 teaspoon bicarbonate of soda

½ teaspoon ground cloves
1 teaspoon ground cinnamon
55 ml | 2 fl oz water
115 g | 4 oz plain chocolate buttons
55 g | 2 oz pistachio nuts, shelled

To finish

icing sugar, sifted

1 Heat the oven to 180°C | 350°F | gas mark 4. Lightly oil a 900 g | 2 lb loaf tin and line the base with a piece of oiled greaseproof paper.
2 Put the squash or courgettes into a clean J–cloth or tea towel and wring out the excess moisture until totally dry. Put into a bowl and fork through to separate the strands.
3 Put the butter, oil and sugar into a mixing bowl and beat until light and fluffy.
4 Separate the eggs and beat the yolks into the creamed mixture.
5 Sift the cocoa powder, flour, baking powder, bicarbonate of soda and spices together on to the butter mixture and fold in, using a large metal spoon. Stir in the water gently.
6 Add the chocolate buttons, squash or courgettes and pistachios and mix well.
7 Whisk the egg whites until stiff but not dry. Fold the whites quickly into the cake mixture, without knocking out too much air. Turn into the prepared tin and smooth the top with a spatula.
8 Bake in the centre of the oven for about 40–45 minutes or until a sharp knife or skewer inserted into the centre of the cake comes out clean.
9 Remove the cake from the oven and allow to cool completely in the tin.
10 When the cake is cold, remove from the tin and serve dusted with icing sugar.

Rich Chocolate and Peach Cake

This cake is a variation of the *Very Rich Chocolate Cake* (see page 305) and can be served as either a cake or a pudding. The cake can be made in advance and frozen; ice the cake once it has defrosted.

MAKES A 20 CM|8 IN CAKE

55 g|2 oz dried peaches, chopped

3 tablespoons orange juice

2 tablespoons Grand Marnier

3 room-temperature eggs, separated

115 g|4 oz caster sugar

2 tablespoons peach conserve

200 g|7 oz plain chocolate, chopped into small pieces

115 g|4 oz butter

55 g|2 oz self-raising flour

85 g|3 oz ground almonds

2 teaspoons sugar

For the icing

115 g|4 oz plain chocolate, chopped into small pieces

100 ml|3½ fl oz double cream

To finish

2 tablespoons peach conserve

2 tablespoons Grand Marnier

1 Soak the dried peaches in the orange juice and Grand Marnier overnight, or for at least 4 hours.

2 Heat the oven to 180°C|350°F| gas mark 4. Grease a deep 20 cm|8 in cake tin and line the base with a disc of baking parchment, cut to fit.

3 Beat the egg yolks with the sugar until pale and mousse-like. Stir in the peach conserve.

4 Melt the chocolate in a heatproof bowl set over a pan of steaming water. Remove from the heat and stir in the butter, piece by piece. Mix until smooth.

5 Sift the flour and mix with the ground almonds.

6 Whisk the egg whites until stiff but not dry, add 2 teaspoons of caster sugar and whisk again until shiny.

7 Fold the chocolate into the egg-yolk mixture, add the flour and almonds and carefully fold in the egg whites. Pour into the prepared tin and bake for 30–40 minutes. The cake should still be moist in the centre; do not overcook it. Remove from the oven and allow to cool in the tin. When cold, remove from the tin and put upside down on the serving plate. Peel off the lining paper.

8 Meanwhile, make the icing. Put the chocolate and cream into a small saucepan and gently heat. As soon as the chocolate is melted, remove from the heat and stir well. Cool completely before using.

9 To finish the cake: mix together the peach conserve and Grand Marnier. Spread over the top and sides of the cake. Leave to soak in for about 1 hour.

10 Spread the chocolate icing over the top and sides of the cake very carefully. Finish by swirling the icing with a palette knife.

Citrus Cakes

Other cakes in this book have some citrus fruit as an ingredient, but those in this section have a particularly tangy, citrus flavour. This is true of the syrup cakes, for example, which are easy to make, taste delicious and freeze well.

Citrus Sponge Cake

MAKES A 23 CM | 9 IN ROUND OR 20 CM | 8 IN SQUARE CAKE

225 g | 8 oz butter

225 g | 8 oz caster sugar

grated zest of 2 limes

grated zest of 1 lemon

grated zest of 1 orange

4 room-temperature eggs, beaten

225 g | 8 oz self-raising flour

55 g | 2 oz ground almonds

For the syrup

juice of 2 limes

juice of 1 lemon

juice of 1 orange

1 tablespoon caster sugar

For the topping

140 g | 5 oz curd cheese

reserved grated zest

icing sugar, sifted

1 Heat the oven to 190°C | 375°F | gas mark 5. Oil a deep 23 cm | 9 in round or 20 cm | 8 in square cake tin and line the base with a piece of baking parchment.

2 Cream the butter and sugar together in a mixing bowl until pale and fluffy. Reserve 1 tablespoon of the mixed citrus zest and beat the remainder into the creamed mixture.

3 Add the eggs gradually, beating well after each addition. Add a little of the flour if necessary, to prevent the mixture from curdling. Beat very well.

4 Fold in the remaining flour and the ground almonds to achieve a reluctant dropping consistency, adding a little water if necessary. Turn into the prepared tin.

5 Bake in the centre of the oven for 20–25 minutes or until well-risen and golden and the top springs back when pressed lightly with a fingertip.

6 Remove from the oven and allow to cool in the tin for a few minutes, then turn out on to a wire rack and pierce the top all over with a skewer.

7 Mix the lime, lemon and orange juices with the sugar in a small bowl and drizzle over the top of the cake while still warm. Leave to cool completely.

8 When the cake is cold, make the topping: put the curd cheese into a bowl with the reserved citrus zest and beat with a wooden spoon until soft and creamy. Add icing sugar to taste. Spread evenly over the cake with a palette knife.

NOTE: For more information on creaming-method cakes, see page 279.

Bitter Orange Cake

This unusual cake, which takes some time to prepare, contains no flour and so is good for people on a gluten-free diet. It is delicious served as a pudding or with orange curd (see *Icings and Fillings*, page 456) as a teatime cake.

MAKES A 23 CM | 9 IN CAKE

2 small, thin-skinned oranges
285 g | 10 oz whole blanched almonds
5 room-temperature eggs
225 g | 8 oz caster sugar
1 teaspoon baking powder

For the syrup

juice of 4 oranges
grated zest of 2 oranges
juice of 1 lemon
115 g | 4 oz caster sugar
150 ml | 5 fl oz water

To serve

icing sugar, sifted
290 ml | 10 fl oz double cream, lightly whipped

1 Boil the oranges in water in a saucepan for about 1 hour or until very soft. Remove from the water and allow to cool. Cut the oranges in half and remove and discard any pips. Purée the skin and pulp in a food processor or push through a sieve.

2 Chop the almonds finely and toast very lightly under the grill, taking care that they do not burn. Allow to cool.

3 Meanwhile, heat the oven to 180°C | 350°F | gas mark 4. Grease a 23 cm | 9 in spring-form cake tin and line the base with a disc of baking parchment.

4 Put the eggs and sugar into a heatproof bowl fitted over, but not in, a saucepan of gently steaming water and whisk with electric beaters until thick and pale.

5 Mix together the orange pulp, almonds and baking powder and fold immediately and quickly into the egg and sugar mixture. Pour into the prepared tin.

6 Bake in the centre of the oven for about 1 hour or until firm to the touch.

7 Remove from the oven and allow to cool in the tin for 20 minutes, then loosen carefully and turn out on to a wire rack. Leave to cool completely.

8 Meanwhile, make the syrup. Put the orange juice and zest with the lemon juice, sugar and water into a small saucepan and bring slowly to the boil. Reduce the heat and simmer for about 20 minutes until syrupy. Remove from the heat and allow to cool.

9 To serve: dust the top of the cake with icing sugar and serve each piece with some syrup and a spoonful of whipped cream.

NOTES: This cake remains moist for some time, but if being kept for more than 1 week it should be frozen. Otherwise keep it in an airtight container in a cool, dry place.

For more information on whisking-method cakes, see page 281.

Summer Lemon Cake

MAKES A 20 CM|8 IN CAKE

6 room-temperature eggs

170 g|6 oz caster sugar

2 tablespoons water

grated zest of 1 lemon

85 g|3 oz plain flour

30 g|1 oz cornflour

For the filling

290 ml|10 fl oz double cream

5 tablespoons lemon curd (see page 456)

115 g|4 oz almonds, toasted and chopped

1 Heat the oven to 180°C|350°F|gas mark 4. Grease 2 × 20 cm|8 in sandwich tins and line the base of each with a disc of baking parchment.

2 Separate the eggs and put the yolks, sugar, water and lemon zest into a heatproof bowl. Fit over, but not in, a saucepan of steaming water and whisk with an electric beater until light and fluffy.

3 Sift the flour and cornflour together and fold into the yolk mixture carefully, using a large metal spoon.

4 Whisk the egg whites until stiff and fold into the mixture. Divide between the prepared tins and spread out evenly.

5 Bake in the centre of the oven for 45 minutes or until the tops spring back when pressed lightly with a fingertip.

6 Remove from the oven and allow to cool in the tins for 10 minutes, then turn out on to a wire rack and leave to cool completely.

7 Meanwhile, make the filling. Whisk the cream until it just holds its shape and add the lemon curd. Continue whisking until stiff, but do not overwhip or the mixture will curdle. Add more lemon curd if you like a pronounced lemony flavour.

8 When the cakes are cold, sandwich them together with some of the filling and spread the top and sides with the remainder. Press the almonds over the top and sides of the cake and keep in the refrigerator until required.

NOTE: For more information on whisking-method cakes, see page 281.

St Clement's Cake

MAKES A 17 CM|7 IN CAKE

170 g|6 oz butter, softened

170 g|6 oz caster sugar

grated zest and juice of 1 medium orange

2 room-temperature eggs, beaten

170 g|6 oz self-raising flour

To finish

3 tablespoons lemon curd (see page 456)

225 g|8 oz icing sugar, sifted

grated zest and juice of 1 lemon

1 Heat the oven to 180°C|350°F|gas mark 4. Grease 2 × 17 cm|7 in sandwich tins and line the bases with baking parchment, cut to fit.

2 Cream the butter with an electric beater and, when soft, add the sugar and beat until pale and fluffy. Add the orange zest.

3 Beat in the eggs a little at a time, beating well between each addition. Fold in the flour and add the orange juice.

4 Divide the mixture between the prepared tins and smooth the tops with a spatula. Bake in the middle of the oven for 20–25 minutes, or until the cakes are well-risen, golden and feel spongy to the fingertips.

5 Allow the cakes to cool for a few minutes in the tins, then turn out on to a wire rack. Peel off the lining paper. Invert the cakes so that they cool the right-side up.

6 Sandwich the cakes together with the lemon curd.

7 Put the icing sugar in a bowl and add the lemon zest and enough lemon juice to make a thick glacé icing. Spread over the top of the cake.

NOTE: For more information on creaming-method cakes, see page 279.

Lemon and Orange-flower Cake

MAKES A 20 CM│8 IN CAKE

5 room-temperature eggs

170 g│6 oz caster sugar

1½ tablespoons orange-flower water

juice and grated zest of 1 lemon

170 g│6 oz plain flour

¼ teaspoon baking powder

55 g│2 oz butter, melted and cooled

To serve

3 tablespoons lemon curd (see page 456)

icing sugar, sifted

1 Heat the oven to 180°C│350°F│gas mark 4. Grease a 20 cm│8 in *moule à manqué* tin and line the base with a disc of baking parchment.

2 Separate the eggs and whisk the yolks and 85 g│3 oz of the sugar in a large bowl until very light and pale. Whisk in the orange-flower water and lemon zest and juice.

3 In a second large bowl whisk the egg whites until stiff. Whisk in the remaining sugar gradually until very thick and shiny.

4 Sift the flour with the baking powder.

5 Half-fold the egg whites into the yolk mixture, using a metal spoon. Add the butter, flour and baking powder and fold together. Pour into the prepared tin.

6 Bake in the centre of the oven for about 35 minutes or until the top springs back when pressed lightly with a fingertip. Loosen the sides of the cake with a knife, turn out on to a wire rack and leave to cool completely.

7 When the cake is cold, split it in half horizontally and sandwich together with the lemon curd. Dust with icing sugar.

Orange and Poppy Seed Cake

MAKES A 23 CM | 9 IN CAKE

115 g | 4 oz butter, softened

225 g | 8 oz sugar

4 room-temperature eggs, beaten

225 g | 8 oz plain flour

2½ teaspoons baking powder

150 ml | 5 fl oz milk

85 g | 3 oz poppy seeds

1 teaspoon vanilla essence

grated zest of 2 oranges

For the glaze

115 ml | 4 fl oz fresh orange juice

115 g | 4 oz granulated sugar

1 Heat the oven to 170°C | 325°F | gas mark 3. Grease a 23 cm | 9 in loose-bottomed cake tin and line the base with a disc of baking parchment.

2 Cream the butter and sugar together in a mixing bowl until pale and fluffy. Add the eggs gradually, beating well after each addition. Add a little of the flour if necessary, to prevent the mixture from curdling.

3 Sift the remaining flour with the baking powder on to the creamed mixture. Using a large metal spoon, fold in carefully, adding the milk, poppy seeds, vanilla essence and orange zest. Pour into the prepared tin.

4 Bake in the centre of the oven for 1–1¼ hours or until the top springs back when pressed with a fingertip. Cover with a piece of greaseproof paper if the top becomes too dark.

5 Meanwhile, make the glaze by combining the orange juice and sugar in a small saucepan. Bring to the boil, then reduce the heat and simmer for 5 minutes.

6 Remove the cake from the oven and allow to cool in the tin for 30 minutes, then turn out on to a wire rack to cool. While still warm, prick holes all over the top with a skewer and pour over the warm glaze. Leave to cool completely.

NOTE: For more information on creaming-method cakes, see page 279.

Yoghurt Cake with Lemon Syrup

This cake is steeped in lemon syrup for up to 24 hours after it has been baked. It tastes fresh and very delicious.

MAKES A 20 CM|8 IN CAKE

85 g|3 oz self-raising flour, sifted

a pinch of salt

1 teaspoon baking powder

225 g|8 oz semolina

140 g|5 oz caster sugar

150 ml|5 fl oz sunflower oil

250 g|9 oz Greek yoghurt

1 teaspoon vanilla essence

1 tablespoon orange-flower water

2 room-temperature eggs, beaten

55 g|2 oz hazelnuts, toasted and finely chopped

For the syrup

170 g|6 oz caster sugar

juice of 1 lemon

290 ml|10 fl oz water

1 Heat the oven to 190°C|375°F|gas mark 5. Lightly oil a 20 cm|8 in cake tin and line the base with a disc of baking parchment.

2 Sift the flour again, with the salt and baking powder, into a large mixing bowl and mix in the semolina and sugar. Make a well in the centre.

3 Mix together the oil, yoghurt, vanilla essence, orange-flower water and eggs and pour into the well. Using a wooden spoon, gradually draw in the dry ingredients from the sides and beat until smooth. Pour into the prepared tin, spread out evenly and sprinkle with the hazelnuts.

4 Bake in the centre of the oven for 35–40 minutes or until a sharp knife inserted into the centre comes out clean. Remove from the oven and leave to cool in the tin for 10 minutes.

5 Meanwhile, make the syrup. Put the sugar and lemon juice into a small saucepan, add the water and stir over a low heat, without boiling, until the sugar has dissolved completely. Bring to the boil, then reduce the heat and simmer for 5 minutes. Turn off the heat but keep the syrup warm.

6 Turn the cake out on to a plate while still warm. Pierce the top with a skewer in about 12–15 different places and spoon over the syrup. Leave the cake to cool and soak up the syrup for 24 hours, spooning the syrup over from time to time so that as much as possible is absorbed.

Passion-fruit and Lime Syrup Cake

MAKES A 20 × 30 CM | 8 × 12 IN CAKE

170 g | 6 oz butter, softened

170 g | 6 oz caster sugar

grated zest of ½ lime

3 large room-temperature eggs, beaten

170 g | 6 oz self-raising flour, sifted

water

For the syrup

juice of 2 limes

3 passion-fruit, halved, juice and seeds reserved

55 g | 2 oz caster sugar

1 Heat the oven to 190°C | 375°F | gas mark 5. Grease a shallow 20 × 30 cm | 8 × 12 in cake tin and line the base with a piece of baking parchment.

2 Cream the butter in a mixing bowl until soft, then add the sugar and beat until pale and fluffy. Add the lime zest.

3 Add the eggs gradually, beating well after each addition. Add a little of the flour if necessary, to prevent the mixture from curdling.

4 Fold in the remaining flour, using a large metal spoon. Add enough water to achieve a dropping consistency. Turn into the prepared tin and spread out evenly.

5 Bake in the centre of the oven for about 20 minutes or until well-risen and golden and the top springs back when pressed lightly with a fingertip.

6 Lay a piece of greaseproof paper on the work surface. Loosen the edges of the cake and turn it out on to the paper. Peel away the lining paper from the bottom of the cake. Turn the right way up on to a wire rack.

7 Make the syrup: put the sugar and lime juice into a small saucepan and stir over a low heat, without boiling, until the sugar has dissolved completely.

8 Bring to the boil and boil until syrupy. Remove from the heat and allow to cool slightly, then add the passion-fruit pulp and seeds.

9 While the cake is still warm, brush the top liberally with the syrup. Leave to cool. The syrup will harden to a crust.

NOTE: For more information on creaming-method cakes, see page 279.

Lime Blueberry Cake

MAKES 16 SQUARES

150 g | 5½ oz butter, softened
150 g | 5½ oz caster sugar
grated zest of 2 limes
2 room-temperature eggs, beaten
250 g | 9 oz plain flour
2 teaspoons baking powder

a pinch of salt
3 tablespoons lemon juice
6 tablespoons milk
150 g | 5½ oz dried, sweetened blueberries
2 tablespoons demerara sugar

1 Heat the oven to 180°C | 350°F | gas mark 4. Line the base and sides of a 20 cm | 8 in square, 3 cm | 1½ in deep cake tin with baking parchment.
2 Cream the butter, sugar and lime zest until pale and fluffy.
3 Gradually beat in the eggs.
4 Sift together the flour, baking powder and salt.
5 Fold the flour into the butter mixture in 3 additions, adding first the lime juice then the milk between additions.
6 Fold in the blueberries, reserving 2 tablespoons to sprinkle over the top.
7 Spread the mixture into the prepared tin and sprinkle with the reserved blueberries and the demerara sugar.
8 Bake in the centre of the oven for 30 minutes. Cool in the tin for 5 minutes then turn out on to a wire rack to finish cooling. Cut into squares to serve.

NOTE: For more information on creaming-method cakes, see page 279.

Ginger Cakes

Ginger has been used as a spice in the West for hundreds of years. It is a rhizome, or underground stem, and in culinary terms we know it as root ginger. It is sold either fresh, as a dried piece of root, dried and powdered, crystallized or in syrup. Originally from the warmer parts of Asia, it has been used in England since before the Norman Conquest. It was used in medieval times in gingerbread, for which there are many old recipes, as well as some for ginger snaps and parkins. As with all spices, it was expensive and so would have been a treat for the rich.

Powdered ginger, candied ginger and ginger in syrup can all be used in cakes and biscuits. It is also possible to grate fresh ginger root in place of powdered ginger. It can be powerful, so care must be taken not to add too much. The flavour of ginger goes particularly well with treacle, which makes a very moist cake that has good keeping qualities. Some ginger cakes are good sliced and spread with butter.

Black Sticky Gingerbread

MAKES 1 LARGE CAKE

225 g | 8 oz butter
225 g | 8 oz soft dark brown sugar
225 g | 8 oz black treacle
290 ml | 10 fl oz milk
340 g | 12 oz plain flour

2 teaspoons ground ginger
1 tablespoon ground cinnamon
2 teaspoons bicarbonate of soda
2 room-temperature eggs, beaten

1 Heat the oven to 150°C | 300°F | gas mark 2.
2 Line the base and sides of a 20 × 30 cm | 8 × 12 in roasting tin with baking parchment.
3 Melt the butter, sugar and treacle in a saucepan. Pour in the milk then cool to room temperature.
4 Sift the flour with the ginger, cinnamon and bicarbonate of soda, then stir in the melted mixture along with the beaten eggs. Stir well and pour into the prepared tin.
5 Bake for about 1 hour, covering the top with the greaseproof paper after 45 minutes. It is cooked when a skewer inserted into the centre comes out clean.
6 When the gingerbread is cold, cut into fingers and store in an airtight container

NOTE: For more information on melting-method cakes, see page 279.

Ginger Cake .

This cake is dark and sticky and keeps very well. It improves if it is kept for a week before serving. Do not open the oven door during baking or the cake will sink. It may sink a little after baking but will be delicious nonetheless.

MAKES A 17 CM|7 IN CAKE

115 g|4 oz butter

115 g|4 oz soft dark brown sugar

225 g|8 oz black treacle

225 g|8 oz plain flour

1 teaspoon ground ginger

2 room-temperature eggs, beaten

55 g|2 oz sultanas

55 g|2 oz preserved stem ginger, chopped into small
  pieces

2 tablespoons milk

½ teaspoon bicarbonate of soda

1 Heat the oven to 170°C|325°F|gas mark 3. Grease a 17 cm|7 in cake tin and line the base with a disc of baking parchment.

2 Melt the butter, sugar and treacle in a saucepan over a low heat. Do not let the mixture boil. Remove from the heat and allow to cool slightly.

3 Sift the flour with the ginger into a mixing bowl and make a well in the centre. Pour in the melted mixture and the eggs. Using a wooden spoon, gradually draw in the flour and mix carefully and well to a smooth batter. Add the sultanas and preserved ginger. Warm the milk to blood heat, stir in the bicarbonate of soda and mix in quickly. Pour into the prepared tin.

4 Bake in the centre of the oven for 1½ hours or until the top springs back when pressed lightly with a fingertip.

5 Remove from the oven and cool in the tin for 15 minutes, then turn out on to a wire rack and leave to cool completely.

NOTES: If the cake is to be kept for a few days before serving, wrap in kitchen foil or store in an airtight cake tin.

For more information on melting-method cakes, see page 279.

Fochabers Gingerbread

Fochabers is a town near Elgin in the north east of Scotland. This gingerbread is made with fruit and beer. Originally it would have been made using half butter and half lard, however, making it with just butter means that vegetarians can enjoy it too. It is good served sliced and spread with butter.

MAKES A 20 CM|8 IN CAKE

225 g|8 oz butter, softened

115 g|4 oz caster sugar

225 g|8 oz black treacle, warmed slightly to make it runny

2 room-temperature eggs, beaten

450 g|1 lb plain flour

2 teaspoons mixed spice

4 teaspoons ground ginger

2 teaspoons ground cinnamon

½ teaspoon ground cloves

85 g|3 oz ground almonds

115 g|4 oz sultanas

115 g|4 oz currants

85 g|3 oz mixed peel

2 teaspoons bicarbonate of soda

290 ml|10 fl oz beer (brown ale)

1 Heat the oven to 150°C|300°F|gas mark 2. Grease and line a deep 20 cm|8 in square cake tin with a piece of baking parchment cut to fit.

2 Using an electric beater, cream the butter and sugar together until they are pale and fluffy. Beat in the slightly warmed treacle (it must be hot).

3 Beat in the eggs a little at a time, beating well between each addition.

4 Sift the flour and the spices together and add to the ground almonds and fruits. Mix into the cake mixture.

5 Dissolve the bicarbonate of soda in the beer and stir into the cake mixture. Transfer the mixture into the cake tin, level the top with a palette knife and place in the centre of the preheated oven. Bake for approximately 1¾ –2 hours. A knife inserted into the centre will come out clean when the cake is cooked. Allow to stand in the tin for 15 minutes before turning it out on to a wire rack to cool completely.

NOTE: For more information on creaming-method cakes, see page 279.

Yorkshire Parkin

Parkin is best stored for about a week before eating. It can be stored in a tin or wrapped in kitchen foil. Serve it cut into squares or thick slices. It is traditionally served on 5 November, Guy Fawkes' Night.

MAKES A 20 × 25 CM | 8 × 10 IN CAKE

225 g | 8 oz plain flour

2 teaspoons baking powder

2 teaspoons ground ginger

55 g | 2 oz butter

55 g | 2 oz lard

225 g | 8 oz medium oatmeal

115 g | 4 oz caster sugar

170 g | 6 oz golden syrup

170 g | 6 oz black treacle

4 tablespoons milk

1 Heat the oven to 180°C | 350°F | gas mark 4. Grease a shallow 20 × 25 cm | 8 × 10 in tin and line the base with a piece of baking parchment.

2 Sift the flour, baking powder and ginger together into a large mixing bowl. Cut the butter and lard into pieces and rub into the flour until the mixture resembles fine breadcrumbs. Stir in the oatmeal and sugar. Make a well in the centre of the mixture.

3 Put the syrup and treacle into a saucepan and warm gently. Pour into the well. Add the milk and mix well until all the flour is incorporated. Turn the mixture into the prepared tin.

4 Bake in the centre of the oven for about 45 minutes or until the sides of the cake have shrunk away from the tin.

5 Turn out on to a wire rack and leave to cool completely.

NOTE: For more information on rubbing-in method cakes, see page 278.

Spiced Ginger Roll

This is a delicious cake to serve as a pudding or for tea.

SERVES 4

For the filling

340 g | 12 oz cooking apples

30 g | 1 oz butter

1 teaspoon ground cinnamon

55 g | 2 oz sugar

For the roll

caster sugar, for dusting

115 g | 4 oz plain flour

1 teaspoon ground mixed spice

1 teaspoon ground ginger

70 g | 2½ oz butter

2 tablespoons black treacle

2 tablespoons golden syrup

1 room-temperature egg

150 ml | 5 fl oz water

1 teaspoon bicarbonate of soda

To serve

150 ml | 5 fl oz double cream, whipped

1 First make the filling: peel and core the apples and slice them thickly.

2 Melt the butter in a saucepan and add the cinnamon, sugar and apples. Cover with a lid and cook over a very gentle heat, stirring occasionally, until the apples are pulpy. Remove from the heat and beat until smooth, adding more sugar if the apples are still tart. Allow to cool.

3 Heat the oven to 180°C|350°F|gas mark 4. Grease a 23 × 30 cm|9 × 12 in Swiss roll tin and line the base with oiled baking parchment. Dust with caster sugar. Tap out the excess.

4 Sift the flour, mixed spice and ginger together into a mixing bowl. Melt the butter in a saucepan with the treacle and syrup. Do not allow to boil. Remove from heat. Whisk the egg with the water and bicarbonate of soda and add to the melted mixture.

5 Pour the mixture into the flour and whisk together for 30 seconds. Pour into the prepared tin.

6 Bake in the centre of the oven for 12–15 minutes or until firm to the touch.

7 Turn out on to a sheet of greaseproof paper dusted with caster sugar. Remove the lining paper. Spread the cake with the apple purée, roll up like a Swiss roll (see page 000) and serve with the cream.

NOTE: For more information on melting-method cakes, see page 279.

Ginger and Banana Cake

MAKES A 20 CM|8 IN SQUARE CAKE

115 g|4 oz butter

115 g|4 oz soft brown sugar

115 g|4 oz treacle

115 g|4 oz plain flour

115 g|4 oz wholemeal flour

2 teaspoons ground ginger

2 teaspoons ground cinnamon

1 room-temperature egg, beaten

1 large ripe banana, mashed

150 ml|5 fl oz milk, warmed slightly

1 teaspoon bicarbonate of soda

1 Heat the oven to 150°C|300°F|gas mark 2. Grease and line a 20 cm|8 in square tin with baking parchment.

2 Melt the butter, sugar and treacle into a saucepan over a low heat; do not allow it to get too hot.

3 Sift the flours together with the spices into a large bowl. Add any bran left in the sieve to the bowl. Make a well in the centre and pour in the cooled melted ingredients and the egg. Mix well and beat to get rid of any floury lumps. Add the mashed banana, milk and bicarbonate of soda. Mix well and pour into the prepared tin.

4 Bake in the centre of the oven for approximately 1 hour. It is cooked if a knife inserted into the centre comes out clean. Allow it to sit in the tin for 15 minutes before turning it out on to a wire rack to cool completely.

NOTE: For more information on melting-method cakes, see page 279.

Ginger and Honey Cake

MAKES A 23 CM|9 IN SQUARE CAKE

225 g|8 oz clear honey

225 g|8 oz butter

170 g|6 oz soft dark brown sugar

225 g|8 oz plain flour

55 g|2 oz self-raising flour

1 tablespoon ground ginger

1 teaspoon ground cinnamon

2 room-temperature eggs, beaten

150 ml|5 fl oz milk

½ teaspoon bicarbonate of soda

For the topping

115 g|4 oz butter

140 g|5 oz icing sugar, sifted

2 tablespoons clear honey

3 tablespoons grated plain chocolate (optional)

1 Heat the oven to 170°C|325°F|gas mark 3. Grease and line a 23 cm|9 in square tin with a piece of baking parchment cut to fit.

2 Put the honey, butter and sugar into a saucepan and place over a low heat to melt. Don't allow it to get too hot. Put to one side to cool until it is just warm.

3 Sift the flours, ginger and cinnamon together into a large mixing bowl. Make a well in the centre and add the eggs. Start to mix with the flour and then add the melted ingredients. Mix well and beat out any lumps that appear. Work quite quickly.

4 Warm the milk slightly and add the bicarbonate of soda. Stir this into the cake mixture. Pour into the prepared cake tin and place in centre of the oven. Bake for approximately 1 hour. It is ready when the top, pressed lightly with a finger, springs back. Alternatively, push a knife into the centre. If it comes out clean, it is cooked. Allow the cake to rest for 5 minutes in the tin before turning out on to a wire rack to cool down completely.

5 To make the honey cream: cream the butter until soft. Gradually add the sugar and finally mix in the honey. When the cake is cold, spread the honey cream over the top and sprinkle with grated chocolate, if using.

NOTE: For more information on melting-method cakes, see page 279.

Ginger and Lemon Cake

This cake is made with grated raw potato. It is very moist, with a slightly chewy crust.

MAKES A 675 G | 1½ LB LOAF

170 g | 6 oz butter, softened

170 g | 6 oz soft dark brown sugar

3 room-temperature eggs, beaten

170 g | 6 oz self-raising flour

2 teaspoons ground ginger

2 teaspoons ground cinnamon

115 g | 4 oz grated raw potato

For the icing

170 g | 6 oz icing sugar, sifted

2 tablespoons lemon juice

1 teaspoon grated lemon zest

1 Heat the oven to 180°C | 350°F | gas mark 4. Grease a 675 g | 1½ lb loaf tin and line the base with a piece of baking parchment.

2 Cream the butter and sugar together in a mixing bowl until pale and fluffy. Add the eggs gradually, beating well after each addition. Add a little of the flour if necessary, to prevent the mixture from curdling.

3 Sift the flour and spices together on to the mixture and fold in, using a large metal spoon. Fold in the grated potato. Turn into the prepared tin.

4 Bake in the centre of the oven for 50–60 minutes or until the top springs back when pressed lightly with a fingertip.

5 When the cake is cold, make the icing: mix the icing sugar with the lemon juice and zest. Spread on top of the cake.

NOTES: The cake will keep well for 4–5 days in a tin or it can be frozen.

For more information on melting-method cakes, see page 279.

Cakes with Nuts

As an ingredient in a cake, nuts can range from being a small addition to give a little texture to being almost the main ingredient. To vary the flavour of the cakes in this section, substitute one kind of nut for another. For example, using hazelnuts instead of walnuts in the *Apricot and Walnut Loaf* will considerably change the flavour but the method and timing will be exactly the same.

Nuts can be ground in a food processor, but if they have been toasted, ensure that they are cold beforehand. Nuts can easily become oily, so in order to absorb some of this oil add a little of the measured sugar from the recipe. This will help to keep the ground nuts from clumping together so that they can be folded into the cake mixture easily. There is more information on nuts in the *Baking Ingredients* section (see page 16). Always use unsalted nuts in the recipes.

Almond Cake

MAKES A 20 CM|8 IN CAKE

140 g|5 oz butter, softened
140 g|5 oz caster sugar
grated zest of 1 lemon
6 room-temperature eggs

85 g|3 oz plain flour
½ teaspoon baking powder
225 g|8 oz blanched almonds, roughly chopped
1 tablespoon water

1 Heat the oven to 190°C|375°F|gas mark 5. Grease a 20 cm|8 in *moule à manqué* tin and line the base with a disc of baking parchment.
2 Cream the butter and sugar together in a large mixing bowl until pale and fluffy. Add the lemon zest. Separate the eggs and beat in the yolks.
3 Sift the flour with the baking powder. Mix with the chopped almonds.
4 Whisk the egg whites until stiff, then fold them into the creamed mixture together with the flour and nut mixture and the water, using a large metal spoon. Pour into the prepared tin.
5 Bake in the centre of the oven for about 35–40 minutes or until the sides have shrunk away from the sides of the tin slightly and the top springs back when pressed lightly with a fingertip.
6 Remove from the oven and allow to cool in the tin for a few minutes, then turn out on to a wire rack and leave to cool completely.

NOTE: For more information on creaming-method cakes, see page 279.

Carrot and Almond Cake

This is a moist cake which is very easy to make.

MAKES A 900 G|2 LB LOAF

170 g|6 oz self-raising flour

1 teaspoon bicarbonate of soda

1 teaspoon mixed spice

½ teaspoon ground ginger

225 g|8 oz soft dark brown sugar

85 g|3 oz raisins

100 g|3½ oz ground almonds

150 ml|5 fl oz sunflower oil

2 room-temperature eggs, lightly beaten

340 g|12 oz carrot, grated (approximately 2 large carrots)

For the icing

55 g|2 oz cream cheese

30 g|1 oz butter, softened

grated zest of 1 orange

140 g|5 oz icing sugar, sifted

45 g|1½ oz flaked almonds, toasted and cooled

1 Heat the oven to 170°C|325°F|gas mark 3. Grease and line the base of a 900 g|2 lb loaf tin with a piece of baking parchment cut to fit.

2 Sift the flour, bicarbonate of soda and spices into a bowl. Add the sugar, raisins and almonds and mix well.

3 Whisk the oil and eggs together and add to the bowl. Mix in well. Add the carrots. Spoon into the prepared loaf tin and bake in the oven for about 1¼ hours. Cover with greaseproof paper if it starts to get too dark. It is ready when the top springs back if touched lightly with a finger. Allow to stand for 5 minutes in the tin before turning out on to a wire rack to cool completely.

4 Meanwhile make the icing. Beat the cream cheese, butter and orange zest together until smooth. Gradually add the icing sugar. Once the cake is cold, spread the icing on top and scatter over the flaked almonds.

Toasted Almond Roulade with Strawberries and Cream

SERVES 6–8

100 g|3½ oz whole blanched almonds
100 g|3½ oz caster sugar
4 room-temperature eggs, separated
a pinch of salt
30 g|1 oz flaked almonds
icing sugar for dusting

For the filling

290 ml|10 fl oz double cream
225 g|8 oz fresh strawberries, hulled and sliced

To decorate

whole strawberries
mint sprigs

1 Heat the oven to 190°C|375°F| gas mark 5. Line a 25 × 35 cm|10 × 14 in roasting tin with baking parchment.

2 Toast the whole almonds on a baking sheet in the oven for 7 minutes until golden-brown then allow to cool. Grind to a fine powder in a food processor with 1 tablespoon of the caster sugar.

3 Reserve 1 tablespoon of the remaining caster sugar for the egg whites and whisk the remainder with the egg yolks in a bowl until light and thick. Fold in the ground–almond mixture.

4 Whisk the egg whites with a pinch of salt until just stiff, then whisk in the reserved sugar. Stir a large spoonful of the whites into the almond mixture. Fold in the remaining egg whites carefully.

5 Turn the mixture into the prepared tin and sprinkle over the flaked almonds. Cook in the oven for 12–15 minutes until golden-brown and risen. Cool on a wire rack.

6 Dust a large piece of greaseproof paper with icing sugar. Turn out the roulade on to the paper. Carefully peel away the baking parchment.

7 Whip the cream until it just holds its shape and spread it over the roulade. Cover the cream with the strawberries, then roll up the roulade and place it on a serving dish. Decorate with the whole strawberries and mint sprigs.

NOTE: For further information on whisking-method cakes, see page 281.

Mandel Cake

This summer cake can be served as a pudding filled with fresh cream and summer berries.

MAKES A 20 CM|8 IN CAKE

6 room-temperature eggs

225 g|8 oz caster sugar

2 tablespoons lemon juice

1 teaspoon grated lemon zest

1 teaspoon ground cinnamon

225 g|8 oz almonds, toasted, cooled and finely ground

55 g|2 oz plain flour

½ teaspoon cream of tartar

For the filling

100 ml|3½ fl oz double cream

2 tablespoons lemon curd (see page 456)

To finish

icing sugar, sifted

1 Heat the oven to 180°C|350°F|gas mark 4. Line the base and sides of 2 × 20 cm|8 in sandwich tins carefully with oiled kitchen foil or non-stick baking parchment paper cases.

2 Separate the eggs. Beat the yolks well with half the sugar until pale and fluffy. Gradually beat in the lemon juice and zest and cinnamon.

3 Mix together the almonds and flour.

4 Whisk the egg whites until stiff. Add the cream of tartar and 2 tablespoons of the remaining sugar. Whisk well until stiff and shiny. Gradually add the remaining sugar, whisking well after each addition.

5 Using a large metal spoon, fold the egg whites quickly into the yolk mixture, then fold in the almonds and flour. Do not overmix or the cake will collapse. Divide between the prepared tins and spread out evenly.

6 Bake for 40 minutes or until the tops spring back when pressed lightly with a fingertip.

7 Remove from the oven and allow to cool in the tins for 5 minutes, then turn out on to a wire rack, carefully peel off the lining foil and leave to cool completely.

8 Meanwhile, make the filling. Whip the cream until it just holds its shape, then fold in the lemon curd.

9 When the cakes are cool, sandwich together with the filling and dust the top with icing sugar.

NOTE: For further information on whisking-method cakes, see page 281.

Orange and Almond Gâteau with Chocolate Ganache

MAKES A 20 CM|8 IN CAKE

4 eggs

115 g|4 oz caster sugar, plus 1 extra teaspoon

grated zest of 2 oranges

55 g|2 oz plain flour

½ teaspoon baking powder

115 g|4 oz ground almonds

For the ganache

125 ml|4 fl oz double cream

170 g|6 oz plain chocolate, chopped into small pieces

For the orange syrup

30 g|1 oz caster sugar

55 ml|2 fl oz water

juice of 1 orange

To finish

icing sugar, sifted

1 Heat the oven to 180°C|350°F|gas mark 4. Grease a 20 cm|8 in *moule à manqué* tin and line the base with a disc of baking parchment.

2 Separate the eggs and put the yolks and 115 g|4 oz sugar into a bowl. Whisk, preferably with an electric beater, until light and creamy. Fold in the orange zest.

3 Whisk the egg whites until stiff. Whisk in the extra teaspoon of sugar. Fold carefully into the egg-yolk mixture, using a large metal spoon.

4 Sift the flour with the baking powder, mix with the ground almonds and fold very carefully and quickly into the cake mixture. Pour into the prepared tin.

5 Bake in the centre of the oven for 35–40 minutes. The sides should shrink away from the tin very slightly and the top spring back when pressed lightly with a fingertip. Do not open the oven door before 30 minutes have passed, as the cake could collapse.

6 Remove the cake from the oven and allow to cool in the tin for 5 minutes, then turn out on to a wire rack and leave to cool completely.

7 Meanwhile, make the ganache. Bring the cream to boiling point in a saucepan, then remove from the heat and stir in the chocolate. Allow the mixture to stand for 2 minutes, then beat until smooth. Set aside to cool at room temperature. Do not refrigerate.

8 Make the orange syrup: put the sugar and water into a small saucepan and heat gently until the sugar has dissolved completely, then bring to the boil. Boil for 1 minute, then remove from the heat and allow to cool. Stir the orange juice into the cooled syrup.

9 When the cake is cold, beat the chocolate ganache with an electric whisk for 2 minutes or until it has lightened in colour and texture.

10 Split the cake in half horizontally. Brush the bottom layer of the cake with half the orange syrup. Spread over a little of the whipped ganache. Cover with the top layer of cake and brush with the remaining syrup.

11 Spread the top and sides of the cake with the remaining ganache, as neatly as possible. Chill for 30 minutes before serving dusted with a little icing sugar.

NOTE: For further information on whisking-method cakes, see page 281.

Pain de Genes (Rich Almond Cake)

This cake is delicious served in small pieces with strong coffee after a meal.

MAKES A 20 CM|8 IN CAKE

115 g | 4 oz blanched almonds

3 room-temperature eggs

140 g | 5 oz caster sugar

55 g | 2 oz potato starch or plain flour

½ teaspoon baking powder

a good pinch of salt

85 g | 3 oz butter

1 tablespoon Amaretto or Kirsch

To finish

icing sugar, sifted

1 Heat the oven to 180°C | 350°F | gas mark 4. Brush a *moule à manqué* or 20 cm | 8 in cake tin with melted butter, line the base with a disc of baking parchment and brush again with melted butter.

2 Grind the almonds slightly less finely than bought ground almonds.

3 Whisk the eggs and sugar together until pale and fluffy.

4 Sift the flour, baking powder and salt together into a mixing bowl. Stir in the ground almonds. Add to the egg and sugar mixture and half-fold in, using a large metal spoon.

5 Melt the butter until runny but not hot and carefully fold it into the cake mixture with the minimum of stirring. Add the Amaretto or Kirsch. Turn the mixture into the prepared tin.

6 Bake in the centre of the oven for 30–35 minutes or until the cake is brown on top and springs back when pressed lightly with a fingertip.

7 Remove the cake from the oven and allow to cool in the tin for 5 minutes, then loosen the sides with a knife and turn out on to a wire rack and leave to cool completely.

8 Serve dusted with icing sugar.

NOTE: For further information on whisking-method cakes, see page 281.

Hazelnut and Apricot Cake

This cake is made without eggs and consequently has a fairly dense texture. The apricot purée makes it very moist and it keeps well. Once iced, it must be kept in the refrigerator.

MAKES A 17 CM | 7 IN CAKE

55 g | 2 oz dried apricots
290 ml | 10 fl oz water
juice of ½ lemon
115 g | 4 oz butter, softened
170 g | 6 oz caster sugar
225 g | 8 oz plain flour
1 teaspoon ground mixed spice

1 teaspoon bicarbonate of soda
115 g | 4 oz toasted hazelnuts, roughly chopped

For the icing

140 g | 5 oz cream cheese
30 g | 1 oz sugar
30 g | 1 oz dried apricots, finely chopped

1 Heat the oven to 180°C | 350°F | gas mark 4. Grease an 17 cm | 7 in cake tin and line the base with a disc of baking parchment.

2 Put the apricots and water into a saucepan and bring to the boil. Reduce the heat, then simmer gently for 20 minutes or until the apricots are very soft.

3 Purée the apricots with the cooking liquid in a food processor or liquidizer, or push it through a sieve. Add the lemon juice and make up to 150 ml | 5 fl oz with water.

4 Meanwhile, cream the butter in a mixing bowl until soft, then add the sugar. Beat together until soft and creamy.

5 Sift the flour together with the mixed spice and bicarbonate of soda.

6 Add the apricot purée to the creamed mixture and fold in the flour and chopped nuts. Mix well. Turn into the prepared tin.

7 Bake in the centre of the oven for about 1 hour. Loosen the edges of the cake with a knife, turn out on to a wire rack and leave to cool completely.

8 Meanwhile, mix together the ingredients for the icing. Taste and add more sugar if necessary.

9 When the cake is cold, spread the icing over the top. Keep in the refrigerator until ready to serve.

NOTE: For more information on creaming-method cakes, see page 279.

Normandy Apple Cake

For the filling

3 cooking apples, total weight about 450 g|1 lb
15 g|½ oz butter
a strip of thinly pared lemon zest
55–85 g|2–3 oz soft light brown sugar

For the cake

125 g|4½ oz caster sugar
40 g|1½ oz toasted hazelnuts, ground
4 egg yolks
50 g|1¾ oz plain flour
50 g|1¾ oz arrowroot
3 egg whites

To serve

icing sugar, sifted
150 ml|5 fl oz double cream, whipped

1 Wash but do not peel the apples, quarter and core them, then slice thinly. Melt the butter in a heavy saucepan and add the apples with the lemon zest and 4 tablespoons water. Cover with a lid and cook over a gentle heat, stirring occasionally, until completely soft. Push through a sieve into a measuring jug.

2 Return the measured purée to the rinsed out pan. Add at least 55 g|2 oz sugar to 570 ml|1 pint purée. Cook rapidly for about 4 minutes until the mixture is of a dropping consistency. Remove from the heat and leave to cool.

3 Heat the oven to 180°C|350°F|gas mark 4. Grease a 20 cm|8 in sandwich tin or *moule à manqué* and dust lightly with flour. Tap out the excess.

4 Beat the sugar, nuts and egg yolks together in a mixing bowl until pale and creamy. Sift the flour with the arrowroot and fold into the creamed mixture, using a large metal spoon.

5 Whisk the egg whites until stiff but not dry, then fold them into the mixture. Turn into the prepared tin and spread out evenly.

6 Bake in the centre of the oven for 40 minutes or until the top springs back when pressed lightly with a fingertip.

7 Remove the cake from the oven and allow to cool in the tin for 10 minutes, then turn out on to a wire rack and leave to cool completely.

8 When the cake is cold, split in half horizontally and sandwich together with the apple filling. Dredge the top with icing sugar and serve with the whipped cream.

NOTE: For further information on whisking-method cakes, see page 281.

Hazelnut Roulade with Mango and Passion-fruit

SERVES 6–8

85 g | 3 oz skinned hazelnuts, toasted

140 g | 5 oz caster sugar

5 room-temperature eggs, separated

2 tablespoons golden syrup

icing sugar, for rolling

For the filling

200 ml | 7 fl oz double cream

2 ripe passion-fruit

1 ripe mango

1 tablespoon icing sugar

1 Heat the oven to 190°C | 375°F | gas mark 5. Line the base and sides of a 23 × 33 cm | 9 × 13 in Swiss roll tin with baking parchment.

2 Finely grind the hazelnuts with 2 tablespoons of the sugar.

3 Whisk the egg yolks with the syrup and half the remaining sugar until pale and thick.

4 Whisk the egg whites until stiff then whisk in the remaining sugar to make a thick meringue.

5 Using a large metal spoon, stir a spoonful of the whites into the yolk/sugar mixture, then carefully fold in the remaining whites alternately with the ground nuts.

6 Gently spread the mixture into the lined tin and bake in the top third of the oven for 12–15 minutes or until firm to the touch.

7 Place on a wire rack in the tin and cover with a damp, clean tea towel to cool.

8 When cool, sprinkle a thick layer of icing sugar on to a piece of greaseproof paper the size of the cake. Working quickly, invert the cake on to the icing sugar and peel away the baking parchment.

9 For the filling, cut the passion-fruit in half and squeeze the pulp and seeds into a bowl. Cut the mango in half to remove the stone then cut the flesh into 1 cm | ½ in dice. Place in the bowl with the passion-fruit.

10 Whip the cream with the icing sugar to the soft-peak stage. Fold the fruit into the cream then spread over the cake.

11 Roll the cake from one of the short ends, using the greaseproof paper to help. Place on a serving dish seam-side down.

Coconut Fruit Cake

This recipe was given to us by David Scott Bradbury, who was the manager of Leiths Restaurant. It is a rich and crumbly cake and will be enjoyed by coconut lovers.

MAKES A 23 CM|9 IN CAKE

225 g | 8 oz butter, softened
340 g | 12 oz caster sugar
4 room-temperature eggs, beaten
450 g | 1 lb self-raising flour, sifted
150 ml | 5 fl oz milk
225 g | 8 oz white or pale sultanas

225 g | 8 oz candied citron or lemon peel, chopped, or chopped mixed peel
225 g | 8 oz candied lemon peel, chopped
450 g | 1 lb tin of pineapple, drained and chopped
450 g | 1 lb brazil nuts, chopped
225 g | 8 oz glacé cherries
225 g | 8 oz fine desiccated coconut

1 Heat the oven to 150°C | 300°F | gas mark 2. Grease and flour a deep 23 cm | 9 in cake tin. Line the base with a disc of baking parchment. Wrap several layers of newspaper around the outside of the tin (see *Preparing a Cake Tin*, page 276).
2 Cream the butter and sugar together in a large mixing bowl until pale and fluffy. Add the eggs gradually, beating well after each addition.
3 Fold in the flour, using a large metal spoon, and add the milk. Stir in all the remaining ingredients and mix well. Turn into the prepared tin.
4 Bake in the oven for about 4 hours or until a sharp knife or skewer inserted into the centre of the cake comes out clean. If the top is getting too dark, cover with a piece of kitchen foil or greaseproof paper.
5 Remove the cake from the oven and allow to cool completely in the tin before turning out.

NOTE: For more information on creaming-method cakes, see page 000.

Peanut Cake

MAKES A 20 CM|8 IN CAKE

3 room-temperature eggs
85 g | 3 oz caster sugar
85 g | 3 oz plain flour
½ teaspoon baking powder
115g | 4 oz peanuts, toasted, skinned and ground
85 g | 3 oz butter, melted and cooled

For the filling

3 tablespoons orange curd (see page 000)
55 g | 2 oz cream cheese, mixed together

To finish

icing sugar, sifted

1 Heat the oven to 180°C | 350°F | gas mark 4. Grease a 20 cm | 8 in *moule à manqué* tin and line the base with a disc of baking parchment.

2 Whisk the eggs with the sugar until light and fluffy.

3 Sift the flour with the baking powder and mix with the ground peanuts. Fold into the egg and sugar mixture, using a large metal spoon. Pour the cool butter on to the mixture and fold in carefully. Pour into the prepared tin.

4 Bake in the centre of the oven for 30–35 minutes or until the top feels firm to the touch.

5 Remove from the oven and allow to cool in the tin for 10 minutes, then turn out on to a wire rack and leave to cool completely.

6 When the cake is cold, split in half horizontally and sandwich together with the orange curd and cream cheese mixed together. Dust the top with icing sugar.

Apricot and Carrot Streusel Cake

Streusel is the German word for crumb.

MAKES A 20 CM|8 IN CAKE

For the streusel topping

115 g|4 oz soft light brown sugar
115 g|4 oz pecan nuts, chopped
55 g|2 oz plain flour
1½ tablespoons ground cinnamon
55 g|2 oz melted butter

225 g|8 oz butter, softened
225 g|8 oz caster sugar
3 room-temperature eggs, beaten
225 g|8 oz plain flour
1 teaspoon bicarbonate of soda
1 teaspoon baking powder
170 ml|6 fl oz milk
115 g|4 oz carrot, grated
140 g|5 oz dried apricots, chopped

1 Make the streusel topping. Put the sugar, pecan nuts, flour and cinnamon into a bowl. Add the melted butter and mix well. Set aside.

2 Heat the oven to 180°C|350°F|gas mark 4. Grease a 20 cm|8 in loose-bottomed cake tin and line the base with a piece of baking parchment cut to fit.

3 Cream the butter and sugar together until pale and fluffy. Add the beaten eggs a little at a time, beating well between each addition.

4 Sift the flour, bicarbonate of soda and baking powder together and fold into the mixture.

5 Add the milk and grated carrot and spread the mixture into the prepared tin.

6 Put the chopped dried apricots on top of the mixture. Scatter over the topping.

7 Place in the centre of the oven for 1–1½ hours. The cake is ready when a knife, inserted into the centre comes out clean. If the cake is not cooked but the top is looking dark, turn the oven down a little and cover with a piece of baking parchment. When cooked, remove from the oven and allow to cool for 10 minutes before removing from the tin and placing on a wire rack to cool completely.

NOTE: For more information on creaming-method cakes, see page 279.

Parsnip and Pecan Cake

This is an all-in-one recipe and therefore quick and easy to make. It does not rise very much. If a deep cake is required, double the quantities, bake in 2 tins and sandwich the cakes together with the icing.

MAKES A 20 CM|8 IN CAKE

140 g|5 oz plain flour

2 teaspoons baking powder

140 g|5 oz parsnips, grated

55 g|2 oz pecan nuts, chopped

1 teaspoon freshly grated root ginger

1 room-temperature egg, lightly beaten

a pinch of salt

150 ml|5 fl oz sunflower oil

140 g|5 oz caster sugar

For the icing

85 g|3 oz unsalted butter, softened

100 g|3½ oz cream cheese

55 g|2 oz icing sugar

2 tablespoons orange juice

peeled zest of 1 orange, cut into thin strips

2 tablespoons sugar

115 ml|4 fl oz water

1 Heat the oven to 180°C|350°F|gas mark 4. Grease a 20 cm|8 in *moule à manqué* or sandwich tin. Line the base with a disc of baking parchment.

2 Put all the cake ingredients into a large mixing bowl and mix together thoroughly. Turn into the prepared tin.

3 Bake in the centre of the oven for about 30 minutes or until a sharp knife or skewer inserted into the centre of the cake comes out clean.

4 Remove the cake from the oven and leave to cool completely in the tin.

5 Meanwhile, make the icing: put the butter into a bowl and beat, then gradually add the cream cheese, beating all the time. Add the icing sugar and orange juice and continue beating until light and fluffy. Chill until ready to use.

6 Put the water and sugar into a small saucepan and heat slowly until all the sugar has dissolved. Add the orange zest, bring to the boil and boil for 5 minutes. Using a slotted spoon, remove the zest and leave on a plate to cool.

7 When the cake is cold, spread with the icing and decorate with the orange zest.

Pecan and Rosemary Génoise

MAKES A 20 CM|8 IN CAKE

4 room-temperature eggs

125 g|4½ oz caster sugar

1 teaspoon vanilla essence

125 g|4½ oz plain flour

85 g|3 oz pecan nuts, finely chopped

1 teaspoon finely chopped fresh rosemary

55 g|2 oz butter, melted and cooled

For the filling

4 tablespoons crème fraiche

To finish

icing sugar, sifted

1 Heat the oven to 190°C|375°F| gas mark 5. Lightly oil a 20 cm|8 in *moule à manqué* or deep sandwich tin and line the base with a disc of oiled baking parchment. Dust first with caster sugar and then with flour. Tap out the excess.

2 Break the eggs into a heatproof bowl, add the sugar and vanilla essence and fit the bowl over, but not in, a saucepan of gently simmering water. Whisk with an electric beater until the mixture has doubled in volume and will leave a ribbon trail on the surface when the whisk is lifted. Remove the bowl from the heat and continue whisking until the mixture has cooled.

3 Sift the flour into the mixture and fold in gently, using a large metal spoon, with the pecan nuts and rosemary. Drizzle the butter around the edge of the bowl and incorporate it just before the nuts and rosemary are completely mixed in.

4 Holding the bowl close to the prepared tin, pour in the mixture, taking care not to lose any volume.

5 Bake in the centre of the oven for 25–30 minutes or until firm to the touch and the sides have shrunk away from the tin slightly.

6 Remove from the oven and allow to cool in the tin for 5 minutes, then turn out on to a wire rack and leave to cool completely.

7 When the cake is cold, split it in half horizontally and sandwich together with the crème fraiche. Dredge the top with icing sugar.

NOTE: For further information on whisking-method cakes, see page 281.

Soured Cream and Pecan Cake

MAKES A 23 CM|9 IN CAKE

225 g|8 oz butter, softened

285 g|10 oz caster sugar

2 room-temperature eggs, beaten

285 g|10 oz self-raising flour, sifted

290 ml|10 fl oz soured cream

2 teaspoons vanilla essence

115 g|4 oz pecan nuts, chopped

1 teaspoon ground cinnamon

1 Heat the oven to 170°C|325°F|gas mark 3. Grease a 23 cm|9 in spring-form or loose-bottomed tin and line the base with a disc of baking parchment.

2 Cream the butter in a mixing bowl and add 225 g | 8 oz of the sugar. Beat until pale and fluffy. Add the eggs gradually, beating well after each addition. Add a little of the flour if necessary, to prevent the mixture from curdling. Fold in the remaining flour and add the soured cream and vanilla essence. Mix well but do not beat.

3 Mix the remaining sugar with the pecan nuts and cinnamon.

4 Put half the cake mixture into the prepared tin. Sprinkle over three-quarters of the pecan mixture. Cover with the remaining cake mixture, spread out evenly and sprinkle over the remaining pecan mixture.

5 Bake in the centre of the oven for 1¼– 1½ hours or until a sharp knife or skewer inserted into the centre of the cake comes out clean.

6 Remove from the oven and allow to cool in the tin for 30 minutes, then turn out on to a wire rack and leave to cool completely.

NOTE: For further information on creaming-method cakes, see page 279.

Cranberry and Pecan Cake

MAKES A 23 CM | 9 IN CAKE

225 g | 8 oz butter

225 g | 8 oz soft light brown sugar

225 g | 8 oz golden syrup

340 g | 12 oz plain flour

½ teaspoon ground cinnamon

½ teaspoon ground coriander

½ teaspoon ground ginger

½ teaspoon ground mace

2 room-temperature eggs, beaten

grated zest of 1 orange

290 ml | 10 fl oz milk

2 teaspoons bicarbonate of soda

225 g | 8 oz fresh cranberries, crushed very lightly with
    a fork

85 g | 3 oz pecan nuts, chopped

1 Heat the oven to 150°C | 300°F | gas mark 2. Grease a deep 23 cm | 9 in cake tin and line the base with a disc of baking parchment.

2 Melt the butter with the sugar and syrup in a saucepan. Do not allow to boil. Remove from the heat and allow to cool.

3 Sift the flour and spices together into a large mixing bowl. Make a well in the centre and pour in the melted mixture, the eggs and orange zest. Mix well.

4 Warm the milk and add the bicarbonate of soda. Mix into the cake mixture with the cranberries and nuts. Turn into the prepared tin.

5 Bake in the centre of the oven for about 2 hours or until a sharp knife or skewer inserted into the centre of the cake comes out clean.

6 Remove the cake from the oven. Allow to cool completely in the tin before turning out.

NOTE: For further information on melting-method cakes, see page 279.

Coffee Walnut Cake

MAKES A 17 CM|7 IN CAKE

170 g|6 oz butter, softened

170 g|6 oz caster sugar

3 large room-temperature eggs, beaten

170 g|6 oz self-raising flour, sifted

2 tablespoons coffee essence or very strong instant coffee

85 g|3 oz walnuts, chopped

water (optional)

For the butter cream

115 g|4 oz softened butter

170 g|6 oz icing sugar

2 teaspoons coffee essence

For the glacé icing

115 g|4 oz icing sugar

boiling water

coffee essence

To decorate

walnut halves

1 Heat the oven to 180°C|350°F|gas mark 4.

2 Lightly grease 2 × 17 cm|7 in sandwich tins and line each with a disc of baking parchment.

3 Cream the butter and sugar together in a mixing bowl until pale and fluffy. Beat the eggs into the creamed mixture a little at a time, beating well after each addition. Add 1 tablespoon of the flour if necessary, to prevent the mixture from curdling.

4 Fold in the remaining flour, using a large metal spoon, and add the coffee essence and chopped walnuts. Add some water if necessary to bring the mixture to a dropping consistency. Divide the mixture between the prepared tins and spread out evenly.

5 Bake in the centre of the oven for about 30 minutes or until the cakes are well-risen and feel spongy to the fingertips.

6 Remove the cakes to cool in the tins for a few minutes, then turn out on to a wire rack and leave to cool completely.

7 Meanwhile, make the buttercream: cream the butter in a bowl and add the icing sugar. Beat well and add the coffee essence.

8 Make the glacé icing: sift the icing sugar into a bowl and add a little boiling water and coffee essence to taste. The icing should be of a very thick pouring consistency.

9 When the cakes are cold, sandwich them together with half the buttercream. Pour the glacé icing over the top and decorate with the remaining buttercream, piped into rosettes, and walnut halves.

NOTE: For more information on creaming-method cakes, see page 279.

Fruit Cakes

The addition of dried fruits such as sultanas, raisins, dates and apricots makes a cake moist and helps with its keeping quality. Any cake that contains a lot of dried fruit generally needs to be baked at a lower oven temperature and for a longer time than other cakes, because of the fruit's high sugar content. The tins should have several layers of newspaper wrapped around them (see *Preparing a Cake Tin*, page 276). It is very important to keep an eye on large fruit cakes during baking, covering them with greaseproof paper and turning down the oven temperature if necessary, to prevent overbrowning the top while the cake cooks through.

See also **Festive Cakes** (page 382) for cake recipes using dried fruits.

Light Fruit Cake

MAKES A 20 CM|8 IN CAKE

170 g|6 oz butter, softened
170 g|6 oz caster sugar
3 room-temperature eggs, beaten
340 g|12 oz self-raising flour
½ teaspoon ground mixed spice

½ teaspoon ground cinnamon
150 ml|5 fl oz milk
225 g|8 oz mixed dried fruit, such as sultanas, raisins, currants, chopped apricots, chopped prunes

1 Heat the oven to 180°C|350°F|gas mark 4. Grease a deep 20 cm|8 in cake tin and line the base with a disc of baking parchment.
2 Cream the butter and sugar together in a large mixing bowl until pale and fluffy. Add the eggs gradually, beating well after each addition.
3 Sift together the flour and spices and fold into the creamed mixture, using a large metal spoon. Add the milk and fruit and mix well. Turn into the prepared tin.
4 Bake in the centre of the oven for 1¼ –1½ hours or until a sharp knife or skewer inserted into the centre of the cake comes out clean.
5 Remove the cake from the oven and allow to cool completely in the tin before turning out.

NOTE: For more information on creaming-method cakes, see page 279.

Dundee Cake

MAKES A 20 CM|8 IN CAKE

225 g|8 oz butter

225 g|8 oz caster sugar

grated zest of 1 lemon

5 room-temperature eggs, beaten

225 g|8 oz plain flour, sifted

340 g|12 oz sultanas

340 g|12 oz currants

170 g|6 oz chopped mixed peel

115 g|4 oz glacé cherries

30 g|1 oz blanched almonds, chopped

85 g|3 oz blanched almonds

1 Heat the oven to 150°C|300°F|gas mark 2. Grease a deep 20 cm|8 in cake tin. Line the base and sides with baking parchment.

2 Cream the butter and sugar together in a large mixing bowl until pale and fluffy. Add the lemon zest.

3 Add the eggs gradually, beating well after each addition. Add a little of the flour if necessary, to prevent the mixture from curdling.

4 Fold in the flour and the dried fruit, peel, cherries and chopped almonds, using a large metal spoon. Mix together carefully. Turn into the prepared tin and spread out evenly.

5 Arrange the almonds in concentric circles on the top of the cake.

6 Bake in the centre of the oven for 3–3½ hours or until a sharp knife or skewer inserted into the centre comes out clean.

7 Remove the cake from the oven and allow to cool completely in the tin before turning out.

NOTE: For more information on creaming-method cakes, see page 279.

Cherry Cake

MAKES A 17 CM|7 IN CAKE

170 g|6 oz butter, softened

170 g|6 oz caster sugar

3 room-temperature eggs, beaten

140 g|5 oz self-raising flour

55 g|2 oz plain flour

225 g|8 oz glacé cherries, halved, washed and dried

85 g|3 oz ground almonds

1 Heat the oven to 180°C|350°F|gas mark 4. Grease a deep 17 cm|7 in cake tin and line the base with a disc of baking parchment.

2 Cream the butter and sugar together in a mixing bowl until pale and fluffy. Add the eggs slowly, beating well after each addition.

3 Sift together the flours and add the cherries and ground almonds. Fold into the creamed mixture, using a large metal spoon. Turn into the prepared tin and make a small dimple in the centre to counteract any tendency to rise in the middle.

4 Bake in the centre of the oven for 1–1½ hours or until a sharp knife or skewer inserted into the centre comes out clean.

5 Remove the cake from the oven and allow to cool in the tin for 20 minutes, then turn out on to a wire rack and leave to cool completely.

NOTE: For more information on creaming-method cakes, see page 279.

Boiled Fruit Cake

This is a less expensive version of the *Old-fashioned Boiled Fruit Cake* on page 388.

MAKES A 20 CM|8 IN CAKE

250 g|9 oz mixed dried fruit (e.g. raisins, mango, peach, apricots, etc.)

125 g|4½ oz butter

170 g|6 oz soft light brown sugar

200 ml|7 fl oz water

340 g|12 oz plain flour

1½ teaspoons baking powder

½ teaspoon mixed spice

a pinch of nutmeg

¼ teaspoon bicarbonate of soda

2 room-temperature eggs, beaten

1 Put the fruit, butter, sugar and water into a saucepan and bring slowly to the boil. Simmer for 10 minutes and allow to cool.

2 Heat the oven to 180°C|350°F|gas mark 4. Grease a deep 20 cm|8 in cake tin and line the base with a disc of baking parchment.

3 Sift together the flour, baking powder and spices. Dissolve the bicarbonate of soda in a little warm water.

4 Stir the beaten eggs into the fruit and add the flour and bicarbonate of soda. Mix well and put into the prepared tin.

5 Bake in the centre of the oven for 50–60 minutes or until a sharp knife inserted into the centre of the cake comes out clean. Remove from the tin on to a wire rack to cool completely.

Cranberry and Cherry Cake

Packets of dried cranberries and cherries are available in supermarkets. They have a sharpness which cuts through the cake well. Mixing the fruit with the flour and almonds before adding to the creamed mixture minimizes the likelihood of the fruit sinking.

MAKES A 20 CM│8 IN CAKE

140 g│5 oz self-raising flour
55 g│2 oz plain flour
85 g│3 oz ground almonds
75 g│2½ oz dried cranberries

75 g│2½ oz dried cherries
170 g│6 oz butter, softened
170 g│6 oz caster sugar
3 room-temperature eggs, beaten

1 Grease a deep 20 cm│8 in cake tin and line the base with a disc of baking parchment cut to fit. Heat the oven to 170°C│325°F│gas mark 3.

2 Sift the flours together and add ground almonds, dried cranberries and dried cherries.

3 Cream the butter and sugar until pale and fluffy. Add the eggs little by little, beating well between each addition.

4 Fold in the flour and fruit mixture and pour into the cake tin. Spread flat.

5 Cook in the centre of the oven for 45–60 minutes. A skewer inserted into the centre should come out clean.

6 Leave in the tin to cool for 10 minutes then turn out on to a wire rack to cool completely.

NOTE: For more information on creaming-method cakes, see page 279.

Bitter-sweet Fruit Cake

MAKES A 15 CM | 6 IN CAKE

225 g | 8 oz raisins

225 g | 8 oz sultanas

grated zest and juice of 1 orange

115 g | 4 oz butter

115 g | 4 oz caster sugar

1½ tablespoons clear honey

140 g | 5 oz plain chocolate, chopped into small pieces

2 room-temperature eggs, beaten

115 g | 4 oz plain wholemeal flour

1 teaspoon ground mixed spice

55 g | 2 oz pine nuts

1 Heat the oven to 170°C | 325°F | gas mark 3. Grease a deep 15 cm | 6 in cake tin and line the base and sides with baking parchment.

2 Put the dried fruit, orange zest and juice, butter, sugar, honey and chocolate into a large saucepan. Heat gently until the chocolate and butter have melted, stirring occasionally. Remove from the heat and allow to cool.

3 Add the eggs and mix thoroughly. Stir in the flour, mixed spice and pine nuts. Turn the mixture into the prepared tin.

4 Bake in the centre of the oven for 40 minutes, then reduce the temperature to 150°C | 300°F | gas mark 2 and bake for a further 50 minutes or until a sharp knife or skewer inserted into the centre of the cake comes out clean.

5 Remove the cake from the oven and allow to cool completely in the tin before turning out.

Coffee and Raisin Cake

MAKES A 20 CM | 8 IN CAKE

140 g | 5 oz soft light brown sugar

225 g | 8 oz golden syrup

225 g | 8 oz butter

2 teaspoons instant coffee

200 ml | 7 fl oz boiling water

340 g | 12 oz plain flour

½ teaspoon freshly grated nutmeg

½ teaspoon ground cloves

½ teaspoon ground cinnamon

1 teaspoon bicarbonate of soda

225 g | 8 oz raisins

2 room-temperature eggs, beaten

1 Heat the oven to 170°C | 325°F | gas mark 3. Grease a deep 20 cm | 8 in cake tin and line with a disc of baking parchment.

2 Put the sugar, syrup and butter into a medium saucepan and melt over a low heat. Do not allow to boil.

3 Mix the coffee with the boiling water and allow to cool.

4 Sift the flour, nutmeg, cloves, cinnamon and bicarbonate of soda together into a large mixing bowl. Add the raisins and make a well in the centre.

5 Pour in the melted mixture, coffee and eggs and mix thoroughly but carefully. Pour into the prepared tin.

6 Bake in the centre of the oven for about 1½ hours or until a sharp knife or skewer inserted into the centre of the cake comes out clean.

7 Remove from the oven and allow to cool in the tin for 10 minutes, then turn out on to a wire rack and leave to cool completely.

NOTES: This cake keeps very well and will be at its best 1–2 weeks after it is baked if stored in an airtight tin.
For more information on melting-method cakes, see page 279.

Wensleydale Fruit Cake

MAKES A 20 CM|8 IN CAKE

225 g|8 oz butter, softened	115 g|4 oz currants
225 g|8 oz soft light brown sugar	115 g|4 oz sultanas
5 room-temperature eggs, beaten	115 g|4 oz raisins
285 g|10 oz plain flour	115 g|4 oz dried apples, chopped
½ teaspoon ground cinnamon	170 g|6 oz Wensleydale cheese, thinly sliced

1 Heat the oven to 170°C|325°F|gas mark 3. Grease a deep 20 cm|8 in cake tin and line the base and sides with baking parchment.

2 Cream the butter in a large mixing bowl, add the sugar and beat until pale and creamy. Add the eggs gradually, beating well after each addition. Add a little of the flour if necessary, to prevent the mixture from curdling.

3 Sift together the flour and cinnamon and add to the creamed mixture with the fruit. Mix well.

4 Put half the mixture into the prepared tin and smooth flat. Cover with the slices of Wensleydale cheese and put the remaining cake mixture on top. Smooth flat.

5 Bake in the centre of the oven for 2–2½ hours or until a sharp knife or skewer inserted into the centre of the cake comes out clean.

6 Remove the cake from the oven and allow to cool completely in the tin before turning out.

NOTES: If the top starts to get too dark during baking, cover with a piece of greaseproof paper or kitchen foil. The cake will keep for a week or so in a tin or can be frozen.
For more information on creaming-method cakes, see page 279.

Date Cake

The date layer in this cake tends to sink to the bottom, making it slightly sticky and delicious.

MAKES A 15 CM|6 IN SQUARE CAKE

For the date layer
115 g|4 oz dried dates, chopped
85 g|3 oz soft light brown sugar
1 tablespoon plain flour
2 teaspoons ground cinnamon
55 g|2 oz butter, melted and cooled

For the cake
115 g|4 oz butter, softened
115 g|4 oz caster sugar

1 room-temperature egg, beaten
1 teaspoon vanilla essence
115 g|4 oz plain flour
1½ teaspoons baking powder
150 ml|5 fl oz milk

For the top
55 g|2 oz hazelnuts, chopped

1 Heat the oven to 180°C|350°F|gas mark 4. Grease a 15 cm|6 in square cake tin and line the base with a piece of baking parchment.

2 Mix together the ingredients for the date layer and set aside.

3 For the cake: cream the butter and sugar together in a mixing bowl until pale and fluffy. Add the egg gradually, beating well after each addition. Add the vanilla essence.

4 Sift the flour with the baking powder and fold into the mixture, using a large metal spoon. Stir in the milk.

5 Spread half the cake mixture in the bottom of the prepared tin. Spoon the date layer mixture carefully on top, spreading it evenly, then spread the remaining cake mixture over that. Sprinkle over the hazelnuts and press down lightly.

6 Bake in the centre of the oven for about 45 minutes or until the top springs back when pressed lightly with a fingertip.

7 Remove the cake from the oven and allow to cool completely in the tin before turning out.

NOTE: For more information on creaming-method cakes, see page 279.

Fruit Cakes: What has gone wrong when . . .

The top of the cake is domed.
- The well in the centre of the cake mixture wasn't large enough.
- The tin was too small.
- The oven was too hot.

The fruit has sunk to the bottom of the cake.
- The cake mixture was too thin.
- The fruit was not mixed in well enough.

The cake has a hard, dark crust around the outside.
- The oven was too hot.
- The cake was overbaked.
- The cake tin was not wrapped in newspaper.

Cakes with Fresh Fruit

Cakes made with fresh fruit are delicious and often make good puddings. Do not be tempted to add too much fruit to the mixture, as fruit produces a lot of liquid during baking which could make the cake soggy and prevent it from rising. Therefore weigh the fruit carefully before adding it.

Apple and Pear Cake

This cake does not contain eggs so it is fairly close-textured. It is moist and keeps and freezes well.

MAKES A 17 CM | 7 IN CAKE

225 g | 8 oz cooking apples

115 g | 4 oz pears

2 tablespoons water

115 g | 4 oz butter, softened

225 g | 8 oz caster sugar

225 g | 8 oz plain flour, sifted

1 teaspoon ground cinnamon

1 teaspoon bicarbonate of soda

170 g | 6 oz dried fruit (e.g. pears, peaches, apricots or raisins)

1 Heat the oven to 180°C | 350°F | gas mark 4. Grease a 17 cm | 7 in cake tin and line the base with a disc of baking parchment.

2 Peel and core the apples and pears and cut into chunks. Put into a saucepan with the water. Cover with a lid and cook over a low heat, stirring occasionally until pulpy. Beat with a wooden spoon to get rid of any large lumps and set aside to cool.

3 Meanwhile, cream the butter and the sugar together until pale and fluffy.

4 Add the cooled fruit purée, flour, cinnamon, bicarbonate of soda and dried fruit. Mix well and turn into the prepared tin.

5 Bake in the centre of the oven for 1–1½ hours or until a sharp knife or skewer inserted into the centre of the cake comes out clean.

6 Remove the cake from the oven and allow to cool in the tin for 10 minutes before turning out on to a wire rack to cool completely.

NOTES: This cake can also be baked in a 900 g | 2 lb loaf tin.

For more information on creaming-method cakes, see page 279.

Apple Sauce Cake

This cake is moist and keeps very well. It does not contain eggs and is therefore fairly close-textured.

MAKES A 17 CM|7 IN CAKE

340 g|12 oz cooking apples

115 g|4 oz butter, softened

225 g|8 oz caster sugar

225 g|8 oz plain flour, sifted

1 teaspoon ground mixed spice

1 teaspoon bicarbonate of soda

170 g|6 oz dried apricots, chopped

To finish

1 tablespoon demerara sugar

1 Heat the oven to 180°C|350°F|gas mark 4. Grease a 17 cm|7 in cake tin and line the base with a disc of baking parchment.

2 Wash but do not peel the apples, core them and cut into chunks. Put them into a saucepan with 1 tablespoon water. Cover with a lid and cook over a low heat, stirring occasionally, until pulpy. Push the apples through a sieve and set aside to cool.

3 Meanwhile, cream the butter and sugar together until pale and fluffy.

4 Add the cooled apple purée, flour, mixed spice, bicarbonate of soda and dried apricots. Mix well. Turn into the prepared tin.

5 Bake in the centre of the oven for about 1½ hours or until a sharp knife or skewer inserted into the centre of the cake comes out clean. 10 minutes before the end of baking time, sprinkle with the demerara sugar.

6 Remove the cake from the oven and allow to cool in the tin for 10 minutes, then turn out on to a wire rack and leave to cool completely.

NOTES: This cake can also be baked in a 900 g|2 lb loaf tin.

For more information on creaming-method cakes, see page 279.

Apple Cake

225 g|8 oz plain flour

2 teaspoons baking powder

115 g|4 oz butter

115 g|4 oz granulated sugar

225 g|8 oz dessert apples, such as Cox's Orange
Pippins, peeled, cored and diced

85 g|3 oz raisins

1 room-temperature egg

100 ml|3½ fl oz milk

To finish

45 g|1½ oz demerara sugar

1 Heat the oven to 180°C|350°F|gas mark 4. Grease a deep 17 cm|7 in cake tin and line the base with a disc of baking parchment.

2 Sift the flour with the baking powder into a large mixing bowl. Cut the butter into small cubes and rub into the flour until the mixture resembles fine breadcrumbs.

3 Add the granulated sugar, apples and raisins and mix thoroughly.

4 Mix together the egg and milk and add to the mixture. It should form a reluctant dropping consistency. Add more milk if necessary. Turn into the prepared tin.

5 Bake in the centre of the oven for 40 minutes, then reduce the temperature to 170°C|325°F|gas mark 3 and bake for a further 50 minutes or until a sharp knife or skewer inserted into the centre of the cake comes out clean.

6 Remove from the oven and immediately sprinkle with the demerara sugar. Allow to cool in the tin for 30 minutes, then turn out on to a wire rack and leave to cool completely.

NOTE: For more information on rubbing-in method cakes, see page 278.

Apple Frangipane Cake

MAKES A 23 CM|9 IN CAKE

2 medium dessert apples

170 g|6 oz butter

170 g|6 oz caster sugar

grated zest of 1 orange

3 room-temperature eggs, beaten

170 g|6 oz self-raising flour, sifted

115 g|4 oz ground almonds

50 mls|2 fl oz milk

To finish

3 tablespoons apricot jam

½ tablespoon orange juice

1 Heat the oven to 190°C|375°F|gas mark 5. Grease a 23 cm|9 in round cake tin and line the base with a piece of baking parchment cut to fit.

2 Peel, quarter and core the apples. Make several cuts in the rounded side of each quarter, but don't cut all the way through.

3 Cream the butter and sugar together until pale and fluffy, then add the orange zest. Add

the eggs a little at a time, beating well between each addition. Mix the flour and almonds together and add to the mixture. Stir well and add the milk.

4 Put the cake mixture into the prepared tin and spread flat. Place the apple quarters at equidistant intervals on the cake mixture, cut sides up. Press them into the mixture slightly.

5 Place in the centre of the oven and bake for 45–60 minutes. The cake is cooked when the top springs back when pressed lightly with a finger. Allow it to cool for 5 minutes in the tin before carefully turning it out on to a wire rack to cool completely.

6 Put the jam and orange juice into a saucepan. Bring to the boil and sieve into a bowl. Cool until it is warm and brush over the top of the cake.

NOTE: For more information on creaming-method cakes, see page 279.

Cinnamon and Apple Cake

This is an easy-to-make, moist cake that keeps and freezes well. It is best if made a day in advance. Store wrapped in clingfilm and foil, at room temperature.

MAKES A 20 CM|8 IN CAKE

200 g|7 oz peeled dessert apples, coarsely grated (about 3)

170 g|6 oz soft light brown sugar

100 ml|3½ fl oz vegetable oil

½ teaspoon vanilla essence

1 room-temperature egg, beaten

225 g|8 oz self-raising flour

1 teaspoon ground cinnamon

¼ teaspoon ground nutmeg

a pinch of salt

170 g|6 oz raisins

1 tablespoon demerara sugar

1 Line the base of a 20 cm|8 in deep tin with baking parchment. Brush the sides with oil.

2 Heat the oven to 180°C|350°F|gas mark 4.

3 Place the grated apples into large bowl and stir in the soft light brown sugar, oil, vanilla and egg.

4 Sift together the flour, cinnamon, nutmeg and salt.

5 Stir into the apple mixture. Stir in the raisins.

6 Spread the mixture into the prepared cake tin and level the top. Sprinkle with the demerara sugar.

7 Bake in the centre of the oven for 35–40 minutes or until well-risen and golden-brown. A skewer inserted in the centre should come out clean.

8 Cool for 10 minutes in the tin then turn out on to a wire rack to finish cooling.

Cheese and Apple Cake

MAKES A 900 G | 2 LB LOAF

115 g | 4 oz butter

170 g | 6 oz caster sugar

2 room-temperature eggs, beaten

225 g | 8 oz cooking apples, cored, grated, with peel and juice

115 g | 4 oz Cheddar cheese, grated

55 g | 2 oz blanched almonds, chopped

450 g | 1 lb plain flour

2 teaspoons baking powder

½ teaspoon bicarbonate of soda

1 Heat the oven to 180°C | 350°F | gas mark 4. Grease a 900 g | 2 lb loaf tin and line the base with a piece of baking parchment.

2 Cream the butter and sugar together in a mixing bowl until pale and fluffy. Add the eggs gradually, beating well after each addition. Stir in the apples, cheese and almonds.

3 Sift together the flour, baking powder and bicarbonate of soda and fold into the mixture, using a large metal spoon.

4 Turn into the prepared tin. Smooth the top with a palette knife.

5 Bake in the centre of the oven for about 1 hour or until a sharp knife or skewer inserted into the centre of the cake comes out clean.

6 Remove the cake from the oven and allow to cool in the tin for 10 minutes, then turn out on to a wire rack and leave to cool completely.

NOTE: For more information on creaming-method cakes, see page 279.

Cider and Apple Cake

MAKES A 900 G | 2 LB LOAF

170 g | 6 oz butter

170 g | 6 oz soft light brown sugar

3 room-temperature eggs, beaten

170 g | 6 oz self-raising flour, sifted

½ teaspoon freshly grated nutmeg

3 tablespoons medium-sweet cider

To finish

2 dessert apples, such as Cox's Orange Pippins, peeled, quartered, cored and sliced

¼ teaspoon ground cinnamon

½ teaspoon demerara sugar

1 Heat the oven to 180°C | 350°F | gas mark 4. Grease a 900 g | 2 lb loaf tin and line the base with a piece of baking parchment.

2 Cream the butter and soft light brown sugar together in a mixing bowl until pale and fluffy. Add the eggs gradually, beating well after each addition. Add a little of the flour if necessary, to prevent the mixture from curdling.

3 Fold the sifted flour and nutmeg into the creamed mixture, using a large metal spoon, and stir in the cider. Turn into the prepared tin and spread out evenly.

4 Bake in the centre of the oven for 20 minutes.

5 Remove the cake from the oven and quickly arrange the sliced apples over the top. Sprinkle with the cinnamon and demerara sugar, mixed together. Work quickly, otherwise the cake will sink.

6 Return the cake to the oven and bake for a further 30 minutes or until a sharp knife or skewer inserted into the centre of the cake comes out clean.

7 Remove the cake from the oven and allow to cool completely in the tin before turning out.

NOTE: For more information on creaming-method cakes, see page 279.

Dutch Spiced Apple Cake

This cake is easy to make and can also be served warm as a pudding, with fresh cream or custard.

MAKES A 20 × 30 CM | 8 × 12 IN CAKE

For the topping	For the cake
3 tablespoons soft light brown sugar	170 g	6 oz butter, softened
2 teaspoons ground cinnamon	170 g	6 oz caster sugar
½ teaspoon grated nutmeg	3 room-temperature eggs, beaten
2 tablespoons plain flour	1 teaspoon vanilla essence
55 g	2 oz butter, melted	225 g	8 oz self-raising flour, sifted
4 dessert apples, peeled, quartered, cored and cut into slices	1–2 tablespoons milk, to mix

1 Heat the oven to 180°C | 350°F | gas mark 4. Grease and line the base of a 20 × 30 cm | 8 × 12 in tin with a piece of baking parchment cut to fit.

2 Make the topping: in a small bowl mix the sugar, cinnamon, nutmeg and flour together. Add the melted butter and mix well. Scatter the mixture over the apples and mix together.

3 Cream the butter and sugar together until they are pale and fluffy. Add the eggs a little at a time, beating well between each addition. Add the vanilla essence.

4 Fold in the flour and add enough milk to make a reluctant dropping consistency.

5 Spread the cake mixture into the prepared tin and cover with the prepared apples. Press down lightly.

6 Bake for 45–60 minutes or until the apples have softened and the cake is cooked.

7 Remove the cake from the oven and allow to cool completely in the tin before turning out.

NOTE: For more information on creaming-method cakes, see page 279.

Apple and Almond Kuchen

SERVES 8

170 g | 6 oz plain flour
55 g | 2 oz ground almonds
115 g | 4 oz cold butter, cut into small pieces
50 g | 1¾ oz caster sugar
grated zest of 1 lemon
½ teaspoon baking powder
a pinch of salt

For the filling

4 red dessert apples
85 g | 3 oz caster sugar
1 teaspoon ground cinnamon
2 egg yolks
½ teaspoon vanilla essence
150 ml | 5 fl oz whipping cream

To serve

ground cinnamon
crème fraiche (optional)

1 Heat the oven to 200°C | 400°F | gas mark 6.
2 Place the flour, ground almonds, butter, sugar, lemon zest, baking powder and salt in a large bowl and rub with your fingers until the mixture resembles fine breadcrumbs. Press into a 23 cm | 9 in tart tin. Chill for 10 minutes.
3 To make the filling, core the apples, cut in half and then slice into 5 mm | ¼ in slices. Arrange the apples over the pastry.
4 Combine the sugar and cinnamon in a bowl, then sprinkle over the apples.
5 Stir the egg yolks and vanilla essence into the cream, then pour over the apples.
6 Bake for 45 minutes, or until the custard is firm and the apples are lightly browned. Dust with ground cinnamon and serve warm with crème fraiche if desired.

NOTE: For more information on rubbing-in method cakes, see page 278.

Farmhouse Apple Cake

MAKES A 20 CM | 8 IN CAKE

225 g | 8 oz wholemeal plain flour
225 g | 8 oz self-raising flour
½ teaspoon ground mixed spice
1 teaspoon ground cinnamon
½ teaspoon bicarbonate of soda

170 g | 6 oz lard or white vegetable fat
225 g | 8 oz soft light brown sugar
250 g | 9 oz dried apple pieces, chopped
2 room-temperature eggs, beaten
150 ml | 5 fl oz milk

1 Heat the oven to 180°C | 350°F | gas mark 4. Grease a deep 20 cm | 8 in tin and line the base with a disc of baking parchment cut to fit.

2 Sift together the flours, mixed spice, cinnamon and bicarbonate of soda into a large bowl. Tip any bran left in the sieve into the bowl.

3 Cut the lard into small pieces and rub into the flour. Add the sugar and dried apple. Mix with the beaten eggs and enough milk to make a soft dropping consistency.

4 Pour into the prepared tin and bake for 1¼ –1½ hours. Cover with greaseproof paper after 1 hour to prevent it from burning. Allow it to stand for 10 minutes before turning out on to a wire rack to cool completely.

NOTE: For more information on rubbing-in method cakes, see page 278.

Fresh Fruit Cake

MAKES A 20 CM|8 IN CAKE

225 g|8 oz mixed fresh fruit, such as apples, pears, plums, nectarines

170 g|6 oz butter, softened

170 g|6 oz caster sugar

3 room-temperature eggs, beaten

170 g|6 oz self-raising flour

2 teaspoons ground cinnamon

1 Heat the oven to 180°C|350°F|gas mark 4. Grease a deep 20 cm|8 in cake tin and line the base with a disc of baking parchment.

2 Peel, core and stone the fruit. Cut into 1 cm|½ in dice.

3 Cream the butter and sugar together in a mixing bowl until pale and fluffy. Add the eggs gradually, beating well after each addition. Add a little of the flour if necessary, to prevent the mixture from curdling.

4 Sift the flour with the cinnamon and fold into the creamed mixture with the chopped fruit. Turn into the prepared tin.

5 Bake in the centre of the oven for 1 hour or until the top feels firm to the touch.

6 Remove the cake from the oven and allow to cool in the tin for 10 minutes, then turn out on to a wire rack and leave to cool completely.

NOTE: For more information on rubbing-in method cakes, see page 278.

Blueberry Streusel Cake

MAKE 9 SQUARES

For the topping
85 g | 3 oz plain flour
a pinch of salt
55 g | 2 oz butter
55 g | 2 oz caster sugar

For the cake
250 g | 9 oz self-raising flour
½ teaspoon bicarbonate of soda

1 teaspoon ground cinnamon
a pinch of salt
115 g | 4 oz butter, softened
115 g | 4 oz soft light brown sugar
2 room-temperature eggs, beaten
1 teaspoon grated lemon zest
140 g | 5 oz soured cream
250 g | 9 oz blueberries

1 For the topping, sift the flour into a bowl with the salt. Cut the butter into small cubes and toss in the flour. Cut in the butter using 2 table knives, scissor-fashion, then rub in with your fingertips until the mixture resembles fine breadcrumbs. Stir in the sugar. Chill.

2 Heat the oven to 190°C | 375°F | gas mark 5. Line the base and sides of a 23 cm | 9 in square cake tin with baking parchment.

3 Sift the flour with the baking powder, bicarbonate of soda, cinnamon and salt into a large bowl.

4 In a separate bowl, cream the butter with the sugar until pale and fluffy. Beat in the eggs gradually then stir in the lemon zest and soured cream.

5 Fold in the sifted flour, taking care not to overstir. Add the blueberries after about 10 strokes. Do not use more than 20 strokes.

6 Spread the mixture into the prepared tin and sprinkle over the topping.

7 Bake in the centre of the oven for 25 minutes or until well-risen and golden-brown. A skewer inserted into the centre should come out clean.

8 Cool on a wire rack in the tin.

NOTE: For more information on creaming-method cakes, see page 279.

Black Cherry Cake

This is a simplified version of a Black Forest Gâteau.

MAKES A 20 CM | 8 IN CAKE

1 × 400 g | 14 oz can of pitted black cherries,
    drained
2 tablespoons Kirsch
290 ml | 10 fl oz double cream
1 chocolate Génoise cake (see page 296)
85 g | 3 oz plain chocolate, chopped into small pieces
3 tablespoons water
115 g | 4 oz icing sugar
55 g | 2 oz flaked almonds, toasted

To finish
icing sugar, for dusting

1 Sprinkle the cherries with the Kirsch. Whip the cream until it just holds its shape.
2 Split the cake into 3 thin rounds. Spread one third of the cream over the bottom layer and sprinkle with half the cherries. Place the next layer on top. Spread on another third of the cream and the rest of the cherries. Place the top layer on and flatten gently with your hands.
3 Place the chocolate in a small, heavy saucepan with the water and stir over a very low heat until smooth, taking care not to get it too hot.
4 Sift the icing sugar into a bowl and blend in the chocolate, adding a little extra water if necessary. Do this drop by drop to create a thick, pouring consistency. Pour over the top of the cake and allow to set and cool.
5 Once the chocolate icing has set, spread the remaining cream around the sides of the cake and press the almonds on to it.
6 Cut 3 strips of greaseproof paper about 25 cm | 10 in long and 2.5 cm | 1 in wide. Place them over the cake about 2.5 cm | 1 in apart and sift over a heavy dusting of icing sugar.
7 Remove the paper strips carefully to reveal a striped brown and white top.

Nectarine Cake

This is a pretty, sticky cake that can also be served warm as a pudding. Peaches can be used instead of nectarines, but they will need to be peeled by dunking them first in boiling water for 20 seconds and then into cold water.

SERVES 4

3 ripe nectarines

1 tablespoon lemon juice

55 g | 2 oz butter, softened

55 g | 2 oz sugar

1 room-temperature egg, beaten

140 g | 5 oz self-raising flour, sifted

55 ml | 2 fl oz milk

To glaze

3 tablespoons apricot jam

1 Heat the oven to 180°C | 350°F | gas mark 4. Grease a 20 cm | 8 in loose-bottomed tart ring.

2 Cut each unpeeled nectarine into about 16 segments. Toss in the lemon juice.

3 Cream the butter and sugar together in a mixing bowl until pale and fluffy. Add the egg gradually, beating well after each addition. Fold the flour into the mixture. Add the milk, mixing carefully.

4 Spread into the prepared tin and arrange the segments of nectarine on top as neatly as possible, pressing them lightly into the cake mixture.

5 Bake in the centre of the oven for 50–60 minutes or until a sharp knife or skewer inserted into the centre comes out clean.

6 Meanwhile, put the apricot jam into a saucepan with 1 tablespoon water. Bring to the boil, then push through a sieve.

7 Remove the cake from the oven and allow to cool in the tin for 15 minutes, then turn out on to a wire rack and leave to cool completely. Brush the top with the warm apricot glaze. Allow to cool.

NOTE: For more information on creaming-method cakes, see page 279.

Banana, Mango and Passion-fruit Cake

The passion-fruit seeds in this cake can be sieved out of the pulp before making the icing.

MAKES A 20 CM|8 IN CAKE

115 g | 4 oz butter, softened
225 g | 8 oz caster sugar
1 room-temperature egg, beaten
2 medium, ripe bananas, mashed
115 g | 4 oz dried mango, cut into cubes
200 ml | 7 fl oz natural yoghurt
200 g | 7 oz self-raising flour, sifted
115 g | 4 oz wholemeal self-raising flour, sifted

For the icing

85 g | 3 oz butter, softened
200 g | 7 oz icing sugar
2 passion-fruit

1 Heat the oven to 180°C | 350°F | gas mark 4. Grease a deep 20 cm | 8 in tin and line the base with a dice of baking parchment cut to fit.
2 Cream the butter and caster sugar together until well-combined. Add the egg and beat well.
3 Stir in the banana, mango, yoghurt and finally the sifted flours. Spread into the prepared tin and place in the centre of the oven for 1 hour. It is ready when the top springs back when pressed lightly with a finger. Leave in the tin for 5 minutes before turning out on to a wire rack to cool down completely.
4 Meanwhile, make the icing. Place the butter in a medium-sized bowl and beat in the icing sugar gradually. Finally, stir in the pulp from the passion-fruit.
5 Once the cake is cold, spread the icing over the top.

NOTE: For more information on creaming-method cakes, see page 279.

Passion-fruit Cake

The passion-fruit in this recipe should be ripe, which means they will have a wrinkled, slightly sunken skin. Unripe passion-fruit are plump and firm and have a very sour taste.

MAKES A 20 CM|8 IN CAKE

225 g|8 oz butter, softened

225 g|8 oz caster sugar

4 room-temperature eggs, beaten

225 g|8 oz self-raising flour, sifted

2 ripe passion-fruit

For the filling

6 tablespoons passion-fruit curd (see page 457)

For the icing

1 quantity passion-fruit icing (see page 455)

1 Heat the oven to 190°C|375°F|gas mark 5. Grease 2 × 20 cm|8 in sandwich tins and line the base of each with a disc of baking parchment.

2 Cream the butter in a mixing bowl, add the sugar and beat together until pale and fluffy.

3 Add the eggs gradually, beating well after each addition. Add a little of the flour if necessary, to prevent the mixture from curdling. Fold in the remaining flour, using a large metal spoon.

4 Cut open the passion-fruit and scoop out the pulp. Fold into the creamed mixture. Divide the mixture between the sandwich tins and spread out evenly.

5 Bake in the centre of the oven for 35–40 minutes or until the tops spring back when pressed lightly with a fingertip.

6 Meanwhile, make the passion-fruit curd and passion-fruit icing.

7 Remove the cakes from the oven and allow to cool in their tins for 5 minutes, then turn out on to a wire rack and leave to cool completely.

8 When the cakes are cold, sandwich together with the passion-fruit curd and spread the top with the passion-fruit icing. Allow to set.

NOTES: This cake will keep for a day or so in a tin in a cool place. It will also freeze quite successfully, but should be iced after defrosting.

For more information on creaming-method cakes, see page 279.

Passion-fruit Syrup Surprise Cake

For the syrup

6 passion-fruit

3 tablespoons caster sugar

1 tablespoon lemon juice

4 tablespoons water

1 tablespoon cornflour

For the cake

340 g|12 oz self raising flour

1 teaspoon mixed spice

115 g|4 oz butter, cut into cubes

115 g|4 oz ground almonds

200 g|7 oz soft light brown sugar

2 room-temperature eggs, beaten

150 ml|5 fl oz milk

1 Cut the passion-fruit in half and spoon the flesh and seeds into a small saucepan. Add the sugar, lemon juice and 2 tablespoons of the water. Bring gently to the boil, dissolving the sugar before it boils. Blend the cornflour with the remaining water and add to the passion-fruit. Bring it to the boil again and allow it to thicken. Put to one side to cool down completely. Passion-fruit come in different sizes, so if the mixture is too thick add a little more water before it cools down.

2 Heat the oven to 190°C|375°F|gas mark 5. Grease a 20 cm|8 in square tin and line the base with a piece of baking parchment cut to fit.

3 Sift the flour and spice into a large bowl. Rub in the butter with your fingertips, until the mixture resembles fine breadcrumbs. Stir in the almonds and sugar. Add the eggs and milk and mix well.

4 Turn the mixture into the cake tin and spread flat. At 2 cm|1 in intervals make holes in the cake mixture and put a teaspoonful of the passion-fruit mixture into each hole. Spread the cake mixture back over the top.

5 Bake in the centre of the oven for 30–40 minutes, or until the top springs back when lightly pressed. Leave in the tin for 10 minutes before carefully removing and placing on a wire rack to cool completely.

NOTE: For more information on rubbing-in method cakes, see page 278.

Passion Cake

MAKES A 20 CM | 8 IN ROUND CAKE

170 ml | 6 fl oz vegetable oil

2 room-temperature eggs, beaten

170 g | 6 oz crushed pineapple, well-drained

100 g | 3½ oz sweetened desiccated coconut

100 g | 3½ oz carrot, finely grated

1 teaspoon vanilla essence

225 g | 8 oz self-raising flour

1 teaspoon bicarbonate of soda

a pinch of salt

1 teaspoon ground cinnamon

½ teaspoon ground ginger

100 g | 3½ oz walnuts, chopped

For the icing

150 g | 5 oz good quality cream cheese, softened

55 g | 2 oz unsalted butter, softened

grated zest of 1 small orange

225 g | 8 oz icing sugar, sifted

1 Heat the oven to 170°C | 325°F | gas mark 3. Line the base and sides of a deep 20 cm | 8 in round cake tin with baking parchment.

2 Mix together the oil, eggs, pineapple, coconut, carrot and vanilla.

3 Sift the flour, bicarbonate of soda, salt, cinnamon and ginger into a large bowl.

4 Stir the wet ingredients into the dry ingredients, then fold in the walnuts.

5 Turn into the prepared tin and bake in the centre of the oven for 1 hour or until a skewer inserted into the centre comes out clean.

6 Cool in the tin for 10 minutes then turn out on to a wire rack to cool completely.

7 For the icing, beat together the cream cheese, butter and orange zest until smooth, then stir in the icing sugar and spread over the cake.

Squashy Rhubarb Cake

This cake can also be served as a pudding, accompanied by crème anglaise or double cream.

SERVES 4

For the crumble topping

55 g | 2 oz butter

85 g | 3 oz plain flour

30 g | 1 oz sugar

For the cake

85 g | 3 oz butter, softened

85 g | 3 oz sugar

2 small room-temperature eggs, beaten

85 g | 3 oz self-raising flour, sifted

a pinch of salt

milk (optional)

For the filling

675 g | 1½ lb rhubarb, cut into 2.5 cm | 1 in pieces

1 tablespoon sugar

To finish

icing sugar, sifted

1 Heat the oven to 190°C | 375°F | gas mark 5. Grease a 20 cm | 8 in loose-bottomed cake tin.

2 Make the topping: rub the butter into the flour in a bowl and add the sugar. Set aside.

3 Make the cake: cream the butter in a mixing bowl until soft. Add the sugar and cream until very pale and fluffy.

4 Add the eggs gradually to the mixture, beating well after each addition. Add a spoonful of the flour if necessary, to prevent the mixture from curdling.

5 Fold in the flour and salt, using a large metal spoon, and add a few dribbles of milk if necessary, to achieve a reluctant dropping consistency.

6 Turn into the prepared tin and spread out evenly. Cover carefully with the rhubarb pieces tossed in the sugar. Sprinkle the crumble mixture over the top.

7 Bake in the centre of the oven for about 45 minutes or until the top feels firm to the touch.

8 Remove the cake from the oven. Cool completely in the tin before turning out.

9 Just before serving, remove the cake from the tin and dust with icing sugar.

NOTES: Tinned rhubarb may be used, without the sugar. You will need a 540 g | 1¼ lb tin, drained.
   For more information on creaming-method cakes, see page 279.

Speciality Cakes

These cakes take more time and skill to make than most of the other cakes in this book. Although they are time-consuming, they are well worth the effort.

Dobez Torte

This is a Hungarian cake in 5 layers. The mixture will not deteriorate if a lack of baking sheets or space in the oven means that all the layers cannot be baked at the same time.

MAKES A 20 CM|8 IN CAKE

4 room-temperature eggs
170 g|6 oz caster sugar
140 g|5 oz plain flour
a pinch of salt

For the buttercream
85 g|3 oz granulated sugar
4–5 tablespoons water
3 room-temperature egg yolks

225 g|8 oz unsalted butter
coffee essence
55 g|2 oz hazelnuts, toasted, skinned and ground

To decorate
140 g|5 oz caster sugar
2 tablespoons toasted chopped almonds or toasted ground hazelnuts
6 whole hazelnuts, browned and skinned

1 Heat the oven to 190°C|375°F|gas mark 5. Mark a 20 cm|8 in circle on each sheet of baking parchment. Place on to baking sheets.

2 Whisk the eggs with an electric beater in a heatproof bowl and gradually whisk in the sugar. Fit the bowl over, but not in, a saucepan of steaming water and whisk until the mixture is thick and mousse-like. Remove from the heat and continue whisking until cool. Sift the flour with the salt and fold into the egg mixture, using a large metal spoon. Divide the mixture between the prepared baking sheets spreading into the circles.

3 Bake in the centre of the oven for 8 minutes or until the cake layers spring back when pressed lightly with a fingertip. Trim the edges neatly and leave to cool on a wire rack.

4 Make the buttercream: put the sugar and water into a saucepan and stir over a low heat until the sugar has dissolved completely. When clear, bring to the boil and boil rapidly until a little syrup forms short, sticky threads when pulled between a wet finger and thumb. Allow to cool slightly, for about 1 minute.

5 Whisk the egg yolks in a bowl and pour on the syrup in a slow, steady stream, whisking constantly. Continue whisking until the mixture is thick and mousse-like. Cream the butter in a bowl until soft, then beat in the egg and sugar mixture.

6 Flavour 2 tablespoons of the buttercream with coffee essence to taste and reserve for decoration. Mix the ground hazelnuts and a little coffee essence into the remaining buttercream.

7 Place one layer of cake on a wire rack set over an oiled baking sheet. Melt the sugar for the caramel in a little water in a saucepan, then boil fiercely until a good caramel colour. Pour immediately over the layer of cake, covering it completely.

8 Allow to harden slightly, then mark into 6 portions with an oiled knife, cutting through the setting caramel but not through the cake. Trim the edges of excess caramel.

9 Sandwich the cake layers together with coffee and hazelnut buttercream, finishing with the caramel layer. Spread the remaining buttercream thinly around the sides and press on the chopped nuts.

10 Fill a piping bag fitted with a large fluted nozzle with the reserved buttercream and pipe a rosette on top of each portion of cake. Decorate each rosette with a whole hazelnut.

NOTE: For more information on whisking-method cakes, see page 281.

Austrian Carrot Cake

MAKES A 23 CM | 9 IN CAKE

5 room-temperature eggs

225 g | 8 oz caster sugar, plus 1 extra teaspoon

225 g | 8 oz carrots, finely grated

225 g | 8 oz ground almonds

2 tablespoons rum

grated zest of 1 lemon

55 g | 2 oz potato flour

1 teaspoon baking powder

1 teaspoon ground cinnamon

a pinch of ground cloves

To finish

icing sugar, sifted

1 Heat the oven to 180°C | 350°F | gas mark 4. Grease a 23 cm | 9 in *moule à manqué* tin and line with a disc of baking parchment. Dust lightly with potato flour and tap out the excess.

2 Separate the eggs. Beat the yolks and sugar together in a large bowl until pale.

3 Whisk the egg whites until stiff. Whisk in the remaining teaspoon of sugar and fold into the yolk and sugar mixture, using a large metal spoon.

4 Carefully fold in the carrots, ground almonds, rum and lemon zest. Sift the flour, baking powder, cinnamon and cloves together into the mixture and combine carefully and thoroughly. Pour into the prepared tin.

5 Bake in the centre of the oven for about 50 minutes or until the top springs back when pressed lightly with a fingertip.

6 Remove the cake from the oven and allow to cool in the tin for 5 minutes, then turn out on to a wire rack and leave to cool completely. Dust lightly with icing sugar before serving.

NOTES: This cake is gluten-free it made using gluten-free baking powder.

For more information on whisking-method cakes, see page 281.

Chocolate Ruffle Cake

This cake will take some time to make, but it keeps well and is good for a special occasion.

MAKES A 23 CM | 9 IN CAKE

115 g | 4 oz plain flour
115 g | 4 oz cornflour
55 g | 2 oz cocoa powder
¼ teaspoon baking powder
6 room-temperature eggs
225 g | 8 oz caster sugar

For the coffee syrup

115 g | 4 oz caster sugar
75 ml | 2½ fl oz water
1 tablespoon espresso powder

For the ganache

450 g | 1 lb good quality plain chocolate, chopped
   into small pieces
425 ml | 15 fl oz double cream
2 tablespoons brandy
55 g | 2 oz unsalted butter

For the chocolate caraque

200 g | 7 oz good quality plain chocolate, chopped
   into small pieces

1 Heat the oven to 190°C | 375°F | gas mark 5. Lightly oil and line 2 × 23 cm | 9 in sandwich tins with baking parchment. Oil again and dust with cocoa powder.

2 Sift together the flour, cornflour, cocoa powder and baking powder. Set aside.

3 Place the sugar and eggs in a bowl and whisk with an electric beater. Place over, but not in, a bowl of steaming water and continue whisking until the mixture forms a ribbon trail.

4 Remove from the heat and continue whisking the mixture until it is cool.

5 Fold in the dry ingredients using a metal spoon. Divide between the prepared tins and bake for 30 minutes or until the cakes start to pull away from the edges of the tin and spring back when tapped in the centre.

6 Allow to cool inverted on a wire rack for 10 minutes, then remove from the tins to cool completely.

7 For the coffee syrup, place the sugar, water, brandy and espresso powder in a saucepan over a low heat to dissolve the sugar. Bring to the boil and boil for 1 minute. Allow to cool.

8 Make the ganache: place the chocolate with the cream and butter in a bowl set over, but not touching, steaming water. Stir occasionally and, when combined, remove from the heat and whisk with an electric mixer until cool and thick.

9 Divide the ganache in half. Place the bottom layer of the cake on a serving dish and brush with some of the coffee syrup. Use half the ganache to fill the cake and the other half to cover the sides and top, first brushing each layer with the coffee syrup.

10 Decorate with chocolate caraque, melt the chocolate in a bowl set over, but not touching, steaming water. Spread the chocolate in a thin layer over a marble, granite or stainless steel surface. Let stand until nearly set and dry-looking on the surface, then scrape a thin, sharp knife through the chocolate at a 45° angle to produce long curls. Arrange these on top of the cake.

NOTES: The chocolate curls will keep in an airtight container for several weeks.

For more information on whisking-method cakes, see page 281z.

Linzer Torte

This is a classic Austrian cake which is often served for dessert. It is best to use a good quality jam.

MAKES A 23 CM | 9 IN CAKE

200 g | 7 oz plain flour
115 g | 4 oz chilled butter, cut into dice
115 g | 4 oz ground hazelnuts or almonds
100 g | 3½ oz caster sugar
1½ teaspoons ground cinnamon
¼ teaspoon ground cloves
grated zest of ½ lemon
2 tablespoons double cream
1 room-temperature egg, beaten
1 room-temperature egg yolk
1 tablespoon lemon juice

For the filling

225 g | 8 oz seedless raspberry jam

To finish

1 egg white
2 tablespoons flaked almonds

1 Grease a 23 cm | 9 in tart tin with a removable base.

2 Sift the flour into a large bowl. Add the butter and rub into the flour until it resembles fine breadcrumbs. Add the nuts, sugar, cinnamon, cloves and lemon zest. Mix well.

3 Mix the cream, egg and egg yolk together. Add the lemon juice and mix into the flour mixture to form a dough.

4 Take just over two thirds of the mixture and push into the base and up the sides of the prepared tin, making sure the corners are not too thick. Spread over the jam. Chill.

5 Meanwhile, take the remaining dough and roll into approximately 10 finger-width sausages. Arrange these in a lattice pattern over the top of the flan. Trim the edges and put back into the refrigerator for 1 hour.

6 Heat the oven to 180°C | 350°F | gas mark 4. Whisk the egg white until frothy.

7 Brush the lattice carefully with the egg white and scatter over the almond flakes. Bake in the centre of the oven for approximately 30 minutes. Turn the oven down to 150°C | 300°F | gas mark 2 and cover the torte with greaseproof paper. Bake for a further 20 minutes. Remove from the oven and allow it to cool before removing from the tin. Serve warm or cold.

Chocolate Rose Leaf Gâteau

This is a relatively simple gâteau to make, but the chocolate rose leaves need to be made in advance. The cake keeps moist for several days, or it can be frozen completely assembled, although the chocolate leaves may develop a white bloom.

MAKES A 20 CM│8 IN CAKE

115 g│4 oz plain chocolate, chopped into small pieces

2 tablespoons water

115 g│4 oz butter, softened

140 g│5 oz caster sugar

3 room-temperature eggs

55 g│2 oz ground almonds

70 g│2½ oz fresh white breadcrumbs

2 teaspoons vanilla essence

For the icing

115 g│4 oz plain chocolate, chopped into small pieces

3 tablespoons strong coffee

15 g│½ oz butter

a few drops of vanilla essence

To decorate

chocolate rose leaves, using 170 g│6 oz plain chocolate (see page 373)

icing sugar, sifted

1 Heat the oven to 190°C│375°F│gas mark 5. Grease a 20 cm│8 in *moule à manqué* tin and line with a disc of baking parchment.

2 Put the chocolate and water into a small, heatproof bowl and melt over but not in a saucepan of steaming water.

3 Meanwhile, cream the butter well in a mixing bowl, add the sugar and beat well until pale and fluffy. Separate the eggs and add the yolks one at a time, beating well after each addition.

4 Stir in the ground almonds, breadcrumbs, vanilla essence and melted chocolate to create a fairly stiff texture.

5 Whisk the egg whites until they form soft-to-medium peaks and stir 1 tablespoon into the cake mixture to loosen it. Fold in the remaining egg whites carefully, using a large metal spoon. Pour into the prepared tin.

6 Bake in the centre of the oven for 30 minutes, then turn the temperature down to 180°C│350°F│gas mark 4 and cover the top of the cake with a piece of damp greaseproof paper. Bake for a further 15–20 minutes or until the top springs back when pressed lightly with a fingertip.

7 Remove the cake from the oven and allow to cool in the tin for 10 minutes, then turn out on to a wire rack and leave to cool completely.

8 Meanwhile, make the icing: put the chocolate, coffee, butter and vanilla essence into a heatproof bowl and place over, but not in, a saucepan of steaming water. Stir until it has melted, but do not allow it to get too hot. Remove the bowl from the pan and leave to cool to a coating consistency, stirring occasionally.

9 When the cake is cold, spread the icing over the top and sides. Arrange the chocolate rose leaves carefully, overlapping in a circular pattern, and dust lightly with icing sugar.

NOTE: For more information on creaming-method cakes, see page 279.

Chocolate Rose Leaves

These make a dramatic decoration for a special cake or gâteau. This amount of chocolate will make 30–40 leaves, depending on their size. Make them in advance and store carefully in a sealed container, in a cool place.

170 g | 6 oz plain chocolate   30–40 rose leaves, well-washed and dried

1 Chop the chocolate into small pieces and place in a heatproof bowl over, but not in, a saucepan of steaming water. Stir occasionally until the chocolate has melted. Do not allow it to get too hot, as this will make the chocolate dull and could give it a white bloom once it has set.

2 Coat the veined underside of each rose leaf carefully, either painting the chocolate on with a pastry brush or dipping the leaf into the chocolate. Place the leaves, chocolate side up, on a wire rack and leave to set. If the room is hot, put them in the refrigerator to set.

3 Once the chocolate has set, peel off the leaves carefully. Put the chocolate leaves back into the refrigerator until ready to use.

Gâteau Opéra

This gâteau freezes well, although it is best to put the chocolate on top once it has defrosted.

MAKES A 20 CM 8 IN SQUARE CAKE

100 g | 3½ oz caster sugar
3 room-temperature eggs
3 room-temperature egg whites
100 g | 3½ oz ground almonds
30 g | 1 oz plain flour
a pinch of baking powder
30 g | 1 oz unsalted butter, melted and cooled

For the buttercream

55 g | 2 oz granulated sugar
100 ml | 3½ fl oz water
2 room-temperature egg yolks
3 teaspoons instant coffee granules
1 tablespoon boiling water
75 g | 2½ oz unsalted butter, softened
75 g | 2½ oz salted butter, softened

For the ganache

170 g | 6 oz plain chocolate, chopped into small pieces
85 ml | 3 fl oz milk
175 ml | 6 fl oz double cream

For the coffee syrup

100 g | 3½ oz granulated sugar
100 ml | 3½ fl oz water
1 teaspoon instant coffee granules

For the topping

140 g | 5 oz plain chocolate, chopped into small pieces

1 Heat the oven to 200°C | 400°F | gas mark 6. Grease a 20 cm | 8 in square cake tin and line the base with a piece of baking parchment.

2 Put 85 g | 3 oz of the sugar and the 3 eggs into a large bowl and beat with an electric whisk until the mixture is light and holds a trail when the whisk is removed from the mixture.

3 Whisk the egg whites until stiff and whisk in the remaining sugar. Fold carefully into the egg and sugar mixture, using a large metal spoon.

4 Mix together the ground almonds, flour and baking powder. Fold the butter and the flour mixture into the cake mixture, using a large metal spoon and being careful not to overfold. Pour into the prepared tin.

5 Bake in the oven for about 15 minutes or until just firm to the touch. Turn out on to a wire rack and leave to cool.

6 When the cake is cold, remove the lining paper and carefully split the cake horizontally into 3 layers.

7 Make the buttercream: dissolve the sugar in the water in a saucepan, then bring to the boil. Boil to the thread stage (when a little syrup is placed between a wet finger and thumb and the fingers are opened, it should form a sticky thread about 2.5 cm | 1 in long).

8 Whisk the egg yolks and pour on to the hot sugar syrup, continuing to whisk until thick.

9 Dissolve the coffee in the water. Whisk the butters gradually into the egg mixture, along with the coffee.

10 Make the chocolate ganache: put the chocolate into a heatproof bowl and melt over, but not in, a saucepan of steaming water.

11 Bring the milk to the boil and add to the melted chocolate. Remove from the heat and allow to cool, stirring occasionally. Whip the cream until it thickens slightly. Fold it into the chocolate mixture.

12 Make the coffee syrup: put the sugar and water into a small saucepan and heat gently until the sugar has dissolved completely, then bring to the boil. Boil for 2 minutes, then add the coffee. Remove from the heat and allow to cool.

13 Assemble the cake: brush the bottom layer with one third of the coffee syrup and spread with all the buttercream. Place the middle layer carefully on top, brush with more syrup and spread with two thirds of the chocolate ganache. Place the final layer on top, brush with the remaining syrup and spread over the remaining ganache in a thin layer. Smooth very well and chill.

14 Put the chocolate for the topping into a heatproof bowl and melt over, but not in, a saucepan of steaming water. Reserving a little for piping, spread the remainder very carefully over the top of the chilled cake, as smoothly as you can.

15 Pipe the word 'Opéra' on top with the remaining melted chocolate.

NOTE: For more information on whisking-method cakes, see page 281.

Sachertorte

This rich chocolate cake originates from Vienna. It is a speciality of the Sacher Hotel and is said to have been invented by Franz Sacher in the mid-1800s. The true recipe is a closely-guarded secret, but this one is a close approximation. It is perfect for a birthday cake, or you can finish it off traditionally by piping 'Sacher' in chocolate across the top.

MAKES A 23 CM|9 IN CAKE

170 g|6 oz plain chocolate, chopped into small pieces

140 g|5 oz butter, softened

115 g|4 oz icing sugar, sifted

6 room-temperature eggs

115 g|4 oz caster sugar

125 g|4½ oz plain flour, sifted

For the glaze

225 g|8 oz apricot jam

½ teaspoon lemon juice

For the icing

285 g|10 oz granulated sugar

290 ml|10 fl oz water

225 g|8 oz plain chocolate, chopped into small pieces

1   Heat the oven to 180°C|350°F|gas mark 4. Grease a 23 cm|9 in spring-form tin and line the base with a disc of baking parchment.

2   Melt the chocolate in a heatproof bowl fitted over, but not in, a saucepan of steaming water. Remove from the heat and allow to cool slightly.

3   Cream the butter in a mixing bowl, add the icing sugar and beat well until pale and fluffy. Separate the eggs and add the yolks one at a time, beating well after each addition.

4   Whisk the egg whites until stiff. Whisk in the caster sugar gradually and whisk again until stiff and shiny.

5   Working quite quickly but carefully, mix the cooled melted chocolate into the creamed mixture, then fold in the egg whites and flour, using a large metal spoon. Pour into the prepared tin.

6   Bake in the centre of the oven for 50 minutes or until a sharp knife or skewer inserted into the centre comes out clean.

7   Remove the cake from the oven and allow to cool in the tin for 10 minutes, then loosen, turn out on to a wire rack and leave to cool completely.

8   Meanwhile, make the glaze: heat the apricot jam with the lemon juice in a saucepan. Bring up to the boil, then push through a sieve and allow to cool slightly. It should be warm when it is used.

9   Make the icing: put the granulated sugar into a thick-bottomed saucepan and add the water. Heat very gently, ensuring that the sugar dissolves before the water boils. Once the sugar has dissolved, bring up to the boil and boil to the thread stage (when a little syrup is placed between a wet finger and thumb and the fingers are opened, it should form a sticky thread about 2.5 cm|1 in long). The temperature will be approximately 105°C|225°F.

10 Remove the sugar syrup from the heat and place the pan in a roasting tin filled with warm water. This will prevent the syrup from cooking further. Leave for 1 minute, then add the chocolate and stir constantly until the chocolate has melted and the icing has cooled and achieved a coating consistency.
11 When the cake is cold, place upside down on a wire rack set over a tray. Paint the top and sides with the warm apricot glaze and allow to cool. Pour the icing quickly over the cake, tilting it as the icing runs over it, to ensure a smooth, even covering. Do not disturb the icing once it is on the cake. Allow to set.

NOTE: For more information on creaming-method cakes, see page 279.

Le Gascon

This is a complicated recipe but the end result justifies all the effort. It is a good alternative to a birthday cake and can also be served as a pudding. It can be made the day before or frozen very successfully.

MAKES A 20 CM|8 IN CAKE

3 egg quantity sponge fingers (see page 201)
3 egg quantity chocolate Génoise (see page 296)
2 tablespoons Armagnac or brandy
150 ml|5 fl oz sugar syrup (see page 475)

3 egg-yolk quantity rich chocolate mousse (see page 378)
2 egg-white quantity prune mousse (see page 378)
115 g|4 oz chocolate quantity glaçage koba (see page 379)

1 Trim one end of the sponge fingers and use to line the sides of a 20 cm|8 in spring-form tin, trimming if necessary to make sure all the fingers are the same height.
2 Split the chocolate Génoise in half horizontally and place one half cut-side up in the bottom of the tin.
3 Add the Armagnac to the sugar syrup. Brush both halves of the cake and the sponge fingers with the syrup.
4 Pour the chocolate mousse into the tin until it comes halfway up the sponge fingers. Allow to set.
5 Place the other half of the Génoise, cut-side up, on top of the set chocolate mousse and brush with the syrup.
6 Pour over the prune mousse, leaving a 5 mm|¼ in space at the top. Allow to set.
7 Pour the glaçage koba over the top and level with a palette knife if necessary. Leave to set.
8 To serve, unclip the tin and carefully ease the cake out on to a serving plate.

Rich Chocolate Mousse

70 g|2½ oz granulated sugar
125 ml|4 fl oz water
3 room-temperature egg yolks

170 g|6 oz plain chocolate, chopped into small
   pieces
350 ml|12 fl oz double cream, lightly whipped

1 Put the sugar and water into a small saucepan and heat gently until the sugar has dissolved completely, then bring to the boil.
2 Boil to the thread stage (when a little syrup is placed between a wet finger and thumb and the fingers are opened, it should form a sticky thread about 2.5 cm|1 in long). Allow to cool slightly.
3 Pour the sugar syrup over the egg yolks, whisking all the time. Continue whisking until the mixture is thick and mousse-like.
4 Melt the chocolate carefully in a heatproof bowl fitted over, but not in, a saucepan of steaming water. Fold the chocolate into the egg mixture, using a large metal spoon.
5 Immediately fold in the cream, carefully. Use as required.

Prune Mousse

115 g|4 oz pitted prunes
150 ml|5 fl oz water
30 ml|1 fl oz Armagnac or brandy
7 g|¾ oz powdered gelatine

115 g|4 oz granulated sugar
150 ml|5 fl oz water
2 egg whites
150 ml|5 fl oz double cream, lightly whipped

1 Soak the prunes in the water and Armagnac for a day, then purée them in a liquidizer or food processor.
2 Soak the gelatine in 3 tablespoons water.
3 Put the sugar and 150 ml|5 fl oz water into a small saucepan and heat gently until the sugar has dissolved completely, then bring to the boil. Boil to the thread stage (when a little syrup is placed between a wet finger and thumb and the fingers are opened, it should form a sticky thread about 2.5 cm|1 in long). Leave to cool for 30 seconds.
4 Whisk the egg whites until stiff and gradually add the sugar syrup, whisking all the time until the mixture has formed a thick, shiny meringue.
5 Dissolve the gelatine over a gentle heat, without boiling. When it is clear, runny and warm, add to the prune purée.
6 Whisk the purée gradually into the meringue mixture. Fold in the cream, using a large metal spoon. Use as required.

Glaçage Koba (Chocolate Icing)

75 ml | 2½ fl oz milk
225 g | 8 oz plain chocolate, chopped into small pieces
30 ml | 1 fl oz double cream

55 g | 2 oz butter
15 g | ½ oz powdered glucose
4 tablespoons sugar syrup (see page 000)

1 Bring the milk to the boil in a heavy saucepan and add the chocolate, cream, butter and glucose. Remove from the heat and stir until well-combined and all the chocolate has melted. Place over a gentle heat if necessary.
2 Stir in the sugar syrup.
3 Allow the icing to cool to a coating consistency at room temperature. Do not refrigerate. If the mixture gets too thick, place over a saucepan of simmering water and stir until the correct consistency is obtained.

NOTE: Use chocolate couverture if available.

Gâteau Nougatine

This classic gâteau takes 1 day to complete.

115 g | 4 oz hazelnuts

4 room-temperature eggs

1 egg white

125 g | 4½ oz caster sugar

55 g | 2 oz butter, softened

100 g | 3½ oz plain flour, sifted

For the royal icing

1 small egg white

170 g | 6 oz icing sugar

a squeeze of lemon juice

For the nougat

45 g | 1½ oz almonds, finely chopped

85 g | 3 oz caster sugar

2 teaspoons powdered glucose or a pinch of cream of
tartar

For the crème au beurre mousseline

85 g | 3 oz granulated sugar

3 tablespoons water

2 room-temperature egg yolks

115–140 g | 4–5 oz unsalted butter

For the chocolate fondant icing

225 g | 8 oz granulated sugar

½ teaspoon liquid glucose or a pinch of cream of
tartar

125 ml | 4 fl oz water

30 g | 1 oz unsweetened plain chocolate, chopped into
small pieces

1 drop of vanilla essence

1 Heat the oven to 180°C | 350°F | gas mark 4.

2 Grease a 20 cm | 8 in *moule à manqué* tin and line with a disc of baking parchment. Dust first with caster sugar and then with flour. Tap out the excess.

3 Spread out the hazelnuts on a baking sheet and brown in the oven for 10–15 minutes. Remove the skins and allow to cool, then grind finely.

4 Make the cake: separate the eggs. Beat the yolks and 1 white with all but 1 tablespoon of the sugar until pale and creamy.

5 Whisk the remaining egg whites until stiff. Whisk in the reserved sugar until stiff and shiny.

6 Quickly add the butter to the egg-yolk mixture. Mix the flour with the ground hazelnuts. Fold the egg whites into the yolk mixture, using a large metal spoon, and then fold in the flour and nuts. Pile into the prepared tin.

7 Bake in the centre of the oven for 40–50 minutes or until the sides have shrunk away from the tin slightly and the top springs back when pressed lightly with a fingertip. Turn out on to a wire rack and leave to cool completely.

8 Make the royal icing: whisk the egg white until frothy. Beat in the icing sugar, with the lemon juice, until very smooth, white and stiff. Cover with a damp cloth until ready for use.

9 Oil a baking sheet.

10 Make the nougat: bake the almonds in the oven until pale brown. Keep warm. Put the

sugar and glucose or cream of tartar into a heavy saucepan and place over a medium heat until melted and golden. Add the almonds and cook for 1 further minute.

11 Pour the mixture on to the oiled baking sheet. Turn it over with an oiled palette knife, using a half-mixing, half-kneading movement. While still warm and pliable, roll the nougat out as thinly as possible, using a lemon coated thinly with vegetable oil.

12 Make the *crème au beurre mousseline*: dissolve the sugar in the water in a heavy saucepan. Boil until a little syrup forms short, sticky threads when pulled between a wet finger and thumb. Whisk the egg yolks and pour on to the sugar syrup in a steady stream, whisking constantly. Continue whisking until thick and mousse-like. Cream the butter in a bowl until soft, then add the mousse and combine thoroughly.

13 Make the chocolate fondant icing: dissolve the sugar and glucose or cream of tartar in the water in a saucepan set over a low heat, without boiling. Cover and bring to the boil. Boil to the soft-ball stage ($110-115°C \mid 230-240°F$). Meanwhile, scrub a stainless steel or heat-resistant work surface and sprinkle with water. Stop the sugar syrup from cooking further by dipping the bottom of the pan into a bowl of very cold water. Cool slightly.

14 Put the chocolate into a heatproof bowl and melt over a saucepan of steaming water. Pour the sugar syrup slowly on to the moistened stainless steel top. Using a wet palette knife, fold the outsides of the mixture into the centre. When opaque but still fairly soft, add the melted chocolate and vanilla essence and continue to turn with a spatula until the fondant becomes fairly stiff. Put into a heatproof bowl and set over, but not in, a saucepan of simmering water to soften.

15 To assemble: when the cake is cold, split horizontally into 3 layers. Crush the nougat with a rolling pin and mix half of it with half the *crème au beurre mousseline*. Sandwich the cake together with the mixture. Pour the melted chocolate fondant icing over the top of the cake. Spread the remaining *crème au beurre mousseline* around the sides and press on the remaining crushed nougat.

16 When the chocolate has set, fill a piping bag fitted with a writing nozzle with the royal icing and pipe the word 'Nougatine' across the top.

NOTE: For more information on whisking-method cakes, see page 281.

Festive Cakes

Cakes often form an important part of a festive occasion, whether it is a *Christmas Cake*, a *Simnel Cake* at Easter, *Black Bun* for Hogmanay in Scotland or the centrepiece at a wedding. Wedding cakes traditionally have been a rich fruit cake of 1–3 tiers, separated by plaster pillars, marzipaned and decorated with royal icing.

In recent years some people have wanted a different look, so they have changed the icing to fondant and placed the tiers directly on top of each other, as in American wedding cakes, or have gone for a different cake entirely. Rich chocolate cakes are now very popular, decorated with chocolate or fresh flowers. Whatever the occasion, a cake can be baked and decorated in celebration of it. The cakes in this section are a few of the well-known festive cakes and also some recipes that can be used for any festive occasion.

Portion Sizes for Celebration Cakes

When making cakes for a celebration such as a wedding, birthday or anniversary, it is useful to know roughly how many portions can be gained from them. The cakes are usually cut into quite small pieces, but as a rough guide you need about 450 g | 1 lb rich fruit cake (weight without the marzipan and icing) for about 10 people. These tables should help to give some indication of how big a cake you will need. Traditionally, with 3 tier cakes, the top tier is not included in the calculations. The top tier is traditionally reserved for the christening of the first child.

2 Tier Cakes

18 and 30 cm	7 and 12 in	160–200 portions
18 and 28 cm	7 and 11 in	125–140 portions
15 and 25 cm	6 and 10 in	100 portions
15 and 23 cm	6 and 9 in	75 portions

3 Tier Cakes

15, 23 and 30 cm	6, 9 and 12 in	225–250 portions
13, 20 and 28 cm	5, 8 and 11 in	175 portions
15, 20 and 25 cm	6, 8 and 10 in	140 portions
13, 18 and 23 cm	5, 7 and 9 in	90 portions

Note: Remember this does not use the top tier.

Simnel Cake

A festive Easter cake: the 11 balls of marzipan are said to represent the apostles (without Judas). Sometimes they are shaped like eggs, the symbol of spring and rebirth.

MAKES A 20 CM│8 IN CAKE

a large pinch each of salt and baking powder
225 g│8 oz plain flour
55 g│2 oz rice flour
115 g│4 oz glacé cherries
225 g│8 oz caster sugar
grated zest of 1 lemon
225 g│8 oz butter, softened
4 room-temperature eggs

225 g│8 oz sultanas
115 g│4 oz currants
30 g│1 oz chopped mixed peel
340 g│12 oz marzipan (see page 461)
1 egg, beaten

To finish
115 g│4 oz glacé icing (see page 455)

1 Heat the oven to 180°C│350°F│gas mark 4. Double-line the base and sides of a 20 cm│8 in cake tin with baking parchment. Wrap the outside of the cake tin with a double thickness of newspaper to insulate the cake from direct heat. Secure with string (see *Preparing a Cake Tin*, page 276).

2 Sift together the salt, baking powder and flours. Cut the cherries in half.

3 Cream the butter in a mixing bowl until soft. Add the sugar and beat until pale and fluffy. Add the lemon zest and mix well.

4 Separate the eggs. Beat the egg yolks into the creamed mixture. Whisk the whites until stiff.

5 Using a large metal spoon, fold three quarters of the flour into the mixture. Fold in the egg whites gradually, alternating with the remaining flour and the cherries, dried fruit and peel.

6 Put half the mixture into the prepared tin.

7 Take just over three quarters of the marzipan paste. Roll it to a smooth 20 cm│8 in diameter round. Place it in the cake tin. Cover with the remaining mixture.

8 Make a small dimple in the centre of the cake to counteract any tendency to rise in the middle.

9 Bake for 2 hours in the centre of the oven, then reduce the oven temperature to 150°C│300°F│gas mark 2. Bake for a further 30 minutes or until a sharp knife or skewer inserted into the centre of the cake comes out clean. Remove from the oven and allow to cool completely in the tin before turning out.

10 Roll the remaining marzipan to a circle the same size as the top of the cake. Cut a piece from the centre about 12.5 cm│5 in in diameter and shape into 11 small, even balls.

11 Heat the grill. Lay the ring of marzipan on top of the cake and brush with beaten egg. Arrange the marzipan balls on top of the ring and brush again with beaten egg. Grill until golden-brown.

12 When the cake is cold, pour a little glacé icing into the centre of the marzipan ring. Tie a ribbon around the sides of the cake.

NOTE: For more information on creaming-method cakes, see page 279.

Christmas Cake

MAKES A 23 CM | 9 IN CAKE

115 g | 4 oz glacé cherries

55 g | 2 oz chopped mixed peel

450 g | 1 lb raisins

285 g | 10 oz sultanas

115 g | 4 oz currants

225 g | 8 oz butter

225 g | 8 oz soft light brown sugar

5 room-temperature eggs, beaten

285 g | 10 oz plain flour, sifted

2 teaspoons ground mixed spice

grated zest of 1 lemon

2 tablespoons black treacle

200 ml | 7 fl oz beer or sherry

115 g | 4 oz ground almonds

1 Heat the oven to 170°C | 325°F | gas mark 3. Line the base and sides of a 23 cm | 9 in round cake tin or a 20 cm | 8 in square cake tin with a double layer of baking parchment. Wrap newspaper around the outside of the tine (see *Preparing a Cake Tin*, page 276).

2 Cut up the cherries and mix with the other dried fruit.

3 Cream the butter in a large mixing bowl until soft. Add the sugar and beat together until light and fluffy.

4 Add the eggs gradually, beating well after each addition. Add 1 teaspoon of the flour if necessary, to prevent the mixture from curdling.

5 Fold in the flour, mixed spice, lemon zest, treacle and beer or sherry, using a large metal spoon.

6 Stir in the ground almonds and the fruit.

7 Turn the mixture into the prepared tin and make a deep hollow in the centre to counteract any tendency to rise in the middle.

8 Bake in the centre of the oven for 2½ hours or until a sharp knife or skewer inserted into the centre of the cake comes out clean.

9 Remove the cake from the oven and allow it to cool completely in the tin before turning out.

NOTES: This cake must now be covered with marzipan (see page 461) before being generously iced with royal icing (see page 466). Alternatively, cover the top with marzipan, rough it lightly with a fork and toast it under the grill until golden-brown.

For more information on creaming-method cakes, see page 279.

Mincemeat Cake

This very moist cake is good for using up leftover mincemeat after Christmas.

MAKES A 17 CM | 7 IN CAKE

225 g | 8 oz sultanas

30 g | 1 oz chopped mixed peel

85 ml | 3 fl oz warm black tea, preferably Indian

170 g | 6 oz butter, softened

170 g | 6 oz demerara sugar

2 room-temperature eggs

225 g | 8 oz self-raising flour

2 teaspoons ground mixed spice

225 g | 8 oz mincemeat

2 tablespoons marmalade

1 Soak the sultanas and mixed peel in the tea for 2 hours.

2 Heat the oven to 150°C | 300°F | gas mark 2. Grease a 17 cm | 7 in cake tin and line the base and sides with baking parchment.

3 Cream the butter and sugar together in a large mixing bowl until pale and fluffy. Add the eggs gradually, beating well after each addition.

4 Sift the flour with the mixed spice and fold into the creamed mixture.

5 Add the soaked sultanas, peel, tea, mincemeat and marmalade. Stir well together and turn into the prepared tin.

6 Bake in the centre of the oven for 2¼ –2½ hours or until a sharp knife or skewer inserted into the centre of the cake comes out clean.

7 Remove the cake from the oven. Cool completely in the tin before turning out.

NOTE: For more information on creaming-method cakes, see page 279.

Rich Fruit Cake

Square cake sizes		15 cm|6 in	17 cm|7 in	20 cm|8 in
Round cake sizes	15 cm|6 in	18 cm|7 in	20 cm|8 in	23 cm|9 in
glacé cherries	45 g|1½ oz	70 g|2½ oz	85 g|3 oz	115 g|4 oz
chopped mixed peel	30 g|1 oz	55 g|2 oz	55 g|2 oz	85 g|3 oz
raisins	140 g|5 oz	225 g|8 oz	340 g|12 oz	450 g|1 lb
sultanas	55 g|2 oz	85 g|3 oz	115 g|4 oz	200 g|7 oz
currants	55 g|2 oz	85 g|3 oz	115 g|4 oz	200 g|7 oz
grated lemon zest	¼ lemon	½ lemon	1 lemon	1 lemon
blanched chopped almonds	30 g|1 oz	55 g|2 oz	55 g|2 oz	85 g|3 oz
butter, softened	85 g|3 oz	140 g|5 oz	170 g|6 oz	285 g|10 oz
soft brown sugar	85 g|3 oz	140 g|5 oz	170 g|6 oz	285 g|10 oz
eggs	2	2½	3	5
plain flour	115 g|4 oz	170 g|6 oz	225 g|8 oz	340 g|12 oz
ground mixed spice	¼ teasp	½ teasp	¾ teasp	1 teasp
black treacle	½ tblsp	¾ tblsp	1 tblsp	1½ tblsp
brandy (can be added after baking)	2 tblsp	3 tblsp	4 tblsp	4½ tblsp
baking time	2 hours	2½ hours	2¾ hours	3¼ hours

Square cake sizes	23 cm|9 in	25 cm|10 in	27 cm|11 in	30 cm|12 in
Round cake sizes	25 cm|10 in	27 cm|11 in	30 cm|12 in	
glacé cherries	140 g|5 oz	225 g|8 oz	285 g|10 oz	340 g|12 oz
chopped mixed peel	115 g|4 oz	140 g|5 oz	200 g|7 oz	250 g|9 oz
raisins	620 g|1 lb 6 oz	790 g|1 lb 12 oz	1.12 kg|2 lb 8 oz	1.35 kg|3 lb
sultanas	225 g|8 oz	370 g|13 oz	425 g|15 oz	500 g|1 lb 2 oz
currants	225 g|8 oz	370 g|13 oz	425 g|15 oz	500 g|1 lb 2 oz
grated lemon zest	1 lemon	1½ lemons	1½ lemons	2 lemons
blanched chopped almonds	115 g|4 oz	140 g|5 oz	200 g|7 oz	250 g|9 oz
butter, softened	340 g|12 oz	500 g|1 lb 2 oz	590 g|1 lb 5 oz	790 g|1 lb 12oz
soft brown sugar	340 g|12 oz	500 g|1 lb 2 oz	590 g|1 lb 5 oz	790 g|1 lb 12oz
eggs	6	9	11	14
plain flour	450 g|1 lb	560 g|1¼ lb	675 g|1½ lb	790 g|1 lb
ground mixed spice	1½ teasp	2 teasp	2½ teasp	2¾ teasp
black treacle	2 tblsp	2½ tblsp	3 tblsp	3½ tblsp
brandy (can be added after baking)	5 tblsp	5½ tblsp	6 tblsp	6½ tblsp
baking time	3½ –4 hours	4–4½ hours	5–5½ hours	6–6½ hours

Rich Fruit Cake

This recipe is ideal to use for a wedding or other celebration cake. The table opposite will give you the ingredient quantities to use for different-sized cakes. *Rich Fruit Cake* is best if allowed to mature for 2–3 months, but it can be used sooner.

1 Heat the oven to 150°C|300°F|gas mark 2. Grease and line the base and sides of the cake tin with a double layer of baking parchment and protect the sides by tying a couple of layers of newspaper around the outside of the tin (see *Preparing a Cake Tin*, page 276).

2 Cut the cherries in half and mix with the mixed peel, raisins, sultanas, currants, grated lemon zest and blanched chopped almonds.

3 Cream the butter until soft, add the sugar and beat well until pale and fluffy. Beat the eggs and add gradually, beating well between each addition. If the mixture looks as if it might curdle, add a spoonful of flour.

4 Sift together the flour and mixed spice and fold into the mixture with the treacle.

5 Fold in the fruit and nut mixture. The brandy can be added now or it can be poured over the cake once it is baked.

6 Put the mixture into the prepared tin and place in the centre of the oven. Bake for the required time (see table). If it is a large cake (i.e. larger than 25 cm|10 in square or 28 cm|11 in round) you should turn the oven temperature down to 140°C|275°F|gas mark 1 after three quarters of the baking time have passed. If the top is getting too dark, cover with a piece of damp greaseproof paper. Test by inserting a sharp knife or skewer into the centre. If it comes out clean, the cake is ready.

7 Remove from the oven and allow to cool completely in the tin. When the cake is cold, remove from the tin but keep it in its greaseproof paper. Make a few holes in the top of the cake and pour over the brandy, if using and not already added. Wrap the cake well in kitchen foil and store in a cool, dry place.

NOTE: For more information on creaming-method cakes, see page 279.

Old-fashioned Boiled Fruit Cake

This cake is not, as the name suggests, boiled instead of baked. The fruit is boiled in water and orange juice and allowed to stand overnight before use, which gives it a wonderful plumpness. Instead of being decorated with marzipan and icing, the cake is finished with a glazed fruit and nut topping and tied with a ribbon. It can be used as a wedding cake (see the table on pages 390–91). Because this cake is packed with dried fruit it is easy to burn, so it is very important to keep a close eye on it when it is cooking and, if in doubt, turn the oven down and cover the cake. However, it is definitely worth the effort.

The table overleaf will give you the ingredient quantities to use for different-sized cakes.

225 g | 8 oz butter
225 g | 8 oz sultanas
225 g | 8 oz raisins
115 g | 4 oz currants
170 g | 6 oz dried apricots, chopped
55 g | 2 oz dried apples, chopped
115 g | 4 oz dried dates, chopped
115 g | 4 oz dried peaches, chopped
115 g | 4 oz dried pears, chopped
55 g | 2 oz chopped mixed peel
55 g | 2 oz glacé cherries, halved
170 g | 6 oz soft dark brown sugar
grated zest and juice of 1 lemon
grated zest and juice of 1 orange
115 ml | 4 fl oz water
85 ml | 3 fl oz orange juice

55 ml | 2 fl oz brandy
½ teaspoon freshly grated nutmeg
1 teaspoon ground cinnamon
1 teaspoon ground allspice
½ teaspoon ground ginger
¼ teaspoon ground cardamom
1 tablespoon black treacle
5 room-temperature eggs, beaten
340 g | 12 oz plain flour
1 teaspoon baking powder

For the fruit and nut topping

340 g | 12 oz apricot jam
340 g | 12 oz mixed dried and glacé fruit and nuts, such as pecans, brazils, almonds, apricots, red and green glacé cherries, prunes, peaches, pears

1 Put the butter into a large saucepan over a low heat, add the dried fruit, peel, cherries, sugar, lemon and orange zest and juice, water and the extra orange juice. Bring slowly up to the boil. Stir with a wooden spoon, cover with a lid, and simmer slowly for 10 minutes.

2 Remove from the heat and allow to cool slightly. Add the brandy and spices and transfer to a large bowl. When the mixture is completely cold, cover and leave in a cool place (not the refrigerator) overnight.

3 Heat the oven to 170°C | 325°F | gas mark 3. Grease a deep 25 cm | 10 in cake tin and double-line the base and sides with baking parchment (see *Preparing a Cake Tin*, page 276). Take 6 layers of newspaper and make into a band to go around the outside of the tin. It should come up 5 cm | 2 in above the top edge of the tin. Tie securely with string. Also, put a newspaper on a baking sheet for the cake to stand on in the oven. This is important as some ovens will colour the base and sides of the cake as well as the top.

4 Stir the treacle into the boiled-fruit mixture and beat in the eggs. Sift the flour with the baking powder and stir into the cake mixture, which will be slightly sloppy. Pour into the prepared tin. Place the tin on top of the newspaper on the baking sheet.

5 Bake on the bottom shelf of the oven for 3 hours (checking after 2 hours that it is not getting too dark). Lower the oven to 150°C|300°F|gas mark 2 and place 3 layers of greaseproof paper or baking parchment over the top to slow down the browning. Cook for a further hour or until a sharp knife or skewer inserted into the centre of the cake comes out clean.

6 Remove the cake from the oven. Cool completely in the tin before turning out.

7 When the cake is cold, wrap carefully in kitchen foil until ready to decorate. The cake will mature well for 2–3 months.

8 To decorate the cake: put the apricot jam into a saucepan with 1 tablespoon water. Heat until boiling, then push through a sieve. Allow to cool slightly, then brush half the glaze over the top of the cake. Arrange the fruit and nuts all over the top of the cake, then brush carefully with the rest of the glaze.

NOTE: Be very careful if cooking this in a fan oven, as the cake may become quite dark and dry. Make sure the oven temperature is lowered according to the manufacturer's instructions. The cake does tend to get quite dark and hard on the top, but this softens after the glaze has been on for an hour or so.

The glaze will remain shiny on the cake for a few days, but after 1 week it will begin to lose its gloss, so it is better not to decorate the cake too early.

Old-fashioned Boiled Fruit Cake

Square cake sizes		15 cm | 6 in	17 cm | 7 in	20 cm | 8 in
Round cake sizes	15 cm | 6 in	18 cm | 7 in	20 cm | 8 in	23 cm | 9 in
sultanas	85 g | 3 oz	115 g | 4 oz	140 g | 5 oz	170 g | 6 oz
raisins	85 g | 3 oz	115 g | 4 oz	140 g | 5 oz	170 g | 6 oz
currants	55 g | 2 oz	55 g | 2 oz	70 g | 2½ oz	85 g | 3 oz
mixed peel	30 g | 1 oz	30 g | 1 oz	45 g | 1½ oz	45 g | 1½ oz
glacé cherries	30 g | 1 oz	30 g | 1 oz	45 g | 1½ oz	45 g | 1½ oz
dried apricots	70 g | 2½ oz	85 g | 3 oz	115 g | 4 oz	140 g | 5 oz
dried apples	30 g | 1 oz	30 g | 1 oz	45 g | 1½ oz	45 g | 1½ oz
dried dates	45 g | 1½ oz	55 g | 2 oz	70 g | 2½ oz	85 g | 3 oz
dried peaches	45 g | 1½ oz	55 g | 2 oz	70 g | 2½ oz	85 g | 3 oz
dried pears	45 g | 1½ oz	55 g | 2 oz	70 g | 2½ oz	85 g | 3 oz
butter	85 g | 3 oz	115 g | 4 oz	140 g | 5 oz	170 g | 6 oz
soft brown sugar	85 g | 3 oz	115 g | 4 oz	140 g | 5 oz	170 g | 6 oz
lemon (juice and zest)	½	½	1	1
orange (juice and zest)	½	½	1	1
water	45 ml | 1½ fl oz	55 ml | 2 fl oz	70 ml | 2½ fl oz	85 ml | 3 fl oz
orange juice	30 ml | 1 fl oz	45 ml | 1½ fl oz	45 ml | 1½ fl oz	55 ml | 2 fl oz
brandy	15 ml | ½ fl oz	30 ml | 1 fl oz	30 ml | 1 fl oz	45 ml | 1½ fl oz
grated nutmeg	⅛ teasp	¼ teasp	¼ teasp	½ teasp
ground cinnamon	¼ teasp	½ teasp	½ teasp	1 teasp
ground allspice	¼ teasp	½ teasp	½ teasp	1 teasp
ground ginger	⅛ teasp	¼ teasp	¼ teasp	½ teasp
ground cardamom	pinch	⅛ teasp	⅛ teasp	¼ teasp
black treacle	¼ tblsp	½ tblsp	½ tblsp	1 tblsp
eggs	2	2½	3	4
plain flour	140 g | 5 oz	170 g | 6 oz	225 g | 8 oz	250 g | 9 oz
baking powder	¼ teasp	½ teasp	½ teasp	1 teasp
baking time	2–2½ hours	2¾ hours	3¼ hours	3½ –4 hours

23 cm | 9 in	25 cm | 10 in	27 cm | 11 in	30 cm | 12 in
25 cm | 10 in	27 cm | 11 in	30 cm | 12 in	
225 g | 8 oz	340 g | 12 oz	500 g | 1 lb 2 oz	750 g | 1 lb 11 oz
225 g | 8 oz	340 g | 12 oz	500 g | 1 lb 2 oz	750 g | 1 lb 11 oz
115 g | 4 oz	170 g | 6 oz	250 g | 9 oz	370 g | 13 oz
55 g | 2 oz	85 g | 3 oz	170 g | 6 oz	250 g | 9 oz
55 g | 2 oz	85 g | 3 oz	170 g | 6 oz	250 g | 9 oz
170 g | 6 oz	285 g | 10 oz	450 g | 1 lb	675 g | 1½ lb
55 g | 2 oz	85 g | 3 oz	170 g | 6 oz	250 g | 9 oz
115 g | 4 oz	170 g | 6 oz	250 g | 9 oz	370 g | 13 oz
115 g | 4 oz	170 g | 6 oz	250 g | 9 oz	370 g | 13 oz
115 g | 4 oz	170 g | 6 oz	250 g | 9 oz	370 g | 13 oz
225 g | 8 oz	340 g | 12 oz	500 g | 1 lb 2 oz	750 g | 1 lb 11 oz
225 g | 8 oz	340 g | 12 oz	500 g | 1 lb 2 oz	750 g | 1 lb 11 oz
1	1	2	3–3½
1	1	2	3–3½
115 ml | 4 fl oz	170 ml | 6 fl oz	250 ml | 9 fl oz	370 ml | 13 fl oz
85 ml | 3 fl oz	125 ml | 4½ fl oz	200 ml | 7 fl oz	250 ml | 9 fl oz
55 ml | 2 fl oz	85 ml | 3 fl oz	125 ml | 4½ fl oz	170 ml | 6 fl oz
½ teasp	1 teasp	1½ teasp	2 teasp
1 teasp	2 teasp	3 teasp	4 teasp
1 teasp	2 teasp	3 teasp	4 teasp
½ teasp	1 teasp	1½ teasp	2 teasp
¼ teasp	½ teasp	1 teasp	1½ teasp
2 tblsp	2 tblsp	3 tblsp	4 tblsp
5	8	11	14
310 g | 11 oz	500 g | 1 lb 2 oz	750 g | 1 lb 11 oz	1 kg | 2¼ lb
1 teasp	2 teasp	2½ teasp	3½ teasp
4–4½ hours	4½–5 hours	5–5½ hours	6–6½ hours

Black Bun

This is a rich, dense fruit cake which is wrapped in pastry and served in Scotland over the Christmas holiday, but particularly at Hogmanay. Serve in small pieces.

MAKES A 900 G | 2 LB LOAF

340 g | 12 oz plain flour

½ teaspoon baking powder

a pinch of salt

55 g | 2 oz lard

115 g | 4 oz butter

170 g | 6 oz plain flour

½ teaspoon baking powder

½ teaspoon cream of tartar

1 teaspoon ground allspice

½ teaspoon ground ginger

½ teaspoon ground cinnamon

½ teaspoon ground nutmeg

½ teaspoon ground black pepper

a pinch of salt

290 ml | 10 fl oz milk

For the filling

450 g | 1 lb currants

340 g | 12 oz raisins

45 ml | 3 tablespoons whisky

55 g | 2 oz mixed peel

55 g | 2 oz chopped almonds

85 g | 3 oz soft dark brown sugar

To glaze

1 egg, beaten with a pinch of salt

1 Heat the oven to 170°C | 325°F | gas mark 3. Grease a 900 g | 2 lb loaf tin, preferably with lard, and line with a strip of baking parchment to help lift the bun out once cooked.

2 Sift the flour with the baking powder and salt. Chop the lard and butter into small pieces and rub into the flour until the mixture resembles fine breadcrumbs. Add enough cold water to bind the pastry together.

3 Roll out three quarters of the pastry and use to line the loaf tin. If it cracks, push it into the tin to seal. Chill for 30 minutes.

4 Soak the currants and raisins in the whisky for 30 minutes. Add the mixed peel, almonds and sugar and mix thoroughly.

5 Sift the flour with the other dry ingredients and stir into the fruit mixture.

6 Add the milk to bind the fruit together and pack it tightly into the prepared pastry case.

7 Roll out the remaining pastry and place on top of the fruit. Crimp the edges and glaze with the beaten egg. Push a skewer right through the bun, making a hole through to the base. Make four holes like this across the bun. Prick the top pastry all over with a fork to stop it rising.

8 Bake in the centre of the oven for 3 hours.

9 Allow to cool before removing from the tin.

NOTE: This cake is best kept for 2 weeks before eating.

Loaf Cakes and Tea Breads

Loaf cakes are cooked in traditional bread loaf tins rather than round cake tins, making them easy to cut and serve. Tea breads are also cooked in loaf tins but they contain dried fruit which has been soaked in tea before mixing with the rest of the ingredients.

The cakes in this section are generally very simple to make, although extra time must be allowed if soaking dried fruit. A loaf tin of whatever size can be lined with baking parchment, greased greaseproof paper or a special paper case chosen to fit the loaf tin. If the recipe is for a 900 g | 2 lb loaf tin the mixture can be put into 2 × 450 g | 1 lb loaf tins, but the cooking time will need to be reduced by roughly 30 per cent, depending on each different recipe. Once the cake is made it will freeze, well-wrapped, for up to 3 months.

Cider Loaf

There is no fat in this recipe apart from that contained in the egg.

MAKES A 450 G | 1 LB LOAF

115 g | 4 oz raisins
115 g | 4 oz dried apricots, chopped
150 ml | 5 fl oz cider
1 dessert apple, cored and grated, including skin
grated zest of 1 lemon

grated zest of 1 orange
85 g | 3 oz soft dark brown sugar
1 room-temperature egg, beaten
150 g | 5½ oz self-raising flour

1 Heat the oven to 180°C | 350°F | gas mark 4. Grease a 450 g | 1 lb loaf tin and line the base with a piece of baking parchment cut to fit.
2 Put the raisins and apricots into a small saucepan. Pour over the cider and bring to the boil. Simmer for 2 minutes and remove from the heat to cool down completely.
3 Put the cider and fruit into a mixing bowl and add the apple, lemon zest, orange zest, sugar and egg. Mix well. Fold in the flour, ensuring there are no lumps in the mixture.
4 Pour into the prepared tin and bake in the centre of the heated oven for 1 hour. The cake is ready when a knife inserted in the centre comes out clean. Allow to stand for 5 minutes in the tin before turning out on to a wire rack to cool completely.

Apple Juice Loaf

150 ml|5 fl oz apple juice

55 g|2 oz raisins

55 g|2 oz dried apricots

55 g|2 oz dried apple

55 g|2 oz dried cranberries

55 g|2 oz butter

85 g|3 oz soft brown sugar

grated zest of 1 orange

grated zest of 1 lime

1 small apple, cored and grated, including skin

1 room-temperature egg, beaten

150 g|5½ oz self-raising flour

1 teaspoon mixed spice

1 Grease a 450 g|1 lb loaf tin or line with baking parchment. Heat the oven to 170°C|325°F|gas mark 3.

2 Put the apple juice, dried fruit, butter, sugar and zest into a saucepan and bring to the boil, stirring well. Pour into a large bowl and allow to cool down. This is important otherwise the flour will cook as it gets mixed into the cake, leading to a leaden result. Add the grated apple and egg.

3 Sift the flour and mixed spice together and stir into the cooled fruit mixture. Put into the prepared loaf tin and bake in the centre of the oven for 1–1¼ hours. It is cooked when a sharp knife inserted into the centre of the cake comes out clean.

4 Remove the loaf from the oven and leave in the tin for 5 minutes before turning out on to a wire rack to cool completely.

Pear and Amaretto Loaf Cake

This recipe is adapted from a delicious cake by Baker and Spice, the London bakery.

MAKES 1 SMALL CAKE

For the topping

55 g|2 oz plain flour

30 g|1 oz butter

15 g|½ oz caster sugar

For the cake

140 g|5 oz ripe pear

1 tablespoon Amaretto

85 ml|3 oz butter, melted

115 g|4 oz caster sugar

1 room-temperature egg, beaten

115 g|4 oz self-raising flour

30 g|1 oz ground almonds

½ teaspoon baking powder

a pinch of ground cinnamon

a pinch of salt

1 egg white

1 Heat the oven to 180°C|350°F|gas mark 4. Line a 450 g|1 lb loaf tin with greaseproof paper and brush lightly with oil.

2 To make the topping, sift the flour into a bowl and rub in the butter until the mixture resembles fine breadcrumbs. Stir in the sugar and set aside.

3 Remove the stem and core from the pear and discard. Peel if desired. Cut the pear into ½ cm|¼ in dice. Place in a bowl and sprinkle with the Amaretto.

4 Beat the butter, caster sugar and egg to combine. Set aside.

5 Sift the flour, ground almonds, baking powder, cinnamon and salt over the butter/sugar mixture and fold in. Fold in the pear and Amaretto.

6 Whisk the egg white to medium peaks and fold in.

7 Turn into the prepared tin and sprinkle over the topping mixture.

8 Bake in the centre of the oven for about 45 minutes or until well-risen and light brown. A wooden skewer inserted in the centre should come out without any wet mixture clinging to it.

9 Cool in the tin for 5 minutes, then remove from the tin and cool on a wire rack.

Lemon Sponge Syrup Loaf

MAKES A 900 G | 2LB LOAF

225 g|8 oz butter, softened
225 g|8 oz caster sugar
grated zest of 2 large lemons
3 room-temperature eggs, beaten
310 g|11 oz self-raising flour
225 ml|8 fl oz buttermilk (or natural yoghurt)

For the syrup
juice of 2 large lemons
115 g|4 oz caster sugar
75 ml|2½ fl oz water

1 Heat the oven to 180°C|350°F|gas mark 4. Grease a 900 g|2 lb loaf tin and line with a piece of baking parchment cut to fit.

2 Cream the butter and sugar in a large bowl using an electric mixer until it is pale and fluffy, then beat in the lemon zest. Add the eggs gradually, beating between each addition.

3 Sift in the flour and mix well. Add the buttermilk.

4 Pour the cake into the prepared tin and bake in the centre of the oven for 1–1¼ hours. Turn the oven down to 170°C|325°F|gas mark 3 after 30 minutes, and if it is getting too dark after 55 minutes cover it with foil. It is cooked when a sharp knife inserted into the centre comes out clean. Leave in the tin.

5 Meanwhile, make the syrup. Put the lemon juice, sugar and water into a saucepan and stir over a low heat until the sugar has dissolved. Bring to the boil, simmer for 2 minutes and remove from the heat.

6 Pour the hot syrup over the hot cake. Allow it to cool in the tin and then remove carefully to a plate.

Lemon Nut Bread

MAKES 2 × 900 G│2 LB LOAVES

450 g│1 lb butter, softened
450 g│1 lb caster sugar
6 room-temperature eggs, beaten
450 g│1 lb plain flour
1 teaspoon salt

grated zest and juice of 3 lemons
225 g│8 oz raisins
225 g│8 oz pecan nuts, chopped
1 teaspoon bicarbonate of soda
1 tablespoon water

1 Heat the oven to 180°C│350°F│gas mark 4. Grease 2 × 900 g│2 lb loaf tins and line the base of each with a piece of baking parchment.

2 Cream the butter in a large mixing bowl until soft. Add the sugar and beat until pale and fluffy. Add the eggs gradually, beating well after each addition. Add a little of the flour if necessary, to prevent the mixture from curdling.

3 Sift the remaining flour with the salt and fold into the mixture, using a large metal spoon. Stir in the lemon zest and juice, raisins and pecan nuts. Mix the bicarbonate of soda with the water and add to the mixture. Turn into the prepared tins.

4 Bake in the oven for 1¼–1½ hours or until the top springs back when pressed lightly with a fingertip.

5 Remove from the oven and allow to cool in the tin for 5 minutes, then turn out on to a wire rack and leave to cool completely.

NOTE: For more information on creaming-method cakes, see page 279.

Date and Orange Loaf

The recipe for this delicious loaf was given to us by Barbara Stevenson, an ex-Principal of Leiths School of Food and Wine. It improves greatly on keeping and is very good served spread with butter.

MAKES A 675 G│1½ LB LOAF

225 g│8 oz dried dates, chopped
125 ml│4 fl oz water
170 g│6 oz soft dark brown sugar
170 g│6 oz butter
grated zest of 1 orange

2 tablespoons orange juice
1 room-temperature egg, beaten
225 g│8 oz plain flour
1 teaspoon baking powder
1 teaspoon ground allspice

1 Heat the oven to 170°C│325°F│gas mark 3. Grease a 675 g│1½ lb loaf tin and line the base with a piece of baking parchment.

2 Put the dates into a small saucepan, add the water and bring to the boil. Cover with a lid and simmer for 5 minutes or until the dates are soft and pulpy.

3 Add the sugar, butter, orange zest and juice and beat well, off the heat, until the butter has melted and everything is well-amalgamated.

4 Allow the melted mixture to cool, then add the egg.

5 Sift together the flour, baking powder and allspice and add gradually to the melted mixture. Mix well until smooth. Pour into the prepared tin.

6 Bake in the centre of the oven for 1–1½ hours or until the top springs back when pressed lightly with a fingertip.

7 Remove the cake from the oven and allow to cool in the tin for 15 minutes, then turn out on to a wire rack and leave to cool completely.

8 Keep the loaf well-wrapped for 1 day to soften before cutting.

Fig and Oat Loaf

MAKES A 900 G | 2 LB LOAF

225 g | 8 oz butter

225 g | 8 oz soft light brown sugar

225 g | 8 oz golden syrup

340 g | 12 oz plain flour

1 teaspoon ground ginger

1 teaspoon ground cinnamon

1 teaspoon ground cardamom

1 teaspoon ground coriander

1 teaspoon freshly grated nutmeg

85 g | 3 oz no-need-to-soak dried figs, chopped

55 g | 2 oz porridge oats

2 room-temperature eggs, beaten

150 ml | 5 fl oz milk

2 teaspoons bicarbonate of soda

1 Heat the oven to 150°C | 300°F | gas mark 2. Grease a 900 g | 2 lb loaf tin and line the base with a piece of baking parchment.

2 Melt the butter, sugar and syrup together in a saucepan.

3 Sift the flour and spices together into a bowl. Add the figs and oats. Make a well in the centre and add the melted mixture and the eggs. Warm the milk to blood temperature, add the bicarbonate of soda, stir well and pour into the well, stirring all the time. Using a wooden spoon, gradually draw in the dry ingredients from the sides and beat until smooth.

4 Bake in the centre of the oven for about 1½ hours or until a sharp knife or skewer inserted into the centre comes out clean.

5 Remove from the oven and allow to cool in the tin for 10 minutes, then turn out on to a wire rack and leave to cool completely.

Honey and Spice Loaf

MAKES A 900 G | 2 LB LOAF

225 g | 8 oz butter, softened
140 g | 5 oz sugar
4 tablespoons clear honey, warmed
4 room-temperature eggs, beaten
450 g | 1 lb plain flour
1½ teaspoons baking powder

1 teaspoon mixed spice
1 teaspoon ground cinnamon
½ teaspoon ground ginger

To finish
170 g | 6 oz glacé icing (see page 455)

1 Heat the oven to 170°C | 350°F | gas mark 3. Grease and line the base of a 900 g | 2 lb loaf tin with a piece of baking parchment cut to fit.

2 Cream the butter and sugar together until they are pale and creamy. Beat in the warm (but not hot) honey. Beat in the eggs a little at a time, beating well between each addition. Add some flour if the mixture begins to curdle.

3 Sift the flour, baking powder and spices together and fold into the cake mixture. Put into the prepared loaf tin, spread flat and bake in the centre of the oven for 50–60 minutes. Check it after 30 minutes and cover with greaseproof paper if it is getting dark. The cake is ready when a sharp knife inserted into the centre comes out clean.

4 Allow to stand in the tin for 5 minutes before turning out on to a wire rack to cool completely. Once cold, cover the top with glacé icing.

Malt Loaf

This is particularly delicious served with plenty of butter.

MAKES 2 × 675 G | 1½ LB LOAVES

450 g | 1 lb plain flour
30 g | 1 oz baking powder
55 g | 2 oz soft dark brown sugar
170 g | 6 oz dried dates, chopped
225 g | 8 oz sultanas

55 g | 2 oz butter
55 g | 2 oz black treacle
115 g | 4 oz malt extract
290 ml | 10 fl oz milk

1 Heat the oven to 180°C | 350°F | gas mark 4. Grease 2 × 675 g | 1½ lb loaf tins and line the base of each with a piece of baking parchment.

2 Sift the flour with the baking powder into a large mixing bowl. Add the sugar, dates and sultanas.

3 Melt the butter, add the treacle and malt extract and heat very gently until the mixture is runny. Add the milk and mix well.

4 Make a well in the flour mixture. Add the liquid ingredients and mix very well to get a smooth soft dough. Spoon into the prepared tins.

5 Bake in the centre of the oven for 1–1½ hours or until a sharp knife or skewer inserted into the centre of the loaves comes out clean.

6 Remove the loaves from the oven and allow to cool in the tins for 10 minutes, then turn out on to a wire rack and leave to cool completely.

Sultana Loaf

MAKES A 900 G | 2 LB LOAF

170 g | 6 oz butter, softened
170 g | 6 oz soft light brown sugar
3 room-temperature eggs, beaten
285 g | 10 oz self-raising flour

340 g | 12 oz sultanas
grated zest of 1 orange
1 teaspoon mixed spice

1 Heat the oven to 180°C | 350°F | gas mark 4. Grease a 900 g | 2 lb loaf tin and line with a piece of baking parchment cut to fit.

2 Cream the butter in a large bowl using an electric beater until it is soft. Add the sugar and beat until pale and fluffy.

3 Add the beaten eggs a little at a time, beating well between each addition. If the mixture starts to curdle, beat in a little of the measured flour.

4 Fold in the flour, sultanas, orange zest and mixed spice. Mix well.

5 Put into the prepared loaf tin and bake in the centre of the oven for 1–1½ hours. If the cake starts to get too dark, cover it with a piece of greaseproof paper and turn the oven down to 150°C | 300°F | gas mark 2. Extend the cooking time if necessary. The cake is ready when a sharp knife inserted into the centre comes out clean. Allow the cake to cool for 10 minutes in the tin and then turn out on to a wire rack to cool completely.

Apricot and Walnut Loaf

MAKES A 900 G|2 LB LOAF

225 g|8 oz dried apricots, roughly chopped
290 ml|10 fl oz water
225 g|8 oz caster sugar
85 g|3 oz butter, melted and cooled
1 room-temperature egg, beaten
55 ml|2 fl oz water

115 ml|4 fl oz orange juice
285 g|10 oz plain flour, sifted
2 teaspoons baking powder
a pinch of salt
85 g|3 oz walnuts, chopped

1 Soak the apricots in the water for 30 minutes.
2 Heat the oven to 180°C|350°F|gas mark 4. Grease a 900 g|2 lb loaf tin and line the base with a piece of baking parchment.
3 Mix the sugar, butter, egg, water and orange juice together in a mixing bowl.
4 Sift together the flour, baking powder and salt and add to the sugar and egg mixture. Mix well. Stir in the drained apricots and the walnuts. Pour into the prepared tin.
5 Bake in the centre of the oven for 1–1¼ hours or until a sharp knife or skewer inserted into the centre of the cake comes out clean.
6 Remove from the oven and leave to cool in the tin for 10 minutes, then turn out on to a wire rack and leave to cool completely.

Cranberry and Banana Walnut Bread

MAKES A 675 G | 1½ LB LOAF

55 ml|2 fl oz orange juice
100 g|3½ oz dried, sweetened cranberries
85 g|3 oz butter, melted and cooled
140 g|5 oz caster sugar
2 room-temperature eggs, beaten

170 g|6 oz peeled weight ripe bananas, mashed
  (about 2 ripe bananas)
250 g|9 oz self-raising flour
1 teaspoon bicarbonate of soda
50 g|1¾ oz walnuts, chopped

1 Line a 10 × 20 cm | 4 × 8 in loaf tin with baking parchment. Heat the oven to 180°C|350°F|gas mark 4.
2 Place the orange juice in a small saucepan then add the cranberries. Heat over a medium heat for 2–3 minutes until the cranberries soften and the orange juice mostly evaporates. Set aside to cool.
3 Stir together the butter, sugar, eggs and bananas.
4 Sift the flour and the bicarbonate of soda over the banana mixture and fold in.
5 Fold in the cranberries and remaining orange juice and the walnuts. Turn into the prepared tin.

6 Bake in the centre of the oven for about 45 minutes–1 hour or until a cocktail stick inserted into the centre comes out clean.

7 Cool in the tin for 15 minutes then transfer to a wire rack to cool completely.

Carrot Cake

MAKES A 900 G | 2 LB LOAF

285 g | 10 oz plain flour

2 teaspoons bicarbonate of soda

a pinch of salt

2 teaspoons ground cinnamon

225 g | 8 oz caster sugar

3 room-temperature eggs

225 g | 8 oz butter, melted and cooled

2 teaspoons vanilla essence

225 g | 8 oz carrots, grated

1 Heat the oven to 170°C | 325°F | gas mark 3. Grease a 900 g | 2 lb loaf tin and line the base with a piece of baking parchment.

2 Sift the flour, bicarbonate of soda, salt and cinnamon together into a large mixing bowl. Add the sugar.

3 Whisk the eggs lightly with the butter and vanilla essence.

4 Make a well in the dry ingredients, add the egg and butter mixture and mix in carefully. Beat well and stir in the carrots. Mix thoroughly. Turn into the prepared tin.

5 Bake in the top of the oven for 1½–2 hours or until the top springs back when pressed lightly with a fingertip.

6 Remove the cake from the oven and allow to cool in the tin for 5 minutes, then turn out on to a wire rack and leave to cool completely.

VARIATION

Carrot and Parsnip Loaf: Use 115g | 4 oz grated parsnip in place of half the grated carrot.

Boiled Carrot and Fruit Cake

This cake is very low in fat.

MAKES A 900 G | 2 LB LOAF

170 g | 6 oz carrots, grated

115 g | 4 oz raisins

55 g | 2 oz dried apricots, chopped

150 ml | 5 fl oz water

200 g | 7 oz caster sugar

30 g | 1 oz butter

225 g | 8 oz self-raising flour

½ teaspoon ground cinnamon

½ teaspoon ground cloves

85 g | 3 oz walnuts, chopped

1 Heat the oven to 170°C | 325°F | gas mark 3. Grease a 900 g | 2 lb loaf tin and line the base with a piece of baking parchment.

2 Put the carrots, raisins, apricots, water, sugar and butter together into a saucepan. Place over a low heat until the sugar has dissolved completely, then bring to the boil, cover with a lid and simmer for 10 minutes. Remove from the heat and allow to cool for about 45 minutes.

3 Sift the flour with the spices and add to the cooled mixture, along with the chopped walnuts, to make a fairly liquid batter. Pour into the prepared tin.

4 Bake in the centre of the oven for 1–1¼ hours or until a sharp knife or skewer inserted into the centre of the cake comes out clean.

5 Remove the cake from the oven and allow to cool for 10 minutes in the tin, then turn out on to a wire rack and leave to cool completely.

Sugarless Carrot Cake

This cake has no added refined sugar. The sweetness comes from the carrots and the apple concentrate. The recipe can be varied by leaving out the nuts and adding dried apricots instead.

MAKES A 900 G | 2 LB LOAF

140 g | 5 oz wholemeal self-raising flour

140 g | 5 oz self-raising flour

½ teaspoon bicarbonate of soda

2 teaspoons ground cinnamon

1 teaspoon ground nutmeg

1 teaspoon mixed spice

285 g | 10 oz carrot grated

30 g | 1 oz desiccated coconut (optional)

55 g | 2 oz walnuts, chopped

85 g | 3 oz sultanas

2 room-temperature eggs, beaten

55 ml | 2 fl oz apple concentrate (available at health-food shops)

250 ml | 9 fl oz milk

1 Heat the oven to 200°C | 400°F | gas mark 6. Grease a 900 g | 2 lb loaf tin and line the base with a piece of baking parchment cut to fit.

2 Sift the flours, bicarbonate of soda and spices into a large bowl. Return the sifted-out bran to the flour mixture. Add the carrot, coconut, nuts and sultanas. Make a well in the centre.

3 Beat the eggs well, add the apple concentrate, beat and mix in the milk. Add to the dry ingredients. Stir until well-mixed and pour the batter into the prepared tin.

4 Bake for 45–50 minutes or until the top springs back lightly when pressed. Cover the cake with foil after 30 minutes to stop the top getting too dark.

5 Allow to cool for 5 minutes in the tin before turning out on to a wire rack to cool completely.

Beetroot And Parsnip Loaf

Root vegetables contain lots of natural sweetness, which works very well in cakes. If possible, use the grating disc on a food processor to prepare the peeled beetroot and parsnip – grating beetroot by hand can be very messy.

MAKES A 900 G | 2 LB LOAF

285 g | 10 oz plain flour

2 teaspoons bicarbonate of soda

a pinch of salt

2 teaspoons ground cinnamon

1 teaspoon ground ginger

225 g | 8 oz caster sugar

3 room-temperature eggs, beaten

225 g | 8 oz butter, melted and cooled

2 teaspoons vanilla essence

115 g | 4 oz grated beetroot

140 g | 5 oz grated parsnips

1 Heat the oven to 170°C | 325°F | gas mark 3. Grease a 900 g | 2 lb loaf tin and line the base with a piece of baking parchment cut to fit.
2 Sift the flour into a large bowl with the bicarbonate of soda, salt, cinnamon and ginger. Add the sugar.
3 Make a well in the centre of the flour and add the eggs, butter and vanilla essence. Mix together and add the beetroot and parsnips. Mix well and put into the prepared loaf tin.
4 Bake in the centre of the oven for 1¼ – 1½ hours, or until a knife inserted into the centre of the cake comes out clean. Remove from the oven and allow to cool for 10 minutes in the tin before turning out on to a wire rack to cool completely.

Courgette Bread

MAKES A 900 G | 2 LB LOAF

170 g | 6 oz plain flour

2 teaspoons baking powder

1 teaspoon bicarbonate of soda

1 teaspoon salt

1 teaspoon ground cinnamon

1 teaspoon ground cloves

a pinch of freshly grated nutmeg

2 room-temperature eggs

170 g | 6 oz sugar

85 ml | 3 fl oz sunflower oil

1 teaspoon vanilla essence

225 g | 8 oz courgettes, grated

85 g | 3 oz walnuts, chopped

1 Heat the oven to 170°C | 325°F | gas mark 3. Grease a 900 g | 2 lb loaf tin and line the base with a piece of baking parchment.
2 Sift the flour, baking powder, bicarbonate of soda, salt and spices together into a large mixing bowl.

3 Beat the eggs lightly and add the sugar, oil and vanilla essence. Add the courgettes and walnuts.

4 Make a well in the centre of the flour and pour in the egg mixture. Mix well. Pour into the prepared tin.

5 Bake in the centre of the oven for about 1½ hours or until a sharp knife or skewer inserted into the centre of the loaf comes out clean.

6 Remove the loaf from the oven and allow to cool in the tin for 10 minutes, then turn out on to a wire rack and leave to cool completely.

NOTE: The bread must be left undisturbed in the oven for 1¼ hours. If the oven door is opened before the bread has set, it will sink in the centre.

Parsnip Bread

MAKES A 900 G | 2 LB LOAF

285 g | 10 oz plain flour
2 teaspoons bicarbonate of soda
a pinch of salt
1 teaspoon ground mixed spice
1 teaspoon ground ginger

225 g | 8 oz caster sugar
3 room-temperature eggs
225 g | 8 oz butter, melted and cooled
2 teaspoons vanilla essence
225 g | 8 oz parsnips, grated

1 Heat the oven to 170°C | 325°F | gas mark 3. Grease a 900 g | 2 lb loaf tin and line the base with a piece of baking parchment.

2 Sift the flour, bicarbonate of soda, salt, mixed spice and ginger together into a large mixing bowl. Add the sugar.

3 Whisk the eggs lightly with the butter and vanilla essence.

4 Make a well in the dry ingredients, add the egg and butter mixture and mix in carefully. Beat well, then stir in the grated parsnips. Mix thoroughly. Turn into the prepared tin.

5 Bake in the top of the oven for 1½–2 hours or until the top springs back when pressed lightly with a fingertip.

6 Remove the loaf from the oven and allow to cool in the tin for 5 minutes, then turn out on to a wire rack and leave to cool completely.

Mocha Loaf

This recipe uses cooked, sieved potatoes, which give the cake a moist, close texture.

MAKES A 900 G | 2 LB LOAF

55 g | 2 oz plain chocolate, chopped

2 teaspoons instant coffee granules

3 tablespoons milk

170 g | 6 oz butter, softened

170 g | 6 oz caster sugar

115 g | 4 oz boiled potatoes, sieved and cooled

3 large room-temperature eggs, beaten

170 g | 6 oz self-raising flour

55 g | 2 oz cocoa powder

1 teaspoon baking powder

For the icing

170 g | 6 oz plain chocolate, chopped into small pieces

30 g | 1 oz butter

2 tablespoons water

1 Heat the oven to 180°C | 350°F | gas mark 4. Grease a 900 g | 2 lb loaf tin and line the base with a piece of baking parchment.

2 Put the chocolate into a heatproof bowl with the coffee and milk. Fit the bowl over, but not touching, a saucepan of gently steaming water and melt the chocolate. Do not allow it to get too hot. Remove from the heat and allow to cool slightly.

3 Cream the butter and the sugar together in a mixing bowl until pale and fluffy. Mix in the potato. Add the eggs gradually with the cooled but still runny chocolate mixture, beating well after each addition.

4 Sift the flour, cocoa and baking powder together on to the mixture and fold in carefully, using a large metal spoon. Turn into the prepared tin.

5 Bake in the centre of the oven for 30–40 minutes or until the top springs back when pressed lightly with a fingertip.

6 Remove the cake from the oven and allow to cool in the tin for a few minutes, then turn out on to a wire rack and leave to cool completely.

7 Make the icing: put the chocolate into a heatproof bowl with the butter and water. Fit over, but not touching, a saucepan of gently steaming water and melt the chocolate, stirring occasionally. Remove from the heat and allow the icing to cool until it will coat the back of a spoon.

8 When the cake is cold, spread the icing over the top and allow to set.

NOTE: This cake freezes well and will become more moist after a couple of days if kept in an airtight tin.

Pumpkin and Banana Bread

MAKES 2 × 900 G | 2 LB LOAVES

450 g|1 lb pumpkin, steamed and cooled *or*
   425 g|15 oz can pumpkin purée
2 ripe bananas
2 room-temperature eggs
340 g|12 oz caster sugar
290 ml|10 fl oz sunflower oil
550 g|1¼ lb plain flour
1 tablespoon baking powder
½ teaspoon ground ginger
2 teaspoons ground cinnamon
1 teaspoon salt
225 g|8 oz walnuts, chopped

For the icing
200 g|7 oz cream cheese
30 g|1 oz caster sugar

To decorate
walnuts, chopped
grated zest of 1 lemon

1 Heat the oven to 180°C|350°F|gas mark 4. Grease 2 × 900 g|2 lb loaf tins and line the base of each with a piece of baking parchment.

2 Mash the pumpkin and banana together in a bowl. Beat in the eggs, sugar and oil.

3 Sift together the flour, baking powder, spices and salt. Beat into the pumpkin mixture until thoroughly mixed. Stir in the walnuts. Divide the mixture between the tins.

4 Bake in the centre of the oven for about 1 hour or until a sharp knife or skewer inserted into the centre of the loaves comes out clean.

5 Meanwhile, make the icing. Mix the cream cheese with the sugar. It may be necessary to add more sugar as some cream cheeses are very salty. The mixture should taste slightly sweet, not savoury.

6 When the loaves are cold, spread the cream–cheese icing over the top and decorate with the walnuts and lemon zest.

Pumpkin and Date Bread

MAKES 2 × 675 G | 1½ LB LOAVES

340 g | 12 oz caster sugar

400 g | 14 oz plain flour

1 teaspoon bicarbonate of soda

¼ teaspoon salt

¼ teaspoon ground cloves

1 teaspoon freshly grated nutmeg

¾ teaspoon ground cinnamon

115 ml | 4 fl oz sunflower oil

2 room-temperature eggs, beaten

225 g | 8 oz canned pumpkin purée

150 ml | 5 fl oz water

85 g | 3 oz walnuts, chopped

115 g | 4 oz dates, chopped

1 Heat the oven to 180°C | 350°F | gas mark 4. Grease 2 × 675 g | 1½ lb loaf tins and line the base of each with a piece of baking parchment.

2 Sift the sugar, flour, bicarbonate of soda, salt and spices together into a large mixing bowl. Make a well in the centre.

3 Add the oil, eggs, pumpkin purée and water and mix very well, beating out any lumps. Stir in the walnuts and dates. Pour into the prepared tins.

4 Bake in the centre of the oven for about 1 hour or until the tops spring back when pressed lightly with a fingertip.

5 Remove the loaves from the oven and allow to cool in the tins for 10 minutes, then turn out on to a wire rack and leave to cool completely.

Chocolate Banana Bread

MAKES A 675 G | 1½ LB LOAF

85 g | 3 oz butter

225 g | 8 oz plain flour

30g | 1oz cocoa powder

3 teaspoons baking powder

½ teaspoon bicarbonate of soda

2–3 large bananas (225 g | 8 oz peeled weight)

115 g | 4 oz caster sugar

2 room-temperature eggs, beaten

140 g | 5 oz plain chocolate chips

1 Heat the oven to 190°C | 375°F | gas mark 5. Grease and line a 10 × 20 cm | 4 × 8 in loaf tin, with a piece of baking parchment cut to fit.

2 Melt the butter in a small saucepan and allow to cool.

3 Sift together the flour, cocoa powder, baking powder and bicarbonate of soda.

4 Mash the bananas with a potato masher or fork and stir in the sugar, eggs and butter.

5 Sift the dry ingredients again over the top and fold in. Stir in the chocolate chips.

6 Turn into the prepared tin. Smooth the top and bake for 45–50 minutes or until a sharp knife inserted into the centre comes out clean.

7 Leave to cool for 5 minutes in the tin before placing on a wire rack.

Pineapple and Banana Loaf

This cake has quite a dense texture due to the amount of fruit it contains, but its flavour is lovely. Serve in slices, spread with butter.

MAKES A 900 G | 2 LB LOAF

225 g | 8 oz plain flour
1 teaspoon ground cinnamon
½ teaspoon ground cloves
½ teaspoon ground nutmeg
½ teaspoon bicarbonate of soda
225 g | 8 oz soft light brown sugar

4 tablespoons sunflower seeds
2 medium bananas, mashed
1 × 425 g | 15 oz can crushed pineapple, drained
115 ml | 4 fl oz sunflower oil
2 room-temperature eggs, beaten

1 Grease a 900 g | 2 lb loaf tin and line the base with a piece of baking parchment cut to fit. Heat the oven to 190°C | 375°F | gas mark 5.
2 Sift the flour, cinnamon, cloves, nutmeg and bicarbonate of soda into a large bowl. Add the sugar and sunflower seeds and mix in. Make a well in the centre.
3 Add the banana, well-drained pineapple, oil and eggs to the well and combine thoroughly.
4 Pour into the prepared tin and bake in the centre of the oven for approximately 1¼– 1½ hours. Allow the cake to stand for 10 minutes in the tin before turning out on to a wire rack to cool.

Fruit Tea Loaf

Soaking the fruit in tea before cooking gives this fatless cake a wonderfully moist texture and an unusual, delicious taste of its own. For the best results, soak the fruit for about 12 hours or overnight.

MAKES A 900 G | 2 LB LOAF

115 g | 4 oz sultanas
115 g | 4 oz raisins
55 g | 2 oz currants
55 g | 2 oz chopped mixed peel

115 g | 4 oz soft dark brown sugar
290 ml | 10 fl oz cold tea (preferably Indian)
225 g | 8 oz self-raising flour
1 room-temperature egg, beaten

1 Soak the dried fruit, peel and sugar in the cold tea overnight.
2 Heat the oven to 170°C | 325°F | gas mark 3. Grease a 900 g | 2 lb loaf tin and line the base with a piece of baking parchment.
3 Stir the flour into the soaked fruit mixture and mix in the egg thoroughly. Turn into the prepared tin. Bake in the centre of the oven for 1¼ hours or until a sharp knife or skewer inserted into the centre of the loaf comes out clean.
4 Remove the cake from the oven and allow to cool in the tin for 10 minutes, then turn out on to a wire rack and leave to cool completely.

Lemon Tea Loaf

This fatless cake contains fruit soaked in a lemon-flavoured tea, which gives a moist and tangy result. For best results, soak the fruit for approximately 12 hours or overnight.

MAKES A 900 G | 2 LB LOAF

115 g | 4 oz sultanas

115 g | 4 oz raisins

55 g | 2 oz chopped mixed peel

55 g | 2 oz dried apricots, chopped

140 g | 5 oz soft light brown sugar

grated zest of 2 lemons

225 ml | 8 fl oz cold tea (preferably Indian and not too strong)

50 ml | 2 fl oz lemon juice

225 g | 8 oz self-raising flour

1 room-temperature egg, beaten

1 Put the sultanas, raisins, mixed peel, apricots, sugar and lemon zest into a large bowl and pour over the tea and lemon juice. Stir well, cover and put in a cool place overnight.

2 Heat the oven to 170°C | 325°F | gas mark 3. Grease a 900 g | 2 lb loaf tin and line the base with a piece of baking parchment cut to fit.

3 Stir the flour into the soaked-fruit mixture and mix in the egg thoroughly. Pour into the prepared tin and bake in the centre of the oven for 1¼ hours or until a sharp knife inserted into the centre comes out clean. You may need to cover it with foil after 50 minutes to ensure that it does not get too dark.

4 Remove the cake from the oven and allow to cool in the tin for 10 minutes, then turn out on to a wire rack to cool completely.

Cinnamon and Apple Tea Loaf

This loaf needs to be prepared 1 day in advance as the apple pieces should soak for at least 8 hours.

MAKES A 900 G | 2 LB LOAF

250 g | 9 oz dried apple pieces, chopped

170 ml | 6 fl oz hot, strained, black tea

85 g | 3 oz butter

170 g | 6 oz caster sugar

2 tablespoons golden syrup

2 room-temperature eggs, beaten

285 g | 10 oz self-raising flour

1 tablespoon ground cinnamon

55 ml | 2 fl oz milk

1 Put the apple pieces into a small bowl and pour over the hot tea. Allow to cool, cover and leave to soak overnight.

2 Heat the oven to 170°C | 325°F | gas mark 3. Grease and line a 900 g | 2 lb loaf tin with a piece of baking parchment cut to fit the base.

3 Put the butter, sugar and syrup together in a small saucepan and melt over a gentle heat.

Do not allow to boil. Cool until just warm and add the soaked fruit with the tea. Sift the flour and cinnamon into the mixture and mix carefully. Add the milk and pour into the prepared tin.

4 Bake in the centre of the oven for approximately 1¼–1½ hours. After 30 minutes turn the oven down to 150°C|300°F|gas mark 2. It is ready when a knife inserted into the centre comes out clean. Allow to stand for 5 minutes before turning out on to a wire rack to cool completely.

Berry Tea Loaf

This loaf uses fruit tea to soak the fruit before mixing with the other ingredients. For best results, soak the fruit for about 12 hours or overnight.

MAKES A 900 G | 2 LB LOAF

75 g|2½ oz dried cranberries
75 g|2½ oz dried blueberries
55 g|2 oz dried pineapple, chopped
55 g|2 oz dried apricots, chopped
115 g|4 oz soft light brown sugar

2 wild berry tea bags, infused with 300 ml|11 fl oz
    boiling water and allowed to cool
225 g|8 oz self-raising flour
1 room-temperature egg, beaten

1 Soak the dried fruit and sugar in the cold tea overnight.
2 Heat the oven to 170°C|325°F| gas mark 3. Grease a 900 g| 2 lb loaf tin and line the base with a piece of baking parchment.
3 Stir the flour into the soaked-fruit mixture and mix in the egg throughly. Turn into the prepared tin. Bake in the centre of the oven for 1¼ hours or until a sharp knife or skewer inserted into the centre of the loaf comes out clean.
4 Remove the cake from the oven and allow to cool in the tin for 10 minutes, then turn out on to a wire rack and leave to cool completely.

Sherry, Date and Walnut Tea Loaf

The fruit in this cake is soaked overnight in tea and sherry, which helps to make a very moist cake. If preferred, leave out the raisins and substitute more dates or chopped apricots.

MAKES A 900 G | 2 LB LOAF

170 g | 6 oz dried dates, chopped

85 g | 3 oz raisins

100 ml | 3½ fl oz hot, strained, black tea

3 tablespoons sweet sherry

140 g | 5 oz butter, softened

140 g | 5 oz caster sugar

2 room-temperature eggs, beaten

140 g | 5 oz plain flour

1 teaspoon bicarbonate of soda

1 teaspoon mixed spice

115 g | 4 oz chopped walnuts

1 Put the dates and raisins into a small bowl and pour over the hot tea. Allow to cool and then add the sherry. Mix well, cover and allow to stand for at least 8 hours or overnight.

2 Heat the oven to 170°C | 325°F | gas mark 3. Grease and line a 900 g | 2 lb loaf tin with a piece of baking parchment cut to fit the base.

3 Cream the butter and sugar together with an electric beater until pale and fluffy. Add the eggs a little at a time, beating well between each addition.

4 Sift the flour, bicarbonate of soda and spice together into the mixture, then add the walnuts, soaked fruit and tea. Mix well and pour into the prepared tin.

5 Bake in the centre of the oven for approximately 1¼ hours. The cake is ready when a knife inserted into the centre comes out clean. Allow it to cool for 5 minutes in the tin before turning it out to cool completely on a wire rack.

Small Cakes

Small cakes are a useful part of the cake-maker's repertoire. The mixture used to make small cakes is usually a creamed mixture and they can have a variety of flavours and/or decorations. Many people who learned cookery at school will have produced fairy cakes or butterfly cakes as an early culinary effort. They are generally baked in patty tins or muffin tins and are much easier to deal with if the tins are first lined with paper cases. The paper cases need no preparation. If you do not have paper cases, grease each patty tin carefully and line with a disc of baking parchment.

Butterfly Cakes

Add 1 tablespoon of cocoa powder to the flour and to the buttercream to make chocolate butterflies.

MAKES 12

115 g│4 oz butter, softened
115 g│4 oz caster sugar
2 room-temperature eggs, beaten
115 g│4 oz self-raising flour
a few drops of vanilla essence

For the buttercream
55 g│2 oz butter
115 g│4 oz icing sugar
a few drops of vanilla essence

1 Put cake cases into patty tins or muffin tins or grease the tins well and line with discs of baking parchment. Heat the oven to 200°C│400°F│gas mark 6.
2 Cream the butter and sugar together until pale and fluffy. Add the beaten egg a little at a time, beating well between each addition. Beat in a little of the flour if the mixture starts to curdle. Stir in the flour and add a few drops of vanilla essence.
3 Three-quarters fill the cases with the cake mixture and bake for 10–15 minutes. Cool on a wire rack.
4 Meanwhile, make the buttercream. Soften the butter with a wooden spoon, then gradually incorporate the icing sugar and add vanilla essence to taste. Add the cocoa powder if used.
5 When the cakes are cold, cut a shallow circle from the top of each cake. Cut the circle in half and fill the cavity with some buttercream. Arrange the 'wings', rounded-side down, in the buttercream.

NOTE: For more information on creaming-method cakes, see page 279.

Fairy Cakes

Fairy cakes can be made using a *Victoria Sandwich* mixture (see page 286), but this recipe gives them a more interesting texture. They can be finished with a variety of different coloured icings and sprinkles.

MAKES 12

85 g | 3 oz butter, softened

85 g | 3 oz caster sugar

1 room-temperature egg, beaten

170 g | 6 oz self-raising flour

55 g | 2 oz ground rice

85 ml–100ml | 3–3½ fl oz milk, to mix

a few drops of vanilla essence

To finish

glacé icing (see page 455)

cake sprinkles, e.g. hundreds and thousands or
  smarties

1 Place cake cases into patty tins or muffin tins or grease well and line with discs of baking parchment. Heat the oven to 200°C | 400°F | gas mark 6.
2 Cream the butter and sugar together until pale and fluffy. Add the egg a little at a time, beating well between each addition. Sift the flour and ground rice together into the mixture and stir well. Add some milk and the vanilla essence to create a dropping consistency.
3 Divide the mixture between the cake cases and bake in the centre of the oven for 15–20 minutes. Allow them to cool on a wire rack.
4 Make up the glacé icing and colour it if desired. Spoon some on the top of each bun and decorate with the sprinkles.

NOTE: For more information on creaming-method cakes, see page 279.

Coconut Buns

MAKES 18

340 g | 12 oz self-raising flour

170 g | 6 oz butter, cut into cubes

170 g | 6 oz caster sugar

115 g | 4 oz desiccated coconut

55 g | 2 oz raisins (optional)

1 room-temperature egg, beaten

290 ml | 10 fl oz milk

1 Heat the oven to 220°C | 425°F | gas mark 7. Line patty tins or muffin tins with cake cases or grease well.
2 Sift the flour into a large bowl and rub in the butter until it resembles fine breadcrumbs.
3 Add the sugar, coconut and raisins and stir well. Add the beaten egg and milk.
4 Spoon into the cake cases and bake in the centre of the oven for 15–20 minutes.
5 Place on a wire rack to cool.

NOTE: For more information on rubbing-in method cakes, see page 278.

Lemon Buns

MAKES 12

225 g | 8 oz self-raising flour

115 g | 4 oz butter, cut into cubes

115 g | 4 oz caster sugar

grated zest of 2 lemons

1 room-temperature egg, beaten

75 ml | 2½ fl oz milk

1 Heat the oven to 200°C | 400°F | gas mark 6. Put paper cases in patty tins or muffin tins or grease well and line with discs of baking parchment.
2 Sift the flour and rub in the butter until it resembles fine breadcrumbs.
3 Add the sugar and lemon zest. Add the beaten egg and milk and mix well to a dropping consistency.
4 Put into the prepared cake cases and bake for 15–20 minutes in the centre of the oven.
5 Place on a wire rack to cool.

Orange Buns

Use the grated zest of 2 oranges instead of lemons.

NOTE: For more information on rubbing-in method cakes, see page 278.

Individual Coffee Walnut Cakes

MAKES 12

115 g | 4 oz butter, softened

115 g | 4 oz caster sugar

2 room-temperature eggs, beaten

115 g | 4 oz self-raising flour

2 teaspoons instant coffee granules

¼ teaspoon vanilla essence

55 g | 2 oz walnuts, chopped

55 g | 2 oz plain chocolate, grated

1 Heat the oven to 180°C | 350°F | gas mark 4. Grease and flour 12 patty tins or muffin tins or put 12 paper cases in the tins.
2 Cream the butter and sugar until pale and fluffy.
3 Beat in the eggs, a little at a time.
4 Fold in the flour, coffee, vanilla essence and walnuts. Add a little water if necessary to make a soft dropping consistency.
5 Two-thirds fill the tin or cases and bake for 15–20 minutes. Leave to cool on a wire rack.
6 Melt the chocolate in a heatproof bowl over, but not touching, a saucepan of steaming water.
7 Spread each bun with a little melted chocolate and leave to cool and harden.

NOTE: For more information on creaming-method cakes, see page 279.

Orange and Almond Buns

These buns have a strong orange flavour. They are fairly close-textured and will freeze well before being iced.

MAKES 12

2 oranges

250 g | 9 oz self-raising flour

115 g | 4 oz butter, cut into small pieces

85 g | 3 oz caster sugar

30 g | 1 oz ground almonds

1 room-temperature egg, beaten

4 tablespoons milk

To finish

85 g | 3 oz icing sugar

30 g | 1 oz flaked almonds, toasted

1 Heat the oven to 190°C | 375°F | gas mark 5. Line 12 patty tins or muffin tins with paper cake cases or grease well and line with discs of baking parchment.
2 Finely grate the zest from the 2 oranges and squeeze the juice from 1.
3 Sift the flour into a large bowl and rub in the butter until it resembles fine breadcrumbs. Add the sugar and almonds.
4 Add the zest, juice, egg and milk to the flour mixture and mix well. The batter should have a reluctant dropping consistency, so if necessary add a little more milk.
5 Divide between the cases and bake for 15–20 minutes. Remove from the oven and cool on a wire rack.
6 When the buns are cold, mix the icing sugar with enough juice squeezed from the remaining orange to make a thick glacé icing. Ice the buns, scatter a few flaked almonds on top and leave to set.

NOTE: For more information on rubbing-in method cakes, see page 278.

English Madeleines

These traditional English cakes are definitely for coconut lovers. They are very different from the French Madeleines (opposite).

MAKES 12

115 g | 4 oz butter, softened

115 g | 4 oz caster sugar

2 room-temperature eggs, beaten

115 g | 4 oz self-raising flour

To finish

4–6 tablespoons seedless raspberry jam

4 tablespoons desiccated coconut

halved glacé cherries

1 Grease 12 dariole moulds and line with discs of baking parchment cut to fit. Heat the oven to 190°C | 375°F | gas mark 5.

2 Cream the butter and sugar together until pale and fluffy. Add the beaten eggs a little at a time, beating well between each addition. If the mixture starts to curdle, beat in a little of the flour.

3 Stir in the remaining flour and three-quarters fill the prepared moulds with the mixture. Place them on a baking sheet and bake in the centre of the oven for 12–15 minutes. Turn the cakes out on to a wire rack to cool.

4 When cold, cut the rounded tops off the cakes (these can be sandwiched together with a little jam to avoid wasting them). Melt the jam and brush all over the cakes. Roll them in the desiccated coconut and place upside down on a plate.

5 Dip a cherry in the jam and place on top of the cakes.

NOTE: For more information on creaming-method cakes, see page 279.

French Madeleines

These are little cakes baked in special scallop shell shaped moulds. They were made famous by Marcel Proust in his book *Remembrance of Things Past* and are a classic Génoise type of cake. If you do not have the correct shaped tins they can be made just as successfully in patty tins. Traditionally plain flour would have been used but using self-raising flour ensures success.

MAKES 12

melted butter and plain flour for lining the tins	1 teaspoon vanilla essence
55 g｜2 oz caster sugar	55 g｜2 oz self-raising flour, well sifted
2 room-temperature eggs	55 g｜2 oz butter, melted but not hot

1 Preheat the oven to 180°C｜350°F｜gas mark 4. Carefully brush the moulds with melted butter and dust with flour.

2 Put the sugar, eggs and vanilla essence into a medium-sized mixing bowl and whisk with an electric whisk until they are very thick and pale and will hold a trail. This will take about 5 minutes.

3 Sift the flour over the top and pour the melted butter round the side of the mixture. Using a large metal spoon, fold them in carefully and quickly, being careful not to knock out any air.

4 Fill the moulds with the mixture and bake in the oven for 10 minutes.

VARIATIONS

For a different flavour, instead of vanilla essence add the grated zest of 1 orange, or the grated zest of 1 lemon, or 1 teaspoon of orange flower-water. Add it to the eggs and sugar before they are whisked together.

Rock Buns

These little cakes suffer from having a name which makes them sound unappetizing. They are supposed to look like little rocks, not to taste like them. Once made they should be eaten straight away or frozen, as they go stale quickly.

MAKES 10

225 g | 8 oz self-raising flour

a pinch of salt

115 g | 4 oz butter

85 g | 3 oz caster sugar

55 g | 2 oz sultanas

55 g | 2 oz raisins

30 g | 1 oz chopped mixed peel

2 room-temperature eggs, beaten

3–4 tablespoons milk

1 Heat the oven to 190°C | 375°F | gas mark 5. Grease a baking sheet.

2 Sift the flour with the salt into a mixing bowl. Cut the butter into pieces and rub in until the mixture resembles fine breadcrumbs. Add the sugar and dried fruit and mix well. Stir in the eggs and enough milk to bind. The mixture should be quite stiff.

3 Use 2 forks to put heaps of the mixture, about the size of a small egg, on to a baking sheet, 5 cm | 2 in apart to allow for spreading.

4 Bake for 15–20 minutes until pale brown. Transfer the buns on to a wire rack and leave to cool completely.

NOTE: For more information on rubbing-in method cakes, see page 278.

Queen Cakes

MAKES 12

115 g | 4 oz butter, softened

115 g | 4 oz caster sugar

2 room-temperature eggs, beaten

115 g | 4 oz self-raising flour

55 g | 2 oz sultanas

a few drops of vanilla essence

1 Place 12 cake cases in patty tins or muffin tins or grease the tins well and line with discs of baking parchment. Heat the oven to 200°C | 400°F | gas mark 6.

2 Cream the butter and sugar together until pale and fluffy. Add the beaten egg gradually, beating well between each addition and adding a little of the flour if the mixture starts to curdle.

3 Stir in the flour, sultanas and a few drops of vanilla essence. Divide the mixture between the cake cases and bake in the centre of the oven for 15–20 minutes or until golden-brown. Remove from the oven and place on a wire rack to cool.

NOTE: For more information on creaming-method cakes, see page 279.

Chocolate Peanut Cakes

These are a cross between a cake and a biscuit.

MAKES ABOUT 20

115 g | 4 oz butter
170 g | 6 oz caster sugar
2 tablespoons cocoa powder

1 egg
170 g | 6 oz self-raising flour
115 g | 4 oz peanuts, toasted, skinned and chopped

1 Heat the oven to 180°C | 350°F | gas mark 4. Grease a baking sheet.
2 Melt the butter in a saucepan, add the sugar and cocoa powder and mix well. Allow to cool, then beat in the egg. Fold in the flour and peanuts.
3 Using wet hands, shape the mixture into balls the size of a ping-pong ball and place on the baking sheet, allowing 2.5 cm | 1 in between them for spreading.
4 Bake in the centre of the oven for about 15 minutes or until they spring back when pressed with a fingertip. Transfer to a wire rack and leave to cool completely. Store in an airtight container.

NOTE: For more information on melting-method cakes, see page 279.

Upside-down Cakes

The cakes in this section are easy to make and can also be used as puddings. Because they have fruit underneath, it is important to ensure that the cake is cooked through: it can remain a little undercooked around the fruit if not carefully checked. If the cake is to be served as a pudding, turn it out directly on to a plate and serve warm.

Wholemeal Apricot Upside-down Cake

MAKES A 17 CM|7 IN SQUARE CAKE

85 g|3 oz butter, melted

2 tablespoons soft light brown sugar

1 × 410 g|14 oz tin of apricots, drained

85 g|3 oz caster sugar

1 egg, beaten

150 ml|5 fl oz milk

a few drops of vanilla essence

170 g|6 oz wholemeal self-raising flour

1 Heat the oven to 180°C|350°F|gas mark 4. Grease a 17 cm|7 in square tin.

2 Mix 30 g|1 oz of the melted butter with the soft brown sugar. Spread into the bottom of the prepared tin and cover with the halved apricots, cut-side down.

3 Mix the remaining melted butter with the caster sugar and egg. Add the milk and vanilla essence and mix well. Stir in the flour.

4 Spread the cake mixture carefully over the apricots and bake for 30–35 minutes. It is ready when the top, pressed lightly with a finger, springs back.

5 Loosen the sides of the cake and turn upside down on to a plate. Serve warm with custard, cream or Greek yoghurt.

Upside-down Toffee Gingerbread

This cake can be served as a very indulgent winter pudding, accompanied by Greek yoghurt.

MAKES A 20 CM|8 IN CAKE

For the toffee topping
55 g|2 oz unsalted butter
85 g|3 oz soft light brown sugar
½ teaspoon ground ginger
6 dried figs, roughly chopped
8 dried pear halves
75 g|2½ oz macadamia nuts

For the gingerbread
115 g|4 oz butter
115 g|4 oz soft light brown sugar
115 g|4 oz black treacle
225 g|8 oz plain flour
2 teaspoons ground ginger
2 eggs, beaten
85 ml|3 fl oz milk
1 teaspoon bicarbonate of soda
2 tablespoons stem ginger, diced

1 Heat the oven to 180°C|350°F|gas mark 4. Grease a 20 cm|8 in *moule à manqué* or round cake tin.

2 Make the toffee topping: melt the butter and stir in the sugar and ginger. Pour into the prepared tin.

3 Arrange the dried fruit and nuts on the toffee.

4 Make the gingerbread: melt the butter, sugar and treacle together in a saucepan over a low heat. Do not let the mixture boil. Remove from the heat and allow to cool.

5 Sift the flour with the ground ginger into a large mixing bowl and make a well in the centre. Pour in the eggs and the melted mixture. Using a wooden spoon, gradually draw in the flour and mix to a smooth batter.

6 Warm the milk to blood temperature, add the bicarbonate of soda and pour into the batter with the stem ginger. Mix well. Pour carefully on to the fruit and nuts in the prepared tin.

7 Bake in the centre of the oven for about 45 minutes or until a sharp knife or skewer inserted into the centre of the cake comes out clean.

8 While the cake is still warm, turn it upside down on to a serving dish and serve. If it is to be served cold, turn on to a wire rack to cool completely.

Pear and Ginger Upside-down Cake

Pears and ginger go very well together and this cake can also be served warm as a pudding.

MAKES A 20 CM | 8 IN CAKE

For the topping

3 dessert pears, peeled, halved and cored

570 ml | 1 pint sugar syrup (see page 475)

55 g | 2 oz butter

55 g | 2 oz soft light brown sugar

For the cake

115 g | 4 oz butter, softened

115 g | 4 oz soft dark brown sugar

170 g | 6 oz black treacle

225 g | 8 oz plain flour

2 teaspoons ground ginger

2 eggs, beaten

85 ml | 3 fl oz milk

1 teaspoon bicarbonate of soda

To serve

290 ml | 10 fl oz Greek yoghurt

1 Heat the oven to 180°C | 350°F | gas mark 4. Grease a deep 20 cm | 8 in cake tin.
2 Make the topping: poach the pears in the sugar syrup in a large saucepan for 30 minutes or until soft.
3 Cream the butter and light brown sugar together in a bowl until pale and fluffy. Spread on the base of the prepared tin. Place the pears, cut-sides down, on top of the butter and sugar mixture with the tops pointing inwards.
4 Make the cake: melt the butter in a saucepan with the dark brown sugar and treacle. Do not allow to boil. Remove from the heat and allow to cool a little.
5 Sift the flour with the ginger into a large mixing bowl. Make a well in the centre and pour in the eggs and the treacle mixture. Carefully mix in the flour to make a smooth batter.
6 Warm the milk gently, add the bicarbonate of soda and pour into the batter. Mix well. Pour the mixture carefully over the pears in the tin, making sure they are not dislodged.
7 Bake in the oven for about 45 minutes or until a sharp knife or skewer inserted into the centre of the cake comes out clean.
8 Remove the cake from the oven and allow to cool in the tin for a few minutes, then turn upside down on to a plate. Serve warm, cut into wedges, with the yoghurt.

Spiced Peach and Almond Upside-down Cake

MAKES A 20 CM|8 IN CAKE

For the topping

55 g|2 oz whole blanched almonds

55 g|2 oz dried peaches

1 × 411 g|14½ oz tin of sliced peaches in natural juice, drained (keep the juice)

6 whole cloves

55 g|2 oz butter, melted

55 g|2 oz soft light muscovado sugar

2 teaspoons ground cinnamon

1 teaspoon grated nutmeg

For the cake

115 g|4 oz butter, softened

115 g|4 oz caster sugar

2 room-temperature eggs, beaten

225 g|8 oz self-raising flour

150 ml|5 fl oz milk

1 Heat the oven to 180°C|350°F|gas mark 4. Grease a 20 cm|8 in square tin.

2 First prepare the topping. Put the almonds on a baking sheet and bake for 5 minutes or until golden-brown. Cut the dried peaches coarsely and put in a saucepan with 55 ml|2 fl oz water, the juice from the tinned peaches and the cloves. Bring to the boil and simmer for 5 minutes. Drain the peaches, discard the cloves and put the juice back in the saucepan. Boil until reduced to approximately 55 ml|2 fl oz and set aside to cool down.

3 Mix the melted butter with the muscovado sugar, cinnamon and nutmeg. Spread into the prepared tin. Arrange the almonds in the tin and place the tinned and dried peaches on top of them.

4 Now make the cake. Cream the butter and sugar together with an electric beater until pale and fluffy.

5 Add the egg a little at a time, beating well between each addition. Mix in half the flour and then add half the milk and stir well. Mix in the rest of the flour and milk.

6 Spread the cake mixture carefully over the peaches and bake in the centre of the oven for about 50 minutes. Check it is cooked by pressing the top with a finger. It should spring back. If you are still not sure, insert a sharp knife into the centre and it should come out clean.

7 Loosen the edges with a knife and turn the cake upside down on to a plate. Spoon over the reserved peach juice. Serve warm with crème fraiche or Greek yoghurt.

Plum Scone

Using a scone dough for the base makes this cake particularly easy to make.

MAKES A 20 CM | 8 IN CAKE

For the topping

140 g | 5 oz caster sugar

2 tablespoons hot water

30 g | 1 oz unsalted butter

55 g | 2 oz toasted almonds, coarsely chopped

400 g | 14 oz plums, halved and stoned

For the scone

140 g | 5 oz self-raising flour

¼ teaspoon ground cinnamon

a pinch of salt

85 g | 3 oz butter

2 tablespoons caster sugar

60 ml | 4 tablespoons milk

extra butter for greasing

extra flour for rolling

To serve

double cream or crème anglaise (see page 474)

1 Heat the oven to 200°C | 400°F | gas mark 6. Butter a 20–23 cm | 8–9 in cake tin.

2 For the topping, place the caster sugar with the water in a clean, heavy-based pan and melt over a low heat. Turn up the heat to boil the sugar then cook to a pale caramel. Wash any crystals of sugar from the sides of the pan using a pastry brush dipped in water. Do not stir. Remove from the heat immediately and add the butter and almonds. Stir in the plums then turn into the buttered tin.

3 Make the scone: sift the flour with the cinnamon and a pinch of salt into a large bowl. Cut the butter into small dice and stir in. Using 2 table knives, scissor-fashion, cut the butter into the flour until it is the size of small peas. The scone can be made in the food processor if desired.

4 Use your fingertips to rub in the butter until the mixture begins to come together. Stir in the sugar then the milk and bring the dough together. On a floured surface, pat into a 20–23 cm | 8–9 in round. Place in the tin, on top of the plums.

5 Bake in the top third of the oven for 25 minutes or until the scone is golden-brown. Carefully invert on to a heatproof serving plate while still hot. Serve warm or at room temperature.

Tray Bakes

Tray bakes are made in shallow rectangular trays or roasting tins. They can have the texture of a biscuit or a cake. Some have a pastry base, a filling and then a topping of icing, crumble or chocolate. They can be cut into squares, bars or triangles and are extremely useful if you are baking for a picnic, cake sale, cricket tea or fête.

They generally freeze very well and, because of their shape, are easy to store. Others, like flapjacks, will store well in a sealed container. If you do not have the size of tin mentioned in the recipe, find a similar one that has sides that add up to the same amount. For example, if the recipe needs a tin that measures 20 × 25 cm | 8 × 10 in, it could be substituted with a tin that is 23 cm | 9 in square or a tin that measures 17 × 27 cm | 7 × 11 in. Otherwise, calculate the area of the tin by multiplying the length of the two adjacent sides and use a tin with a similar area.

Flapjacks

MAKES 18

170 g | 6 oz butter
115 g | 4 oz demerara sugar

55 g | 2 oz golden syrup
225 g | 8 oz porridge oats

1 Heat the oven to 190°C | 375°F | gas mark 5. Grease a shallow 22 × 30 cm | 9 × 12 in tin.
2 Melt the butter in a saucepan. Add the sugar and syrup and heat through.
3 Remove the pan from the heat and stir in the oats. Spread the mixture evenly in the prepared tin.
4 Bake in the centre of the oven for about 30 minutes or until golden-brown.
5 Remove from the oven and cut immediately into bars. Allow to cool completely in the tin.

Fruit Flapjacks

Adding a little flour to a flapjack mixture gives a softer texture than the traditional flapjack.

MAKES 24

170 g | 6 oz butter
115 g | 4 oz soft light brown sugar
55 g | 2 oz golden syrup
225 g | 8 oz porridge oats
55 g | 2 oz plain flour

a pinch of salt
100 g | 3½ oz raisins
55 g | 2 oz dried cranberries
30 g | 1 oz chopped mixed peel

1 Heat the oven to 190°C | 375°F | gas mark 5.
2 Place the butter, sugar and golden syrup in a small pan (the syrup can be weighed directly into the pan to avoid mess) and melt over a low heat to combine.
3 Mix the oats, flour and salt in a large bowl.
4 Stir the butter/sugar mixture into the flour and add the fruit.
5 Press into a shallow 30 × 35 cm | 10 × 12 in baking tin and bake in the centre of the oven for 30 minutes or until golden-brown.
6 Cut into fingers while still warm.

Apricot Squares

These are a variation on flapjacks. Any combination of nuts and seeds can be used, or, leave them out and make up the weight with other dried fruits such as raisins, cranberries or apples.

MAKES 9

3 tablespoons golden syrup
85 g | 3 oz butter, softened
30 g | 1 oz soft light brown sugar
170 g | 6 oz dried apricots, chopped

170 g | 6 oz porridge oats
30 g | 1 oz almonds, chopped
15 g | ½ oz sunflower seeds
15 g | ½ oz pumpkin seeds

1 Heat the oven to 170°C | 325°F | gas mark 3. Grease and line the base of a shallow 20 cm | 8 in square cake tin with a piece of baking parchment cut to fit.
2 In a large bowl mix the syrup into the softened butter. Mix in the rest of the ingredients and press into the prepared tin.
3 Bake in the centre of the oven for 20–30 minutes. Allow to cool for a few minutes in the tin, then turn out, cut into 9 squares and cool on a wire rack.

Orange Oatmeal Squares

MAKES 24

290 ml|10 fl oz orange juice
115 g|4 oz porridge oats
115 g|4 oz butter, softened
170 g|6 oz soft dark brown sugar
2 room-temperature eggs, beaten
225 g|8 oz self-raising flour
½ teaspoon ground cinnamon
55 g|2 oz walnuts, chopped

For the topping

115 g|4 oz soft dark brown sugar
55 g|2 oz butter
150 ml|5 fl oz orange juice
55 g|2 oz walnuts, chopped
55 g|2 oz flaked almonds

1 Heat the oven to 180°C|350°F|gas mark 4. Grease a shallow 22 × 30 cm|9 × 12 in tin and line the base with a piece of baking parchment.

2 Put the orange juice into a saucepan and bring to the boil. Reduce the heat and allow to simmer for 2 minutes. Pour over the oats in a bowl and stir well to mix. Set aside to cool.

3 Cream the butter in a mixing bowl. Add the sugar and beat well together until pale and fluffy. Add the eggs gradually, beating well after each addition.

4 Sift the flour with the cinnamon. Fold half the flour mixture into the creamed mixture. Blend in the cool, soaked oats and orange juice. Mix carefully to ensure there are no lumps. Fold in the remaining flour and stir in the walnuts. Pour into the prepared tin and spread out evenly.

5 Bake in the centre of the oven for 30 minutes or until the top springs back when pressed lightly with a fingertip. Remove from the oven and allow to cool in the tin.

6 Meanwhile, make the topping. Put the sugar, butter and orange juice into a saucepan. Bring to the boil and dissolve the sugar, then reduce the heat and allow to simmer for 8 minutes. Add the walnuts and almonds and simmer for 1 further minute, taking care that the mixture does not burn. Remove from the heat and allow to cool for 10 minutes.

7 Heat the grill to its highest setting.

8 Spread the topping over the cooled base and place under the grill for about 1 minute or until bubbling on top. Watch carefully in case it shows signs of burning. Allow to cool in the tin, then cut into squares.

NOTE: The topping becomes very hot when it is grilled. Do not be tempted to pick a piece off the top until it has cooled.

Blueberry and Sultana Bars

MAKES 16

200 g | 7 oz butter

115 g | 4 oz soft light brown sugar

115 g | 4 oz sultanas

75 g | 2½ oz dried blueberries

85 g | 3 oz porridge oats

140 g | 5 oz plain flour

1 Heat the oven to 180°C | 350°F | gas mark 4. Grease a shallow 20 × 30 cm | 8 × 12 in tin.

2 Melt the butter and add the sugar, sultanas, cranberries, oats and flour. Mix well and press into the prepared tin.

3 Bake for about 25 minutes. A knife pressed into the centre should come out clean. Leave to cool in the tin until just warm and then cut into 16 pieces. The bars are easier to cut whilst warm, but leave them in the tin until cold before removing.

Crunchy Chocolate Bars

MAKES 16

225 g | 8 oz butter, softened

140 g | 5 oz soft light brown sugar

140 g | 5 oz self-raising flour

1½ tablespoons cocoa powder

85 g | 3 oz porridge oats

85 g | 3 oz crushed corn flakes

To finish

140 g | 5 oz plain (or milk) chocolate, chopped into small pieces

1 Heat the oven to 180°C | 350°F | gas mark 4. Grease and line a 18 × 28 cm | 7 × 11 in tin with a piece of baking parchment paper cut to fit.

2 Cream the butter and sugar together with a wooden spoon until pale and fluffy. Sift the flour and cocoa together and add to the butter mixture with the oats and corn flakes. Mix well. The mixture will be quite dry.

3 Press into the prepared tin (a potato masher can help with this) and bake in the centre of the oven for 20 minutes. The mixture should still seem a little soft when in the oven.

4 Mark into 16 bars while still hot then allow to cool completely in the tin.

5 Melt the chocolate in a bowl placed over but not in a pan of steaming water. Spread the chocolate over the top and remark into the bars. When the chocolate has set, cut the bars with a large, sharp knife.

Coffee Streusel Bars

MAKES 16

For the base

115 g | 4 oz butter, softened

55 g | 2 oz caster sugar

170 g | 6 oz plain flour

For the topping

170 g | 6 oz plain flour

115 g | 4 oz butter

2 teaspoons ground cinnamon

55 g | 2 oz soft light brown sugar

For the filling

1 × 400 g | 14 oz can sweetened condensed milk

30 g | 1 oz butter

2 tablespoons golden syrup

3 teaspoons instant coffee granules

55 g | 2 oz walnuts, chopped

1 Heat the oven to 180°C | 350°F | gas mark 4. Grease a shallow 22 × 30 cm | 9 × 12 in tin.

2 Make the base: cream the butter and sugar together in a mixing bowl until pale and fluffy. Stir in the flour and bring together to form a dough.

3 Press the dough evenly into the prepared tin, using the back of a spoon.

4 Bake in the centre of the oven for 10 minutes.

5 Meanwhile, make the filling. Put the condensed milk, butter, syrup and coffee into a saucepan and stir together over a medium heat. Bring to the boil, then reduce the heat and simmer for about 3 minutes or until thick. Stir in the walnuts and leave to cool.

6 Remove the base from the oven and spread evenly with the filling mixture.

7 Make the topping: sift the flour into a bowl. Cut the butter into the flour and rub in carefully with the fingertips, ensuring the butter does not get too soft. Stir in the cinnamon and sugar.

8 Sprinkle the topping over the surface of the filling. Return to the oven and bake for a further 15 minutes or until firm to the touch.

9 Remove from the oven and allow to cool completely in the tin before cutting into slices.

Nut Squares

These squares have the sticky consistency of pecan pie. They can be made using pecan nuts or hazelnuts or a combination of the two. They keep for about 5 days in a tin or will freeze very well.

MAKES 24

For the base

85 g | 3 oz butter, softened

85 g | 3 oz sugar

1 egg, beaten

a few drops of vanilla essence

1 teaspoon grated lemon zest

170 g | 6 oz plain flour

For the topping

170 g | 6 oz nuts, such as pecan nuts, hazelnuts or a combination of both, chopped

340 g | 12 oz soft light brown sugar

55 g | 2 oz plain chocolate, grated

3 eggs, beaten

2 tablespoons plain flour

1　Heat the oven to 180°C | 350°F | gas mark 4. Grease a 22 × 30 cm | 9 × 12 in roasting tin.

2　Make the base: cream the butter in a mixing bowl and add the sugar. Beat together until pale and fluffy. Add the egg, vanilla essence and lemon zest and beat well. Stir in the flour.

3　Spread the mixture evenly in the prepared tin. Chill for 10 minutes.

4　Bake the base in the centre of the oven for 10 minutes.

5　Meanwhile, make the topping. Mix together the nuts, sugar, chocolate and eggs. Beat well and stir in the flour.

6　Remove the biscuit base from the oven and pour over the nut topping. Turn the oven up to 190°C | 375°F | gas mark 5 and bake for 30 minutes.

7　Remove from the oven and allow to cool completely in the tin. Cut into even squares or fingers.

Walnut and Coconut Slices

MAKES 12

For the base

85 g | 3 oz self-raising flour

55 g | 2 oz caster sugar

55 g | 2 oz butter, melted and cooled

45 g | 1½ oz desiccated coconut

For the topping

2 eggs

½ teaspoon vanilla essence

85 g | 3 oz desiccated coconut

85 g | 3 oz walnuts, chopped

225 g | 8 oz soft light brown sugar

½ teaspoon baking powder

1　Heat the oven to 180°C | 350°F | gas mark 4. Grease a shallow 20 × 25 cm | 8 × 10 in tin.

2　Make the base: mix the flour, sugar, melted butter and coconut together in a mixing bowl. This will produce a crumbly mixture, so use your hands to bring it together and then press it into the base of the prepared tin, using the back of a spoon to make sure it is level and pressed into the corners. Chill for 10 minutes.

3 Bake in the centre of the oven for about 10 minutes or until beginning to brown. Remove from the oven and allow to cool in the tin for 10–15 minutes.

4 Meanwhile, make the topping. Beat the eggs with the vanilla essence until they are well-broken up. Add all the remaining ingredients and mix well.

5 Spread the mixture over the base and return to the oven. Bake for 15 minutes, then turn the oven temperature down to 170°C|325°F|gas mark 3 and bake for a further 20 minutes or until the topping is brown and still feels slightly soft when pressed lightly with a fingertip.

6 Remove from the oven and allow to cool in the tin for 15 minutes. Mark the cake into 12 even pieces. Transfer to a wire rack and leave to cool completely. When cold, cut into the marked pieces.

Date Bars

MAKES 18

For the filling

250 g|9 oz dried dates, chopped

grated zest and juice of 1 orange

For the base and topping

115 g|4 oz butter, softened

85 g|3 oz caster sugar

a few drops of almond essence

170 g|6 oz plain flour

55 g|2 oz ground almonds

a pinch of salt

1 Heat the oven to 170°C|325°F|gas mark 3.

2 For the filling: place the dates, orange zest and juice into a small pan and heat over a low-to-medium heat for 5–10 minutes or until mushy. Set aside to cool.

3 For the base and topping: mix together the butter, caster sugar and almond essence, then stir in the flour and salt. You will need to bring the mixture together with your fingers.

4 Press two thirds of the mixture into a 28 cm|9 in square tin then chill for 10 minutes. Squeeze the remaining mixture into small clumps then chill.

5 Bake the base for 20 minutes then remove from the oven and turn the oven up to 190°C|375°F|gas mark 5.

6 Spread the date mixture over the base then sprinkle over the topping.

7 Bake for 20 minutes in the centre of the oven or until the topping is golden-brown.

8 Cut into bars while still warm.

Millionaire's Shortbread

For the shortbread

200 g|7 oz butter, softened
115 g|4 oz caster sugar
285 g|10 oz plain flour

For the filling

115 g|4 oz butter
115 g|4 oz caster sugar
2 tablespoons golden syrup
1 × 400 g|14 oz can condensed milk

For the topping

115 g|4 oz plain chocolate, chopped into small
  pieces

1 Heat the oven to 180°C|350°F|gas mark 4. Grease a 22 × 30 cm|9 × 12 in Swiss roll tin.

2 Make the shortbread: cream the butter in a mixing bowl, add the sugar and beat until pale and fluffy. Add the flour and bring together to form a dough.

3 Press the dough evenly into the prepared tin, using the back of a spoon.

4 Bake in the centre of the oven for 20 minutes or until golden-brown. Remove from the oven and allow to cool completely in the tin.

5 Make the filling: put all the ingredients into a saucepan and heat gently to melt the butter and dissolve the sugar, stirring occasionally. Increase the heat and boil rapidly for 5 minutes, stirring constantly. Take care not to touch the filling. It is very hot. Remove from the heat and allow to cool for 1 minute. Pour over the cooled shortbread. Allow to cool and set.

6 Make the topping: melt the chocolate in a small, heatproof bowl set over, but not touching, a saucepan of gently steaming water. Spread the melted chocolate carefully over the cold, set caramel. Mark into fingers and leave to set before removing from the tin. Cut into fingers only once they are cold.

Chocolate Almond Squares

MAKES 24

225 g|8 oz flour quantity rich shortcrust pastry (see
  Pastry, page 46)
100 g|3½ oz butter, softened
100 g|3½ oz caster sugar
1 egg, beaten
1 egg yolk
100 g|3½ oz ground almonds
2 tablespoons plain flour

55 g|2 oz blanched almonds, roughly chopped
100 g|3½ oz plain chocolate chunks or drops
1 teaspoon almond essence

For the icing

150 g|5½ oz plain chocolate, chopped into small
  pieces
30 g|1 oz butter

1 Grease a shallow tin measuring 20 × 30 cm|8 × 12 in and about 2.5 cm|1 in deep. Roll out the pastry and line the base and sides of the tin. Chill until firm.

2 Heat the oven to 200°C|400°F|gas mark 6.

3 Cream the butter and, when soft, add the sugar and beat again until the mixture is pale and fluffy.

4 Gradually add the egg and egg yolk, beating well after each addition. Stir in the ground almonds, flour, chopped almonds, chocolate and almond essence.

5 Spread the almond mixture on top of the pastry and smooth with a palette knife.

6 Bake in the centre of the oven for 35–45 minutes or until the filling is set and the pastry crisp. If it is getting too dark, cover with greaseproof paper or foil and turn the oven down to 170°C|325°F|gas mark 3. Leave in the tin to cool down.

7 When cold, make the icing: put the chocolate in a bowl with the butter and place over, but not in, a pan of gently simmering water. Once the chocolate and butter have melted, mix well and carefully spread over the cooked almond pastry. Leave to set, or put in the refrigerator if necessary, and then mark into squares with a sharp knife.

Banana Chocolate Chip Bars

MAKES 20

300 g|10½ oz plain flour

2 teaspoons baking powder

a pinch of salt

170 g|6 oz unsalted butter, softened

115 g|4 oz caster sugar

115 g|4 oz soft light brown sugar

275 g|9½ oz ripe bananas (peeled weight), about 3 bananas

1 egg, beaten

½ teaspoon vanilla essence

225 g|8 oz chocolate chips

1 Heat the oven to 190°C|375°F|gas mark 5.

2 Line a 20 × 25 cm|8 × 10 in roasting tin or baking tin with baking parchment.

3 Sift together the flour, baking powder and salt. Set aside.

4 Beat the butter until soft, then add the sugars and beat again until pale and fluffy.

5 Stir in the bananas, egg and vanilla essence.

6 Fold in the flour mixture and the chocolate chips.

7 Spread into the prepared tin and bake for 45–50 minutes or until the mixture is golden-brown and springs back when the top is lightly pressed.

8 Leave to cool on a wire rack and cut into slices while still warm.

Chocolate Peppermint Bars

These can be cut into larger pieces, but they are very rich and a little will go a long way.

MAKES 27

For the base

200 g | 7 oz butter, softened
115 g | 4 oz caster sugar
290 g | 10 oz plain flour

For the chocolate layer

150 g | 5½ oz plain chocolate, chopped into small pieces
15 g | ½ oz butter

For the peppermint layer

115 g | 4 oz butter, softened
450 g | 1 lb icing sugar
1 tablespoon milk
1½ teaspoons peppermint essence

1 Heat the oven to 180°C | 350°F | gas mark 4. Grease a 22 × 30 cm | 9 × 12 in tin.

2 First make the base. Cream the butter until soft. Add the sugar and continue to beat until pale and fluffy. Add the flour and bring together to form a dough. Press the dough into the prepared tin and flatten with the back of a metal spoon. Bake for 20 minutes. Remove from the oven and allow to cool down in the tin.

3 Next make the peppermint filling. Cream the butter in a small bowl using an electric beater until it is pale and fluffy. Gradually beat in the icing sugar, then the milk and peppermint essence. Add more essence if liked. Spread the filling over the cooled base and chill for 1 hour.

4 Finally, melt the chocolate and butter in a small bowl over, but not touching, a pan of gently steaming water. Stir the chocolate well and spread carefully over the peppermint layer. Chill until set. Cut using a sharp knife.

Spiced Fruit Shortcake

MAKES 16

For the filling

450 g | 1 lb mixed dried fruit (peaches, cranberries, dates, raisins)

45 g | 1½ oz brown sugar

1 teaspoon ground nutmeg

1 teaspoon ground cinnamon

2 teaspoon grated lemon zest

juice of 1½ lemons

1 tablespoon cornflour

290 ml | 10 fl oz water

1 apple (Granny Smith), cored and grated, including skin

1 banana, mashed

For the shortcake

225 g | 8 oz butter, softened

115 g | 4 oz caster sugar

1 room-temperature egg

1 tablespoon lemon juice

225 g | 8 oz plain flour

150 g | 5½ oz self-raising flour

To finish

caster sugar

1 Make the filling: combine the fruit, sugar, nutmeg, cinnamon, zest and juice in a large saucepan. Blend the cornflour with the water and add to the pan. Bring up to the boil, stirring all the time, and allow it to simmer for 3 minutes until very thick. Remove from the heat, add the apple and banana and allow to get completely cold before using.

2 Heat the oven to 200°C | 400°F | gas mark 6. Grease a shallow 20 × 28 cm | 8 × 11 in tin.

3 Cream the butter, sugar, egg and lemon juice in a bowl with an electric beater until pale and fluffy.

4 Sift the flours and stir into the mixture. Turn it on to a floured board and knead with more flour until it is no longer sticky.

5 Divide into 2 and chill for 5 minutes. Roll out and line the prepared tin with half the pastry, pushing up the sides. Chill for 20 minutes.

6 Spoon the filling into the pastry case and roll out the remaining dough to fit the top. Pinch the edges together and make a few holes in the top. Bake for 10 minutes, then reduce the oven temperature to 170°C | 325°F | gas mark 3 for a further 30 minutes. Cover the top with greaseproof paper if it gets too dark. Whilst still warm, dust the top with caster sugar. Cut into bars.

Fig and Chocolate Bars

These bars are very rich and you may want to cut them in half to make 24 small squares.

MAKES 12

For the base

140 g | 5 oz plain flour

85 g | 3 oz butter

55 g | 2 oz soft light brown sugar

For the filling

1 lemon

250 g | 9 oz no-soak dried figs

115 ml | 4 fl oz water

1 teaspoon ground cinnamon

30 g | 1 oz soft light brown sugar

For the topping

115 g | 4 oz plain chocolate, chopped into small pieces

1 Heat the oven to 180°C | 350°F | gas mark 4. Line a shallow 20 cm | 8 in square tin with baking parchment cut to fit.

2 Sift the flour and rub in the butter. Add the sugar and mix to a firm dough. Press into the tin and prick with a fork. Bake for 30–35 minutes or until golden-brown. Allow to cool in the tin.

3 Meanwhile, make the filling. Wash the lemon, cut into quarters and remove any pips. Slice each quarter into thin slices. Put the sliced lemon into a saucepan with the figs, water and cinnamon. Bring to the boil and simmer gently, covered, for 15 minutes. Add the sugar and cook, covered, for another 5 minutes. Process until smooth in a food processor – it will be quite thick – and allow to cool completely.

4 Spread the filling over the base. Put the chocolate in a bowl over a pan of steaming water. Stir until it is just melted; do not allow it to get too hot. Carefully spread over the filling, chill for 10 minutes and cut into 12 pieces when it is nearly set. Leave for about 1 hour for the flavours to develop.

Cranberry and Raisin Squares

MAKES 16

115 g | 4 oz butter, softened

115 g | 4 oz soft light brown sugar

2 room-temperature eggs, beaten

75 g | 2½ oz dried cranberries

75 g | 2½ oz raisins

115 g | 4 oz self-raising flour

55 g | 2 oz ground almonds

To finish

icing sugar

1 Heat the oven to 170°C | 325°F | gas mark 3. Grease and line a 20 cm | 8 in square tin with a piece of baking parchment cut to fit.

2 Cream the butter and sugar together until pale and fluffy. Add the eggs a little at a time, beating between each addition.

3 Add the cranberries, raisins, flour and almonds. Mix well and put into the prepared tin. Spread flat with a palette knife and bake in the centre of the oven for 25–30 minutes.

4 Turn out on to a wire rack to cool. Once cold, cut into squares and dust with icing sugar.

Fruit Slices

MAKES 18

85 g|3 oz butter, softened
55 g|2 oz caster sugar
2 room-temperature eggs
225 g|8 oz plain flour
1 teaspoon baking powder
½ teaspoon vanilla essence
½ teaspoon ground mixed spice
a pinch of ground cloves
115 g|4 oz dried dates, chopped
55 g|2 oz pitted prunes, chopped
55 g|2 oz dried apricots, chopped

55 g|2 oz chopped mixed peel
115 g|4 oz hazelnuts, toasted, skinned and chopped
55 g|2 oz plain chocolate, chopped
85 g|3 oz raisins
grated zest and juice of 1 orange
100 ml|3½ fl oz milk

For the icing

115 g|4 oz plain chocolate, chopped into small pieces
20 g|¾ oz butter

1 Heat the oven to 180°C|350°F|gas mark 4. Grease a small roasting tin measuring about 22.5 × 28 cm|9 × 11 in and line the base with a piece of baking parchment.

2 Cream the butter and sugar together in a mixing bowl until pale and fluffy. Add the eggs gradually, beating well after each addition. Sift together the flour and baking powder and fold into the mixture with the vanilla essence, mixed spice and cloves. Stir in the chopped fruit, nuts, chocolate, raisins, orange zest and juice and the milk. Turn into the prepared tin and spread evenly.

3 Bake for 45 minutes. Remove from the oven and allow to cool in the tin.

4 When the cake is cold, make the icing: melt the chocolate and butter in a heatproof bowl over, but not touching, a saucepan of gently steaming water. Allow to cool slightly, then spread over the top of the cake. Allow to set, then cut into 18 even pieces.

Brownies and Blondies

Brownies are so called because of their deep brown colour and are an American speciality. The first brownie recipe is thought to have appeared in the Sears, Roebuck Catalogue in 1897. These were small, individual cakes made from molasses. A recipe in the 1906 edition *Boston School Cookbook* has chocolate added, but they were still cooked in small tins. Brownies became particularly popular in the 1920s.

Blondie recipes predate brownies, although with a different name. They were made from brown sugar or molasses with butter, flour and a raising agent. In the 1950s these butterscotch or vanilla brownies were called 'blonde brownies' and from there they became blondies. Although some blondies now contain white chocolate, they don't have to. The texture is important. They should be chewy and dense, a cross between a cake and a cookie. Some recipes contain nuts, but these can be left out if preferred or substituted with dried fruit.

Overcooked brownies are dry so it is probably preferable to slightly undercook rather than overcook them.

Brownies

MAKES 16

140 g | 5 oz unsalted butter

200 g | 7 oz plain chocolate, chopped into small pieces

225 g | 8 oz caster sugar

2 teaspoons vanilla essence

2 large eggs, at room temperature

1 large egg yolk, at room temperature

85 g | 3 oz plain flour

a pinch of salt

1 Heat the oven to 180°C | 350°F | gas mark 4.
2 Line a 20 cm | 8 in square tin with baking parchment.
3 Place the chocolate and butter in a bowl set over, but not touching, a saucepan of steaming water. Allow to melt, stirring occasionally.
4 Remove the bowl from the water and allow to cool so that it does not feel warm.
5 Stir in the sugar and the vanilla. The mixture will be slightly grainy.
6 Beat the eggs and yolks and stir into the chocolate mixture.
7 Sift the flour and salt over the mixture then fold in. Turn into the prepared tin.
8 Bake in the centre of the oven for 35–35 minutes or until a knife inserted into the centre comes out with moist crumbs (but not wet batter) clinging to it.
9 Allow to cool in the tin then cut into squares. Wrap in foil and store in the refrigerator.

Chocolate and Walnut Brownies

MAKES 12

115 g|4 oz plain chocolate, chopped into small pieces
115 g|4 oz butter
225 g|8 oz caster sugar
2 eggs, beaten

115 g|4 oz plain flour
½ teaspoon baking powder
115 g|4 oz walnuts, chopped
a pinch of salt

1 Heat the oven to 180°C|350°F|gas mark 4.

2 Grease a shallow 18 × 28 cm|7 × 11 in tin.

3 Put the chocolate into a heatproof bowl with the butter. Fit the bowl over, but not touching, a saucepan of gently steaming water.

4 When the chocolate and butter have melted, remove the bowl from the heat and stir in all the remaining ingredients. Pour the mixture into the prepared tin.

5 Bake in the centre of the oven for 30 minutes or until the centre is firm to the touch. Remove the cake from the oven and allow to cool in the tin for 10 minutes, then cut into 12, transfer to a wire rack and leave to cool completely.

Pecan Brownies

These brownies are very dark and less sweet than many recipes; definitely for adults only.

MAKES 36 PETITS FOURS OR 16 LARGE BROWNIES

115 g|4 oz butter
140 g|5 oz good quality plain chocolate, chopped into small pieces
170 g|6 oz caster sugar
2 eggs, beaten

½ teaspoon vanilla essence
55 g|2 oz plain flour
30 g|1 oz cocoa powder
100 g|3½ oz pecan nuts, roughly chopped

1 Heat the oven to 180°C|350°F|gas mark 4. Line a 18 cm|7 in square tin with baking parchment.

2 Melt the butter and chocolate over a very low heat, stirring occasionally.

3 Stir in the sugar, then remove from the heat and allow to cool to room temperature.

4 Stir in the eggs and vanilla.

5 Sift together the flour and cocoa and fold into the chocolate mixture. Stir in the nuts.

6 Spread the mixture out evenly in the tin and bake for 30 minutes or until just set in the centre. A skewer inserted into the centre should have a small amount of crumbs, but not wet mixture, stuck to it.

7 Allow to cool for 20 minutes, then cut into squares.

8 When completely cool, wrap in foil and store in the refrigerator for up to 3 days.

Cocoa Brownies

Using cocoa powder is easy and is less expensive than using melted plain chocolate.

MAKES 16 SQUARES

115 g | 4 oz butter

45 g | 1½ oz cocoa powder

2 eggs, beaten

225 g | 8 oz caster sugar

1 teaspoon vanilla essence

55 g | 2 oz self-raising flour

115 g | 4 oz walnuts, chopped

55 g | 2 oz chocolate chips

1 Heat the oven to 180°C | 350°F | gas mark 4. Grease and line the base of a 20 cm | 8 in square tin.
2 Melt the butter over a low heat, then stir in the cocoa powder. Leave to cool.
3 Beat the eggs with the caster sugar until pale, then fold in the cocoa mixture.
4 Stir in the vanilla then sift the flour over the mixture and fold in.
5 Spread half the mixture into the prepared tin and sprinkle with half the walnuts and chocolate chips. Cover with the remaining mixture then the rest of the walnuts and chocolate chips.
6 Bake in the centre of the oven for 30 minutes or until set. A wooden cocktail stick inserted into the centre should come out damp but should not have any uncooked mixture clinging to it.
7 Place the tin on a wire rack to cool before cutting into squares.

Fruit and Nut Brownies

MAKES 12

140 g | 5 oz butter, cut into pieces

200 g | 7 oz plain chocolate, chopped into small pieces

225 g | 8 oz soft light brown sugar

115 g | 4 oz plain flour

30 g | 1 oz self-raising flour

2 tablespoons cocoa powder

2 eggs, beaten

55 g | 2 oz skinned hazelnuts, lightly chopped

55 g | 2 oz raisins

To finish

extra cocoa powder

1 Heat the oven to 180°C | 350°F | gas mark 4. Grease and line a 23 cm | 9 in square tin with a piece of baking parchment cut to fit.
2 Melt the butter and chocolate in a medium-to-large saucepan. Stir over a low heat until both have just melted. Cool down until it is only slightly warm.
3 Stir in the sugar, sift the flours and cocoa powder together and add to the pan. Mix in the eggs, hazelnuts and raisins.
4 Spread into the prepared tin and place in the centre of the oven. Bake for approximately 25 minutes. It should still be a little soft in the centre.
5 Cool in the tin and then turn out and cut into 12 squares. Dust with sifted cocoa powder.

Chocolate and Mango Brownies

MAKES 16

85 g | 3 oz butter

250 g | 9 oz plain chocolate, chopped into small pieces

2 teaspoon vanilla essence

200 g | 7 oz soft light brown sugar

2 eggs

70 g | 2½ oz plain flour

115 g | 4 oz dried mango, chopped into small pieces

75 ml | 2½ fl oz soured cream

1 Heat the oven to 180°C | 350°F | gas mark 4. Grease and line a 20 cm | 8 in square tin with a piece of baking parchment cut to fit.

2 Melt the butter in a saucepan, add the chocolate and continue to melt over a very low heat, stirring all the time. Allow to cool.

3 Put the vanilla, sugar and eggs into a large bowl and beat until light and fluffy. Stir in the sifted flour, followed by the chocolate mixture, mango and soured cream.

4 Spread the mixture into the prepared tin and bake in the centre of the oven for 40–50 minutes.

5 Allow to cool in the tin before turning out and cutting into squares.

Triple Chocolate Brownies

MAKES 24

115 g | 4 oz butter

200 g | 7 oz plain chocolate, chopped into small pieces

115 g | 4 oz caster sugar

2 eggs, lightly beaten

225 g | 8 oz plain flour

140 g | 5 oz white chocolate, chopped into small pieces

85 g | 3 oz milk chocolate, chopped into small pieces

1 Heat the oven to 180°C | 350°F | gas mark 4. Grease a deep 20 cm | 8 in cake tin and line the base with a piece of baking parchment.

2 Melt the butter and plain chocolate in a saucepan over a low heat. Remove from the heat and allow to cool slightly, then stir in the sugar and eggs.

3 Mix together the flour and white and milk chocolates and fold into the plain-chocolate mixture. Pour into the prepared tin.

4 Bake in the centre of the oven for 35 minutes or until the centre is firm to the touch.

5 Remove the cake from the oven and allow to cool completely in the tin, then turn out and cut into squares.

NOTE: 85 g | 3 oz chopped pecan nuts can be substituted for the milk chocolate.

Macadamia Nut Brownies

Macadamia nuts are delicious in this recipe, but if you have difficulty finding them you can use brazil nuts, hazelnuts or almonds instead. The brownies can be kept in the refrigerator for a couple of days.

MAKES 16

115 g | 4 oz unsalted butter
115 g | 4 oz plain chocolate, chopped into small
  pieces
2 eggs
170 g | 6 oz caster sugar
55 ml | 2 fl oz dark rum
115 g | 4 oz plain flour
115 g | 4 oz macadamia nuts, chopped

For the icing

115 ml | 4 fl oz double cream
1 tablespoon dark rum
115 g | 4 oz plain chocolate, chopped into small
  pieces

1 Heat the oven to 180°C | 350°F | gas mark 4. Grease a shallow 20 cm | 8 in square tin and line with a piece of baking parchment.
2 Melt the butter and chocolate in a saucepan over a low heat without allowing it to get too hot. Remove and allow to cool.
3 Beat the eggs and sugar together until light and thick. Stir in the cooled chocolate mixture and the rum.
4 Sift the flour and add to the mixture with the macadamia nuts. Fold in carefully and thoroughly, using a large metal spoon.
5 Bake in the centre of the oven for 30 minutes or until firm to the touch.
6 Remove from the oven and allow to cool completely in the tin, then turn out on to a wire rack.
7 Meanwhile, make the icing. Put the cream into a saucepan and bring to the boil. Remove from the heat and add the rum and chocolate. Stir until the chocolate melts. Allow to cool until the icing thickens.
8 When the cake is cold, spread the icing over the top and chill to set. Cut into small squares to serve.

Chocolate and Peanut Butter Brownies

MAKES 16

140 g│5 oz plain chocolate, chopped into small
  pieces
115 g│4 oz butter
225 g│8 oz caster sugar

170 g│6 oz plain flour
½ teaspoon baking powder
170 g│6 oz crunchy peanut butter
3 eggs, beaten

1 Heat the oven to 170°C│325°F│gas mark 3. Line a 20 cm│8 in square cake tin with baking parchment.

2 Melt the chocolate, butter and sugar together over a low heat to combine. Do not allow to get too hot.

3 Sift the flour and baking powder together into a large bowl.

4 Mix the peanut butter into the chocolate mixture.

5 Make a well in the centre of the flour. Incorporate the eggs and the chocolate mixture, using a whisk to beat out any floury lumps. Put into the prepared tin and spread flat. Bake for 20 minutes. The brownies are ready when the crust has set on the top but if you push a sharp knife into the centre there is still a little wet mixture left on it. Remove from the oven and allow to cool in the tin before cutting into squares.

NOTE: These brownies are better undercooked. If cooked for too long, they become very dry.

Chocolate Raspberry Brownies

MAKES 9

2 eggs

200 g | 7 oz golden caster sugar

115 g | 4 oz butter, melted and cooled

1 teaspoon vanilla essence

55 g | 2 oz self-raising flour

45 g | 1½ oz cocoa powder

115 g | 4 oz fresh or frozen raspberries (defrosted)

For the icing

85 g | 3 oz plain chocolate, chopped into small pieces

15 g | ½ oz butter

1 Heat the oven to 180°C | 350°F | gas mark 4. Line the base of an 17 cm | 7 in square tin with baking parchment.

2 Beat the eggs and the sugar together until pale and fluffy, then beat in the cooled butter and vanilla essence.

3 Sift the flour and cocoa powder together then fold into the egg mixture. Fold in half the raspberries.

4 Spread the brownie mixture into the tin then scatter the remaining berries over the top.

5 Bake for 30–35 minutes until risen and set. A skewer inserted into the brownies should come out slightly sticky. Allow to cool.

6 Make the icing: place the chocolate and the butter in a small bowl set over, but not touching, steaming water. Melt, then stir together. Spread over the cooled brownies.

7 Chill until required. Cut into 9 pieces before serving.

Marbled Chocolate Brownie Cake

MAKES 12 PIECES

For the marbling mixture

200 g | 7 oz good quality cream cheese, at room
   temperature

1 teaspoon orange zest

85 g | 3 oz caster sugar

1 egg yolk

2 tablespoons plain flour

For the brownie mixture

200 g | 7 oz plain chocolate, chopped into small
   pieces

140 g | 5 oz unsalted butter

225 g | 8 oz caster sugar

2 teaspoons vanilla essence

2 large room-temperature eggs

1 large room-temperature eggs

85 g | 3 oz plain flour

a pinch of salt

To serve

vanilla ice cream, slightly softened

1 Heat the oven to 180°C | 350°F | gas mark 4.

2 Line a 20 cm | 8 in round sandwich tin with baking parchment.

3 Make the marbling mixture: beat the cream cheese, orange zest and sugar until smooth. Stir in the egg yolk then the flour. Set aside.

4 For the brownie mixture: place the chocolate and butter in a bowl set over, but not touching, a saucepan of steaming water. Allow to melt, stirring occasionally.

5 Remove the bowl from the steaming water and allow to cool until it does not feel warm.

6 Stir in the sugar and vanilla. The mixture will be slightly grainy.

7 Beat the eggs and egg yolk and stir into the chocolate mixture.

8 Sift the flour and salt over the mixture then fold in. Turn the mixture into the lined tin.

9 Drop teaspoonfuls of the marbling mixture over the chocolate mixture. Drag a table knife through it to create a marbled effect.

10 Bake in the centre of the oven for 50 minutes or until a knife inserted into the centre comes out with moist crumbs (but not wet batter) clinging to it. Cover the cake halfway through the baking time so that it does not overbrown.

11 Allow to cool for 15 minutes in the tin then turn out carefully. Cut into wedges.

12 Serve warm with ice cream or wrap in foil and store in the refrigerator.

White Chocolate and Apricot Blondies

MAKES 24

170 g | 6 oz butter, softened
300 g | 10½ oz soft light brown sugar
3 room-temperature eggs, beaten
1 teaspoon vanilla essence
200 g | 7 oz plain flour

1 teaspoon baking powder
100 g | 3½ oz dried apricots, coarsely chopped
100 g | 3½ oz white chocolate chips
100 g | 3½ oz walnuts, chopped

1 Heat the oven to 180°C | 350°F | gas mark 4. Line the base and sides of a 3 cm | 1¼ in deep 20 × 30 cm | 8 × 12 in tin with baking parchment.
2 Beat the butter with the sugar until pale and fluffy, then beat in the eggs gradually. Stir in the vanilla.
3 Sift the flour with the baking powder and fold into the butter/sugar mixture. Fold in the apricots, white chocolate chips and walnuts.
4 Spread into the prepared tin and bake for 30–35 minutes or until just set in the centre. Take care not to overbake as the blondies will become dry and hard.
5 Cut into squares while still warm.

Pecan Blondies

This 'plain vanilla' version of brownies is filled with toasted nuts and chocolate chunks, making it anything but plain.

MAKES 24

170 g | 6 oz butter, softened
170 g | 6 oz caster sugar
170 g | 6 oz soft light brown sugar
3 room-temperature eggs, beaten
1 teaspoon vanilla essence

200 g | 7 oz plain flour
1 teaspoon baking powder
100 g | 3½ oz pecan nuts, toasted and coarsely chopped
170 g | 6 oz plain chocolate chips

1 Heat the oven to 180°C | 350°F | gas mark 4. Line the base and sides of a 20 × 30 cm | 8 × 12 in deep tin with baking parchment.
2 Beat the butter with the sugars until pale and fluffy, then beat in the eggs gradually. Stir in the vanilla.
3 Sift the flour with the baking powder and fold into the butter/sugar mixture. Fold in half the pecan nuts and chocolate chips.
4 Spread into the prepared tin and scatter over the remaining pecan nuts and chocolate chips. Bake for 30–35 minutes or until just set. Take care not to overbake as the blondies will become dry and hard.
5 Cut into squares while still warm.

Icings and Fillings

This chapter gives recipes for icings and fillings suitable for sponge cakes and pâtisserie. Along with the traditional fillings and buttercreams for sandwiching and icing cakes there are also find ideas for fruit curds, cheeses and jams.

When finishing a cake with the icings and fillings in this section it is important to follow a few rules to get a good result. Make sure the work surface and the cake are clear of crumbs (use a pastry brush if necessary to clear them away). If the cake needs to be cut in half horizontally do this carefully, following the instructions on page 000. If 2 cakes have been baked in sponge tins, sandwich the bases together and choose the best-looking cake to be the top or presentation side.

A palette knife is best for spreading on icing, as it is flexible and will give a good finish. Palette knives are available in several different sizes and it is worthwhile buying a small one as well as a normal-sized one.

Store unused icing in the refrigerator, covered, for 2–7 days. The length of time an icing can be kept depends on its ingredients. If it contains cream it will keep for a couple of days, but a butter icing will keep for much longer. Glacé icings, even if covered, tend to form a skin which needs a teaspoon or so of boiling water added to break it down. You may then need to add some extra sifted icing sugar to thicken the icing again.

Butter Icings

Vanilla Butter Icing

This is a useful and easy topping and/or filling for a *Victoria Sandwich* (see page 286). It can be flavoured to give variety (see below).

FILLS 17 CM | 1 IN CAKE

55 g | 2 oz butter
115 g | 4 oz icing sugar, sifted

a few drops of vanilla essence
1 tablespoon warm water

Cream the butter until soft and gradually beat in the icing sugar. Add the vanilla essence and water and use as required.

VARIATIONS

Omit the vanilla essence and add the following:

Almond butter icing: 1 tablespoon finely chopped toasted almonds.

Coffee butter icing: 1½ teaspoons instant coffee granules mixed with 1 tablespoon boiling water, allowed to cool until lukewarm.

Orange or lemon butter icing: 1 teaspoon grated orange or lemon zest and 1 teaspoon orange or lemon juice.

Chocolate butter icing: 2 teaspoons cocoa powder or 30 g | 1 oz melted chocolate.

Mocha butter icing: 1 teaspoon cocoa powder and 1 teaspoon instant coffee granules mixed with 1 tablespoon boiling water, allowed to cool until lukewarm.

Rich Chocolate Butter Icing

FILLS A 17 CM | 7 IN CAKE

115 g	4 oz plain chocolate, chopped into small pieces	55 g	2 oz unsalted butter, softened
1 tablespoon water	115 g	4 oz icing sugar, sifted
	1 egg yolk

1 Melt the chocolate with the water in a bowl placed over, but not touching, steaming water, stirring constantly.
2 Beat together the butter and sugar until light and fluffy.
3 Beat in the egg yolk followed by the melted chocolate.

NOTE: Make double this recipe to cover the outside of the cake as well as filling the layers.

Soured Cream and Chocolate Icing

TO ICE A 17 CM | 7 IN CAKE

140 g	5 oz plain chocolate	2 teaspoons caster sugar
140 ml	5 fl oz soured cream	

1 Break up the chocolate and place in a bowl set over, but not touching, steaming water.
2 Add the soured cream and sugar. Melt together over a low heat. Leave to cool and thicken.

Buttercreams

The following buttercreams are cooked icings and require more skill and time than the butter icings. The buttercreams, with their rich flavour and light texture, are used for filling and icing Génoise cakes (see page 296).

Coffee Custard Buttercream

Toasted flaked almonds pressed on to the sides of the cake complement the coffee flavouring in this buttercream.

Have a bowl and a sieve ready to strain the custard before beginning to cook.

FILLS AND COVERS A 20 CM | 8 IN CAKE

225 ml	8 fl oz milk	3 egg yolks
170 g	6 oz caster sugar	170 g	6 oz salted butter, softened
2 tablespoons instant coffee granules	170 g	6 oz unsalted butter, softened

1 Place the milk with half the sugar and the coffee granules in a small saucepan and heat until it steams.
2 Place the egg yolks in a bowl with the remaining sugar and stir until pale and thick.
3 Slowly pour the hot milk in a thin stream on to the yolks, whilst stirring.
4 Rinse the saucepan and return the mixture to the pan. Cook the custard over a low heat, stirring until thickened. It should coat the back of a wooden spoon.
5 Strain the custard to remove any eggy threads and allow to cool.
6 Beat the butter until it is very soft, rather like soft margarine.
7 Beat the cooled custard into the butter 1 tablespoonful at a time. The buttercream is ready to use.

NOTE: If the mixture curdles when the custard is beaten into the butter, it is likely that it has become too cold. Place the bowl over a saucepan of steaming water and beat vigorously.

Crème au Beurre Meringue

This filling has a cooked meringue base which makes it very light and fluffy. It is particularly suitable for flavouring with chocolate. For a dark, fudgy chocolate icing use ganache (see page 370).

FILLS AND COVERS A 20 CM|8 IN CAKE

3 egg whites

170 g|6 oz icing sugar

140 g|5 oz salted butter, softened

140 g|5 oz unsalted butter, softened

Suggested flavourings

140 g|5 oz plain chocolate, melted, *or*

grated zest of 2–3 oranges, lemons or limes *or*

strong coffee essence, to taste

1 Place the egg whites in a large bowl and sift the icing sugar over the top. Stir to combine.

2 Place the bowl over a saucepan of simmering water and beat, preferably with an electric hand whisk, until the mixture is thick and glossy.

3 Remove from the heat and continue to whisk until the mixture is thick enough to hold a teaspoon upright.

4 Beat the butter with the whisk to bring it to the consistency of soft margarine. If using chocolate, substitute the chocolate for half of the butter. Beat the cooled melted chocolate into the butter.

5 Gradually beat the butter into the meringue.

6 If using citrus or coffee flavourings instead of chocolate, these should be added at this point. The buttercream is ready to use.

Crème au Beurre Mousseline

This is a rich, creamy cake filling. It is particularly suitable for flavouring with citrus juice and zest.

FILLS AND COVERS A 20 CM|8 IN CAKE

170 g|6 oz granulated sugar

170 ml|6 fl oz citrus juice or water

4 egg yolks

grated zest of 1 lemon and 1 orange

225 g|8 oz unsalted butter, softened

1 Place the sugar and juice or water in a small saucepan over a low heat. Stir gently to help the sugar dissolve. If desired, a sugar thermometer can be placed in the pan at this point.

2 Place the yolks in a large bowl and stir in the zest.

3 When the sugar has dissolved, increase the heat and boil the mixture until it reaches the short thread stage (108°C|225°F).

4 Immediately pour the boiling syrup on to the yolks, whilst whisking, taking care not to pour the syrup over the whisk. Continue whisking until the mixture is thick and cool.

5 Beat the butter with the whisk until it has the consistency of soft margarine.

6 To combine the yolk mixture with the butter, gradually whisk the thinner of the two mixtures into the other mixture.

To decorate with citrus peel

Cakes flavoured with citrus can be decorated with strips of peel called 'needleshreds'. Remove 5 cm│2 in strips of peel from the fruit, taking care not to cut into the bitter white pith. Scrape any pith from the back of the zest with a knife. Cut the zest into 1 mm│1¹⁄₁₆ in thin, 5 cm│2 in long strips called 'julienne'. Boil the zest until just tender, about 3 minutes, in a sugar syrup made with 150 ml│5 fl oz water and 75 g│2½ oz granulated sugar. Drain in a sieve then separate the shreds and roll them in caster sugar.

Buttercreams: What has gone wrong when . . .

The mixture splits.

- The butter was too cold.
- The flavouring liquid was added too quickly.
- The flavouring liquid was too cold.

To correct, place the bowl over a second bowl of steaming water and beat vigorously.

Sugar Icings

American Frosting

This classic American icing is in fact an uncooked meringue. The sugar syrup must reach the correct temperature: if it is not hot enough, the frosting will not thicken; if it is too hot, the frosting will crack and be very dry. The quantities given here make sufficient to cover the Angel Cake on page 293.

170 g│6 oz granulated sugar
85 ml│3 fl oz water
a pinch of cream of tartar

1 egg white
1 teaspoon vanilla essence

1 Put the sugar, water and cream of tartar into a saucepan. Dissolve the sugar carefully over a low heat before the water comes to the boil, then cover with a lid and boil for 3 minutes. Uncover and boil to the 'soft ball' stage. That is when a small amount of syrup dropped into a cup of cold water will come together to form a soft ball. The syrup temperature will be 120°C│235°F.
2 When the sugar syrup is ready, whisk the egg white until stiff and pour on the very hot syrup, whisking constantly. Add the vanilla essence.
3 Continue to whisk until the frosting is cool and firm enough to spread. If it gets too thick, add ½ teaspoon boiling water.

Feather Icing

Feather icing is a technique used to decorate the top of a cake or pastry.

TO ICE A 17 CM | 7 IN CAKE

225 g | 8 oz icing sugar   food colouring or melted chocolate
boiling water

1 Sift the icing sugar into a bowl.
2 Add enough boiling water to mix to a fairly stiff coating consistency. The icing should hold a trail when dropped from a spoon but gradually finds its own level.
3 Take 2 tablespoons of the icing and colour it with food colouring or chocolate. Place in a piping bag fitted with a fine writing nozzle.
4 Spread the remaining icing smoothly and evenly over the top of the cake, using a warm palette knife.
5 While the icing is still wet, quickly pipe lines, about 2.5 cm | 1 in apart, across the top of the cake.
6 Now draw more lines at right angles to the piped lines with a pin or a sharp knife, dragging the tip through the piped lines to pull them into points. If the pin is dragged in one direction through the icing lines, pattern A will result; if the pin is dragged alternately in opposite directions through the icing lines, pattern B will result.

NOTE: Smooth melted jam can be used instead of coloured icing for the feathering.

Pattern A

Pattern B

Glacé Icing

TO ICE A 17CM|7 IN CAKE
225 g|8 oz icing sugar   boiling water

1 Sift the icing sugar into a bowl.
2 Add enough boiling water to mix to a fairly stiff coating consistency. The icing should hold a trail when dropped from a spoon but gradually finds its own level. It needs surprisingly little water.
3 Spread the icing smoothly and evenly over the top of the cake, using a warm palette knife.

NOTE: Hot water produces a shinier result than cold. Also, on drying, the icing is less likely to craze, crack or become watery if made with boiling water.

Chocolate Glacé Icing

TO ICE A 17 CM | 7 IN CAKE
200g | 7 oz icing sugar   boiling water
30g | 1 oz cocoa powder

1 Sift the icing sugar and cocoa powder into a bowl.
2 Add enough boiling water to mix to the consistency of thick double cream.
3 Spread or pour over the cake and smooth with a warm palette knife. Allow to set.

Passion-fruit Icing

TO ICE A 17CM | 7 IN CAKE
15 g|½ oz butter   1 teaspoon lemon juice
juice of 1 passion-fruit, strained   8–10 tablespoons icing sugar, sifted

1 Melt the butter and add the passion-fruit juice and lemon juice.
2 Stir in enough icing sugar to make a coating consistency.
3 Spread or pour over the cake and smooth with a warm palette knife. Allow to set.

Fruit Fillings

All curds keep well in the refrigerator for up to 3 weeks, and they freeze very successfully.

Lemon Curd

MAKES 450 G | 1 LB

zest and juice of 2 large lemons
85 g | 3 oz unsalted butter, chopped

225 g | 8 oz granulated sugar
3 eggs, lightly beaten

1 Place the juice, butter, sugar and eggs into a heavy saucepan or double boiler and cook over a low heat, stirring constantly, until the mixture is thick.
2 Pass through a sieve to remove any egg-y threads, then stir in the zest.
3 Strain into jam jars and cover with waxed discs and cellophane covers.

NOTE: Lime curd can be made using the same recipe. Substitute the lemons for limes, but as limes are generally smaller you will need to use 3 or 4 limes. You can also use a combination of lemons and limes.

Orange Curd

MAKES 450 G | 1 LB

juice of 1 lemon
juice of 1 orange
grated zest of 2 oranges

85 g | 3 oz unsalted butter, chopped
170 g | 6 oz granulated sugar
3 eggs, lightly beaten

1 Put the juices, zest, butter, sugar and eggs into a heavy saucepan or double boiler and cook over a low heat, stirring constantly, until the mixture is thick.
2 Strain into jam jars and cover with waxed discs and cellophane covers.

NOTE: If the curd is boiled, no great harm is done. The acid and sugar will prevent the eggs from scrambling, but the curd will have a grainy texture.

Passion-fruit Curd

MAKES ABOUT 6–8 TABLESPOONS

4 passion-fruit

85 g│3 oz granulated sugar

30 g│1 oz unsalted butter

2 tablespoons lemon juice

1 egg, beaten

1 Cut the passion-fruit open and remove the pulp. Sieve it and discard the pips.
2 Put the sugar, butter, lemon juice, egg and passion-fruit purée together into a heavy saucepan and cook over a low heat, stirring constantly, until the mixture is thick. Strain and allow to cool.

NOTE: If the curd is boiled, no great harm is done. The acid and sugar prevent the eggs from scrambling, but the curd will have a grainy texture.

Raspberry Compote

This recipe is halfway towards being a jam, but because it is not boiled for a long time it keeps its fresh-fruit flavour. It must be kept in the refrigerator or it may be frozen. It's a little more runny than a jam and can be used as a filling for a cake or served with scones or with natural yoghurt as a quick pudding.

MAKES ABOUT 450 G│1 LB

450 g│1 lb raspberries

170 g│6 oz caster sugar

juice of half a lemon

1 Check the raspberries and remove any bruised or bad fruit. Wash them quickly, being careful not to damage them. Drain very well.
2 Put the raspberries into a bowl and cover with the sugar. Cover and leave in a cool place for 4–6 hours. This helps to prevent them from breaking up later.
3 Put the raspberries and sugar into a saucepan and add the lemon juice. Bring to the boil. Remove from the heat before they break up.
4 If there is a lot of extra liquid, strain the raspberries very carefully through a sieve. Put the reserved juice back into the saucepan and bring to the boil. Reduce until slightly sticky and add to the raspberries.
5 Store in sterilized pots or in a bowl in the refrigerator.

Damson Cheese

Traditionally this cheese is served as an accompaniment to lamb or game, when it needs to be put into a straight-sided jar or bowl so that it can be turned out and sliced. However, it is also delicious spread on scones or used as a filling for cakes.

MAKES ABOUT 900 G | 2 LB

1 kg | 2 lb damsons
150 ml | 5 fl oz water

450 g | 1 lb granulated sugar to each 570 ml | 1 pint purée

1 Wash the damsons and remove the stalks. Put them into a saucepan with the water. Cook over a low heat until the fruit is very soft.

2 Sieve the fruit and discard the stones.

3 Measure the purée and use 450 g | 1 lb granulated sugar for every 570 ml | 1 pint.

4 Put the damson pulp and sugar into a large saucepan. Set over a low heat until the sugar has dissolved completely, then bring to the boil.

5 Boil steadily until you can make a clear track through the purée with a wooden spoon, showing the base of the pan. Keep stirring, otherwise the cheese will burn on the bottom of the pan.

6 Pour into warmed jars and cover with waxed discs and cellophane circles.

Crème Pâtissière (Pastry Cream)

Crème Pâtissière is a custard thickened with flour or cornflour to a smooth, heavy consistency. Crème pâtissière is spread thickly on the base of blind-baked tart shells before decorating the tart with glazed fresh fruit, or spread thinly between wafer-thin layers of puff pastry for millefeuille. Crème pâtissière is also piped into choux buns and meringues or spread on to enriched sweet doughs, such as Danish Pastries, before they are baked.

The following recipe makes a very thick crème pâtissière. It is best lightened with an equal quantity of lightly whipped cream and/or flavoured with liqueur, chocolate, coffee or the zest of citrus fruits. Crème pâtissière can also be lightened with whisked egg whites to make a Crème St Honoré, a filling for the choux-pastry dessert Gâteau St-Honoré.

The starch in the mixture allows it to boil without curdling, but it is necessary to stir it continuously to prevent lumps from forming. It is important to boil the mixture or an enzyme in the egg yolks could make the mixture runny.

Crème Pâtissière

290 ml|10 fl oz milk

2 egg yolks

55 g|2 oz caster sugar

20 g|¾ oz plain flour

20 g|¾ oz cornflour

a few drops of vanilla essence

150 ml|5 fl oz double cream, lightly whipped

1 Scald the milk by bringing it to just below boiling point in a saucepan.

2 Cream the egg yolks with the sugar. Add a little of the hot milk to the yolks to warm them gradually, then mix in the flours. Pour on the remaining milk and mix well.

3 Rinse out the saucepan to remove the coagulated milk proteins, pour the mixture into the pan and bring slowly to the boil, stirring continuously.

4 Boil for 1 minute to thicken while stirring. Pass through a sieve into a cold bowl.

5 Stir in the vanilla to taste.

6 Place a piece of dampened greaseproof paper directly on the surface to prevent a skin from forming and allow to cool.

7 The crème pâtissière will become very stiff when cold. To use, place it in a food processor and whizz for about 30 seconds, or pass through a sieve, then fold in the lightly whipped cream.

VARIATIONS

Crème pâtissière can be flavoured with melted chocolate, liqueurs, dissolved coffee powder, ground macaroons or almonds. The flavouring ingredient is added once the custard is thickened.

Storing Crème Pâtissière: Refrigerate, covered with greaseproof paper then clingfilm, for up to 2 days. Freezing is not recommended.

Crème Pâtissière: What has gone wrong when . . .

The crème pâtissière is lumpy.

- The mixture was not stirred sufficiently when it started to thicken. To correct, pass through a sieve or whizz in a food processor.

The mixture becomes thinner upon standing.

- The sauce was not brought back up to the boil to denature the enzyme found in egg yolk which breaks down the thickening properties of starch. Discard the mixture.

The crème pâtissière is too thin.

- The crème pâtissière was not brought to the boil. To correct, return to the saucepan and bring to the boil whilst stirring.

Formal Icing

Once a cake has been made for a formal occasion – i.e. a wedding, birthday, anniversary, etc. – it needs to be decorated. Full details are given here on covering a cake with marzipan before applying royal or fondant icing, making icing bags and using them to pipe decoratively.

The simplest way to decorate a formal cake is to cover it with fondant or ready-to-roll icing and then decorate the top. This can involve piping royal icing over the top or simply decorating with fresh flowers. Alternatively the cake can be covered in marzipan, which is allowed to dry and then covered carefully with smooth layers of royal icing. The very formal, highly decorated wedding cakes of the past are now out of fashion and just a small amount of decoration on a cake can look very effective, but it does mean that the icing and decoration must be of very good quality. The techniques and tips in this section are designed to provide you with as much information as you may need to decorate a cake.

Marzipan

Marzipan is used on rich fruit cakes to form a barrier between the cake and the icing, whether it is royal icing or fondant/ready-to-roll icing: it stops the colour from the cake leaching into the icing. The ground almonds that are used in the marzipan should be of a high quality, so that very little of the outer skin remains. Too much of this ground-up skin can cause brown specks to discolour the icing.

When applied to a cake, home-made marzipan should be left for at least 3 days and up to 1 week in a dry, cool place before applying the icing. Do not store it in a humid area nor in the refrigerator. The quantity of sugar in the marzipan preserves it and means that bacteria cannot grow. Marzipan is also sometimes added as a layer inside cakes such as Simnel Cake.

Uncooked Marzipan

MAKES 450 G|1 LB

115 g|4 oz sugar

115 g|4 oz icing sugar

225 g|8 oz ground almonds

1 egg yolk

1 whole egg

lemon juice (optional)

1 Sift the sugars together into a bowl and mix with the ground almonds.

2 Mix together the egg yolk and whole egg and add to the sugar mixture.

3 Mix well and knead briefly. If the paste is too dry, add a little lemon juice. If it is too wet, add more icing sugar.

4 Wrap well and store in a cool, dry place until ready to use.

Cooked Marzipan

This recipe gives a softer, easier-to-handle paste than the more usual, uncooked marzipan.

MAKES 900 G|2 LB

3 small eggs

225 g|8 oz caster sugar

225 g|8 oz icing sugar

450 g|1 lb ground almonds

4 drops of vanilla essence

1½ teaspoons lemon juice

sifted icing sugar for kneading

1 Beat the eggs lightly in a heatproof bowl.

2 Sift together the sugars and mix with the eggs.

3 Set the bowl over, but not touching, a saucepan of boiling water and whisk until light and creamy. Remove from the heat and allow to cool.

4 Add the ground almonds, vanilla essence and lemon juice and stir well to combine.

5 Lightly dust a work surface with icing sugar. Knead the paste carefully until just smooth, (overworking will draw out the oil from the almonds, giving a too greasy paste). Wrap well and store in a cool, dry place.

Marzipan Quantities

This table shows the made-up weight of marzipan needed for each size of cake. The *Uncooked Marzipan* recipe (see above) makes 450 g | 1 lb; the *Cooked Marzipan* recipe (see above) makes 900 g | 2 lb.

Square		15 cm|6 in	17 cm|7 in	20 cm|8 in	23 cm|9 in	25 cm|10 in	27 cm|11 in	30 cm|12 in
Round	15 cm|6 in	17 cm|7 in	20 cm|8 in	23 cm|9 in	25 cm|10 in	27 cm|11 in	30 cm|12 in	
Marzipan	340 g|12 oz	450 g|1 lb	565 g|1¼ lb	790 g|1¾ lb	900 g|2 lb	1 kg|2¼ lb	1.2 kg|2½ lb	1.35 kg|3 lb

Covering a Cake with Marzipan

Once the cake is ready to be covered with marzipan, make up the marzipan (whether uncooked or cooked) and the apricot glaze. Ensure that the work surface is very clean. Even tiny spots of fruit cake collected on the outside of the marzipan can leach colour through the finished icing. Also, ensure that the marzipan is not overkneaded, otherwise oil will escape from the almonds and leave greasy marks on the icing. Once the cake has been covered with marzipan leave it to dry, uncovered, in a cool, dry place for at least 2 days but preferably for 1 week.

Covering a Round Cake with Uncooked Marzipan

FOR A 23 CM|9 IN CAKE

uncooked marzipan made with 450 g|1 lb ground almonds (see page 461)

apricot glaze (see page 474)

icing sugar

1 If the cake is not level, carefully shave off a little of the top. Turn it upside down.
2 Measure around the side with a piece of string.
3 Dust a very clean work surface lightly with icing sugar and roll out two thirds of the marzipan to a strip the length of the piece of string and the depth of the cake. Trim it neatly.
4 Roll out the remaining marzipan to a circle the size of the cake top.
5 Brush the sides of the cake with the apricot glaze and, holding the cake firmly between both hands, turn it on to its side and roll it along the prepared strip of marzipan. Turn the cake right-side up again. Wash your hands. Smooth the join with a round-bladed knife. Take a jam jar or straight-sided tin and roll it around the side of the cake.
6 Brush the top of the cake with apricot glaze and, using a rolling pin, lift the circle of marzipan on to the cake. Seal the edges with the knife and smooth the top with the rolling pin. Place on a cake board and leave to dry.

NOTE: Round cakes can also be covered using a cooked marzipan (see below), but square cakes are normally covered with uncooked marzipan. The cooked marzipan is too pliable to get perfectly square corners.

Covering a Square Cake with Uncooked Marzipan

FOR A 20 CM|8 IN SQUARE CAKE

uncooked marzipan made with 450 g|1 lb ground almonds (see page 461)

apricot glaze (see page 474)

icing sugar

1 If the cake is not level, carefully shave off a little of the top. Turn it upside down.
2 Measure one side of the cake with a piece of string.
3 Dust a very clean work surface lightly with icing sugar and roll out two thirds of the marzipan into 4 strips the length of the piece of string and the depth of the cake. Trim neatly.
4 Roll out the remaining marzipan, with any trimmings, to a square the size of the cake top.
5 Brush one side of the cake with apricot glaze. Turn the cake on to its side and, holding it firmly between both hands, place the glazed edge on a strip of marzipan. Trim the edges and repeat with the other 3 sides. Wash your hands. Smooth the joins at the corners with a round-bladed knife. Take a jam jar or straight-sided tin and roll it around the sides of the cake, keeping the corners square.
6 Brush the top of the cake with apricot glaze and, using a rolling pin, lift the square of marzipan on to the cake. Seal the edges with the knife and smooth the top with the rolling pin. Place on a cake board and leave to dry.

Covering a Round Cake with Cooked Marzipan

FOR A 23 CM|9 IN CAKE

cooked marzipan made with 450 g|1 lb ground almonds (see page 461)

apricot glaze (see page 474)

icing sugar

1 If the cake is not level, carefully shave off a little of the top. Turn it upside down. Brush lightly with apricot glaze.
2 Dust a very clean work surface lightly with icing sugar and roll out the marzipan to a circle 10 cm|4 in larger in diameter than the cake.
3 Place the glazed cake upside down in the centre of the marzipan and, using your hands, carefully work the marzipan up the sides of the cake.
4 Take a jam jar or straight-sided tin and roll it around the sides of the cake to make sure that they are quite straight, and the edges square.
5 Turn the cake the right way up, place on a cake board and leave to dry.

Fondant Icing or Moulding Paste

Fondant icing can be applied directly to sponge cakes and fruit cakes or it can be put on top of a layer of marzipan. The top of the cake must be spread with a little apricot glaze to make the icing stick, or if the cake has been covered in marzipan, a little egg white can be used instead of apricot glaze.

The icing should be rolled out on a surface that has been sprinkled with a mixture of icing sugar and cornflour. Once it is on the cake it can be smoothed into position, using hands dipped in icing sugar and cornflour. It can also be polished to a shine with the hands.

Fondant icing can be coloured very easily by kneading colour (preferably paste or gel colours rather than liquid) into it. It is very good for making flowers or to mould other shapes.

If you are making a tiered wedding cake and wish to use fondant icing, it is better to pile the cakes directly on top of each other, as for an American wedding cake, rather than try to use pillars to separate the tiers. It is difficult to make fondant icing hard enough to support the weight of the cakes when using pillars.

Fondant Icing

This soft, easy-to-cut icing is similar to the 'ready-to-roll' icing available in supermarkets and specialist food shops. It is very useful for covering single-tier cakes or for modelling flowers, and can be used with or without a layer of marzipan. Liquid glucose is available from larger chemists or specialist cake-decorating shops.

TO ICE A 20 CM|8 IN CAKE

450 g|1 lb icing sugar, plus extra if necessary	1 egg white, lightly whisked until frothy
3 tablespoons liquid glucose	1 teaspoon lemon juice

1 Sift the icing sugar into a mixing bowl. Warm the liquid glucose by standing the jar in a saucepan of hot water. Make a well in the centre of the sugar and add the egg white, glucose and lemon juice.
2 Using first a round-bladed knife and then the fingers of one hand, mix well and add more icing sugar if necessary to make a stiff paste. Knead well.
3 Use immediately or store, wrapped thoroughly, in a plastic bag, ensuring that all air is excluded.

Covering a Cake with Fondant Icing

1 Brush the cake with apricot glaze (see page 474), or egg white if it is already covered with marzipan.
2 Sprinkle the work surface and rolling pin with a mixture of icing sugar and cornflour.
3 Roll out the icing until it is about 10 cm|4 in larger than the top of the cake.

4 Using a rolling pin to lift up the icing, and transfer it on to the top of the cake.

5 Press the icing over the top and sides of the cake with your hands dipped into a mixture of icing sugar and cornflour. Trim off extra icing from the base of the cake and continue smoothing the icing into place, removing any wrinkles or folds as you do so. For a square cake, cut a piece out of each corner and then pinch the corners together to hide the join.

6 Leave to dry for 24 hours before decorating.

Royal Icing

Royal icing is traditionally used over a layer of marzipan for the coating and decoration of special occasion fruit cakes. It can be made and stored in an airtight container in the refrigerator for a couple of days. It should always be stirred thoroughly before use and a little extra sifted icing sugar added if it has gone thin.

To make royal icing you should allow 1 egg white to each 340–450g|12–16oz icing sugar. It is possible to use egg albumen powder, which is available from specialist cake decorating shops. This will give a more uniform result than using the whites of a number of different eggs. Glycerine can be added to the icing to prevent it from becoming rock-hard. However, on a wedding cake it is advisable to leave glycerine out of the first 2 coats of icing on the bottom and middle tiers, as a certain amount of strength is needed to take the weight of the tiers above. Use ½ teaspoon glycerine to every 225g|8oz icing sugar.

Colouring
A drop of blue colouring added to the icing will help to make the icing bright white. If you are planning to make a cream-coloured wedding cake to go with a cream or ivory wedding dress, make up all the icing you will need at the beginning and colour with some golden-yellow (if you only have primrose yellow, add a touch of orange as well). Be very sparing with the amount of colouring added until you have exactly the right shade. Store the unused icing, covered, in the refrigerator.

Bubbles
When making the icing (see recipe on page 464), mix the sugar into the egg white carefully, avoiding beating it for too long, as this will create bubbles which will be very difficult to get rid of later. If you get a lot of bubbles in the icing, leave it to stand, covered, overnight in the refrigerator. The following day, stir carefully to burst the bubbles which have risen to the surface. The thicker the icing, the more difficult it is to get rid of the bubbles.

Consistency
A cake is normally covered with 2–3 coats of icing and then decorated with piping or 'run-out' work (see page 470). The consistency varies for each coat and for the top and sides. The icing for the sides should always be a little thicker so that it will not slide down and form a bulge near the board. The first coating should be thick, and the icing should stand in peaks when the spoon is lifted from the bowl. The second and third coatings should be a

little thinner, and the icing should form very soft peaks. The consistency required for piping also varies. When using a writing pipe, the icing needs to be a little thinner than when using a star pipe.

Royal Icing

TO ICE A 17 CM|7 IN CAKE

1 egg white

450 g|1 lb icing sugar, sifted

1 tablespoon glycerine (optional)

1 teaspoon lemon juice (optional)

1 Mix the egg white with 3 tablespoons of the icing sugar in a large bowl and add the glycerine and lemon juice, if using.

2 Add the remaining icing sugar gradually and mix very well until the icing will hold its shape. Do not overbeat, or bubbles will form which will be difficult to get rid of. Add more or less icing sugar, depending on the consistency required.

3 Cover with a damp cloth until ready to use.

NOTE: The glycerine will keep the icing from becoming rock hard when it has set, and the lemon juice helps to take away some of the intense sweetness from the icing sugar.

Royal Icing Quantities

This table gives the approximate quantities of icing sugar needed for applying 2 thin coats of royal icing to different sizes of cakes. Remember, between 340 g|12 oz and 450 g|1 lb of icing sugar is needed for each egg white. This will vary slightly depending on the size of the eggs and the thickness of the icing required.

Square	–	15 cm|6 in	17 cm|7 in	20 cm|8 in	23 cm|9 in	25 cm|10 in	27 cm|11 in	30 cm|12 in
Round	15 cm|6 in	17 cm|7 in	20 cm|8 in	23 cm|9 in	25 cm|10 in	27 cm|11 in	30 cm|12 in	–
Icing sugar	450 g|1 lb	565 g|1¼ lb	675 g|1½ lb	900 g|2 lb	1 kg|2¼ lb	1.2 kg|2 7oz	1.4 kg|3 lb	1.7 kg|3½ lb

Covering a Cake with Royal Icing

It is important to put several thin coats of icing on a cake rather than one thick one. It is better to apply the icing to the top of the cake first. Allow it to dry and then ice the sides. Once the sides are dry, apply another layer to the top, and so on until you have a result with which you are happy. Before you apply a second or third coat, remove any lumpy bits of icing with a serrated knife, otherwise the icing ruler or comb will catch on them and draw a line through the icing.

Place a small spoonful of icing on a cake board and put the cake on top. It will now stick to the board. Spoon some icing on to the top of the cake and, using a palette knife, spread to the edges. Then put an icing ruler or straight edge on top of the centre of the cake and draw it backwards and forwards across the surface until the icing is perfectly smooth and level. Carefully remove any icing that has fallen down the sides of the cake. Leave to dry for 24 hours.

Applying royal icing to the top of a cake

Smoothing the royal icing on a turntable

To flat-ice the sides of the cake, put the cake and board on an icing turntable and spread the icing evenly around the sides, using a special icing scraper or comb held at an angle of 45° to the cake. Try to turn the cake around in one movement as you ice, in order to ensure a smooth finish. For a square cake, ice 2 of the opposite sides, leave them to dry, then ice the other 2 sides.

Put another 2 coats of icing on the top and sides of the cake. The last coat should be quite thin. Leave to dry. The cake should be stored in a cool, dry place. If it is to be kept for a few weeks, cover with tissue paper. If the storage area is damp the icing will not dry. If it is too warm the cake will 'sweat' and oil from the marzipan will be drawn into the icing.

Applying Icing to the Cake Board

Sometimes it is a good idea to ice the cake board, particularly if the cake has been put on a large board or if it is part of a tiered wedding cake. Finish icing the cake on both the top and sides and make sure it has been stuck to the centre of the board and all the icing is dry. Thin the icing slightly with egg white, lemon juice or water: this will make it easier to apply. Put the cake on a turntable and spread the icing carefully on the board. Using a palette knife or icing comb, spread the icing in a flat, even finish on the board. Remove any surplus icing carefully from the sides. If you are applying lace-work (see page 470) to the cake you could put this on the board too, either on top of the iced board or the uniced board. The board can be finished with a ribbon around the edge, secured with pins.

Decorating Techniques

Making an Icing Bag

There are a number of different ways of making a greaseproof paper icing bag. The type you make depends on the type of icing pipes (nozzles) you have. Some pipes are quite long and narrow and you should make a type A bag (see below). Other pipes are much fatter and need a type B bag (see opposite). Some pipes have a special screw-on connector, to be used with a plastic or nylon icing bag. These are fine if you are not using too many different colours of icing, but obviously the more colours used, the more nylon bags will be needed. Icing pumps are also available but are quite difficult to use and control and are not advisable for use in delicate royal icing work.

Type A bag
1 Cut a 23 × 30 cm|9 × 12 in rectangle of greaseproof paper (if you want a smaller bag you can use a smaller rectangle).
2 Fold the paper diagonally in half, as shown. Cut the paper in half along the folded line. This will make 2 bags.
3 If you are right-handed, take hold of the piece of paper in your left hand with the small cut edge at the top and your left thumb opposite the point.
4 Twist the bag to form a point at your thumb and secure with your right hand. Fold the rest of the bag around the back and fold the points together.
5 To use, snip off the tip with a pair of scissors and put the pipe into the bag.

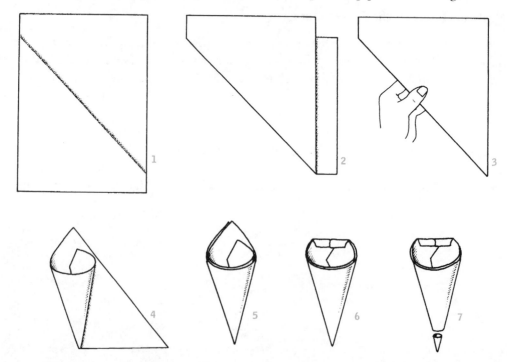

1 Cut a 25 cm | 10 in square of greaseproof paper. Fold the paper diagonally in half, to form a triangle.

2 Fold point A up to point B, as shown.

3 Fold again to point C.

4 Fold point D up to points A and B.

5 Secure the bag by folding the top of the bag down.

6 To use, snip off the tip with a pair of scissors and put the pipe into the bag.

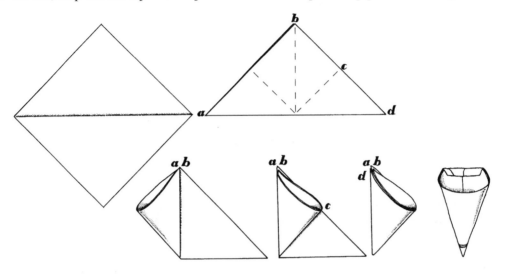

Decorating with Royal Icing

Decorating a cake with royal icing is an advanced skill and it is best to practise with smaller cakes before embarking on an ambitious project such as a tiered wedding cake. These notes are intended as guidelines for those who have already iced a cake or two.

1 It is vital to clear up as you go along. Keep the work surface as clean and tidy as possible. Get all the pipes ready and make as many bags as you think you may need before you start icing.

2 Never overfill the piping bag. This leads to the icing squeezing out of the top.

3 Keep all piping bags that you are using in a plastic bag to prevent the icing from drying in the nozzle.

4 Always keep the icing covered with a damp cloth to prevent it from drying out.

5 Clean the pipes well after use. Use a small paintbrush to help with this and dry them carefully in a warm oven.

6 Work out the pattern before you start icing and prick out the design using a template and pin. Practise icing on a work surface before tackling the cake. If you are not very experienced, keep to the simpler designs.

Direct Piping

Straight lines

Using a plain pipe, put the tip where the line is to begin. Press out the icing and hold the pipe about 4 cm | 1½ in above the surface of the cake. Move your hand in the direction you want to make the line, pressing out the icing gently. Use your other hand to steady the pipe but do not press with it or you will cause air bubbles to form in the bag.

Lattice or trellis work

Using a plain pipe, pipe parallel lines. Pipe a second layer over the top at right angles or at an angle of 45° to the first. Then pipe another layer as closely as possible over the first set of lines and another over the second layer and so on until you have the desired height of trellis. 6 layers (3 in each direction) is usual for an elaborate cake.

Star piping

Use a star pipe. Hold the pipe upright, immediately above and almost touching the top of the cake, and squeeze gently from the top of the bag. Stop pressing and then lift the bag away.

Shells

Use a star or special shell-shaped pipe. Hold the bag at an angle of about 45°. Pipe a shell, release the pressure on the bag, allow the icing to tail off to make a point, and begin a new shell over the point of the first one so that each new shell overlaps its predecessor.

Scrolls

Use a star or shell pipe and hold the bag at an angle of 45° to the cake surface. Pipe in a question-mark shape, pushing out more icing at the beginning and allowing it to tail off at the end. The next one is started over the point of the last.

Dots or pearl piping

Use a plain pipe and pipe as for stars. If the dots are too small, do not try to increase their size by piping out more icing; use a larger nozzle.

Lace-work

Use a plain pipe and hold it just above the cake surface at a slight angle. Press out the icing and, using a movement like scribbling with a pen, cover the cake surface. Generally a fine plain pipe is used, although a medium pipe could be used for the bottom tier of a wedding cake.

Flooding Techniques for Decorating with Royal Icing ('Run-outs')

Run-outs are used when a raised design on a cake is required. They can also be used to create a 3-dimensional shape, for example butterflies or swans.

Trace the chosen shapes on to a piece of greaseproof paper. Cut strips of waxed or silicone paper. Make up the icing. The outline icing should be of a consistency thick enough for writing, i.e. it should form medium peaks. The flooding icing should just about find its own level. If it is too thick, it will not; if it is too thin, it is likely to crack when dry. Colour any of the icings if necessary.

Using a medium writing pipe, put a little icing on to the greaseproof paper and stick the strips of waxed or silicone paper on the top. Carefully pipe the outlines, using the design underneath as a guide. Try to press the icing down only at the start and finish of the outline, lifting the pipe up so that the icing forms a continuous line. Lift up the waxed paper, move it along and repeat more outlines.

Using another piping bag filled with the flooding icing, fill in the piped shapes. The piping bag does not need a pipe, simply snip the end off the bag with a pair of scissors. Flood each shape as full as the outline will take. Leave on a flat surface to dry for 48 hours. Make more shapes than you need, as some will probably break.

If separation of sections is needed, allow each part to dry before flooding the next. This is essential if different colours are used.

Templates

If you are going to put an iced design on top of a cake, it is a very good idea to draw a template first. This means that you can plan your design properly and ensure that it is symmetrical before putting the design on to the cake. Templates are used for cakes iced with royal or fondant icing.

Draw the design you wish to use on greaseproof paper cut to the exact size of the top of the cake. To ensure that the design is symmetrical, use rulers and compasses. It is possible to buy plastic or metal symmetrical rings which will help to make curves on the cake. For a tiered wedding cake, each template will need to be in proportion with the others.

To use the template, place it on top of the cake and secure with pins. Using a longish pin, prick out the design through the paper. Remove the paper and pipe over the pin marks with your design.

Templates can also be made for the sides of cakes.

Piping with Royal Icing: what has gone wrong when . . .

The lines are broken.
- The icing was too thick.
- The icing was pulled along rather than being allowed to flow from the nozzle.
- The icing contained air bubbles.

The lines are wobbly.
- The icing was squeezed out of the bag too quickly.
- The icing was too liquid.
- The icing was too stiff and therefore too much pressure was applied when pressing out the icing.

The lines are flattened.
- The icing was too liquid.
- The nozzle was held too near to the surface of the cake.

Glazes and Sauces

Some cakes and pâtisserie call for something a little different from the icings and fillings discussed in the previous chapter. Almost any cake or tart can be transformed into a delicious pudding with the addition of a sauce such as *Crème Anglaise* or *Raspberry Coulis*, whilst *Sugar Syrup* can be used in a number of ways, whether to poach fruit or to use as a suspension to add alcohol before soaking a sponge cake.

Jam glazes are used to give a finished sheen to a cake or a pastry. In France pâtisserie is glazed very thickly, so be bold when using the glaze. You can use a pastry brush or a spoon to apply the glaze, but care should be taken to put it on evenly. When put on top of fresh fruit, a glaze should be lukewarm, as if it is too hot it will cause the fruit to weep and make the finished product soggy.

Glazing Tarts and Other Pâtisserie with Jam

Warmed jam is used to glaze fruit tarts and certain types of pâtisserie. The jam glaze adds sweetness and flavour to the tart and helps keep the fruit from drying out.

Apricot jam is used to glaze yellow, orange and green fruit. Either apricot jam or redcurrant jelly is used to glaze red fruit. It does not make sense to use good-quality jam that is full of fruit for glazing because the fruit is sieved from the jam before it is used.

Redcurrant Glaze

SUFFICIENT FOR A 20 CM|8 IN RED FRUIT TART

250 g |9 oz redcurrant jelly
1 strip of lemon zest

lemon juice, to taste

1 Melt the jelly with the zest over a low heat.
2 Add lemon juice to reduce the over-sweet jam flavour.
3 Do not boil or the colour will become murky.
4 Pass through a fine sieve and use as required.

Apricot Glaze

SUFFICIENT FOR A 20 CM|8 IN FRUIT TART

250 g|9 oz apricot jam
2 tablespoons water

1 strip of lemon peel
lemon juice, to taste

1 Place the jam in a heavy-based saucepan together with the water and lemon peel.
2 Warm over a low heat to melt, then bring to the boil.
3 Pass through a fine sieve into a clean saucepan. Discard any fruit left in the sieve.
4 Add lemon juice to reduce the over-sweet jam flavour.
5 For a fruit tart, the jam glaze should have a thick coating consistency but be runny enough to flow off a pastry brush. As the glaze cools it will thicken. Rewarm the glaze over a low heat. It must not be too hot or it will cook the fruit.
6 The fruit must be dry or the glaze will run off.
7 Starting in the centre of the tart and working towards the edges, dab the fruit with a pastry brush loaded with the glaze. Be sure to cover the fruit completely but do not glaze fruit twice or the glaze is liable to form lumps. Do not glaze the pastry.
8 Unused glaze can be kept indefinitely in the refrigerator as long as it does not contain crumbs.

Glazing: What has gone wrong when . . .

The glaze runs off the fruit.
- The fruit is wet.
- Too much water has been added.
- The glaze was too hot when applied.

The glaze is lumpy.
- The glaze is too cool.
- The glaze has not been sieved.
- The glazed areas have been reglazed.

Sauces

Crème Anglaise

MAKES 290 ML|10 FL OZ

290 ml|10 fl oz milk
1 vanilla pod, split lengthways, or a few drops of
  vanilla essence

2–3 egg yolks
2–3 tablespoons caster sugar

1 Heat the milk with the vanilla pod, if using, until steaming. Leave to stand for 20 minutes to allow the flavour to infuse, then scrape the seeds from the vanilla pod and stir into the milk.

2 Beat the egg yolks with the sugar in a bowl. Slowly pour the milk on to the yolks in a thin stream, stirring constantly. Rinse out the saucepan then return the milk to the pan.

3 Stir over a low-to-medium heat until the mixture thickens sufficiently to coat the back of a spoon. Do not allow it to boil.

4 Strain into a bowl to remove any fragments of cooked egg. Add the vanilla essence, if using. Place a piece of greaseproof paper directly on to the surface of the custard to prevent a skin from forming.

5 Serve warm or cold. Store in the refrigerator.

Raspberry Coulis

250 g | 9 oz raspberries, defrosted
55 g | 2 oz caster sugar

55 ml | 3 tablespoons water
lemon juice to taste

1 Place the raspberries in the bowl of a food processor or liquidizer.

2 Put the sugar and water into a small pan over a medium heat. Allow the sugar to dissolve then bring to the boil for 2 minutes.

3 Pour the boiling syrup on to the raspberries and process to a purée. Pass through a sieve to remove the seeds. Adjust the seasoning with a little lemon juice, if desired.

Sugar Syrup

This is used for moistening layers of sponge in rich gâteaux such as *Le Gascon* (see page 377).

MAKES 290 ML | 10 FL OZ

140 g | 5 oz granulated sugar
290 ml | 10 fl oz water

thinly pared zest of 1 lemon (optional)

1 Put the sugar, water and lemon zest (if using) into a saucepan and set over a low heat until the sugar has dissolved completely.

2 Bring to the boil and boil for 3–4 minutes. Remove from the heat and allow to cool.

3 Strain the syrup. Keep covered in a cool place until needed.

NOTE: Sugar syrup will keep unrefrigerated for about 5 days, and for several weeks if kept chilled.

Stages of Bread-making

The following stages apply to making most types of yeast bread. It is important to understand the various stages and to know when it is time to move from one stage to the next.

- **Mixing** is the combining of the yeast, flour, salt and liquid. Fat and sugar are also sometimes added at this stage.

- **Kneading** is the manipulation of the dough in order to develop the gluten and distribute the yeast. A yeast bread dough is kneaded until it is smooth and elastic. Test the dough by shaping it into a tight ball and pressing it. It should feel springy.

- **Rising** is when the dough is left to rest for a period of time so that the yeast can reproduce and thereby stretch the gluten. A dough is risen when it has doubled in size and the indentation will remain when the dough is prodded.

- **Knocking back/Shaping** means kneading the dough for a short time, then forming it into the shape required for the finished bread. Knocking back is done to even out the texture of the bread and to redistribute the yeast. If nuts, herbs or fruit are to flavour the bread, they are added at this stage.

- **Proving** is the last rising before the dough is baked. It allows the shaped dough to rise again to nearly its final size. When the dough is proved it will feel soft and pillowy and when prodded the indentation will spring back only about half-way.

- **Baking** is the cooking of the dough to make it edible. Bread is baked in a hot oven to kill the yeast and set the dough. It is done when the dough is well-browned and feels light and in most cases sounds hollow when tapped on the underside.

Bread

Wheat has been a staple part of the diet of the Western world for centuries. For a very long time wheat grain was coarsely ground, mixed with a little water, then baked or dried on a hearth. It was not until a method for rising the dough was discovered, probably by accidentally leaving a dough to stand for longer than usual before baking, that the slightly raised 'flat' breads, such as Middle Eastern pitta breads, were made.

Natural yeasts are present in the environment, so a dough left to stand for a length of time would capture these wild yeasts. The yeast would grow in the dough, making the loaf lighter and nicer to eat than the usual hard, unleavened bread. Perhaps the dough had been mixed with wine, fruit juice or ale. It is recorded that thousands of years ago the Egyptians used the froth on the top of beer, the barm, which is full of yeast, to leaven their bread.

In the 1800s, naturally leavened bread became popularly known as sourdough (see *Sourdough Bread*, page 587). Although loaves made by this method were a staple of many European countries including France and Poland, the sourdough method of bread-making became associated with the gold miners in the western states of the US and with ranchers in the Australian outback. The sourdough method is a way of leavening bread when baker's yeast is not available and is a method that is still used today. A piece of dough is set aside from a loaf before it is baked, then used as a 'starter' to leaven the next loaf. This piece of dough was often stored in the saddlebag and gave the name 'sourdoughs' to the gold miners.

By the mid-1800s a method for growing yeast commercially was developed, allowing bakers to produce a dough that would rise reliably to make an acceptable loaf. With the advent of factory-made bread, bread-making almost became a lost art amongst home cooks for a while. It has been rediscovered in recent years, prompted by the fashion for exotic, flavoured breads. Frequently, making a successful loaf ignites a passion for bread-making and it becomes part of the pattern of life, if only to recapture the unequalled smell and intense pleasure of eating a freshly-baked loaf.

Bread-making is as much a science as a craft and the product can be improved by understanding the process and the ingredients. The basic ingredients for making a loaf of bread are flour, yeast, salt and liquid. These can be varied to produce bread of different flavours and textures. Each of these ingredients and their effects on the finished loaf are discussed in detail below.

Flour

Wheat flour, used either alone or in combination with other types of flour, is the main ingredient in bread. Wheat flour has a higher protein content than flours made from other grains, so it is the most suitable flour to use for yeast-risen (leavened) bread.

Although the percentage protein content listed on the side of the flour will not tell you exactly how a flour will behave when made into bread, it can be used to give a rough indication as to whether or not the flour should be used for bread or pastry. Soft flour usually will have a protein percentage between 7 and 9 per cent. All-purpose flour ranges from 10 to 11.5 per cent and strong flour will have a protein percentage of 11.5–15 per cent. The notable exception to this is durum wheat flour, which has a high protein content but not a high gluten-forming protein content.

The strong flour used for making bread is produced from the hard winter wheat grown principally in northern regions of the US and Canada. Commercial flours are usually blended to give a uniform product. Today white flour is often enriched with vitamins and minerals in order to replace those extracted during milling and sifting. For example, Vitamin C is added because it has been found to help strengthen gluten. Some flours contain certain enzymes that have an effect on gluten development and yeast activity.

Wholemeal flour is again very popular due to its higher nutritional value, having been very much the 'poor relation' to white flour for centuries. Wholemeal flour has a slightly lower gluten content than white flour due to the presence of the bran and the wheatgerm in the flour. The fat and the abrasive qualities of the bran and wheatgerm have a softening effect on gluten development, so a loaf made with wholemeal flour will require a slightly longer kneading time. A loaf made entirely of wholemeal flour will be very dense and heavy so equal quantities of wholemeal and strong flour can be mixed to produce a more palatable loaf.

Two proteins in the flour called glutenin and gliadin bond with the liquid in the recipe to form a substance called gluten. When the dough is kneaded the gluten is developed and forms elastic strands. The dough becomes firmer and has a smooth, almost satiny appearance when the gluten is fully developed. When the yeast reproduces and gives off carbon dioxide gas, the gas stretches these strands of gluten, rather like a bubble blown in chewing gum. Baking the dough sets the open network of bubbles in place and air replaces the carbon dioxide gas. It is the gluten which is chiefly responsible for giving the bread its open, chewy texture. Kneading strengthens gluten. Although it is unlikely that a dough would ever become over kneaded by hand, it is possible to over knead a dough when using a machine. When this happens, the gluten strands are stretched so much that they break and the dough disintegrates into a soft, runny mass.

Yeast

Yeast is a single-celled micro-organism of the fungus family, which is used in bread-making to raise (leaven) the dough and give the finished loaf a lighter, more open texture. In order to raise the dough the yeast needs to grow or reproduce. Yeast requires warmth, moisture and food to reproduce. Too much heat will kill it, so care must be taken to ensure the liquid added to the yeast is not too hot. When the yeast reproduces it gives off carbon dioxide and alcohol and stretches the strands of gluten in the dough.

The yeast uses the starch available in the flour for food as well as any sugar or sweetening ingredient in the recipe. However, too high concentrations of sugar, salt, alcohol or fat will inhibit the reproduction of the yeast, slowing down the rising. If the dough is high in any of these ingredients it is wise to use a greater amount of yeast, and/or expect a longer rising time.

Either fresh baker's yeast or dried yeast can be used to make bread. The recipes in this book have been written using fresh yeast, but they can be converted for dried or fast action yeast using the conversion information on page 480. Any timings given in the recipes are likely to differ if dried yeast is used in place of fresh yeast.

Fresh yeast comes in a block and is a creamy, pale, beige colour. It has a pleasant, slightly yeasty smell. The texture should be smooth and it should break with a clean snap. On no account should it smell 'beery' or feel slimy. When it is old it discolours and eventually dries out. Old yeast is not reliable for raising bread and will produce a loaf with an unpleasant yeasty flavour.

Fresh yeast can be purchased from the bread counter of large supermarkets and many independent bakeries.

Storing Yeast

Fresh yeast can be stored in the refrigerator for up to 1 week. It seems happiest when stored in a jar or other lidded container with enough space to allow for air circulation. If wrapped tightly in clingfilm it can be frozen for up to 1 month. To freeze yeast, divide it into 30 g | 1 oz pieces, wrap individually, then overwrap. The yeast will liquefy upon defrosting so it should be used immediately. Yeast is generally less active after being frozen, so increase the quantity of yeast in the recipe by 25 per cent.

Using Yeast

In most bread recipes the yeast is first mixed with some of the liquid and a little sweetener in order to make a smooth cream. For fresh yeast, the liquid is usually warmed to blood heat, 37°C | 100°F, which feels slightly warm to the touch. If you do not have a thermometer and are uncertain about the liquid temperature, one part boiling water mixed with two parts cool tap water will produce a temperature of about 37°C | 100°F.

Dried yeast is sold in granular form in foil packages that will normally have a 'use by' date. It should be kept in a cool, dry place. It will usually keep for about 6 months but it should be discarded if the 'use by' date has passed.

Dried yeast requires a slightly higher temperature than fresh yeast – about 39°C | 110°F – in order to be reconstituted successfully. It is very important, though, that the temperature of the liquid is not too hot as too high a heat will kill the yeast and the dough will not rise. Mix the yeast with some of the liquid and a little of the flour, then leave to stand and become frothy before mixing with the remaining flour.

'Fast-action' or 'easy-blend' yeast is dried yeast that has been designed to be mixed in its dry form directly with flour, making it somewhat easier to use than the other types of yeast. This yeast has been very finely milled so that it disperses well when mixed with the flour. The method of making bread using fast-action yeast can be abbreviated because the yeast is so reliable and so active. A dough made with this yeast only needs to be kneaded once after mixing and is then placed directly into the prepared tin to rise. As soon as the dough has doubled in size it can be baked immediately. It does not need to be knocked back and risen again before baking. The texture is only very slightly coarser than the texture of a loaf that has had the usual rising and proving.

Fast-action yeast can be used in recipes that require the yeast to be reconstituted with liquid before it is added to the flour. It will dissolve in liquid of a cooler temperature than standard dried yeast, slightly lower than blood temperature, although the warmer temperature of 37°C | 100°F will help it rise more quickly. As with all yeast, too high a heat will kill it.

The quantity of yeast recommended to raise 225 g | 8 oz flour in a standard bread recipe is as follows:

    10 g | ⅓ oz fresh yeast *or*
    3.5 g | ⅛ oz fast-action yeast = 1½ teaspoons fast-action yeast *or*
    5 g | ⅕ oz dried active yeast = 2 teaspoons dried active yeast

For converting US recipes:

    1 cake of fresh yeast = 15 g | ½ oz fresh yeast *or* 2¼ teaspoons fast-action yeast

The type of yeast used to make a dough will affect the rising time of the dough, although by making the relevant conversion using the quantities table above you should get similar results from the various types.

Salt

Salt is an essential ingredient to make bread palatable. Without salt, bread would taste stale and dull and the texture would be coarse. Tuscan bread is made without salt, but as it is customarily served with very salty food, the salt in the food compensates for the lack of salt in the bread.

Either ordinary table salt or sea salt can be used. Sea salt is popular with chefs as it has a more complex flavour than table salt – it contains flavourful minerals in addition to sodium chloride. Coarse salt should be ground finely or dissolved in liquid before adding to the flour.

The presence of salt in the flour also helps gluten development. A dough mixed and kneaded without salt will have a softer, more elastic texture than a dough made with salt. This is noticeable in starter recipes where the dough is mixed, kneaded and risen before the salt is added in order to promote yeast growth.

It is important to measure the salt accurately. Too much salt in a dough will inhibit the growth of the yeast and result in a dense, badly risen loaf. The standard amount required for a savoury loaf is 1 teaspoon per 225 g|8 oz flour. Use a level 5 ml spoon. Salt also can be measured using bakers' percentages (see below).

Liquid

Water, or other liquids, such as milk, cream or juice, is an essential ingredient in bread-making. Water makes a loaf with an open texture and a hard crust. Milk will produce a loaf with a finer crumb than water due to the fat in the milk. Bread made with milk will keep better than a loaf made with water.

It is thought that the serum proteins in milk interact with the proteins in the flour, inhibiting the development of gluten producing a weak, slack dough. For this reason it is recommended to scald the milk then remove the scum that forms on the surface before using it to make bread.

Beer makes a flavourful bread but it must be boiled to drive away the alcohol before use as the alcohol would interfere with yeast activity. When adding liquid to flour, most of the liquid should be added all at once. It is better to have slightly wet dough than a dry one, but if the dough is too sticky, add flour as necessary.

Weighing is the most accurate method of measuring the liquid for bread.

Fat

Fat is not an essential ingredient in bread-making but it is used in many recipes for flavour, to help the browning of the crust and to produce a finer texture. The most usual types of fat for making bread are butter, olive oil, eggs and milk. The bran found in flour also adds to the fat content.

Butter gives a good flavour and a well-browned crust as well as improving the keeping qualities of the loaf. If it is rubbed into the flour before the liquid in the recipe is added, the fat will coat the starch and inhibit gluten development when the dough is kneaded. This will produce a loaf with a softer, finer texture. Sweet yeasted breads often require the butter to be rubbed into the flour before the liquid is added.

Alternatively the butter can be melted and cooled to lukewarm, then added as part of the liquid ingredients. A loaf made with the butter added in liquid form will have a comparatively more open, chewier texture. This difference is particularly noticeable in recipes for brioche, where the butter content is high.

Oil makes dough easy to knead and produces a slightly chewy loaf. More than 30 ml|1 fl oz oil per 250 g|9 oz flour will produce a bread with a slightly oily crumb. An oil with a neutral flavour such as sunflower oil can be used, or a stronger oil such as olive or walnut oil will provide additional flavour.

Fat slows the action of the yeast and softens the gluten in the flour. Too much fat in a dough can result in bread with a fine, cake-like texture. Doughs with a significant proportion of fat often have more yeast added and/or require longer or additional periods of rising.

Sugar

Sugar is not absolutely necessary in a dough but a small amount, 1–2 teaspoonfuls per 225 g|8 oz flour, is often included as a source of food for the yeast. The presence of sugar in a dough will help the bread to brown in the oven.

White, demerara and brown sugar can be used in doughs as well as honey, molasses, treacle, golden syrup or malt extract.

A high concentration of sugar will inhibit the growth of the yeast, so for sweet breads the quantity of yeast is often increased. The sugar in a sweet bread makes the bread more moist and extends the keeping time.

Sugar also has a softening effect on gluten, so doughs with a high sugar content often require two risings to give the yeast longer to stretch the gluten, which will result in bread with a better texture.

Enriched Doughs

Enriched doughs are yeast-raised doughs made richer by the addition of noticeable quantities of fat and/or sugar. The fat is usually butter or oil, but lard is sometimes used. Milk, cream, eggs and the bran and wheatgerm in wholemeal flour also contain fat.

Bread made from an enriched dough has a softer, finer texture because the fat weakens the gluten in the flour. For this reason enriched doughs often require a longer kneading time and are frequently allowed to rise twice before knocking back and shaping.

Enough sugar or honey is often added to enriched doughs to give them a sweet taste. A large amount of sweetening ingredients in a dough inhibits yeast growth, so these breads are often made with a greater quantity of yeast to compensate. Examples of breads made from enriched doughs are hot cross buns, brioche, Chelsea buns and panettone.

Baker's Percentages

Commercial bakers use a system called 'bakers' percentages' to develop their recipes and to make their bread on a daily basis. This system enables the baker to assess recipes relative to each other, to mix large quantities of dough more easily and to scale recipes to produce different-sized batches of bread. The amount of flour is expressed as 100 per cent. The other ingredients are expressed as percentages as they relate to the amount of flour. In bread making there are set ratios of ingredients that vary within certain parameters. For example, a basic white loaf would look something like this if expressed in bakers' percentages:

Strong white flour	100%	250 g
Water	65%	170 ml
Yeast, fresh	5%	12 g
Butter	10%	25 g
Salt	2%	5 g

The water quantity is referred to as the 'percentage hydration'. Each type of bread has a characteristic percentage hydration. A baguette, for example, would normally have 70 per cent hydration.

The Stages of Bread-making

Almost all cooks would agree that yeast cookery is a particularly satisfying craft. Whether it evokes the homely folk memory of a floury-handed grandma or the noble notion that one is producing the staff of life, the smell of baking bread unquestionably produces one of the most appealing kitchen environments. But for all its inherent romance, bread-making is a scientific process. By understanding how this process works it is possible to create reliable results time after time, even when conditions change. Bread-making can be broken down into the 6 stages below. To help our students remember these stages, we remind them to think of the sentence *Mary knits red knickers pretty badly*, where the initials stand for *mixing*, *kneading*, *rising*, *knocking back and shaping*, *proving* and *baking*.

Mixing

This is the process of combining the basic ingredients. Many recipes will call for 'creaming the yeast'. This means mixing the yeast with some of the liquid specified in the recipe and, perhaps, a little of the sugar or other sweetener to the consistency of thin cream. Creaming the yeast makes it easier to distribute the yeast evenly throughout the flour. If the yeast is active it should start to go frothy within about 10–15 minutes of creaming. If it does not, it is likely that the yeast has died, so it is advisable to start again, with some fresh yeast.

Some recipes specify mixing a little of the flour with the yeast liquid to make a sponge or starter, then leaving the sponge to stand for at least 20 minutes or up to several days. This process is discussed under *Sourdough Bread* (see page 000). Even a short period of standing, say 20 minutes, will improve the flavour of the finished bread.

The dough can be mixed in a large bowl with a wooden spoon or in an electric mixer fitted with a dough hook or in a food processor with a plastic paddle.

There are two basic methods for mixing the dough. One method is to sift the flour into a large bowl with the salt and make a well in the centre. The yeast mixture is poured into the well along with enough liquid to make a soft dough. At least three quarters of the liquid should be added immediately and stirred in quickly with the remaining liquid added as required. The amount of liquid required will vary depending on the flour used and the humidity of the weather.

The other method, called the fountain method, is to place the liquid and the yeast in the bowl then stir in enough flour to make a soft dough.

A relatively modern approach to mixing which is sometimes used by artisan bakers is the autolyse process. Developed by the baker Raymond Calvel in the 1970s, it is now widely used by artisan bread-bakers throughout the world. Mr Calvel discovered that by roughly mixing the flour and liquid for the bread and allowing the mixture to stand undisturbed for at least 20 minutes, the gluten would form more quickly when the dough is kneaded. During this rest period, enzymes in the flour help to align the jumbled bonds of gluten. This will help to form stronger bonds when the dough is kneaded.

Some artisan bread-makers will leave their autolyse for several hours, particularly when a very high-protein flour is being used. While the dough is standing the gluten begins to align itself, making kneading more efficient.

After the autolyse period has finished, the yeast and salt are added to the dough and it is mixed and kneaded in the usual manner.

Kneading

Kneading is the process of manipulating the dough in order to distribute the yeast and develop the gluten. When the liquid is added to the flour, the water molecules combine with the protein in the flour to form gluten. When the dough is kneaded these protein strands are stretched and toughened.

To knead bread by hand, place the heel of your hand on the top of the dough and push away from you, moving from one side of your body to the other. (a) With your fingertips, flip the ball of dough over, pulling the dough back towards you. (b) Give the dough a quarter turn. Repeat the process with your other hand. Continue to knead, alternating hands. (c)

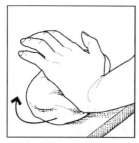

Kneading yeast dough (a)   Kneading yeast dough (b)

The majority of doughs will require kneading for 10–15 minutes by hand or 5–10 minutes in a mixer with a dough hook. If mixing in a free-standing machine, start on the lowest speed then gradually turn the mixer to a medium speed. The dough should wrap itself around the dough hook and will eventually produce a 'slapping' noise against the side of the bowl. If the dough will not form around the hook it is either too wet or too dry and the proportion of ingredients should be adjusted.

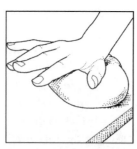
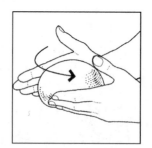

Kneading yeast dough (c)   Circular kneading (d)

To tell if a dough has been kneaded enough, roll it into a tight ball (d) and prod it with your finger. It should spring back readily and will also be smooth and satiny in appearance. The dough will also be stretchy and should form a 'gluten window' if a small piece of it is stretched (see photograph).

Food processors can be used to knead dough if the paddle or stirring blade is used. The cutting blade will cut through the strands of gluten and is not recommended. A dough kneaded in a food processor will only need 30 seconds to 1 minute on the lowest speed. The food processor does not knead as well as a free-standing machine or by hand, so it is best to use it only for flat breads, such as pizza dough, where the texture of the finished bread is less important. The food processor is suitable for mixing and kneading very wet doughs. The food processor does produce a lot of heat, however, so it is not suitable for doughs that should be kept cool, such as baguette dough.

Although it is unlikely that a dough will become overheated when kneading by hand, it is possible that a strong, efficient machine will overheat the dough. When this happens, the dough becomes overheated and too much air is beaten into the dough, causing it to oxidize. The finished bread will have a flat, dull flavour and a poor crust colour.

Kneading method for soft doughs

Soft doughs, such as fougasse and brioche, are made more easily using a standing electric mixer. However, if you do not have one of these mixers the dough can be kneaded by hand.

Place the dough on the work surface. Grab a handful of the dough and pull it upwards as far as you can without breaking it, then push it back down on to the work surface. Continue this motion until the dough becomes smooth and satiny. You will be able to stretch the dough to nearly shoulder-height when it has been thoroughly kneaded.

Kneading method for soft doughs

Soft doughs can also be 'kneaded' by the turning method. With this process, the dough is not kneaded in the conventional sense; instead it is lifted and stretched, then folded like a business letter before being returned to the bowl. This process needs to be repeated several times over a period of several hours. The baked loaf will have an open texture with large holes.

Rising

This is the stage at which the dough is allowed to stand in order for the yeasts to reproduce. As the yeasts reproduce they emit carbon dioxide gas, which stretches the gluten in the dough, and causes it to expand. This process will give the final loaf its texture.

Usually the dough is allowed to rise until it has doubled its original size and an indentation made in the dough will not spring back. Place it in a lightly oiled bowl or a large oiled plastic bag. Turn the dough to coat the surface with the oil. This keeps the dough from developing a dry outer layer, which might inhibit rising. If using a bowl, cover it with lightly oiled clingfilm and place in a warm, but not hot, place.

At a room temperature of 22°C|75°F – an ideal temperature for rising dough – the dough should double in size in approximately 1 hour. Many of the following recipes do not specify an exact time for rising as this will vary, depending on many factors such as room temperature. It is best to look for confirmation that the dough has doubled in size rather than adhere to a specified time. The dough can be risen at a cooler temperature than this, but obviously it will take longer. Some recipes call for a long, cool rise, often in the refrigerator, for 8 hours or more. This procedure will produce bread with a more complex flavour due to enzyme activity and bacterial growth in the dough.

Bread that is risen at too high a temperature or for too long can have an unpleasant beery taste and smell. The dough might collapse if left for too long. If this happens, knead the dough for a few minutes, then shape it as required.

If making bread in a very hot climate, it will be best to reduce the amount of yeast used and to place the dough in the refrigerator to slow the rising time down to that specified in the recipe. The rising can be retarded by placing the dough in a cool room or refrigerator to rise. Rising at a low temperature will take much longer than at a warm temperature. The baker can use this to their advantage and control the rate of rising to help ensure the dough is ready for baking when they are ready to bake it. Another advantage of cool-rising is that the by-products of cool fermentation are pleasantly flavourful, whereas the by-products of fast fermentation can be unpleasantly sour. Retardation is used frequently for enriched doughs and for hearth-type breads, such as sourdough.

To tell if the dough has risen sufficiently, prod it with your finger. It should feel soft and pillowy and the indentation made by your fingertip should remain. This indicates that the gluten in the dough has been stretched to its full capacity.

Knocking Back and Shaping

Knocking back redistributes the yeast in the dough after it has risen and doubled in size, and evens out the texture of the bread by kneading out the air bubbles that have formed during rising. It is done by the same procedure as *kneading* (see the description above).

Generally, knocking back needs to be done for only one to two minutes. In certain speciality breads an uneven texture with large holes is desirable, so the dough does not require knocking back. The recipe will indicate if this is the case. Do not cut into the dough to check the texture because this cuts the strands of gluten and will interfere with the final texture of the bread.

Some bread recipes will call for a second rising. The dough needs to be knocked back after the first rise, then left to rise again in the manner described above. Two risings are often called for with *enriched doughs* (see page 482). Dough that has been allowed to rise twice will have a finer texture.

For recipes which have additional ingredients such as fruit or nuts, add these ingredients after the dough has been knocked back and before the final shaping.

Shaping is the process by which the dough is given its final shape, whether it be a traditional loaf in a tin, a free-form bloomer or dinner rolls. As knocking back can cause the gluten in the bread to tighten, it may be necessary to let the dough stand for up to 10 minutes to allow the gluten to relax before shaping. Cover the dough with oiled clingfilm or a clean tea towel while it is standing.

Once the bread is shaped it should be put in the oiled tins or on an oiled baking sheet immediately and allowed to prove. Bread is best baked in a dull metal loaf tin that has been lightly oiled. Rolls should be baked on lightly oiled or floured dull metal trays. Shiny trays will make the rolls brown too much.

Baking or pizza stones are good for baking pizza or free-form loaves as they slow down the crusting process and produce a thicker, chewier crust. The dough must first be proved on a baking sheet, then transferred on to the hot pizza stone which has been preheated in the oven. To make transferring the risen loaf easier, dredge the baking sheet with polenta or rice flour before placing the shaped dough on to it.

Examples of bread shapes are as follows:

Plain loaf: Cup both hands around the edges of the dough and roll the dough on the work surface using a circular movement, for about 10 seconds. This movement aligns the gluten, giving the finished bread a more even texture.

Using both hands, pull the dough towards you over the work surface. This should smooth the surface of the dough. (a) Gently roll the ends of the dough with both hands to form a slightly elongated shape. Place in the prepared tin. Flatten into the corners, using your fingers. (b)

Plaited loaf: Divide the dough into 3 equal pieces and shape each piece into a sausage about 40 cm | 16 in long. Place 2 of the pieces parallel to each other, about 2.5 cm | 1 in apart. Put the third piece perpendicularly across the middle, over one piece and under the other, to form an 'H'. (a) Starting from the middle, take the left-hand piece and place it in the centre of the 2 other pieces and proceed to plait the dough. (b) At the end, squeeze the pieces together to secure, then turn the whole plait over. (c) Proceed from the middle with the unplaited pieces as before. Turn the ends underneath to secure and place on a lightly oiled baking sheet. To bake in a tin, fold the long plait into thirds, rather like a business letter, and place in the lightly oiled tin.

4-Strand plaited loaf: This method is used for *Challah* (see **Festive Breads**, page 618).

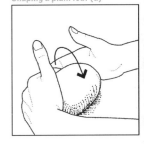

Bloomers are large oval loaves. Shape as for a plain loaf, then roll the dough at the ends to taper. Slash the loaf 3 times with a serrated knife or single-edged razor blade before proving.

Bloomer

Cottage loaf: Divide the dough into 2 pieces, one 3 times larger than the other. Shape both pieces into balls as for *dinner rolls* (see 547). Make a small indentation in the centre of the top of the large ball and place the smaller ball on it. Using a floured finger or a wooden spoon handle, press a hole through both rolls to the baking sheet below, thus fixing the top to the bottom.

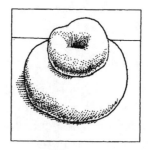

Cottage loaf

Baguettes are shaped using rice flour on a dry work surface. The dough should be gently pulled into a rectangle then cut lengthways into thirds. Each piece of dough should be folded along the cut edge and pinched together to seal (see photographs).

Proving

Proving is the last rising before the dough is baked. During this last rising the dough assumes its final shape and most of its final size. Proving can be done in a slightly warmer environment than rising to speed up the process: 25°C|80°F is the recommended temperature. Usually proving will take approximately half the time of rising because the previous rising will have stretched the gluten strands, making the dough more elastic.

The shaped dough needs to be loosely covered with lightly oiled clingfilm to keep the surface from drying out.

The dough is ready to be baked when it has incresed in size by 75–100 per cent. If the dough is prodded gently, in a discreet spot, the indentation made will spring back about halfway. The dough will feel soft and pillowy.

Dough that has been underproved will result in a bread that has a close, heavy texture and a thick crust. 'Oven-spring', a crack in the bread where the crust has separated from the body of the loaf, may result. If the dough proves for too long, i.e. over-proves, the bread will have large bubbles under the surface of the crust and may collapse in the oven.

Slashing

Loaves are sometimes slashed before baking to give a rustic appearance and to help prevent oven-spring. Slashing also avoids the formation of bubbles under the crust which can form when the steam in a baking loaf is trapped under the crust. Slashing is best done with a sharp, serrated knife or a single-edged razor about 10 minutes before the bread is due to go into the oven.

Glazing

Before the dough is baked it is often glazed to improve the appearance of the crust. Beaten egg will give the crust a shine and help it brown. Milk will also help the crust brown but will produce a softer crust with a matt appearance. It is important to apply the glaze thinly, using a pastry brush. The glaze should not be allowed to drip into the crack between the dough and the tin or it may act as glue once cooked and the finished loaf will be difficult to remove from the tin. Dough can also be dusted with flour before baking to give the bread a dusty, rustic appearance with a soft crust.

Baking

Baking cooks the dough in its final shape. During baking the dough continues to rise for a short while due to the formation of steam and continued action of the yeast. It will stop rising when the dough hardens and the yeast dies – when the internal temperature of the dough reaches 60°C|140°F. This usually happens within the first 10 minutes of baking. The moisture in the dough and the alcohol from the yeast reproduction evaporates and is replaced by air, leaving a network of fine bubbles in the dough that gives the bread its open texture.

It is important to preheat the oven before baking. Most bread is baked at 200°C|400°F|gas mark 6, near the top of the oven, the hottest part. Some recipes may call for preheating the oven to 220°C|425°F|gas mark 7, then turning the oven temperature down to 200°C|400°F|gas mark 6 when the dough is put in the oven, as a falling oven temperature is well suited to bread-baking. Other recipes, particularly those for *enriched doughs* (see page 482), may call for a baking temperature of 190°C|375°F|gas mark 5.

Many hearth-type breads call for the addition of steam when the dough is first placed in the oven. The steam slows the crusting of the dough and results in a lighter-textured loaf. Steam can be created by splashing a cupful of iced water on to the floor of the oven or into a hot roasting tin placed near the bottom of the oven. Alternatively, boiling water from the kettle can be poured into a hot roasting tin placed at the bottom of the oven. The dough and the sides of the oven can also be misted with a plant mister to create a moist environment. The dough benefits from the steam for the first 5 minutes of baking, after which time the crust has formed.

A loaf of bread is baked until it is golden-brown all over and it sounds hollow when tapped on the underside. If the top crust has browned well but the sides are still pale, the bread can be turned on its side and returned to the oven to continue baking for about 5 minutes until brown all over.

Occasionally the crust of the bread will crack in the oven. This cracking is called *oven-spring*. It happens when the loaf forms a crust before the yeast has died so the crust cracks during the final rise in the oven. It can be avoided by proving the dough completely and/or slashing the loaf before baking.

When the bread is done, remove it from the tin immediately and cool on a wire rack. The bread is still cooking during the cooling process, so it is important to leave it to cool completely before consuming. This can take up to 2 hours.

Storing Bread

Wrap the cooled loaf in greaseproof paper. Placing bread in a plastic bag will cause it to sweat, making the crust soft. Bread is best stored at room temperature because it stales more quickly if stored in the refrigerator. However, if the weather is very warm and there is a risk that the bread will go mouldy, it can be refrigerated.

Bread-making: What has gone wrong when . . .

The bread has risen only a little.
- The dough was too dry.
- The shaped dough was proved for too short a time.
- Too much salt or sugar was added to the dough.
- The yeast was stale and not sufficiently active.
- The dough was overproved and collapsed in the oven.
- The liquid was too warm and some of the yeast was killed.

The bread has a cake-like texture.
- The kneading was insufficient for the gluten to develop properly.
- The dough was proved for too short a time.
- The dough was too dry.
- The dough contained too much salt.
- Plain flour was used instead of strong flour.
- The recipe contains a lot of fat.

The bread has a coarse texture.
- Too little salt was added to the dough.
- Too much liquid was added to the dough.
- The dough was risen for too short a time.
- The dough was overproved.

The bread has an uneven texture and/or holes.

- The dough was not knocked back sufficiently.
- The dough was overproved.
- The dough was too wet.

The bread has a sour and/or yeasty flavour.

- The dough was risen for too long a time.
- The dough was risen/proved at too high a temperature.
- The yeast was stale.
- Too much yeast was used.

The bread has a cracked crust (oven-spring).

- The dough was proved for too short a time.
- The oven was too hot.
- The dough formed a leathery crust when it was proving because it was not covered properly. Slashing the loaf during proving, before the loaf is baked, will help prevent oven-spring.

The bread has a wrinkled crust.

- The bread was cooled too quickly. Cover it with a tea towel while cooling.
- The dough was overproved.

The bread has holes underneath the crust.

- The dough was overproved.
- The oven was too hot so the crust formed too quickly. Slash the proved loaf before baking.

Basic Breads

Basic White Bread

MAKES 1 LOAF OR 12 DINNER ROLLS

225 g | 8 oz strong white flour

1 teaspoon salt

10 g | ⅓ oz fresh yeast*

1 teaspoon caster sugar

150 ml | 5 fl oz lukewarm water

30 g | 1 oz butter, melted and cooled

extra flour for kneading oil for greasing

To glaze

1 egg, beaten with a pinch of salt

1 Sift the flour with the salt into a large bowl and make a well in the centre.

2 Place the fresh yeast in a small bowl and add the sugar. Mix to a smooth cream with 2 tablespoons of the water.

3 Tip the yeast mixture into the well. Rinse the yeast bowl with a little of the water, then tip all of the water and the butter into the well.

4 Stir the mixture with a wooden spoon to make a soft dough, adding more water or flour as necessary.

5 Turn the dough out on to a floured work surface. Knead for 10–15 minutes by hand or for 5–7 minutes in an electric mixer, adding extra flour if the dough is too sticky, until the dough is smooth and elastic.

6 Place the dough in an oiled bowl, turning it over to coat the surface with the oil. Cover the bowl with oiled clingfilm and leave to rise in a warm place, about 22°C | 75°F.

7 When the dough has doubled in bulk, punch your fist into the centre of the dough to deflate it. Turn it on to the work surface and knead for 30 seconds to knock it back. Let the dough rest for 5 minutes before shaping as required. For a plain loaf, lightly oil a small loaf tin.

8 Heat the oven to 200°C | 400°F | gas mark 6.

9 Cover the dough loosely with oiled clingfilm and leave to prove (rise again) until nearly doubled in size.

10 Glaze the dough with the beaten egg, taking care not to let the glaze drip into the tin. (This would seal the bread into the tin, making it difficult to remove after baking.)

11 Place the dough in the top third of the oven (the hottest part). Bake for 30 minutes or until the loaf is golden-brown and sounds hollow when tapped on the underside. Cool on a wire rack before slicing.

* If using fast-action or dried yeast, see page 480.

Basic Wholemeal Bread

MAKES 1 LOAF OR 12 DINNER ROLLS

115 g | 4 oz strong white flour

115 g | 4 oz strong wholemeal flour

1 teaspoon salt

170 ml | 6 fl oz water

10 g | ⅓ oz fresh yeast*

1 teaspoon caster sugar

30 g | 1 oz butter, melted and cooled

extra flour for kneading

oil for greasing

To glaze

1 egg, beaten with a pinch of salt

1 Sift the flours with the salt into a large bowl. Reserve any bran left in the sieve for the topping. Make a well in the centre of the flour.

2 Warm the water to 37°C | 100°F (blood temperature). Place the fresh yeast in a small bowl and add the sugar. Mix to a smooth cream with 2 tablespoons of the water.

4 Tip the yeast mixture into the well. Rinse the yeast bowl with a little of the water, then tip all of the water and the butter into the well.

5 Stir the mixture with a wooden spoon to make a soft dough, adding more water or flour as necessary.

6 Turn the dough out on to a floured work surface. Knead for 10–12 minutes by hand or for 5–7 minutes in an electric mixer, adding extra flour if the dough is too sticky, until the dough is smooth and elastic.

7 Place the dough in an oiled bowl, turning it over to coat the surface with the oil. Cover the bowl with oiled clingfilm and leave to rise in a warm place, about 22°C | 75°F.

8 When the dough has doubled in bulk, punch your fist into the centre of the dough to deflate it. Turn it on to the work surface and knead for 30 seconds to knock it back. Let the dough rest for 5 minutes before shaping as required. For a plain loaf, lightly oil a small loaf tin.

9 Heat the oven to 200°C | 400°F | gas mark 6.

10 Cover the dough loosely with oiled clingfilm and leave to prove (rise again) until nearly doubled in size.

11 Glaze the dough with the beaten egg, taking care not to let the glaze drip into the tin. (This would seal the bread into the tin, making it difficult to remove after baking.) Sprinkle over the reserved bran.

13 Place the dough in the top third of the oven (the hottest part). Bake for 30 minutes or until the loaf is golden-brown and sounds hollow when tapped on the underside. Cool on a wire rack before slicing.

* If using fast-action or dried yeast, see page 480.

Ballymaloe Brown Bread

MAKES 1 LOAF

30 g | 1 oz fresh yeast*

1 teaspoon black treacle

290–340 ml | 10–12 fl oz lukewarm water

450 g | 1 lb wholemeal flour

1 teaspoon salt

1 tablespoon sesame seeds

1 Grease a 13 × 20 cm | 5 × 8 in loaf tin.

2 Mix the yeast with the treacle and 150 ml | 5 fl oz of the water, and leave in a warm place for about 5 minutes, by which time it should look creamy and slightly frothy on top.

3 Sift the flour with the salt into a large mixing bowl. Make a well in the centre and add the yeast mixture and enough of the remaining liquid to make a wettish dough that would be just too wet to knead by hand.

5 Heat the oven to 220°C | 425°F | gas mark 7.

4 Put the dough into the loaf tin and smooth down the surface. Sprinkle with the sesame seeds and pat down. Place the tin in a warm place and cover with oiled clingfilm. Leave to rise for 15–30 minutes or until nearly doubled in size.

6 Bake the bread for 30 minutes, then remove the loaf from the tin and return it to the oven to bake for a further 15–25 minutes. When cooked, the bread should sound hollow when tapped on the underside.

* If using fast-action or dried yeast, see page 480.

Easy Wholemeal Bread

This wholemeal bread is simple to make as it has only one rising. As with all bread made from 100 per cent wholemeal flour, it will be heavier than bread made from a mixture including white flour. The flour and water quantities are approximations, as wholemeal flours vary enormously in the amount of water they absorb. The dough should be moist but not sticky. Use the smaller quantity of flour and water called for and then add extra flour or water as necessary.

MAKES 2 SMALL LOAVES

550–600 g | 1 lb 4 oz–1 lb 6 oz stoneground 100 per cent wholemeal flour

2 teaspoons salt

3 tablespoons buttermilk

290–340 ml | 10–12 fl oz lukewarm water

20 g | ⅔ oz fresh yeast*

1 tablespoon black treacle

1 Warm the flour with the salt in a large mixing bowl in the bottom of a low oven for about 5 minutes. Oil 2 × 675 g | 1½ lb loaf tins.

2 Mix the buttermilk with the warm water. Mix the yeast with 2 tablespoons of the liquid and the treacle.

3 Make a well in the centre of the flour; pour in the yeast mixture and nearly all the water and buttermilk. Mix to a dough. Add extra flour or liquid as required.

Knead well for 10 minutes by hand or 6 minutes by machine.

4 Divide the dough between the tins. Smooth the tops and cover with a piece of lightly oiled clingfilm. Leave in a warm place for 45 minutes, or until the dough has risen to the top of the tins.

5 Meanwhile, heat the oven to 220°C|425°F|gas mark 7.

6 Place the loaf tins in the top third of the oven and bake for 15 minutes. Turn down the oven temperature to 190°C|375°F|gas mark 5 and bake for a further 25 minutes. Remove from the tins.

7 The bread should sound hollow when it is tapped on the underside. If it does not or feels squashy and heavy, then return to the oven, without the tins, for a further 5–10 minutes. Leave to cool on a wire rack.

* If using dried or fast-action yeast, see page 480.

Spelt Bread

Spelt flour is an ancient flour that was brought to England by the Romans. It has a pale brown colour and a nutty flavour and is reputed to be easily digestible.

MAKES 1 LOAF

225 ml|8 fl oz lukewarm water

1 tablespoon clear honey

15 g|½ oz fresh yeast*

400 g|14 oz spelt flour

1½ teaspoons salt

30 g|1 oz butter

1 Place the water and honey in a bowl and whisk in the yeast.

2 In a large bowl, sift together the flour and salt then rub in the butter.

3 Stir the water mixture into the flour to make a soft dough, adding more flour or water as required.

4 Knead for about 10 minutes by hand or 6 minutes by machine, until smooth and elastic.

5 Place in an oiled bowl and turn the dough to coat in the oil. Cover with clingfilm and allow to rise until doubled in size.

6 Knock back the dough by kneading lightly then shape into a loaf. Place in an oiled 675 g|1½ lb loaf tin and cover with oiled clingfilm.

7 Heat the oven to 200°C|400°F|gas mark 6.

8 Allow the dough to rise until nearly doubled in size, then bake for 30 minutes or until risen and well-browned. Check after 20 minutes; if the crust is becoming too dark, cover with a tent of foil.

9 Turn out of the tin and cool on a wire rack.

* If using fast-action or dried yeast, see page 480.

Enriched White Bread

MAKES 1 LOAF

290 ml | 10 fl oz milk

450 g | 1 lb strong plain flour

2 teaspoons salt

30 g | 1 oz butter

20 g | ⅔ oz fresh yeast*

1 teaspoon caster sugar

1 egg, lightly beaten

oil for greasing

To glaze

1 egg, beaten

1   Place the milk in a small saucepan and heat gently until steaming. Allow to cool to tepid then skim.

2   Sift the flour with the salt into a large mixing bowl and rub in the butter.

3   Dissolve the yeast with a little of the milk and the sugar in a small bowl.

4   Pour the yeast mixture, the milk and the beaten egg into the flour and mix to a soft dough.

5   Add flour if the dough is too sticky. When the dough will leave the sides of the bowl, press it into a ball and tip it out on to a work surface.

6   Knead until it is elastic, smooth and shiny, about 10 minutes by hand or 6 minutes by machine.

7   Put the dough back into a lightly oiled bowl and turn to coat with the oil. Cover the bowl with a piece of lightly oiled clingfilm.

8   Put it in a warm, draught-free place and leave to rise until it has doubled in size, about 1 hour.

9   Knock back the dough and knead for 1 further minute. Heat the oven to 200°C | 400°F | gas mark 6.

10 Shape the dough into an oblong and put it into a 900 g | 2 lb loaf tin.

11 Cover again with oiled clingfilm and prove (allow to rise again) until it has nearly doubled in size. Brush with beaten egg.

12 Bake the loaf for 30 minutes or until it is golden and sounds hollow when tapped on the underside. If it does not, or feels squashy and heavy, return it to the oven, without the tin, for a further 5 minutes.

13 Place the loaf on a wire rack to cool.

* If using fast-action or dried yeast, see page 480.

White Sandwich Bread

MAKES 1 LOAF

225 ml|8 fl oz milk

15 g|½ oz fresh yeast*

1 tablespoon clear honey

1 tablespoon sunflower oil

1½ teaspoons salt

340 g|12 oz strong white flour

extra milk for brushing

1 Heat the milk until it steams heavily, then cool to lukewarm. Skim.
2 Mix 2 tablespoons of the milk with the yeast to form a thin cream.
3 Sift the flour and salt into a large bowl and make a well in the centre. Add the yeast mixture, honey and oil.
4 Stir to a soft but not sticky dough, adding more milk or flour as required.
5 Knead by hand for 10 minutes or by machine for 6 minutes or until the dough is smooth and elastic.
6 Place the dough into an oiled bowl and turn to coat with the oil. Cover with oiled clingfilm and leave in a warm place to rise for 1½ hours or until doubled in size. Turn the dough out on to a worksurface and knead for 30 seconds.
7 Heat the oven to 200°C|400°F|gas mark 6.
8 Shape into a loaf and place in an oiled 900 g|2 lb loaf tin. Cover with oiled clingfilm and leave in a warm place to prove (rise again) until nearly doubled. An indentation made in the dough will spring back about halfway.
9 Brush the top of the loaf with a little milk. Using a sharp knife, cut several slits lengthways down the centre of the dough, ¼ cm|⅛ in deep.
10 Bake in the top third of the oven for 30 minutes or until golden-brown. The loaf should sound hollow when tapped on the underside.
11 Cool on a wire rack.

* If using fast-action or dried yeast, see page 480.

Wholesome Loaf

This recipe uses a new flour which is a combination of white and wholemeal flour. It works well in a bread machine if fast-action yeast is used in place of the fresh yeast.

MAKES 3 LOAVES

400 g | 14 oz 'wholesome' flour

1½ teaspoons salt

15 g | ½ oz fresh yeast*

250 ml | 9 fl oz lukewarm water

2 tablespoons sunflower or vegetable oil

1 tablespoon clear honey

1 Sift the flour and salt into a large bowl. Reserve any leftover bran in the sieve to top the loaf. Make a well in the centre of the flour.

2 Mix the yeast with 2 tablespoons of the water, then tip into the flour along with the oil and honey.

3 Stir in enough water to make a soft but not sticky dough,

4 Turn out on to a work surface and knead for 10 minutes by hand. If kneading in a machine with a dough hook, knead for 6 minutes or until the dough is smooth.

5 Place in an oiled bowl and turn to coat the dough in the oil. Cover with oiled clingfilm and leave in a warm place for 1½ hours or until doubled in size.

6 Heat the oven to 200°C | 400°F | gas mark 6.

7 Knock back by kneading for 30 seconds.

8 Shape into a loaf and place in a 675 g | 1½ lb loaf tin. Cover with oiled clingfilm and set in a warm place to prove (rise again) until an indentation made in the side of the dough with your finger will spring back just halfway.

9 Sprinkle over the reserved bran. Bake the loaf in the top third of the oven for 30 minutes, or until well-risen and golden-brown. Turn the loaf out of the tin. It should sound hollow when tapped on the underside. Cool on a wire rack.

* If using fast-action or dried yeast, see page 480.

Flavoured Breads

The breads in this section are made from basic bread dough, using the same method described in the introduction to the **Bread** chapter. They have additional ingredients, however, which give them their unique flavours. Many of these flavoured breads are modern concoctions.

Some of the recipes that follow contain seeds and nuts, while others have dried fruit added. Usually these ingredients are added after the dough has had its first rising and before it is shaped. The easiest way to add these firm ingredients is to roll the dough out as flat as possible using a rolling pin and sprinkle over the additions. Then roll up the dough to encase the additional ingredients. The dough should then be kneaded lightly to incorporate these additions and to prevent a 'spiral effect'. It is important not to knead the dough heavily at this stage or the added ingredients will tear the gluten and/or break down in the dough. Try to avoid having dried fruit on the outside of your dough as it will burn in the oven and take on a bitter taste.

A few of the recipes, such as *Apple Bread* and *Sun-dried Tomato Bread*, incorporate fruit or vegetables in the dough when it is mixed. In these recipes the fruit/vegetable breaks down in the dough when it is kneaded and adds moisture as well as flavour to the bread.

Multigrain Malthouse Bread

Malthouse flour is a blend of wheat flour, rye flour and malt flour with added malted grains of wheat. It is nutty-flavoured and delicious. If you can't find it in the shop, substitute wholewheat flour and add another teaspoon of malt extract to the dough.

MAKES 1 SMALL LOAF

15 g | ½ oz fresh yeast*
180–200 ml | 6–7 fl oz lukewarm water
1 teaspoon malt extract
115 g | 4 oz strong white flour
85 g | 3 oz malthouse flour
55 g | 2 oz rye flour
30 g | 1 oz porridge oats

2 tablespoons polenta
1 rounded teaspoon sea salt
30 g | 1 oz softened butter

To glaze
1 egg, beaten and sieved

1 For the starter, mix the yeast with 2 tablespoons of the water, the malt extract and 2 tablespoons of the white flour. Allow to stand at room temperature for 20 minutes.
2 For the dough, sift the remaining flours into a large bowl, reserving any large grains left in the sieve. Add the oats and polenta.
3 Stir in enough water to make a soft dough. Cover with a clean tea towel and let stand at room temperature for 20 minutes.
4 Work together the yeast mixture, dough, salt and butter to make a soft but not too sticky dough. Add more flour if necessary. Knead for 10 minutes by hand or 6 minutes by machine until the dough is smooth.
5 Place in an oiled bowl, turning to coat in the oil. Cover with oiled clingfilm and set in a warm place to rise until doubled in size.
6 Knock back the dough by kneading for 30 seconds, then shape into a loaf.
7 Place in an oiled 450 g | 1 lb loaf tin and cover with oiled clingfilm. Place in a warm place to prove until nearly doubled in size.
8 While the dough is proving, heat the oven to 200°C | 400°F | gas mark 6.
9 Brush with the dough with beaten egg and sprinkle over the reserved grains.
10 Bake in the top third of the oven for 30–35 minutes or until golden-brown. The bread will sound hollow when tapped on the underside.
11 Cool on a wire rack.

* If using fast-action or dried yeast, see page 480.

Herb Fougasse

Stages of Bread-making

Mixing

Kneading

Rising

Knocking back

Shaping

Slashing and proving

The baked loaf

Stromboli

Forming a gluten window

Shaping Ciabatta

Ciabatta

Sun-dried Tomato Bread (Breadmaker)

Mediterranean Vegetable Pizzas

Poaching Soft Pretzels

Pretzels and Beer

Bagels

Garlic Butter Fan Tan Rolls
and Butterhorns

Making Baguettes

Cutting the dough with a bread scraper

Shaping the dough

Proving

Baguettes for breakfast

Sourdough starters in jars

Sourdough on a peel

Using a peel to transfer the dough to a baking stone

Baked Sourdough Loaf

Pumpkin Seed Bread

Oatmeal Bread

This is a light loaf that has a nutty flavour. It is good for both sandwiches and toast and keeps well for several days.

MAKES 1 LOAF

200 ml | 7 fl oz milk

55 g | 2 oz porridge oats

1 tablespoon clear honey

15 g | ½ fresh yeast*

1 egg, beaten

30 g | 1 oz butter, melted

170 g | 6 oz strong white flour

85 g | 3 oz strong wholemeal flour

1¼ teaspoons salt

To glaze and finish

1 egg, beaten and sieved

2 tablespoons porridge oats

1 Heat the milk until steaming. Place the oats in a bowl then stir in the hot milk. Allow to cool to blood temperature.

2 Stir in the remaining ingredients in the order listed and mix to a soft dough, adding a little more milk or flour if necessary.

3 Knead for 10 minutes by hand or 6 minutes by machine until the dough is smooth and elastic.

4 Place in an oiled bowl and turn the dough to coat in a thin film of oil. Cover with oiled clingfilm and place in a warm place (22°C | 75°F) to rise until doubled in size, about 1½ hours.

5 Knock the dough back by kneading lightly for 30 seconds. Grease a 675 g | 1½ lb loaf tin. Shape the loaf into a neat oblong and place in the tin. Cover with oiled clingfilm and leave in a warm place to prove until nearly doubled in size, about 45 minutes.

6 Heat the oven to 220°C | 425°F | gas mark 7.

7 Brush the top of the loaf with a little of the egg, taking care not to let it drip between the side of the dough and the tin. Sprinkle with the porridge oats.

8 Place the loaf in the centre of the oven then turn the temperature down to 200°C | 400°F | gas mark 6. Bake for 30 minutes. The loaf might need to be covered loosely with greaseproof paper halfway through the cooking time in order to keep it from over browning. The bread is done when it is golden-brown and sounds hollow when tapped on the underside. Cool on a wire rack.

* If using fast-action or dried yeast, see page 480.

Cornmeal Bread

This popular New England bread is also known as 'Anadama' Bread, supposedly because a fisherman, tiring of the usual cornmeal mush, baked it into a loaf whilst muttering about his wife, 'Anna, damn her.'

The dough is very sticky, so it is best to use a free-standing machine fitted with a dough hook or a breadmaker to knead it. Use a plastic scraper to remove the dough from the bowl and put it into the tin.

MAKES 1 LARGE LOAF OR 2 SMALL LOAVES

55 g | 2 oz polenta

200 ml | 7 fl oz boiling water

1 tablespoon black treacle or molasses

15 g | ½ oz fresh yeast*

1 egg, beaten

30 g | 1 oz butter, melted

170 g | 6 oz strong white flour

85 g | 3 oz strong wholemeal flour

1½ teaspoons salt

To glaze

1 egg, beaten and sieved

2 tablespoons polenta (cornmeal)

1 Place the polenta in a bowl then stir in the boiling water. Allow to cool to blood temperature.

2 Stir in the remaining ingredients in the order listed and mix to a soft dough, adding a little more water or flour if necessary.

3 Knead for 6 minutes by machine until the dough is smooth and elastic.

4 Place in an oiled bowl and turn the dough to coat in a thin film of oil. Cover with oiled clingfilm and place in a warm place (22°C | 75°F) to rise until doubled in size, about 1½ hours.

5 Knock back the dough by kneading it lightly for 30 seconds. Grease a 675 g | 1½ lb loaf tin and sprinkle it with a little polenta. Shape the loaf into a neat oblong and place in the tin. Cover with oiled clingfilm and leave in a warm place to prove until nearly doubled in size, about 45 minutes.

6 Heat the oven to 220°C | 425°F | gas mark 7.

7 Brush the top of the loaf with a little of the egg, taking care not to let it drip between the side of the dough and the tin. Sprinkle with the polenta.

8 Place the loaf in the centre of the oven then turn the temperature down to 200°C | 400°F | gas mark 6. Bake for 30 minutes. The loaf may need to be covered loosely with greaseproof paper halfway through the cooking time in order to keep it from overbrowning. The bread is done when it is golden–brown and sounds hollow when tapped on the underside. Cool on a wire rack.

TO MAKE IN A BREADMAKER: Mix the polenta with the boiling water as per step 1 and place in the machine. When cooled to lukewarm, add the remaining ingredients to the machine in the order listed, omitting the glaze, and make as for a standard wholemeal loaf loaf. Do not use the 'delay' setting.

*   If using fast-action or dried yeast, see page 480.

Potato Bread

The potato, with its starch and moisture, provides the ideal climate for the yeast to feed upon: this gives a soft, moist dough that rises quickly.

MAKES 3 LOAVES

450 g | 1 lb floury potatoes, peeled
30 g | 1 oz fresh yeast*
425 ml | 15 fl oz luke-warm water

1 tablespoon malt extract
675 g | 1½ lb strong white flour
4 teaspoons salt

1 Cut the potatoes into 5 cm | 2 in chunks. Cover with water then boil until tender. Drain, saving the water for the bread. Mash the potatoes and cool until lukewarm.
2 Dissolve the yeast in a little of the warm water. Stir in the malt extract. Mix it with the mashed potatoes.
3 Sift the flour with the salt into a large mixing bowl. Add the potato mixture and enough water to mix to a soft dough. Mix well. When the mixture will leave the sides of the bowl, press it into a ball and tip it out on to a floured surface.
4 Knead for about 15 minutes by hand or 10 minutes by machine, until elastic, smooth and shiny.
5 Put the dough into an oiled bowl and turn to coat with the oil. Cover with lightly oiled clingfilm.
6 Leave it in a warm place to rise until doubled in size, at least 1 hour.
7 Knock back and knead for 1 further minute. Heat the oven to 220°C | 425°F | gas mark 7.
8 Shape into 3 oval loaves, place on a greased baking sheet and cover again with oiled clingfilm. Leave to prove (rise again) until 1½ times their original size. Dust lightly with flour. Slash the tops of the loaves.
9 Bake the loaves in the oven for 10 minutes. Turn the oven temperature down to 190°C | 375°F | gas mark 5 and bake for a further 25 minutes, or until golden-brown. The bread should sound hollow when tapped on the underside.
10 Turn out on to a wire rack to cool.

* If using fast-action or dried yeast, see page 480.

Three Seed Bread

MAKES 1 LOAF

15 g | ½ oz fresh yeast*
1 teaspoon caster sugar
290 ml | 10 fl oz lukewarm water
225 g | 8 oz strong white flour
225 g | 8 oz strong wholemeal flour
2 teaspoons salt
2 tablespoons olive oil

oil for greasing
6 tablespoons mixed seeds, such as poppy, sesame,
    millet, sunflower

To glaze
1 egg, beaten

1 Cream the yeast with the sugar and a little warm water.
2 Sift the flours and salt into a large bowl and make a well in the centre. Add the yeast mixture to the well.
3 Add the oil and the rest of the water to the flour and stir to make a soft dough, adding additional water or flour as required. Knead the dough for about 8–10 minutes or until smooth and elastic.
4 Place the dough in a large oiled bowl, turning it so it is coated with a thin film of oil. Cover with clingfilm and leave in a warm place to rise for about 1 hour, or until doubled in size.
5 Heat the oven to 200°C | 400°F | gas mark 6.
6 Knock back the dough by pushing it down and pulling the edges into the centre. Knead for 30 seconds, then roll out on a floured work surface about 2.5 cm | 1 in thick. Reserve 2 tablespoons of the seeds and sprinkle the remainder over the dough. Fold the dough over itself to encase the seeds and continue to knead for 10 seconds.
7 Shape the dough into a plait (see page 487) and place on an oiled baking sheet. Cover with oiled clingfilm and leave in a warm place to prove (rise again) until soft and pillowy.
8 Glaze with the beaten egg, sprinkle with the reserved seeds and bake for 30–35 minutes. When done, the bread will feel light and sound hollow when tapped on the underside. Transfer to a wire rack and leave to cool.

* If using fast-action or dried yeast, see page 480.

Five Grain Bread

MAKES 2 SMALL LOAVES OR 1 LARGE LOAF

225 g | 8 oz strong white flour

55 g | 2 oz spelt flour

55 g | 2 rye flour

2 teaspoons salt

55 g | 2 oz polenta

55 g | 2 oz porridge oats

20 g | ⅔ oz fresh yeast*

250 ml | 9 fl oz lukewarm water

1 tablespoon malt extract

To finish

1 egg, beaten with a pinch of salt

1 tablespoon porridge oats

1   Sift the flours with the salt into a large bowl and return the bran left in the sieve to the flour. Stir in the polenta and the oats. Make a well in the centre.

2   In a small bowl, mix the yeast with 2 tablespoons water and the malt extract. Pour into the well in the flour.

3   Stir enough water into the flour to make a soft but not sticky dough. Add more flour or water, if necessary.

4   Knead for 10 minutes by hand or 6 minutes by machine or until smooth and elastic.

5   Place in an oiled bowl and turn the dough to coat it in a thin film of oil. Cover with oiled clingfilm and leave to rise in a warm place until doubled in size about 1 ½ hours.

6   Knead the dough for 30 seconds to knock it back. Cover with the clingfilm and allow to stand for 10 minutes.

7   Lightly oil 1 × 900 g | 2 lb or 2 × 450 g | 1 lb loaf tins.

8   Shape the dough into a loaf or loaves. Place in the tin(s) and cover with oiled clingfilm. Allow to prove (rise again) until nearly doubled in size. If the dough is prodded, the indentation should spring back just halfway.

9   Meanwhile, heat the oven to 200°C | 400°F | gas mark 6.

10   Brush the top of the loave(s) with the beaten egg, taking care not to let the egg drip between the dough and the side of the tin. Sprinkle over the oats.

11   Bake for 30 minutes in the top third of the oven or until golden-brown. The bread is done when it sounds hollow when tapped on the underside.

12   Remove from the tin(s) and cool on wire rack.

* If using fast-action or dried yeast, see page 480.

Walnut Bread

MAKES 2 LOAVES

290 ml | 10 fl oz milk

225 g | 8 oz strong plain flour

225 g | 8 oz malted brown flour

1 teaspoon salt

15 g | ½ oz fresh yeast*

2 tablespoons walnut or olive oil

170 g | 6 oz walnuts, coarsely chopped

To glaze

1 tablespoon clear honey

1 Place the milk in a small saucepan and heat gently until steaming. Allow to cool to tepid, then skim.

2 Sift the flours and salt into a large mixing bowl and make a well in the centre.

3 Mix the yeast with 2 tablespoons of the milk. Pour into the well with the remaining milk and the oil.

3 Mix together to make a soft but not sticky dough.

4 Knead until smooth, about 10 minutes by hand or 6 minutes by machine, using more flour if necessary.

5 Put the dough into a lightly oiled bowl and turn to coat with a thin film of oil. Cover with a piece of lightly oiled clingfilm. Put in a warm place to rise until the dough has doubled in size, about 1 hour.

6 Heat the oven to 190°C | 375°F | gas mark 5.

7 Knock back the dough and knead the walnuts into it. Divide the dough into 2 equal pieces and shape into ovals. Place on a baking sheet. Slash the tops with a sharp knife.

8 Cover the loaves with lightly oiled clingfilm and leave in a warm place until they are 1½ times their original size.

9 Bake in the oven for 30 minutes, or until they sound hollow when tapped on the underside. Brush the honey evenly over the loaves. Return to the oven for 5 minutes.

10 Place on a wire rack and leave to cool.

* If using fast-action or dried yeast, see page 480.

Seaweed Bread

This speckled, salty bread is good to serve with a fish first course.

MAKES 2 SMALL LOAVES OR 20 DINNER ROLLS

10 g | ⅓ oz nori seaweed

340 g | 12 oz strong white flour

115 g | 4 oz wholemeal flour

1 teaspoon sea salt

290 ml | 10 fl oz lukewarm water

20 g | ⅔ oz fresh yeast*

1 tablespoon clear honey

1 tablespoon sunflower oil

To finish

extra oil

coarse sea salt

1 Heat the oven to 180°C | 350°F | gas mark 4. Cut the seaweed into ½ cm | ¼ in strips. Place on a baking sheet and bake in the oven for 5 minutes or until dry and crisp. Cool, then process the seaweed in a blender or coffee grinder to small pieces. Set aside.

2 Sift the flours and salt into a large bowl, returning any bran left in the sieve to the bowl. Stir in the seaweed and make a well in the centre of the flour.

3 Mix 2 tablespoons of the water with the yeast to a thin cream and place in the well in the flour, along with the honey and oil.

4 Add the remaining water then stir to a soft but not sticky dough. If required, add a little more water or flour.

5 Knead by hand for 10 minutes or by machine for 6 minutes or until the dough is smooth and elastic.

6 Place the dough into an oiled bowl and turn to coat with the oil. Cover with oiled clingfilm and leave in a warm place to rise for 1½ hours or until doubled in size.

7 Turn the dough out on to a work surface and knead for 30 seconds.

8 Heat the oven to 200°C | 400°F | gas mark 6.

9 Shape into 2 loaves and place into 2 oiled 450 g | 1 lb loaf tins. If making rolls, divide the dough into 20 equal-sized pieces and shape as desired. Cover with oiled clingfilm and leave in a warm place to prove (rise again) until nearly doubled in size. An indentation made in the dough should spring back about halfway.

10 Brush the tops of the loaves or rolls with a little oil and sprinkle with the coarse sea salt. Using a sharp, serrated knife, cut a slit lengthways down the centre of the dough, ¼ cm | ⅛ in deep.

11 Bake in the top third of the oven for 30 minutes or until golden-brown. When done, the bread should sound hollow when tapped on the underside.

12 Cool on a wire rack.

NOTE: If using fast-action or dried yeast, see page 480.

Austrian Rye Bread

If you like rye bread to be heavier and darker, use proportionally more rye flour than white flour.

MAKES 1 LOAF

150 ml | 5 fl oz lager

115 ml | 4 fl oz cold water

30 g | 1 oz fresh yeast*

1 teaspoon brown sugar

225 g | 8 oz strong white bread flour

1 teaspoon salt

225 g | 8 oz rye flour

1 tablespoon pumpkin seeds

1 tablespoon sunflower seeds

1 teaspoon caraway seeds

1 egg, beaten

1 Bring the lager to the boil and add the cold water. Allow to cool until lukewarm.

2 Mix the yeast and sugar together and add a little of the lukewarm liquid.

3 Sift the white flour together with the salt into a large bowl. Add the rye flour and seeds. Make a well in the centre and add the egg, yeast and liquid. Mix to make a soft but not wet dough. If necessary add some more water. Knead for 10 minutes by hand or 6 minutes by machine.

4 Place in an oiled bowl and turn the dough to coat it in the oil. Cover with a piece of oiled clingfilm. Leave in a warm place to rise until the dough has doubled in size. This will take between 30 minutes and 1 hour, depending on the temperature of the room.

5 Heat the oven to 200°C | 400°F | gas mark 6.

6 Remove the dough from the bowl and knock back to remove any large air pockets. Shape into a large oval loaf, put on to an oiled baking sheet and make a slash down the length of the loaf with a serrated knife. Cover with a piece of oiled clingfilm and leave to prove for 15–20 minutes or until the loaf is 1½ times its original size.

7 Remove the clingfilm and sprinkle with some white flour. Bake in the top of the oven for 25 minutes or until the loaf sounds hollow when tapped underneath. Put on a wire rack to cool down.

* If using fast-action or dried yeast, see page 480.

Wholemeal Polenta Bread

MAKES 1 LARGE LOAF

15 g | ½ oz fresh yeast*
1 teaspoon caster sugar
200–250 ml | 7–9 fl oz lukewarm water
115 g | 4 oz strong white flour
200 g | 7 oz strong wholemeal flour

1½ teaspoons salt
55 g | 2 oz polenta
15 g | ½ oz butter
extra oil for brushing

1 Place the yeast in a small bowl with the caster sugar. Add the water and whisk to combine. Stir in the white flour and set aside.

2 Sift the wholemeal flour and salt into a large bowl and stir in the polenta.

3 Rub in the butter then make a well in the centre. Add the yeast mixture and enough additional water to make a soft but not sticky dough.

4 Knead for 10 minutes by hand or 6 minutes by machine or until the dough is smooth.

5 Place the dough in a lightly oiled bowl and turn the dough to coat it in a thin film of oil. Leave the dough in the bowl and cover with oiled clingfilm. Leave to rise at warm room temperature until doubled in size, about 1 hour.

6 Knead the dough lightly to knock it back, then shape it into a loaf.

7 Heat the oven to 200°C | 400°F | gas mark 6.

8 Place in an oiled 900 g | 2 lb loaf tin. Cover with oiled clingfilm and let rise until nearly doubled, about 30 minutes. Brush with oil and sprinkle with a little polenta.

9 Bake in the top third of the oven (the hottest part) for 30 minutes or until a deep brown. The loaf should sound hollow when tapped on the underside.

10 Turn out on to a wire rack to cool.

* If using fast-action or dried yeast, see page 480.

Cheese Gannat

This recipe is based on a cheese brioche originally from Gannat, a small town in the Auvergne.

MAKES 1 LOAF

100 ml | 3½ fl oz milk
15 g | ½ oz fresh yeast*
⅓ teaspoon sugar
225 g | 8 oz wholemeal flour
1 teaspoon salt
a pinch of cayenne pepper
a pinch of dry English mustard
freshly ground black pepper

55 g | 2 oz butter
2 eggs, beaten
115 g | 4 oz cheese, preferably strong Cheddar or
    Gruyère, grated

To glaze
a little milk

1 Scald the milk, then allow to cool until lukewarm. Skim.
2 Mix the yeast with the sugar and 2 tablespoons of milk to create a smooth cream.
3 Sift the flour with the salt, cayenne, mustard and pepper into a warmed mixing bowl and make a well in the centre.
4 Melt the butter, remove from the heat and add the milk. Mix with the eggs and the yeast. Pour this liquid into the flour and mix to a soft dough. Knead until just smooth.
5 Cover and leave to rise in a warm place. Do not worry if it does not rise very much; it will during baking.
6 Heat the oven to 200°C | 400°F | gas mark 6.
7 Mix all but 2 tablespoons of the cheese into the dough.
8 Divide the dough into 8 pieces and form each piece into balls. Place into a well-greased 20 cm | 8 in sandwich tin. Cover with oiled clingfilm and put in a warm place to prove (rise again) for 10–15 minutes.
9 Remove the clingfilm and bake in the oven for 25–30 minutes.
10 Brush lightly with the milk and sprinkle with the remaining cheese, then return the loaf to the oven for a further 5 minutes. Turn out on to a wire rack to cool.

* If using fast-action or dried yeast, see page 480.

Savoury Brioche

Less rich than the sweet brioche on page 600, this brioche is best cooked as a large loaf. It is ideal to use for toasting, to serve with pâtés and terrines.

MAKES 1 LOAF

10 g|⅓ oz fresh yeast*

1 tablespoon caster sugar

2 tablespoons lukewarm water

225 g|8 oz plain white flour

½ teaspoon salt

2 eggs, beaten

55 g|2 oz melted butter, cooled

To glaze

1 egg, mixed with 1 tablespoon water and sieved

1 Butter and flour a 450 g|1 lb loaf tin.

2 Mix the yeast with 1 teaspoon of the sugar and the water.

3 Sift the flour with the salt into a mixing bowl. Sprinkle over the rest of the sugar. Make a well in the centre. Drop in the eggs, yeast mixture and melted butter and mix to a soft but not sloppy paste.

4 Knead on an unfloured surface for 5 minutes or until smooth (see page 000 for method). Put into a clean bowl, cover with a damp cloth or lightly oiled clingfilm and leave to rise in a warm place until doubled in size (about 1 hour).

5 Turn out and knead again on an unfloured surface for 30 seconds.

6 Place the dough in the prepared loaf tin (it should not come more than halfway up the sides).

7 Cover with lightly oiled clingfilm and leave to prove (rise again) until risen to the top of the tin (about 30 minutes for the large brioche, 15 minutes for individual ones).

8 Meanwhile, heat the oven to 200°C|400°F|gas mark 6.

9 Brush the brioche with the egg glaze. Bake for 20–25 minutes. Leave to stand in the tin for 5 minutes then turn on to a wire rack to cool.

* If using fast-action or dried yeast, see page 480.

Oatmeal Seed Bread

MAKES 1 LARGE LOAF

450g | 1 lb strong white flour
225 g | 8 oz oatmeal
1 teaspoon salt
30 g | 1 oz butter
290 ml | 10 fl oz lukewarm milk
20 g | ⅔ oz fresh yeast*

1 teaspoon caster sugar
1 egg, beaten
30 g | 1 oz pumpkin seeds
30 g | 1 oz sesame seeds
30 g | 1 oz sunflower seeds
30 g | 1 oz pine nuts

1 Grease a baking sheet. Heat the oven to 200°C | 400°F | gas mark 6.

2 Sift the flour into a large bowl, then add the oatmeal and salt. Melt the butter and add to the milk. Cream the yeast with the sugar until liquid.

3 Make a well in the centre of the flour and pour in the milk, yeast and beaten egg. Mix to make a soft but not wet dough, adding more flour or milk as necessary.

4 Put the dough on to a floured surface and knead for 10 minutes by hand or 6 minutes by machine, or until very elastic.

5 Put the dough into an oiled bowl and turn the dough to coat in the oil. Cover with oiled clingfilm. Leave in a warm place until it has doubled in size.

6 Take the dough out of the bowl and place on a floured surface. Scatter over the seeds and knead them into the dough.

7 Shape the dough into an oval. Place on the greased baking sheet. Cover with oiled clingfilm and return to a warm place until it has risen to 1½ times its original size.

8 Dust with a little flour and put in the oven for 40 minutes. The loaf is cooked when it sounds hollow when tapped on the underside. Cool on a wire rack.

* If using fast-action or dried yeast, see page 480.

Apple Bread

MAKES 2 SMALL LOAVES

375 g | 12 oz Bramley apples (peeled and cored weight)
15 g | ½ oz fresh yeast*
1 teaspoon sugar
225 g | 8 oz wholemeal flour

225 g | 8 oz strong white flour
½ teaspoon salt
85 g | 3 oz dried apple, chopped
extra strong white flour for dusting

1 Cut the peeled and cored apples into chunks and put in a saucepan with 2 tablespoons water. Put over a low heat, cover with a lid and cook gently, stirring occasionally until the apple has become a smooth pulp. Allow it to cool until just warm.

2 Cream the yeast with the sugar. Sift the flours and salt into a large bowl. Add any bran left in the sieve to the bowl.

3 Mix the yeast and apple purée with the flour and bring together to form a soft dough. It may be necessary to add some water or extra flour, depending on the apples.

4 Turn the dough out on to a floured surface and knead for 10 minutes by hand or 6 minutes by machine or until smooth and elastic. Place in an oiled bowl and turn the dough to coat in the oil. Cover with a piece of oiled clingfilm. Put into a warm, draught-free place and leave to rise until it has doubled in size (at least an hour).

5 Remove the dough from the bowl and put on a floured work surface. Sprinkle over the dried apple pieces. Knock back the dough and knead in the apple pieces for another minute. Heat the oven to 200°C|400°F| gas mark 6. Grease a baking sheet.

6 Divide the dough in half and shape into 2 round loaves. Place on the baking sheet approximately 7.5 cm|3 in apart. Cover with the oiled clingfilm and leave to prove for approximately 15–20 minutes or until the loaves are 1½ times their original size.

7 Dust with flour and place in the oven. Bake for 30 minutes or until they sound hollow when tapped on their undersides. Cool on a wire rack.

* If using fast-action or dried yeast, see page 480.

Apricot and Orange Bread

MAKES 1 LARGE LOAF

225 g|8 oz strong white bread flour	290 ml|10 fl oz lukewarm milk
225 g|8 oz wholemeal flour	1 tablespoon olive oil
1 teaspoon salt	grated zest of 1 orange
15 g|½ oz fresh yeast*	115 g|4 oz dried apricots, chopped

1 Sift the flours and salt into a large mixing bowl and make a well in the centre.

2 Mix the yeast with 1 tablespoon of the milk. Pour into the well with the remaining milk and the oil. Mix to make a soft but not wet dough.

3 Knead for 10 minutes by hand or 6 minutes by machine, until smooth and elastic.

4 Place the dough into an oiled bowl and turn to coat in the oil. Cover with a piece of lightly oiled clingfilm. Leave in a warm place until doubled in size (about 1 hour).

5 Heat the oven to 190°C|375°F|gas mark 5.

6 Knock back the dough and knead the orange zest and apricots into it. Shape into a round loaf and place on a baking sheet. Score a lattice pattern on the top with a knife.

7 Cover the loaf with lightly oiled clingfilm and leave in a warm place to prove until it is 1½ times its original size. Dust the top with a little flour.

8 Bake the loaf for 30 minutes or until it sounds hollow when tapped on the underside.

9 Place the loaf on a wire rack and leave to cool.

* If using fast-action or dried yeast, see page 480.

Beer Bread

2 teaspoons soft light brown sugar

290 ml|10 fl oz brown ale

55 g|2 oz butter

30 g|1 oz fresh yeast*

1 egg

225 g|8 oz wholemeal flour

225 g|8 oz strong plain white flour

2 teaspoons salt

1 Oil a 900 g|2 lb loaf tin.

2 Bring the sugar and beer to boiling point, allow to boil for 1 minute then add the butter then allow to cool until lukewarm.

3 Use 2 tablespoonfuls of this liquid to mix with the yeast. Add the yeast and lightly beaten egg to the beer mixture.

4 Sift the flours and salt into a large mixing bowl. Make a well in the centre and pour in the liquid. Mix to a soft but not too sticky dough. Knead for 10 minutes by hand or 6 minutes by machine or until smooth, a little shiny and very elastic.

5 Put the dough into an oiled bowl and turn to coat with the oil. Cover with a piece of oiled clingfilm. Leave in a warm place until it has doubled in size.

6 Take the dough out of the bowl, knock it back and knead until smooth again. Shape the dough into a loaf shape and put into the tin. Cover again with oiled clingfilm and return to the warm place to prove (rise again) until nearly doubled in size.

7 Meanwhile, heat the oven to 200°C|400°F|gas mark 6. Bake the loaf in the top third of the oven for 35 minutes, or until it is brown on top and sounds hollow when tapped on the underside. Cool on a wire rack.

* If using fast-action or dried yeast, see page 480.

Carrot Bread

225 g|8 oz strong white flour

225 g|8 oz wholemeal flour

1 teaspoon salt

115 g|4 oz carrots, grated

2 tablespoons chopped fresh thyme

2 tablespoons chopped fresh chives

1 tablespoon chopped fresh dill

2 tablespoons sunflower seeds

15 g|½ oz fresh yeast*

½ teaspoon sugar

225 ml|8 fl oz lukewarm water

1 tablespoon olive oil

1 egg, beaten

1 Sift the flours and salt into a large bowl. Add any bran left in the sieve. Add the carrot, thyme, chives, dill and sunflower seeds.

2 Mix the yeast with the sugar and 1 tablespoon of the water and add with the oil, beaten egg and rest of the water to the flour mixture.

3 Mix to make a soft but not wet dough.

4 Put on to a floured surface and knead for 10 minutes by hand or 6 minutes by machine, or until smooth and elastic.

5 Place in an oiled bowl and turn the dough to to coat in the oil. Cover with oiled clingfilm and leave to rise in a warm place until doubled in size.

6 Heat the oven to 200°C|400°F|gas mark 6. Grease a baking sheet.

7 Knock back the dough and shape into an oval loaf. Place on the greased baking sheet. Make 3 or 4 slashes across the bread, cover with the oiled clingfilm and leave to prove in a warm place until it is 1½ times its original size.

8 Dust with flour and bake for approximately 35 minutes or until the loaf sounds hollow when tapped on the underside. Cool on a wire rack.

* If using fast-action or dried yeast, see page 480.

Pumpkin Seed Bread

MAKES 1 LARGE LOAF

450 g|1 lb pumpkin or butternut squash, peeled, seeded and cut into chunks	1 teaspoon salt
15 g|½ oz fresh yeast*	4 tablespoons pumpkin seeds
2 teaspoons clear honey	**To finish**
30 ml|1 fl oz lukewarm water	1 egg, beaten
450 g|1 lb strong white flour	½ tablespoon pumpkin seeds

1 Steam the pumpkin until very soft and purée in a food processor or blender. Allow it to cool. Alternatively you could use a 425 g|15 oz tin of pumpkin purée (unsweetened).

2 Mix the yeast with the honey and water. Sift the flour and salt into a large bowl, then add the yeast and pumpkin purée. Mix to a soft but not wet dough, adding more flour or water as necessary.

3 Put the dough on to a floured surface and knead for 10 minutes by hand or 6 minutes by machine, or until it is smooth and elastic. Place in an oiled bowl and turn the dough to coat in the oil. Cover with a piece of oiled clingfilm. Leave in a warm, draught-free place for 1 hour or until it has doubled in size.

4 Put the dough on to a floured surface and scatter over the pumpkin seeds. Work them into the dough, knocking it back at the same time.

5 Heat the oven to 200°C|400°F|gas mark 6. Grease a baking sheet.

6 Shape the dough into an oblong loaf and place on the baking sheet. Cover with oiled clingfilm and leave to prove for 20 minutes or until it is 1½ times its original size. Brush with the beaten egg and scatter over the remaining pumpkin seeds. Slash the centre 1 cm|½ in deep. Bake for 40–45 minutes or until it sounds hollow when tapped on the underside. Cool on a wire rack.

* If using fast-action or dried yeast, see page 480.

Walnut, Rosemary and Raisin Bread

MAKES 1 LOAF

225 g | 8 oz strong white flour

1 teaspoon salt

15 g | ½ oz fresh yeast*

150 ml | 5 fl oz lukewarm water

2 tablespoons olive oil

2 tablespoons chopped fresh rosemary

100 g | 3½ oz walnuts, chopped

100 g | 3½ oz raisins

coarse sea salt for sprinkling

1 Sift the flour with the salt into a large bowl and make a well in the centre.

2 Mix the yeast with 2 tablespoons of the warm water to make a thin cream. Pour the mixture into the well then rinse any remaining yeast from the container with a little additional water.

3 Pour the oil into the well.

4 Pour three quarters of the remaining water into the well, then stir vigorously with a wooden spoon to make a soft dough. As the dough comes together, add more water as needed to any dry flour in the bowl. The dough should be soft and pliable but not too sticky.

5 Knead the dough for 8–10 minutes by hand or 6 minutes by machine, until smooth.

6 Place the dough in an oiled bowl and turn the dough to coat it in a thin film of oil. Cover with oiled clingfilm. Allow to rise until doubled in size, approximately 1 hour.

7 Heat the oven to 220°C | 425°F | gas mark 7.

8 Turn the dough out of the bowl on to a lightly floured work surface and roll flat with a rolling pin. Sprinkle with the rosemary, walnuts and raisins, then roll up tightly. Knead a few times then shape in to a rugby-ball shape. Slice with a serrated knife on the diagonal several times across the top.

9 Place on an oiled baking sheet and cover with oiled clingfilm. Allow to rise again in a warm place until nearly doubled in size. Sprinkle with sea salt.

10 Place the dough on the baking sheet in the top third of the oven. Turn the oven temperature down to 200°C | 400°F | gas mark 6.

11 Bake the bread for about 25 minutes or until well-risen and golden-brown. Remove the bread from the baking sheet and place directly on the oven shelf, so that the underside of the bread can brown. This will take an additional 5–10 minutes.

12 The bread is done when it feels light and sounds hollow when tapped on the underside. Cool on a wire rack.

* If using fast-action or dried yeast, see page 480.

Sun-dried Tomato Bread

The tomatoes break down when the dough is kneaded to produce an orange-coloured loaf flecked with red. This bread is delicious sliced for sandwiches. This recipe works well in a bread machine.

MAKES 1 LOAF

15 g | ½ oz fresh yeast*
2 teaspoons caster sugar
200 ml | 7 fl oz lukewarm water
340 g | 12 oz strong white flour

1½ teaspoons salt
2 tablespoons oil from sun-dried tomato jar
55 g | 2 oz sun-dried tomatoes, cut into ½ cm | ¾ in pieces

1 Place the yeast in a small bowl with the sugar and 2 tablespoons of the water. Mix to a smooth cream.
2 Sift the flour and salt into a large bowl and make a well in the centre.
3 Add the oil to the well, along with the sun-dried tomatoes and yeast mixture, and mix with enough water to make a soft but not too sticky dough.
4 Knead by hand for 10 minutes or by machine for 6 minutes. The dough should be smooth and satiny.
5 Place the dough in an oiled bowl and turn the dough to coat it in a thin film of oil. Cover with oiled clingfilm. Leave in a warm place to rise until doubled in size, about 1¼ hours.
6 Heat the oven to 220°C | 425°F | gas mark 7.
7 Knock back the dough by kneading lightly and shape into a loaf.
8 Place in an oiled 675 g | 1½ lb loaf tin and cover with oiled clingfilm. Leave in a warm place to prove until risen just over the top of the tin, about 40 minutes.
9 Place the dough in the top third of the oven and immediately turn the oven temperature to 200°C | 400°F | gas mark 6. Bake for 30 minutes or until golden-brown. The loaf should sound hollow when tapped on the underside. Remove the loaf from the tin and cool on a wire rack.

* If using fast-action or dried yeast, see page 480.

Sun-dried Tomato Couronne

20 g | ⅔ oz fresh yeast*
170 ml | 6 fl oz lukewarm water
340 g | 12 oz strong white flour
1 teaspoons salt
2 tablespoons olive oil

For the filling

3 tablespoons sun-dried tomato pesto
50 g | 1¾ oz pine nuts, toasted

1 Whisk the yeast into the water. Stir in half the flour and allow to stand for 20 minutes.

2 Stir in the remaining flour, salt and olive oil. Add more water or more flour if required to make a soft dough.

3 Knead for 10 minutes by hand or 6 minutes by machine.

4 Place in an oiled bowl and turn the dough to coat it in a thin film of oil. Cover with oiled clingfilm and leave to rise in a warm place until doubled in size.

5 On a floured surface roll the dough into a rectangle measuring 20 × 30 cm | 8 × 12 in.

6 Spread with the sun-dried tomato pesto and sprinkle over the pine nuts. Roll up from one of the long sides. **(a)** Pinch the dough where it joins to seal. **(b)**

7 Cut the log in half lengthways and turn each piece cut-side up. **(c)** Make a loose twist with the two pieces **(d)** and shape into a ring on a baking sheet. **(e)**

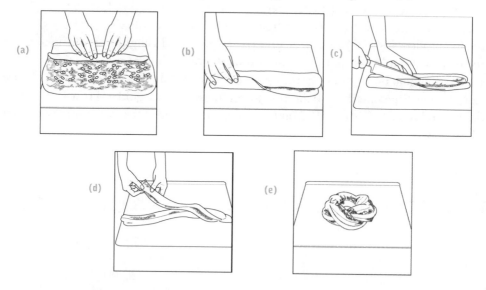

8 Cover with oiled clingfilm and leave to prove (rise again) at room temperature. Heat the oven to 200°C | 400°F | gas mark 6.

9 Bake the couronne in the top third of the oven for 30 minutes or until golden-brown. Cool on a wire rack, but serve warm. The bread can be reheated before serving.

* If using fast-action or dried yeast, see page 480.

Fig and Walnut Loaves

This bread makes a delicious accompaniment to cheese.

MAKES 2 × 450 G|1 LB LOAVES

For the starter

290 ml|10 fl oz lukewarm water

20 g|⅔ oz fresh yeast*

1 tablespoon clear honey

100 g|3½ oz malted brown flour

For the dough

1½ teaspoons salt

2 tablespoons walnut oil

340–400 g|12–14 oz malted brown flour

115 g|4 oz walnuts, coarsely chopped

115 g|4 oz dried figs, cut into eighths

To glaze

extra clear honey

1 For the starter, place the water in a large bowl and whisk in the yeast, honey and flour. Allow to stand at room temperature for 1 hour.

2 To make the dough, stir in the salt, walnut oil and enough flour to make a soft but not sticky dough.

3 Turn out on to a work surface and knead for 10 minutes by hand or in a machine for 6 minutes, or until the dough is smooth and elastic.

4 Place the dough in an oiled bowl and turn to coat in the oil. Cover with clingfilm and allow to rise at room temperature until doubled in size.

5 Turn the dough on to the work surface and knead for 30 seconds. Cover the dough with clingfilm again and allow to stand for 15 minutes to relax.

6 Roll the dough into a sheet about 1 cm|½ in thick, then scatter over the nuts and figs. Roll up the dough then knead lightly.

7 Cut the dough in half, then shape into 2 oval loaves. Place on a greased baking sheet. Slash each loaf 5 times, about ½ cm|¼ in deep, then cover with oiled clingfilm.

8 Heat the oven to 200°C|400°F|gas mark 6.

9 Allow the dough to rise in a warm place until soft and pillowy, about 30 minutes.

10 Remove the clingfilm and place the bread in the top third of the oven. Bake for 20 minutes then turn the loaves over and bake for a further 10 minutes. The loaves should sound hollow when tapped on the underside.

11 Place on a wire rack and brush with a little honey to glaze. Cool.

* If using fast-action or dried yeast, see page 480.

Wholemeal Raisin Bread

MAKES 1 LOAF

290 ml | 10 fl oz lukewarm milk
225 g | 8 oz strong white flour
225 g | 8 oz wholemeal flour
1 teaspoon salt
15 g | ½ oz fresh yeast*

1 tablespoon oil
115 g | 4 oz raisins

1   Scald the milk and allow to cool to room temperature. Skim. Sift the flours and salt into a large mixing bowl and make a well in the centre.
2   Mix the yeast with 2 tablespoons of the milk. Pour into the well with the remaining milk and the oil.
3   Mix to a soft dough, adding more flour if necessary.
4   Knead until smooth and elastic, about 10 minutes by hand or 6 minutes by machine.
5   Put the dough into a large, lightly oiled bowl and turn to coat. Cover with a piece of lightly oiled clingfilm. Leave in a warm place to rise until doubled in size, about 1 hour.
6   Heat the oven to 190°C | 375°F | gas mark 5.
7   Knock back the dough and gently knead the raisins into it. Shape into a round loaf and place on a greased baking sheet.
8   Cover the loaf with lightly oiled clingfilm and leave in a warm place until it is 1½ times its original size. Dust the top with a little flour. Make 3 slashes ½ cm | ¼ in deep with a serrated knife.
9   Bake the loaf in the oven for 30 minutes, or until it sounds hollow when tapped on the underside.
10   Place the loaf on a wire rack and leave to cool.

* If using fast-action or dried yeast, see page 480.

Olive Oil Breads

Bread doughs made with the addition of olive oil are native to the Mediterranean region. Focaccia and ciabatta are among the best-known of the olive oil breads and have become very popular in Britain and the US.

Breads made with olive oil are usually best on the day of baking, although they can be frozen successfully for up to 1 month if tightly wrapped in clingfilm. Unwrap to defrost then warm in a hot oven for 5–10 minutes before serving.

If you want to increase the olive oil content of a loaf it is best to drizzle additional olive oil over the loaf after it comes out of the oven. This way it will absorb the oil and maintain its chewy texture without becoming greasy.

Italian Bread

This is a basic olive oil bread which can be easily adapted by adding a variety of herbs, such as rosemary or sage, grated cheese, olives or sun-dried tomatoes.

MAKES 1 LARGE OR 2 SMALL LOAVES

30 g|1 oz fresh yeast*
225 ml|8 fl oz lukewarm water
450 g|1 lb strong white flour

2 teaspoons salt
4 tablespoons olive oil
coarse sea salt (optional)

1 Dissolve the yeast in the warm water.
2 Sift the flour with the salt into a large bowl and make a well in the centre. Pour in the dissolved yeast and 2 tablespoons of oil. Add enough water to mix to a soft but not sticky dough.
3 Knead for 10 minutes by hand or 6 minutes by machine, or until the dough is smooth. Cover the dough with oiled clingfilm and leave to rest for 10 minutes.
4 Oil a baking sheet. Roll the dough with a rolling pin into 1 or 2 ovals about 2 cm|¾ in thick and place on the baking sheet. Cover with oiled clingfilm and leave in a warm place to rise.
5 Heat the oven to 200°C|400°F|gas mark 6.
6 When the dough feels soft and pillowy, make about 8 indentations in the dough with your finger. Drizzle with the remaining olive oil and sprinkle with sea salt if using.
7 Bake for 20 minutes. Remove the loaf from the baking sheet and place directly on the oven shelf. Bake for a further 10 minutes. Transfer to a wire rack to cool.

* If using fast-action or dried yeast, see page 480.

Red Onion Focaccia

MAKES 1 LOAF

For the dough

450 g | 1 lb strong flour

2 teaspoons sea salt

30 g | 1 oz fresh yeast*

4 tablespoons olive oil

290 ml | 10 fl oz lukewarm water

For the topping

2 tablespoons olive oil

285 g | 10 oz red onions, sliced

2 cloves of garlic, peeled and crushed

sea salt

1 Sift the flour into a large bowl with the salt. Make a well in the centre.

2 Place the yeast in a small bowl and stir in a little warm water until dissolved.

3 Add the yeast to the flour, along with the olive oil and enough warm water to make a soft but not sticky dough.

4 Turn the dough out on to a lightly floured surface and knead for 10 minutes by hand or 6 minutes by machine. Transfer the dough to a lightly oiled bowl and turn to coat it in oil. Cover with oiled clingfilm and leave in a warm place to rise until doubled in size, about 1 hour.

5 Line a 25 × 30 cm | 10 × 12 in roasting tin with baking parchment and oil it lightly. Gently lift the dough from the bowl and place in the roasting tin, stretching it to fit. Cover with oiled clingfilm and leave the dough at room temperature until almost doubled in size.

6 Meanwhile, heat the oven to 200°C | 400°F | gas mark 6.

7 To make the topping, place the oil in a sauté pan, stir in the onions and cover them with a piece of damp greaseproof paper. Cook over a low heat for 10 minutes.

8 Remove the paper, stir in the garlic and continue to cook for 1 minute. Turn on to a plate to cool.

9 Top the bread with the cooled onions and garlic. Sprinkle with sea salt. Bake in the top third of the oven for 30–35 minutes, until golden-brown. Serve warm.

* If using fast-action or dried yeast, see page 480.

Herb Fougasse

Fougasse is a traditional French hearth bread from the Provence region, shaped like a fern or leaf, hence the name.

MAKES 1 LARGE LOAF OR 2 SMALL LOAVES

For the starter

10 g | ⅓ oz fresh yeast*
150 ml | 5 fl oz lukewarm water
½ teaspoon caster sugar
140 g | 5 oz strong white flour

For the dough

10 g | ⅓ oz fresh yeast*

150 ml | 5 fl oz lukewarm water
340 g | 12 oz strong white flour
2 teaspoons salt
4 tablespoons olive oil
2 tablespoons rice flour
1 tablespoon dried herbes de Provence or dried
  mixed herbs
coarse sea salt

1 Make the starter: whisk the yeast into the water, then stir in the sugar and the flour. Cover with clingfilm and leave in a cool place overnight.
2 Make the dough: whisk the yeast into the water. Sift the flour into a large bowl with the salt and make a well in the centre.
3 Tip the starter into the well along with the new yeast mixture and 2 tablespoons olive oil.
4 Stir to make a soft dough, adding a little more water or more flour if required.
5 Knead the dough for 10 minutes by hand or for 6 minutes by machine to make a smooth, elastic dough.
6 Place the dough in an oiled bowl and turn to coat with a thin film of oil. Cover with oiled clingfilm. Leave to rise in a warm place until doubled in size, about 1 hour.
7 Heat the oven to 200°C | 400°F | gas mark 6. Place a roasting pan on the lower shelf of the oven.
8 Sprinkle the rice flour on to a baking sheet. Carefully lift the risen dough out of the bowl and place on the baking sheet, stretching it into 1 or 2 ovals. Cut slits in the dough where the veins in a leaf would be found.
9 Brush the dough with 1 tablespoon olive oil. Cover with clingfilm and leave to prove (rise again) until it is pillowy and springs back only a little when prodded.
10 Sprinkle the dough with the dried herbs and a little salt. Splash a little cold water into the roasting pan to create a steamy environment. Bake in the top third of the oven (the hottest part) for 20–30 minutes.
11 Remove the bread from the baking sheet after 20 minutes and place it directly on the oven shelf so that the base can brown. Bake for a further 5–10 minutes. The bread is done when it is golden-brown, feels light and sounds hollow when tapped on the underside.
12 Transfer to a wire rack and drizzle with the remaining oil. Allow to cool.

* If using fast-action or dried yeast, see page 480.

Caramelized Onion and Thyme Focaccia

For maximum flavour the biga (see page 566) should be made 1 day in advance.

MAKES 1 LOAF

For the biga

1 large onion, chopped

2 tablespoons olive oil

1 teaspoon clear honey

150 ml|5 fl oz cool water

10 g|⅓ oz fresh yeast*

1 teaspoon black onion seeds

1 teaspoon coarsely chopped fresh thyme

100 g|3½ oz strong white flour

For the dough

140 g|5 oz strong white flour

1 teaspoon salt

To finish

1 tablespoon olive oil

7 sprigs fresh thyme

1 Place the onion in a saucepan with the olive oil. Cover with a piece of dampened greaseproof paper and cover with a lid. Cook over a low heat until softened, stirring occasionally. This will take about 20 minutes.

2 Remove the lid and paper from the onion and stir in the honey. Cook over a medium heat, stirring, until golden-brown. Place in a bowl.

3 Add the water to the onion then whisk in the yeast. Stir in the onion seed, thyme and flour. Cover with clingfilm and leave at room temperature until doubled in size. Chill overnight.

4 To make the dough, stir the flour and salt into the biga, adding additional water or flour to make a soft dough.

5 Knead for 10 minutes by hand or 6 minutes by machine.

6 Place the dough in an oiled bowl and turn to coat it in a thin film of oil. Cover with oiled clingfilm and leave in a warm place to rise until doubled in size. This will take about 2 hours.

7 To knock back the dough, oil your hands and gently lift the dough. Stretch it to about 50 cm|20 in then fold it in 3, like a business letter. Replace in the bowl.

8 Heat the oven to 200°C|400°F|gas mark 6. Line the base and sides of a 23 × 30 cm|9 × 12 in baking tin with baking parchment.

9 Using oiled hands, lift the dough into the tin. Gently pull it to reach the edges of the tin.

10 Drizzle with the olive oil and scatter over the sprigs of thyme. Cover with oiled clingfilm and leave to rise until doubled in size, about 1 hour.

11 Bake for 30 minutes or until golden-brown. Transfer to a wire rack to cool.

* If using fast-action or dried yeast, see page 480.

Onion, Red Pepper and Herb Bread

This bread can also be made successfully using the jars of grilled or roasted peppers in oil that are available from supermarkets. To vary the filling, crumble 85 g | 3 oz feta cheese into the cold filling before placing it on the dough.

MAKES APPROXIMATELY 12 SQUARES

For the bread
30 g | 1 oz fresh yeast*
225 ml | 8 fl oz lukewarm water
450 g | 1 lb strong white flour
2 teaspoons salt
2 tablespoons olive oil
extra sprigs of thyme
salt and freshly ground black pepper

For the filling
3 red peppers
2 tablespoons olive oil
1 large onion, sliced
1 clove of garlic, crushed
½ teaspoon caster sugar
2 teaspoons balsamic vinegar
2 tablespoons chopped fresh thyme
2 tablespoons chopped fresh basil

1 Dissolve the yeast in the warm water. Sift the flour and salt into a large bowl and make a well in the centre. Pour in the dissolved yeast and the oil. Quickly mix the ingredients to form a dough and then knead for 10 minutes by hand or 6 minutes by machine.

2 Place the dough in an oiled bowl and turn to coat it in oil. Cover with oiled clingfilm and put in a warm, draught-free place to rise for 1 hour or until it has doubled in size.

3 Cut the peppers into quarters and remove their seeds. Grill until their skins are black and blistered then put them into a plastic bag or in a bowl and cover with a plate. Leave to steam for 10 minutes.

4 Heat the olive oil in a saucepan and add the sliced onions. Cover with a lid and cook on a low heat, stirring occasionally until the onions are soft but not coloured. This will take about 25 minutes. Add the garlic and cook for a further 2 minutes.

5 Peel the peppers and cut into slices. Add them to the onions, with the sugar, turn up the heat and allow the peppers and onions to caramelize a little. Add the balsamic vinegar, herbs and some salt and pepper. Boil off any liquid. Put to one side and allow to cool.

6 Grease a roasting tin measuring approximately 20 × 30 cm | 8 × 12 in. Cut the risen dough in half and roll out one half to a rectangle the size and shape of the roasting tin. Cover with the peppers and onions and roll the other piece of dough to the same size. Carefully lay it on top, excluding as much air as possible. Press down and pinch to seal the edges. Cover with oiled clingfilm and leave to prove for 15 minutes.

7 Heat the oven to 200°C | 400°F | gas mark 6. When the dough feels soft and pillowy, make several indentations with your fingers. Drizzle oil into the holes and place sprigs of thyme in the oil. Bake for 30–40 minutes. It should sound hollow when tapped on the underside.

8 Carefully remove from the tin and place on a wire rack to cool. Serve cut into squares.

* If using fast-action or dried yeast, see page 480.

Roasted Pepper Bread

MAKES 12 ROLLS OR 1 LOAF

2 red or yellow peppers

450 g | 1 lb strong white bread flour

1 teaspoon salt

1 teaspoon caster sugar

30 g | 1 oz fresh yeast*

3 tablespoons olive oil

290 ml | 10 fl oz lukewarm water

2 tablespoons shredded fresh basil

2 tablespoons grated Parmesan cheese

1 Heat the oven to 200°C | 400°F | gas mark 6. Grease and line the base of a 23 cm | 9 in square tin with baking parchment cut to fit.

2 Cut the peppers into quarters, remove and discard the seeds. Grease a baking sheet and place the peppers on it, skin-side up. Cook in the oven for 20 minutes or until the skin is blistered and beginning to blacken. Remove from the baking sheet and put in a bowl, covered with a plate, to cool.

3 Sift the flour and salt together into a large bowl. Cream the sugar and yeast together until it becomes liquid. Mix 2 tablespoons of the oil with the water. Add the water and yeast to the flour and mix to form a soft but not wet dough.

4 Using a little flour, knead the dough for 10 minutes by hand or 6 minutes by machine, or until it is smooth and elastic. Place in an oiled bowl and turn the dough to coat it in the oil. Cover with oiled clingfilm and leave in a warm place to rise until it has doubled in size. This will take about 1 hour.

5 Meanwhile, peel the peppers and cut into fine dice. Mix with the basil and Parmesan cheese.

6 Take the dough from the bowl and roll out to a 30 cm | 12 in square. Spread over the peppers, basil and Parmesan, making sure they go right up to the edges.

7 Roll up as tightly as possible and rest on its seam. Cut into 12 slices and lay side by side, cut-side up, in the prepared tin. Cover with the oiled clingfilm and leave in a warm place to prove for approximately 20 minutes or until it is about 1½ times its original size.

8 Remove the clingfilm and put into the oven for 10 minutes. Reduce the heat to 190°C | 375°F | gas mark 5 and continue to bake for a further 20 minutes or until the centre of the bread is cooked.

9 Remove the bread from the oven, turn it out of the tin and place on a wire rack to cool. Brush the top with olive oil to make it shine.

NOTE: This bread is batch-baked in rolls that look like Chelsea buns. Try to ensure that most of the red pepper is tucked into the rolls so that it doesn't burn. Alternatively the red-pepper filling could be kneaded into the dough at stage 6, which could then be baked as a loaf.*

If using fast-action or dried yeast, see page 480.

Ciabatta

MAKES 2 LOAVES

For the biga (see page 566)

15 g | ½ oz fresh yeast*

340 ml | 12 fl oz still mineral water, at room
  temperature

225 g | 8 oz organic strong white flour

For the dough

2 tablespoons olive oil

2 teaspoons fine sea salt

225 g | 8 oz organic strong white flour

To shape

2 tablespoons rice flour, ground rice or polenta

1 For the biga, place the yeast in a large bowl and whisk in the water. Stir in the flour and cover with clingfilm. Leave to stand at a cool room temperature for at least 1 hour or overnight. The longer the starter is left, the more complex the flavour of the finished loaf.

2 For the dough, mix the oil, salt and flour into the starter. The dough will be wet, so it should be kneaded either by machine for 6 minutes until smooth and elastic or by the method described for kneading soft doughs on page 000.

3 Cover the dough with oiled clingfilm and leave at cool room temperature until doubled in size, about 2 hours.

4 To turn the dough, oil your hands to prevent the dough from sticking and scoop the dough from underneath, then fold into thirds, rather like folding a business letter. Return the dough to the bowl and cover with oiled clingfilm for 30 minutes.

5 Meanwhile, heat the oven to 220°C | 425°F | gas mark 7. If using a baking stone, place it in the oven when you turn it on. Place an empty roasting tin in the bottom third of the oven.

6 Sprinkle a peel or baking sheet with the rice flour, ground rice or polenta so that it is thickly and evenly covered.

7 Pour the dough on to the peel or baking sheet. Stretch the dough into a rectangle about 16 × 32 cm | 7 × 14 in, then cut the dough in half lengthways using an oiled knife.

8 Cover the dough with oiled clingfilm and allow to rest for 15 minutes.

9 Remove the clingfilm. If using a baking stone, carefully tip the loaves on to the stone; otherwise, leave the loaves on the baking sheet to bake.

10 Toss a cupful of iced water into the hot roasting tin to produce steam, then bake the loaves in the top third of the oven for 25–30 minutes or until golden-brown. The bread may need to be turned over for the last 5 minutes of baking. The bread will feel light when done and should sound hollow when tapped on the underside. Cool on a wire rack.

* If using fast-action or dried yeast, see page 480.

Sun-dried Tomato Ciabatta

Ciabatta dough is very wet so it must be kneaded by machine. The bubbles are formed by the yeast stretching large holes in the wet dough. It is not knocked back as that would deplete the large bubbles. Instead it is lifted gently with oiled hands then stretched and folded to capture even more air. For the best flavour, make the biga the night before baking and leave at cool room temperature or in the refrigerator.

MAKES 1 LOAF

For the biga (see page 566)

10 g | ⅓ fl oz fresh yeast*
100 ml | 3½ fl oz still mineral water, at room
  temperature
100 g | 3½ oz organic strong white flour

For the dough

2 tablespoons sun-dried tomato oil
140 g | 5 oz strong white flour
1 teaspoon sea salt
55 g | 2 oz oil-packed sundried tomatoes, chopped
2–3 tablespoons rice flour

1 To make the biga, place the yeast and water in a large bowl and whisk to combine. Stir in the flour. Don't worry about lumps. Cover with clingfilm and leave at cool room temperature for at least 2 hours or overnight.

2 To make the dough, mix the oil, flour and salt into the biga. Knead by machine for 6 minutes or by hand for 10 minutes, using the technique for kneading soft doughs on page 485. You should be able to form a gluten window (see photograph) when the dough has been kneaded sufficiently.

3 Cover the bowl with oiled clingfilm and leave to rise until doubled in size, about 1½ hours.

4 Sprinkle the sun-dried tomatoes over the dough. Oil your hands and slip them under the dough. Lift the dough and stretch and fold it into three, like a business letter, to incorporate the sun-dried tomatoes.

5 Return the dough to the bowl and cover with oiled clingfilm for 30 minutes.

6 Meanwhile, heat the oven to 220°C | 425°F | gas mark 7. Sprinkle a baking sheet with the rice flour.

7 Lift the dough from the bowl with oiled hands and place on the rice flour. Stretch the dough into a long loaf shape.

8 Bake in the top third of the oven for 30 minutes. Spray with a plant mister 3 times during the first 5 minutes of baking. Cool on a wire rack.

* If using fast-action or dried yeast, see page 480.

VARIATION

Olive Ciabatta: Substitute olive oil for the sun-dried tomato oil and 55 g | 2 oz pitted black olives, halved, for the sun-dried tomatoes in the recipe above.

Stromboli

Stromboli is a delicious olive oil bread, filled with cheese and ham, which is almost a meal in itself. This recipe was inspired by a cookery demonstration by Ursula Ferrigno.

MAKES 1 LARGE LOAF

For the dough
20 g | ⅔ oz fresh yeast*
200 ml | 7 fl oz lukewarm water
1 teaspoon malt extract
340 g | 12 oz strong white flour
1 teaspoon salt
2 tablespoons olive oil

For the filling
150 g | 5 oz mozzarella
150 g | 5 oz Parma ham
10 g | ⅓ oz fresh basil, stems removed

For the topping
1 tablespoon olive oil
4 sprigs of rosemary
coarse sea salt

1 Place the yeast in a small bowl and mix to a thin cream with a little of the water. Stir in the malt extract. Leave to stand for 5 minutes.
2 Sift the flour and salt into a large bowl and make a well in the centre.
3 Pour the yeast mixture and the olive oil into the well. Stir in, adding enough of the remaining water to make a soft dough.
4 Knead until smooth and satiny, about 10 minutes by hand or 6 minutes by machine.
5 Place in an oiled bowl. Turn the dough to coat it in a thin film of oil. Cover with oiled clingfilm and leave to rise in a warm place until doubled in size, about 1 hour.
6 Lightly flour a work surface. Lift the risen dough out of the bowl and place on the work surface. Pat and stretch the dough into a 20 × 40 cm | 8 × 16 in rectangle.
7 Scatter the cheese, ham and basil over the dough and roll up from one of the long sides. Squeeze the join together to seal the filling inside the dough.
8 Place on an oiled baking sheet and pat to flatten slightly. Cover with oiled clingfilm and leave to prove (rise again) until soft and pillowy. An indentation made with your finger should only spring back about halfway.
9 Meanwhile, heat the oven to 220°C | 425°F | gas mark 7.
10 Brush the risen dough with the olive oil. Divide the rosemary sprigs in two and press on to the top of the dough. Sprinkle with sea salt.
11 Place the dough in the top third of the oven (the hottest part) and bake for 10 minutes, then turn the temperature down to 200°C | 400°F | gas mark 6 and bake for a further 25–30 minutes. The bread will sound hollow when tapped on the underside.
12 Cool on a wire rack for 1 hour before serving.

* If using fast-action or dried yeast, see page 480.

Flat Breads and Pizzas

Flat breads are the most ancient type of bread: similar breads were made by the Egyptians, dating back to 4000 BC. These breads were a simple mixture of coarsely ground grain and water that was baked on a stone hearth. At some point the Egyptians discovered that this bread could be leavened using barm, the foam that rises to the top of a fermenting brew. This making of loaves and rolls is illustrated in the hieroglyphics of Egyptian tombs.

Flat breads are still eaten today in the countries bordering the Mediterranean, as well as throughout the Middle East and India. These flat breads, such as pita, naan and wraps, are also popular in the UK and the USA. The recipes in this book use bakers' yeast as a leavening but do not allow the dough to rise much, as baking the breads in a very hot oven helps them puff up. Flat breads make excellent 'scoops' for eating dips, mezze and curries with your fingers.

Pizza is thought to have evolved from Egyptian flat bread. Translated literally, 'pizza' means 'pie'; however, traditionally this popular food is made with a yeast-leavened flat bread and topped with tomatoes and mozzarella cheese. Soldiers returning home brought pizza from Italy following World War II and now it is eaten throughout the world with every imaginable type of topping.

In restaurants, pizzas are baked in very hot ovens that give a crisp, chewy crust. The best pizzas are baked in wood-fired ovens which impart a delicious smoky flavour. Although this is tricky to duplicate at home, a pizza does benefit from being baked on a pizza or baking stone, a flat ceramic disc which is placed in the oven to heat when it is turned on. The pizza stone will help produce a chewy crust. A large, unglazed ceramic tile can also be used, or you can place a baking sheet in the oven to heat before baking. To transfer your pizza to the stone or tile, slip it from a floured baking sheet or peel (see page 32) on to the hot stone. If you have an Aga, the pizza can be placed directly on to the hot plate for a few seconds after baking, to slightly char and crisp the base.

Middle Eastern Flat Bread with Zahtar

Zahtar is a mixture of dried thyme, sesame seeds and dried, ground sumac that is used in the Middle East and North Africa to flavour bread, meats and vegetables (see **Suppliers**, page 655).

MAKES 8

For the dough
450 g | 1 lb strong white flour
1 teaspoon salt
15 g | ½ oz fresh yeast*
a pinch of sugar
310 ml | 11 fl oz lukewarm water
4 tablespoons olive oil

For the topping
2 tablespoons olive oil
20 g | ⅔ oz zahtar
coarse sea salt

1 Sift the flour with the salt into a large bowl. Make a well in the centre.
2 Place the yeast in a small bowl with the sugar and mix to a thin cream with 3 tablespoons of the water. Add the mixture to the flour.
3 Place the olive oil in the well then add enough water to make a soft dough.
4 Knead until smooth and elastic, about 6 minutes in a machine or 10 minutes by hand.
5 Place the dough in an oiled bowl and turn to coat it in a thin film of oil. Cover with oiled clingfilm and leave to rise at warm room temperature until doubled in size, about 1½ hours.
6 Turn the dough out on to a floured surface and knead for 30 seconds to knock back.
7 Heat the grill to its highest setting and place a baking sheet under the grill about 10 cm | 4 in from the heat source.
8 Divide the dough into 8 equal pieces. Roll each piece as thinly as possible then brush with the olive oil and sprinkle with the zahtar and salt.
9 Bake the bread in batches on the hot baking sheet for about 3–4 minutes. Serve immediately or reheat for 5 minutes in a warm oven before serving.

* If using fast-action or dried yeast, see page 480.

Pitta Bread

MAKES 8

15 g | ½ oz fresh yeast*
1 teaspoon caster sugar
150 ml | 5 fl oz lukewarm water
250 g | 9 oz strong white flour

1 teaspoon salt
2 tablespoons olive oil
2 tablespoons polenta

1 Mix the yeast and sugar with 2 tablespoons of the warm water.
2 Sift the flour and salt into a large bowl and make a well in the centre.
3 Tip the yeast mixture into the well, add the olive oil and enough warm water to make a soft but not too sticky dough.
4 Knead the dough by hand for 10 minutes or by machine for 6 minutes, until smooth.
5 Place the dough in an oiled bowl and turn to coat it in the oil. Cover with oiled clingfilm and leave to rise until doubled in size, about 1 hour.
6 Place the dough on a lightly floured work surface and knock back by kneading for 30 seconds.
7 Divide the dough into 8 balls. Place the polenta on a plate and roll each ball in it. Roll the dough balls into rounds 12 cm | 5 in in diameter.
8 Heat the grill on its highest setting until very hot. Place the dough rounds on to a greased baking sheet (you will need to do this in 2 batches or use 2 baking sheets).
9 Grill the dough about 7.5 cm | 3 in from the heat source for 2 minutes per side, or until puffed and golden-brown. Serve warm. The bread can be reheated, if required, before serving.

* If using fast-action or dried yeast, see page 480.

Pebble Bread

The crevasses in this bread, named after its bumpy surface, are perfect for absorbing the garlic-scented olive oil.

MAKES 1 LOAF

225 g | 8 oz strong white flour
1 teaspoon salt
10 g | ⅓ oz fresh yeast*
150 ml | 5 fl oz lukewarm water

2 tablespoons olive oil
2 cloves of garlic, crushed
coarse sea salt for sprinkling

1 Sift the flour with the salt into a large bowl. Make a well in the centre.
2 In a small bowl, mix the yeast to a thin cream with 2 tablespoons of the water.
3 Pour it into the well, along with 1 tablespoon of the oil. Add enough water to mix to a soft but not sticky dough.
4 Knead for 10 minutes by hand or 6 minutes in a food mixer with a dough hook or for 3 minutes in a food processor.
5 Place in an oiled bowl and turn the dough to coat it in a thin film of oil. Cover with oiled

clingfilm and leave to rise until doubled in size. The dough can be kneaded lightly and chill at this point for up to 24 hours.

6 Mix the garlic with the remaining oil.

7 Place the dough on a lightly floured work surface and pull it into a 30 cm | 12 in round. Place on an oiled baking sheet.

8 Heat the oven to 220°F | 425°C | gas mark 7.

9 Spread the dough with the remaining oil and garlic. Sprinkle over the salt. Allow to prove (rise again) in a warm place for 30 minutes. Push your fingertips into the dough all over to make a dimpled surface.

10 Bake in the top third of the oven for 25 minutes or until golden-brown. Serve warm.

* If using fast-action or dried yeast, see page 480.

Chickpea Flat Bread

This bread has been adapted from a Jamie Oliver recipe. It is delicious served with spicy dips and curries.

MAKES 8

15 g	½ oz fresh yeast*	140 g	5 oz cooked chickpeas, drained and roughly
1 teaspoon sugar	crushed
150 ml	5 fl oz lukewarm water	2 tablespoons chopped fresh coriander
250 g	9 oz strong unbleached white flour	1 teaspoon cumin seeds
1 teaspoon salt	2 tablespoons vegetable oil
	2 tablespoons rice flour

1 Mix the yeast and sugar with the warm water. Sift the flour and salt into a large bowl. Mix in the chickpeas, coriander and cumin seeds then make a well in the centre.

2 Place the yeast liquid and oil into the well and stir to make a soft, slightly sticky dough. Add more water or flour as necessary.

3 Knead until smooth and elastic, about 8–10 minutes by hand or 5–6 minutes in a machine. Place in an oiled bowl and turn to coat in the oil. Cover with oiled clingfilm. Leave in a warm place for about 1 hour or until doubled in size.

4 Place a baking stone or baking sheet in the top third of an oven heated to 220 8C | 425°F | gas mark 7.

5 Sprinkle the work surface with the rice flour. Divide the dough into 8 pieces and place on the rice flour. Pat each piece of dough into a round about 2.5 cm | 1 in thick. Keep the dough covered with clingfilm or a tea towel to keep it from drying out.

6 As the dough starts to puff again, after about 5–10 minutes, place it on the hot baking stone or baking sheet and bake in the top third of the oven for 15 minutes or until golden-brown. You will probably need to bake the breads in several batches.

7 Cool slightly on a wire rack. Serve warm.

* If using fast-action or dried yeast, see page 480.

Pide Dough

These Turkish flat breads, pronounced *pee-day*, are served as a base for a topping, much like pizza. They make a delicious snack or lunch.

SERVES 4

15 g | ½ oz fresh yeast*

1 teaspoon caster sugar

115–150 ml | 4–5 fl oz lukewarm water

2 tablespoons plain yoghurt

250 g | 9 oz strong white flour

1 teaspoon salt

1 tablespoon olive oil

1 egg, beaten

2 teaspoons sesame seeds or black onion seeds

1 Place the yeast in a bowl with the caster sugar. Stir in the water, yoghurt and 50 g | 1¾ oz flour. Cover with clingfilm and leave to stand at room temperature for 30 minutes.

2 Sift the remaining flour with the salt into a large bowl. Make a well in the centre and add the olive oil and yeast mixture. Stir to a soft but not sticky dough.

3 Knead for 10 minutes by hand or 6 minutes by machine until the dough is smooth.

4 Place in an oiled bowl and turn to coat in the oil. Cover with clingfilm and leave to rise until doubled in size, about 1½ hours.

5 Meanwhile heat the oven to 220°C | 425°F | gas mark 7.

6 Knock back the dough by kneading lightly for 30 seconds. Return to the bowl, cover with clingfilm and leave to rest for 15 minutes.

7 Divide the dough into 4 pieces. Roll each piece into a flat oval 15 cm | 6 in long, 10 cm | 4 in wide and ½ cm | ¼ in thick.

8 Place on an oiled baking sheet. Cover with oiled clingfilm. Leave to prove (rise again) for 30 minutes. Remove the clingfilm and press your fingers firmly into the centre of the pide to flatten the centres, leaving a border of 2.5 cm | 1 in.

9 Brush the pide with the beaten egg and sprinkle with the seeds.

10 Bake for 10–15 minutes, then place your desired topping in the centre and return to the oven for a further 10 minutes. Serve warm.

* If using fast-action or dried yeast, see page 480.

Feta and Herb Pide

These Peynirli pide can be made in miniature for cocktail canapés.

MAKES 4

1 recipe pide dough (see above)

For the topping

1 egg, beaten

100 g | 3½ oz feta cheese, roughly crumbled

3 tablespoons finely chopped fresh dill

2 tablespoons finely chopped flat-leaf parsley

freshly ground black pepper

ground cayenne pepper (optional)

1 Heat the oven to 200°C|400°F|gas mark 6.

2 Make and half-bake the pide according to the recipe on page 534.

3 For the filling, place the egg in a bowl and stir in the cheese and herbs. Season with pepper and cayenne pepper, if using.

4 Divide the filling between the pide, spreading the mixture 1 cm|½ in from the edge.

5 Bake for a further 10 minutes for large pide or 5 minutes for cocktail-size pide. Serve warm.

Spicy Lamb Pide

MAKES 4

1 recipe pide dough (see page 534)

For the filling

2 tablespoons olive oil

1 small onion, chopped

1 clove of garlic, crushed

225 g|8 oz minced lamb

55 ml|2 fl oz white wine

1 teaspoon ground coriander

1 teaspoon ground cumin

½ teaspoon ground ginger

a pinch of ground cinnamon

a pinch of ground cayenne pepper

200 g|7 oz chopped tomatoes

150 ml|5 fl oz water

salt and freshly ground black pepper

To serve

2 tablespoons chopped fresh coriander

1 Heat the oven to 200°C|400°F|gas mark 6.

2 Make and half-bake the pide according to the recipe on page 000.

3 For the filling, place half the olive oil in a sauté pan and stir in the onion. Cover with a dampened piece of greaseproof paper and cook over a low heat until softened, about 10–15 minutes. Remove the paper and turn up the heat slightly to brown the onions. Stir in the garlic and cook for a further 30 seconds. Remove from the pan and set aside.

4 Place the remaining olive oil in the sauté pan and brown the lamb over a medium heat. Remove with a slotted spoon and place in a sieve over a bowl to drain away any excess fat. Remove any excess fat from the pan.

5 Add the wine to the hot pan and scrape the bottom to remove the brown colour. Return the meat to the pan, stir in the spices and cook for a further minute then add the tomatoes and water. Add the onions and garlic.

6 Transfer to a small saucepan and cook at a low simmer, uncovered, for 1 hour or until the meat is tender and the sauce is no longer watery. Season with salt and pepper.

7 Divide the filling between the pide, spreading the mixture 1 cm|½ in from the edge.

8 Bake for a further 10 minutes and serve warm. Garnish with the fresh coriander.

Naan

This flat bread is served as an accompaniment to Indian curries and grilled meats.

MAKES 8

450g | 1 lb strong white flour

2 teaspoons salt

15 g | ½ oz fresh yeast*

1 teaspoon sugar

90–150ml | 3–5 fl oz lukewarm milk

2 tablespoons sesame oil

150 ml | 3–5 fl oz plain yoghurt

1 egg, beaten

1 Sift the flour and salt into a bowl.

2 Mix the yeast with the sugar, then mix with the milk, oil, yoghurt and egg.

3 Mix the yeast mixture into the flour to form a soft but not sticky dough. Knead by hand for 5 minutes or until smooth.

4 Put the dough into an oiled bowl and turn to coat with a thin film of oil. Cover with oiled clingfilm and leave to rise in a warm place until doubled in size.

5 Turn the dough on to a floured surface and knead for 1 further minute.

6 Divide the dough into 8 equal pieces and roll each piece into an oval measuring about 12.5 × 20 cm | 5 × 8 in. Place on a greased baking sheet, cover with clingfilm and leave to rise for about 15 minutes or until 1½ times their original size.

7 Heat the grill to its highest setting.

8 Brush the bread with water and grill on each side for 3 minutes or until well-browned. Serve warm.

* If using fast-action or dried yeast, see page 480.

Peshwari Naan

MAKES 4

For the dough

170 ml | 6 fl oz water

10 g | ⅓ oz fresh yeast*

1 tablespoon natural yoghurt

15 g | ½ oz butter or ghee, melted and cooled

50 g | 1¾ oz creamed coconut

300 g | 10½ oz strong white flour

1 teaspoon salt

For the filling

4 tablespoons sweetened desiccated coconut

2 tablespoons raisins or sultanas

2 tablespoons flaked almonds

additional melted butter or ghee for brushing

1 Place the water in a large bowl and stir in the yeast, yoghurt and butter. Crumble the creamed coconut into the water.

2 Stir in the flour and salt then knead until smooth and elastic, about 10 minutes by hand or 6 minutes by machine.

3 Place the dough in an oiled bowl and turn to coat it in a thin film of oil. Cover with oiled clingfilm and leave to rise in a warm place until doubled in size, about 1 hour.

4 Heat the grill to its highest setting. Place a baking sheet under the grill, about 12 cm | 5 in from the heat source.

5 Divide the dough into 8 pieces and roll each piece as thinly as possible into rounds. Divide the coconut, raisins and flaked almonds between four of the rounds, leaving a border of about 1 cm | ½ in.

6 Place a second round of dough on top of the filling and press with your fingers to seal. Cover with oiled clingfilm and leave to stand for 15 minutes.

7 Brush the naan on both sides with the melted butter or ghee and place on the heated baking sheet to grill for 2–3 minutes per side or until golden-brown. Wrap in a tea towel and serve warm.

* If using fast-action or dried yeast, see page 480.

Coriander and Onion Seed Naan

MAKES 4

170 ml | 6 fl oz water
10 g | ⅓ oz fresh yeast*
1 tablespoon natural yoghurt
15 g | ½ oz butter or ghee, melted and cooled
300 g | 10½ oz strong white flour

1 teaspoon salt
1 teaspoon black onion seeds
3 tablespoons chopped fresh coriander
additional melted butter or ghee for brushing

1 Place the water in a large bowl and stir in the yeast, yoghurt and butter.

2 Stir in the flour, salt, onion seeds and coriander, then knead until smooth and elastic, about 10 minutes by hand or 5 minutes by machine.

3 Place the dough an oiled bowl and turn to coat in a thin film of oil. Cover with oiled clingfilm and leave to rise in a warm place until doubled in size, about 1 hour.

4 Heat the grill to its highest setting. Place a baking sheet under the grill, about 12 cm | 5 in from the heat source.

5 Divide the dough into 4 pieces and roll each piece into an oval about 1 cm | ½ in thick. Cover with oiled clingfilm and leave to stand for 15 minutes.

6 Brush the naan on both sides with the melted butter or ghee and place on the heated baking sheet to grill for 2–3 minutes per side or until golden-brown. Wrap in a tea towel and serve warm.

* If using fast-action or dried yeast, see page 480.

Sheet Music Bread

This thin, crisp flat bread is a traditional Sardinian bread. It is a good accompaniment to mezze or a cheese course.

MAKES ABOUT 12 PIECES

20 g|⅔ oz fresh yeast*

a pinch of sugar

200 ml|7 fl oz luke-warm water

340 g|12 oz strong white flour

1 teaspoon sea salt

2 tablespoons olive oil

olive oil for brushing

sea salt for sprinkling

1 tablespoon coarsely chopped fresh rosemary

1 Place the yeast and sugar in a small bowl and mix with 2 tablespoons of the warm water to form a thin cream.

2 Sift the flour with the salt into a large bowl and make a well in the centre.

3 Pour the yeast mixture into the well and add the olive oil and enough water to make a soft but not sticky dough.

4 Turn the dough on to a floured surface and knead for 10 minutes by hand, adding more flour if the dough is too sticky, to make a smooth dough. If using a machine, knead for 6 minutes.

5 Place the dough in an oiled bowl and turn to coat in the oil. Chill for at least 10 minutes.

6 Meanwhile, heat the oven to 230°C|450°F|gas mark 8. Place an oiled baking sheet in the oven.

7 Divide the dough into 12 pieces. Using one piece of dough at a time and keeping the other pieces covered with clingfilm, roll as thinly as possible. Brush with oil then sprinkle with sea salt and rosemary.

8 Place the thin dough on to the hot baking sheet and bake for 5–7 minutes or until golden and slightly puffed.

9 Cool slightly on a wire rack before serving.

* If using fast-action or dried yeast, see page 480.

Seed Crackers

MAKES ABOUT 20

20 g | ⅔ oz fresh yeast*

a pinch of sugar

150 ml | 5 fl oz lukewarm water

225 g | 8 oz strong white flour

1 teaspoon sea salt

1 tablespoon olive oil

olive oil for brushing

sea salt for sprinkling

2 tablespoons sesame and/or onion seeds

1 Place the fresh yeast and the sugar in a small bowl and mix with 2 tablespoons warm water to form a thin cream.

2 Sift the flour with the salt into a large bowl and make a well in the centre.

3 Pour the yeast mixture into the well and add the olive oil and enough water to make a soft but not sticky dough.

4 Turn the dough on to a floured surface and knead for 10 minutes by hand or 6 minutes by machine, adding more flour if the dough is too sticky, to make a smooth dough.

5 Place the dough in an oiled bowl and turn to coat in the oil. Chill for at least 10 minutes.

6 Meanwhile, heat the oven to 230°C | 450°F | gas mark 8. Place an oiled baking sheet in the oven.

7 Divide the dough into 20 pieces. Using one piece of dough at a time and keeping the other pieces covered with clingfilm, roll as thinly as possible. A pasta machine is useful for this if you have one. Brush the pieces of dough with oil then sprinkle with sea salt and seeds.

8 Place the thin dough on to the hot baking sheet and bake for 5 minutes or until golden and slightly puffed.

9 Cool slightly on a wire rack before serving.

* If using fast-action or dried yeast, see page 480.

Grissini

MAKES 20

7 g|¼ oz fresh yeast*

2 teaspoons sugar

3 tablespoons lukewarm water

1 teaspoon sea salt

150 ml|5 fl oz boiling water

225 g|8 oz strong white flour

1 tablespoon olive oil

1 egg, beaten

1 Heat the oven to 150°C|300°F|gas mark 2.
2 Dissolve the yeast and sugar in the lukewarm water.
3 Dissolve the sea salt in the boiling water then allow to cool to blood temperature.
4 Sift the flour into a large bowl. Make a well in the centre and pour in the yeast mixture, the salted water and the oil. Mix to a soft dough.
5 Tip the dough on to a floured surface and knead for 3–4 minutes or until smooth and elastic. Cover with a damp cloth and leave for 5 minutes. Knead for 3 minutes and then divide into 20 equal pieces.
6 Roll out each piece of dough until it is ½ cm|¼ in thickness. Place on oiled baking sheets and prove (allow to rise again) for 10–15 minutes.
7 Sprinkle with sea salt and bake in the oven for about 45 minutes or until crisp and golden-brown.

* If using fast-action or dried yeast, see page 480.

Black and White Sesame Bread Sticks

MAKES 16

7 g|¼ oz fresh yeast*

a pinch of caster sugar

150 ml|5 fl oz luke warm water

225 g|8 oz strong white flour

1 teaspoon sea salt

3 tablespoons olive oil

3 tablespoons black sesame seeds

3 tablespoons white sesame seeds

1 egg white, beaten

coarse sea salt for sprinkling

1 Mix the yeast with the sugar and water.
2 Sift the flour and salt into a large bowl and make a well in the centre. Pour in the yeast liquid and the olive oil and mix to a soft dough, adding more flour or water as required.
3 Knead for 10 minutes by hand or 6 minutes by machine to a smooth dough.
4 Cover the dough with oiled clingfilm and leave to rise for 20 minutes.
5 Meanwhile, heat the oven to 150°C|300°F|gas mark 2.
6 Divide the dough in half. Knead 1 tablespoon of each type of sesame seeds into each half

of the dough then divide them into 8 equal-sized pieces. Roll with your fingers into 30 cm | 12 in long sticks. Place on lightly greased baking sheets.

7 Brush the sticks with the egg white then sprinkle with the remaining seeds and sea salt.

8 Bake in the top third of the oven for 45 minutes or until golden-brown and firm to the touch.

9 Cool on a wire rack and store in an airtight container.

* If using fast-action or dried yeast, see page 480.

Parmesan Grissini

These can be mixed in a food processor for 30 seconds, if desired.

MAKES 20

7 g | ¼ oz fresh yeast*

2 teaspoons sugar

3 tablespoons lukewarm water

½ teaspoon sea salt

150 ml | 5 fl oz boiling water

225 g | 8 oz strong white flour

1 tablespoon olive oil

55 g | 2 oz Parmesan cheese, finely grated

coarse sea salt for sprinkling

1 Heat the oven to 150°C | 300°F | gas mark 2.

2 Dissolve the yeast and sugar in the lukewarm water.

3 Dissolve the sea salt in the boiling water then leave to cool to blood temperature.

4 Sift the flour into a large bowl. Make a well in the centre and pour in the yeast mixture, the salted water, oil and Parmesan cheese. Mix to a soft dough.

5 Tip the dough on to a floured work surface and knead for 3–4 minutes or until smooth and elastic. Cover with oiled clingfilm and leave for 5 minutes. Knead for 30 seconds and then divide into 20 equal pieces.

6 Roll out each piece of dough until it is a thin finger thickness. Place on oiled baking sheets and prove (allow to rise again) for 10–15 minutes.

7 Sprinkle with sea salt and bake in the oven for about 45 minutes or until crisp and golden-brown.

* If using fast-action or dried yeast, see page 480.

Pizza

MAKES 1 × 25 CM|10 IN PIZZA

For the dough

200 g|7 oz plain flour

½ teaspoon salt

10 g|⅓ oz fresh yeast*

a pinch of sugar

115 ml|4 fl oz lukewarm water

2 tablespoons olive oil

For the topping

1 small onion, chopped

2 tablespoons olive oil

2 cloves of garlic, crushed

1 × 400 g|14 oz tin plum tomatoes

1 tablespoon tomato purée

1 teaspoon dried oregano

½ teaspoon dried basil

1 bay leaf

1 teaspoon sugar

115 g|4 oz grated mozzarella cheese

1 tablespoon freshly grated Parmesan cheese

salt and freshly ground black pepper

1 For the topping, place the onion in a small saucepan and stir in the oil. Cover with a piece of dampened greaseproof paper and a lid and cook over a low to medium heat until softened.

2 Remove the lid and paper, stir in the garlic and cook for a further minute.

3 Stir in the plum tomatoes and crush them with a wooden spoon. Stir in the tomato purée, oregano, basil, bay leaf and sugar. Cook over a low heat for 1 hour. Remove the bay leaf and season to taste. Allow to cool.

4 For the dough, sift the flour and salt into a bowl. Make a well in the centre.

5 Mix the yeast to a thin cream with the sugar and 2 tablespoons of the water. Pour into the well. Add the olive oil to the well then add enough water to make a soft dough.

6 Knead for 10 minutes by hand or 6 minutes by machine.

7 Place in an oiled bowl and turn to coat in the oil. Cover with oiled clingfilm and leave to rise in a warm place until doubled in size, about 1 hour.

8 Meanwhile, heat the oven to 220°C|425°F|gas mark 7.

9 Turn out the dough and knead for 30 seconds.

10 Roll into a 25 cm|10 in circle and place on a greased baking sheet or pizza stone.

11 Spread with the sauce then sprinkle with the cheeses.

12 Bake for 20–25 minutes or until the crust is golden-brown.

* If using fast-action or dried yeast, see page 480.

Mediterranean Vegetable Pizzas

This is a wet dough that needs to be made in a food processor or with a free-standing mixer. The vegetables can be grilled if preferred.

MAKES 4 MINI PIZZAS OR 1 LARGE PIZZAS

For the dough

250 g | 9 oz strong white flour

1 teaspoon salt

10 g | ⅓ oz fresh yeast*

2 tablespoons olive oil

170 ml | 6 fl oz lukewarm water

For the topping

1 small aubergine, sliced into 1 cm | ½ in thick, 5 cm | 2 in long strips

1 red pepper, cored and sliced into 1 cm | ½ in × 3 cm | 1 ½ strips

1 yellow pepper, cored and sliced into 1 cm | ½ in × 3 cm | 1 ½ strips

1 medium courgette, halved and sliced into ½ cm | ¼ in strips

2 red onions, peeled, halved and sliced into ½ cm | ¼ in pieces

4 tablespoons olive oil

1 clove of garlic, crushed

100 g | 3½ oz feta cheese, crumbled

10 g | ⅓ oz fresh basil, chopped

freshly ground black pepper

4 tablespoons sun-dried tomato paste

1 Place the flour and salt in the bowl of a food processor fitted with the mixing blade or a free-standing mixer fitted with a dough hook.

2 Whisk together the yeast, olive oil and water and tip into the bowl. Pour into the flour. Process for 1 minute in a food processor or knead for 5 minutes by machine.

3 Cover with oiled clingfilm and leave to rise until doubled in size.

4 Knead the dough for 30 seconds to knock back, then shape the dough into 4 × 15 cm | 6 in diameter discs or a disc measuring 30 cm | 12 in diameter, using extra flour as required. Place on a floured peel or rimless baking sheet.

5 Prick the centre all over to 2.5 cm | 1 in of the rim then brush with olive oil. Cover with clingfilm and leave to rise for 30 minutes.

6 Meanwhile, heat the oven to 220°C | 425°F | gas mark 7. Place a pizza stone in the oven.

7 Toss the vegetables with 2 tablespoons of the oil and the garlic and place in a single layer in a roasting tin.

8 Roast for 15 minutes, turning occasionally, until soft and lightly browned. Place on a plate to cool.

9 Slide the pizzas from the peel or baking sheet on to the pizza stone and bake for 15 minutes. Spread with the sun-dried tomato paste.

10 Scatter the roasted vegetables over the pizzas then top with the cheese, basil and freshly ground black pepper. Return to the oven for a further 5 minutes. Serve warm.

* If using fast-action or dried yeast, see page 480.

Deep Pan Pizza

This recipe makes a very wet dough, so it is best made in a food processor. The wet dough results in a very light base. There is enough sauce for two pizzas, so double up the dough recipe if you wish or save the sauce for another time. The sauce can be frozen for up to 6 months.

MAKES 1 × 35 CM | 14 IN PIZZA

For the dough

300 g | 10½ oz strong white flour

1 teaspoon salt

1 teaspoon fast-action yeast

1 tablespoon olive oil

200 ml | 7 fl oz lukewarm water

For the topping

1 small red onion

1 tablespoon olive oil

170 g | 6 oz chorizo, diced

1 clove of garlic, crushed

1 × 400 g | 14 oz tin plum tomatoes in tomato juice

a pinch of caster sugar

1 tablespoon tomato purée

1 teaspoon dried oregano

2 large leaves of fresh basil, shredded

85 g | 3 oz grated mozzarella (enough for 1 pizza)

1 For the dough, place all the ingedients in the food processor and process for 30 seconds on the lowest speed. Liberally oil a large bowl then scrape the dough into the bowl using a plastic spatula. Turn the dough several times with the spatula to smooth the surface.

2 Cover the dough with oiled clingfilm and leave in a warm place to rise until doubled in size, about 45 minutes.

3 Meanwhile, make the sauce. Place the onion and oil in a sauté pan and cook over a low heat until softened. Alternatively, place in a small bowl and microwave on high for 3 minutes and leave to stand for 2 minutes before turning into the sauté pan.

4 When the onion is soft, add the chorizo and fry over a medium heat for 5 minutes. Add the garlic and cook for 1 further minute.

5 Add the tomatoes and juice. Bash the tomatoes with a spoon to break them up. Add the sugar, tomato purée and oregano. Cook over a medium heat, stirring frequently until thick and paste-like. Set aside.

6 Oil a baking sheet or a shallow 35 cm | 14 in pizza plate. Heat the oven to 220°C | 425°F | gas mark 7.

7 Scrape the dough on to the baking sheet or tin and smooth a little oil over the top, using your fingers. Flatten the dough to 35 cm | 14 in by pushing it gently with your fingers. Cover with oiled clingfilm and leave in a warm place to rise for 20 minutes or until puffy.

8 Pat the dough again all over, except for a 2.5 cm | 1 in rim. Place the pizza in the oven and bake for 5 minutes or until a crust has formed on the top.

9 Remove from the oven and spread over half of the tomato sauce and sprinkle with the basil and cheese. Return to the oven for 15–20 minutes or until well-browned. Serve immediately.

Spiced Beef Calzone

The spiced filling for these calzone was inspired by the calzone at Sally Clarke's wonderful bakery.

MAKES 4

For the dough

250 g | 9 oz strong white flour

1 teaspoon salt

10 g | ⅓ oz fresh yeast*

2 tablespoons olive oil

170 ml | 6 fl oz lukewarm water

For the filling

2 tablespoons olive oil

1 small onion, chopped

1 clove of garlic, crushed

225 g | 8 oz minced beef

55 ml | 2 fl oz red wine

1 teaspoon dried oregano

½ teaspoon dried basil

a pinch of ground cinnamon

a pinch of ground cayenne

200 g | 7 oz chopped tomatoes

150 ml | 5 fl oz water

55 g | 2 oz raisins

55 g | 2 oz toasted pine nuts

salt and freshly ground black pepper

1 To make the dough, place the flour and salt into the bowl of a food processor fitted with the mixing blade or a mixer fitted with a dough hook.

2 Whisk together the yeast, olive oil and water and tip into the bowl. Pour into the flour. Process for 1 minute in a food processor or knead for 5 minutes by machine.

3 Cover with oiled clingfilm and leave to rise until doubled in size.

4 For the filling, place half the olive oil in a sauté pan and stir in the onion. Cover with a dampened piece of greaseproof paper and cook over a low heat until softened. Remove the paper and turn up the heat slightly to brown the onions. Stir in the garlic and cook for a further 30 seconds. Remove from the pan and set aside.

5 Place the remaining olive oil in the sauté pan and brown the beef over a medium heat. Remove with a slotted spoon and place in a sieve over a bowl to drain away any excess fat. Remove any excess fat from the pan.

6 Add the wine to the hot pan and scrape the bottom to remove the brown colour. Return the meat to the pan along with the tomatoes, herbs and water. Add the onions and garlic.

7 Transfer to a small saucepan and cook at a low simmer, uncovered, for 1 hour or until the meat is tender and the sauce is no longer watery. Season with salt and pepper.

8 Stir in the raisins and pine nuts and leave to cool.

9 Meanwhile, heat the oven to 220°C | 425°F | gas mark 7.

10 Turn the dough out on to a lightly floured surface and divide into 4 pieces. Roll out each piece to 15 cm | 6 in in diameter.

11 Divide the filling between the 4 rounds, placing it on one half of each round. Fold over the other half of the dough to make a half-moon shape. Fold and twist the edges together.

12 Place on a greased baking sheet and brush with a little olive oil. Make a couple of small slits in the top of the calzones to let out the steam.

13 Bake in the top of the oven for 15–20 minutes or until golden-brown. Serve warm.

* If using fast-action or dried yeast, see page 480.

Ricotta Calzone

This dough is sticky and is most easily made in a food processor or free-standing mixer.

MAKES 4

For the dough

250 g | 9 oz strong white flour

1 teaspoon salt

10 g | ⅓ oz fresh yeast*

2 tablespoons olive oil

170 ml | 6 fl oz lukewarm water

For the filling

1 tablespoon olive oil

1 clove of garlic, crushed

250 g | 9 oz full-fat ricotta

140 g | 5 oz grated mozzarella

30 g | 1 oz Parmesan cheese, freshly grated

1 tablespoon chopped fresh basil

salt and freshly ground black pepper

1 To make the dough, place the flour and salt into the bowl of a food processor fitted with the mixing blade or a free-standing mixer fitted with a dough hook.

2 Whisk together the yeast, olive oil and water and tip into the bowl. Pour into the flour. Process for 1 minute in a food processor or knead for 5 minutes by machine.

3 Cover with oiled clingfilm and leave to rise until doubled in size.

4 Meanwhile, make the filling. Place the olive oil in a small saucepan and stir in the garlic. Cook over a low heat for 2 minutes. Leave to cool.

5 Mix together the ricotta, mozzarella, Parmesan and basil. Stir in the cooled garlic then season to taste with salt and pepper.

6 Heat the oven to 220°C | 425°F | gas mark 7.

7 Turn the dough out on to a lightly floured surface and divide into 4 pieces. Roll each to in a diameter of 10 cm | 4 in.

8 Divide the filling between the rounds of dough, placing it on one half of each round. Fold over the other half of the dough to make a half-moon shape. Twist the edges together like a Cornish pasty.

9 Place on a greased baking sheet and brush with a little olive oil. Make a couple of small slits in the top of the calzones to let out the steam.

10 Bake in the top third of the oven for 15–20 minutes or until golden-brown. Serve warm.

* If using fast-action or dried yeast, see page 480.

Rolls, Baps and Buns

The recipes in this section are for breads that are baked in individual serving sizes. They can be served as dinner rolls to accompany a first course or cheese, or they can be split and filled to eat as a sandwich. Bagels are also included here: they are delicious toasted and spread with cream cheese for breakfast, or filled and eaten like a sandwich.

Sizing

Dinner rolls are usually made using 35–40 g | 1 ¼ – 1 ½ oz of dough, while baps are normally larger, using 55–60 g | 2–2 ¼ oz of dough. Baps can be served for breakfast or lunch, and they are of course the ubiquitous holder for hamburgers.

When shaping these individual breads it is important to make them all the same size. This way they bake at the same rate and each person will have the same size serving.

Shaping

Dinner rolls are made using approximately 35 g | 1 ¼ oz dough. Place the dough on a smooth work surface and, working around the circumference of the dough, **(a)** bring the edges up to meet in the centre. **(b)** Cup your hand over the dough ball and roll gently on the surface. Turn the ball over so that the smooth side is uppermost.

Shaping dinner rolls (a)

Shaping dinner rolls (b)

Baps are made using 55 g | 2 oz dough and are shaped in the same manner as for dinner rolls (above). They should be flattened with the palm of the hand once placed on the baking sheet.

Plain roll

Bap

Knot

Knots are made by rolling 45 g | 1½ oz dough for each knot into a 10 cm | 4 in sausage shape which is then tied into a knot with the ends tucked underneath.

Soft White Dinner Rolls

MAKES 24 ROLLS

290 ml | 10 fl oz milk
450 g | 1 lb strong plain flour
2 teaspoons salt
20 g | ⅔ oz fresh yeast*
1 teaspoon caster sugar

30 g | 1 oz butter
1 egg, lightly beaten

To glaze
1 egg, beaten

1 Place the milk in a small saucepan and heat gently until steaming. Allow to cool until lukewarm then skim.
2 Sift the flour with the salt into a large mixing bowl and rub in the butter.
3 Dissolve the yeast with a little of the milk and the sugar in a small bowl.
4 Pour the yeast mixture, milk and beaten egg into the flour and mix to a soft dough. Add flour if the dough is too sticky. When the dough will leave the sides of the bowl, press it into a ball and tip out on to a work surface.
5 Knead the dough until it is elastic, smooth and shiny, about 10 minutes by hand or 6 minutes by machine.
6 Put the dough back into a lightly oiled bowl and turn to coat with the oil. Cover the bowl with a piece of lightly oiled clingfilm.
7 Put it in a warm, draught-free place and leave the dough to rise until it has doubled in size, about 1 hour.
8 Knock back the dough and knead for 30 seconds. Heat the oven to 200°C | 400°F | gas mark 6. Lightly oil 2 baking sheets.
9 Divide the dough into 24 pieces of equal size (ideally they should weigh 35 g | 1 ¼ oz each) and shape into dinner rolls. Place on the baking sheets. Cover with oiled clingfilm.
10 Prove (allow to rise again) until they are soft and pillowy. Brush with beaten egg, taking care not to let the egg drip on to the baking sheet or the rolls will stick to the sheet.
11 Bake for 15–18 minutes or until the rolls are golden and sound hollow when tapped on the underside.
12 Place on a wire rack. Cover the rolls with a clean tea towel whilst they are still warm to keep them soft. Serve warm.

* If using fast-action or dried yeast, see page 480.

Bridge Rolls

These delicate rolls are delicious filled with soft, savoury fillings for tea.

MAKES 18

200 ml | 7 fl oz milk

340 g | 12 oz strong white flour

1 teaspoon fine sea salt

30 g | 1 oz butter

10 g | ⅓ oz fresh yeast*

1 tablespoon caster sugar

1 egg, beaten

To glaze

additional milk

1 Place the milk in a saucepan and heat until it steams. Cool until lukewarm then skim.

2 Sift the flour and salt into a bowl. Using your fingertips, rub the butter into the flour.

3 Mix the yeast and sugar with 2 tablespoons of the milk.

4 Make a well in the centre of the flour and add the yeast mixture, milk and egg. Stir to make a soft dough, adding additional milk or flour as required.

5 Knead the dough by hand for 10 minutes or by machine for 5 minutes.

6 Place the dough in an oiled bowl and turn to coat it with oil. Cover with oiled clingfilm and leave in a warm place to rise for 1½ hours or until doubled in size.

7 Knead the dough lightly to knock it back then divide it into 18 equal-sized pieces.

8 Heat the oven to 200°C | 400°F | gas mark 6.

9 Shape each piece into an oval then place on a greased baking sheet. Cover with lightly oiled clingfilm and prove at room temperature for 30–45 minutes or until nearly doubled in size. Brush with milk.

10 Place in the top third of the oven and bake for 15–20 minutes or until golden-brown.

11 Cool on a wire rack covered with a clean, dry tea towel.

* If using fast-action or dried yeast, see page 480.

Baps

MAKES 8

450 g | 1 lb strong white flour

2 teaspoons salt

15 g | ½ oz fresh yeast*

1 teaspoon caster sugar

150 ml | 5 fl oz lukewarm water

150 ml | 5 fl oz lukewarm milk

To glaze

1 tablespoon milk

1 Sift the flour and salt into a large bowl. Cream the yeast with the sugar and a little of the water. Add the yeast mixture, water and milk to the flour. Mix to make a soft but not wet dough. Add extra flour if necessary.

2 Knead for 10 minutes by hand or 6 minutes by machine, or until it is smooth and elastic. Place the dough in an oiled bowl and turn it to coat in the oil. Cover with oiled clingfilm and leave in a warm place to rise for 1 hour or until it has doubled in size.

3 Heat the oven to 200°C | 400°F | gas mark 6. Grease a large baking sheet.

4 Knock back the dough on a floured work surface and divide into 8 pieces. Shape each piece into a round roll and flatten with your hand. Place on the baking sheet. Repeat with the other 7 pieces, using 2 baking sheets if necessary. Cover with oiled clingfilm and allow to prove for 20 minutes or until the rolls have risen by 1½ times their original size.

5 Glaze with the milk, lightly dust with sifted white flour and make an indentation in the centre of each one with your thumb to about 1 cm | ½ in deep. This helps to keep them flat during baking.

6 Bake the rolls for 15–20 minutes or until they sound hollow on the underside when tapped. Place on a wire rack and cover with a clean tea towel to cool and soften the top.

* If using fast-action or dried yeast, see page 480.

VARIATION

Wholemeal baps: To make wholemeal baps use 225g | 8oz strong white flour and 225g | 8oz strong wholemeal flour. Glaze the proved baps with beaten egg and sprinkle with sesame seeds.

Hard Rolls

These popular, crusty rolls, ubiquitous in American restaurants and supermarkets, are like small baguettes.

MAKES 16

For the starter

150 ml|5 fl oz cool water

5 g|⅙ oz fresh yeast*

1 teaspoon caster sugar

140 g|5 oz organic strong white flour

For the dough

340 g|12 oz organic strong white flour

2 teaspoons salt

10 g|⅓ oz fresh yeast*

2 tablespoons vegetable oil

1 teaspoon caster sugar

150 ml|5 fl oz lukewarm water

To finish

melted butter

1 For the starter, place the water in a bowl and whisk in the yeast. Stir in the sugar and flour then cover with clingfilm and allow to stand at room temperature for 24 hours.

2 For the dough, sift the flour into a large bowl with the salt. Make a well in the centre. Scrape the starter into the well then crumble in the yeast and add the vegetable oil, sugar and water.

3 Mix to a soft but not sticky dough, adding more water or flour as required.

4 Knead for 6 minutes by machine or 10 minutes by hand to make a smooth, elastic dough.

5 Place in an oiled bowl, turning the dough to coat it in a thin film of oil. Cover with oiled clingfilm then leave to rise until doubled in size, about 1½ hours.

6 Turn the dough out on to the work surface and knead for 30 seconds to knock back.

7 Divide the dough into 16 equal-sized pieces. Shape each piece into an oval. Press the handle of a wooden spoon lengthways into each oval to form a crease. Pinch the ends and pull to elongate.

8 Place on to two greased baking sheets and brush with melted butter.

9 Cover with oiled clingfilm. Allow to prove (rise again) until soft and pillowy.

10 Meanwhile heat the oven to 200°C|400°F|gas mark 6.

11 Bake the rolls in the top third of the oven for 20 minutes or until golden-brown. Cool on a wire rack.

* If using fast-action or dried yeast, see page 480.

Parkerhouse Rolls

These buttery rolls take their name from a famous Boston restaurant.

MAKES 16

For the starter

150 ml | 5 fl oz cool water
5 g | ⅙ fresh yeast*
1 teaspoon caster sugar
140 g | 5 oz organic strong white flour

For the dough

150 ml | 5 fl oz milk
340 g | 12 oz organic strong white flour
2 teaspoons salt
10 g | ⅓ oz fresh yeast*
2 tablespoons vegetable oil
1 teaspoon caster sugar

To finish

melted butter

1　For the starter, place the water in a bowl and whisk in the yeast. Stir in the sugar and flour then cover with clingfilm and allow to stand at room temperature for 24 hours.

2　For the dough, heat the milk in a small saucepan until steaming then allow to cool until lukewarm. Skim.

3　Sift the flour into a large bowl with the salt. Make a well in the centre. Scrape the starter into the well then crumble in the yeast and add the vegetable oil and sugar.

4　Mix to a soft but not sticky dough, adding more water or flour as required.

5　Knead for 6 minutes by machine or 10 minutes by hand to make a smooth dough.

6　Place in an oiled bowl, turning the dough to coat it in a thin film of oil. Cover with oiled clingfilm then leave to rise until doubled in size, about 1½ hours.

7　Turn the dough out on to a work surface and knead for 30 seconds to knock back.

8　Divide the dough into 16 equal-sized pieces. Roll into 10 cm | 4 in rounds. Brush with melted butter then fold over, keeping the top half slightly short of the bottom half.

9　Place on 2 greased baking sheets and brush with melted butter. Cover with oiled clingfilm. Allow to prove (rise again) until soft and pillowy.

10　Meanwhile, heat the oven to 200°C | 400°F | gas mark 6.

11　Bake the rolls for 20 minutes or until golden-brown. Cool on a wire rack.

* If using fast-action or dried yeast, see page 480.

Potato and Spring Onion Baps

These light, flavourful baps are perfect for filling with grated Cheddar and pickle.

MAKES 6 BAPS OR 12 DINNER ROLLS

225 g | 8 oz floury potatoes, peeled

15 g | ½ oz butter

10 g | ⅓ oz fresh yeast*

115 g | 4 oz buttermilk

4 spring onions, finely chopped

225–250 g | 8–10 oz strong white flour

1¼ teaspoons salt

For shaping

6 tablespoons rice flour

1 Cut the potatoes into even-sized chunks and place in a saucepan. Cover with cold water and a pinch of salt. Bring to the boil and simmer until tender.

2 Drain the potatoes then pass them through a sieve. Stir in the butter. Let the potatoes cool until just warm to the touch. Crumble the yeast over the potatoes.

3 Stir in the buttermilk, spring onions, flour and salt into the potatoes.

4 Mix to a soft dough then knead by machine for 6 minutes or by hand for 10 minutes. The dough will be soft, so kneading in a machine is recommended.

5 Place in an oiled bowl and turn the dough to coat in the oil. Cover with oiled clingfilm and leave in a warm place to rise for 1½ hours or until doubled in size.

6 Sprinkle a work surface with the rice flour then turn the dough out and divide into 12 equal-sized pieces. Shape into rounds.

7 Heat the oven to 200°C | 400°F | gas mark 6.

8 Place the baps on a lightly greased baking sheet and cover with oiled clingfilm.

9 Leave to prove (rise again) until soft and pillowy, about 30 minutes.

10 Bake in the top third of the oven for 20 minutes.

11 Place on a wire rack and cover with a clean tea towel while cooling.

* If using fast-action or dried yeast, see page 480.

Bagels

Bagels originated in eastern Europe and were brought to the US by Jewish immigrants. They are eaten toasted for breakfast or are used in place of bread for sandwiches. A traditional way of serving bagels is to split and toast them then spread thickly with cream cheese and top with smoked salmon.

MAKES 12

450 g | 1 lb strong white flour

1½ teaspoons salt

15 g | ½ oz yeast*

225 ml | 8 fl oz mixed milk and water, at room
   temperature

1 teaspoon caster sugar

1 teaspoon malt extract

30 g | 1 oz butter, melted and cooled

1 egg, beaten

To poach

1 tablespoon malt extract

To glaze

2 tablespoons sesame seeds or poppy seeds

1 Sift the flour with the salt into a large bowl and make a well in the centre.

2 Whisk the yeast into the milk and water. Add the sugar and malt extract.

3 Pour the yeast mixture into the flour and salt. Add the melted butter and egg.

4 Mix to a dough and knead for 10 minutes by hand or 6 minutes by machine, until smooth and elastic.

5 Place in an oiled bowl and turn to coat in the oil. Cover with oiled clingfilm and leave in a warm place for about 1½–2 hours or until doubled in size.

6 Knead the dough for 30 seconds then divide into 12 equal-sized balls. Shape each ball into a neat round. Make a hole in the centre of each ball and swing each one around your finger to increase the size of the hole to a diameter of at least 4 cm | 1½ in.

7 Place the bagels on a greased baking sheet and cover with oiled clingfilm. Leave for 20 minutes in a warm place or until soft and pillowy.

8 Meanwhile, fill a large saucepan with water and add 1 tablespoon malt extract. Bring to the boil, then turn down the temperature so an occasional bubble rises to the surface.

9 Heat the oven to 220°C | 425°F gas mark 7. Place a baking stone, if using, in the top third of the oven and a roasting tin on the shelf below the baking stone.

10 Drop the bagels one or two at a time into the saucepan. Poach for about 10 seconds per side. Remove with a slotted spoon and place on a tea towel to drain. If the bagels collapse after poaching you have poached them for too long. Do not leave them on the tea towel for more than 5 minutes or they will stick to the towel.

11 Place the bagels on the baking stone or a lightly greased baking sheet and sprinkle with poppy or sesame seeds. Bake for 20 minutes. Add iced water to the roasting tin and spray the bagels with a plant mister during the first 5 minutes of baking.

12 Place on a wire rack to cool.

* If using fast-action or dried yeast, see page 480.

Onion Bagels

MAKES 12

2 tablespoons vegetable oil

1 Spanish onion, finely chopped

450 g | 1 lb strong white flour

1½ teaspoons salt

15 g | ½ oz yeast*

225 ml | 8 fl oz mixed milk and water, at room
   temperature

1 teaspoon caster sugar

2 tablespoons butter, melted and cooled

1 egg, beaten

To poach

1 tablespoon malt extract

To finish

2 tablespoons onion seeds

1 Place the oil in a sauté pan and stir in the onions. Cover with a piece of dampened greaseproof paper and a lid. Cook over a low heat until soft and golden-brown, stirring occasionally. Allow to cool.

2 Sift the flour with the salt into a large bowl and make a well in the centre.

3 Whisk the yeast into the milk and water. Add the sugar.

4 Pour the yeast mixture into the flour and salt. Add the melted butter, egg and cooled onions.

5 Mix to a dough and knead for 10 minutes by hand or 6 minutes by machine until smooth and elastic.

6 Place in an oiled bowl and turn to coat in the oil. Cover with oiled clingfilm and leave in a warm place for about 1½–2 hours or until doubled in size.

7 Knead the dough for 30 seconds then divide into 12 equal-sized balls. Shape each ball into a neat round. Make a hole in the centre of each ball and swing each one around your finger to increase the size of the hole to a diameter of at least 4 cm | 1½ in.

8 Place the bagels on a greased baking sheet and cover with oiled clingfilm. Leave for 20 minutes in a warm place or until soft and pillowy.

9 Meanwhile, fill a large saucepan with water and add 1 tablespoon malt extract. Bring to the boil, then turn down the temperature so an occasional bubble rises to the surface.

10 Heat the oven to 220°C | 425°F gas mark 7. Place a baking stone, if using, in the top third of the oven and a roasting tin on the shelf below the baking stone.

11 Drop the bagels one a time into the saucepan. Poach for about 10 seconds per side. Remove with a slotted spoon and place on a tea towel to drain. If the bagels collapse after poaching you have poached them for too long.

12 Sprinkle the bagels with the onion seeds.

13 Place on the baking stone or a lightly greased baking sheet and bake for 20 minutes. Add iced water to the hot roasting tin and spray the bagels with a plant mister once or twice during the first 5 minutes of baking.

14 Place on a wire rack to cool.

* If using fast-action or dried yeast, see page 480.

Cinnamon Raisin Bagels

Serve these split, toasted and spread with lots of butter.

MAKES 12

450 g | 1 lb strong white flour

2 teaspoons salt

2 teaspoons ground cinnamon

15 g | ½ oz yeast*

225 ml | 8 fl oz mixed milk and water, at room
temperature

1 teaspoon malt extract

2 tablespoons butter, melted and cooled

1 egg, beaten

115 g | 4 oz raisins

To poach

1 tablespoon malt extract

1 Sift the flour with the salt and cinnamon into a large bowl and make a well in the centre.
2 Whisk the yeast into the milk and water. Add the malt extract.
3 Pour the yeast mixture into the flour and salt. Add the melted butter and egg.
4 Mix to a dough and knead for 10 minutes by hand or 6 minutes by machine until smooth and elastic.
5 Place in an oiled bowl and turn to coat in the oil. Cover with oiled clingfilm and leave in a warm place for about 1½–2 hours or until doubled in bulk.
6 Turn the dough out on to a work surface and roll flat. Sprinkle over the raisins and roll up. Knead to incorporate the raisins.
7 Divide into 12 equal-sized balls. Shape each ball into a neat round. Make a hole in the centre of each of the balls and swing each one around your finger to increase the size of the hole to a diameter of at least 4 cm | 1½ in.
8 Place the bagels on a greased baking sheet and cover with oiled clingfilm. Leave for 20 minutes in a warm place or until soft and pillowy.
9 Meanwhile, fill a large saucepan with water and add 1 tablespoon malt extract. Bring to the boil, then turn down the temperature so an occasional bubble rises to the surface.
10 Heat the oven to 220°C | 425°F gas mark 7. Place a baking stone, if using, in the top third of the oven and a roasting tin on the shelf below the stone.
11 Drop the bagels one a time into the saucepan. Poach for about 10 seconds per side. Remove with a slotted spoon and place on a tea towel to drain. If the bagels collapse after poaching you have poached them for too long. Place on a clean tea towel after poaching, but not for more than a few minutes or they will stick.
12 Place on the baking stone or a lightly greased baking sheet and bake for 20 minutes. Add iced water to the hot roasting tin and spray the bagels with a plant mister once or twice during the first 5 minutes of baking.
13 Place on a wire rack to cool.

* If using fast-action or dried yeast, see page 480.

Bialys

Bialys are very similar to bagels, but without the hole. Originating from Bialystock, Poland, but now favoured in the US, they are served for breakfast or brunch or can be filled with thinly sliced roasted meat for a delicious sandwich. Bialys are usually scented with onion and are always served toasted.

MAKES 16

4 tablespoons vegetable oil

2 Spanish onions, finely chopped

20 g|⅔ oz fresh yeast*

570 ml|1 pint lukewarm water

1 tablespoon malt extract

1 teaspoon freshly ground black pepper

775 g|1lb 12 oz strong white flour

4 teaspoons salt

2 tablespoons polenta

1 tablespoon poppy seeds

1 Place the oil in a sauté pan and stir in the onions. Cover with a piece of dampened greaseproof paper and a lid. Cook over a low to medium heat until soft and golden-brown. Allow to cool.

2 Meanwhile, put the water into a bowl and beat in the yeast to dissolve. Stir in the malt extract and pepper.

3 Stir 6 tablespoons of the onions into the water and reserve the rest for the topping.

4 Add 340 g|12 oz flour to the water. Beat to combine, then cover with clingfilm and leave to rise at room temperature for 1 hour.

5 Beat in the salt and as much additional flour as required to make a soft dough. Knead in the mixer for 5 minutes or by hand for 10 minutes until the dough is smooth and elastic.

6 Cover the dough with oiled clingfilm and leave to rise at room temperature until doubled in size, about 1 hour.

7 Heat the oven to 220°C|425°F|gas mark 7. Place a roasting tin on a shelf in the bottom third of the oven. Sprinkle 2 baking sheets with the polenta.

8 Divide the dough into 16 equal-sized pieces. Shape each piece into a round about 6 cm|2½ in in diameter, then make a dip in the centre to create a thick rim. Place the bialys on the baking sheets. Prick the centre of each bialy with a fork several times.

9 Mix the poppy seeds with the remaining onion and distribute between the centres of the bialys.

10 Cover with oiled clingfilm and leave to rise until soft and pillowy, about 20 minutes.

11 Prick the centres of the bialys again then bake in the top third of the oven for about 15–20 minutes, until golden, adding iced water to the roasting tin when the bialys are put in the oven. The bialys can be baked on a baking stone if desired.

12 Serve on the day of baking or freeze for up to 1 month.

* If using fast-action or dried yeast, see page 480.

Soft Pretzels

Pretzels are originally from Germany, where they are a traditional accompaniment to beer. There they are called *bretzelen*, meaning 'crossed arms', in reference to the shape of the pretzels.

Like bagels, pretzels are poached before baking in water with added bicarbonate of soda. The poaching ensures that the pretzels have a thin crust and a chewy texture, while the bicarbonate of soda helps browning. It is best to knead the dough in a machine as it is quite stiff.

MAKES 16

For the starter

5 g | ⅙ oz fresh yeast*

a pinch of caster sugar

50 ml | 1¾ fl oz cool water

4 tablespoons strong white flour

For the dough

10 g | ⅓ oz fresh yeast*

2 teaspoons caster sugar

115 ml | 4 fl oz lukewarm water

115 ml | 4 fl oz lukewarm milk

30 g | 1 oz butter, melted

450 g | 1 lb strong white flour

1½ teaspoons salt

To poach

2 tablespoons bicarbonate of soda

To finish

coarse sea salt

1 For the starter, place the yeast and sugar in a small bowl and stir in the water then the flour. Cover with clingfilm. Leave to stand at room temperature for 2 hours.

2 For the dough, stir the additional yeast, sugar, water, milk and butter into the starter. Sift the flour with the salt and add enough flour to the liquid mixture to make a dough.

3 Knead for 10 minutes by hand or 6 minutes by machine.

4 Place in an oiled bowl and turn the dough to coat with a thin film of oil. Cover with clingfilm and leave to rise until doubled in size, about 1 hour.

5 When the dough has nearly doubled, heat the oven to 190°C | 375°F | gas mark 5. Half-fill a large saucepan with water and add the bicarbonate of soda. Bring to the simmer. Lightly oil 3 baking sheets.

6 Knead the dough for 30 seconds to knock it back, then divide it into 16 equal-pieces. Work with one piece of dough at a time, keeping the others covered with oiled clingfilm.

7 Roll each piece of dough into a thin log about 40 cm | 16 in long. Fold the ends towards the middle, twist together about 5 cm | 2 in from each end then fold through the middle.

Shaping Pretzels (a)   Shaping Pretzels (b)   Shaping Pretzels (c)

Press the ends on to the centre of the piece of dough to make a pretzel shape. Place on the baking sheets and cover with oiled clingfilm to rest while shaping the other pieces of dough.

8 To poach the pretzels, drop them a few at a time into the simmering water. Poach on each side for 10 seconds then remove with a fish slice. Place on a clean tea towel to drain. Immediately sprinkle with coarse sea salt then place the poached pretzels on to the baking sheets.

9 Bake for 12–15 minutes or until golden-brown. Cool on a wire rack.

* If using fast-action or dried yeast, see page 480.

Fan Tan Rolls

The dough for these buttery dinner rolls is layered so that the rolls look like fans when they are baked.

MAKES 16

225 ml | 8 fl oz milk

15 g | ½ oz fresh yeast*

2 teaspoons caster sugar

450 g | 1 lb strong white flour

2 teaspoons salt

30 g | 1 oz vegetable shortening or lard

1 egg, beaten

55 g | 2 oz butter, softened

1 Scald the milk and set aside to cool to blood temperature. Skim.

2 Mix the yeast with the caster sugar and two tablespoons of the milk.

3 Sift the flour with the salt into a large bowl. Cut the vegetable shortening into small pieces and rub into the flour.

4 Make a well in the centre of the flour and pour in the yeast mixture, the egg and most of the remaining milk. Mix to a soft but not sticky dough, adding more milk or flour as necessary.

5 Knead for 6 minutes by machine or 10 minutes by hand until satiny.

6 Place the dough in an oiled bowl and turn to coat it in a thin film of oil. Cover with oiled clingfilm and leave to rise until doubled in size.

7 Knock back the risen dough by kneading for 30 seconds. Roll the dough into a rectangle 80 × 30 cm | 32 × 12 in.

8 Heat the oven to 190°C | 375°F | gas mark 5. Lightly butter 16 muffin tins.

9 Spread the remaining butter over the dough. Cut the dough lengthways into 6 strips. Stack the strips then cut them into 16 × 5 cm | 2 in pieces. Place the pieces in the muffin tins and cover with oiled clingfilm. Leave to prove until soft and pillowy, about 30 minutes.

10 Bake in the centre of the oven for 20–25 minutes or until golden-brown. Serve warm.

11 To reheat, place the rolls on a baking sheet in an oven preheated to 180°C | 350°F | gas mark 4 for 10 minutes.

* If using fast-action or dried yeast, see page 480.

Garlic Butter Fan Tan Rolls

MAKES 16

225 ml | 8 fl oz milk

15 g | ½ oz fresh yeast*

2 teaspoons caster sugar

450 g | 1 lb strong white flour

2 teaspoons salt

30 g | 1 oz vegetable shortening or lard

1 egg, beaten

55 g | 2 oz butter, softened

2 cloves of garlic, crushed

2 tablespoons chopped flat-leaf parsley

1 Scald the milk and set aside to cool to blood temperature. Skim.

2 Mix the yeast with the caster sugar and 2 tablespoons of the milk.

3 Sift the flour with the salt into a large bowl. Cut the vegetable shortening into small pieces and rub into the flour.

4 Make a well in the centre of the flour and pour in the yeast mixture, egg and most of the remaining milk. Mix to a soft but not sticky dough, adding more milk or flour as necessary.

5 Knead for 6 minutes by machine or 10 minutes by hand until satiny.

6 Place the dough in an oiled bowl and turn the dough to coat it in a thin film of oil. Cover with oiled clingfilm and leave to rise until doubled in size.

7 Knock back the risen dough by kneading for 30 seconds then roll it into a rectangle measuring 80 × 30 cm | 32 × 12 in.

8 Heat the oven to 190°C | 375°F | gas mark 5. Lightly butter 16 muffin tins.

9 Mix the garlic and parsley with the remaining butter and spread over the dough. Cut the dough lengthways into 6 strips. Stack the strips then cut them into 16 × 5 cm | 2 in pieces. Place the pieces in the muffin tins and cover with oiled clingfilm. Leave to prove until soft and pillowy, about 30 minutes

10 Bake in the centre of the oven for 20 minutes or until golden-brown. Serve warm.

11 To reheat, place the rolls on a baking sheet in an oven preheated to 180°C | 350°F | gas mark 4 for 10 minutes.

* If using fast-action or dried yeast, see page 480.

Butterhorns

These tender crescent rolls are ideal for a special dinner. Add an extra tablespoon of sugar to the dough and they can be served for breakfast.

MAKES 12

150 ml|5 fl oz buttermilk

55 ml|2 fl oz lukewarm water

2 teaspoons caster sugar

10 g|⅓ oz fresh yeast*

285 g|10 oz strong white flour

1 teaspoon salt

30 g|1 oz butter, softened

To glaze

1 egg, beaten

1   Place the buttermilk and water in a small saucepan and warm over a low heat to blood temperature. Do not boil. Pour into a bowl and stir in the sugar, yeast and 2 tablespoons of the flour. Allow to stand for 15 minutes to become bubbly.

2   Sift the remaining flour into a large bowl with the salt. Cut in the butter using 2 table knives, scissor-fashion, then rub in with your fingertips.

3   Stir the yeast mixture into the flour to make a soft but not too sticky dough. Add more water or more flour if required.

4   Knead for 6 minutes by machine or 10 minutes by hand until the dough is smooth.

5   Place the dough in a lightly oiled bowl and turn to coat it with the oil. Cover with oiled clingfilm and leave in a warm place to rise until doubled in size, about 1½ hours.

6   Knead the dough for 30 seconds to knock it back then return it to the bowl and cover with the clingfilm. Chill for 2 hours.

7   Turn the dough out on to a floured work surface and pat into a 23 cm|9 in round.

8   Cut into 12 equal-sized triangular wedges, like the spokes of a wheel. Roll each wedge with a rolling pin to flatten so that the triangle is about 5 cm|2 in wide and 15 cm|6 in long, then roll up the dough to shape it like a croissant.

9   Place on an oiled baking sheet and cover with oiled clingfilm. Allow to prove (rise again) until soft and pillowy, about 1 hour.

10 Brush lightly with the beaten egg and bake for 15–20 minutes or until golden-brown. Cool on a wire rack.

* If using fast-action or dried yeast, see page 480.

Pumpkin Seed Rolls

These rolls are quick to make as they have only 1 rising. The dough is sticky and so should be kneaded in a food processor or free-standing machine fitted with a dough hook.

MAKES 12

170 g | 6 oz strong white flour

170 g | 6 oz strong wholemeal flour

1 teaspoon salt

15 g | ½ oz fresh yeast*

290 ml | 10 fl oz buttermilk

1 tablespoon malt extract or clear honey

45 g | 1½ oz butter, softened

100 g | 3½ oz pumpkin seeds

1 Sift the flours and salt into a large bowl. Rub in the butter then make a well in the centre.

2 Warm the buttermilk to lukewarm then whisk in the yeast. Place in the well. Add the malt extract or honey to the well.

3 Stir to combine then knead for 6 minutes with a free-standing machine or 30 seconds in a food processor. Add all but 2 tablespoons of the pumpkin seeds and mix briefly to combine.

4 Grease 12 muffin cups and divide the dough between them. Sprinkle with the remaining seeds. Cover with oiled clingfilm and leave to rise until the mixture is soft and pillowy, about 1 hour.

5 Meanwhile, heat the oven to 200°C | 400°F | gas mark 6.

6 Bake in the top third of the oven for 15–20 minutes or until golden-brown. Remove from the muffin tins and place on a wire rack to cool.

* If using fast-action or dried yeast, see page 480.

Potato and Rosemary Rolls

MAKES 3 LOAVES

225 g | ½ lb potatoes, peeled

225 ml | 8 fl oz lukewarm water

15 g | ½ oz fresh yeast*

1 tablespoon malt extract

340 g | 12 oz strong white flour

2 teaspoons salt

1 tablespoon chopped fresh rosemary

To shape

2 tablespoons polenta

1 Cut the potatoes into 5 cm | 2 in chunks. Cover with water then boil until tender. Drain, saving the water for the bread. Mash the potatoes and cool until lukewarm.

2 Combine the yeast with 2 tablespoons of the warm water. Stir in the malt extract. Mix it with the mashed potatoes.

3 Sift the flour with the salt into a large mixing bowl. Add the potato mixture, rosemary and enough water to mix to a soft dough. Mix well. When the mixture will leave the sides of the bowl, press it into a ball and tip out on to a floured surface.

4 Knead until elastic, smooth and shiny, about 15 minutes by hand or 10 minutes by machine.

5 Put the dough into an oiled bowl and turn to coat with the oil. Cover with lightly oiled clingfilm.

6 Leave in a warm place to rise until doubled in size, at least 1 hour.

7 Knock down and knead for a further 30 seconds. Heat the oven to 220°C|425°F| gas mark 7.

8 Shape into 20 rolls. Dip the bases in the polenta then place on a greased baking sheet and cover again with oiled clingfilm. Leave to prove (rise again) until soft and pillowy. Dust lightly with flour.

9 Bake the rolls in the top third of the oven for 15–20 minutes. Bake until golden-brown. The rolls should sound hollow when tapped on the underside.

10 Place on a wire rack to cool.

* If using fast-action or dried yeast, see page 480.

English Muffins

MAKES 8–10

450 g | 1 lb strong white flour

1 teaspoon salt

15 g | ½ oz fresh yeast*

½ teaspoon sugar

340 ml | 12 fl oz lukewarm milk

rice flour or ground rice for dusting baking sheets

1 Sift the flour with the salt into a large mixing bowl. Cream the yeast with the sugar and a little of the milk. Make a well in the flour and add the yeast mixture and the remaining milk. Mix to make a soft but not wet dough.

2 Knead for 10 minutes by hand or 6 minutes by machine, or until the dough is smooth and elastic. Place the dough in an oiled bowl and turn to coat it in the oil. Cover with oiled clingfilm or a clean damp cloth and leave in a warm place to rise until doubled in size. This will take about 1 hour, depending on the warmth of the room.

3 Knock back the risen dough and knead again for a couple of minutes. Cover again, return to the warm place and leave to rise for a further 30 minutes. Sprinkle 2 baking sheets with rice flour or ground rice.

4 Without knocking it back, divide the dough into 8–10 pieces and shape into balls. Place them on the prepared baking sheets. Sprinkle the balls of dough with more rice flour or ground rice and flatten them slightly with the palm of your hand. Cover again, return to the warm place and leave to rise for 30 minutes.

5 Heat an ungreased griddle or heavy frying pan until moderately hot, cook the muffins, a few at a time, over a very low heat for 15–20 minutes on each side or until golden-brown and the sides spring back when pressed.

6 Keep warm in the folds of a clean tea towel while cooking the remaining muffins in the same way.

* If using fast-action or dried yeast, see page 480.

NOTE: If making 8 muffins, they may take nearer to 20–25 minutes on each side. Do not be tempted to rush the cooking process or the outside will burn while the inside remains doughy.

Artisan Breads: Points to Remember

- Use organic flour, stoneground if possible.
- Use non-chlorinated water, i.e. filtered or mineral water.
- Use a starter or biga or, at the very least, fresh yeast.
- Make the dough with a small amount of yeast and let it ferment in a cool environment for a longer time. Take a day or two to make your bread, rather than an hour or two.
- Try to become accustomed to handling wetter doughs. At Leiths we say, 'The wetter, the better.' Your loaves will be larger and lighter.
- Use a free-standing machine to knead the dough or the turning method described on page 484.
- Use a natural sea salt.
- Use a pizza or baking stone.
- Create steam by adding either iced cold water or boiling water to a roasting tin placed at the bottom of your oven.
- Spray your dough with water from a plant mister during the first 5 minutes of cooking.
- Don't expect identical results every time you bake. A bread dough is a living thing and it changes from day to day.
- Have fun and don't be afraid to experiment.

Artisan Breads

The recipes in this section are for breads popularly known as 'artisan' or 'hearth' breads. These are breads made using somewhat different methods from those in the previous chapter, methods that are similar to those used hundreds of years ago. In recent years these breads have become popular again, because they are delicious. Although they often take longer to make than basic breads, they have a much more complex and better flavour and have the added benefit of keeping for longer without going stale or mouldy. The longer fermentation process, as well of the use of a smaller amount of yeast in this type of bread, is thought to produce loaves that are more easily digestible.

Many years ago bread was baked by being placed directly on the floor of a wood-fired oven, much like some pizzas are today. Every household would prepare their own dough, with their own starter or leavening, and take it to the communal oven in the village to be baked. The dough was slashed in different patterns so each family could identify their bread. This method of baking produced loaves with thick crusts and an incomparable flavour.

Bar building a wood-fired hearth oven in the garden, it is difficult to reproduce these loaves today. There are some steps that can be taken, however, to produce similar loaves. See the box opposite for tips.

What is a Starter?

There are many different terms used to describe a mixture of flour, water and yeast, in varying proportions, used to leaven dough to produce breads with more complex flavours and chewier textures. These are some of the more frequently encountered terms:

Sourdough starter

Sourdough starter is a mixture of organic flour and mineral water which produces a thick batter that is allowed to ferment the wild yeasts present in the flour and air. One of the most well-known sourdough breads, San Francisco sourdough, is made with a starter containing *Lactobacillus sanfrancisco*, a bacteria that is unique to the San Francisco area.

Poolish

The term 'poolish' came to prominence in the central European countries in the nineteenth century. It is made from equal weights of flour and water and a very small amount of yeast. It has the consistency of a thick batter.

Pâte fermentée or old dough starter

This starter is a portion of dough, with all its ingredients, that is reserved and kept chilled before being used to leaven the next batch of dough.

Biga

A biga is a firm starter made with a small amount of commercial yeast which was developed in Italy in order to strengthen the gluten in loaves made with low-protein Italian flour. Many bigas are now made quite wet, rather like a poolish.

The biga is a combination of water, flour and fresh yeast which is allowed to ferment at a cool temperature (12–$14°C | 55$–$60°F$) overnight or for up to 2 days. The fermentation produces acetic acid which, when kneaded into a dough, strengthens the gluten. If you have a larder or wine cellar the temperature there will be ideal for fermenting your biga. If your kitchen is too warm it is best to place the biga in the refrigerator.

Sponge or levain or chef

This is a firm starter, similar to a pâte fermentée, containing flour, water and yeast. However, it is made specifically for a recipe rather than being reserved from a prior loaf.

Mixed starter or levain de pâte

This method is used to produce 'sourdough'-flavoured bread, using a combination of an old dough starter and a small amount of commercial yeast. It is easier to use than a traditional sourdough starter because the fermentation time is more predictable.

Adapting a Bread Recipe for the Starter Method

Most bread recipes can be altered to produce a starter by mixing the liquid with half of the yeast, any sugar or sweetening called for in the recipe and enough flour to make a batter. The batter is then left to stand for at least 20 minutes and as long as 3 days in a cool kitchen or larder. The longer the starter is left to stand, the more intense the tangy flavour will be. This starter is also called a pre-ferment.

To make the dough, add the starter to the remaining flour along with the salt and any fat called for in the recipe. Cream the remaining half of the yeast with a little warm liquid of the type specified in the recipe and add to the flour. Mix to form a soft dough. Knead, rise, prove and bake in the usual way.

The finished bread should have a more complex flavour and a more open, chewy texture. The crust should be thicker and chewier. This method of mixing the dough is particularly suitable for olive oil breads where an open texture and thicker crust is particularly desirable.

Mediterranean Country Bread

150 ml | 5 fl oz lukewarm water

85 g | 3 oz plain yoghurt

2 tablespoons clear honey

15 g | ½ oz fresh yeast*

1 tablespoon olive oil

340 g | 12 oz strong white flour

55 g | 2 oz strong wholemeal flour

1½ teaspoons sea salt

2 tablespoons polenta or rice flour

1 Place the water in a bowl and whisk in the yoghurt, honey, yeast and oil.

2 Sift the flours and salt into a second large bowl, adding back any bran remaining in the sieve. Make a well in the centre.

3 Pour in the wet mixture and stir to make a soft but not too sticky dough. Add more flour or water if necessary.

4 Knead by machine for 6 minutes or by hand for 10 minutes or until the dough is smooth and elastic.

5 Place the dough in an oiled bowl and turn to coat in a thin film of oil. Cover with oiled clingfilm and leave to rise until doubled in size, about 1½ hours.

6 Sprinkle a rimless baking sheet or peel with the polenta or rice flour. Lift the dough from the bowl and shape into a round. Place on the baking sheet.

7 Cover with clingfilm and allow to prove (rise again) until nearly doubled in size, about 45 minutes.

8 Meanwhile, heat the oven to 220°C | 425°F | gas mark 7. Place a baking stone in the top third of the oven to heat.

9 Slide the dough on to the hot baking stone. Turn the heat to 200°C | 400°F | gas mark 6. Spray the dough with water 3 times during the first 5 minutes of baking, using a plant mister.

10 Bake for 35 minutes or until the loaf sounds hollow when tapped on the underside.

11 Cool on a wire rack.

* If using fast-action or dried yeast, see page 480.

Pain de Campagne

Pain de campagne is a round, rustic loaf with a floury crust and a slightly grey crumb. Found throughout France, it varies in size and composition from place to place, though it invariably contains wholemeal flour.

    This bread is made from a starter known as a chef. Usually the chef is a dryish sourdough starter, made from wild yeast, which gives the bread a sour flavour (see *Pain Levain*, page 572). This recipe uses a small amount of baker's yeast to speed the process of producing the loaf, hopefully without compromising too much on flavour. The bread will take 2 days to produce but it keeps very well.

MAKES 1 LARGE LOAF

For the chef

1 teaspoon fresh yeast*

85 ml | 3 fl oz mineral water, at room temperature

85 g | 3 oz organic wholemeal flour

Place the yeast in a bowl and whisk in the water. Stir in the flour. Cover with clingfilm and leave to stand at room temperature for 2 hours.

For the refreshment

chef (above)

55 g | 2 fl oz mineral water, at room temperature

115 g | 4 oz organic wholemeal flour

1 Stir the refreshment water into the chef and then stir in the flour.

2 Cover with clingfilm.

3 Leave to stand at room temperature for 4 hours. It is now ready to use to make bread. If you are not ready to use the chef immediately it can be chilled for up to 1 week.

For the dough

chef that has been refreshed and standing at room
   temperature for 4 hours

85 ml | 3 oz mineral water, at room temperature

10 g | ⅓ oz fresh yeast*

55 g | 2 oz organic rye flour

170 g | 6 oz organic strong white flour

1 tablespoon vegetable oil

1 tablespoon caster sugar or honey (optional)

1½ teaspoons fine sea salt

rice flour, polenta or additional flour for dusting

1 For the dough, stir the water and the yeast into the refreshed chef. Stir in the flours, but do not knead. Cover the dough closely with oiled clingfilm and leave to stand for 20 minutes.

2 Add the oil and sugar or honey, if using, to the dough and knead for 6 minutes by machine or 10 minutes by hand, adding more water or flour as necessary to make a soft but not too sticky dough.

3 Place the dough in an oiled bowl and turn the dough to coat it in a thin film of oil. Cover with clingfilm and allow to rise to 1½ times its original size. Chill for 8 hours or overnight.

4 Remove the dough from the refrigerator and reserve 100 g | 3½ oz dough for the next loaf. Store the reserved dough in a glass jar and keep in the refrigerator for up to 1 week.

5 Turn the dough out on to a work surface. Sprinkle with the sea salt. Knead for 20 seconds to combine then shape the dough into a round.

6 Place the dough into a basket or banneton lined with a heavily floured tea towel. Cover the top of the dough with oiled clingfilm.

7 When the dough has nearly doubled in size, place a baking stone on a rack in the oven and place a roasting pan at the bottom of the oven. Heat the oven to 220°C|425°F|gas mark 7.

8 Dust a peel (see page 32) or baking sheet with rice flour, polenta or white flour. Turn out the dough on to the flour or polenta, then make several slashes with a serrated knife or single-edged razor. Allow the dough to stand for a further 10 minutes then slide the dough on to the hot baking stone.

9 Add a cupful of iced water to the roasting tin. Bake the bread for 35–40 minutes or until a deep golden-brown. The bread can be sprayed with water from a plant mister 3 times during the first 5 minutes of baking.

10 When done, the loaf should sound hollow if tapped on the underside.

11 Place on a wire rack to cool before slicing.

* If using fast-action or dried yeast, see page 480.

NOTE: When making another loaf using the reserved *chef* from step 5, begin the recipe with the refreshment.

Pugliese

This Italian bread is from the Apulia region of Italy. The durum wheat flour makes this dough particularly stretchy. The finished loaf has a chewy texture with a brittle, shiny crust. The biga needs to be made the day before the bread is baked. This bread is best made using a machine.

MAKES 1 LOAF

For the biga

150 ml | 5 fl oz mineral water, at room temperature

1 teaspoon fresh yeast*

115 g | 4 oz organic strong white flour

For the dough

170 g | 6 oz organic strong white flour

115 g | 4 oz durum wheat flour (pasta flour)

1½ teaspoons fine sea salt

10 g | ⅓ oz fresh yeast*

100 ml | 3½ fl oz mineral water, at room temperature

extra durum wheat flour or rice flour for sprinkling

1 For the biga, place the water in a bowl and crumble in the yeast. Whisk to combine then stir in the flour. Cover with clingfilm and allow to stand at a cool room temperature overnight or for up to 3 days.
2 For the dough, sift the flours and the salt into a bowl and make a well in the centre.
3 Scrape the starter into the well then crumble in the yeast. Add the water and stir to make a soft dough.
4 Knead for 6 minutes by machine to a smooth, stretchy dough.
5 Place in an oiled bowl and turn the dough to coat it in a thin film of oil. Cover with oiled clingfilm.
6 Allow to rise until doubled in size, then oil your hands and forearms and gently lift the dough. As it stretches fold it into 3, like a business letter, and return to the bowl. Repeat this stretching and folding two more times at 20-minute intervals.
7 Heavily sprinkle a rimless baking sheet or peel with the extra durum wheat or rice flour and set aside.
8 To shape the dough, sprinkle the work surface with extra flour. Oil your hands and forearms again and place the dough on the flour. Shape into a round using the circular kneading or rounding technique (see page 484) then pat the dough down to flatten it slightly.
9 Set the dough on the floured baking sheet.
10 Slash a circle in the dough 3 cm | 1¼ in from the edge. Cover with oiled clingfilm.
11 Heat the oven to 220°C | 425°F | gas mark 7. Place a baking stone on a shelf in the top third of the oven. On a shelf in the bottom of the oven place an empty roasting tin.
12 Allow the dough to prove (rise again) until an indentation made in the side springs back only halfway.
13 Slide the dough on to the baking stone and splash a cupful of iced water into the roasting tin to create steam.
14 Bake for 30 minutes, spraying with a plant mister twice during the first 5 minutes of

baking. After 10 minutes turn the oven down to 200°C|400°F|gas mark 6. When done, the loaf will sound hollow when tapped on the underside.

* If using fast-action or dried yeast, see page 480.

Light Rye Bread

This recipe uses the starter method to make a light, slightly tangy bread that is good for sandwiches. It keeps well.

MAKES 1 LOAF

For the starter

10 g|⅓ oz fresh yeast*
1 tablespoon clear honey
150 ml|5 fl oz lukewarm water
140 g|5 oz organic natural yoghurt
100 g|3½ oz rye flour

For the dough

100 g|3½ oz spelt flour
140 g|5 oz strong white flour
1½ teaspoons salt
15 g|½ oz soft butter
extra flour for sprinkling

1 Mix together the ingredients for the starter in a large bowl and let stand at room temperature until light and foamy, about 1 hour.
2 Stir the ingredients for the dough into the starter ingredients to make a soft dough. Add more flour if the mixture is too sticky.
3 Knead until smooth and satiny, about 10 minutes by hand or 6 minutes by machine.
4 Place in an oiled bowl and turn to coat in the oil. Cover with clingfilm. Leave to rise until doubled in size, either at room temperature or in the refrigerator overnight.
5 Heat the oven to 200°C|400°F|gas mark 6.
6 Knock back the dough by kneading for 30 seconds. Shape into a loaf and place in an oiled 675 g|1½ lb loaf tin. Cover with clingfilm and leave to prove until nearly doubled in size.
7 About 5 minutes before the dough is ready to go into the oven, sprinkle the top with extra flour and slash the top 1 cm|½ in deep in 3 places.
8 Bake for 30 minutes or until well-browned. The loaf will sound hollow when tapped on the underside.
9 Turn out on a wire rack to cool.

* If using fast-action or dried yeast, see page 480.

Pain Levain

The master Parisian baker Lionel Poilâne was renowned for his pain levain. This bread is made using an 'old dough' starter or leavening: a piece of dough is kept back and reserved to rise the next loaf, and so on. The starter is sometimes referred to as the levain or the chef.

Loaves of pain levain are not as sour as a classic sourdough (see page 588). Pain levain is good for sandwiches and morning toast. It makes an excellent accompaniment to wine and cheese. The moist loaves keep well for up to 5 days.

MAKES 1 LOAF
For the chef
Day 1

50 ml | 1¾ fl oz still mineral water   100 g | 3½ oz organic wholemeal flour

Mix together the water and flour. Place in a jar or glass bowl and leave to stand uncovered at room temperature for 24 hours.

Day 2

100 g | 3½ oz chef from day 1   100 g | 3½ oz organic wholemeal flour
100 ml | 3½ oz still mineral water

1 Break the chef from day 1 into 5 pieces (discard the remainder) and place in a glass bowl.
2 Pour over the water and allow to stand for 10 minutes to soften.
3 Stir in the flour. Cover with clingfilm and allow to stand uncovered for 24 hours at room temperature.

Days 3 and 4

100 g | 3½ oz chef from previous day   100 g | 3½ oz organic wholemeal flour
100 g | 3 fl oz mineral water

4 Break the chef into 5 pieces and pour over the water. Let stand for 10 minutes then stir in the flour to make a soft dough.
5 Place in a glass bowl or jar and cover with clingfilm. Mark a line on the bowl level with the top of the dough in order to monitor its growth.
6 Let stand uncovered at room temperature until it triples in size in 24 hours. It is now ready to use to make bread.

For the dough

chef that has been refreshed and has been standing at room temperature for 4 hours

115 ml | 4 oz mineral water

100 g | 3½ oz organic rye flour

200 g | 7 oz organic strong white flour

15 g | ½ oz butter, softened (optional)

2 teaspoons caster sugar or honey (optional)

2 teaspoons fine sea salt

rice flour, polenta or additional flour for dusting

1 Break the chef into walnut-sized pieces and place in a bowl. Pour over the water and let stand for 10 minutes at room temperature.

2 Stir in the flours, but do not knead. Cover the dough closely with clingfilm and let stand for 20 minutes.

3 Add the butter and sugar or honey, if using, to the dough and knead for 6 minutes by machine or 10 minutes by hand, adding more water or flour as necessary to make a soft but not too sticky dough.

4 Place the dough in an oiled bowl and turn the dough to coat it in a thin film of oil. Cover with clingfilm and allow to rise to 1½ times its original size. Chill for 8 hours or overnight.

5 Remove the dough from the refrigerator and reserve 100 g | 3½ oz dough for the next loaf. Store the reserved dough in a glass jar and keep in the refrigerator. Refresh before using, as for instructions for days 3–4 above.

6 Turn the dough out on to a work surface. Sprinkle with 1½ teaspoons fine sea salt. Knead for 20 seconds to combine, then shape the dough into a round.

7 Place the dough into a basket or banneton lined with a heavily floured tea towel. Cover the top of the dough with oiled clingfilm.

8 When the dough has nearly doubled in size, place a baking stone on a rack in the oven and place a roasting pan at the bottom of the oven. Heat the oven to 220°C | 425°F | gas mark 7.

9 Dust a peel or baking sheet with rice flour, polenta or white flour. Turn the dough out on to the flour or polenta, then slash with a serrated knife or single-edged razor. Allow the dough to stand for a further 10 minutes, then slide the dough on to the hot baking stone. Bake for 35–40 minutes or until a deep golden-brown. The loaf should sound hollow when done.

10 Place on a wire rack to cool for 2 hours before slicing.

100% Rye Bread

As rye flour is very low in gluten, many rye bread recipes contain wheat flour to give the bread a lighter texture. However, this recipe produces a moist, dense loaf using only rye flour. It is a difficult dough to knead by hand because it is sticky, so use a free-standing mixer or food processor fitted with the stirring paddle. Do not knead for more than 5 minutes. It is best not to leave the dough in a refrigerator overnight, as the cold will slow the yeast activity too much and prevent it from rising well. This bread is particularly delicious with a strong-flavoured soft cheese.

MAKES 1 SMALL LOAF

For the starter

140 g | 5 oz organic plain yoghurt

15 g | ½ oz fresh yeast*

1 tablespoon black treacle

55 g | 2 oz organic rye flour

For the dough

170 g | 6 oz organic rye flour

1 teaspoon salt

45–75 ml | 3–5 tablespoons lukewarm water

½ -1 teaspoon caraway seeds (optional)

1 For the starter, place the yoghurt in a bowl to fill it no more than half-full. Stir in the yeast, treacle and rye flour.

2 Cover with clingfilm and leave to stand at room temperature until it has risen and just started to drop. This will take about 2 hours.

3 For the dough, sift the flour and salt into a large bowl and make a well in the centre. Scrape the starter into the centre.

4 Add the caraway seeds to the dough or reserve to sprinkle on the top.

5 Knead for 4 minutes in a free-standing machine or 2 minutes in a food processor, adding enough water to bring the mixture together into a dough. The dough will be sticky and crumbly.

6 Place the dough in an oiled bowl and cover directly on the surface with oiled clingfilm. Leave to rise until doubled in size.

7 Scrape the dough into a 450 g | 1 lb loaf tin lined on the base and sides with baking parchment. Dampen your fingers with water and tap the surface of the dough to level it. Sprinkle with the caraway seeds, if desired.

8 Cover with oiled clingfilm and leave to rise until about 1½ times its original size.

9 Heat the oven to 220°C | 450°F | gas mark 7.

10 Fill a 900 g | 2 lb loaf tin halfway with warm water (bain-marie). Wrap the tin containing the dough in foil, folding the ends securely over the top. Place the smaller loaf tin in the larger one (the bain-marie) and bake in the oven for 40 minutes.

11 Remove the small loaf tin from the bain-marie and return it to the oven, still wrapped in the foil, to bake for another 40 minutes.

12 Remove the loaf from the oven and unwrap it. Use the baking parchment to lift the loaf from the tin. Cool on a wire rack for half an hour then wrap in foil while still slightly warm.

* If using fast-action or dried yeast, see page 480.

Sunflower Rye Bread

MAKES 1 LOAF

For the starter

100 g | 3½ oz rye flour

225 ml | 8 fl oz boiling water

20 g | ⅔ oz fresh yeast*

1 tablespoon clear honey

For the dough

100 g | 3½ oz rye flour

140 g | 5 oz strong white flour

1½ teaspoons salt

30 g | 1 oz butter, melted and cool

¼ teaspoon ground caraway seed or ground cumin

100 g | 3½ oz sunflower seeds

To glaze

1 egg white, lightly beaten

1 To make the starter, place the flour in a heatproof bowl and pour over the boiling water. Stir to combine and allow to cool until lukewarm.

2 Stir in the yeast and honey. Cover with clingfilm and allow to stand at room temperature for 2 hours or until puffy.

3 For the dough, stir together the flours, salt, butter and ground caraway or cumin into the starter to make a soft dough. Add more water if the dough is dry. Knead for 5 minutes in a machine at low speed.

4 Cover with oiled clingfilm and allow to rise until doubled in size, about 2 hours.

5 Tip the dough on to a floured work surface and knead in all but 1 tablespoon of the sunflower seeds.

6 Oil a 675 g | 1½ lb loaf tin. Shape the dough into a loaf and press into the prepared tin. Cover with oiled clingfilm and allow to rise until doubled in size.

7 Heat the oven to 200°C | 400°F | gas mark 6.

8 Brush the risen dough with the egg white and sprinkle with the remaining sunflower seeds.

9 Bake the loaf in the centre of the oven for 35–40 minutes. The loaf should sound hollow when tapped on the underside.

10 Cool on a wire rack. Wrap in greaseproof paper then place in a plastic bag. Keep for at least 1 day before slicing.

* If using fast-action or dried yeast, see page 480.

Seeded Black Bread

MAKES 1 LARGE LOAF

For the starter

170 g|6 oz floury potatoes, peeled and boiled

250 ml|9 fl oz water (saved from cooking the potatoes)

1 teaspoon fresh yeast*

1 tablespoon black treacle

100 g|3½ oz rye flour

For the dough

225 g|8 oz strong white flour

225 g|8 oz strong wholemeal flour

2¼ teaspoons salt

10 g|⅓ oz fresh yeast*

1 tablespoon vegetable oil

8 tablespoons mixed seeds (pumpkin, poppy, sesame, sunflower, linseed)

1 For the starter, push the potatoes through a sieve to mash, then stir in the potato water. Allow to cool until lukewarm then stir in the yeast, treacle and flour. Cover with clingfilm and leave in a cool place to rise overnight.

2 For the dough, sift the flours and salt into a large bowl and make a well in the centre. Scrape in the starter, then crumble in the yeast. Add the oil and stir to make a soft but not too sticky dough, adding more flour or warm water as required.

3 Knead the dough for 6 minutes by machine. Place the dough in a lightly oiled bowl and turn to coat in the oil. Cover with oiled clingfilm and leave to rise until doubled in size, about 1½ hours.

4 Place the dough on a lightly floured work surface and roll to flatten with a rolling pin. Sprinkle over the seeds, reserving 2 tablespoons for the outside of the dough. Roll up the dough and knead lightly to incorporate the seeds. Knead briefly then roll the outside of the dough in the reserved seeds.

5 Shape into a round and place on a lightly greased baking sheet. Cover with oiled clingfilm and leave to prove (rise again) until soft and pillowy.

6 Meanwhile, heat the oven to 200°C|400°F|gas mark 6. Place a roasting tin on a shelf in the bottom of the oven and a baking stone on a shelf set in the top third of the oven.

7 When the dough has proved, slide it on to the baking stone. Pour about half a pint of boiling water into the roasting tin. Bake for 30 minutes or until a deep brown. The loaf will sound hollow when tapped on the bottom. Cool on a wire rack.

* If using fast-action or dried yeast, see page 480.

Pumpernickel Bread

Pumpernickel bread is made from a combination of rye and wholemeal flour, enriched with chocolate and molasses. There is no such thing as a pumpernickel grain. This bread is excellent with strong cheeses and smoked meats. The dough is very heavy and sticky, so it is a good idea to use a machine for kneading.

MAKES 2 LOAVES

For the starter

290 ml | 10 fl oz water

1 teaspoon instant espresso coffee powder

30 g | 1 oz plain chocolate, chopped into small pieces

1 tablespoon treacle or molasses

125 g | 4½ fl oz plain organic yoghurt

10 g | ⅓ oz fresh yeast*

225 g | 8 oz rye flour

For the dough

340 g | 12 oz strong wholemeal flour, preferably organic

115 g | 4 oz rye flour

1 tablespoon sea salt

1 teaspoon caraway seeds, toasted and ground

55 g | 2 oz unsalted butter, melted and cooled

20 g | ⅔ oz fresh yeast*

150 ml | 5 fl oz lukewarm water

2 tablespoons polenta (optional)

To finish

1 egg white, beaten lightly with a fork

1 tablespoon caraway or sesame seeds

1 Make the starter: place the water, espresso powder, chocolate and treacle in a small saucepan and heat, stirring, to melt the chocolate and combine the ingredients. Remove from the heat.

2 Stir in the yoghurt. When the mixture has reached 37°C | 100°F (blood temperature), stir in the yeast. Turn into a large bowl.

3 Stir in the flour and allow to stand at a cool room temperature overnight.

4 Make the dough: sift the flours, salt and caraway seeds into a large bowl. Make a well in the centre and tip in the cooled melted butter and the starter.

5 Mix the yeast with 2 tablespoons of the warm water and pour into the well.

6 Stir to make a sticky dough, adding warm water or flour as necessary.

7 Knead for 5 minutes in a machine until smooth. Place in an oiled bowl and cover with oiled clingfilm. Leave to rise at normal room temperature until doubled in size. This can take 2–3 hours.

8 Knock the dough back by kneading for 30 seconds, then cover with oiled clingfilm and allow to rise again for another 2–3 hours.

9 Heat the oven to 200°C | 400°F | gas mark 6.

10 Divide the dough in half and shape each piece to fit into a large oiled loaf tin, or shape into ovals and place on a greased baking sheet sprinkled with polenta, if using. Cover with oiled clingfilm and allow to prove (rise again) until nearly doubled in size.

11 Brush with the egg white and sprinkle with the seeds. Make 3–5 slashes about 1 cm | ½ in deep on the tops of the loaves.

12 Bake in the top third of the oven (the hottest part) for 10 minutes. Turn the oven temperature down to 180°C | 350°F | gas mark 4 and bake for a further 30–40 minutes. The loaves should sound hollow when tapped on the underside. Turn out on to a wire rack and leave to cool.

* If using fast-action or dried yeast, see page 480.

Raisin Rye Bread

This recipe is similar to a Russian black bread. The rye flour, cocoa powder and treacle give it a nearly-black colour. The raisins add a sweetness to this bread which contrasts well with the bitterness of the rye flour. Serve with a soft, tangy cheese.

MAKES 1 LOAF

For the starter

1 teaspoon fresh yeast*
150 ml | 5 fl oz lukewarm water
2 tablespoons black treacle or molasses
115 g | 4 oz strong white flour
55 g | 2 oz rye flour
50 g | 1¾ oz raisins

For the dough

55 g | 2 oz strong white flour
55 g | 2 oz wholemeal flour
55 g | 2 oz rye flour
30 g | 1 oz cocoa powder
1½ teaspoons salt
10 g | ⅓ oz fresh yeast*
30 g | 1 oz butter, melted and cooled
2 tablespoons dark muscovado sugar
55–85 g | 2–3 fl oz lukewarm water
100 g | 3½ oz raisins

1 For the starter, whisk the yeast into the water then stir in the treacle or molasses, the flours and the raisins. Cover with clingfilm and leave to stand in a cool place overnight.

2 For the dough, sift together the flours, cocoa powder and salt into a large bowl. Make a well in the centre. Scrape the starter into the well then crumble in the additional fresh yeast.

3 Add the butter and sugar and stir together with enough additional water to make a soft dough.

4 Knead for 6 minutes in a free-standing mixer or 2 minutes in a food processor.

5 Place the dough in a lightly oiled bowl and turn the dough to coat it into a thin film of oil. Cover with oiled clingfilm and leave in a warm place to stand until doubled in size.

6 Turn the dough on to a work surface and sprinkle over the raisins. Knead lightly to incorporate them, then shape the dough into a rugby-ball shape. Place on an oiled baking sheet and cover with oiled clingfilm.

7 Allow to prove (rise again) until soft and pillowy.

8 Heat the oven to 190°C | 375°F | gas mark 5.

9 Slash the bread on the diagonal about 1 cm | ½ in deep and 2.5 cm | 1 in apart.

10 Bake in the top third of the oven for 35–40 minutes or until the loaf sounds hollow when tapped on the underside.

11 Cool on a wire rack. Wrap in foil and keep for 1 day before slicing.

* If using fast-action or dried yeast, see page 480.

Cinnamon, Hazelnut and Raisin Bread

Make a starter with organic apple juice and honey to give this bread a delicious fruity flavour.

MAKES 2 LOAVES

For the starter

150 ml|5 fl oz organic apple juice

1 tablespoon organic clear honey

10 g|⅓ oz fresh yeast*

115 g|4 oz strong wholemeal or rye flour

10 g|⅓ oz fresh yeast

2 eggs, beaten

55 g|2 oz butter, melted and cooled

150 g|5 oz toasted hazelnuts

200 g|7 oz raisins or sultanas

For the dough

225 g|8 oz strong white flour

1 teaspoon salt

2 teaspoons ground cinnamon

To glaze

2 tablespoons clear honey

1 Make the starter: place the apple juice in a bowl and whisk in the honey and yeast. When the yeast has dissolved, stir in the flour. Cover with clingfilm and allow to stand at room temperature for 2–3 hours or until well-risen and bubbly. The starter can be chilled overnight after rising, if desired.

2 To make the dough, sift together the flour, salt and cinnamon into a large bowl. Make a well in the centre.

3 Tip the starter mixture into the well. Crumble in the yeast then add the eggs and butter. Quickly stir to combine, adding more warm water or flour if necessary to make a soft dough.

4 Turn out on to a floured work surface and knead until smooth and elastic, about 10 minutes. Alternatively, the dough can be kneaded in a machine for 6 minutes.

5 Place in an oiled bowl and cover with oiled clingfilm. Leave to rise in a warm place until doubled in size, about 1 hour.

6 Heat the oven to 220°C|425°|gas mark 7. Oil 2 × 450 g|1 lb loaf tins.

7 Turn the dough on to the work surface and pat down into a large rectangle about 2.5 cm|1 in thick.

8 Scatter the hazelnuts and raisins over the dough then knead gently to incorporate. Try not to let the raisins and nuts break through the surface of the dough as they could burn during baking.

9 Place the bread into the oiled loaf tins. Cover with oiled clingfilm. Leave in a warm place to prove to their final shape, about 45 minutes.

10 Place in the top third of the oven and turn the temperature down to 190°C|375°F|gas mark 5. Bake for 35–40 minutes or until golden-brown. The bread will sound hollow if tapped on the underside.

11 Remove the bread from the tins and place on a wire rack to cool. Whilst still warm, brush with the honey to glaze.

* If using fast-action or dried yeast, see page 480.

Baguettes

In France, baguettes are made using type 55 flour, a finely milled low-protein flour which makes an elastic dough. Use plain organic flour as a substitute. The dough for this bread is soft and sticky, so it is easier to knead it with a machine. If you do not have one, use the technique for kneading soft doughs, on page 485. It is important to keep all the ingredients cool.

MAKES 3 BAGUETTES

For the starter

200 ml | 7 fl oz mineral water, at cool room
   temperature
1 teaspoon fresh yeast*
100 g | 3½ oz organic plain white flour

For the sponge

the starter above, risen and collapsed
100 ml | 3½ fl oz mineral water, at cool room
   temperature
100 g | 3½ oz organic plain white flour

For the dough

285 g | 10 oz organic plain white flour
2 teaspoons fine sea salt

For shaping

3 tablespoons rice flour

1 For the starter, place the water in a bowl and stir in the yeast and flour. Cover with clingfilm and leave to rise at cool room temperature (18°C | 65°F) until it has risen fully and collapsed. This will take about 4 hours. Place in the refrigerator overnight.

2 To make the sponge, mix the mineral water and flour into the collapsed starter. Cover with clingfilm and leave to stand at cool room temperature or in the refrigerator until it has risen and just started to collapse. If this sponge is kept in the refrigerator, it can be used up to 2 weeks after making.

3 To make the dough, mix the flour and salt into the sponge. Knead until smooth and elastic, about 6 minutes in a machine.

4 Place the dough in an oiled bowl and turn to coat it with a thin film of oil. Cover the bowl with oiled clingfilm and leave to rise at cool room temperature until nearly tripled in size. This will take about 4 hours.

5 Oil your hands and gently lift the dough then fold it into 3 like a business letter, taking care not to knock out all of the air. Return it to the bowl, cover with oiled clingfilm and leave to stand for half an hour.

6 To shape the baguettes, sprinkle the rice flour on a dry work surface to cover an area measuring 20 × 40 cm | 8 × 16 in. Lift the dough from the bowl and place on the flour. Gently pull the dough into a rectangle measuring 15 × 35 cm | 6 × 14 in. Cut the dough lengthways into thirds, using a sharp, oiled knife. Fold along the cut edge of the dough to enclose that edge.

7 Pinch the dough together gently to seal. Place the baguettes on an oiled baking sheet or baguette tin with the join underneath. Slash the dough lightly on the diagonal in several places using a very sharp knife or single-edged razor blade.

8 Cover with oiled clingfilm and leave to rise until doubled in size. This can take 1–2 hours. If the dough is prodded gently the indentation will only spring back halfway.

9 Meanwhile heat the oven to 230°C|450°F|gas mark 8. Place a roasting tin in the bottom of the oven to heat.

10 Remove the clingfilm and place the loaves in the top third of the oven to bake. Add iced water to the roasting tin to create steam. Turn the oven temperature down to 200°C|400°F|gas mark 6. Bake for 20–25 minutes or until golden, then turn the baguettes over and bake for a further 5 minutes. Cool on a wire rack.

* If using fast-action or dried yeast, see page 480.

Italian Sesame Loaf

MAKES 1 LOAF

For the biga

10 g|⅓ oz fresh yeast*

150 ml|5 fl oz mineral water, at room temperature

100 g|3½ oz durum wheat flour

For the dough

1 tablespoon olive oil

140 g|5 oz strong white flour

1 teaspoon sea salt

2 tablespoons sesame seeds

2–3 tablespoons rice flour

1 To make the biga, place the yeast and water in a large bowl and whisk to combine. Stir in the flour. Don't worry about lumps. Cover with clingfilm and leave at cool room temperature for at least 1 hour or overnight.

2 To make the dough, mix the oil, flour and salt into the biga. Knead by machine for 6 minutes or by hand for 5 minutes using the technique for kneading soft doughs on page 000. You should be able to form a gluten window (see page 000) when the dough has been kneaded sufficiently.

3 Cover the bowl with oiled clingfilm and leave to rise until doubled in size, about 1½ hours.

4 Return the dough to the bowl and cover with oiled clingfilm for 30 minutes.

5 Meanwhile, heat the oven to 220°C|425°F|gas mark 7. Sprinkle a baking sheet with the sesame seeds.

6 Lift the dough from the bowl with oiled hands and place on the sesame seeds. Stretch the dough into a long loaf shape, about 10 × 40 cm|4 × 16 in, and roll to coat in the sesame seeds.

7 Move the dough to one side then sift the rice flour on to the baking sheet. Place the dough on top of the rice flour and cover with oiled clingfilm.

8 Leave to prove (rise again) until soft and pillowy, about 30 minutes.

9 Place in the top third of the oven and bake for 30 minutes. Spray with a plant mister 3 times during the first 5 minutes of baking.

10 Cool on a wire rack.

* If using fast-action or dried yeast, see page 480.

Bâtard

This bread is made using an 'old dough' starter, a method that produces a chewy loaf with a thick crust and lots of flavour. It is similar to a baguette but is shorter and fatter.

MAKES 2 LOAVES

For the first-stage starter

15 g|½ oz piece fully risen white bread dough

55 ml|2 fl oz lukewarm mineral water

85 g|3 oz organic strong white flour

For the second-stage starter

the first-stage starter

55 ml|2 fl oz lukewarm mineral water

115 g|4 oz organic strong white flour

For the dough

the second-stage starter

290 ml|10 fl oz cool water

10 g|⅓ oz fresh yeast*

340–400 g|12 oz-14 oz organic strong flour

2½ teaspoons sea salt

To shape

3 tablespoons rice flour

First stage

1 Cut the dough into small pieces and drop into the water. Leave to soften for 5 minutes.
2 Gradually mix in the flour. Stir to make a dough.
3 Cover with clingfilm and leave to rise at room temperature for 8 hours.

Second stage

4 Combine all the ingredients as for the first-stage starter.
5 Leave to rise at room temperature for 4 hours. It should more than double in size. Chill for at least 1 hour or up to 8 hours.

For the dough

6 Deflate the second-stage starter, break into pieces and add to the water. Crumble in the yeast. Leave to stand for 5 minutes.
7 Using a freestanding mixer, mix in the flour then leave to stand for 10 minutes.
8 Sprinkle the salt over the dough and knead for 5–8 minutes.
9 Transfer the dough to a clean, oiled bowl, cover with oiled clingfilm and leave to rise for 1½ hours or until doubled in size.
10 Using oiled hands, gently lift the dough from the bowl, stretch it to about 60 cm|24 in then fold it over itself into 3, like a business letter. Return to the oiled bowl and leave to rise again for 45 minutes.
11 To shape: sprinkle the rice flour over a work surface to cover 40 × 60 cm|12 × 24 in. Using oiled hands, lift the risen dough from the bowl and place on the rice flour. Cut the dough in half lengthways, using an oiled knife. Cover with oiled clingfilm.
12 Leave the dough to prove for 1 hour or until the dough will spring back only very slightly when prodded.
13 Place a baking stone in the top third of the oven. Place a roasting tin with water in the bottom of the oven and heat it to 200°C|400°F|gas mark 6.
14 Add half a cup of iced water to the roasting tin to create steam. Bake the loaves on the

baking stone for 30 minutes. Spray the bread with water using a plant mister 3 times during the first 5 minutes of baking. The loaves may need to be turned over for the last 5 minutes of baking to fully brown the undersides.

15 Cool on a wire rack.

* If using fast-action or dried yeast, see page 480.

Pain d'Epi

The name of this traditional harvest bread translates as 'wheat ear'. It is shaped by cutting into the dough for a large baguette at a 45° angle, first on one side then on the other, down the length of the dough. The pieces are then pulled sideways and twisted so that the finished loaf resembles a stalk of wheat.

MAKES 1 LARGE LOAF

For the starter
10 g|⅓ oz fresh yeast*
150 ml|5 fl oz lukewarm water
½ teaspoon caster sugar
140 g|5 oz strong white flour

For the dough
10 g|⅓ oz fresh yeast*
150 ml|5 fl oz lukewarm water
340 g|12 oz strong white flour
2 teaspoons salt
2 tablespoons olive oil
2 tablespoons rice flour

1 Make the starter: whisk the yeast into the water, then stir in the sugar and the flour. Cover with clingfilm and leave in a cool place overnight.

2 Make the dough: whisk the yeast into the water. Sift the flour into a large bowl with the salt and make a well in the centre.

3 Tip the starter into the well along with the new yeast mixture and 1 tablespoon oil.

4 Stir to make a soft dough, adding a little more water or more flour if required.

5 Knead the dough for 10 minutes by hand or for 6 minutes by machine to make a smooth, elastic dough.

6 Place the dough in an oiled bowl and turn to coat with a thin film of oil. Cover with oiled clingfilm. Leave to rise in a warm place until doubled in size, about 1 hour.

7 Heat the oven to 200°C|400°F|gas mark 6. Place a roasting pan on the lower shelf of the oven.

8 Sprinkle the rice flour on to a baking sheet. Carefully lift the risen dough out of the bowl, place on the baking sheet and stretch to 40 cm|16 in.

9 Brush the dough with 1 tablespoon oil. Make cuts 5 cm|2 in apart down both sides of the dough at a 45° angle, nearly to the centre of the dough. (a) Twist the pieces of dough made by the cuts so that the cut side is uppermost. (b) Cover with oiled clingfilm and leave to prove (rise again) until it is pillowy and springs back only a little when prodded. (c)

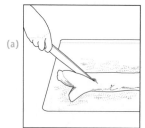 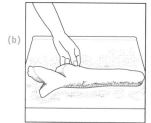 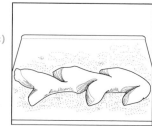

(a)   (b)   (c)

10 Splash a little cold water into the roasting pan to create a steamy environment. Bake the loaf in the top third of the oven (the hottest part) for 20–30 minutes. Spray twice with a plant mister during the first 5 minutes of baking.

11 After 20 minutes, remove the bread from the baking sheet and place it directly on the oven shelf so that the base can brown. Bake for a further 5–10 minutes. The bread is done when it is golden-brown, feels light and sounds hollow when tapped on the underside.

12 Transfer to a wire rack to cool.

* If using fast-action or dried yeast, see page 480.

Sfilatino

This bread is also made using an 'old dough' starter, producing a flavoursome, crusty loaf. Begin the recipe the day before baking.

MAKES 3 SMALL BAGUETTES

For the first-stage starter
15 g | ½ oz piece fully risen white bread dough
55 ml | 2 fl oz lukewarm mineral water
85 g | 3 oz organic strong white flour

For the second-stage starter
the first-stage starter
55 ml | 2 fl oz lukewarm mineral water
115 g | 4 oz organic strong white flour

For the dough
the second-stage starter
250 ml | 9 fl oz cool water
10 g | ⅓ oz fresh yeast*
3 tablespoons olive oil
340–400 g | 12–14 oz organic strong white flour
1 tablespoon sea salt

To shape
3 tablespoons rice flour

First stage
1 Cut the dough into small pieces and drop into the water. Leave to soften for 5 minutes.
2 Gradually mix in the flour. Stir to make a dough.
3 Cover with clingfilm and leave to rise in a warm place for 8 hours.

Second stage

4 Combine all the ingredients as for the first-stage starter.

5 Leave to rise in a warm place for 4 hours. It should more than double in size. Chill for at least 1 hour or up to 8 hours.

For the dough

6 Deflate the second-stage starter, break into pieces and add to the water. Leave to stand for 5 minutes.

7 Using a freestanding mixer, mix in the flour and the olive oil then leave to stand for 10 minutes.

8 Sprinkle the salt over the dough and knead for 5–8 minutes.

9 Transfer the dough to a clean, oiled bowl, cover with oiled clingfilm then and leave to rise for 1½ hours or until doubled in size.

10 Using oiled hands, gently lift the dough from the bowl, stretch it to about 60 cm | 24 in then fold it over itself into 3, like a business letter. Return to the oiled bowl and leave rise again for 45 minutes.

To shape

11 Sprinkle the rice flour over a work surface to cover 40 × 60 cm | 12 × 24 in. Using oiled hands, lift the risen dough from the bowl and place on the rice flour. Cut the dough in half lengthways, using an oiled knife. Cover with oiled clingfilm.

12 Leave the dough to prove for 1½ hours or until the dough will spring back only very slightly when prodded.

13 Place a baking stone in the top third of the oven. Place a roasting tin with water in the bottom of the oven and heat it to 230°C | 450°F | gas mark 8.

14 Slide the loaves on to the baking stone and bake for 30 minutes.

15 Cool on a wire rack.

* If using fast-action or dried yeast, see page 480.

Tuscan Bread

Historically, Tuscan bread has always been made without salt because salt was heavily taxed by the government in ancient times. However, it is served with salty food, such as olives and cured meats, which compensate for the lack of salt in the bread. Slices of this bread toasted and rubbed with olive oil and garlic make the perfect base for crostini.

The absence of salt means that the yeast will be very active, causing the bread to rise rapidly. As the dough is very wet, the finished loaf will have large uneven holes, a thick crust and a chewy texture.

The biga needs to be started the day before baking.

MAKES 1 LOAF

For the biga
1 teaspoon fresh yeast*
290 ml | 10 fl oz mineral water
150 g | 5 oz organic strong white flour

For the dough
10 g | ⅓ oz fresh yeast*
250 g | 9 oz organic strong white flour
2 tablespoons polenta

1 For the starter, place the yeast in a bowl and whisk in the water. Stir in the flour then cover the bowl with clingfilm and leave to stand at cool room temperature overnight.

2 For the dough, crumble the yeast into the starter then stir in the flour. Allow the dough to stand for 20 minutes at room temperature, then knead for 6 minutes by machine.

3 Place the dough in a lightly oiled bowl and turn to coat it in a thin film of oil. Cover with oiled clingfilm and leave in a warm place to rise until doubled in size, about 1 hour.

4 Sprinkle the polenta in a thin, even layer on to a baking sheet.

5 Oil your hands and gently lift the dough from the bowl. It will be sticky and stretchy. Fold it over on itself several times to form it into a round. Place on the polenta-covered baking sheet. Using oiled hands, pat the dough down so that it is about 2.5 cm | 1 in thick. Cover with oiled clingfilm. Allow to prove (rise again) until an indentation made on the side of the dough only springs back halfway.

6 Meanwhile, heat the oven to 200°C | 400°F | gas mark 6. Place one shelf in the top third of the oven and another shelf with a roasting tin on it in the bottom third. Place a baking stone on the top shelf of the oven.

7 Remove the clingfilm and dust the top of the dough with flour.

8 Slide the dough from the baking sheet on to the hot baking stone and bake in the top third of the oven for 30 minutes, adding iced water to the hot roasting tin to create steam when the dough is placed in the oven. The baked loaf should sound hollow when tapped on the underside.

9 Cool on a wire rack.

* If using fast-action or dried yeast, see page 480.

Sourdough Bread

The sourdough method of making bread produces a dense, chewy loaf with a thick crust and a sour tang. The loaves are frequently made either partially or wholly from wholemeal flour, sometimes with the addition of rye flour, and are shaped into a free-form loaf that is slashed several times. In Europe, sourdough bread is very popular in central Europe and in France, where it is known as La Poilâne, after a famous family bakery in Paris. The bread keeps well and is particularly good served with a strong-flavoured cheese.

Sourdough bread was widely made in the American West and in the Australian outback, where it is still popular today. San Francisco is renowned for its sourdough bread, which is made with a white starter and white flour. It owes its particular taste to a strain of bacterium, *Lactobacillus sanfrancisco*, which is unique to that city.

The original sourdough breads were made using the wild yeast present in the environment to leaven the flour, following a process that was used for centuries to produce a raised loaf, long before bakers' yeast became available commercially. It is thought that the first raised loaf was made by accidentally capturing these yeasts, probably on the inside of a vessel used for wine.

Sourdough bread is leavened with a starter. Originally a piece of bread dough was kept back from the loaf being baked. This piece of dough was stored in the flour sack and then mixed with fresh water and flour to make the next loaf. This type of starter is known as a 'dry' or 'firm' starter. Today it is a useful way to add flavour to bread.

A second type of starter, called a 'wet' starter, is made by mixing organic flour and water to the consistency of a batter or thick cream, then allowing it to stand uncovered for about 3 days to capture the wild yeast present in the air. The starter should become foamy and smell sweetly yeasty. If it smells 'off' it is best to discard it and start again. Organic yoghurt, honey, grapes and even beer can be used to help feed the starter. A starter can be made more successfully in a rural environment, rather than in a city where the air is polluted. It is important to use organic ingredients when making sourdough bread. Bleached flour and chlorinated water contain chemicals that inhibit yeast growth.

A loaf raised entirely by a natural yeast starter can take up to 24 hours to make (not including the time required to make the starter) from the time the loaf is mixed to the time it is baked because of the relatively small amount of yeast in the dough. Obviously this method of bread-making is time-consuming, but the flavour of the finished loaf is much more complex and interesting and the texture of the loaf is chewier and the crust crustier. There is the added advantage that the bread made using a starter is more moist and keeps longer than ordinary bread. Many bakers today add a small amount of commercial baker's yeast to the flour along with the starter. This produces a loaf with a flavour similar to a sourdough bread in a much shorter time.

Sourdough Bread

A natural yeast starter for sourdough bread will take about 1 week to become active. To be active enough to raise a dough, a starter should double in 4 hours when fed and left at room temperature. A traditional sourdough loaf will take about 1½ days to produce. To make a loaf more quickly, follow the *Modern Sourdough Loaf* recipe opposite. Whole wheat grain can be found in health-food shops.

MAKES 1 LOAF

For the starter

225 g | 8 oz organic wheat grain or strong white organic flour
225 ml | 8 fl oz lukewarm mineral water
225 g | 8 oz strong white organic flour
1 tablespoon organic barley malt syrup
290 ml | 10 fl oz lukewarm mineral water

For the dough

225 g | 8 oz starter (see left)
55–115ml | 2–4 fl oz lukewarm mineral water
1 tablespoon clear organic honey or barley malt syrup
170 g | 6 oz strong white organic flour
55 g | 2 oz organic rye flour or wholemeal flour
1½ teaspoons fine sea salt

For the starter

1 If using wheat grain, grind it in a clean coffee grinder to make flour. Place this flour or 225 g | 8oz strong white organic flour in a bowl and stir in 225 ml | 8 fl oz water to make a paste. Leave to stand uncovered for 3 days at room temperature. A few whole unwashed grapes can be added to the mixture, which should start to bubble and smell sweetly yeasty. If it smells unpleasant, throw it away and start again.

2 On the third day stir in the second quantity of flour, the barley malt syrup and the 290 ml | 10 fl oz water. Leave to stand, uncovered, for a further 3 days. Discard the grapes, if using. Remove 225 g | 8 oz of the starter to make the bread. Feed the remaining starter by mixing in 100 ml | 3½ fl oz mineral water and 100 g | 3½ oz strong white organic flour, then cover and store in the refrigerator.

For the bread

3 Place 225 g | 8 oz of the starter in a large bowl and stir in the water and honey or malt syrup. Sift the flours together, then add enough flour to make a soft but not too sticky dough.

4 Knead for 10 minutes by hand or 6 minutes by machine. Place in an oiled bowl and turn to coat with a thin film of oil. Cover with oiled clingfilm and leave to stand at room temperature until doubled in size. This will take up to 8 hours.

5 Knock back the dough and knead for 1 minute. Return to the oiled bowl, cover with oiled clingfilm and chill overnight.

6 Sprinkle the salt over the dough then knead to knock back for 2 minutes. Cover the dough with clingfilm and leave it to rest for 10 minutes. Heavily flour a 20 cm | 8 in diameter basket or line a bowl with a heavily floured tea towel.

7 Shape the dough into a smooth round and place in the basket or bowl. Cover with oiled clingfilm and leave to prove (rise again) in a warm place until nearly doubled in size, about 3 hours.

8 Meanwhile, place a baking stone on a rack placed in the top third of the oven and heat

the oven to 220°C | 425°F | gas mark 7. Place an empty roasting tin on a rack in the bottom third of the oven.

9 When the dough has proved, sprinkle a baking sheet or peel liberally with flour. Carefully turn the dough on to the baking sheet or peel, then slash it with a razor or serrated knife in a noughts and crosses grid pattern. Boil some water for steam.

10 Slide the dough from the baking sheet on to the baking stone, then pour a cup of boiling water into the roasting tin to create a steamy environment. Spray the dough with a plant mister during the first 5 minutes of baking. Bake for 35–40 minutes or until the loaf is well-browned and sounds hollow when tapped on the underside. Transfer to a wire rack and leave to cool for 1 hour before slicing.

Modern Sourdough Bread

This recipe uses sourdough starter plus fresh yeast to speed the rising and proving times.

MAKES 1 LOAF

10 g | ⅓ oz fresh yeast*
100 ml | 3½ fl oz lukewarm water
1 tablespoon malt extract or clear honey
225 g | 8 oz sourdough starter (see page 588), at
  room temperature

225 g | 8 oz strong white flour
1 teaspoon salt
rice flour

1 Whisk the yeast into the water and stir in the malt extract or honey.
2 Stir in the sourdough starter.
3 Sift the flour and salt over the top and stir to make a soft but not too sticky dough.
4 Knead for 6 minutes by machine or 10 minutes by hand then place in a lightly oiled bowl. Turn the dough to coat it in the oil then cover with oiled clingfilm.
5 Allow the dough to rise in a warm place until doubled in size, about 2 hours.
6 Knock back the dough by kneading lightly by hand then shaping into a round. Place on a baking sheet or peel sprinkled with rice flour. Cover with oiled clingfilm and leave in a warm place to rise until soft and pillowy, about 45 minutes.
7 Meanwhile, heat the oven to 220°C | 425°F | gas mark 7. Place a baking stone in the top third of the oven and an empty roasting tin in the bottom third.
8 When the dough is nearly ready to go into the oven, slash in 3 places using a serrated knife. Allow the dough to recover for 5 minutes. Boil the kettle.
9 Slide the dough on to the hot baking stone in the oven. Pour a cupful of boiling water into the roasting tin to create steam.
10 Turn the oven temperature down to 200°C | 400°F | gas mark 6. Bake the loaf for 30–40 minutes or until it sounds hollow when tapped on the underside.
11 Transfer to a wire rack to cool.

* If using fast-action or dried yeast, see page 480.

Fruit and Nut Sourdough

MAKES 2 LOAVES

225 g | 8 oz sourdough starter (see page 588), at room temperature

225 ml | 8 fl oz lukewarm mineral water

10 g | ⅓ oz fresh yeast or 1 teaspoon fast-action yeast

30 g | 1 oz caster sugar

30 g | 1 oz butter, melted and cooled to room temperature

115 g | 4 oz organic rye flour

1½ teaspoons salt

300 g | 10½ oz strong organic white flour

250 g | 9 oz mixed dried fruit

100 g | 3½ oz whole almonds, toasted

1 Place the sourdough starter in a large bowl and mix in the mineral water, yeast, sugar and butter.

2 Stir in the rye flour, salt and enough white flour to make a soft dough. Knead for 10 minutes by hand or 6 minutes by machine.

3 Place in an oiled bowl and turn the dough to coat in a thin film of oil. Cover with oiled clingfilm and leave to rise in a warm place until doubled in size, about 2 hours.

4 Flatten the dough to 1 cm | ½ in thick on a floured work surface and sprinkle over the dried fruits and the almonds. Roll up the dough and knead lightly to incorporate the fruit and nuts.

5 Divide into 2 loaves and shape into rounds, keeping the fruit to the interior of the loaf to avoid burning. Place on 2 greased baking sheets.

6 Make slashes ½ cm | ¼ in deep and cover with oiled clingfilm. Leave to rise until nearly doubled in size in a warm place for 1 hour or in the refrigerator overnight. Allow the dough to come to room temperature before baking.

7 Heat the oven to 200°C | 400°F | gas mark 6. Bake the loaves in the top third of the oven for 35–40 minutes or until a deep brown. The loaves may need to be covered halfway through baking to prevent overbrowning. Turn the bread over for the last 5 minutes of baking time, to brown the underside. When done, the bread should sound hollow when tapped on the underside. Cool on a wire rack.

Sweet Yeast Breads and Rolls

The breads in this section are enriched with the addition of fat, in the form of extra butter, eggs and/or milk, and they include more sugar than recipes for basic breads. Many of the recipes are for regional specialities and also include various spices, dried fruits and nuts. They are yeast-raised and are lower in fat and sugar than a cake, so can be considered a 'healthy alternative'.

The addition of extra fat and sugar to a bread dough will slow the action of the yeast and therefore lengthen the rising and proving times. Fat and sugar will also soften the gluten, resulting in a bread with a finer, softer texture that is rather more like a cake. The added fat will help the bread to keep for several days.

Bara Brith

The name for this Welsh cake means 'speckled bread'. It is a popular teatime treat.

MAKES 1 LARGE LOAF

225 ml | 8 fl oz milk
450 g | 1 lb strong white flour
1 teaspoon salt
55 g | 2 oz butter, softened
1 teaspoon mixed spice

55 g | 2 oz light muscovado sugar
20 g | ⅔ oz fresh yeast*
1 egg, beaten
250 g | 9 oz mixed dried fruit

1 Heat the milk in a small saucepan until it steams heavily, then set aside to cool until lukewarm. Skim.
2 Sift the flour and salt into a large bowl then rub in the butter. Stir in the mixed spice and the sugar. Make a well in the centre.
3 Mixed the yeast to a cream with 2 tablespoons of the milk and pour into the well. Add the egg and enough milk to make a soft but not too sticky dough.
4 Knead for 6 minutes by machine or 10 minutes by hand or until smooth and satiny.
5 Place the dough in an oiled bowl and turn to coat it in the oil. Cover with oiled clingfilm and leave to rise at warm room temperature until doubled in size, about 1½ hours.
6 Turn the dough out on to a lightly floured work surface and roll to a flat rectangle. Sprinkle over the fruit then roll up. Knead lightly to incorporate the fruit but try not to let it break through the surface of the dough.
7 Shape the dough into a round and place on an oiled baking sheet. Cover with oiled clingfilm and leave to prove (rise again) until soft and pillowy.

8 Meanwhile, heat the oven to 190°C|375°F|gas mark 5.

9 Bake in the centre of the oven for 35–40 minutes, covering with greaseproof paper halfway through cooking if the loaf is becoming too brown. Cool on a wire rack.

* If using fast-action or dried yeast, see page 480.

Spiced Orange Sweet Bread

Like most sweet yeast breads, this can be served for breakfast, 'elevenses' or at teatime in place of a cake.

MAKES 1 LARGE LOAF

30 g|1 oz fresh yeast*

55 g|2 oz sugar

200 ml|7 fl oz lukewarm milk

85 ml|3 fl oz orange juice

30 g|1 oz unsalted butter, melted

1 egg, beaten

550 g|1 lb 4 oz strong white flour

grated zest of 1 orange

½ teaspoon salt

For the filling

85 g|3 oz demerara sugar

1 teaspoon ground cinnamon

1 teaspoon mixed spice

30 g|1 oz unsalted butter, melted

1 Mix the yeast with a teaspoon of the sugar and 2 tablespoons of the milk. Mix the rest of the milk with the orange juice, butter and egg.

2 Sift the flour into a large bowl, then add the rest of the sugar, the orange zest and salt. Make a well in the centre and add the yeast and liquid. Mix to make a soft but not wet dough, adding more flour if necessary.

3 Knead for 10 minutes by hand or 6 minutes by machine, or until the dough is smooth and elastic. Place the dough in an oiled bowl and turn to coat it in the oil. Cover with oiled clingfilm and leave to rise in a warm place for 45–60 minutes or until it has doubled in size.

4 Meanwhile, mix together the demerara sugar, spices and melted butter.

5 Heat the oven to 190°C|375°F|gas mark 5. Grease a baking sheet.

6 Remove the dough from the bowl and roll out to a rectangle measuring 20 × 30 cm| 8 × 12 in. Spread over the spiced sugar mixture, taking it right to the edges. Roll up as tightly as possible and place seam-side down on the greased baking sheet. Cover with oiled clingfilm and put in a warm place to prove for 15–20 minutes or until it is 1½ times its original size.

7 Dust with flour and put in the oven. Bake for 30–40 minutes or until the loaf sounds hollow when tapped on the underside. Remove from the baking sheet and put on a wire rack to cool.

* If using fast-action or dried yeast, see page 480.

Saffron Cake

Saffron cake is particularly popular in Cornwall. This is because the Phoenicians traded saffron for Cornish tin. Nowadays saffron is so expensive that these cakes sold in bakeries usually contain only a very little saffron and are instead coloured with yellow food dye. Only cakes labelled 'genuine saffron cake' contain the real thing.

MAKES 1 LARGE LOAF

30 saffron strands
150 ml | 5 fl oz boiling water
115 g | ½ oz fresh yeast*
115 g | 4 oz caster sugar
85 ml | 3 fl oz lukewarm milk
450 g | 1 lb plain flour
½ teaspoon salt
¼ teaspoon freshly grated nutmeg
¼ teaspoon ground cinnamon

85 g | 3 oz butter
85 g | 3 oz lard
115 g | 4 oz sultanas
115 g | 4 oz currants
30 g | 1 oz mixed peel

To glaze

1 egg, beaten

1 Soak the strands of saffron in the boiling water for about 2 hours.
2 Cream the yeast with 1 teaspoon of the sugar and add the milk.
3 Sift the flour, salt and spices together into a large mixing bowl. Cut the butter and lard into pieces and rub in with your fingertips.
4 Make a well in the centre and add the yeast mixture, saffron and saffron-flavoured water. Mix to make a soft but not wet dough. Knead for 10 minutes by hand or 6 minutes by machine, or until the dough is smooth and elastic. Place the dough in an oiled bowl and turn to coat in the oil. Cover with oiled clingfilm or a clean damp cloth and leave in a warm place to rise until doubled in size.
5 Heat the oven to 190°C | 375°F | gas mark 5 and grease a 900 g | 2 lb loaf tin.
6 Take the risen dough out of the bowl, scatter over the remaining sugar and the dried fruit and peel. Knock back the dough and knead in the fruit, distributing evenly throughout the dough.
7 Shape into a loaf and put into the prepared tin. Cover, return to the warm place and leave until 1½ times its original size. This will take about 15 minutes, depending on the warmth of the room.
8 Glaze the top of the loaf with beaten egg and bake in the oven for 20 minutes, then turn the oven temperature down to 180°C | 350°F | gas mark 4 and bake for a further 25 minutes or until the cake sounds hollow when tapped on the underside.
9 Turn out on to a wire rack and leave to cool completely.

* If using fast-action or dried yeast, see page 480.

Selkirk Bannock

This is a round, flat, yeasted fruit loaf.

MAKES 1 LOAF

15 g | ½ oz fresh yeast*
115 g | 4 oz sugar
55 g | 2 oz butter
55 g | 2 oz lard
290 ml | 10fl oz lukewarm milk

450 g | 1 lb plain flour
a pinch of salt
85 g | 3 oz sultanas
85 g | 3 oz raisins
55 g | 2 oz chopped mixed peel

1 Cream the yeast with 1 teaspoon of the sugar.
2 Melt the butter and lard until liquid but not hot. Add to the milk with the yeast mixture.
3 Sift the flour with the salt into a large mixing bowl. Make a well in the centre to expose the bottom of the bowl. Pour the yeast mixture slowly into the well, mixing with a round-bladed knife and gradually drawing in the surrounding flour until you have a smooth, softish batter.
4 Cover the bowl with a piece of oiled clingfilm or a clean damp cloth and leave in a warm place to rise until doubled in size. This should take about 1 hour, depending on the warmth of the room.
5 Heat the oven to 200°C | 400°F | gas mark 6.
6 Tip the risen dough on to a floured work surface and work in the dried fruits, peel and the remaining sugar, kneading carefully until the fruits are evenly distributed. Shape into a large round. Place on a floured baking sheet.
7 Cover the dough once again with the clingfilm or cloth, return to the warm place and leave until 1½ times its original size. This will take about 15 minutes.
8 Bake in the oven for 35–40 minutes or until the loaf sounds hollow when tapped on the underside. If the bannock shows signs of becoming too brown, turn the oven temperature down to 170°C | 325°F | gas mark 3.
9 Transfer the bannock to a wire rack and leave to cool.

* If using fast-action or dried yeast, see page 480.

Iced Cinnamon Swirl Bread

MAKES 1 SMALL LOAF

10 g|⅓ oz fresh yeast*
45 g|1½ oz caster sugar
225 g|8 oz strong white flour
½ teaspoon salt
45 g|1½ oz butter
1 egg
125 ml|4 fl oz lukewarm milk

1 teaspoon ground cinnamon
55 g|2 oz sultanas
55 g|2 oz raisins
55 g|2 oz dried apricots, chopped
55 g|2 oz hazelnuts, toasted, skinned and chopped
115 g|4 oz icing sugar quantity glacé icing (see page 455)

1 Cream the yeast with 1 teaspoon of the sugar.
2 Sift the flour with the salt into a warmed mixing bowl. Rub in half the butter with the fingertips and stir in half the remaining sugar.
3 Beat the egg and add to the yeast mixture with the milk.
4 Make a well in the centre of the flour and pour in the yeast liquid. Mix to make a soft but not wet dough and knead until smooth.
5 Cover the bowl with oiled clingfilm and leave in a warm place to rise until doubled in size. This will take about 1 hour, depending on the warmth of the room.
6 Knock back the risen dough and knead again on a floured surface. Roll out to a 15 × 25 cm|6 × 10 in rectangle.
7 Heat the oven to 200°C|400°F|gas mark 6. Grease a 450 g|1 lb loaf tin.
8 Soften the remaining butter, mix with half the remaining sugar and spread over the dough. Toss the fruit and nuts in the remaining sugar and the spice and sprinkle over the butter and sugar mixture.
9 Roll up the dough like a Swiss roll and pinch the ends to seal. Place in the prepared tin, return to the warm place and leave to rise for about 15 minutes or until 1½ times its original size.
10 Bake in the centre of the oven for 30–40 minutes or until the loaf sounds hollow when tapped on the underside.
11 Turn out on to a wire rack and leave to cool completely.
12 When the loaf is cold, pour the glacé icing over the top and allow to set.

* If using fast-action or dried yeast, see page 480.

Monkey Bread

This is a funny name for a sweet bread to pull apart and share.

SERVES 8–10

For the dough
200 ml | 7 fl oz milk

30 g | 1 oz fresh yeast*

500 g | 1 lb 2 oz strong white flour

1 teaspoon cinnamon

1½ teaspoons salt

55 g | 2 oz unsalted butter

2 eggs, beaten

2 tablespoons clear honey

For the filling
100 g | 3½ oz light brown muscovado sugar

1½ teaspoons ground cinnamon

85 g | 3 oz unsalted butter, melted

100 g | 3½ oz pecan nuts or walnuts, toasted and
chopped

For the icing
115 g | 4 oz icing sugar, sifted

2 tablespoons boiling water

1 Heat the milk until it steams then leave to stand until it is lukewarm. Skim.

2 Place the yeast in a small bowl and mix to a smooth cream with 2 tablespoons of the milk.

3 Sift together the flour, cinnamon and salt into a large bowl. Cut the butter into small pieces then rub into the flour using your fingertips. Make a well in the centre of the flour.

4 Tip the yeast, eggs and honey into the well then add enough milk to make a soft but not sticky dough.

5 Knead for 10 minutes by hand or 6 minutes by machine.

6 Place in an oiled bowl then turn to coat in the oil. Cover with oiled clingfilm and allow to rise until doubled in size.

7 Knock back the dough by kneading lightly.

8 Mix together the muscovado sugar and cinnamon and place on a plate. Put the melted butter into a bowl.

9 Line the base and sides of an angel food tin or a deep 20 cm | 8 in round cake tin with baking parchment and oil it lightly. If using a cake tin, place an empty, clean 400 g | 14 oz tin in the centre of the tin so that the bread will cook in a ring shape.

10 Break off walnut-sized lumps of dough and dip in the butter then roll in the cinnamon sugar. When you have completed one layer of dough balls, sprinkle with half the nuts. Continue making dough balls until all the dough is used. Sprinkle with the remaining nuts. Cover with clingfilm and allow to nearly double in size.

11 Meanwhile, heat the oven to 180°C | 350°F | gas mark 4. Bake the bread for 35–40 minutes or until golden. The bread will need to be covered with greaseproof paper or foil about halfway through the cooking time to prevent overbrowning.

12 Remove from the tin while warm and place on a serving plate.

13 Mix half the icing sugar with the boiling water then gradually stir in the remaining icing sugar to make a smooth, slightly runny icing. Use a tablespoon to drizzle the icing over the bread.

* If using fast-action or dried yeast, see page 480.

Croatian Walnut Bread

These loaves are ubiquitous in the bakeries of Croatia. They are a great treat for breakfast or with a cup of tea.

MAKES 1 LOAF

For the dough

150 ml | 5 fl oz milk
20 g | ⅔ oz fresh yeast*
30 g | 1 oz caster sugar
340 g | 12 oz strong white flour
½ teaspoon salt
1 egg, beaten
30 g | 1 oz butter, melted and cooled

For the filling

140 g | 5 oz walnuts
85 g | 3 oz soft light brown sugar
85 g | 3 oz butter, softened
1 teaspoon cinnamon

To glaze

1 tablespoon milk
2 tablespoons icing sugar

1 Warm the milk until it steams then cool until lukewarm. Skim.

2 Mix the yeast to a thin cream with 2 tablespoons of the milk and a teaspoon of the caster sugar.

3 Sift the flour and salt into a large bowl and stir in the remaining sugar. Make a well in the centre of the flour and add the milk, yeast mixture, egg and butter.

4 Mix to a soft but not sticky dough, adding more milk or flour as required.

5 Knead for 10 minutes by hand or 6 minutes in a machine until smooth and satiny.

6 Place the dough in an oiled bowl and turn to coat it in the oil. Cover with oiled clingfilm and leave at room temperature to rise until doubled in size.

7 Meanwhile, make the filling. Chop the walnuts very finely either by hand or in the food processor. If chopping in the food processor, add a couple of tablespoons of the sugar to help keep the nuts free-flowing.

8 Mix the nuts, sugar, butter and cinnamon and set aside.

9 When the dough has doubled in size, place it on a lightly floured surface and roll into a 20 × 40 cm | 8 × 16 in rectangle. Spread over the walnut paste then roll up tightly from each of the short ends towards the middle. Pinch the ends together to keep the filling from spilling out.

10 Place the dough, smooth side down, into a lightly oiled 900 g | 2 lb tin. Cover with oiled clingfilm and leave to rise until soft and pillowy, about 45 minutes.

11 Meanwhile, heat the oven to 190°C | 375°F | gas mark 5.

12 Bake the loaf in the top third of the oven for 35 minutes. It will sound hollow when tapped on the underside.

13 Place the warm loaf on to a wire rack and brush the top and sides whilst still warm with the milk and sift over the icing sugar.

* If using fast-action or dried yeast, see page 480.

Schiacciata

This bread from the Chianti region of Italy makes the most of their famous indigenous ingredient, the grape. It can be served as a snack or as a dessert. This recipe needs to be started 1½ days before serving.

SERVES 8–10

For the sponge
290 ml | 10 fl oz lukewarm water
30 g | 1 oz fresh yeast*
100 g | 3½ oz organic strong white flour

For the dough
340 g | 12 oz organic strong white flour
1 teaspoon salt

2 tablespoons olive oil
150 ml | 5 oz lukewarm water

For the topping
1 kg | 2¼ lb seedless red grapes
115 g | 4 oz caster sugar
½ teaspoon fennel seeds

1 Make the sponge: place the water in a bowl and mix in the yeast. Stir in the flour and cover the bowl with clingfilm. Leave to stand in a cool place for 24 hours.
2 Make the dough: sift together the flour and salt into a large bowl. Make a well in the centre and tip in the sponge and the olive oil. Stir together, adding enough additional water to make a soft but not too sticky dough.
3 Knead for 10 minutes by hand or 6 minutes by machine to a smooth dough.
4 Place the dough in an oiled bowl and turn to coat in a thin film of oil. Cover with oiled clingfilm and leave in a warm place until doubled in size.
5 Wash and dry the grapes, removing any stems. Mix the grapes with the sugar and fennel seeds and set aside.
6 Oil a 30 cm | 12 in pizza pan.
7 Carefully remove the dough from the bowl and divide into 2 equal-sized pieces.
8 Heat the oven to 190°C | 375°F | gas mark 5.
9 Stretch one piece of dough to fit the pizza pan. Place in the oiled pan and top with half the grapes. Stretch the second piece of dough to cover the first. Press over the top then cover with the remaining grapes. Cover with oiled clingfilm and leave to rise until almost doubled in size.
10 Bake for 1 hour. Serve warm.

* If using fast-action or dried yeast, see page 480.

Spiced Tea Ring

MAKES 1 RING

15 g | ½ oz fresh yeast*
30 g | 1 oz sugar
150 ml | 5 fl oz lukewarm milk
1 egg, beaten
225 g | 8 oz plain flour
½ teaspoon salt
½ teaspoon ground mixed spice
½ teaspoon ground cinnamon
30 g | 1 oz butter

30 g | 1 oz sultanas
30 g | 1 oz chopped mixed peel
grated zest of 1 lemon

To finish
115 g | 4 oz icing sugar
boiling water
15 g | ½ oz flaked almonds, toasted

1   Cream the yeast with the sugar and a little of the milk.

2   Mix the egg with the remaining milk.

3   Sift the flour, salt and spices together into a large mixing bowl. Rub the butter into the flour with the fingertips until the mixture resembles fine breadcrumbs.

4   Make a well in the centre and pour in the liquid gradually. Mix to make a soft but not wet dough. Knead for 10 minutes by hand or 6 minutes by machine, or until the dough is elastic and shiny.

5   Place the dough in an oiled bowl and turn to coat it in the oil. Cover with a piece of oiled clingfilm and leave in a warm place to rise until doubled in size. This will take about 1 hour, depending on the warmth of the room.

6   Heat the oven to 200°C | 400°F | gas mark 6. Grease a 570 ml | 1 pint ring mould.

7   Knock back the dough and knead in the sultanas, peel and lemon zest until evenly distributed.

8   Divide the dough into 5 pieces, shape into balls and place in the ring mould (they should barely touch each other). Return to the warm place and leave until nearly doubled in size.

9   Bake in the centre of the oven for 30–40 minutes or until brown and firm to the touch. Transfer to a wire rack and leave to cool completely.

10 When the tea ring is cold, mix the icing sugar with a little boiling water to a just-runny consistency. Drizzle the icing all over the tea ring and scatter over the almonds while the icing is still wet. Allow to set.

* If using fast-action or dried yeast, see page 480.

Barm Brack

'Barm' means yeast and 'brack' means speckled. Barm Brack is a sweet Irish yeast bread traditionally served at Hallowe'en. The speckles are the caraway seeds.

MAKES 1 LARGE LOAF

675 g | 1½ lb plain flour
½ teaspoon salt
15 g | ½ oz fresh yeast*
½ teaspoon caster sugar
290 ml | 10 fl oz lukewarm water

2 eggs, lightly beaten
55 g | 2 oz butter, melted and cooled
85 g | 3 oz caster sugar
30 g | 1 oz caraway seeds

1 Heat the oven to 200°C | 400°F | gas mark 6. Grease a baking sheet.
2 Sift the flour with the salt into a large mixing bowl. Make a well in the centre.
3 Cream the yeast with the sugar and some of the water.
4 Add the yeast mixture, eggs and remaining water to the well in the flour. Mix to make a soft but not wet dough. Knead for 10 minutes by hand or 6 minutes by machine, or until the dough is smooth and elastic. Place the dough in an oiled bowl and turn to coat it in the oil. Cover with oiled clingfilm and leave in a warm place to rise until doubled in size. This will take about 1 hour, depending on the warmth of the room.
5 Knock back the risen dough and knead in the butter, sugar and caraway seeds. Shape into a round loaf and place on the prepared baking sheet. Cover with oiled clingfilm or a clean cloth, return to the warm place and leave for about 20 minutes or until 1½ times its original size.
6 Dust with a little flour, then bake in the centre of the oven. Bake for 30 minutes or until the loaf sounds hollow when tapped on the underside. Transfer to a wire rack to cool.

* If using fast-action or dried yeast, see page 480.

Brioche

Brioche can be sweetened or not, depending on how the finished product is to be used. Plain flour produces a brioche with a fine, cake-like texture, whilst strong flour produces a brioche with a more open, bread-like texture.

MAKES 1 LARGE OR 12 SMALL BRIOCHE

85 ml | 3 fl oz milk
15 g | ½ oz fresh yeast*
30g | 1 oz caster sugar
500g | 1 lb 2 oz flour (see above for type)
1½ teaspoons salt
6 eggs, beaten

340 g | 12 oz unsalted butter, softened
extra melted butter and flour for the tins

To glaze
1 egg yolk, beaten with 1 tablespoon milk

1. Scald the milk, then allow to cool to blood temperature. Skim.
2. Cream the yeast with the milk and a pinch of the sugar.
3. Sift the flour with the salt into a large bowl and make a well in the centre.
4. Place the milk, yeast mixture and eggs in the well, then stir to make a soft, very sticky dough.
5. Beat the dough in an electric mixer or by hand. If kneading by hand, take a lump of the dough and pull it up vertically, then push it back down and away from you (see page 485). Continue this process until the dough becomes smooth and elastic and forms a cohesive ball.
6. Place the dough in an oiled bowl. Cover the dough with lightly oiled clingfilm and leave in a warm place to rise until doubled in size.
7. Beat the butter and rest of the sugar together to dissolve the sugar and to bring the mixture to the same texture as the dough.
8. To add the butter to the dough using a mixer, beat 1 tablespoon of the butter at a time into the dough, only adding more butter when the previous addition has been incorporated. To add the butter by hand, turn the dough on to a work surface. Bury the butter 1 tablespoon at a time in the centre of the dough, then knead the dough as above until it becomes a smooth, silky mass. Continue adding butter in this way until it has all been incorporated.
9. Place the dough in a bowl and cover with oiled clingfilm. Allow to rise until doubled in size. It should not be risen in a very warm place, i.e. no more than 21°C|70°F, or the butter could become too soft, which would result in a greasy brioche.
10. When the dough has risen, gently knock it back by folding the edges of the dough over the centre and patting it down lightly.
11. Cover the dough with oiled clingfilm and chill for at least 8 hours or overnight.
12. Generously grease the brioche tins with 2 coatings of butter and dust with flour, tapping out any excess flour on to the work surface.
13. Half-fill the prepared tins with the cold brioche dough. For *brioche à tête*, make a hole in the centre of the dough all the way to the bottom, using the floured handle of a wooden spoon. Place an elongated 'head' of dough into the hole and secure it by pressing through the centre of the 'head' with the spoon handle.
14. Heat the oven to 190°C|375°F|gas mark 5. Cover the brioche tins with oiled clingfilm and leave to rise until the dough is mounding slightly over the top of the tins.
15. Brush the dough with the egg-yolk glaze, taking care not to let any of the glaze drip between the edge of the dough and the tin or the glaze could 'glue' the dough to the tin, making the brioche difficult to remove.
16. Bake in the top third of the oven (the hottest part) for 8–10 minutes for individual brioches, or 30–40 minutes for a large mould. Larger brioches will need to be covered with greaseproof paper after about 15 minutes' baking to prevent them from over-browning. The brioche is done when it is a deep brown on the top and a pale golden-brown and firm where it was covered by the tin. It should feel light for its size.
17. Allow to cool on a wire rack. Eat within 1 day or freeze for up to 1 month.

* If using fast-action or dried yeast, see page 480.

Peach Brioche Tart

Buttery brioche makes a delicious base for a fruit tart. The dough needs to be cold when it is shaped so it must be prepared in advance. It can be kept in the refrigerator for up to 2 days or frozen for 1 month. As the dough is very sticky, it is easier to make the brioche in a machine. However, it can be made by hand (see *Kneading Soft Doughs*, page 485). Use a baking stone for the best results. If the peaches are not ripe enough to peel, immerse them in boiling water for 30–60 seconds then plunge them into cold water. The skins should slip off.

SERVES 8–10

For the sponge

150 ml | 5 fl oz milk

20 g | ¾ oz fresh yeast*

170 g | 6 oz strong white flour

For the dough

55 g | 2 oz caster sugar

1 teaspoon salt

4 eggs, beaten

300 g | 10½ oz plain flour

170 g | 6 oz unsalted butter, softened

2 tablespoons rice flour

For the topping

1 egg white, beaten

6–8 ripe peaches, peeled and sliced

2 tablespoons caster sugar

To serve

200 ml | 7 fl oz crème fraiche

1–2 tablespoons icing sugar

a few drops of vanilla essence

1 Scald the milk then allow to cool until lukewarm. Skim.

2 Mix in the yeast and strong flour and leave to stand for 30 minutes at warm room temperature.

3 Stir the sugar, salt and eggs into the mixture. Add enough plain flour to make a soft, sticky dough. Beat in a machine until smooth, about 10 minutes.

4 Cover the dough with oiled clingfilm and leave to rise until doubled in size.

5 Using a free-standing mixer, beat the dough again to knock it back, then beat in the butter a tablespoonful at a time. Continue to beat until smooth. Chill overnight.

6 Sprinkle a baking sheet liberally with rice flour.

7 Pat the brioche dough on to the baking sheet into a round about 25 cm | 10 in diameter, keeping the edge a little thicker than the middle, rather like a pizza.

8 Brush the brioche with the egg white then arrange the peaches in overlapping concentric circles over the brioche base. Sprinkle the tart with caster sugar. Allow to prove until the brioche dough is soft and pillowy, about 1 hour

9 Meanwhile, place a baking stone in the oven and heat it to 180°C | 350°F | gas mark 4.

10 Remove the baking stone from the oven and slide the brioche on to the stone. Bake in the top third of the oven for 30–40 minutes or until golden-brown and cooked through. Serve warm with crème fraiche flavoured with a little icing sugar and vanilla essence.

* If using fast-action or dried yeast, see page 480.

Brioche Tart with Grapes and Mascarpone

SERVES 8–10

450 g | 1 lb flour quantity brioche dough (see page 600)

170 g | 6 oz raisins (optional)

200 g | 7 oz mascarpone cheese

225 g | 8 oz seedless grapes

115 g | 4 oz soft dark brown sugar

1 Heat the oven to 190°C | 375°F | gas mark 5.

2 Knock back the risen brioche dough and roll out to a circle 28 cm | 11 in in diameter. Place on a baking sheet.

3 If using raisins, sprinkle them over the surface of the dough and press in lightly.

4 Spread the mascarpone over the surface, leaving a 2.5 cm | 1 in border around the edge.

5 Scatter the grapes on top and press firmly into the mascarpone. Sprinkle over the sugar.

6 Bake the tart in the centre of the oven for 30–40 minutes or until golden-brown. Reduce the oven temperature if the tart shows signs of becoming too dark.

7 Serve the tart warm.

NOTE: Other soft fruits can be used in place of the grapes, for example pitted cherries, peaches or plums.

Gugelhopf

This light yeast cake from Austria and Germany is filled with raisins and nuts.

MAKES 1 CAKE

340 g | 12 oz plain flour

1 teaspoon salt

30 g | 1 oz fresh yeast*

225 ml | 8 fl oz lukewarm milk

30 g | 1 oz caster sugar, plus extra for the tin

2 small eggs, beaten

115 g | 4 oz butter, softened

115 g | 4 oz mixed raisins and currants

30 g | 1 oz flaked almonds

1 Sift the flour with the salt. Make a well in the centre.

2 Dissolve the yeast in the milk with the sugar. Mix with the eggs and butter.

3 Add the yeast liquid to the well and mix gradually with the flour. Stir in the fruit and almonds.

4 Butter a gugelhopf tin, dust with caster sugar and tap out the excess.

5 Put the mixture into the tin, which should be three-quarters full. Cover with oiled clingfilm or a clean damp cloth and leave in a warm place to rise until the mixture reaches the top of the tin. This will take about 20 minutes, depending on the warmth of the room.

6 Meanwhile, heat the oven to 190°C | 375°F | gas mark 5.

7 Place the tin on a baking sheet and bake in the centre of the oven for 35–45 minutes or until golden and firm to the touch.

8 Allow the cake to cool in the tin for 10 minutes, then turn out carefully on to a wire rack and leave to cool completely.

* If using fast-action or dried yeast, see page 480.

Fruit Gugelhopf

This is an extra rich version of the preceding basic Gugelhopf recipe.

MAKES 1 CAKE

For the fruit

225 g | 8 oz good-quality mixed dried fruit, such as
    peaches, apricots, apples, pears and prunes,
    chopped
1 tablespoon Calvados
570 ml | 1 pint cold tea, preferably Indian
2 cloves
1 × 5 cm | 2 in cinnamon stick
¼ teaspoon ground mixed spice
thinly pared zest of 1 lemon
1 star anise pod

For the dough
250 g | 9 oz plain flour

85 g | 3 oz semolina
1 teaspoon salt
30 g | 1 oz fresh yeast*
30 g | 1 oz caster sugar, plus extra for the tin
225 ml | 8 fl oz lukewarm milk
2 small eggs, beaten
115 g | 4 oz butter, softened
grated zest of ½ lemon

To finish
115 g | 4 oz icing sugar, sifted
2 teaspoons boiling water
lemon juice
30 g | 1 oz flaked almonds, toasted

1 Prepare the fruit: soak the mixed dried fruit in the Calvados and tea overnight.
2 Pour the fruit and soaking liquid into a saucepan and add the cloves, cinnamon, mixed spice, lemon zest and star anise. Bring to the boil, then reduce the heat and simmer slowly for up to 20 minutes until the fruit is soft.
3 Drain the fruit, reserving the liquid. Remove the cloves, cinnamon stick, lemon zest and star anise.
4 Pour the liquid into a small saucepan and boil rapidly until reduced to a syrup of thick coating consistency.
5 Heat the oven to 190°C | 375°F | gas mark 5. Butter a gugelhopf tin or ring mould and dust lightly with sugar. Tap out the excess.
6 Sift the flour, semolina and salt together into a warm mixing bowl. Make a well in the centre.
7 Cream the yeast and sugar with a little of the milk. Mix with the eggs, butter and lemon zest.
8 Pour the yeast and egg mixture into the well and mix in, adding enough milk to make a very thick batter. Add the fruit and stir well.
9 Pour the mixture into the prepared tin, which should be three-quarters full. Cover with oiled clingfilm.
10 Leave in a warm place for about 30 minutes, until slightly risen.
11 Place the tin on a baking sheet and bake for 45 minutes in the centre of the oven or until golden and firm to the touch.
12 Allow the cake to cool in the tin for 10 minutes, then turn out, brush with the fruit syrup and leave on a wire rack to cool until tepid.

13 Make the glacé icing: put the icing sugar into a bowl and stir in the boiling water and lemon juice, to taste, until smooth.

14 Sprinkle the gugelhopf with almonds and drizzle trails of icing over the top. Allow to set.

* If using fast-action or dried yeast, see page 480.

Almond and Raisin Brioche Loaf

This brioche loaf is excellent toasted and buttered for breakfast. It is best made using a machine.

MAKES 1 LARGE LOAF

300 g | 10½ oz strong white flour

½ teaspoon salt

15 g | ½ oz fresh yeast*

100 ml | 3½ fl oz lukewarm water

55 g | 2 oz caster sugar

2 eggs, beaten

85 g | 3 oz unsalted butter, softened

115 g | 4 oz flaked almonds

200 g | 7 oz raisins

extra butter and flour for tins

1 Sift the flour and salt into a large bowl.

2 In a small bowl, crumble the yeast then whisk in the water. Stir in 1 teaspoon of the caster sugar then add the remaining sugar to the flour. Make a well in the centre of the flour and tip in the yeast mixture, eggs and butter.

3 Beat with a machine until smooth and satiny, about 6 minutes.

4 Cover with oiled clingfilm and allow to rise in the refrigerator overnight.

5 The following day, turn the dough out on to a lightly floured surface and pat into a flat rectangle. Sprinkle over all but 1 tablespoon of the flaked almonds and all of the raisins. Roll up the dough (if it is very sticky oil your hands lightly).

6 Place the dough in a buttered and floured 900 g | 2 lb loaf tin and sprinkle with the reserved almonds.

7 Cover with oiled clingfilm and leave to rise at room temperature until near to the top of the tin, about 1½ hours.

8 Meanwhile, heat the oven to 190°C | 375°F | gas mark 5.

9 Bake the loaf in the centre of the oven for about 40 minutes or until well-browned. The loaf will need to be covered with greaseproof paper halfway through the cooking time to prevent overbrowning.

10 Release from the tin with a palette knife and cool on a wire rack.

* If using fast-action or dried yeast, see page 480.

Sweet Yeast Rolls

Sweet yeast rolls are individually baked breads made from dough enriched with eggs, milk, butter and sugar. They are normally served for breakfast, as a snack or at teatime. Certain recipes are traditionally served during times of religious festivals, such as Hot Cross Buns at Easter.

The rising and proving times will be longer for these enriched doughs because the additional fat slows the action of the yeast. The extra sugar in the recipes will cause the rolls to brown quickly in the oven, so it is best to watch them carefully and cover them with greaseproof paper if they are browning too rapidly.

Chelsea Buns

MAKES 12

225 ml | 8 fl oz milk

15 g | ½ oz fresh yeast*

85 g | 3 oz caster sugar

450 g | 1 lb strong white flour

1 teaspoon salt

½ teaspoon ground cinnamon

85 g | 3 oz butter

1 egg

½ teaspoon ground mixed spice

55 g | 2 oz sultanas

55 g | 2 oz currants

sugar for sprinkling

To glaze

apricot glaze (see page 474)

1 Scald the milk. Cool until lukewarm then skim.
2 Mix the yeast with 1 teaspoon of the sugar and 2 tablespoons warm milk.
3 Sift the flour with the salt and cinnamon into a mixing bowl. Rub in half the butter and stir in half the sugar.
4 Beat the egg and add to the flour with the lukewarm milk and yeast mixture. Mix to a soft dough, then knead for 10 minutes by hand or 6 minutes by machine.
5 Place the dough in a lightly oiled bowl and turn to coat with a thin film of oil. Cover with oiled clingfilm and leave to rise in a warm place until doubled in size, about 1 hour.
6 Knock the dough down and knead for 1 minute. Roll in to a 30 cm | 12 in square.
7 Mix the remaining butter with the remaining sugar and the mixed spice and spread over the dough. Sprinkle with the fruit.
8 Heat the oven to 200°C | 400°F | gas mark 6.
9 Roll up the dough like a Swiss roll and cut into 12 × 2.5 cm | 1 in slices.
10 Arrange the buns cut-side up on the baking sheet and cover with oiled clingfilm. Leave at room temperature to prove (rise again) until soft and pillowy.
11 Sprinkle with sugar. Bake in the oven for 20–25 minutes. Brush with apricot glaze.
12 Leave the buns to cool on a wire rack before separating.

* If using fast-action or dried yeast, see page 480.

Tea Cakes

MAKES 10

450 g | 1 lb plain flour
1 teaspoon salt
45 g | 1½ oz butter
15 g | ½ oz fresh yeast*
200 ml | 7 fl oz lukewarm milk
75 ml | 2½ fl oz water
1 egg, beaten

45 g | 1½ oz sugar
45 g | 1½ oz sultanas
45 g | 1½ oz currants

To glaze

1 egg, beaten
a pinch of sugar

1 Sift the flour with the salt into a large mixing bowl and rub in the butter.
2 Cream the yeast with a little of the milk. Make a well in the centre of the flour and add the yeast, the remaining milk, the water and egg. Mix to make a soft but not wet dough. Knead for 10 minutes by machine or 6 minutes by hand, or until the dough is smooth and elastic.
3 Place the dough in an oiled bowl and turn to coat it in the oil. Cover with oiled clingfilm or a clean damp cloth and leave in a warm place to rise until doubled in size. This will take about 1 hour, depending on the warmth of the room.
4 Heat the oven to 190°C | 375°F | gas mark 5.
5 Place the risen dough on a lightly floured work surface. Sprinkle over the sugar, sultanas and currants and knock back, kneading the fruit and sugar evenly into the dough. Be careful not to knead too vigorously or the fruit will break through the dough.
6 Divide the dough into 10 equal-sized pieces and shape into flat round rolls. Place on baking sheets, cover with a clean cloth and return to the warm place to rise until 1½ times their original size. This will take approximately 10–15 minutes, depending on the warmth of the room.
7 Mix the egg with the sugar for the glaze. Brush the risen tea cakes carefully with the glaze.
8 Bake in the oven for 15–20 minutes or until the tea cakes sound hollow when tapped on the underside. Serve warm, with butter, or toasted with butter.

* If using fast-action or dried yeast, see page 480.

NOTE: For spiced tea cakes, add ½–1 teaspoon ground mixed spice to the flour.

Orange Scented Rolls

These fruited rolls are baked together in a tin and then pulled apart to serve.

MAKES 14

450 g | 1 lb strong white flour
1 teaspoon salt
45 g | 1½ oz butter
15 g | ½ oz fresh yeast*
1 teaspoon caster sugar
290 ml | 10 fl oz lukewarm milk

1 egg, beaten
grated zest of 1 orange
225 g | 8 oz dried orange fruits (e.g. apricots,
    peaches, mango), chopped
2 tablespoons orange-flower water

1 Sift the flour and salt into a large mixing bowl. Rub half the butter into the flour.
2 Cream the yeast and sugar together with a little of the milk. Add the yeast, milk and egg to the flour. Mix to make a soft but not wet dough.
3 Knead for 10 minutes by hand or 6 minutes by machine, until it is smooth and elastic. Place the dough in an oiled bowl and turn it to coat in the oil. Cover with a piece of oiled clingfilm. Leave in a warm place to rise for 1 hour or until it has doubled in size.
4 Put the orange zest and dried fruits into a bowl and pour over the orange-flower water. Mix well and leave to stand for 30 minutes.
5 Heat the oven to 200°C | 400°F | gas mark 6. Line a 23.5 cm | 9 in round cake tin with baking parchment.
6 Remove the dough from the bowl to a floured surface. Use a rolling pin to roll the dough into a 30 × 35 cm | 12 × 14 in round.
7 Soften the remaining butter and spread over the surface of the dough. Scatter over the soaked fruit. Roll up the dough like a Swiss roll and use a serrated bread knife to cut it into 2 cm | 1 in slices.
8 Arrange the buns cut-side up and slightly apart in the tin. Cover with the oiled clingfilm and leave in a warm place to prove for 15 minutes or until they are 1½ times their original size.
9 Bake in the top of the oven for 25–35 minutes. Remove from the tin and put on a wire rack to cool before separating the buns.

* If using fast-action or dried yeast, see page 480.

Pecan Sticky Buns

Pecan Sticky Buns are an American classic. An over-the-top version of Chelsea buns, made from a dough enriched with butter, sugar and eggs then filled with brown sugar and nuts, they are served for breakfast or brunch with a cup of coffee or tea. The base dough is often referred to by bakers as a 'foundation dough' because it can be used as a base for many sweet breads. Like many sweet doughs, it requires 2 risings.

MAKES 16

For the dough

450 g | 1 lb strong white flour

1 teaspoon salt

55 g | 2 oz caster sugar

1 teaspoon ground cinnamon, (optional)

30 g | 1 oz fresh yeast*

150–200 ml | 5–7 fl oz milk, scalded and cooled

2 eggs, beaten

85 g | 3 oz butter, softened

For the filling

55 g | 2 oz caster sugar

1 teaspoon ground cinnamon

100 g | 3½ oz pecan nuts, chopped

1 egg, beaten

For the topping

225 g | 8 oz unsalted butter

170 g | 6 oz soft light brown sugar

200 g | 7 oz whole pecan nuts

1   Sift together the flour, salt, sugar and cinnamon into a large bowl. Make a well in the centre.

2   Cream the yeast with 2 tablespoons of the milk and pour into the well.

3   Add the eggs and butter to the well then stir in with enough milk to make a soft dough.

4   Turn the dough out on to a work surface and knead for 10–15 minutes or until the dough becomes soft and elastic. Add additional flour if the dough is too sticky to knead.

5   Place the dough in an oiled bowl and cover with oiled clingfilm. Leave to rise in a warm place until doubled in size, about 1 hour.

6   Turn the edges of the dough into the middle to deflate it, then knead for 1 minute. Return to the oiled bowl, cover and leave to rise again until doubled, about 30 minutes.

7   For the filling mix together the sugar, cinnamon and nuts. Set aside.

8   Prepare 2 shallow 23 cm | 9 in round cake tins, or 2 shallow 20 cm | 8 in source tins or 16 muffin cups, by spreading with the topping butter, then sprinkle with the sugar and nuts.

9   Knock the dough back as in step 6 then divide into 2 equal pieces. Roll each piece into a rectangle measuring 25 × 35 cm | 10 × 14 in.

10   Brush each rectangle with the beaten egg then sprinkle over the filling. Roll lightly with a rolling pin to press in the filling.

11   Roll each rectangle from one of the long ends into a tight log. Pinch the edge to secure. (The logs can be frozen at this point for up to 1 month.)

12   Heat the oven to 180°C | 350°F | gas mark 4.

13   Cut each log into 8 equal pieces. Place one piece in the centre of each tin then place the remaining 7 pieces around the edge. Cover with oiled clingfilm and leave to prove until risen to 1½ times its original size. Chill for 20 minutes.

14   Bake the buns for 35–40 minutes or until golden-brown.

15   Remove from the oven and immediately turn out on to a serving dish. Allow to cool until just warm. Serve on the day of making.

* If using fast-action or dried yeast, see page 480.

Cornish Splits

MAKES 12–16

20 g | ⅔ oz fresh yeast*
1 teaspoon sugar
450 g | 1 lb plain flour
2 teaspoons salt
45 g | 1½ oz lard
290 ml | 10 fl oz lukewarm milk
15 g | ½ oz butter, melted and cooled

For the filling
290 ml | 10 fl oz double cream, whipped, or clotted
 cream
fresh raspberries or seedless raspberry jam

To finish
icing sugar, sifted

1 Grease 2 baking sheets and dredge lightly with flour.
2 Cream the yeast with the sugar. Sift the flour with the salt into a large mixing bowl and rub in the lard with your fingertips.
3 Add the milk to the yeast mixture.
4 Make a well in the centre of the flour and pour in the yeast mixture. Stir the liquid to make a soft but not wet dough.
5 Knead until the dough is soft, shiny and elastic, 10 minutes by hand or 5 minutes by machine.
6 Place the dough in an oiled bowl and turn to coat it in the oil. Cover with a piece of oiled clingfilm and leave in a warm place to rise until doubled in size. This will take about 1 hour, depending on the warmth of the room.
7 Knock back the risen dough and knead for about 10 minutes. Shape into 12–16 balls and flatten them slightly. Place on the prepared baking sheets and cover with clingfilm. Return to the warm place and leave until nearly doubled in size.
8 Heat the oven to 200°C | 400°F | gas mark 6.
9 Bake in the centre of the oven for 20–25 minutes or until the rolls sound hollow when tapped on the underside. Transfer to a wire rack, brush with the melted butter and leave to cool.
10 To serve: cut the Cornish splits diagonally across the top. Fill with cream and raspberries or raspberry jam and dust with icing sugar.

* If using fast-action or dried yeast, see page 480.

Rum Baba

SERVES 4

For the sugar syrup
170 g | 6 oz granulated sugar
225 ml | 8 fl oz water
2 tablespoons rum

For the baba
115 g | 4 oz plain flour
15 g | ½ oz fresh yeast*
15 g | ½ oz caster sugar

85 ml | 3 fl oz lukewarm milk
2 egg yolks
grated zest of ½ lemon
55 g | 2 oz unsalted butter

To decorate (optional)
225 g | 8 oz fresh fruit, e.g. grapes and raspberries
150 ml | 5 fl oz double cream, sweetened with 1
    tablespoon icing sugar and lightly whipped

1 Make the sugar syrup: dissolve the sugar in the water and boil rapidly for 3 minutes. The syrup should be boiled 'to the thread' (when a little syrup is put between finger and thumb and the fingers are opened, the syrup should form a short thread). Add the rum.

2 Sift the flour into a bowl. Mix the yeast with ½ teaspoon sugar, 1 teaspoon flour and enough milk to make a batter consistency.

3 Whisk the egg yolks, remaining sugar and lemon zest until fluffy. Melt the butter, but do not allow it to get too hot.

4 Make a well in the centre of the flour and add the yeast and beaten eggs. With your fingers, mix together and gradually draw in more flour from the sides, adding more milk as you take in the flour. When all the flour has been incorporated, beat with your hand until soft and smooth.

5 Gradually add the cooled melted butter, kneading and slapping the dough until it looks like very thick batter and no longer sticks to the palm of your hand.

6 Put in a clean bowl, cover and leave in a warm place to rise for about 45 minutes. It should double in size.

7 Heat the oven to 190°C | 375°F | gas mark 5. Grease a 1 litre | 1½ pint ring mould with butter.

8 When the dough has risen, beat it down again and use to fill the mould. It should half-fill the tin. Cover and leave to prove (rise again) in a warm place until it is 1½ times its original size. This may take 10–20 minutes.

9 Bake in the oven for 30–35 minutes.

10 Turn out on to a wire rack and prick with a skewer whilst still warm, and brush with plenty of rum syrup until the baba is soaked and shiny. Place on a serving dish.

11 Serve plain or pile the whipped cream in the centre and surround with fruit.

* If using fast-action or dried yeast, see page 480.

Doughnuts

MAKES 8

225 g|8 oz plain flour
a pinch of salt
10 g|⅓ oz fresh yeast*
45 g|1½ oz sugar
30 g|1 oz butter
2 egg yolks

150 ml|5 fl oz lukewarm milk
vegetable oil for deep-frying

To finish
3 tablespoons caster sugar
1 tablespoon ground cinnamon

1 Grease a baking sheet. Sift the flour and salt into a mixing bowl.

2 Cream the yeast with 1 teaspoon of the sugar. Set aside

3 Rub the butter into the flour with your fingertips. Make a well in the centre.

4 Mix together the egg yolks, yeast mixture, remaining sugar and milk. Pour into the well in the flour. Mix to make a soft but not wet dough.

5 Place the dough in an oiled bowl and turn to coat it in the oil. Cover with oiled clingfilm. Leave in a warm place to rise for 45 minutes.

6 Knock back the risen dough and knead well for 5 minutes. Roll out on a floured surface to 1 cm|½ in thick. Using a 5 cm|2 in plain cutter, press out small rounds. Place on the prepared baking sheet, cover with the clingfilm, return to the warm place and leave to rise again until nearly doubled in size.

7 Heat the oil in a deep-fryer until a cube of bread sizzles vigorously in it. Put the doughnuts into the fryer basket, a few at a time, and lower into the oil. Fry until golden-brown, then drain on absorbent paper. See safety note below.

8 Toss, while still hot, in the sugar and cinnamon mixture.

* If using fast-action or dried yeast, see page 480.

NOTES: Deep fat frying is a potentially dangerous activity. The oil is extremely hot. Only half fill the fryer or saucepan with oil. Do not drop the food into the oil. Never leave hot fat unattended or attempt to move a container of hot fat. If the oil begnis to smoke, turn off the heat. Never splash water on to hot fat. A fire should be extinguished with a fire blanket or cover.

Festive Breads and Buns

The breads in this chapter are a collection from around the world and traditionally appear as part of religious celebrations. Such breads are enriched with butter and usually contain additional dried fruits and/or nuts, making them a relatively expensive treat.

These enriched doughs take longer to rise than basic bread doughs. As most of the recipes are quite complicated, they are best attempted by well-practised bakers.

Stollen

This is the traditional Christmas cake of Germany.

MAKES 2 SMALL LOAVES

30 g | 1 oz fresh yeast*
45 g | 1½ oz caster sugar
200 ml | 7 fl oz lukewarm milk
450 g | 1 lb strong plain flour
1 teaspoon grated lemon zest
1 large egg, beaten
115 g | 4 oz butter, melted and cooled
115 g | 4 oz sultanas

55 g | 2 oz currants
30 g | 1 oz chopped mixed peel
85 g | 3 oz blanched almonds, chopped

To finish

55 g | 2 oz butter, melted
icing sugar, sifted

1 Cream the yeast with 1 tablespoon of the sugar and a little of the milk.
2 Sift the flour into a large mixing bowl. Add the remaining sugar and the lemon zest. Make a well in the centre and add the egg, yeast mixture and butter. Adding as much milk as is necessary, mix to a soft but not wet dough. Knead for 10 minutes by hand or 6 minutes by machine, or until smooth, shiny and elastic.
3 Place in an oiled bowl and turn the dough to coat it in the oil. Cover with oiled clingfilm and leave in a warm place to rise until doubled in size. This will take about 1 hour, depending on the warmth of the room.
4 Heat the oven to 190°C | 375°F | gas mark 5. Grease a baking sheet.
5 Place the risen dough on the work surface. Sprinkle over the fruit and almonds and knead carefully into the dough until they are evenly distributed.
6 Divide in half and shape into 2 oval loaves with tapered ends.
7 Place the loaves on the prepared baking sheet. Cover with the clingfilm and leave to rise until 1½ times their original size, about 1 hour.
8 Brush the loaves with melted butter and bake in the top of the oven for 45–50 minutes or until they sound hollow when tapped on the underside.
9 Transfer to a wire rack and leave to cool. Dust with icing sugar while still warm.

* If using fast-action or dried yeast, see page 480.
NOTE: The stollen can be stuffed with either 85 g | 3 oz halved glacé cherries or 225 g | 8 oz marzipan (see page 461). Roll out both pieces of dough and place the cherries and marzipan in the middle of each. Bring up the sides to cover the stuffing and place seam-side down on the baking sheet. Continue as from step 7.

Hot Cross Buns

MAKES 16

200 ml | 7 fl oz milk
20 g | ⅔ oz fresh yeast*
55 g | 2 oz caster sugar
450 g | 1 lb strong white flour
½ teaspoon salt
4 teaspoons ground mixed spice
2 eggs, beaten
85 g | 3 oz butter
115 g | 4 oz currants
30 g | 1 oz mixed peel, finely chopped

To glaze
a little sweetened milk
apricot jam (optional)

For the crosses
115 g | 4 oz plain flour
water

1 Scald the milk and leave to cool to blood temperature. Skim.
2 Mix the yeast with 1 teaspoon of the sugar and 2 tablespoons of the warm milk.
3 Sift the flour with the salt and spice into a large mixing bowl. Rub in the butter. Add the remaining sugar. Make a well in the centre of the flour. Tip in the yeast, eggs and enough warm milk to make a soft dough.
4 Knead until the dough is smooth, about 10 minutes by hand or 6 minutes by machine.
5 Place in a lightly oiled bowl and turn to coat with a thin film of oil. Cover with oiled clingfilm. Leave to rise in a warm place until doubled in size, about 1½ hours.
6 Heat the oven to 200°C | 400°F | gas mark 6.
7 Turn out on to a work surface and knead again for a few seconds. Roll out to ½ cm | ¼ in thick and sprinkle over the fruit. Knead lightly to ensure that it is distributed evenly.
8 Divide into 16 equal-sized pieces and shape into small round buns. Mark a cross on top of each bun with a knife. Place on baking trays and cover with oiled clingfilm. Leave to prove (rise again) until doubled in size. Brush the tops with the sweetened milk.
9 Mix 115 g | 4 oz plain flour with enough water to make a smooth paste the consistency of toothpaste. Place the paste in a piping bag with a ¼ cm | ⅛ in nozzle and pipe a cross over the marks on the tops of the buns.
10 Bake in the oven for about 20 minutes. Brush again with sweetened milk, bake for a further 5 minutes, then cool on a wire rack. For a shiny finish, brush the buns with a little melted apricot jam.

* If using fast-action or dried yeast, see page 480.

Panettone

This is the celebration cake sold in Italy over the Christmas period. It is time-consuming to make but worth the effort. Any that is left over makes a delicious variation in a bread and butter pudding.

MAKES 1 LARGE CAKE

For the base batter

20 g | ⅔ oz fresh yeast*
115 ml | 4 fl oz lukewarm water
4 teaspoons sugar
140 g | 5 oz plain flour
30 g | 1 oz unsalted butter
1 egg, beaten

For the fruit mixture

55 g | 2 oz unsalted butter, softened
55 g | 2 oz caster sugar
1 egg

2 egg yolks
1 teaspoon vanilla essence
2 teaspoons clear honey
a pinch of salt
grated zest of 1 orange
grated zest of 1 lemon
2 tablespoons chopped candied orange peel
2 tablespoons chopped candied lemon peel
85 g | 3 oz raisins, soaked in hot water for 30 minutes
    and drained
115 g | 4 oz plain flour

1 Make the base batter: cream the yeast with the water and sugar. Sift the flour into a medium bowl. Rub in the butter with the fingertips. Make a well in the centre and add the egg and yeast mixture. Mix to a smooth batter. Cover with oiled clingfilm and leave in a warm place to rise for 1 hour.

2 Meanwhile, make the fruit mixture. Beat the butter and sugar together until light and creamy. Add the whole egg and egg yolks and beat well again. Mix in the vanilla essence, honey, salt, orange and lemon zest, candied orange and lemon rind and raisins.

3 Add the fruit mixture to the risen base batter and beat to distribute well. Mix in the remaining flour. Return to the warm place and leave to rise for 1 hour.

4 Heat the oven to 200°C | 400°F | gas mark 6. Grease a deep 900 g | 2 lb cake tin or a 2.25 litre | 4 pint charlotte mould and line the base with a disc of baking parchment.

5 Knock back the risen dough quickly and place in the tin. Mark a cross 1 cm | ½ in deep across the top of the cake, cover with clingfilm, return to the warm place and leave to rise until it has doubled in size, about 1 hour.

6 Mark the cross again and bake in the centre of the oven for 10 minutes. Turn the temperature down to 180°C | 350°F | gas mark 4 and bake for a further 40 minutes or until a sharp knife or skewer inserted into the centre comes out clean.

7 Remove from the oven and allow to cool in the tin for 30 minutes, then turn out on to a wire rack and leave to cool completely.

* If using fast-action or dried yeast, see page 480.

Bremen Sweet Bread

Germany has many recipes for sweet breads that are made around Christmas time and sold at markets throughout the country.

MAKES 1 LARGE LOAF

30 g | 1 oz fresh yeast*

55 g | 2 oz caster sugar

400 ml | 14 fl oz lukewarm milk

675 g | 1½ lb strong white bread flour

1 teaspoon salt

55 g | 2 oz butter, cut into pieces

½ teaspoon ground cardamom

grated zest of 2 lemons

85 g | 3 oz raisins

30 g | 1 oz currants

30 g | 1 oz sultanas

55 g | 2 oz flaked almonds

To finish

milk

30 g | 1 oz butter, melted

1 Cream the yeast with a teaspoon of the sugar and 2 tablespoons of the warm milk.

2 Sift the flour and salt into a large bowl, rub in the butter and add the cardamom and lemon zest. Make a well in the centre and add the milk. Mix to make a soft but not wet dough.

3 Knead for 10 minutes by hand or 6 minutes by machine, or until it is smooth and elastic. Place the dough in an oiled bowl, turning it to coat in the oil. Cover with a piece of oiled clingfilm and put in a warm place to double in size. This will take between 45 minutes and 1 hour.

4 Remove the risen dough from the bowl and put on to a floured work surface. Sprinkle over the fruit and 30 g | 1 oz of the almonds. Knead well to knock out any large air bubbles and to distribute the fruit. Heat the oven to 190°C | 375°F | gas mark 5. Grease a baking sheet.

5 Shape into a roll approximately 30 cm | 12 in long. Put on to the baking sheet, cover and put in a warm place to prove until it has not quite doubled in size. This may take 20–30 minutes.

6 Brush with milk and scatter on the remaining almonds. Bake for 45–60 minutes. It is ready when the underside sounds hollow when tapped. If it gets too dark during the cooking process, turn the oven down to 150°C | 300°F | gas mark 2 and cover loosely with foil.

7 Remove from the oven, brush with melted butter and place on a wire rack to cool.

* If using fast-action or dried yeast, see page 480.

Christmas Wreath

This cinnamon and raisin-filled bread can be served for breakfast on Christmas Day. It freezes well before icing and can be defrosted on Christmas Eve to be reheated in the morning.

MAKES 16 PIECES

For the dough

170 ml | 6 fl oz milk

340 g | 12 oz strong white flour

½ teaspoon ground cinnamon

1 teaspoon salt

30 g | 1 oz butter, softened

30 g | 1 oz caster sugar

30 g | 1 oz fresh yeast*

1 egg, beaten

For the filling

55 g | 2 oz butter, softened

55 g | 2 oz caster sugar

30 g | 1 oz soft light brown sugar

1 teaspoon ground cinnamon

50 g | 1¾ oz raisins

50 g | 1¾ oz walnuts, chopped

30 g | 1 oz candied peel, chopped

For the icing

100 g | 3½ oz icing sugar

8 glacé cherries, halved (optional)

1 Heat the milk in a saucepan until it steams heavily. Do not boil. Allow the milk to cool until just warm. Skim.

2 Sift the flour with the cinnamon and salt into a large bowl.

3 Cut the butter into small pieces and add to the flour. Rub in the butter then stir in the caster sugar. Make a well in the centre.

4 Mix the yeast with 2 tablespoons of the milk. Add to the well in the flour.

5 Add the egg to the well then stir into the flour with enough milk to make a soft dough.

6 Knead for 10 minutes by hand or 6 minutes by machine, until smooth and elastic.

7 Place the dough in an oiled bowl and turn to coat it in a thin film of oil. Cover with oiled clingfilm and leave to rise at room temperature until doubled in size, about 2 hours.

8 On a lightly floured work surface roll the dough into a rectangle about 30 × 40 cm | 12 × 16 in.

9 Make the filling: mix together the butter, caster sugar, brown sugar and cinnamon. Spread over the dough then sprinkle over the raisins, walnuts and candied peel.

10 Roll the dough tightly from one of the long sides and pinch it together where it joins. Trim the ends of the roll to neaten.

11 Shape into a circle and place on a lightly oiled baking sheet, seam-side down.

12 Cut slits in the dough, from the outside of the roll to ½ cm | 1¼ from the centre, to make 16 flaps.

13 Twist each piece so that it lies flat on the baking sheet, with a cut side uppermost, in slightly overlapping slices. Cover with oiled clingfilm and allow to rise until pillowy.

14 Heat the oven to 180°C | 350°F | gas mark 4.

15 Bake for 25–30 minutes or until golden-brown. Allow to cool on a wire rack.

16 To finish, pour 20 ml | 4 teaspoons boiling water into a bowl and sift the icing sugar on top. Stir to make a smooth cream. Drizzle over the wreath and decorate with the glacé cherries.

* If using fast-action or dried yeast, see page 480.

Challah

Similar to brioche, challah is a bread enriched with eggs. It is prepared for Jewish religious days and is made using vegetable oil so that it can be served after a meat meal. If you prefer, melted butter can be substituted for the oil. It is traditionally shaped making a plait with 4 strands of dough. Leftover challah makes a particularly delicious bread and butter pudding.

MAKES 1 LARGE LOAF

For the starter

55 ml | 2 fl oz room-temperature water

1 teaspoon fresh yeast*

3 eggs, beaten

1 tablespoon clear honey

85 ml | 3 oz strong white flour

For the dough

250 g | 9 oz strong white flour

1 teaspoon salt

45 g | 1½ oz caster sugar

55 ml | 2 fl oz vegetable oil

10 g | ⅓ oz fresh yeast*

To glaze

1 egg, beaten with 2 tablespoons water

1 Make the starter: place the water in a bowl and whisk in the yeast. Stir in the eggs, honey and flour. Cover with clingfilm and leave at cool room temperature for 2 hours.

2 Make the dough: sift the flour with the salt into a large bowl. Stir in the sugar.

3 Make a well in the centre of the flour and add the starter and oil. Crumble in the yeast. Stir to make a soft but not sticky dough, adding more flour or water as required.

4 Knead for 6 minutes by machine or 10 minutes by hand.

5 Place a sheet of oiled clingfilm directly on to the surface of the dough and leave to rise at room temperature until doubled. This will take 2–3 hours.

6 Turn the dough out on to a lightly floured work surface and knead for 10 seconds to knock back. Divide the dough into 3 or 4 equal pieces.

7 Roll each piece into a strand about 40 cm | 16 in long, with tapering ends. Shape into a 4-stranded plait.

To make the 4-stranded plait:

1 Pinch together the ends of the 4 x 40 cm | 16 in long pieces of dough. (a)

2 Slip the first strand on the left beneath the 2 strands to its right. (b)

3 Wrap the second strand to the left under the third strand. (c)

4 Slip the strand on the right underneath the 2 middle strands and bring it over the top and into the middle. (d)

5 Take the strand on the left and bring it underneath the two adjacent strands. Bring it over the top and into the middle of the 2 strands on the left. (e)

6 Slip the strand on the right over the strand to its left, and under the next left strand to that. (f)

7 Repeat from step 2 until the dough is fully plaited. Pinch the ends together. (g)

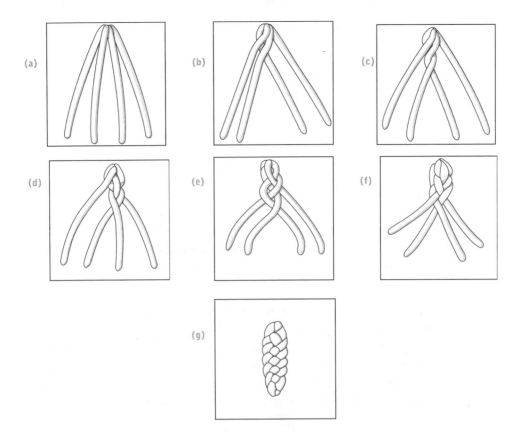

8 Place the plait on a lightly oiled baking sheet and cover with oiled clingfilm.

9 Leave to rise again at room temperature until soft and pillowy.

10 Heat the oven to 190°C|375°F|gas mark 5.

11 When the dough is nearly ready to bake, glaze it thoroughly with the beaten egg and water. Allow the glaze to dry then glaze again.

12 Bake in the centre of the oven for 25–30 minutes, covering with foil after 20 minutes if the crust is becoming too brown.

13 Place on a wire rack to cool.

* If using fast-action or dried yeast, see page 480.

Kulich

This is a Russian Easter bread which is traditionally cooked in a very tall, straight-sided mould like a coffee tin. It is often served with Pashka (a curd cheese dessert that contains dried fruit, chocolate and nuts) and painted eggs at an Easter celebration.

MAKES 2 CAKES

565 g | 1¼ lb plain flour, sifted

2 teaspoons fast-action yeast

170 ml | 6 fl oz lukewarm milk

¼ teaspoon salt

3 egg yolks

140 g | 5 oz caster sugar

3 cardamom pods, seeded and crushed

140 g | 5 oz butter, softened

3 egg whites

75 g | 2½ oz raisins

30 g | 1 oz each candied fruit, chopped

30 g | 1 oz blanched almonds, chopped

To decorate (optional)

blanched almonds, chopped candied fruit and peel

or white glacé icing

1 Mix 225 g | 8 oz of the flour with the yeast in a mixing bowl then stir in the milk. Cover with oiled clingfilm and leave in a warm place until spongy and doubled in size (about 1 hour).

2 Mix in the salt, 3 egg yolks, sugar, cardamom and butter. Whisk the egg whites until stiff and fold in with 225 g | 8 oz more flour. The dough will be on the wet and sticky side. Add the remaining flour gradually until the dough leaves the sides of the bowl. Do not worry if it is sticky. Cover with clingflim. Put in a warm place and leave to rise again (about 2–3 hours).

3 Knock back the dough using a wooden spoon or your oiled hands and add the fruits and almonds. Divide between 2 buttered and floured tall round moulds, such as large brioche tins. If you have no suitable moulds, use coffee tins or 2 × 20 cm | 8 in unglazed flower pots washed and lined with baking parchment. The dough should come half or two thirds of the way up the tins. Leave in a warm place to prove for about 1 hour.

4 Heat the oven to 180°C | 350°F | gas mark 4. Bake the kulichs for about 45 minutes. Check after 35 minutes by inserting a cocktail stick or thin skewer, which should come out clean. When the dough is cooked, the cakes should have the appearance of chefs' hats.

5 Turn out and and decorate, if you like, with chopped fruit and nuts. Alternatively, use icing, pouring it on so that it dribbles down the sides. At Easter time, stick a candle in the top of each cake.

Baking with Breadmakers

At Leiths we think the breadmaker is a great invention. They have spurred a renewed interest in bread-making and they allow anyone to make fresh bread with relative ease at almost any time. One very positive result of the popularity of breadmakers has been the increased variety of flours available to the home baker.

Although the instructions given in this book are not specifically for bread-making machines, many of the recipes can be adapted for use in breadmakers by following the general guidelines given.

Baking with Breadmakers: Points to Remember

- Use 'fast-action' or 'easy-blend' yeast. Convert the fresh yeast quantity given in the recipe using this formula: 10 g | ⅓ oz fresh yeast = 1 level 5 ml teaspoon fast-action yeast. Bake according to the manufacturer's directions for a loaf type similar to the one in the recipe.
- Many breadmaker recipes call for an unnecessarily large amount of sugar. A sugar/honey/malt extract amount of 1 tablespoon per 400 g | 14 oz flour is adequate. The recipes also call for a lower amount of salt than usual. Again, the salt quantity can be changed to suit your taste: 1½ teaspoons per 400 g | 14 oz flour will be in line with the recipes in this book.
- Weigh the water when adding it to the breadmaker. This is the most accurate means of measuring. If using fresh milk do not use the delay setting as the milk could sour. If you do need to use the delay setting, use water or dried milk powder. Keep the dried milk powder separate from the water.
- We recommend having a look at the dough once mixing has begun, to ensure that the liquid quantity is correct for the type of flour being used. You can always add a little more flour or liquid if need be. It is also a good idea to scrape down the corners of the bread-making basket so that any flour left in the corners is mixed into the dough.
- The loaf should be removed from the breadmaker about 5 minutes after baking has finished, if possible. This prevents the bread from steaming in its own heat, which makes the crust soft. Remember to protect your hands with oven gloves when removing the basket and bread from the machine. Cool the baked loaf on a wire rack.
- Use the 'dough only' setting for loaves baked on a baking sheet or baking stone.

In addition to the recipes given in this chapter, the following recipes also work well in a breadmaker:

Spelt Bread (see page 495)
Wholesome Loaf (see page 498)
Wholemeal Polenta Bread (see page 509)
Three Seed Bread (see page 504)
Five Grain Bread (see page 505)
Sun-dried Tomato Bread (see page 517)
Bob's Bread (see page 631)

Basic White Breadmaker Loaf

MAKES 1 MEDIUM LOAF

250 ml | 9 fl oz lukewarm water
30 g | 1 oz butter or 2 tablespoons oil
1½ teaspoons salt
1 tablespoon clear honey

2 tablespoons dried skimmed milk powder
450 g | 1 lb strong white flour
2 teaspoons fast-action yeast

Place the ingredients in the breadmaker basket in the order listed and set the breadmaker for a basic white loaf.

Basic Brown Breadmaker Loaf

270 ml | 9½ fl oz water
1 tablespoon malt extract or honey
15 g | ½ butter or 1 tablespoon oil
225 g | 8 oz strong white flour

225 g | 8 oz strong wholemeal or granary flour
2 teaspoons fast-action yeast
1½ teaspoons sea salt

If your machine has a warming function on the wholemeal bread setting the water can be added as it comes from the cold tap, otherwise use warm water by mixing ⅓ boiled water with ⅔ cold water.

Place the ingredients in the bread-making basket in the order listed and set the machine for a wholemeal loaf.

Baking with Breadmakers: What has gone wrong when . . .

The bread collapses.
- Too much yeast was added to the dough.
- The dough was too wet.

The bread is craggy on top.
- The dough was too dry.

The bread has risen too much.
- Too much yeast was added to the dough.
- Too much sugar was added to the dough.

The bread is soggy.
- The loaf was left in the machine for too long after baking.
- The dough was too wet.
- Too much low-gluten and/or coarse flour was used in the dough.

Gluten-free Baking

Gluten is the gummy substance formed in wheat flour when it is mixed with liquid. Small amounts of gluten are also present in oats, rye and barley. Gluten-free baking is of particular interest to people with coeliac disease, a disease of the intestine which makes them ill if they eat gluten. There are also many people who are sensitive to wheat and gluten-containing foods who choose not to eat these foods. In the UK, an estimated 1 per cent of people are intolerant of gluten.

There are now many gluten-free products in supermarkets and health-food shops, including gluten-free flour, bread, cakes, cookies and pasta. Many of these products are excellent. The flour is very good for substituting in traditional recipes calling for wheat flour, although it is a good idea to use xanthan gum in addition to gluten-free flour, as this helps the baked product stick together. This gum can be bought in most supermarkets or health-food shops, or alternatively it can be found on the Internet. Xanthan gum is produced from the fermentation of corn sugar. It is used as a thickener, emulsifier and stabilizer in foods. Add 1 teaspoon of xanthan gum per 225 g|8 oz gluten-free flour.

The recipes in this chapter have been made using a combination of gluten-free flours such as rice flour, potato flour, buckwheat flour, soya flour and gram flour. By using different combinations of these flours you can vary the flavour and texture of your baked goods. The only 'rule' is to use at least 50 per cent rice flour. Remember to add xanthan gum (see above). The recipes will probably need a bit more liquid than a wheat-flour recipe. The result is also likely to be denser and more crumbly, but it is worth experimenting to find recipes that you like. To use the other recipes in this book you can substitute one of the gluten-free flours for the wheat flour called for in the recipe, or mix your own by combining different gluten-free flours.

In most of the gluten-free bread recipes yeast has not been used, as yeast requires gluten to give traditional bread its texture. Although yeast also imparts a particular flavour to bread recipes, many people find this flavour unpleasant so we have provided bread recipes without gluten and without yeast.

When using chemical raising agents, ensure that the baking powder you use is gluten-free. Alternatively, you can make your own by combining bicarbonate of soda with cream of tartar in a ratio of 1:2.

In addition to the recipes given in this chapter, the following recipes are also gluten-free:
Meringues (see pages 173–187)
New York Cheesecake (see page 190)
Chocolate Polenta Cake (see page 311)
Chocolate Roulade (see page 308)
Toasted Almond Roulade with Strawberry and cream (see page 331)
Hazelnut Roulade with Mango and Passion-fruit (see page 337)
Bitter Orange Cake (see page 315)
Austrian Carrot Cake (see page 369)

Gluten-free White Bread

MAKES 1 SMALL LOAF

140 g | 5 oz rice flour

55 g | 2 oz potato flour

30 g | 1 oz soya flour

2 teaspoons gluten-free baking powder

1 teaspoon xanthan gum

½ teaspoon bicarbonate of soda

1¼ teaspoons salt

3 eggs, separated

1 teaspoon clear honey

150 ml | 5 fl oz milk

30 g | 1 oz butter, melted and cooled

1 Heat the oven to 200°C | 400°F | gas mark 6. Line the base and sides of a 450 g | 1 lb loaf tin with baking parchment.
2 Sift together the rice flour, soya flour, baking powder, xanthan gum, bicarbonate of soda and salt into a large bowl. Make a well in the centre.
3 Mix together the egg yolks, honey, milk and butter. Pour into the well in the flour and stir quickly to make a soft dough. The dough will be sticky.
4 Whisk the egg whites until they are just stiff and fold into the dough one third at a time.
5 Pile into the prepared loaf tin and bake in the centre of the oven for 40 minutes or until a cocktail stick inserted into the centre comes out clean. The loaf may need covering with foil after 30 minutes to avoid overbrowning.
6 Place on a wire rack and cover with a clean tea towel to cool.

Polenta and Seed Bread

This gluten-free bread can be varied with the addition of different seeds, herbs or grated cheese.

MAKES 1 SMALL LOAF

140 g|5 oz fine cornmeal or polenta
140 g|5 oz rice flour or ground rice
1 teaspoon bicarbonate of soda
1 teaspoon salt
1 tablespoon sunflower seeds

1 tablespoon poppy seeds
2 tablespoons olive oil
2 teaspoons lemon juice
350 ml|12 fl oz milk

1 Heat the oven to 200°C|400°F|gas mark 6. Grease a 450 g|1 lb loaf tin and line with baking parchment.
2 Mix the cornmeal, rice flour, bicarbonate of soda, salt, sunflower seeds and poppy seeds together in a large mixing bowl. Add the olive oil, lemon juice and milk. Mix well. Place into the prepared loaf tin and smooth the surface. Bake in the centre of the oven for 30 minutes. The loaf is ready when it sounds hollow when tapped.
3 Remove from the tin and cool on a wire rack.

Buckwheat Bread

This recipe makes a tender brown bread with a slighty nutty flavour. It is good both plain and toasted.

MAKES 1 SMALL LOAF

100 g|3½ oz buckwheat flour
100 g|3½ oz rice flour
30 g|1 oz soya flour
2 teaspoons gluten-free baking powder
1 teaspoon xanthan gum
½ teaspoon bicarbonate of soda

1¼ teaspoons salt
3 eggs, separated
1 teaspoon clear honey
150 ml|5 fl oz milk
30 g|1 oz butter, melted and cooled

1 Heat the oven to 200°C|400°F|gas mark 6. Line the base and sides of a 450 g|1 lb loaf tin with baking parchment.
2 Sift together the buckwheat flour, rice flour, soya flour, baking powder, xanthan gum, bicarbonate of soda and salt into a large bowl. Make a well in the centre.
3 Mix together the egg yolks, honey, milk and butter. Pour into the well in the flour and stir quickly to make a soft dough.
4 Whisk the egg whites until they are just stiff and fold into the dough one third at a time.
5 Pile into the prepared loaf tin and bake in the centre of the oven for 40 minutes or until a cocktail stick inserted into the centre comes out clean. The loaf may need covering with foil after 30 minutes to avoid overbrowning.
6 Place on a wire rack and cover with a clean tea towel to cool.

Gluten-free Parsnip Bread

Brown rice flour is usually available at health-food shops. Alternatively use white rice flour or ground rice, although the result will be a little different. Parsnips are a winter vegetable and you will get a better flavour from this bread when they are in season. If available in the summer months, they tend to be woody and have less flavour and sweetness.

MAKES 1 SMALL LOAF

170 g | 6 oz brown rice flour

2 teaspoons bicarbonate of soda

½ teaspoon salt

½ teaspoon grated nutmeg

2 tablespoons sunflower seeds

2 eggs, beaten

5 tablespoons natural yoghurt

150 ml | 5 fl oz sunflower oil

225 g | 8 oz parsnip, grated (approximately 2 large parsnips)

1 Heat the oven to 170°C | 325°F | gas mark 3. Grease and line the base of a 450 g | 1 lb loaf tin with a piece of baking parchment cut to fit.

2 Put the rice flour, bicarbonate of soda, salt, nutmeg and sunflower seeds into a bowl. Make a well in the centre and add the eggs, yoghurt and oil. Mix well, then stir in the grated parsnip and transfer to the prepared tin.

3 Bake for 1 hour or until the top springs back when pressed or a sharp knife comes out clean when pushed into the centre. Turn out on to a wire rack to cool.

Gluten-free Pizza

MAKES A 30 CM | 12 IN PIZZA

For the base

115 g | 4 oz rice flour

85 g | 3 oz potato flour

30 g | 1 oz soya flour

1 tablespoon gluten-free baking powder

1 teaspoon xanthan gum

a pinch of salt

30 g | 1 oz butter, softened

30 g | 1 oz Parmesan cheese, grated

1 egg, beaten

30 ml | 2 tablespoons milk

For the sauce

½ recipe pizza topping, (see page 000)

85 g | 3 oz grated mozzarella

1 Heat the oven to 200°C | 400°F | gas mark 6. Grease a baking sheet.

2 Sift the flours together into a large bowl with the baking powder, xanthan gum and salt.

3 Cut the butter into the flour using 2 table knives, scissor-fashion, then rub in lightly with your fingertips until the mixture resembles fine breadcrumbs. This can be done in a food processor, if prefered.

4 Stir in the Parmesan. Mix together the egg and milk then stir into the flour mixture using the blade of a table knife.

5 Bring the mixture together with your fingers and flatten on the baking sheet into a 30 cm | 12 in disc.

6 Bake for 10 minutes, then remove from the oven and spread over the tomato sauce and sprinkle with the mozzarella. Return to the oven for 5 minutes then serve.

Gluten-free Pastry

FOR A 20 CM | 8 IN TART TIN

100 g | 3½ oz rice flour

100 g | 3½ oz potato flour

30 g | 1 oz soya flour

1 teaspoon xanthan gum

¼ teaspoon salt

115 g | 4 oz butter

1–2 tablespoons beaten egg

1 Sift the flours together into a large bowl and stir in the xanthan gum and salt. Cut the butter into small dice and stir in. Using 2 table knives, scissor-fashion, cut the butter into the flour until it is the size of small peas. The pastry can be made in the food processor.

2 Use your fingertips to rub in the butter until the pastry begins to come together. Stir in enough egg to bring the pastry together. Place the pastry between 2 sheets of clingfilm and roll into a 25 cm | 10 in disc. Chill until just firm.

3 Remove the top sheet of the clingfilm and turn the pastry over. Press into a 20 cm | 8 in tart tin, using the clingfilm to help. Remove the second piece of clingfilm. Chill until firm. Use as required.

VARIATION

Sweet gluten-free pastry: Stir 2 tablespoons caster sugar into the flour before adding the butter.

Brown Gluten-free Pastry

FOR A 20 CM|8 IN TART TIN

85 g|3 oz rice flour

55 g|2 oz buckwheat flour

30 g|1 oz potato flour

1 teaspoon xanthan gum

¼ teaspoon salt

85 g|3 oz butter

1–2 tablespoons beaten egg

1 Sift the flours together into a large bowl and stir in the xanthan gum and salt. Cut the butter into small dice and stir in. Using 2 table knives, scissor-fashion, cut the butter into the flour until it is the size of small peas. The pastry can be made in the food processor, if preferred.

2 Use your fingertips to rub in the butter until the pastry begins to come together or combine in the food processor using the pulse setting. Stir in enough egg to bring the pastry together. Place the pastry between 2 sheets of clingfilm and roll into a disc the thickness of a £1 coin. Chill until firm but slightly pliable.

3 Remove the top sheet of clingfilm, then press the pastry into the tart tin, using the second piece of clingfilm to protect the pastry from your hand. Chill until firm.

4 Bake blind as for *Shortcrust Pastry* (see page 44).

Gluten-free Banana Bread

MAKES 1 LOAF

1 large ripe banana (100 g|3½ oz peeled weight)

2 eggs, separated

50 ml|1¾ fl oz vegetable oil or melted butter

100 g|3½ oz soft light brown sugar

85 g|3 oz rice flour

55 g|2 oz potato flour

30 g|1 oz buckwheat flour

1 teaspoon xanthan gum

1 tablespoon gluten-free baking powder

1½ teaspoons bicarbonate of soda

85 g|3 oz walnuts, chopped

1 Heat the oven to 190°C|375°F|gas mark 5. Line the base and sides of a 450 g|1 lb loaf tin with baking parchment.

2 Place the banana in a large bowl and mash. Stir in the yolks, oil or butter and sugar.

3 Sift together the flours, xanthan gum, baking powder and bicarbonate of soda.

4 Whisk the egg whites until just stiff.

5 Fold the dry ingredients into the wet ingredients, then fold in the walnuts and the whisked egg whites one third at a time.

6 Turn into the prepared tin and bake for 45 minutes or until a cocktail stick inserted into the centre comes out clean.

7 Leave to stand in the tin for 5 minutes then remove and place on a wire rack to cool.

Bob's Bread

Bob Zappacosta developed this breadmaker recipe for his 3 coeliac sons. It makes great toast and keeps well for several days.

MAKES 1 LOAF

Wet ingredients

2 eggs, beaten

½ teaspoon white wine vinegar

1 tablespoon sunflower oil

225 ml | 8 fl oz milk

15 g | 4 teaspoons xanthan gum

2 tablespoons caster sugar

1¼ teaspoons salt

30 g | 1 oz mixed nuts or seeds

1¼ teaspoons fast-action yeast

Dry ingredients

250 g | 9 oz rice flour

55 g | 2 oz potato flour

45 g | 1½ oz buckwheat flour

1 Mix together the wet ingredients and place in the breadmaker.
2 Mix together the dry ingredients and add to the breadmaker.
3 Set the breadmaker to the wholemeal program, which should take about 3½ hours. Do not use the delay setting.
4 Turn out and cool on a wire rack before slicing and toasting.

Rice Cake

MAKES A 17 CM | 7 IN CAKE

115 g | 4 oz butter, softened

225 g | 8 oz caster sugar

grated zest of ½ lemon

4 eggs

225 g | 8 oz ground rice

1 Heat the oven to 180°C | 350°F | gas mark 4. Double-line a 17 cm | 7 in cake tin with greased and floured greasproof paper.
2 Cream the butter until soft in a mixing bowl. Beat in the sugar until light and fluffy. Add the lemon zest and mix well.
3 Separate the eggs. Add the yolks to the creamed mixture one at a time, beating hard all the time.
4 Whisk the egg whites until fairly stiff but not dry. Take 1 spoonful of egg white and mix it into the creamed mixture. Stir in half the ground rice. Add half the remaining egg whites. Add the remaining ground rice, then the remaining egg white.
5 Turn the mixture into the prepared tin. Make a slight dip in the centre to counteract any tendency to rise in the middle.

6 Bake in the centre of the oven for 45 minutes or until slightly shrunken at the edges and firm to the touch.

7 Remove the cake from the oven and allow to cool in the tin for 5 minutes, then turn out on to a wire rack and leave to cool completely.

Toffee, Banana and Walnut Upside-down Tart

SERVES 6

For the pastry

55 g | 2 oz rice flour

55 g | 2 oz potato flour

30 g | 1 oz soya flour

1 teaspoon xanthan gum

¼ teaspoon salt

75 g | 2½ oz butter

2 tablespoons caster sugar

1 tablespoon beaten egg

For the topping

140 g | 5 oz caster sugar

2 tablespoons hot water

30 g | 1 oz unsalted butter

55 g | 2 oz walnuts, coarsely chopped

4 large bananas, peeled and sliced into 1 cm | ½ in slices

1 For the pastry, sift the flours together into a large bowl and stir in the xanthan gum and salt. Cut the butter into small dice and stir in. Using 2 table knives, scissor-fashion, cut the butter into the flour until it is the size of small peas. The pastry can be made in the food processor, if preferred.

2 Use your fingertips to rub in the butter until the pastry begins to come together. Stir in the sugar then enough egg to bring the pastry together. Place the pastry between 2 sheets of clingfilm and roll into a 20 cm | 8 in disc. Chill until firm.

3 Heat the oven to 200°C | 400°F | gas mark 6. Place a round 20 cm | 8 in ovenproof dish in the oven to warm.

4 For the topping, put the caster sugar with the water into a clean, heavy-based pan and melt over a low heat. Turn up the heat to boil the mixture then cook to a deep caramel. Wash any crystals of sugar from the sides of the pan using a pastry brush dipped in water. Do not stir. Take care not to touch the caramel as it is extremely hot. Remove from the heat immediately and carefully add the butter and walnuts. Pour into the warmed ovenproof dish.

5 Arrange the bananas in a single layer over the caramel. Remove the clingfilm from the pastry. Place the pastry on top of the bananas. Bake in the top third of the oven for 30 minutes or until the pastry is golden-brown. Carefully invert on to a heatproof serving plate while still hot. Serve warm or at room temperature, with cream if desired.

Chocolate Nut Cake

This gluten-free cake is perfect for a special occasion.

SERVES 8–10

200 g|7 oz good quality plain chocolate, chopped

2 tablespoons brandy (optional)

115 g|4 oz soft butter, diced

140 g|5 oz caster sugar

3 eggs, separated

75 g|2½ oz hazelnuts, skinned, toasted and ground

45 g|1½ oz chestnut flour

1 teaspoon gluten-free baking powder

To serve

whipping cream, lightly whipped

1 punnet fresh raspberries

1 Heat the oven to 180°C|350°F|gas mark 4. Line the base of a 20 cm|8 in diameter *moule à manqué* tin with baking parchment and lightly butter the paper and the tin.

2 Put the chocolate into a bowl with the brandy or 2 tablespoons of water and set over a pan of steaming water. When the chocolate has just melted, take it off the heat and stir in the butter.

3 Whisk 115 g|4 oz sugar and egg yolks in a large bowl until pale and thick, stir in the chocolate mixture and then fold in the hazelnuts. Sift over the chestnut flour and baking powder and fold in.

4 Whisk the egg whites until just stiff then whisk in the remaining 30 g|1 oz caster sugar. Fold a spoonful of the whites into the chocolate mixture, then fold in the remainder.

5 Turn the mixture into the tin and bake in the centre of the oven for about 40 minutes (cover with greaseproof paper if the cake is browning too quickly). A cocktail stick inserted into the centre of the cake should come out without any cake mixture adhering to it.

6 Leave the cake to cool in the tin for 10 minutes, then remove the tin and place the cake on a wire rack to cool completely.

7 Serve with whipped cream and fresh raspberries, if desired.

Gluten-free Scones

MAKES 7–8

115 g | 4 oz rice flour

85 g | 3 oz potato flour

30 g | 1 oz soya flour

1 tablespoon gluten-free baking powder

1 teaspoon xanthan gum

a pinch of salt

55 g | 2 oz butter, softened

30 g | 1 oz caster sugar

1 egg, beaten

4 tablespoons milk

To glaze

1 egg, beaten

1 Heat the oven to 200°C | 400°F | gas mark 6. Grease a baking sheet.

2 Sift the flours together into a large bowl with the baking powder, xanthan gum and salt.

3 Cut the butter into the flour using 2 table knives, scissor-fashion, then rub in lightly with your fingertips until the mixture resembles fine breadcrumbs. This process can be done in a food processor, if preferred.

4 Stir in the sugar. Mix together the egg and milk and stir into the flour mixture using the blade of a table knife.

5 Bring the mixture together with your fingers and flatten on a work surface into a 2.5 cm | 1 in thick disc. Cut out the scones using a 7 cm | 2¾ in cutter and place on the prepared baking sheet. The mixture will need to be squeezed together in order to cut out all the scones.

6 Brush the tops with the beaten egg and bake for 12–15 minutes or until well-risen and golden-brown.

7 Cool on a wire rack.

8 Serve slightly warm or at room temperature, cut in half and spread with butter, clotted cream and / or jam, as desired.

Gluten-free Fruit Cake

MAKES 1 LARGE LOAF

250 g | 9 oz mixed dried fruit

290 ml | 10 fl oz orange juice

50 g | 1¾ oz glacé cherries

1 tablespoon black treacle

115 g | 4 oz butter, softened

115 g | 4 oz soft dark brown sugar

3 eggs, separated

140 g | 5 oz buckwheat flour

1 teaspoon xanthan gum

1 teaspoon mixed spice

50 g | 1¾ oz ground almonds

1 Place the mixed dried fruit and orange juice in a small saucepan over a low to medium heat and simmer for 10 minutes, stirring occasionally. Stir in the treacle and allow to cool.

2 Line a 900 g | 2 lb loaf tin with a double thickness of baking parchment. Heat the oven to 170°C | 325°F | gas mark 3.

3 Beat the butter with the sugar until fluffy then add the egg yolks.

4 Sift together the flour, xanthan gum, mixed spice and ground almonds, then fold into the butter mixture. Fold in the cherries, fruit and any remaining juice.

5 Whisk the egg whites until just stiff then fold into the mixture, one third at a time.

6 Spread into the prepared tin and bake for 2 hours or until a cocktail stick inserted into the centre comes out clean. Cover the cake with greaseproof paper after 1 hour if it is becoming too brown.

7 Cool in the tin for 10 minutes then remove from the tin and cool on a wire rack.

8 Wrap in foil when cool and store for at least 1 day before slicing.

Ginger Loaf

MAKES 1 LOAF

85 g | 3 oz butter

85 g | 3 oz dark muscovado sugar

85 g | 3 oz black treacle

55 ml | 2 fl oz milk

85 g | 3 oz buckwheat flour

85 g | 3 oz rice flour

30 g | 1 oz soya flour

2 teaspoons gluten-free baking powder

1 teaspoon xanthan gum

½ teaspoon bicarbonate of soda

a pinch of salt

1½ teaspoons ground cinnamon

1 teaspoon ground ginger

a pinch of ground cloves

3 eggs, separated

3 pieces of stem ginger, finely chopped

1 Heat the oven to 200°C | 400°F | gas mark 6. Line the base and sides of a 10 × 20 cm | 4 × 8 in loaf tin with baking parchment.

2 Place the butter, sugar and treacle in a small saucepan and warm over a low heat to melt the butter and sugar. Stir to combine and add the milk. Allow to cool until barely warm.

3 Sift together the flours with the baking powder, xanthan gum, bicarbonate of soda, salt, cinnamon, ginger and cloves into a large bowl. Make a well in the centre.

4 Beat the egg yolks into the butter/sugar mixture and pour into the well. Stir quickly to make a soft dough.

5 Whisk the egg whites until they are just stiff and fold into the dough, one third at a time, along with the chopped stem ginger.

6 Pile into the prepared loaf tin and bake in the centre of the oven for 40 minutes or until a cocktail stick inserted into the centre comes out clean. The loaf may need covering with foil after 30 minutes to avoid overbrowning.

7 Place on a wire rack and cover with a clean tea towel to cool. Wrap in foil and keep for 1 day before slicing.

Citrus Polenta Cake

This moist cake keeps well for up to 5 days and can be frozen for up to 1 month. For a special dessert, serve slices with a little crème fraiche or whipped cream and garnish with fresh raspberries and mint.

SERVES 10

4 eggs, separated
170 ml | 6 fl oz sunflower oil
170 g | 6 oz caster sugar
grated zest of 1 orange
grated zest of 1 lemon
140 g | 5 oz ground almonds
100 g | 3½ oz polenta

1 teaspoon gluten-free baking powder
2 tablespoons poppy seeds (optional)

For the syrup
150 ml | 5 fl oz orange and lemon juice
55 g | 2 oz caster sugar

1 Heat the oven to 180°C | 350°F | gas mark 4. Lightly oil a 23 cm | 9 in spring-form tin and line the base and sides with baking parchment.

2 Beat the egg yolks, oil, 150 g | 5 oz caster sugar and the orange and lemon zest until smooth.

3 Mix together the ground almonds, polenta, baking powder and poppy seeds, if using, then fold into the egg mixture.

4 Whisk the egg whites to stiff peaks in a clean bowl then beat in the remaining caster sugar. Fold into the cake mixture in three additions.

5 Turn into the prepared tin and bake in the centre of the oven for 35–40 minutes. A wooden cocktail stick inserted into the centre should come out clean when the cake is cooked.

6 Cool in the tin while making the syrup. Place the orange and lemon juice in a small saucepan with the caster sugar over a low heat. Heat until the sugar dissolves, stirring all the time, then bring the mixture to the boil. Boil for 1 minute. Allow to cool for 10 minutes.

7 Pierce the cake all over through to the bottom with a skewer then drizzle the warm syrup over the cake. Allow to cool completely before serving.

Orange and Almond Cake

This delicious, moist cake is best eaten the day after it is made.

MAKES A 23 CM|9 IN CAKE

400 g|14 oz whole oranges

1 lemon

225 g|8 oz caster sugar

6 eggs

250 g|9 oz ground almonds

2 teaspoons gluten-free baking powder

1 Place oranges and lemon in a large saucepan. Cover with cold water and bring to boil. Simmer for 2 hours then drain and allow to cool.

2 Cut each fruit in half and remove any pips. Purée to a pulp in a food processor.

3 Heat the oven to 190°C|375°F|gas mark 5. Grease the base and sides of a 23 cm|9 in spring-form tin and line with baking parchment.

4 Whisk the eggs and the sugar until thick and foamy and the mixture forms a ribbon trail from the beaters.

5 Stir together the ground almonds, baking powder and pulped fruit.

6 Fold a large spoonful of the egg/sugar mixture into the fruit pulp to loosen it, then fold in the remainder.

7 Turn into the prepared tin and bake in the centre of the oven for 1 hour or until a skewer inserted into the centre comes out clean. Check the cake after 40 minutes of baking; however, as it may need to be covered with greaseproof paper or foil to prevent the top from burning.

8 Remove from the oven and place the tin on a wire rack. Allow to cool completely before removing from the tin.

NOTE: Alternatively, you can replace the oranges with an equal weight of clementines (probably 4–5). If replacing with lemons, increase the sugar to 250 g|9 oz and, if you like, add a lemon juice and icing-sugar glaze.

High Altitude Baking

The altitude of your kitchen can have a marked effect on your baking. Low atmospheric pressure will cause baked items to rise more easily and liquids to evaporate more quickly. This results in a change in the ratio of the remaining ingredients. For example, the percentage of sugar will be greater if the liquid ingredients have evaporated, and too much sugar in a cake can prevent it from setting. When the gas bubbles in a batter rise to the surface and pop they are no longer there to give the cake a light texture. Without them the cake will fall.

If the altitude of your kitchen is higher than 900 m | 3,000 feet, adjustments need to be made to ensure acceptable results. A certain amount of experimentation will be needed to adjust individual recipes.

Above 3,000 feet the oven temperature should be increased by 10°C | 25°F in any baking recipe.

The air at higher altitudes tends to be drier than normal, which results in drier flour and therefore recipes will often need a little more liquid. If a recipe does not list a liquid ingredient, use egg white.

- At 900 m | 3,000 ft increase the liquid amount by 1 tablespoon.
- At 1,500 m | 5,000 ft increase the liquid amount by 2½ tablespoons.
- At 2,000 m | 7,000 ft increase the liquid amount by 3½ tablespoons.

The sugar content in recipes should also be adjusted to compensate for the higher concentration created by the evaporating liquid.

- At 900 m | 3,000 feet reduce the sugar content by half.
- At 2,000 m | 7,000 feet reduce the sugar content by two thirds.

For baked goods such as cakes and biscuits that require a chemical raising agent, the following guidelines are recommended in addition to the guidelines above for liquid and sugar alterations:

- At 900 m | 3,000 feet reduce the amount of chemical raising agent by ⅛ teaspoon per teaspoon.
- Altitudes above 1,500 m | 5,000 feet generally require slightly higher baking temperatures. Increase by an additional 10°C | 20°F.

- At 2,000 m|7,000 feet and above reduce the chemical raising agent by ¼ teaspoon per teaspoon.

For whisked cakes and soufflés (in addition to the above recommendations for liquid and sugar alterations):
- Do not whisk egg whites to stiff peaks as they will rise too much. Whisk only to the soft-peak stage.

For yeast bread recipes (in addition to the above recommendations for liquid and sugar alterations):

- Use slightly more liquid.
- Allow the bread to rise and prove for a shorter time than at sea level. Only allow the bread to just double when rising.
- Yeast breads will have a coarser texture. Allow the dough to have an extra rising.

Part Three
TERMS AND TABLES

Baking Terminology

Autolyze: The resting period of at least 20 minutes for a mixture of flour and liquid when making bread which allows even hydration and aids gluten formation.

Bain-marie: A water bath either hot or cold. A roasting tin half-filled with hot water which is used to protect food, such as cheesecakes, from the fierce heat of the oven. The steamy atmosphere will also keep the food from drying out. A cold bain-marie consists of ice set in a bowl of water and is used to cool food quickly or keep food cold.

Batter: A farinaceous mixture of thick liquid consistency used to make drop scones (pancakes) and crêpes.

Barm: A leavening from the froth produced during beer fermentation.

Beat: To work a substance or mixture energetically using a spoon, electric hand mixer or free-standing mixer.

Beurre noisette: Butter cooked over a medium heat until the milk solids turn nut-brown in colour and delicately toasted in flavour.

Biga: An Italian term for a dough starter made from commercial yeast, flour and water.

Biscuit: Derived from the French term meaning twice-cooked (biscotti in Italian). Used to describe individual small, crisp, sweet or savoury pastries.

Blend: To mix two or more substances together, either by hand, using a spoon, or in a food processor or liquidizer.

Blind bake: To bake an empty pastry case so that the pastry is cooked through and will be crisp when filled (see *Pastry*, page 44).

Blood temperature: 37°C|98.6°F.

Cake: A raised, sweet, baked mixture of flour, sugar or other sweeteners, fat and eggs with a moist, tender texture and small crumb.

Canapé: A small bread or biscuit base, sometimes fried and spread with savoury paste, or garnished with a wide variety of ingredients. Used for cocktail nibbles or as an accompaniment to meat dishes. Sometimes used to denote the base only.

Caramel: The stage at which melted and heated sugar crystals turn deep brown, 174°C|345°F.

Caramelize: To turn sugar into caramel by gently heating it.

Caraque: Chocolate curls used to decorate cakes and desserts (see page 370).

Cartouche: A piece of greaseproof paper used to line an uncooked pastry case before weighing it down with beans to bake blind (see page 44). Also a dampened piece of greaseproof paper placed directly on the surface of vegetables, such as onions, during cooking to help them soften more quickly.

Chef: A French term for a dry dough starter made with wild yeast held back from a previous loaf.

Coating consistency: A term to describe the consistency of a liquid or sauce when it coats the back of a spoon lightly and evenly.

Cookie: An American term meaning biscuit, derived from the Dutch word *koekje*. Cookies are normally softer and/or chewier than biscuits.

Coulis: A thick sauce made from the puréed cooked or raw fruit, such as summer berries.

Couverture: Plain dark chocolate with a relatively high proportion of cocoa butter, meaning 'blanket' or 'covering'. Used mainly for confectionery as it becomes shiny and brittle once tempered.

Cream: To beat ingredients together to incorporate air, such as butter and eggs when making a sponge cake.

Cream yeast: To mix yeast with a little liquid (water or milk) and sometimes a pinch of sugar to break it down to a creamy consistency before it is added to dry ingredients.

Croûte: French for crust. Sometimes a pastry case, to contain a fillet of beef or fish en croûte. Croûte also describes bread sliced and cut into squares or rounds, dipped in butter, baked and topped with savoury mixtures for hors d'oeuvres.

Crush: To reduce a solid ingredient to very small pieces using a mortar and pestle, a food processor or the end of a rolling pin.

Crystallize: A preserving technique most frequently applied to fruit, flowers and nuts (see **Baking Ingredients**, page 15).

Curd: The coagulated semi-solid protein and fat constituents of separated milk.

Curdle: When the solid and liquid components of an emulsion separate (e.g. cake mixture).

Cut: To incorporate solid fat into dry ingredients only until lumps of the desired size remain, using 2 knives or a food processor.

Détrempe: The dough base for layered pastry, consisting of flour and a little fat and water.

Dredge: To coat food lightly and evenly with a powdered ingredient such as flour or icing sugar.

Dropping consistency: The consistency of a mixture that drops reluctantly from a spoon, neither pouring off nor obstinately adhering. Describes cake mixtures and uncooked choux pastry.

Egg wash: Beaten raw egg, sometimes with salt added, used for glazing pastry or bread to give it a shine when baked.

Emulsion: A suspension of a fat in liquid or liquid in fat such as butter and eggs for a creamed cake.

Enrich: To increase the fat and protein content of a mixture by adding cream, butter, eggs or egg yolk.

Feather ice: To decorate a cake or sauce with an icing or sauce of a contrasting colour by dragging a skewer or cocktail stick through it (see page 454).

Firm ball: The stage of a boiled sugar syrup where a small amount of syrup will form a firm ball when dropped into cold water, 122°C|250°F.

Fold: To combine whisked or beaten ingredients with dry ingredients, using a gentle lifting motion to retain as much of the air in the mixture as possible.

Fraiser: To mix butter, eggs and flour together with a chopping and smearing motion when making French pastry.

Freeze: To cool solid or liquid food quickly to −18°C|0°F or lower in order to preserve it or to make iced foods such as ice cream and sorbets.

Ganache: A filling for cakes and chocolates made from plain chocolate and double cream.

Ghee: Butter that has been melted and had the milk solids and salt removed then cooked until all the moisture is evaporated. The butter starts to brown slightly, giving it a nutty flavour.

Glaze: To create a glossy surface on food to enhance its appearance and to prevent discoloration caused by contact with the air. Desserts such as fruit tarts are glazed with a fruit glaze of finely sieved apricot jam or redcurrant jelly and rum baba is glazed with flavoured sugar syrup. Also refers to a stock that has been reduced until thick and sticky.

Gluten: The elastic substance formed in wheat flour by the proteins glutenin and gliadin when worked with a liquid.

Grate: To reduce a solid food to coarse or fine threads (cheese, fruit zest, etc.) or powder (nutmeg) by repeatedly rubbing it over one of the various faces of a grater.

Grill: To cook or brown food quickly under the intense heat of an electric element or gas flame.

Ice: To decorate the surface of sweet foods, cakes and biscuits with sugar-based toppings known as icing.

Infuse: To steep or flavour a liquid with an aromatic ingredient by slowly heating to boiling point and then allowing to cool. The resulting flavoured liquid is called an infusion.

Julienne: Citrus peel or vegetables cut into thin matchsticks or very fine shreds, strictly 1–2 mm|$\frac{1}{25}$–$\frac{1}{12}$ in wide and 3 cm|2$\frac{1}{4}$ in long.

Knead: To manipulate dough by pushing it across a work surface, flipping it over and pulling it back. Also an efficient way of incorporating additional ingredients once the dough has risen.

Knock back: To punch down or knead out the carbon dioxide in risen dough so that it resumes its original size.

Knock up: To separate the layers of raw puff pastry with the blade of a knife around the cut edge of the pastry to facilitate rising while it is baked.

Leaven: To incorporate a leavening (raising) agent (e.g. yeast, baking powder, eggs) to a batter, cake mixture or dough to make it rise.

Let down or thin: To add water or a liquid to a sauce to thin its consistency.

Levain: French term for leavening. A fully developed dough starter made from wild yeast, and containing wholemeal and rye flours, usually of a very thick batter consistency.

Lighten: To incorporate air and lighten the texture of a mixture with whisked double cream or egg whites.

Loosen: To stir a spoonful of whisked egg white into a mixture to make it easier to incorporate the remaining egg white by folding. A technique used to retain as much of the foam's volume as possible.

Lukewarm: Tepid, at blood temperature 37°C|98.6°F.

Macerate: To soak raw, dried or preserved foods, such as dried fruits, in liqueur, brandy or sugar syrups, sometimes infused with aromatic spices. As the food absorbs the liquid it improves in flavour and softens in texture.

Marble: An incomplete combination of mixtures of different colours achieved by folding the mixtures together or by feather–icing.

Millefeuille: French for a thousand layers. A term used to describe the characteristic appearance of a traditional French layered dessert made with puff pastry.

Mise en place: Literally, to put in place. Preparing and setting out ingredients and utensils in an organized manner prior to preparing and serving a meal.

Mix: The process of combining two or more ingredients.

Molasses: Also known as black treacle.

Mousse: A French term meaning foam or froth, used to describe the light, airy consistency of savoury or sweet mousses obtained by the addition of whisked egg whites.

Napper: To coat, mask or cover a prepared food evenly.

Needleshreds: Fine, evenly cut shreds (or julienne) of citrus zest, generally used as a garnish.

Noisette: French for hazelnut. Usually means nut-brown, as in beurre noisette, i.e. butter browned over heat, to a nut colour.

Oven-spring: A crack in baked bread where the crust has separated from the body of the loaf.

Panade or panada: The name given to the choux pastry base before the eggs are added.

Pastry: A combination of flour, fat and usually liquid to make a dough which is shaped and baked. Pastry is used to hold, cover or support other ingredients.

Pâtisserie: Sweet or savoury pastries and cakes. The name also applies to the shop where the pastries are made and sold.

Peel: To remove thinly the skin of fruits and vegetables, using a knife or vegetable peeler. Also a flat paddle with a long handle used to place bread dough and pizza in the oven.

Petits fours: Bite-sized items of pâtisserie, such as tartlets, little cakes and biscuits, or chocolates and candied fruit, served after a meal with coffee.

Pinch: A very small quantity, amounting to approximately 3–5 g | ⅛ teaspoon of a dry powdered ingredient, such as salt, pepper or spice, taken between the thumb and forefinger and added directly to the food being prepared.

Pipe: To press a soft substance, such as meringue, icing or whipped cream through a piping bag fitted with a shaped metal or plastic nozzle to produce decorative details on a cake, or to form a food into an interesting shape for presentation purposes.

Pith: The soft white layer under the outer skin of citrus fruit. When zesting or peeling the zest of citrus fruit, be careful to leave the pith behind as it has an unpleasant bitter taste.

Poach: To cook food gently by immersing it in liquid moving with the barest tremble.

Praline: Almonds cooked in boiling sugar until the sugar caramelizes to a rich brown colour. The mixture is then cooled and crushed to a powder. Used for flavouring desserts and ice cream.

Prove: The last rising of a bread dough into its final shape before it is baked.

Purée: Fruit or vegetables, delicate meats and fish liquidized, sieved or finely mashed to a smooth consistency.

Quenelle: To shape soft, smooth foods (such as whipped cream or ice cream) with 2 spoons into egg-shaped portions.

Raising agent: An ingredient or substance that causes a mixture or dough to rise and increase in volume when cooked. Natural raising agents include eggs, which trap expanding air and steam. Yeast and the chemical raising agents baking powder and sodium bicarbonate, used in conjunction with an acid such as cream of tartar, produce the raising agent carbon dioxide.

Reduce: To reduce the amount of a liquid by rapid boiling, to concentrate the flavour and colour and to thicken its consistency.

Refresh: To pass boiled fruit or vegetables under cold, running water or to immerse them in iced water to prevent them cooking further and to set their colour.

Relax or rest: To set aside pastry or pasta dough in a cool place to allow the gluten (which will have tightened during rolling) to soften. Batters are also set aside to allow the starch cells to swell with liquid, giving a lighter result when cooked.

Roux: Equal amounts of butter and flour cooked together and used as a liaison to thicken sauces and soups.

Rub in: To mix flour and fat together lightly with the fingertips until the mixture resembles breadcrumbs.

Sabayon: A light, foamy sauce or dessert made with eggs whisked over heat with sugar, sweet wine or liqueur.

Sauté: To cook small pieces of food quickly by shaking and tossing in very little hot oil and/or butter until brown, using a wide, shallow pan called a sauté pan.

Scald: To immerse food briefly in boiling water to kill micro-organisms on its surface, or to loosen the skins of fruit and vegetables for easier peeling. To scald milk means to heat milk until just before the point of boiling, when some movement can be seen at the edges of the pan but there is no overall bubbling.

Score: To make shallow, long cuts, using a small knife, along the surface without cutting through.

Season: To use small quantities of salt, pepper, spices, sugar and other flavourings such as lemon, vinegar and oil to balance, enhance but not dominate the flavour of a dish or food. Also describes the preparation of new cooking equipment, such as crêpe pans, to prevent subsequent rusting and sticking.

Separate: To separate egg yolks from the whites.

Setting point: The point at which a mixture containing gelatine starts to set and thicken.

Shape dough: To give a prepared dough its final shape before baking.

Shred: To slice or tear food into long, thin strips.

Sift: To pass one or more dry ingredients through a wire mesh sieve to remove lumps and combine and aerate ingredients. Drum sieves are used for sifting large quantities of ingredients.

Simmer: To cook food in liquid that is just below its boiling point (around 98°C|208°F) so that the liquid's surface trembles, with small bubbles breaking the surface.

Skim: To remove impurities from the surface of a simmering liquid using a ladle.

Skin: To remove the skin from fish, poultry, meat and game.

Slake: To mix thickening ingredients such as flour, arrowroot or corn flour to a thin paste with a small quantity of cold water, before adding to a sauce or soup, to prevent lumps forming.

Soft ball: The term used to describe sugar syrup reduced by boiling to a viscosity that when dropped into cold water and squeezed gently between finger and thumb forms a soft ball, 115°C|235°F.

Soufflé: French term, meaning puff, used to describe a light, sweet or savoury dish, either hot or cold, enriched with egg yolks; lightened with whisked egg whites and flavoured with vegetables, fish, cheese, fruit, chocolate or alcohol.

Spice: Seeds, roots, leaves and stems of plants with a powerful, sharp aroma, used to flavour food.

Sponge gelatine: To sprinkle powdered gelatine over cool water or liquid, leaving it to absorb the liquid until it becomes spongy in texture.

Sponge yeast: To mix yeast with a little water, flour and sometimes sugar then let it stand to become active before using in a dough.

Steam: To cook food by direct steaming in hot vapours in a perforated container over boiling liquid (usually water). Alternatively, foods such as steamed puddings may be indirectly steamed by cooking them in a sealed container (usually a pudding basin) placed on a trivet, half-submerged in a pan of boiling water.

Steep: To saturate fruit and cakes such as a savarin or baba with syrup, or liqueur to flavour and moisten them.

Stock: Liquid flavoured through cooking with aromatic vegetables, such as onion, carrot and celery, and sometimes meat or fish bones.

Strain: To separate pieces of raw or cooked food from water, a marinade or cooking liquid, using a sieve, colander or strainer.

Suet: Saturated fat taken from around the kidneys of animals, usually cattle. Used for making steamed suet puddings, dumplings and suet pastry.

Sweat: To cook gently, usually in butter or oil, but sometimes in the food's own juices, to soften and to concentrate the food's flavour without frying or browning.

Syrupy: A term used to describe the consistency of a liquid or sauce when it is thickened to the viscosity of a thin sugar syrup and will evenly coat the back of a spoon.

Temper: To heat, cool, then warm chocolate to precise temperatures so that it is shiny when set (see page 5).

Tepid: Lukewarm temperature, 37°C|98.6°F.

To the ribbon: The stage at which whisked egg yolks become sufficiently thick to leave a trail on their surface when dribbled from the whisk held above the bowl.

To the thread: Term used to denote degree of viscosity achieved when reducing sugar syrup, i.e. the syrup will form threads if tested between a wet finger and thumb.

Toss: To agitate food gently in order to mix ingredients or coat delicate food in a dressing or sauce.

Vol au vent: A large pastry case (15–20 cm | 6–8 in in diameter) with a lid, made from puff pastry with high, raised sides and a deep, hollow centre which is filled after baking.

Well: A large, bowl-like hollow made in the centre of a pile of flour, either on a work surface or in a bowl, to hold liquid ingredients.

Whisk: To beat a substance (or substances) together vigorously to incorporate air, using a whisk or an electric mixer with whisking attachment.

Yeast: Single-celled micro-organism of the fungus family used to leaven bread, yeasted pastry and cakes. Fast-action yeast is a fine-textured dry yeast that is manufactured to mix directly with flour. It is also known as easy-blend yeast or instant yeast (see page 480).

Zest: The outer skin of citrus fruit, containing aromatic oils, used for flavouring.

Glossary of British and American Terms

aubergine	eggplant
baking sheet	baking tray
bicarbonate of soda	baking soda
broad beans	fava beans
cheese biscuits	crackers
cornflour	cornstarch
coriander	cilantro
courgette	zucchini
caster sugar	superfine sugar
demerara sugar	turbinado sugar
digestive biscuits	graham crackers
double cream	heavy cream
fish slice	pancake turner
greaseproof paper	*use* wax paper
grill	broiler
to grill	to broil
hazelnuts	filberts
icing sugar	confectioners' sugar
knock back	punch down
mixed spice	apple pie spice
plain flour	all-purpose flour
plain chocolate	semi-sweet chocolate
polenta	fine cornmeal
prawn	jumbo shrimp
prove	last rising before bread is baked
red pepper	red bell pepper
sauté pan	frying pan or skillet
scones	biscuits
scone cutter	plain biscuit cutter about 7.5 cm|3 in in diameter
self-raising flour	*use* 4 oz|1 cup cake flour plus 2 teaspoons baking powder
single cream	light cream
silicon paper	baking parchment
spring onions	green onions/scallions
sponge (the yeast)	proof
stock	broth
strong flour	bread flour

tap	faucet
tin	pan
unsalted butter	sweet butter
wholemeal flour	wholewheat flour

Conversion Tables

Weights

Imperial	Metric	Imperial	Metric
5 g	1/6 oz	240 g	8½ oz
7–8 g	¼ oz	250 g	9 oz
15 g	½ oz	270 g	9½ oz
20 g	¾ oz	285 g	10 oz
30 g	1 oz	300 g	10½ oz
45 g	1½ oz	315 g	11 oz
55 g	2 oz	340 g	12 oz (¾ lb)
70 g	2½ oz	370 g	13 oz
85 g	3 oz	400 g	14 oz
100 g	3½ oz	425 g	15 oz
115 g	4 oz (¼ lb)	450 g	16 oz (1 lb)
125 g	4½ oz	500 g	1 lb 2 oz
140 g	5 oz	600 g	1 lb 5 oz
155 g	5½ oz	675 g	1½ lb
170 g	6 oz	700 g	1 lb 9 oz
185 g	6½ oz	800 g	1 lb 12 oz
200 g	7 oz	900 g	2 lb
215 g	7½ oz	1 kg	2 lb 4 oz
225 g	8 oz (½ lb)	1.35kg	3 lb

Lengths

Imperial	Metric
1 in	2.5 cm
2 in	5 cm
4 in	10 cm
6 in	15 cm
8 in	20 cm
9 in	23 cm
10 in	25 cm
12 in	30 cm

Liquid Measures

Imperial	American	ml	fl oz
½ teaspoon		2.5	1/12
1 teaspoon		5	1/6
1 tablespoon		15	½
2 tablespoons		30	1
4 tablespoons	¼ cup	55	2
¼ pint (1 gill)		150	5
	1 cup	225	8
½ pint	1¼ cups	290	10
¾ pint	2 cups	450	15
	1 pint	450	16
1 pint	2½ cups	570	20
	1 quart (2 pints)	900	32
2 pints	2½ pints (5 cups)	1.1 litres	40
8 pints	10 pints	4.5 litres	160

Oven Temperatures

°C	°F	Gas mark	AMERICAN	AUSTRALIAN
70	150	¼	COOL	VERY SLOW
80	175	¼	COOL	VERY SLOW
100	200	½	COOL	VERY SLOW
110	225	½	COOL	VERY SLOW
130	250	1	VERY SLOW	SLOW
140	275	1	VERY SLOW	SLOW
150	300	2	SLOW	SLOW
170	325	3	MODERATE	MODERATELY SLOW
180	350	4	MODERATE	MODERATELY SLOW
190	375	5	MODERATELY HOT	MODERATE
200	400	6	FAIRLY HOT	MODERATE
220	425	7	HOT	MODERATELY HOT
230	450	8	VERY HOT	MODERATELY HOT
240	475	8	VERY HOT	HOT
250	500	9	EXTREMELY HOT	HOT
270	525	9	EXTREMELY HOT	VERY HOT
290	550	9	EXTREMELY HOT	VERY HOT

Suppliers

Food

Billington's Unrefined Sugar
Tel. 020 8838 9670
www.billingtons.co.uk

The Chocolate Society
Tel. 01423 322230
www.chocolate.co.uk

Doves Farm Foods
Salisbury Road
Hungerford
Berkshire RG17 0RF
www.dovesfarm.co.uk
Organic flours, gluten free flour.

Green & Blacks
Tel. 020 7633 8113
www.greenandblacks.co.uk
Organic Chocolate.

The Flour Bin
www.flourbin.com
Flour, dried yeast.

Seasoned Pioneers
Tel. 0800 0682348
www.seasonedpioneers.co.uk
Dried herbs and spices, spice mixes.

Shipton Mill Ltd
Long Newton
Tetbury
Gloucestershire GL8 8RP
Tel. 01666 505050
www.shipton-mill.com

Equipment

Cookware Online
Tel. 01877 339900
www.cookware-online.co.uk

Divertimenti
Tel. 020 7730 4259
www.divertimenti.co.uk

John Lewis
Tel. 020 7629 7711
www.johnlewis.com

Lakeland Ltd
Tel. 015394 88100
www.lakelandlimited.co.uk

Nisbets
Tel. 0845 140 5555
www.nisbets.co.uk

Squire's Kitchen
Tel. 0845 225 5671
www.squires-shop.com
Cake decorating supplies.

Select Bibliography

David, Elizabeth, *English Bread and Yeast Cookery*, 1st ed. 1977, Penguin Books, London, 2001

Dinah, Alison, *Totally Flour Free Baking*, Avital Books, Andover, Hampshire, 2005

Galli, Franco, *The Il Fornaio Baking Book*, Chronicle Books, San Francisco, California, 1993

Kimball, Christopher, *Baking Illustrated*, Cook's Illustrated, Boston Common Press, Boston, Massachusetts, 2004

Lepard, Dan and Whittington, *Baking with Passion*, Quadrille Publishing, London, 1999

Maglieri, Nick, *How to Bake*, HarperCollins, New York, 1995

McFadden, Christine and Christine France, *Chocolate Bible*, Lorenz Books, London, 2003

Reinhart, Peter, *Crust and Crumb*, Ten Speed Press, Berkeley, California, 1998

Roux, Michel and Albert Roux, *The Roux Brothers on Pâtisserie*, 1st ed. 1986, Little Brown and Company, London, 1993

Wing, Daniel and Alan Scott, *The Bread Builders*, Chelsea Green Publishing, Vermont, 1999

Index

A Note on the Authors

Susan Spaull is a freelance cookery author and editor, food stylist, teacher and demonstrator. She is the author of *Ideal Home Entertaining*, the award-winning *Leiths Techniques Bible* and was a contributor to the *Leiths Cookery Bible*. After training at the Cordon Bleu School in London and Leiths School of Food and Wine she ran her own catering and cookery demonstration business for ten years. In 1995 she returned to Leiths as a teacher and demonstrator. Susan was born in New York and currently lives in London and Colchester.

Fiona Burrell trained at Queen Margaret College, Edinburgh. After leaving college she worked with *Woman and Home* magazine's cookery school in Edinburgh before setting up her own catering business. She joined Leiths School of Food and Wine in 1983 and was co-principal with Caroline Waldegrave from 1991 until 1995. She is the author of *Leiths Book of Cakes*, the co-author of *Leiths Complete Christmas* with Prue Leith and Caroline Waldegrave, and was a contributor to *Leiths Cookery Bible* and *Leiths Vegetarian Bible*. She lives in Edinburgh with her husband and three daughters.